THE WORLD OF

Henry Lawson

THE WORLD OF

Henry Lawson

EDITED BY WALTER STONE

PAUL HAMLYN
SYDNEY
LONDON
NEW YORK
TORONTO

Published by Paul Hamlyn Pty. Limited, 176 South Creek Road,
Dee Why West, NSW 2099
First Published 1974
© Copyright Paul Hamlyn Pty. Limited 1974
Produced in Australia by the Publisher
Typeset in Australia by Smith and Miles Ltd.
Printed in Hong Kong.
National Library of Australia Registry number
and ISBN 0 600 07073 5

CONTENTS

ACKNOWLEDGEMENTS are made to all those who have talked to me about Lawson, to all those whose written words I have read about him, to all those who helped in any way. They were and are legion. In particular to Beatrice Davis and the late John Abernethy, to Phillip Mathews, publisher's editor, with whom I have an affinity in suffering, but gladly, the enthusiasm of writers, and 'last, but not least', to my wife, Jean, and she alone knows why.

W.S.

HENRY LAWSON

A Discursive Biography

Henry Lawson holds a unique place in Australian and possibly in world literature. Alone of creative writers in this country, he lived to see the emergent nation adopt his interpretation of its way of life as equivalent to a sense of identity. By a singular and fortuitous combination of author, time, place and circumstance he welded his ideal of mateship, as a code, to the world's most sparsely settled continent—a land in which men measured distance not in miles but in time and tribulation, as perhaps they measured life itself. He achieved it in poetry and the short story, in forms that went straight to the hearts of his readers, as they have done ever since.

Out of the welter of legends that have come down from those who were his friends, or those who magnified a single meeting with him into a life-long mateship, few stories rise above the level of the homespun, and none take him into the heroic folklore class. They have served merely to confound biographers and to please listeners. No idolatrous Boswell sat in Lawson's salon. He had neither. When his friend, patron and publisher, George Robertson of Sydney, made him an advance of one hundred pounds ($200) against royalties to write his autobiography, the result was disastrous. Two instalments of 'A Fragment of Autobiography', with a break of some years in the composition, were all that Lawson wrote, or felt that he could or would write. Unsupported by written records of any kind—he never kept a journal—they were little more than reminiscences laced with fact and fantasy and a sure snare for unwary biographers who drew upon the variously published excerpts from the manuscript, lately published in full for the first time.

In other and later biographical excursions Lawson never really grappled with the last, long, sad years of his decline—years which were to be schismatic on the Australian literary scene and to remain so for forty years, with the open book of Lawson's private life the basic cause.

It is almost impossible to be objective on the question of a definitive biography of Lawson. The results of the minute and extensive research by Professor Colin Roderick will, by the time they are finalized, leave little to be discovered. This is not to say that reinterpretation will be barred, any more than it was when, in 1963, the first substantial biography of any value as a source book, but limited to the facts and legends of the day, appeared from the pen of 'Denton Prout'. Its title, *The Grey Dreamer,* was inspired by a verse from Lawson's poem 'The Wander-Light' (1902):

And my dreams are strange dreams, are day dreams, are grey dreams,
And my dreams are wild dreams, and old dreams and new,
They haunt me and taunt me with fears of the morrow—
My brothers they doubt me—but my dreams come true.

Much stress has been put on Lawson's ancestry as an explanation or excuse for his waywardness, his emotional instability and even for his literary talent. His mother's side of the family bore the brunt of it for many years, even having to suffer the slur, as they imagined, of a gypsy strain, a dream which Lawson invented and clung to, much to the family's annoyance. But a balance has been struck of late, in the discovery that his Norwegian father's family had also contributed to his behaviour patterns.

At one time his father was summarily dismissed, by those who tinkered with the Lawson saga, as a Norwegian sailor who happened to call at Melbourne during the height of the goldrushes and deserted his ship in quest of an easy fortune. Research triggered by the enthusiasm of a Norwegian scholar, Odd Bjørge, who was in Tasmania as a teacher in the 1950s, and came under the spell of Henry's writing, brings Niels Hertzberg Larsen more fully into the picture. Known to his mates in Australia as 'Peter Larsen' he was born in 1832 into a good family at Flademoen in Tromoy, Norway, where he received a sound education before completing his training in navigation. In 1853 he left Norway as mate on his cousin's ship; a blighted romance, according to Professor Roderick's researches, may have led him to vow that he would never return. From the same sources we do know that he came to Melbourne on December 27, 1855 on the *Pedro V* which sailed on January 22, 1856. With his shipmate, John Slee, Niels Hertzberg Larsen deserted ship to become a gold seeker.

About ten years later he went to the goldrush at New Pipeclay (later known as Eurunderee) near Mudgee, and in July 1866 married Louisa Albury, daughter of a local bushworker, turned shanty-keeper.

Louisa was one of the family of six daughters and a son of Harriet Wynn and Henry Albury, both from England, who had married at Mulgoa, NSW, in 1845. According to family tradition Louisa showed much promise as a student, with a marked interest in literature. She also had a promising concert voice, both attributes of little value to one of a large family in a small country town in central New South Wales in the 1860s. Formal education ended at the primary level and for girls the only future lay in marriage.

She was eighteen when she married Niels (alias 'Peter') Larsen who was then thirty-four. For the romantic, high spirited Louisa any prospects she had of escaping from the monotony of a life in the bush were soon shattered. Family gossip says that she knew within a fortnight that her marriage to Peter was a mistake. Perhaps for Louisa marriage itself was.

Soon Peter was on the move again and took Louisa to a small town near the Weddin Mountains where a new rush had, to use an expression of the time, 'broken out'. Henry Lawson, was born on June 17, 1867, at Grenfell, an event now celebrated there by an annual festival.

Whether Henry Lawson was born in a tent on the goldfield, as he believed or whether through the good offices of his father's friend, John Slee, Louisa was admitted to the Grenfell hospital, a building not then officially opened, is uncertain. Whether the night was wintry-dark and stormy as Henry believed, or as Professor Roderick claims in an interesting surmise, it was a fine night, truth remains silent.

No record of his baptism has ever been found but generations of school children have listened, without question, to the incongruous story of that apocryphal event. Reviewing his first book *Short Stories in Prose and Verse* in the issue of January 5, 1895, the *Bulletin* had this to say:

'The 'Archibald' is a somewhat humorous misunderstanding on the part of the minister who officiated at the christening, and who being rather deaf, mistook 'Hertzberg' for Archibald and sent the young Australian through the world with an English, instead of a Norse middlename, much to his father's disgust.'

The legend was further embellished in the schools with credit being given to the mythical parson for the change from 'Larsen' to 'Lawson'. When Louisa registered his birth at the town of Forbes on July 22 his name was simply entered as 'Henry Lawson'. Later she added 'Archibald' to the line in the Family Bible and Henry used it on occasion varying it to 'Hertzberg' as the mood took him.

The Grenfell diggings proving no different from other alluvial goldfields were soon washed out and by the end of the year Louisa, with her husband and family, was back at her father's shanty near which Peter built a two roomed hut in which the second son, Charles, was born in 1869. With her husband frequently absent for periods as a bush worker in the district she looked back to this lonely time with bitterness. It may have been to placate her that Peter next took up a selection of land for farming and built a cottage which was to be the family home. Today only the brick fireplace and chimney still stand and are the nucleus of Eurunderee's shrine to the memory of Henry Lawson.

Peter's choice of a most unlikely piece of farmland was said to have been based on the presence of what his son was later to describe as 'a little, stony, scrubby, useless ridge' which might have been auriferous. It wasn't and Peter, in 1871, was happy to leave it and join the goldrush to nearby Gulgong.

Barely four years old when this happened Henry conjured up an imaginative and exciting description of the move for his 'Fragment of Autobiography':

'We didn't seem to live in the new house any time before a tremendous thing happened.
We were in a cart with bedding and a goat, and a cat in a basket, and fowls in a box, and there were great trees all along, and teams with loads of bark and rafters, and tables upside down with bedding and things between the legs, and baskets and pots hanging around and gold-cradles, gold-dishes, windlass, bales and picks and shovels; and there were more drays and carts, and women and children, and goats—some tied behind the carts—and men on horses and men walking. All the world was shifting as fast as it ever could.'

The excitement did not end there. The next couple of years were highwater marks in the lore of the family. Peter for once struck gold, Louisa's venture as a dressmaker paid off, there was a trip to Sydney and a Christmas with money to spend—they were in truth 'The Roaring Days' and Lawson built the family tales into his own store of experiences and, in the fullness of time, graphically drew on them for inspiration.

But Gulgong failed. For Peter and Louisa the return to Eurunderee was something of an anti-climax. Louisa, expecting her third child, Peter, born in 1873, was once again in the original hut. Peter had overlooked the legal complexities of property ownership and was some time regaining possession of the cottage on the selection. Louisa sought refuge in a nervous breakdown.

Louisa's discontent, fed by the failure of her marriage to take her out of the monotony of small-town bush life, had made her difficult to live with and the continuous domestic quarrels had a marked effect on the sensitive Henry, in the period before his twin sisters were born. His story, 'A Child in the Dark—and a Foreign Father' first published in England, comes to mind and the reference to 'a foreign father' may have interesting implications as to Louisa's attitude towards her husband. It must be remembered, since we rely so heavily on Louisa and her family for background material, that her husband has had no one except Henry to state his case.

Local agitation, in which Peter and Louisa played an active part, resulted in a provisional school being opened at Eurunderee on October 2, 1876. Henry Lawson, already nine, was among the first students enrolled by John Tierney, the one teacher for the 45 pupils. 'The Old Bark School', as Lawson wrote of it, was replaced later by a permanent structure for which Peter had the building contract.

In the rather terse account of his schooldays, Henry saw himself as an object of pity, overcome with disappointment and frustration, looked askance at by other children as well as by his relatives. His youngest brother, Peter, recalled many years later that Henry at school was 'morose, somewhat irritable and characteristically unobservant...about the last Eurunderee urchin one would have nominated for future greatness'.

His apparent unsocial attitudes are consistent with the onset of his deafness, the symptoms of which became obvious when he was nine and at the very time he began his formal schooling. In his 'Fragment of Autobiography' he described his deafness as 'a thing which was to cloud my whole life, to drive me into myself and to be, perhaps, in a great measure responsible for my writing...I was fourteen when I became as deaf as I am now'. Within their limited means his parents sought, unavailingly, as he himself did in later life, the best medical treatment and advice.

His failure as a scholar was a more likely reason for Louisa's moving him from school to school in the district than her warring with the teachers on personal grounds. At the time she believed, as did Henry, that the fault lay with his teachers rather than in his deafness. The one subject that bought him any meed of praise was 'English composition' and his promise in this respect led to the District School Inspector, Charles Kevin, discussing literary matters with the boy and encouraging him to think of authorship as a career. Some of Louisa's obsession with literature and writing, which led to members of the family accusing her of neglecting her family duties, rubbed off on the children and it is to

Henry Lawson   A Crayon Portrait from Life by Reg Russom, August 1922.

her that credit must go for Henry's interest in Dickens, Marryat, Poe, Marcus Clarke, Bret Harte and Defoe by the time he was ready to leave school.

He was fourteen when his schooldays ended and he joined his father, now a full-time builder and contractor, whose work took him away from home for days or weeks at a time and Louisa's misgivings as she saw her son leave home for the first time, may be imagined.

In 1883 Louisa and Peter agreed that she should take the family and settle in Sydney and the Eurunderee property was let to a tenant. It is clear that the marriage had broken up but Peter Lawson was shown in the Street Directories as the nominal tenant of the houses in which Louisa lived before settling at 138 Phillip Street. Free at last, she lost no time in sending for Henry and it was from this house, not far from Circular Quay, that the impressionable youth walked to Redfern Station to take a train to Clyde where he was apprenticed to the carriage building firm of Hudson Bros. The dire poverty, distress and despair which he saw on all sides of the city and inner suburbs were not forgotten when he came to write the indignant 'Faces in the Street' and the pathetic 'Arvie Aspinall' stories. But these achievements were still in the future.

Ambitiously he attended night school in the hope of matriculating but the strain of working long hours and his poor grounding in mathematics and other subjects told against him. Nor did he complete his indentures with Hudson Bros. for not much time passed before he was employed by William Kerridge as a 'painter's improver' at thirty shillings ($3) per week.

Louisa had lost no time in becoming involved in the rabid political life of the city and her home was soon a hot-bed of Radicalism of all kinds. Her opening gambit had been the inauguration of a successful movement to provide a fitting memorial to Henry Kendall—a venture from which she was excluded when it was taken over at a social level. She did manage to buy the poet's original grave-site as well as the adjoining plot—the former to be her own last resting place.

The legend that her son, Henry, was a timid or simple youth when he first took his poems to the office of the *Bulletin* is hardly likely as at home he was already on speaking terms with one and another of its staff journalists, each proclaiming a panacea for social problems. Out of the dynamic and exciting ideas he chose as his creed that of revolutionary republicanism, a movement with tradition extending as far back as the First Fleet.

Lawson's youthful militancy was fired by the Republican Riots of 1887. At a public meeting convened by the Mayor of Sydney to consider 'feasting the school children . . . in honour of Queen Victoria's Jubilee' a resolution vetoing the proposal as 'unwise and calculated to injure the democratic spirit of the colony' was carried. The Mayor ignored such a display of disloyalty, closed the meeting, and called a further meeting for the following week—admission to be by ticket only.

Crowds converged on the Town Hall for the second meeting; some had official tickets, others had forged tickets, but the great majority had none. The doors opened at 7pm and within minutes there was not even standing room in the hall. The *Bulletin* reporter wrote:

'Then followed a scene hard to describe in language we permit ourselves to use . . . the room was tightly packed with men in whose faces the occupants of the platform could plainly read the elements of failure for their little game of snivel. One would suppose that with such men as Chief-Justice Darley, Lieutenant-Governor Stephen, Premier Parkes, Justice Manning and other of the station in the minority, the undoubted rights of the majority would have been readily recognized and respected ... The assembled citizens called loudly on Mr John Norton and Mr Frederic Jones to propose a resolution in opposition to the scheme which had already been considered and negatived, and if these gentlemen had been permitted to obey the calls of the meeting the business would have been over in a few minutes. But the *soi-disant* 'loyalists', the friends *par excellence* of what they are pleased to call law and order, who held possession of the platform, violently assaulted the speakers selected by the people, and roughly ejected them from the chamber!'

The *Sydney Morning Herald* took another view:

'... a successful attempt was made by a number of individuals to thwart the object of the gathering and to turn the proceedings into an absolute chaos of uproar, confusion, faction-fighting, and ruffianism of the most disgraceful and unprecedented character in the history of the colony ...

Premier Henry Parkes took the sting out of the radicals' victory by ordering the closure on Sunday nights of Sydney's theatres, a time when they were used as lecture halls and in some of which Lawson heard 'a host of Yankee free-thought and socialistic lecturers'. Despite protests, public meetings and a cable to the Queen from his opponents, Parkes did not withdraw his edict and Sydney Domain on Sunday afternoons became the safety valve of agitators. Lawson said that after the Republican Riots he 'had to write then or burst—the *Bulletin* saved me from bursting'.

In its issue of June 18, 1887, Lawson joined the army of writers who first saw themselves in print in the 'Answers to Correspondents' column in the *Bulletin*. To be noticed and have four lines of verse published with an encouraging comment from J. F. Archibald, its editor, was almost a short-cut to Parnassus. The anxious poet called and saw Archibald who informed him that his poem 'Sons of the South' was being held over for a special issue. On Eight Hour Day, 1887, it appeared, editorially re-titled 'A Song of the Republic', and a singularly important result of the Republic Riots.

A fortnight later the young poet saw his first published prose piece, 'Australian Loyalty Sentimental and Political' in the monthly *Republican,* with which he was to be closely associated as editor and nominal proprietor in 1888, shortly after a visit to Melbourne in 1887 seeking treatment for his deafness. His duties on the *Republican,* later the *Australian Nationalist,* included the actual printing. For some reason his four political articles were not included in his collected prose until recently.

In July 1888, on the appearance of 'Faces in the Street' in the *Bulletin* the emotional impact of the verses on the reading public brought him nation-wide fame in which he was to bask for the rest of his life. His acceptance as a short story writer came with 'His Father's Mate' in the Christmas issue of the *Bulletin,* an annual for which Archibald saved what he held to be the cream of the year's contributions. He spent part of his time assisting Louisa who was now editing and publishing *Dawn,* a suffragette newspaper, under the *nom de plume* of 'Dora Falconer'. It kept her busy for 17 years and except for a foreman, was entirely produced by women. But the successes of the year were dampened for Henry by the death on December 31 of his father with whom he had kept in close contact.

Lawson did not take the short story very seriously until the 1890s preferring to write verses for a number of papers besides the *Bulletin* and *Truth,* the latter then under the editorship of W. H. Traill one of the early proprietors of former.

Early in 1890 he met Mary Jane Cameron—later Dame Mary Gilmore—who after some years teaching in the country had been posted to Neutral Bay. Her mother, also a journalist, was friendly with Louisa and the way was easy for a close friendship to develop between the two young people.

Although he was already an established writer when they first met, she was in the vanguard of those who, in later years, asserted that they had been major contributors to the making of Lawson as an author. Not only, she claimed, had she tutored him in the minor mysteries of ballad writing and introduced him to the work of the great English poets, she had in fact come to an agreement with him that since there was such a similarity between their respective points of view and writing styles that there was no room for both of them in the pages of the *Bulletin* she would leave the field to him—an immeasurable sacrifice, surely!

It is only fair to add that she did become a poet of importance in time and her friendship with Lawson, which lasted until his death, was sincere. Whether or not she would have married him in 1890, and there is such a legend, I recall an afternoon in 1944 when the talk having turned on Lawson, she said with great emotion, 'My poor, *poor* Henry Lawson' and paused to look wistfully across half a century of spent years to the time when she had first met him.

Whether Louisa was concerned at the possible outcome of the romance, or at her son's growing problem with alcohol, for which she blamed some of his friends, she somewhat drastically shipped him and his brother Peter to Western Australia in search of employment. Five months of battling in the West, with little to show for it except some journalism for the *Albany Observer*, which would have yielded little if any money, was enough for Henry and he returned to Sydney and intermittent work as a builder's labourer.

The 1890s were ten long and bitter years in Australia. The spacious vision of the 1880s had begun to narrow. Confrontations between Capital and Labour took place with dire results for the apostles of Revolution. The unexpected and sudden emergence of the Labor Party as a force, almost before it was ready for such responsibility, raised the hopes of many radicals that political and constitutional action were a way to social justice, and Lawson was among those who hymned the Millenium. He no longer dreamed of heroically mounting the barricades but saw mateship in their stead. The pamphleteers and the politicians turned to the wordy crusade for Federation, their victory tempered to some extent by the outbreak of the Boer War and Australia's readiness to participate, a sentiment which Lawson and his friends did not share.

Lawson wrote his way into the 1890s as a social commentator in verse, always on the attack, and aware of the impact his words had on his readers and on the editors of country and other papers who reprinted his verses with an acknowledgement to the author as the only reward. As a man with a message, as the people's poet, this was enough. After all, if the initial payment for verse was 'a-penny-a-line' (almost one cent) and never much more, what was a reprint worth?

He was also one of a number of writers churning out work for a penny a line, always hopeful of a permanent position as an editor or journalist on one of the established newspapers or periodicals. He had begun writing for William Lane's Queensland *Worker* and the *Boomerang*, a Brisbane weekly on which in 1891 he was offered and accepted his first full-time journalistic post.

Niels Hertzberg Larsen ('Peter Lawson'), Henry's father, from a photograph taken in 1867, a year after his marriage.

From all accounts Peter Lawson seems to have been an easy going, reasonably well educated ship's mate, with a good family background, who having tried his luck on the gold fields in the 1850s, liked what he saw of Australia and remained to become a bush carpenter and builder. He died at Mount Victoria, NSW, on New Year's Eve, 1888, a few days after the appearance of his son's first published short story 'His Father's Mate' in the *Bulletin*.

Gresley Lukin, the versatile editor was a friend of Louisa—she seemed forever in the background of her wayward son's movements.

He versified, briefly, news from the outback in a column headed 'Country Crumbs', for which he was paid two pounds ($4) per week. Despite Lukin's courage and ability the economic stringency of the period led to Lawson's retrenchment and the ultimate end of what he recalled as 'the fighting, dying *Boomerang*'. Among those whom Lukin had employed at the same time as Lawson was a compositor from Gympie, A. G. Stephens, whose critical acumen as literary editor of the *Bulletin's* 'Red Page' in later years profoundly influenced local writers who feared, as much as they came to appreciate, his judgement.

Lawson, dispirited and downcast, once more unemployed, for a time drifted hopelessly round Sydney, but the strange, charismatic attraction he had for his friends and fellow writers led E. J. Brady to have Archibald induce Lawson to go to Bourke, a railhead town over 500 miles from Sydney, to comment on local conditions. It was a scheme to get him away from his drinking mates.

Here he met up with the unionism of the shearers and bush workers, saw their creed of mateship in practice, and nationalized it so that men came to believe in it as something wholly Australian, which like his best prose and verse could have been inspired nowhere else in the world. The shattering experience of his walk from Bourke to Hungerford in search of work in the searing heat of the drought years of 1892-3 strengthened his faith in mateship as an essential factor in the struggle of men against their environment. Those who have at times belittled Lawson as a bogus bushman should remember that he spent most of his first twenty years in various parts of the country.

A short spell in Sydney was followed by a period in New Zealand where he worked in the bush as a telegraph linesman. This ended suddenly with an offer as editor of a new Labor Party paper about to begin in Sydney. Back on the first available boat, he arrived two days before it ceased publication. Fortune was never with him. An appointment as provisional editor of the *Worker* at Sydney lasted one month although he was retained as an exclusive contributor at twelve shillings and sixpence ($1.25) a prose column and the usual penny-a-line for verse. It was truly a time when if you didn't work you didn't eat. [Fifty years later freelance rates were little better on quite prestigious papers —in 1955 a sonnet returned the hopeful poet exactly half a guinea ($1.05).]

Lawson never lost sight of himself as a professional author and waited for the day when a published volume of his work would be in the bookshops alongside those already published for some of his friends.

Again Louisa rose to the occasion—for probably the last time. From her own press, at the office of the *Dawn,* still a female sanctuary, she published *Short Stories in Prose and Verse Henry Lawson Price One Shilling.* An unpretentious little book, Henry himself referred to it as no more than a pamphlet, scarcely to be called a volume, it ranks today high on the priorities of Australian book-collectors. Whether or not he did, in fact, suppress it, as he claimed later in brushing it aside, it is now scarce, even rare. This may be accounted for by its inherently physical shortcomings. Despite everything, it takes its place in Australian literature as surely as Poe's *Tamerlane* in America and Coleridge and Wordworth's *Lyrical Ballads 1798* in the English context. This is not to be construed as setting Lawson up as an Australian Poe or Wordsworth, but simply that it had a catalytic effect on contemporary literature. On this very point he used the preface to *Short Stories in Prose and Verse* as a personal, if not a national manifesto, still with some relevance:

'THIS is an attempt to publish, in Australia, a collection of sketches and stories at a time when everything Australian, in the shape of a book, must bear the imprint of a London publishing firm before our critics will condescend to notice it, and before the 'reading public' will think it worth its while to buy nearly so many copies as will pay for the mere cost of printing a presentable volume.

The Australian writer, until he gets a 'London hearing', is only accepted as an imitator of some recognized English or American author; and, so soon as he shows signs of coming to the front, he is labelled 'The Australian Southey', 'The Australian Burns', or 'The Australian Bret Harte', and lately, 'The Australian Kipling'. Thus, no matter how original he may be, he is branded, at the very start, as a plagiarist, and by his own country, which thinks, no doubt, that it is paying him a compliment and encouraging him, while it is really doing him a cruel and an almost irreparable injury.

But, mark! So soon as the Southern writer goes 'home' and gets some recognition in England, he is 'So-and-So, the well-known Australian author whose work has attracted so much attention in London lately'; and we first hear of him by cable, even though he might have been writing at his best for ten years in Australia.

The same paltry spirit tried to dispose of the greatest of modern short story writers as 'The Californian Dickens', but America wasn't built that way—neither was Bret Harte!

To illustrate the above growl: a Sydney daily paper, reviewing the *Bulletin's Golden Shanty* when the first edition came out, said of my story, 'His Father's Mate', that it stood out distinctly as an excellent specimen of that kind of writing which Bret Harte set the world imitating in vain, and, being 'full of local colour, it was no unworthy copy of the great master'. That critic evidently hadn't studied the 'great master' any more than he did my yarn, or Australian goldfield life.

Then he spoke of another story as also having the 'Californian flavor'. For the other writers I can say that I feel sure they could point out their scenery, and name, or, in some cases, introduce 'the reader' to their characters in the flesh. The first seventeen years of my life were spent on the goldfields, and, therefore, I didn't need to go back, in imagination, to a time before I was born, and to a country I had never seen, for literary material.'

Every freelance author's dream of publication between the covers of a book was realized for Lawson when in 1895 he signed a contract with Angus & Robertson, then a rapidly expanding firm of publishers and booksellers, to provide them with the copy not for one volume, but for two—*In the Days When the World was Wide* and *While the Billy Boils*. It was the beginning of a love-hate relationship which was possibly unique in Australian literary annals relating to author and publisher. On the one hand was George Robertson, Scot and canny, with an implicit faith in the future of the literature of his adopted country and on the other Henry Lawson, completely devoid of a knowledge of the financial side of publishing and, in fact, irresponsible in money matters. Many stories are told, and some have been written, of the happenings, which Lawson was to satirize (with nostalgic overtones) in his long poem, posthumously published in 1923, as *The Auld Shop and the New*. It was to George Robertson that Lawson turned for help when in his deepest trouble, and he never knew how far indebted he was to 'G.R.' or 'the Chief' for financial help which found no place on Lawson's ledger sheet in the Angus & Robertson files.

The preparation and editing of the prose and verse for his two books imposed a heavy strain on Lawson. He did not take kindly to the textual changes proposed by George Robertson and his staff but it was a publishing experience that was to be frequently repeated, and as frequently resented. This is borne out in part in *Henry Lawson Letters* which has been edited by Professor Roderick and published by Angus & Robertson (1970).

About this time he met Bertha Bredt, a trainee nurse on a visit to her mother, who after her first husband's death had married W. H. T. McNamara, bookseller, publisher and arch-radical whose shop in Castlereagh Street has been referred to as 'the cradle of the Labor Party'. Bertha McNamara, his future mother-in-law, born Bertha Kalkstein in Germany, was a pioneer in the Australian suffragette movement, as active in politics as her husband, and to whom there is a memorial plaque in Sydney's Trades Hall. A personality in her own right, she counted as friends and customers at her shop many who later became political leaders, among them W. M. Hughes and W. A. Holman. And in the year that Lawson and young Bertha Bredt met, a future Premier of New South Wales, John Thomas Lang, married her sister, Hilda Bredt.

In the Days When the World was Wide was acclaimed by the critics and the public on publication in February, 1896 and Lawson, for once optimistic about his future, married Bertha in April against the well-founded and well-meaning advice of their friends, including George Robertson.

The pattern of Lawson's life was now becoming predictable. Any deep emotional upset stirred his latent restlessness into making a fresh start in another place, but the 'place' was always one that he had previously visited. Within a few weeks of marriage he and his wife were in Western Australia. A few months were enough and the inevitable return to Sydney was followed by a year in New Zealand where Bertha spent some time teaching at a Maori school at Maungamanu. It was during this period that he began the 'Joe Wilson' stories which he hoped to work on and publish as a novel. In *My Henry Lawson* (1943), Bertha's discreet account of their lives together—not factually reliable—leaves the reader with the impression that Henry was relying or leaning on Bertha as much as he had leant on his mother. Her various stratagems to keep him from going into Kaikoura paid off, but the loneliness and the imminent birth of their first child, Jim, hastened a return to the city of Wellington.

Bland Holt, a prominent theatrical producer and actor, who had known Lawson in Australia met him there and commissioned him to write a play, which was unplayable, and since it has never been published, is probably unreadable but Holt paid up and Lawson, Bertha and their month-old son were back in Sydney in March 1898.

A sinecure in the New South Wales Government Statistician's office, at three pounds and ten shillings ($7) per week, with freedom to write at the office, lasted only a few weeks and Lawson, drinking heavily, was by the end of the year to have treatment at a home for inebriates.

In January 1899 his bitter article, 'Pursuing Literature in Australia', was published in the *Bulletin*. The nationalistic strain so noticeable in the preface to *Short Stories in Prose and Verse* had given way to desperation engendered by a sense of failure, for which he accepted none of the blame but passed it on to publishers, whether of books, journals or newspapers. In the concluding paragraph, he urged any young Australian writer 'to go steerage, stow away, swim, and seek London, Yankeeland or Timbuctoo rather than stay in Australia till his genius has turned to gall or beer . . .'. Lawson's plaintive story of his meagre returns from writing took no account of his own lack of business acumen, nor of the way in which he traded his copyright in his books, nor of the generosity of Robertson and the *Bulletin*.

Professor Walter Murdoch, a leading essayist and critic, who championed Lawson's work and remembered the pleasurable excitement of his fellow students at the University of Western Australia whenever a new story by him appeared.

James R. Tyrrell, Sydney bookseller and publisher, had a fund of stories about Henry Lawson, a number of which he published in various books and journals. He is here looking at Low's famous cartoon of Lawson which he published, having had it printed by E. H. Shea at the Sunnybrook Press.

James Vance Marshall, to whose book *Jail from Within,* Henry Lawson contributed a preface in 1919, writing it with a sense of fellow-feeling for the young radical who had served a gaol sentence during the Conscription Campaigns of the World War I period, 'for having made utterances likely to cause disaffection to His Majesty the King.' A second sentence was served for 'having made a speech likely to prejudice recruiting'.

Jail from Within was followed by *The World of the Living Dead* and created a mild sensation by drawing attention to the treatment of gaol inmates, and set Marshall on the way to writing as part of a busy career, mainly spent in England.

In what was a long preface for him, Lawson wrote, *inter alia,* 'Vance Marshall also asked me to give some detail concerning the composing "One Hundred and Three" in gaol. There was no "composing"; the idea, and the body of it came in very short time — probably in one night, as a thing of its kind might come to any writer in a state of high mental tension.

'The jotting down of what I call "key lines", or notes of the subject matter of the verses (for we are not allowed pen and ink or pencils — or even lady typistes in our cells) and the smuggling out of these notes is a matter which, for obvious reasons, I cannot dwell upon.'

The wide controversy following the article was mild compared with the reaction that came after his announcement later in the year that he was going to follow his own advice and seek wider fame and fortune in London.

Consciously or subconsciously, Lawson's mind was made up for him by a number of factors. Bertha was becoming heartily tired of the life she had led since marriage, with its continuous uncertainty and unhappiness. Generous reviews of his books in the English press had led to some promising correspondence with publishers of the standing of William Blackwood, and an offer from the editor of *Chambers Journal.* The comparison with Kipling in reviews was seen as praise of a high order and no longer mere patronage. Nor did he interpret as patronage the financial help of his publisher, George Robertson, the wealthy book collector, David Scott Mitchell (already negotiating the gift of his Library to the people of New South Wales) and the bohemian-minded State Governor, Earl Beauchamp, whose involvement with such people as poets and authors caused eyebrows to rise as high as they did when as a newly arrived, brash, young Viceroy he referred to the 'birthstains' of a Colony which many people were then anxious to forget.

In April 1900 Henry and Bertha, now with two children—the baby, Bertha, being two months old—sailed for London in the *Damascus.* In Melbourne Lawson sat for the fine portrait by John Longstaff, commissioned by the Trustees of the National Art Gallery of New South Wales. On board ship Lawson continued to drink heavily and Bertha's misgivings on first hearing of Henry's plan to go to England were confirmed. After arriving in England, and with his affairs in the hands of J. B. Pinker, a leading English literary agent, he appeared to prosper. Contracts for books were arranged with William Blackwood and the short stories he had saved for the English market were sold at good prices. But it was not long before he began seeking further advances against royalties or speedy payment on acceptance for stories and articles. His Australian way of life had carried over to England and the letters which passed between Pinker and Lawson's publishers indicate their concern for the author and his wife and young family. Problems arising from insecurity, added to Henry's alcoholic retreat from reality, broke Bertha's nerve. She spent months in hospital recovering and alarming reports of Lawson's behaviour reached Australia.

Mary Gilmore, with her husband William, whom she had married in Paraguay, and an infant son, called on the hapless Lawsons in London whilst on the way home following the demoralising failure of the New Australia movement. Here she met Louisa for the first time and it did not take her long to prevail upon Henry to allow Bertha and the children to return with her to Australia. To raise the fares he fell back on the usual expedient of mortgaging his future. He contracted with Blackwood for another book and was to follow as soon as he had completed some publishing business in London with Methuen's.

Lawson's imminent return to Australia was announced in the *Bulletin* in a typical piece of his public relations writing (although they didn't call it that in those days):

'...Have been wonderfully successful from a literary point of view—work in Blackwood's, Cassell's, Chambers's, etc.—and offers from most of the publishers—but my health has completely broken down and I must come home for a year or so. Some of my stories are being translated into German. I know London as well as the Bush and propose to write of London for Australian papers, of Australia for the London papers.'

How green always were the hills that Lawson saw in the distance.

Among his achievements in England there has to be counted the launching of Miles Franklin as an author. With her permission, and possibly at her request, he had taken the script of her first novel *My Brilliant Career* to London, hoping to find a publisher for it. Neither J. B. Pinker nor William Blackwood were enthusiastic about it but Blackwood agreed to publish it on condition that Lawson contribute a preface, which he finally did. In 1901 the book was published and A. G. Stephens reviewed it very favourably in the *Bulletin*.

Lawson was to write bitterly in later years of 'the run to London that wrecked and ruined me'. He might, as justifiably, have written those words of the return voyage. Bertha and the children, together with the Gilmores, had embarked on the *Karlsruhe* at Antwerp and Lawson followed a fortnight later in her sister-ship, the *Gera*. Damaged in an accident near Suez, the *Karlsruhe* reached Colombo four days after the *Gera* and Lawson was waiting to join his family there, a transfer having been arranged with the shipping company.

Whatever happened between the Lawsons and the Gilmores on board ship from Colombo to Adelaide, personal relationships had reached breaking point, or worse. Lawson left the ship at Adelaide and went by train to Melbourne, alone.

At this point the story of Hannah Thornburn weaves its way into the legendary fabric of Lawson's life. How intimate or deep their attachment to each other was—they had met about 1898—Hannah Thornburn was to join the 'loves' that Lawson was to incorporate into his stories and verses. In an exhaustive editorial note to the poem 'Hannah Thornburn' in *Henry Lawson Collected Verse,* Vol 2 (Angus & Robertson 1968), Professor Colin Roderick points out that she was the daughter of a Sydney bookseller, that she had been a friend of Lawson's, and that she had suffered a tragic death.

He adds a long and careful transcript of a letter by Mary Gilmore to George Robertson, written in 1924, detailing much of the legend. There are, too, some curious implications in that she insists that a copy of the original must be given to her son Billy: '....Some day an evil mind may assail his mother's name, and he, for want of documents, not be in a position to have a suitable reply made.' There is the circumstantial and melodramatic account of Hannah Thornburn's death, 'His name was the last word said.'

Whatever the real reason was for Lawson's haste to get to Melbourne before Bertha, two accounts are given. Was one, as the Lawson family believe, that he was hoping to enlist the aid of relatives in effecting a reconciliation between himself and his wife? Or was it, as Mary Gilmore would have had us think, that he was hoping to see Hannah Thornburn who was seriously ill?

The unfortunate Hannah had died in Melbourne about six weeks before Henry's alleged mad dash to be at her bedside. It is doubtful if he ever knew she had been in Melbourne and the sad circumstances of her death are hardly indicative of a deep and undying faithfulness to the absent Henry—indeed, one of his friends, unnamed, is suggested as having been responsible for her condition. The whole sorry episode surrounding Hannah Thornburn became for Lawson the great love of the dream world to which he so often escaped, the love that might have been, the 'Spirit Girl' whom he incorporated into some of his writing. And the tale of it loses nothing in the telling by Mary Gilmore.

Lawson at Leeton, 1917.

In August 1922 Lawson made his last round of the places he knew so well in North Sydney and McMahon's Point. He was accompanied by Mr Reg Russom, Head of the Art Department at Newcastle Technical College, who took a number of photographs of the writer, which he used as basis for two crayon sketches, one of which is reproduced in this book. This one, taken at the farrier's shop in Blues Point Road, McMahon's Point, on the way up from the ferry wharf, can scarcely be called 'happy'.

Lawson's work has been internationally known for many years as is indicated by the above titles in Hebrew, Russian and Roumanian. Some of these editions are printed in runs of 250,000 copies. French, German, Indian and South American editions are also in print.

Lawson's optimism as expressed in the letter to the *Bulletin* evaporated on his return to Sydney. Within a few months Bertha and he were judicially separated. No matter how low he had fallen, she and the family had given him some sense of responsibility. Now, with that gone, he drifted aimlessly. His mother, whose ambition for him and pride in his early achievements had been justified, had come to the point of bitterly disowning him.

It must be admitted that by 1904, not yet forty, Lawson's best years were behind him. He was left only with the dreams of the man he might have been. He could add to his grudge against Fate, Bertha's final decision to be rid of him, as well as the personal affront he undoubtedly suffered each time she had him gaoled for non-compliance with the alimony agreement made at the time of the judicial separation. Her actions in this respect set in train years of fierce partisanship in Australia's literary world, which only objective judgement in time will resolve.

Lawson, now more hopeless and helpless than ever, drinking heavily, drifted around Sydney and the inner suburbs living as best he could. He was in a sorry plight when Mrs Isabel Byers, an elderly widow, shocked at his pathetic and destitute circumstances, took him to live at her home in North Sydney. It was an association that was to continue for the best part of the next twenty years.

At its beginning Mrs Byers had owned some property which she sold to help maintain herself and Lawson, but it was not long before she was in want. Helped surreptitiously by friends she devotedly maintained a home to which he returned from the frequent, but voluntary, periods of treatment for inebriety or from the involuntary spells in Darlinghurst gaol. She was waiting, too, when he returned from occasional holidays in the country which had been arranged for him by his mates. Lawson was not ungrateful and as early as September 3, 1905, he made a will leaving her 'all my papers and effects to keep and do with what she likes'.

Sister A. de V. MacCallum, sister-in-charge of the Mental Hospital at Darlinghurst, 1908-1922, where Lawson frequently sought 'drying out' treatment, was kind and patient with him, and more than sympathetic towards Mrs Byers. In a letter to Professor Roderick, published in *The Later Life of Henry Lawson* (Wentworth Press, 1961), she wrote:

'She was the most faithful and devoted of all Lawson's friends—though perhaps the least spectacular; and any account of his association with the Mental Hospital would be incomplete without some record, however inadequate, of her unfailing loyalty through all the years I knew them both; a time that held more disappointment than success for him and much suffering and sacrifice for her, especially those last sad years of which I can never think without pain. She was a tiny creature, and in all the time I knew her I always seem to remember her wearing the same shabby little snuff-coloured dress, and always reminded me of a little brown bird—a mother wren—as she fluttered, brisk and alert up the garden to the Hospital, or perched on the edge of a chair in my office chirping happily of some new and wonderful plan for Henry, or of some recognition he had received, or fluffing up her plumage in indignation at some criticism or slight. When I think of her and Lawson I am reminded of Alice Meynell and Francis Thompson, though her devotion was far greater and far less rewarded... I must confess that on more than one occasion, one of the reasons for keeping Lawson at the Hospital despite his outrageous behaviour and flagrant breaking of rules, was to make things temporarily easier for the Little Brown Bird. I really loved her and I am sure that Lawson loved her too, though he caused her so much anguish of spirit: he often spoke of her as 'The Little Mother'.'

By 1906 dissipation had begun to take its toll not only of him but of his writing, and work of any lasting importance only occasionally appeared. Much of his work had been better lost and not given the permanence of print in minor journals and newspapers, the respective editors of which showed little discernment so long as they could blithely announce him as a contributor.

Brian Matthews aptly entitled his analytical study of these years of Lawson's life as those of *The Receding Wave* (1972, M.U.P.), a title taken from a poem by W. B. Yeats, referring to the 'last great song' returning no more. So it was with Lawson. Save for an occasional flicker in poems such as 'One-hundred-and-three', based on his prison experiences, and 'My Army, O My Army', the fire had burned low. To his friends and to anyone who might listen he poured forth his personal troubles and in one telling cartoon he is depicted as 'the picture of Misery'. The single-minded firebrand of the 1890s and earlier had given way, not to the mellowness of age, but to a confused and disgruntled misanthropy.

The outbreak of World War I stirred the Australian people as nothing before had done. For Lawson it halted the ebbing of the tide of inspiration, but briefly. At beginning he both praised and denigrated the war, but as the years went by he was pleading in verse for Conscription, even before it was a national issue. For many this was outright and unforgivable apostasy; his friends, more in sorrow than in anger, could do no more than gently chide him.

In 1916, following an appeal to the Premier, W. A. Holman, by a group of his friends, Lawson agreed to go to Yanco in the Murrumbidgee Irrigation Area where the sale of liquor was, at the time, prohibited. Provided with a small literary grant and a rent-free cottage he was to act as a publicity man for the Area. Mrs Byers accompanied him as housekeeper and after the first few months there was a marked improvement in both his health and literary output. Besides writing stories and poems he spent much time in revising verses for a volume of *Selected Poems,* finally published in 1918 with an Introduction by David McKee Wright, in which he was hailed as 'the first articulate voice of the real Australia'.

Lawson's concern at the editorial emendations to his work, referred to earlier, is well in evidence in his correspondence with Robertson during the preparation of this book for publication. He did however agree to a number of changes so that in this present volume, readers will perhaps see lines that they do not recall in the versions they once memorized. In the exhaustive edition of Lawson's *Collected Verse* prepared by Colin Roderick (1967-70, Angus & Robertson) textual variants are carefully listed. Lawson himself was responsible for some, editors and printers for others.

His appointment at Leeton was terminated during an unauthorized trip to Sydney and on his return his improved health failed for the usual reasons. A steady decline culminated three years later in a cerebral haemorrhage. Whilst recuperating he was cheered by the wide public interest in his health —particularly on the part of school children.

His mother's death in 1920 moved him to a few indifferent lines to her memory. Louisa, her wish ignored or forgotten, was buried at Rookwood Cemetery near Sydney, and not in her chosen plot at Waverley.

Lawson's health deteriorated rapidly in the next couple of years and on the night of September 2, 1922, he died suddenly at Abbotsford—a Sydney suburb—aged 55. On the table at which he had been working was an unfinished story intended for the monthly journal, *Aussie,* edited by his friend, Phil Harris.

When the news broke in the press that 'the People's Poet' was dead, a nation mourned. The Prime Minister, William Morris Hughes, joined in the flood of tributes and at the end of a panegyric said: 'The Commonwealth decrees him a public funeral, and in the name of Australia, I invite all to pay him their last respects.'

During the religious ceremony at St. Andrews' Anglican Cathedral, Bertha, as chief mourner, beckoned Mrs Byers from the public pews to sit by her— a proper tribute to Henry's staunchest friend. Crowds lined the streets to see the pomp and ceremony of what was the first Commonwealth ordained funeral for a local author. Henry's wish, expressed many years before, that his country should 'shout' him the price of a brass band at his funeral was granted.

At Waverley Cemetery Henry Lawson was buried in one of the plots bought by his mother—but not in Kendall's erstwhile grave as was reported with solemn melodrama in at least one of Sydney's newspapers.

Bertha survived him for many years and lived long enough to see and take part in many lasting tributes paid to his memory and to know that he was assured of immortality as a poet, short story writer, journalist and patriot. She died in July, 1957, and her ashes were mingled with the soil on his grave by members of her family at a private ceremony.

Lawson belongs to the select band of authors who did not have to be rescued from obscurity by scholars and critics, although their abiding interest and, sometimes bewilderment, has followed in the wake of generations of readers who continue to read him for the simple pleasure it gives them. To write one's way into the hearts and minds of a people is given to few authors— Lawson is one of them.

Walter Stone

HIS FATHER'S MATE

Lawson's first published short story, it appeared in the *Bulletin's* Christmas Number, December 22, 1888. Reprinted in 'A Golden Shanty' (1890), the *Bulletin* anthology, compiled by J. F. Archibald and comprising literary contributions that he considered 'of more than ephemeral merit'.

It was Golden Gully still, but golden in name only, unless indeed the yellow mullock heaps or the bloom of the wattle-trees on the hillside gave it a claim to the title. But the gold was gone from the gully, and the diggers were gone, too, after the manner of Timon's friends when his wealth deserted him. Golden Gully was a dreary place, dreary even for an abandoned goldfield. The poor, tortured earth, with its wounds all bare, seemed to make a mute appeal to the surrounding bush to come up and hide it, and, as if in answer to its appeal, the shrub and saplings were beginning to close in from the foot of the range. The wilderness was reclaiming its own again.

The two dark, sullen hills that stood on each side were clothed from tip to hollow with dark scrub and scraggy box-trees; but above the highest row of shafts on one side ran a line of wattle-trees in full bloom.

The top of the western hill was shaped somewhat like a saddle, and standing high above the eucalypti on the point corresponding with the pommel were three tall pines. These lonely trees, seen for many miles around, had caught the yellow rays of many a setting sun long before the white man wandered over the ranges.

The predominant note of the scene was a painful sense of listening, that never seemed to lose its tension—a listening as though for the sounds of digger life, sounds that had gone and left a void that was accentuated by the signs of a former presence. The main army of diggers had long ago vanished to new rushes, leaving only its stragglers and deserters behind. These were men who were too poor to drag families about, men who were old and feeble, and men who had lost their faith in fortune. They had dropped unnoticed out of the ranks, and remained to scratch out a living among the abandoned claims. Golden Gully had its little community of fossickers who lived in a clearing called Spencer's Flat on one side and Pounding Flat on the other, but they lent no life to the scene; they only haunted it. A stranger might have thought the field entirely deserted until he came on a coat and a billy at the foot of saplings amongst the holes, and heard, in the shallow ground underneath, the thud of a pick, which told of some fossicker below rooting out what little wash remained.

One afternoon towards Christmas, a windlass was erected over an old shaft of considerable depth at the foot of the gully. A greenhide bucket attached to a rope on the windlass was lying next morning near the mouth of the shaft, and beside it, on a clear-swept patch, was a little mound of cool, wet wash-dirt.

A clump of saplings near at hand threw a shade over part of the mullock heap, and in this shade, seated on an old coat, was a small boy of eleven or twelve years, writing on a slate.

He had fair hair, blue eyes, and a thin old-fashioned face—a face that would scarcely alter as he grew to manhood. His costume consisted of a pair of moleskin trousers, a cotton shirt, and one suspender. He held the slate rigidly with a corner of its frame pressed close against his ribs, whilst his head hung to one side, so close to the slate that his straggling hair almost touched it. He was regarding his work fixedly out of the corners of his eyes, whilst he painfully copied down the head line, spelling it in a different way each time. In this laborious task he appeared to be greatly assisted by a tongue that lolled out of the corner of his mouth and made an occasional revolution round it, leaving a circle of temporarily clean face. His small clay-covered toes also entered into the spirit of the thing, and helped him not a little by their energetic wriggling. He paused occasionally to draw the back of his small brown arm across his mouth.

Little Isley Mason, or, as he was called, "His Father's Mate," had always been a favourite with the diggers and fossickers from the days when he used to slip out first thing in the morning and take a run across the frosty flat in his shirt. Long Bob Sawkins would often tell how Isley came home one morning from his run in the long, wet grass as naked as he was born, with the information that he had lost his shirt.

Later on, when most of the diggers had gone, and Isley's mother was dead, he was to be seen about the place with bare, sunbrowned arms and legs, a pick and shovel, and a gold dish about two-thirds of his height in diameter, with which he used to go "a-speckin'" and "fossickin'" amongst the old mullock heaps. Long Bob was Isley's special crony, and he would often go out of his way to lay the boy "onter bits o' wash and likely spots," lamely excusing his long yarns with the child with the explanation that it was "amusin' to draw Isley out."

Isley had been sitting writing for some time when a deep voice called out from below:

"Isley!"

"Yes, father."

"Send down the bucket."

"Right."

Isley put down his slate, and going to the shaft, dropped the bucket down as far as the slack rope reached; then, placing one hand on the bole of the windlass and holding the other against it underneath, he let it slip round between his palms until the bucket reached bottom. A sound of shovelling was heard for a few moments, and presently the voice cried, "Wind away, sonny."

"Thet ain't half enough," said the boy, peering down. "Don't be frightened to pile it in, father. I kin wind up a lot more'n thet."

A little more scraping, and the boy braced his feet well upon the little

32

mound of clay which he had raised under the handle of the windlass to make up for his deficiency in stature.

"Now then, Isley!"

Isley wound slowly but sturdily, and soon the bucket of "wash" appeared above the surface; then he took it in short lifts and deposited it with the rest of the wash-dirt.

"Isley!" called his father again.

"Yes, father."

"Have you done that writing lesson yet?"

"Very near."

"Then send down the slate next time for some sums."

"All right."

The boy resumed his seat, fixed the corner of the slate well into his ribs, humped his back, and commenced another wavering line.

Tom Mason was known on the place as a silent, hard worker. He was a man of about sixty, tall, and dark bearded. There was nothing uncommon about his face, except, perhaps, that it had hardened, as the face of a man might harden who had suffered a long succession of griefs and disappointments. He lived in a little hut under a peppermint-tree at the far edge of Pounding Flat. His wife had died there about six years before, and though new rushes broke out and he was well able to go, he never left Golden Gully.

Mason was kneeling in front of the "face" digging away by the light of a tallow candle stuck in the side. The floor of the drive was very wet, and his trousers were heavy and cold with clay and water; but the old digger was used to this sort of thing. His pick was not bringing out much today, however, for he seemed abstracted and would occasionally pause in his work, while his thoughts wandered far away from the narrow streak of wash-dirt in the "face."

He was digging out pictures from a past life. They were not pleasant ones, for his face was stony and white in the dim glow of the candle.

Thud, thud, thud—the blows became slower and more irregular as the fossicker's mind wandered off into the past. The sides of the drive seemed to vanish slowly away, and the "face" retreated far out beyond an horizon that was hazy in the glow of the southern ocean. He was standing on the deck of a ship and by his side stood a brother. They were sailing southward to the Land of Promise that was shining there in all its golden glory! The sails pressed forward in the bracing wind, and the clipper ship raced along with its burden of the wildest dreamers ever borne in a vessel's hull! Up over long blue ocean ridges, down into long blue ocean gullies; on to lands so new, and yet so old, where above the sunny glow of the southern skies blazed the shining names of Ballarat! and Bendigo! The deck seemed to lurch, and the fossicker fell forward against the "face" of the drive. The shock recalled him, and he lifted his pick once more.

But the blows slacken again as another vision rises before him. It is Ballarat now. He is working in a shallow claim at Eureka, his brother by his side. The brother looks pale and ill, for he has been up all night dancing and drinking. Out behind them is the line of the blue hills; in front is the famous Bakery Hill, and down to the left Golden Point. Two mounted troopers are riding up over Specimen Hill. What do they want?

They take the brother away, handcuffed. Manslaughter last night. Cause—drink and jealousy.

The vision is gone again. Thud, thud, goes the pick; it counts the years that follow—one, two, three, four, up to twenty, and then it stops for the next scene—a selection on the banks of a bright river in New South Wales. The little homestead is surrounded by vines and fruit-trees. Many swarms of bees work under the shade of the trees, and a crop of wheat is nearly ripe on the hillside.

A man and a boy are engaged in clearing a paddock just below the homestead. They are father and son; the son, a boy of about seventeen, is the image of his father.

Horses' feet again! Here comes Nemesis in mounted troopers' uniform.

The mail was stuck up last night about five miles away, and a refractory passenger shot. The son had been out "possum shooting" all night with some friends.

The troopers take the son away handcuffed: "Robbery under arms."

The father was taking out a stump when the troopers came. His foot is still resting on the spade, which is half driven home. He watches the troopers take the boy up to the house, and then, driving the spade to its full depth, he turns up another sod. The troopers reach the door of the homestead; but still he digs steadily, and does not seem to hear his wife's cry of despair. The troopers search the boy's room and bring out some clothing in two bundles; but still the father digs. They have saddled up one of the farm horses and made the boy mount. The father digs. They ride off along the ridge with the boy between them. The father never lifts his eyes; the hole widens round the stump; he digs away till the brave little wife comes and takes him gently by the arm. He half rouses himself and follows her to the house like an obedient dog.

Trial and disgrace follow, and then other misfortunes, pleuro among the cattle, drought, and poverty.

Thud, thud, thud again! But it is not the sound of the fossicker's pick—it is the fall of sods on his wife's coffin.

It is a little bush cemetery, and he stands stonily watching them fill up her grave. She died of a broken heart and shame. "I can't bear disgrace! I can't bear disgrace!" she had moaned all these six weary years—for the poor are often proud.

But *he* lives on, for it takes a lot to break a man's heart. He holds up his head and toils on for the sake of a child that is left, and that child is—Isley.

And now the fossicker seems to see a vision of the future. He seems to be standing somewhere, an old, old man, with a younger one at his side; the younger one has Isley's face. Horses' feet again! Ah, God! Nemesis once more in troopers' uniform!

The fossicker falls on his knees in the mud and clay at the bottom of the drive, and prays Heaven to take his last child ere Nemesis comes for him.

Long Bob Sawkins had been known on the diggings as "Bob the Devil." His profile, at least from one side, certainly did recall that of the sarcastic Mephistopheles; but the other side, like his true character, was by no means a devil's. His physiognomy had been much damaged, and one eye removed by the premature explosion of a blast in some old Ballarat mine. The blind eye was covered with a green patch, which gave a sardonic appearance to the remaining features.

He was a stupid, heavy, good-natured Englishman. He stuttered a little, and had a peculiar habit of wedging the monosyllable "why" into his conversation at times when it served no other purpose than to fill up the pauses caused by his stuttering; but this by no means assisted him in his speech, for he often stuttered over the "why" itself.

The sun was getting low down, and its yellow rays reached far up among the saplings of Golden Gully when Bob appeared coming down by the path that ran under the western hill. He was dressed in the usual costume—cotton shirt, moleskin trousers, faded hat and waistcoat, and blucher boots. He carried a pick over his shoulder, the handle of which was run through the heft of a short shovel that hung down behind, and he had a big dish under his arm. He paused opposite the shaft with the windlass, and hailed the boy in his usual form of salutation.

"Look, see here Isley!"

"What is it, Bob?"

"I seed a young—why—magpie up in the scrub, and yer oughter be able to catch it."

"Can't leave the shaft; father's b'low."

"How did yer father know there was any—why—wash in the old shaft?"

"Seed old Corney in town Saturday, 'n he said thur was enough to make it worth while bailin' out. Bin bailin' all the mornin'."

Bob came over, and letting his tools down with a clatter he hitched up the knees of his moleskins and sat down on one heel.

"What are yer—why—doin' on the slate, Isley?" said he, taking out an old clay pipe and lighting it.

"Sums," said Isley.

Bob puffed away at his pipe a moment.

"'Tain't no use!" he said, sitting down on the clay and drawing his knees up. "Edication's a failyer."

"Listen at 'im!" exclaimed the boy. "D'yer mean ter say it ain't no use learnin' readin' and writin' and sums?"

"Isley!"

"Right, father."

The boy went to the windlass and let the bucket down. Bob offered to help him wind up, but Isley, proud of showing his strength to his friend, insisted on winding by himself.

"You'll be—why—a strong man some day, Isley," said Bob, landing the bucket.

"Oh, I could wind up a lot more'n father puts in. Look how I greased the handles! It works like butter now," and the boy sent the handles spinning round with a jerk to illustrate his meaning.

"Why did they call yer Isley for?" queried Bob, as they resumed their seats. "It ain't yer real name, is it?"

"No, my name's Harry. A digger useter say I was a isle in the ocean to father 'n mother, 'n then I was nicknamed Isle, 'n then Isley."

"You hed a—why—brother once, didn't yer?"

"Yes, but thet was afore I was borned. He died, at least mother used ter say she didn't know if he was dead; but father says he's dead as fur's he's concerned."

"And your father hed a brother, too. Did yer ever—why—hear of him?"

"Yes, I heard father talkin' about it wonst to mother. I think father's brother got into some row in a bar where a man was killed."

"And was yer—why—father—why—fond of him?"

"I heard father say that he was wonst, but thet was all past."

Bob smoked in silence for a while, and seemed to look at some dark clouds that were drifting along like a funeral out in the west. Presently he said half aloud something that sounded like "All, all—why—past."

"Eh?" said Isley.

"Oh, it's—why, why—nothin'," answered Bob, rousing himself. "Is that a paper in yer father's coat-pocket, Isley?"

"Yes," said the boy, taking it out.

Bob took the paper and stared hard at it for a moment or so.

"There's something about the new goldfields there," said Bob, putting his finger on a tailor's advertisement. "I wish you'd—why—read it to me, Isley; I can't see the small print they uses nowadays."

"No, thet's not it," said the boy, taking the paper, "it's something about——"

"Isley!"

"'Old on, Bob, father wants me."

The boy ran to the shaft, rested his hands and forehead against the bole of the windlass, and leant over to hear what his father was saying.

Without a moment's warning the treacherous bole slipped round; a small body bounded a couple of times against the sides of the shaft and fell at Mason's feet, where it lay motionless!

"Mason!"

"Ay?"

"Put him in the bucket and lash him to the rope with your belt!"

A few moments, and——

"Now, Bob!"

Bob's trembling hands would scarcely grasp the handle, but he managed to wind somehow.

Presently the form of the child appeared, motionless, and covered with clay and water. Mason was climbing up by the steps in the side of the shaft.

Bob tenderly unlashed the boy and laid him under the saplings on the grass; then he wiped some of the clay and blood away from the child's forehead, and dashed over him some muddy water.

Presently Isley gave a gasp and opened his eyes.

"Are yer—why—hurt much, Isley?" asked Bob.

"Ba-back's bruk, Bob!"

"Not so bad as that, old man."

"Where's father?"

"Coming up."

Silence a while, and then—

"Father, father! be quick, father!"

36

Mason reached the surface and came and knelt by the other side of the boy.

"I'll, I'll—why—run fur some brandy," said Bob.

"No use, Bob," said Isley. "I'm all bruk up."

"Don't yer feel better, sonny?"

"No—I'm—goin' to—die, Bob."

"Don't say it, Isley," groaned Bob.

A short silence, and then the boy's body suddenly twisted with pain. But it was soon over. He lay still a while, and then said quietly:

"Good-bye, Bob!"

Bob made a vain attempt to speak. "Isley!" he said, "——"

The child turned and stretched out his hands to the silent, stony-faced man on the other side.

"Father—father, I'm goin'!"

A shuddering groan broke from Mason's lips, and then all was quiet.

Bob had taken off his hat to wipe his forehead, and his face, in spite of its disfigurement, was strangely like the face of the stone-like man opposite.

For a moment they looked at one another across the body of the child, and then Bob said quietly:

"He never knowed."

"What does it matter?" said Mason gruffly; and, taking up the dead child, he walked towards the hut.

It was a very sad little group that gathered outside Mason's hut next morning. Martin's wife had been there all the morning cleaning up and doing what she could. One of the women had torn up her husband's only white shirt for a shroud, and they had made the little body look clean and even beautiful in the wretched little hut.

One after another the fossickers took off their hats and entered, stooping through the low door. Mason sat silently at the foot of the bunk with his head supported by his hand, and watched the men with a strange abstracted air.

Bob had ransacked the camp in search of some boards for a coffin.

"It will be the last I'll be able to—why—do for him," he said.

At last he came to Mrs Martin in despair. That lady took him into the dining-room, and pointed to a large pine table, of which she was very proud.

"Knock that table to pieces," she said.

Taking off the few things that were lying on it, Bob turned it over and began to knock the top off.

When he had finished the coffin one of the fossicker's wives said it looked too bare, and she ripped up her black riding-skirt, and made Bob tack the cloth over the coffin.

There was only one vehicle available in the place, and that was Martin's old dray; so about two o'clock Pat Martin attached his old horse Dublin to the shafts with sundry bits of harness and plenty of old rope, and dragged Dublin, dray and all, across to Mason's hut.

The little coffin was carried out, and two gin-cases were placed by its side in the dray to serve as seats for Mrs Martin and Mrs Grimshaw, who mounted in tearful silence.

Pat Martin felt for his pipe, but remembered himself and mounted on the shaft. Mason fastened up the door of the hut with a padlock. A couple of blows on one of his sharp points roused Dublin from his reverie. With a lurch to the right and another to the left he started, and presently the little funeral disappeared down the road that led to the "town" and its cemetery.

About six months afterwards Bob Sawkins went on a short journey, and returned with a tall, bearded young man. He and Bob arrived after dark, and went straight to Mason's hut. there was a light inside, but when Bob knocked there was no answer.

"Go in; don't be afraid," he said to his companion.

The stranger pushed open the creaking door, and stood bareheaded just inside the doorway.

A billy was boiling unheeded on the fire. Mason sat at the table with his face buried in his arms.

"Father!"

There was no answer, but the flickering of the firelight made the stranger think he could detect an impatient shrug in Mason's shoulders.

For a moment the stranger paused irresolute, and then stepping up to the table he laid his hand on Mason's arm, and said gently:

"Father! Do you want another mate?"

But the sleeper did not—at least, not in this world.

FACES IN THE STREET

They lie, the men who tell us, for reasons of their own,
That want is here a stranger, and that misery's unknown;
For where the nearest suburb and the city proper meet
My window-sill is level with the faces in the street—
   Drifting past, drifting past,
    To the beat of weary feet—
While I sorrow for the owners of those faces in the street.

And cause I have to sorrow, in a land so young and fair,
To see upon those faces stamped the marks of Want and Care;
I look in vain for traces of the fresh and fair and sweet
In sallow, sunken faces that are drifting through the street—
   Drifting on, drifting on,
    To the scrape of restless feet;
I can sorrow for the owners of the faces in the street.

In hours before the dawning dims the starlight in the sky
The wan and weary faces first begin to trickle by,
Increasing as the moments hurry on with morning feet,
Till like a pallid river flow the faces in the street—
   Flowing in, flowing in,
    To the beat of hurried feet—
Ah! I sorrow for the owners of those faces in the street.

The human river dwindles when 'tis past the hour of eight,
Its waves go flowing faster in the fear of being late;
But slowly drag the moments, whilst beneath the dust and heat
The city grinds the owners of the faces in the street—
   Grinding body, grinding soul,
    Yielding scarce enough to eat—
Oh! I sorrow for the owners of the faces in the street.

Lawson's bitter denunciation of the poverty of the under-privileged took the Radical movement by storm. In its day, it assumed almost the status of a revolutionary verse anthem.

And then the only faces till the sun is sinking down
Are those of outside toilers and the idlers of the town,
Save here and there a face that seems a stranger in the street
Tells of the city's unemployed upon their weary beat—
　　　　　Drifting round, drifting round,
　　　　　To the tread of listless feet—
Ah! my heart aches for the owner of that sad face in the street.

And when the hours on lagging feet have slowly dragged away,
And sickly yellow gaslights rise to mock the going day,
Then, flowing past my window, like a tide in its retreat,
Again I see the pallid stream of faces in the street—
　　　　　Ebbing out, ebbing out,
　　　　　To the drag of tired feet,
While my heart is aching dumbly for the faces in the street.

And now all blurred and smirched with vice the day's sad end
　　　is seen,
For where the short "large hours" against the longer "small hours"
　　　lean,
With smiles that mock the wearer, and with words that half entreat,
Delilah pleads for custom at the corner of the street—
　　　　　Sinking down, sinking down,
　　　　　Battered wreck by tempests beat—
A dreadful, thankless trade is hers, that Woman of the Street.

But, ah! to dreader things than these our fair young city comes,
For in its heart are growing thick the filthy dens and slums,
Where human forms shall rot away in sties for swine unmeet
And ghostly faces shall be seen unfit for any street—
　　　　　Rotting out, rotting out,
　　　　　For the lack of air and meat—
In dens of vice and horror that are hidden from the street.

I wonder would the apathy of wealthy men endure
Were all their windows level with the faces of the Poor?
Ah! Mammon's slaves, your knees shall knock, your hearts in terror
    beat,
When God demands a reason for the sorrows of the street,
            The wrong things and the bad things
            And the sad things that we meet
In the filthy lane and alley, and the cruel, heartless street.

I left the dreadful corner where the steps are never still,
And sought another window overlooking gorge and hill;
But when the night came dreary with the driving rain and sleet,
They haunted me—the shadows of those faces in the street,
            Flitting by, flitting by,
            Flitting by with noiseless feet,
And with cheeks that scarce were paler than the real ones in
    the street.

Once I cried: "O God Almighty! if Thy might doth still endure,
Now show me in a vision for the wrongs of Earth a cure."
And, lo, with shops all shuttered I beheld a city's street,
And in the warning distance heard the tramp of many feet,
            Coming near, coming near,
            To a drum's dull distant beat—
'Twas Despair's conscripted army that was marching down the
    street!

Then, like a swollen river that has broken bank and wall,
The human flood came pouring with the red flags over all,
And kindled eyes all blazing bright with revolution's heat,
And flashing swords reflecting rigid faces in the street—
            Pouring on, pouring on,
            To a drum's loud threatening beat,
And the war-hymns and the cheering of the people in the street.

THE ARMY OF THE REAR

I listened through the music and the sounds of revelry,
And all the hollow noises of the year of Jubilee;
I heard behind the music and beyond the loyal cheer
The steady tramp of thousands who were marching in the rear.
       Tramp! tramp! tramp!
       They seemed to shake the air,
Those never-ceasing footsteps of the outcasts in the rear.

I hate the wrongs I read about, I hate the wrongs I see—
The tramping of that army sounds as music unto me!
A music that is terrible, that frights the anxious ear,
Is beaten from the weary feet slow-tramping in the rear.
       Tramp! tramp! tramp!
       In dogged, grim despair—
They have a goal, those footsteps of the Army of the Rear!

I looked upon the nobles, with their lineage so old,
I looked upon their mansions, on their acres and their gold,
I saw their women radiant in jewelled robes appear—
And then I joined the army of the outcasts in the rear.
       Tramp! tramp! tramp!
       We'll show what Want can dare,
My brothers and my sisters of the Army of the Rear!

I looked upon the mass of poor, in filthy alleys pent,
And on the rich men's Edens, that are built on grinding rent;
I looked o'er London's miles of slums—I saw the horrors here,
And swore to die a soldier of the Army of the Rear.
       Tramp! tramp! tramp!
       I've sworn to do and dare,
I've sworn to die a soldier of the Army of the Rear!

"They're brutes," so say the wealthy, "and by steel must be dis-
    mayed"—
Be there brutes among us, nobles, they are brutes that *ye* have
    made;
We want what God hath given us, we want our portion here.
And that is why we're marching—and we'll march beyond the rear!
            Tramp! tramp! tramp!
            Awake and have a care,
Ye proud and haughty spurners of the wretches in the rear.

We'll nurse our wrongs to strengthen us, our hate that it may grow,
For, outcast from society, society's our foe.
Beware! who grind out human flesh, for human life is dear!
There's menace in the marching of the Army of the Rear.
            Tramp! tramp! tramp!
            There's danger in despair,
There's danger in the marching of the Army of the Rear!

The wealthy care not for our wants, nor for the pangs we feel;
Our hands have clutched in vain for bread, and now they clutch
    for steel!
Come, men of rags and hunger, come! There's work for heroes here!
There's room still in the vanguard of the Army of the Rear!
            Tramp! tramp! tramp!
            O men of want and care!
There's glory in the vanguard of the Army of the Rear!

THE BLUE MOUNTAINS

Above the ashes straight and tall,
  Through ferns with moisture dripping,
I climb beneath the sandstone wall,
  My feet on mosses slipping.

Like ramparts round the valley's edge
  The tinted cliffs are standing,
With many a broken wall and ledge,
  And many a rocky landing.

And round about their rugged feet
  Deep ferny dells are hidden
In shadowed depths, whence dust and heat
  Are banished and forbidden.

The stream that, crooning to itself,
  Comes down a tireless rover,
Flows calmly to the rocky shelf,
  And there leaps bravely over.

Now pouring down, now lost in spray
  When mountain breezes sally,
The water strikes the rock midway,
  And leaps into the valley.

Now in the west the colours change,
  The blue with crimson blending;
Behind the far Dividing Range
  The sun is fast descending.

And mellowed day comes o'er the place,
  And softens ragged edges;
The rising moon's great placid face
  Looks gravely o'er the ledges.

PAYABLE GOLD

Among the crowds who left the Victorian side for New South Wales about the time Gulgong broke out was an old Ballarat digger named Peter McKenzie. He had married and retired from the mining some years previously and had made a home for himself and family at the village of St Kilda, near Melbourne; but as was often the case with old diggers, the gold fever never left him, and when the fields of New South Wales began to blaze he mortgaged his little property in order to raise funds for another campaign, leaving sufficient behind him to keep his wife and family in comfort for a year or so.

As he often remarked, his position was now very different from what it had been in the old days when he first arrived from Scotland, in the height of the excitement following on the great discovery. He was a young man then with only himself to look after, but now that he was getting old and had a family to provide for he had staked too much in this venture to lose. His position did certainly look like a forlorn hope, but he never seemed to think so.

Peter must have been very lonely and low-spirited at times. A young or unmarried man can form new ties, and even make new sweethearts if necessary, but Peter's heart was with his wife and little ones at home, and they were mortgaged, as it were, to Dame Fortune. Peter had to lift this mortgage off.

Nevertheless, he was always cheerful, even at the worst of times, and his straight grey beard and scrubby brown hair encircled a smile which appeared to be a fixture. He had to make an effort in order to look grave, such as some men do when they want to force a smile.

It was rumoured that Peter had made a vow never to return home until he could take sufficient wealth to make his all-important family comfortable, or, at least, to raise the mortgage from the property, for the sacrifice of which to his mad gold fever he never forgave himself. But this was one of the few things which Peter kept to himself.

The fact that he had a wife and children at St Kilda was well known to all the diggers. They had to know it, and if they did not know the age, complexion, history and peculiarities of every child and of the "old woman" it was not Peter's fault.

He would cross over to our place and talk to the mother for hours about his wife and children. And nothing pleased him better than to discover peculiarities in us children wherein we resembled his own. It pleased us also for mercenary reasons. "It's just the same with my old woman," or "It's just the same with my youngsters," Peter would exclaim boisterously, for he looked upon any little similarity between the two families as a remarkable coincidence. He liked us all, and was always very kind to us, often standing between our backs and the rod that spoils the child—that is, I mean, if it isn't used. I was very short-tempered, but this failing was more than condoned by the fact that Peter's "eldest" was given that way also. Mother's second son was very good-natured; so was Peter's third. Her "third" had a great aversion for any duty that threatened to increase his muscles; so had Peter's "second." Our baby was very fat and heavy and was given to sucking her own thumb vigorously, and, according to the latest bulletins from home, it was just the same with Peter's "last."

I think we knew more about Peter's family than we did about our own. Although we had never seen them, we were as familiar with their features as the photographer's art could make us, and always knew their domestic history up to the date of the last mail.

We became interested in the McKenzie family. Instead of getting bored by them as some people were, we were always as much pleased when Peter got a letter from home as he was himself, and if a mail were missed, which seldom happened—we almost shared his disappointment and anxiety. Should one of the youngsters be ill, we would be quite uneasy, on Peter's account, until the arrival of a later bulletin removed his anxiety, and ours.

It must have been the glorious power of a big true heart that gained for Peter the goodwill and sympathy of all who knew him.

Peter's smile had a peculiar fascination for us children. We would stand by his pointing forge when he'd be sharpening picks in the early morning, and watch his face for five minutes at a time, wondering sometimes whether he was always *smiling inside,* or whether the smile went on externally irrespective of any variation in Peter's condition of mind.

I think it was the latter case, for often when he had received bad news from home we have heard his voice quaver with anxiety, while the old smile played on his round, brown features just the same.

Little Nelse (one of those queer old-man children who seem to come into the world by mistake, and who seldom stay long) used to say that Peter "cried inside."

Once, on Gulgong, when he attended the funeral of an old Ballarat mate, a stranger who had been watching his face curiously remarked that McKenzie seemed as pleased as though the dead digger had bequeathed him a fortune. But the stranger had soon reason to alter his opinion, for when another old mate began in a tremulous voice to repeat the words "Ashes to ashes, an' dust to dust," two big tears suddenly burst from Peter's eyes, and hurried down to get entrapped in his beard.

Peter's goldmining ventures were not successful. He sank three duffers in succession on Gulgong, and the fourth shaft, after paying expenses, left a little over a hundred to each party, and Peter had to send the bulk of his share home. He lived in a tent (or in a hut when he could get one) after the manner of diggers, and he "did for himself," even to washing his own clothes. He never drank nor "played," and he took little enjoyment of any kind, yet there was not a digger on the field who would dream of calling old Peter McKenzie "a mean man." He lived, as we know from our own observations, in a most frugal manner. He always tried to hide this, and took care to have plenty of good things for us when he invited us to his hut; but children's eyes are sharp. Some said that Peter half-starved himself, but I don't think his family ever knew, unless he told them so afterwards.

Ah, well! the years go over. Peter was now three years from home, and he and Fortune were enemies still. Letters came by the mail, full of little home troubles and prayers for Peter's return, and letters went back by the mail, always hopeful, always cheerful. Peter never gave up. When everything else failed he would work by the day (a sad thing for a digger), and he was even known to do a job of fencing until such time as he could get a few pounds and a small party together to sink another shaft.

Talk about the heroic struggles of early explorers in a hostile country; but for dogged determination and courage in the face of poverty, illness, and distance, commend me to the old-time digger—the truest soldier Hope ever had!

In the fourth year of his struggle Peter met with a terrible disappointment. His party put down a shaft called the Forlorn Hope near Happy Valley, and after a few weeks' fruitless driving his mates jibbed on it. Peter had his own opinion about the ground—an old digger's opinion, and he used every argument in his power to induce his mates to put a few days' more work in the claim. In vain he pointed out that the quality of the wash and the dip of the bottom exactly resembled that of the "Brown Snake," a rich Victorian claim. In vain he argued that in the case of the above-mentioned claim, not a colour could be got until the payable gold was actually reached. Home Rule and The Canadian and that cluster of fields were going ahead, and his party were eager to shift. They remained obstinate, and at last, half-convinced against his opinion, Peter left with them to sink the "Iawatha," in Log Paddock, which turned out a rank duffer—not even paying its own expenses.

A party of Italians entered the old claim and, after driving it a few feet farther, made their fortune.

We all noticed the change in Peter McKenzie when he came to Log Paddock, whither we had shifted before him. The old smile still flickered, but he had learned to "look" grave for an hour at a time without much effort. He was never quite the same after the affair of Forlorn Hope, and I often think how he must have "cried" sometimes "inside."

However, he still read us letters from home, and came and smoked in the evening by our kitchen-fire. He showed us some new portraits of his family which he had received by a late mail, but something gave me the impression that the portraits made him uneasy. He had them in his possession for nearly a week before showing them to us, and to the best of our knowledge he never showed them to anybody else. Perhaps they reminded him of the flight of time—perhaps he would have preferred his children to remain just as he left them until he returned.

But stay! there was one portrait that seemed to give Peter infinite pleasure. It was the picture of a chubby infant of about three years or more. It was a fine-looking child taken in a sitting position on a cushion, and arrayed in a very short shirt. On its fat, soft, white face, which was only a few inches above the ten very podgy toes, was a smile something like Peter's. Peter was never tired of looking at and showing the picture of his child—the child he had never seen. Perhaps he cherished a wild dream of making his fortune and returning home before *that* child grew up.

McKenzie and party were sinking a shaft at the upper end of Log Paddock, generally called "the other end." We were at the lower end.

One day Peter came down from "the other end" and told us that his party expected to "bottom" during the following week, and if they got no encouragement from the wash they intended to go prospecting at the "Happy Thought," near Specimen Flat.

47

The shaft in Log Paddock was christened "Nil Desperandum." Towards the end of the week we heard that the wash in the "Nil" was showing good colours.

Later came the news that "McKenzie and party" had bottomed on payable gold, and the red flag floated over the shaft. Long before the first load of dirt reached the puddling machine on the creek, the news was all round the diggings. The "Nil Desperandum" was a "Golden Hole!"

We will not forget the day when Peter went home. He hurried down in the morning to have an hour or so with us before Cobb & Co. went by. He told us all about his little cottage by the bay at St Kilda. He had never spoken of it before, probably because of the mortgage. He told us how it faced the bay—how many rooms it had, how much flower garden, and how on a clear day he could see from the window all the ships that came up to the Yarra, and how with a good telescope he could even distinguish the faces of the passengers on the big ocean liners.

And then, when the mother's back was turned, he hustled us children round the corner, and surreptitiously slipped a sovereign into each of our dirty hands, making great pantomimic show for silence, for the mother was very independent.

And when we saw the last of Peter's face setting like a good-humoured sun on the top of Cobb & Co.'s, a great feeling of discontent and loneliness came over all our hearts. Little Nelse, who had been Peter's favourite, went round behind the pig-sty, where none might disturb him, and sat down on the projecting end of a trough to "have a cry," in his usual methodical manner. But old "Alligator Desolation," the dog, had suspicions of what was up, and, hearing the sobs, went round to offer whatever consolation appertained to a damp and dirty nose and a pair of ludicrously doleful yellow eyes.

HENRY
LAWSON
1900

John Longstaff (1862-1941)   *Henry Lawson* (1900)
91 x 78.5 cm   Oil on canvas
Reproduced with the kind permission of the Art Gallery Of New South Wales, Sydney

Florence Rodway (1881-1971)   *Henry Lawson* (1913)
62.3 x 48 cm   Pastel drawing
Reproduced with the kind permission of the Dixson Gallery, The Library of New South Wales, Sydney

ARVIE ASPINALL'S ALARM-CLOCK

In one of these years a paragraph appeared in a daily paper to the effect that a constable had discovered a little boy asleep on the steps of Grinder Bros' factory at four o'clock one rainy morning. He awakened him, and demanded an explanation.

The little fellow explained that he worked there, and was frightened of being late; he started work at six, and was apparently greatly astonished to hear that it was only four. The constable examined a small parcel which the frightened child had in his hand. It contained a clean apron and three slices of bread and treacle.

The child further explained that he woke up and thought it was late, and didn't like to wake mother and ask her the time "because she'd been washin'." He didn't look at the clock, because they "didn't have one." He volunteered no explanations as to how he expected mother to know the time, but, perhaps, like many other mites of his kind, he had unbounded faith in the infinitude of a mother's wisdom. His name was Arvie Aspinall, please sir, and he lived in Jones's Alley. Father was dead.

A few days later the same paper took great pleasure in stating, in reference to that "Touching Incident" noticed in a recent issue, that a benevolent society lady had started a subscription among her friends with the object of purchasing an alarm-clock for the little boy found asleep at Grinder Bros' workshop door.

Later on it was mentioned, in connection with the touching incident, that the alarm-clock had been bought and delivered to the boy's mother, who appeared to be quite overcome with gratitude. It was learned, also, from another source, that the last assertion was greatly exaggerated.

The touching incident was worn out in another paragraph, which left no doubt that the benevolent society lady was none other than a charming and accomplished daughter of the House of Grinder.

It was late in the last day of the Easter Holidays, during which Arvie Aspinall had lain in bed with a bad cold. He was still what he called "croopy." It was about nine o'clock, and the business of Jones's Alley was in full swing.

"That's better, mother, I'm far better," said Arvie, "the sugar and vinegar cuts the phlegm, and the both'rin' cough gits out." It got out to such an extent for the next few minutes that he could not speak. When he recovered his breath, he said:

"Better or worse, I'll have to go to work to-morrow. Gimme the clock, mother."

"I tell you you shall not go! It will be your death."

"It's no use talking, mother; we can't starve—and—s'posin' somebody got my place! Gimme the clock, mother."

"I'll send one of the children round to say you're ill. They'll surely let you off for a day or two."

"'Tain't no use; they won't wait; I know them—what does Grinder Bros care if I'm ill! Never mind, mother, I'll rise above 'em all yet. *Give me the clock,* mother."

She gave him the clock, and he proceeded to wind it up and set the alarm.

"There's somethin' wrong with the gong," he muttered, "it's gone wrong two nights now, but I'll chance it. I'll set the alarm at five, that'll give me time to dress and git there early. I wish I hadn't to walk so far."

He paused to read some words engraved round the dial:

Early to bed and early to rise
Makes a man healthy and wealthy and wise.

He had read the verse often before, and was much taken with the swing and rhyme of it. He had repeated it to himself, over and over again, without reference to the sense or philosophy of it. He had never dreamed of doubting anything in print—and this was engraved. But now a new light seemed to dawn upon him. He studied the sentence a while, and then read it aloud for the second time. He turned it over in his mind again in silence.

"Mother!" he said suddenly, "I think it lies." She placed the clock on the shelf, tucked him into his little bed on the sofa, and blew out the light.

Arvie seemed to sleep, but she lay awake thinking of her troubles. Of her husband carried home dead from his work one morning; of her eldest son who only came to loaf on her when he was out of jail; of the second son, who had feathered his nest in another city, and had no use for her any longer; of the next—poor delicate little Arvie—struggling manfully to help, and wearing his young life out at Grinder Bros when he should be at school; of the five helpless younger children asleep in the next room: of her hard life—scrubbing floors from half-past five till eight, and then starting her day's work—washing!—of having to rear her children in the atmosphere of the slums, because she could not afford to move and pay a higher rent; and of the rent.

Arvie commenced to mutter in his sleep.

"Can't you get to sleep, Arvie?" she asked. "Is your throat sore? Can I get anything for you!"

"I'd like to sleep," he muttered, dreamily, "but it won't seem more'n a moment before—before——"

"Before what, Arvie?" she asked, quickly, fearing that he was becoming delirious.

"Before the alarm goes off!"

He was talking in his sleep.

She rose gently and put the alarm on two hours. "He can rest now," she whispered to herself.

Presently Arvie sat bolt upright, and said quickly, "Mother! I thought the alarm went off!" Then, without waiting for an answer, he lay down as suddenly and slept.

The rain had cleared away, and a bright, starry dome was over sea and city, over slum and villa alike; but little of it could be seen from the hovel in Jones's Alley, save a glimpse of the Southern Cross and a few stars round it. It was what ladies call a "lovely night," as seen from the house of Grinder —"Grinderville"—with its moonlit terraces and gardens sloping gently to the water, and its windows lit up for an Easter ball, and its reception-rooms thronged by its own exclusive set, and one of its charming and accomplished daughters melting a select party to tears by her pathetic recitation about a little crossing sweeper.

There *was* something wrong with the alarm-clock, or else Mrs Aspinall had made a mistake, for the gong sounded startlingly in the dead of the night. She woke with a painful start, and lay still, expecting to hear Arvie get up; but he made no sign. She turned a white, frightened face towards the sofa where he lay—the light from the alley's solitary lamp on the pavement above shone down through the window, and she saw that he had not moved.

Why didn't the clock wake him? He was such a light sleeper! "Arvie!" she called; no answer. "Arvie!" she called again, with a strange ring of remonstrance mingling with the terror in her voice. Arvie never answered.

"Oh! my God!" she moaned.

She rose and stood by the sofa. Arvie lay on his back with his arms folded —a favourite sleeping position of his; but his eyes were wide open and staring upwards as though they would stare through ceiling and roof to the place where God ought to be.

A VISIT OF CONDOLENCE

"Does Arvie live here, old woman?"

"Why?"

"Strike me dead! carn't yer answer a civil queschin?"

"How dare you talk to me like that, you young larrikin! Be off! or I'll send for a policeman."

"Blarst the cops! D'yer think I cares for 'em? Fur two pins I'd fetch a push an' smash yer ole shanty about yer ears—y'ole cow! *I only arsked if Arvie lived here!* Holy Mosis! carn't a feller ask a civil queschin?"

"What do *you* want with Arvie? Do you know him?"

"My oath! Don't he work at Grinder Brothers? I only come out of my way to do him a good turn; an' now I'm sorry I come—damned if I ain't—to be barracked like this, an' shoved down my own throat. (*Pause*) I want to tell Arvie that if he don't come ter work termorrer, another bloke'll collar his job. I wouldn't like to see a cove collar a cove's job an' not tell a bloke about it. What's up with Arvie, anyhow? Is he sick?"

"Arvie is dead!"

"Christ! (*Pause*) Garn! What-yer-giv'n-us? Tell Arvie Bill Anderson wants-ter see him."

"My God! haven't I got enough trouble without a young wretch like you coming to torment me? For God's sake go away and leave me alone! I'm telling you the truth, my poor boy died of influenza last night."

"My oath!"

The ragged young rip gave a long, low whistle, glanced up and down Jones's Alley, spat out some tobacco-juice, and said:

"Swelp me Gord! I'm sorry, mum. I didn't know. How was I to know you wasn't havin' me?"

He withdrew one hand from his pocket and scratched the back of his head, tilting his hat as far forward as it had previously been to the rear, and just then the dilapidated side of his right boot attracted his attention. He turned the foot on one side, and squinted at the sole; then he raised the foot to his left knee, caught the ankle in a very dirty hand, and regarded the sole-leather critically, as though calculating how long it would last. After which he spat desperately at the pavement, and said:

"Kin I see him?"

He followed her up the crooked little staircase with a who's-afraid kind of swagger, but he took his hat off on entering the room.

He glanced round, and seemed to take stock of the signs of poverty—so familiar to his class—and then directed his gaze to where the body lay on the sofa with its pauper coffin already by its side. He looked at the coffin with the critical eye of a tradesman, then he looked at Arvie, and then at the coffin again, as if calculating whether the body would fit.

The mother uncovered the white, pinched face of the dead boy, and Bill came and stood by the sofa. He carelessly drew his right hand from his pocket, and laid the palm on Arvie's ice-cold forehead.

"Poor little cove!" Bill muttered, half to himself; and then, as though ashamed of his weakness, he said:

"There wasn't no post mortem, was there?"

"No," she answered; "a doctor saw him the day before—there was no post mortem."

"I thought there wasn't none," said Bill, "because a man that's been post mortemed always looks as if he'd been hurt. My father looked right enough at first—just as if he was restin'—but after they'd had him opened he looked as if he'd been hurt. No one else could see it, but I could. How old was Arvie?"

"Eleven."

"I'm twelve—goin' on for thirteen. Arvie's father's dead, ain't he?"

"Yes."

"So's mine. Died at his work, didn't he?"

"Yes."

"So'd mine. Arvie told me his father died of something with his heart!"

"Yes."

"So'd mine; ain't it rum? You scrub offices an' wash, don't yer?"

"Yes."

"So does my mother. You find it pretty hard to get a livin', don't yer, these times?"

"My God, yes! God only knows what I'll do now my poor boy's gone. I generally get up at half-past five to scrub out some offices, and when that's done I've got to start my day's work, washing. And then I find it hard to make both ends meet."

"So does my mother. I suppose you took on bad when yer husband was brought home?"

"Ah, my God! Yes. I'll never forget it till my dying day. My poor husband had been out of work for weeks, and he only got the job two days before he died. I suppose it gave your mother a great shock?"

"My oath! One of the fellows that carried father home said: 'Yer husband's dead, mum,' he says; 'he dropped off all of a suddint,' and mother said, 'My God! my God!' just like that, and went off."

"Poor soul! poor soul! And—now my Arvie's gone. Whatever will me and the children do? Whatever will I do? Whatever will I do? My God! I wish I was under the turf."

"Cheer up, mum!" said Bill. "It's no use frettin' over what's done."

He wiped some tobacco-juice off his lips with the back of his hand, and regarded the stains reflectively for a minute or so. Then he looked at Arvie again.

"You should ha' tried cod liver oil," said Bill.

"No. He needed rest and plenty of good food."

"He wasn't very strong."

"No, he was not, poor boy."

"I thought he wasn't. They treated him bad at Grinder Brothers; they didn't give him a show to learn nothing; kept him at the same work all the time, and he didn't have cheek enough to arsk the boss for a rise, lest he'd be sacked. He couldn't fight, an' the boys used to tease him; they'd wait outside the shop to have a lark with Arvie. I'd like to see 'em do it to me. *He* couldn't fight; but then, of course, he wasn't strong. They don't bother me while I'm strong enough to heave a rock; but then, of course, it wasn't Arvie's fault. I s'pose he had pluck enough, if he hadn't the strength." And Bill regarded the corpse with a fatherly and lenient eye.

"My God!" she cried, "if I'd known this, I'd sooner have starved than have my poor boy's life tormented out of him in such a place. He never complained.

My poor, brave-hearted child! He never complained! Poor little Arvie! Poor little Arvie!"

"He never told yer?"

"No—never a word."

"My oath! You don't say so! P'raps he didn't want to let you know he couldn't hold his own; but that wasn't his fault, I s'pose. Y'see, he wasn't strong."

An old print hanging over the bed attracted his attention, and he regarded it with critical interest for a while:

"We've got a pickcher like that at home. We lived in Jones's Alley wunst —in that house over there. How d'yer like livin' in Jones's Alley?"

"I don't like it at all. I don't like having to bring my children up where there are so many bad houses; but I can't afford to go somewhere else and pay higher rent."

"Well, there *is* a good many night-shops round here. But then," he added, reflectively, "you'll find them everywheres. An', besides, the kids git sharp, an' pick up a good deal in an alley like this; 'twon't do 'em no harm; it's no use kids bein' green if they wanter get on in a city. You ain't been in Sydney all yer life, have yer?"

"No. We came from the bush, about five years ago. My poor husband thought he could do better in the city. I was brought up in the bush."

"I thought yer was. Well, men are sich fools. I'm thinking about gittin' a billet up-country, myself, soon. Where's he goin' ter be buried?"

"At Rookwood, to-morrow."

"I carn't come. I've got ter work. Is the Guvmint goin' to bury him?"

"Yes."

Bill looked at the body with increased respect. "Kin I do anythin' for you? Now, don't be frightened to arsk!"

"No. Thank you very much, all the same."

"Well, I must be goin'; thank yer fur yer trouble, mum."

"No trouble, my boy—mind the step."

"It *is* gone. I'll bring a piece of board round some night and mend it for you, if you like; I'm learnin' the carpenterin'; I kin nearly make a door. Tell yer what, I'll send the old woman round to-night to fix up Arvie and lend yer a hand."

"No, thank you. I suppose your mother's got work and trouble enough; I'll manage."

"I'll send her round, anyway; she's a bit rough, but she's got a soft gizzard; an' there's nothin' she enjoys better than fixin' up a body. Good-bye, mum."

"Good-bye, my child."

He paused at the door, and said:

"I'm sorry, mum. Swelp me God! I'm sorry. S'long, an' thank yer."

An awe-stricken child stood on the step, staring at Bill with great brimming eyes. He patted it on the head and said:

"Keep yer pecker up, young 'un!"

JONES'S ALLEY

She lived in Jones's Alley. She cleaned offices, washed, and nursed from daylight until any time after dark, and filled in her spare time cleaning her own place (which she always found dirty—in a "beastly filthy state," she called it—on account of the children being left in possession all day), cooking, and nursing her own sick—for her family, though small, was so in the two senses of the word, and sickly; one or another of the children was always sick, but not through her fault. She did her own, or rather the family washing, at home too, when she couldn't do it by kind permission, or surreptitiously in connection with that of her employers. She was a haggard woman. Her second husband was supposed to be dead, and she lived in dread of his daily resurrection. Her eldest son was at large, but, not being yet sufficiently hardened in misery, she dreaded his getting into trouble even more than his frequent and interested appearances at home. She could buy off the son for a shilling or two and a clean shirt and collar, but she couldn't purchase the absence of the father at any price—*he* claimed what he called his "conzugal rights" as well as his board, lodging, washing and beer. She slaved for her children, and nag-nag-nagged them everlastingly, whether they were in the right or in the wrong, but they were hardened to it and took small notice. She had the spirit of a bullock. Her whole nature was soured. She had those "worse troubles" which she couldn't tell to anybody, but had to suffer in silence.

She also, in what she called her "spare time", put new cuffs and collar-bands on gentlemen's shirts. The gentlemen didn't live in Jones's Alley—they boarded with a patroness of the haggard woman; they didn't know their shirts were done there—had they known it, and known Jones's Alley, one or two of them, who were medical students, might probably have objected. The landlady charged them twice as much for repairing their shirts as she paid the haggard woman, who, therefore, being unable to buy the cuffs and collar-bands ready-made for sewing on, had no lack of employment with which to fill in her spare time.

Therefore, she was a "respectable woman," and was known in Jones's Alley as "Misses" Aspinall, and called so generally, and even by Mother Brock, who kept "that place" opposite. There is implied a world of difference between the "Mother" and the "Misses," as applied to matrons in Jones's Alley; and this distinction was about the only thing—always excepting the everlasting "children"—that the haggard woman had left to care about, to take a selfish, narrow-minded sort of pleasure in—if, indeed, she could yet take pleasure, grim or otherwise, in anything except, perhaps, a good cup of tea and time to drink it in.

Times were hard with Mrs Aspinall. Two coppers and two half-pence in her purse were threepence to *her* now, and the absence of one of the half-pence made a difference to her, especially in Paddy's Market—that eloquent advertisement of a young city's sin and poverty and rotten wealth—on Saturday night. She counted the coppers as anxiously and nervously as a thirsty dead-beat does. And her house was "falling down on her" and her troubles, and she couldn't get the landlord to do a "han'stern" to it.

At last, after persistent agitation on her part (but not before a portion of the plastered ceiling had fallen and severely injured one of her children) the landlord caused two men to be sent to "effect necessary repairs" to the three square, dingy, plastered holes—called "three rooms and a kitchen"—for the privilege of living in which, and calling it "my place," she paid ten shillings a week.

Previously the agent, as soon as he had received the rent and signed the receipt, would cut short her reiterated complaints—which he privately called her "clack"—by saying that he'd see to it, he'd speak to the landlord; and, later on, that he *had* spoken to him, or could do nothing more in the matter—that it wasn't his business. Neither it was, to do the agent justice. It was his business to collect the rent, and thereby earn the means of paying his own. He had to keep a family on his own account, by assisting the Fat Man to keep his at the expense of people—especially widows with large families, or women, in the case of Jones's Alley—who couldn't afford it without being half-starved, or running greater and unspeakable risks which "society" is not supposed to know anything about.

So the agent was right, according to his lights. The landlord had recently turned out a family who had occupied one of his houses for fifteen years, because they were six weeks in arrears. He let them take their furniture, and explained: "I wouldn't have been so lenient with them only they were such old tenants of mine." So the landlord was always in the right according to *his* lights.

But the agent naturally wished to earn his living as peacefully and as comfortably as possible, so, when the accident occurred, he put the matter so persistently and strongly before the landlord that he said at last: "Well, tell her to go to White, the contractor, and he'll send a man to do what's to be done; and don't bother me any more."

White had a look at the place, and sent a plasterer, a carpenter, and a plumber. The plasterer knocked a bigger hole in the ceiling and filled it with mud; the carpenter nailed a board over the hole in the floor; the plumber stopped the leak in the kitchen, and made three new ones in worse places; and their boss sent the bill to Mrs Aspinall.

She went to the contractor's yard, and explained that the landlord was responsible for the debt, not she. The contractor explained that he had seen the landlord, who referred him to her. She called at the landlord's private house, and was referred through a servant to the agent. The agent was sympathetic, but could do nothing in the matter—it wasn't his business; he also asked her to put herself in his place, which she couldn't, not being any more responsible than such women are in such cases. She let things drift, being powerless to prevent them from doing so; and the contractor sent another bill, then a debt collector and then another bill, then the collector again, and threatened to take proceedings, and finally took them. To make matters worse, she was two weeks in arrears with the rent, and the wood-and-coal man (she had dealt with them for ten years) was pushing her, as also were her grocers, with whom she had dealt for fifteen years and never owed a penny before.

She waylaid the landlord, and he told her shortly that he couldn't build houses and give them away, and keep them in repairs afterwards.

She sought for sympathy and found it, but mostly in the wrong places. It was comforting, but unprofitable. Mrs Next-door sympathized warmly, and offered to go up as a witness—she had another landlord. The agent

58

sympathized wearily, but not in the presence of witnesses—he wanted her to put herself in his place. Mother Brock, indeed, offered practical assistance, which offer was received in breathlessly indignant silence. It was Mother Brock who first came to the assistance of Mrs Aspinall's child when the plaster accident took place (the mother being absent at the time), and when Mrs Aspinall heard of it, her indignation cured her of her fright, and she declared to Mrs Next-door that she would give "that woman"— meaning Mother Brock—"in charge the instant she ever *dared* to put her foot inside her (Mrs A.'s) respectable door-step again. She was a respectable, honest, hard-working woman, and—" etc.

Whereat Mother Brock laughed good-naturedly. She was a broad-minded bad woman, and was right according to *her* lights. Poor Mrs A. was a respectable, haggard woman, and was right according to *her* lights and to Mrs Next-door's, perfectly so—they being friends—and vice versa. None of them knew, or would have taken into consideration, the fact that the landlord had lost all his money in a burst financial institution, and half his houses in the general depression, and depended for food for his family on the somewhat doubtful rents of the remainder. So they were all right according to their different lights.

Mrs Aspinall even sought sympathy of "John," the chinaman (with whom she had dealt for four months only), and got it. He also, in all simplicity, took a hint that wasn't intended. He said: "Al li'. Pay bimeby. Nexy time Flyday. Me Tlust." Then he departed with his immortalized smile. It would almost appear that he was wrong—according to our idea of Chinese lights.

Mrs Aspinall went to the court—it was a small local court. Mrs Next-door was awfully sorry, but she couldn't possibly get out that morning. The contractor had the landlord up as a witness. The landlord and the P.M. nodded pleasantly to each other, and wished each other good morning. . . . Verdict for plaintiff with costs. . . . "Next case!" . . . "You mustn't take up the time of the court, my good woman." . . . "Now, Constable!" . . . "Arder in the court!" . . . "Now, my good woman," said the policeman in an undertone, "you must go out; there's another case on—come now." And he steered her—but not unkindly—through the door.

"My good woman" stood in the crowd outside and looked wildly round for a sympathetic face that advertised sympathetic ears. But others had their own troubles, and avoided her. She wanted someone to relieve her bursting heart to; she couldn't wait till she got home.

Even "John's" attentive ear and mildly idiotic expression would have been welcome, but he was gone. He *had* been in court that morning, and had won a small debt case, and had departed cheerfully, under the impression that he lost it.

"Y'aw Mrs Aspinall, ain't you?"

She started, and looked round. He was one of those sharp, blue or grey-eyed, sandy or freckled complexioned boys-of-the-world whom we meet everywhere and at all times, who are always going on towards twenty, yet never seem to get clear out of their teens, who know more than most of us have forgotten, who understand human nature instinctively—perhaps unconsciously—and are instinctively sympathetic and diplomatic; whose satire is quick, keen, and dangerous, and whose tact is often superior to that of many educated men-of-the-world. Trained from childhood in the great school of poverty, they are full of the pathos and humour of it.

"Don't you remember me?"

"No; can't say I do. I fancy I've seen your face before somewhere."

"I was at your place when little Arvie died. I used to work with him at Grinder Bros', you know."

"Oh, of course I remember you! What was I thinking about? I've had such a lot of worry lately that I don't know whether I'm on my head or my heels. Besides, you've grown since then, and changed a lot. You're Billy—Billy——"

"Billy Anderson's my name."

"Of course! To be sure! I remember you quite well."

"How've you been gettin' on, Mrs Aspinall?"

"Ah! Don't mention it—nothing but worry and trouble—nothing but trouble. This grinding poverty! I'll never have anything else but worry and trouble and misery so long as I live."

"Do you live in Jones's alley yet?"

"Yes."

"Not bin there ever since, have you?"

"No; I shifted away once, but I went back again. I was away nearly two years."

"I thought so, because I called to see you there once. Well, I'm goin' that way now. You goin' home, Mrs Aspinall?"

"Yes."

"Well I'll go along with you, if you don't mind."

"Thanks. I'd be only too glad of company."

"Goin' to walk, Mrs Aspinall?" asked Bill, as the tram stopped in their way.

"Yes. I can't afford trams now—times are too hard."

"Sorry I don't happen to have no tickets on me!"

"Oh, don't mention it. I'm well used to walking. I'd rather walk than ride."

They waited till the tram passed.

"Some people"—said Bill, reflectively, but with a tinge of indignation in his tone, as they crossed the street—"some people can afford to ride in trams.

"What's your trouble, Mrs Aspinall—if it's a fair thing to ask?" said Bill, as they turned the corner.

This was all she wanted, and more; and when, about a mile later, she paused for breath, he drew a long one, gave a short whistle, and said:

"Well, it's red-hot!"

Thus encouraged, she told her story again, and some parts of it for third and fourth and even fifth time—and it grew longer, as our stories have a painful tendency to do when we re-write them with a view to condensation.

But Bill heroically repeated that it was "red-hot."

"And I dealt off the grocer for fifteen years, and the wood-and-coal man for ten, and I lived in that house nine years last Easter Monday and never owed a penny before," she repeated for the tenth time.

"Well, that's a mistake," reflected Bill. "I never dealt off nobody more'n twice in my life. . . . I heerd you was married again, Mrs Aspinall—if it's a right thing to ask?"

"Wherever did you hear that? I did get married again—to my sorrow."

"Then you ain't Mrs Aspinall—if it's a fair thing to ask?"

"Oh, yes! I'm known as Mrs Aspinall. They all call me Mrs Aspinall."

"I understand. He cleared, didn't he? Run away?"

"Well, yes—no—he——"

"I understand. He's s'posed to be dead?"

"Yes."

"Well, that's red-hot! So's my old man, and I hope he don't resurrect again."

"You see, I married my second for the sake of my children."

"That's a great mistake," reflected Bill. "My mother married my step-father for the sake of me, and she's never been done telling me about it."

"Indeed! Did *your* mother get married again?"

"Yes. And he left me with a batch of step-sisters and step-brothers to look after, as well as mother; as if things wasn't bad enough before. We didn't want no help to be pinched, and poor, and half-starved. I don't see where my sake comes in at all."

"And how's your mother now?"

"Oh, she's all right, thank you. She's got a hard time of it, but she's pretty well used to it."

"And are you still working at Grinder Bros'?"

"No. I got tired of slavin' there for next to nothing. I got sick of my step-father waitin' outside for me on pay-day, with a dirty, drunken, spieler pal of his waitin' round the corner for him. There wasn't nothin' in it. It got to be too rough altogether. . . . Blast Grinders!"

"And what are you doing now?"

"Sellin' papers. I'm always tryin' to get a start in something else, but I ain't got no luck. I always come back to sellin' papers."

Then after a thought, he added reflectively: "Blast papers!"

His present ambition was to drive a cart.

"I drove a cart twice, and once I rode a butcher's horse. A bloke worked me out of one billet, and I worked myself out of the other. I didn't know when I was well off. Then the banks went bust, and my last boss went insolvent, and one of his partners went into Darlinghurst for suicide, and the other went into Gladesville for being mad; and one day the bailiff seized the cart and horse with me in it and a load of timber. So I went home and helped mother and the kids to live on one meal a day for six months, and keep the bum-bailiff out. Another cove had my news-stand."

Then, after a thought:

"Blast reconstruction!"

"But you surely can't make a living selling newspapers?"

"No, there's nothing in it. There's too many at it. The blessed women spoil it. There's one got a good stand down in George Street, and she's got a dozen kids sellin'—they can't be all hers—and then she's got the hide to come up to my stand and sell in front of me. . . . What are you thinkin' about doin' Mrs Aspinall?"

"I don't know," she wailed. "I really don't know what to do."

And there still being some distance to go, she plunged into her tale of misery once more, not forgetting the length of time she had dealt with her creditors.

Bill pushed his hat forward and walked along the edge of the kerb.

"Can't you shift? Ain't you got no people or friends that you can go to for a while?"

"Oh, yes; there's my sister-in-law; she's asked me times without number to come and stay with her till things got better, and she's got a hard enough struggle herself, Lord knows. She asked me again only yesterday."

"Well, that ain't too bad," reflected Bill. "Why don't you go?"

"Well, you see, if I did they wouldn't let me take my furniture, and she's got next to none."

"Won't the landlord let you take your furniture?"

"No, not him! He's one of the hardest landlords in Sydney—the worst I ever had."

"That's red-hot! . . . I'd take it in spite of him. He can't do nothin'."

"But I daren't; and even if I did I haven't got a penny to pay for a van."

They neared the alley. Bill counted the flagstones, stepping from one to another over the joints. "Eighteen—nineteen—twenty—twenty-one!" he counted mentally, and came to the corner kerbing. Then he turned suddenly and faced her.

"I'll tell you what to do," he said decidedly. "Can you get your things ready by to-night? I know a cove that's got a cart."

"But I daren't. I'm afraid of the landlord."

"The more fool you," said Bill. "Well, I'm not afraid of him. He can't do nothin'. I'm not afraid of a landlady, and that's worse. I know the law. He can't do nothin'. You just do as I tell you."

"I'd want to think over it first, and see my sister-in-law."

"Where does your sister-'n-law live?"

"Not far."

"Well, see her, and think over it—you've got plenty of time to do it in—and get your things ready by dark. Don't be frightened. I've shifted mother and an aunt and two married sisters out of worse fixes than yours. I'll be round after dark, and bring a push to lend a hand. They're decent coves."

"But I can't expect your friend to shift me for nothing. I told you I haven't got a——"

"Mrs Aspinall, I ain't that sort of a bloke, neither is my chum, and neither is the other fellows—'relse they wouldn't be friends of mine. Will you promise, Mrs Aspinall?"

"I'm afraid—I—I'd like to keep my few things now. I've kept them so long. It's hard to lose my few bits of things—I wouldn't care so much if I could keep the ironin' table."

"So you could by law—it's necessary to your living, but it would cost more'n the table. Now, don't be soft, Mrs Aspinall. You'll have the bailiff in any day, and be turned out in the end without a rag. The law knows no 'necessary.' You want your furniture more'n the landlord does. He can't do nothin'. You can trust it all to me.... I knowed Arvie.... Will you do it?"

"Yes, I will."

At about eight o'clock that evening there came a mysterious knock at

62

Mrs Aspinall's door. She opened, and there stood Bill. His attitude was business-like, and his manner very impressive. Three other boys stood along by the window, with their backs to the wall, deeply interested in the emptying of burnt cigarette-ends into a piece of newspaper laid in the crown of one of their hats, and a fourth stood a little way along the kerb casually rolling a cigarette, and keeping a quiet eye out for suspicious appearances. They were of different makes and sizes, but there seemed an undefined similarity between them.

"This is my push, Mrs Aspinall," said Bill; "at least," he added apologetically, "it's part of 'em. Here, you chaps, this is Mrs Aspinall, what I told you about."

They elbowed the wall back, rubbed their heads with their hats, shuffled round, and seemed to take a vacant sort of interest in abstract objects, such as the pavement, the gas-lamp, and neighbouring doors and windows.

"Got the thing ready?" asked Bill.

"Oh, yes."

"Got 'em downstairs?"

"There's no upstairs. The rooms above belong to the next house."

"And a nice house it is," said Bill, "for rooms to belong to. I wonder," he reflected, cocking his eye at the windows above; "I wonder how the police manage to keep an eye on the next house without keepin' an eye on yours— but they know."

He turned towards the street end of the alley and gave a low whistle. Out under the lamp from behind the corner came a long, thin, shambling, hump-backed youth, with his hat down over his head like an extinguisher, dragging a small bony horse, which, in its turn, dragged a rickety cart of the tray variety, such as is used in the dead marine trade. Behind the cart was tied a mangy retriever. This affair was drawn up opposite the door.

"The cove with a cart," was introduced as "Chinny." He had no chin what-ever, not even a receding chin. It seemed as though his chin had been cut clean off horizontally. When he took off his hat he showed to the mild surprise of strangers a pair of shrewd grey eyes and a broad high forehead. Chinny was in the empty bottle line.

"Now, then, hold up that horse of yours for a minute, Chinny," said Bill briskly, " 'relse he'll fall down and break the shaft again." (It had already been broken in several places and spliced with strips of deal, clothes-line, and wire.) "Now, you chaps, fling yourselves about and get the furniture out."

This was a great relief to the push. They ran against each other and the door-post in their eagerness to be at work. The furniture—what Mrs A. called her "few bits of things"—was carried out with elaborate care. The ironing table was the main item. It was placed top down in the cart, and the rest of the things went between the legs without bulging sufficiently to cause Chinny any anxiety.

Just then the picket gave a low, earnest whistle, and they were aware of a policeman standing statue-like under the lamp on the opposite corner, and apparently unaware of their existence. He was looking, sphinx-like, past them towards the city.

"It can't be helped; we must put on front an' go on with it now," said Bill.

"He's all right, I think," said Chinny. "He knows me."

"He can't do nothin'," said Bill; "don't mind him, Mrs Aspinall. Now, then (to the push), tie up. Don't be frightened of the dorg—what are you frightened of? Why! he'd only apologize if you trod on his tail."

The dog went under the cart, and kept his tail carefully behind him.

The policeman—he was an elderly man—stood still, looking towards the city, and over it, perhaps, and over the sea, to long years agone in Ireland when he and the boys ducked bailiffs, and resisted evictions with "shticks," and "riz" sometimes, and gathered together at the rising of the moon, and did many things contrary to the peace of Gracious Majesty, its laws and constitutions, crown and dignity; as a reward for which he had helped to preserve the said peace for the best years of his life, without promotion; for he had a great aversion to running in "the boys"—which included nearly all mankind—and preferred to keep, and was most successful in keeping, the peace with no other assistance than that of his own rich fatherly brogue.

Bill took charge of two of the children; Mrs Aspinall carried the youngest.

"Go ahead, Chinny," said Bill.

Chinny shambled forward, sideways, dragging the horse, with one long, bony, short-sleeved arm stretched out behind holding the rope reins; the horse stumbled out of the gutter, and the cart seemed to pause a moment, as if undecided whether to follow or not, and then, with many rickety complaints, moved slowly and painfully up on to the level out of the gutter. The dog rose with a long, weary, mangy sigh, but with a lazy sort of calculation, before his rope (which was short) grew taut—which was good judgment on his part for his neck was sore; and his feet being tender, he felt his way carefully and painfully over the metal, as if he feared that at any step he might spring some treacherous, air-trigger trap-door which would drop and hang him.

"Nit, you chaps," said Bill, "and wait for me." The push rubbed its head with its hat, said "Good night, Mrs Ashpennel," and was absent, spook-like.

When the funeral reached the street, the lonely "trap" was, somehow, two blocks away in the opposite direction, moving very slowly, and very upright, and very straight, like an automaton.

64

J. F. Archibald and John Haynes in 1882 during a six-week period spent in the Debtors' Quarters in Darlinghurst Gaol for non-payment of legal expenses incurred in a libel suit brought against the Sydney *Bulletin,* of which they were the co-founders and editors. The imprisonment in no way curbed their crusading spirit.

The action had been brought against the journal following publication of an article, written by W. H. Traill, later one of the editors, in which the proprietors of a pleasure ground at Clontarf, near Sydney, were attacked for allowing the 'larrikin residuum' to turn the spot into a 'saturnalia of vice'.

A farthing damages for the plaintiffs left the *Bulletin* responsible for costs which amounted to £1,500 ($3,000), a sum raised finally by public subscription.

Whilst incarcerated they continued to edit the *Bulletin* and so foster Australian nationalism. Archibald's lifetime assistance to Henry Lawson was just one of the services he rendered to literature in this country.

ANDY'S GONE WITH CATTLE

Our Andy's gone with cattle now—
  Our hearts are out of order—
With drought he's gone to battle now
  Across the Queensland border.

He's left us in dejection now;
  Our thoughts with him are roving;
It's dull on this selection now,
  Since Andy went a-droving.

Who now shall wear the cheerful face
  In times when things are slackest?
And who shall whistle round the place
  When Fortune frowns her blackest?

Oh, who shall cheek the squatter now
  When he comes round us snarling?
His tongue is growing hotter now
  Since Andy crossed the Darling.

Oh, may the showers in torrents fall,
  And all the tanks run over;
And may the grass grow green and tall
  In pathways of the drover;

And may good angels send the rain
  On desert stretches sandy;
And when the summer comes again
  God grant 'twill bring us Andy.

Sir Arthur Streeton (1867-1943)   *The Railway Station, Redfern* (1893)
40.8 x 61 cm   Oil on canvas   Gift of Lady Denison
Reproduced with the kind permission of the Art Gallery Of New South Wales, Sydney

Robert Wakelin (1887-1971) *Down the Hills to Berry's Bay* (1916)
68 x 122 cm Oil on canvas, mounted on hard board
Reproduced with the kind permission of the Art Gallery Of New South Wales, Sydney

THE ROARING DAYS

A brilliant evocation
of the excitement
and romance of the
gold rushes of
the 1860s in
Australia. Events,
people and places
would have
become alive to
Lawson as he
listened to his
elders re-living
the period.

The night too quickly passes
  And we are growing old,
So let us fill our glasses
  And toast the Days of Gold;
When finds of wondrous treasure
  Set all the South ablaze,
And you and I were faithful mates
  All through the Roaring Days!

Then stately ships came sailing
  From every harbour's mouth,
And sought the Land of Promise
  That beaconed in the South;
Then southward streamed their streamers
  And swelled their canvas full
To speed the wildest dreamers
  E'er borne in vessel's hull.

Their shining Eldorado
  Beneath the southern skies
Was day and night for ever
  Before their eager eyes.
The brooding bush, awakened,
  Was stirred in wild unrest,
And all the year a human stream
  Went pouring to the West.

The rough bush roads re-echoed
  The bar-room's noisy din,
When troops of stalwart horsemen
  Dismounted at the inn.
And oft the hearty greetings
  And hearty clasp of hands
Would tell of sudden meetings
  Of friends from other lands.

And when the cheery camp-fire
  Explored the bush with gleams,
The camping-grounds were crowded
  With caravans of teams;
Then home the jests were driven,
  And good old songs were sung,
And choruses were given
  The strength of heart and lung.

Oft when the camps were dreaming,
  And fires began to pale,
Through rugged ranges gleaming
  Swept on the Royal Mail.
Behind six foaming horses,
  And lit by flashing lamps,
Old Cobb and Co., in royal state,
  Went dashing past the camps.

Oh, who would paint a goldfield,
  And paint the picture right,
As we have often seen it.
  In early morning's light?
The yellow mounds of mullock
  With spots of red and white,
The scattered quartz that glistened
  Like diamonds in light;

The azure line of ridges,
  The bush of darkest green,
The little homes of calico
  That dotted all the scene.
The flat straw hats, with ribands,
  That old engravings show—
The dress that still reminds us
  Of sailors, long ago.

I hear the fall of timber
  From distant flats and fells,
The pealing of the anvils
  As clear as little bells,
The rattle of the cradle,
  The clack of windlass-boles,
The flutter of the crimson flags
  Above the golden holes.

Ah, then their hearts were bolder,
  And if Dame Fortune frowned
Their swags they'd lightly shoulder
  And tramp to other ground.
Oh, they were lion-hearted
  Who gave our country birth!
Stout sons, of stoutest fathers born,
  From all the lands on earth!

Those golden days are vanished,
  And altered is the scene;
The diggings are deserted,
  The camping-grounds are green;
The flaunting flag of progress
  Is in the West unfurled,
The mighty Bush with iron rails
  Is tethered to the world.

BALLAD OF THE DROVER

Generations of
readers know this
poem as 'Harry
Dale, the Drover'.

Across the stony ridges,
　Across the rolling plain,
Young Harry Dale, the drover,
　Comes riding home again.
And well his stock-horse bears him,
　And light of heart is he,
And stoutly his old packhorse
　Is trotting by his knee.

Up Queensland way with cattle ·
　He's travelled regions vast,
And many months have vanished
　Since home-folks saw him last.
He hums a song of someone
　He hopes to marry soon;
And hobble-chains and camp-ware
　Keep jingling to the tune.

Beyond the hazy dado
　Against the lower skies
And yon blue line of ranges
　The station homestead lies.
And thitherward the drover
　Jogs through the lazy noon,
While hobble-chains and camp-ware
　Are jingling to a tune.

An hour has filled the heavens
　With storm-clouds inky black;
At times the lightning trickles
　Around the drover's track;
But Harry pushes onward,
　His horses' strength he tries,
In hope to reach the river
　Before the flood shall rise.

The thunder, pealing o'er him,
　Goes rumbling down the plain;
And sweet on thirsty pastures
　In torrents falls the rain;
Then every creek and gully
　Sends forth its little flood—
The river runs a banker,
　All stained with yellow mud.

Now Harry speaks to Rover,
    The best dog on the plains,
And to his hardy horses,
    And strokes their shaggy manes:
"We've breasted bigger rivers
    When floods were at their height,
Nor shall this gutter stop us
    From getting home tonight!"

The thunder growls a warning
    The ghastly lightnings gleam;
The drover turns his horses
    To swim the fatal stream.
But, oh! the flood runs stronger
    Than e'er it ran before;
The saddle-horse is failing,
    And only half-way o'er!

When flashes next the lightning,
    The flood's grey breast is blank;
A cattle-dog and packhorse
    Are struggling up the bank.
But in the lonely homestead
    The girl shall wait in vain—
He'll never pass the stations
    In charge of stock again.

The faithful dog a moment
    Lies panting on the bank,
Then plunges through the current
    To where his master sank.
And round and round in circles
    He fights with failing strength,
Till, gripped by wilder waters,
    He fails and sinks at length.

Across the flooded lowlands
    And slopes of sodden loam
The packhorse struggles bravely
    To take dumb tidings home;
And mud-stained, wet, and weary,
    He goes by rock and tree,
With clanging chains and tinware
    All sounding eerily.

THE DROVER'S WIFE

One of Lawson's best known stories, this bitter, rather than tragic picture of a woman of the bush has been published in many anthologies and dramatized. I would say that it could have been written nowhere else but in Australia and by nobody else but Lawson.

The two-roomed house is built of round timber, slabs, and stringy-bark, and floored with split slabs. A big bark kitchen standing at one end is larger than the house itself, veranda included.

Bush all round—bush with no horizon, for the country is flat. No ranges in the distance. The bush consists of stunted, rotten native apple-trees. No undergrowth. Nothing to relieve the eye save the darker green of a few she-oaks which are sighing above the narrow, almost waterless creek. Nineteen miles to the nearest sign of civilization—a shanty on the main road.

The drover, an ex-squatter, is away with sheep. His wife and children are left here alone.

Four ragged, dried-up-looking children are playing about the house. Suddenly one of them yells: "Snake! Mother, here's a snake!"

The gaunt, sun-browned bushwoman dashes from the kitchen, snatches her baby from the ground, holds it on her left hip, and reaches for a stick.

"Where is it?"

"Here! gone into the wood-heap!" yells the eldest boy—a sharp-faced urchin of eleven. "Stop there, mother! I'll have him. Stand back! I'll have the beggar!"

"Tommy, come here, or you'll be bit. Come here at once when I tell you, you little wretch!"

The youngster comes reluctantly, carrying a stick bigger than himself. Then he yells, triumphantly:

"There it goes—under the house!" and darts away with club uplifted. At the same time the big, black, yellow-eyed dog-of-all-breeds, who has shown the wildest interest in the proceedings, breaks his chain and rushes after the snake. He is a moment late, however, and his nose reaches the crack in the slabs just as the end of its tail disappears. Almost at the same moment the boy's club comes down and skins the aforesaid nose. Alligator takes small notice of this, and proceeds to undermine the building; but he is subdued after a struggle and chained up. They cannot afford to lose him.

The drover's wife makes the children stand together near the dog-house while she watches for the snake. She gets two small dishes of milk and sets them down near the wall to tempt it to come out; but an hour goes by and it does not show itself.

It is near sunset, and a thunderstorm is coming. The children must be brought inside. She will not take them into the house, for she knows the snake is there, and may at any moment come up through a crack in the rough slab floor; so she carries several armfuls of firewood into the kitchen, and then takes the children there. The kitchen has no floor—or, rather, an earthen one—called a "ground floor" in this part of the bush. There is a large, roughly-made table in the centre of the place. She brings the children in, and makes them get on this table. They are two boys and two girls—mere babies. She gives them some supper, and then, before it gets dark, she goes into the house, and snatches up some pillows and bedclothes—expecting to see or lay her hand on the snake any minute. She makes a bed on the kitchen table for the children, and sits down beside it to watch all night.

She has an eye on the corner, and a green sapling club laid in readiness on the dresser by her side; also her sewing basket and a copy of the *Young Ladies' Journal*. She has brought the dog into the room.

Tommy turns in, under protest, but says he'll lie awake all night and smash that blinded snake.

His mother asks him how many times she has told him not to swear.

He has his club with him under the bedclothes, and Jacky protests:

"Mummy! Tommy's skinnin' me alive wif his club. Make him take it out."

Tommy: "Shet up, you little ——! D'yer want to be bit with the snake?"

Jacky shuts up.

"If yer bit," says Tommy, after a pause, "you'll swell up, an' smell, an' turn red an' green an' blue all over till yer bust. Won't he, mother?"

"Now then, don't frighten the child. Go to sleep," she says.

The two younger children go to sleep, and now and then Jacky complains of being "skeezed." More room is made for him. Presently Tommy says: "Mother! listen to them (adjective) little possums. I'd like to screw their blanky necks."

And Jacky protests drowsily.

"But they don't hurt us, the little blanks!"

Mother: "There, I told you you'd teach Jacky to swear." But the remark makes her smile. Jacky goes to sleep.

Presently Tommy asks:

"Mother! Do you think they'll ever extricate the (adjective) kangaroo?"

"Lord! How am I to know, child? Go to sleep."

"Will you wake me if the snake comes out?"

"Yes. Go to sleep."

Near midnight. The children are all asleep and she sits there still, sewing and reading by turns. From time to time she glances round the floor and wall-plate, and, whenever she hears a noise, she reaches for the stick. The thunderstorm comes on, and the wind, rushing through the cracks in the slab wall, threatens to blow out her candle. She places it on a sheltered part of the dresser and fixes up a newspaper to protect it. At every flash of lightning, the cracks between the slabs gleam like polished silver. The thunder rolls, and the rain comes down in torrents.

Alligator lies at full length on the floor, with his eyes turned towards the partition. She knows by this that the snake is there. There are large cracks in that wall opening under the floor of the dwelling house.

She is not a coward, but recent events have shaken her nerves. A little son of her brother-in-law was lately bitten by a snake, and died. Besides, she has not heard from her husband for six months, and is anxious about him.

He was a drover, and started squatting here when they were married. The drought of 18— ruined him. He had to sacrifice the remnant of his flock and go droving again. He intends to move his family into the nearest town when he comes back, and, in the meantime, his brother, who keeps a shanty on the main road, comes over about once a month with provisions. The wife has still a couple of cows, one horse, and a few sheep. The brother-in-law kills one of the latter occasionally, gives her what she needs of it, and takes the rest in return for other provisions.

She is used to being left alone. She once lived like this for eighteen months. As a girl she built the usual castles in the air; but all her girlish hopes and aspirations have long been dead. She finds all the excitement and recreation she needs in the *Young Ladies' Journal,* and Heaven help her! takes a pleasure in the fashion-plates.

Her husband is an Australian, and so is she. He is careless, but a good enough husband. If he had the means he would take her to the city and keep her there like a princess. They are used to being apart, or at least she is. "No use fretting," she says. He may forget sometimes that he is married; but if he has a good cheque when he comes back he will give most of it to her. When he had money he took her to the city several times—hired a railway sleeping compartment, and put up at the best hotels. He also bought her a buggy, but they had to sacrifice that along with the rest.

The last two children were born in the bush—one while her husband was bringing a drunken doctor, by force, to attend to her. She was alone on this occasion, and very weak. She had been ill with a fever. She prayed to God to send her assistance. God sent Black Mary—the "whitest" gin in all the land. Or, at least, God sent King Jimmy first, and he sent Black Mary. He put his black face round the door post, took in the situation at a glance, and said cheerfully: "All right, missus—I bring my old woman, she down alonga creek."

One of the children died while she was here alone. She rode nineteen miles for assistance, carrying the dead child.

It must be near one or two o'clock. The fire is burning low. Alligator lies with his head resting on his paws, and watches the wall. He is not a very beautiful dog, and the light shows numerous old wounds where the hair will not grow. He is afraid of nothing on the face of the earth or under it. He will tackle a bullock as readily as he will tackle a flea. He hates all other dogs—except kangaroo-dogs—and has a marked dislike to friends or relations of the family. They seldom call, however. He sometimes makes friends with strangers. He hates snakes and has killed many, but he will be bitten some day and die; most snake-dogs end that way.

Now and then the bushwoman lays down her work and watches, and listens, and thinks. She thinks of things in her own life, for there is little else to think about.

The rain will make the grass grow, and this reminds her how she fought a bush-fire once while her husband was away. The grass was long, and very dry, and the fire threatened to burn her out. She put on an old pair of her husband's trousers and beat out the flames with a green bough, till great drops of sooty perspiration stood out on her forehead and ran in streaks down her blackened arms. The sight of his mother in trousers greatly amused Tommy, who worked like a little hero by her side, but the terrified baby howled lustily for his "mummy." The fire would have mastered her but for four excited bushmen who arrived in the nick of time. It was a mixed-up affair all round; when she went to take up the baby he screamed and struggled convulsively, thinking it was a "blackman;" and Alligator, trusting more to the child's sense than his own instinct, charged furiously, and (being old and slightly deaf) did not in his excitement at first recognize his mistress's voice, but continued to hang on to the moleskins until choked off by Tommy with a saddle-strap. The dog's sorrow for his blunder, and his anxiety to let it be known that it was all a mistake, was as evident as his ragged tail and a twelve-inch grin could make it. It was a glorious time for the boys; a day to look back to, and talk about, and laugh over for many years.

She thinks how she fought a flood during her husband's absence. She stood for hours in the drenching downpour, and dug an overflow gutter to save the dam across the creek. But she could not save it. There are things that a bushwoman cannot do. Next morning the dam was broken, and her heart was nearly broken too, for she thought how her husband would feel when he came home and saw the result of years of labour swept away. She cried then.

She also fought the pleuro-pneumonia—dosed and bled the few remaining cattle, and wept again when her two best cows died.

Again, she fought a mad bullock that besieged the house for a day. She made bullets and fired at him through cracks in the slabs with an old shot-gun. He was dead in the morning. She skinned him and got seventeen-and-sixpence for the hide.

She also fights the crows and eagles that have designs on her chickens. Her plan of campaign is very original. The children cry "Crows, mother!" and she rushes out and aims a broomstick at the birds as though it were a gun, and says "Bung!" The crows leave in a hurry; they are cunning, but a woman's cunning is greater.

Occasionally a bushman in the horrors, or a villainous-looking sundowner, comes and nearly scares the life out of her. She generally tells the suspicious-looking stranger that her husband and two sons are at work below the dam, or over at the yard, for he always cunningly inquires for the boss.

Only last week a gallows-faced swagman—having satisfied himself that there were no men on the place—threw his swag down on the veranda, and demanded tucker. She gave him something to eat; then he expressed his intention of staying for the night. It was sundown then. She got a batten from the sofa, loosened the dog, and confronted the stranger, holding the batten in one hand and the dog's collar with the other. "Now you go!" she said. He looked at her and at the dog, said "All right, mum," in a cringing tone, and left. She was a determined-looking woman, and Alligator's yellow eyes glared unpleasantly—besides, the dog's chawing-up apparatus greatly resembled that of the reptile he was named after.

She has few pleasures to think of as she sits here alone by the fire, on guard against a snake. All days are much the same to her; but on Sunday afternoon she dresses herself, tidies the children, smartens up baby, and goes for a lonely walk along the bush-track, pushing an old perambulator in front of her. She does this every Sunday. She takes as much care to make herself and the children look smart as she would if she were going to do the block in the city. There is nothing to see, however, and not a soul to meet. You might walk for twenty miles along this track without being able to fix a point in your mind, unless you are a bushman. This is because of the everlasting, maddening sameness of the stunted trees—that monotony which makes a man long to break away and travel as far as trains can go, and sail as far as ship can sail—and further.

But this bushwoman is used to the loneliness of it. As a girl-wife she hated it, but now she would feel strange away from it.

She is glad when her husband returns, but she does not gush or make a fuss about it. She gets him something good to eat, and tidies up the children.

She seems contented with her lot. She loves her children, but has no time to show it. She seems harsh to them. Her surroundings are not favourable to the development of the "womanly" or sentimental side of nature.

It must be near morning now; but the clock is in the dwelling-house. Her candle is nearly done; she forgot that she was out of candles. Some more wood must be got to keep the fire up, and so she shuts the dog inside and hurries round to the wood-heap. The rain has cleared off. She seizes a stick, pulls it out, and—crash! the whole pile collapses.

Yesterday she bargained with a stray blackfellow to bring her some wood, and while he was at work she went in search of a missing cow. She was absent an hour or so, and the native black made good use of his time. On her return she was so astonished to see a good heap of wood by the chimney, that she gave him an extra fig of tobacco, and praised him for not being lazy. He thanked her, and left with head erect and chest well out. He was the last of his tribe and a King; but he had built that wood-heap hollow.

She is hurt now, and tears spring to her eyes as she sits down again by the table. She take up a handkerchief to wipe the tears away, but pokes her eyes with her bare fingers instead. The handkerchief is full of holes, and she finds that she has put her thumb through one, and her forefinger through another.

This makes her laugh, to the surprise of the dog. She has a keen, very keen, sense of the ridiculous; and some time or other she will amuse bushmen with the story.

She had been amused before like that. One day she sat down "to have a good cry," as she said—and the old cat rubbed against her dress and "cried too." Then she had to laugh.

It must be near daylight now. The room is very close and hot because of the fire. Alligator still watches the wall from time to time. Suddenly he becomes greatly interested; he draws himself a few inches nearer the partition, and a thrill runs through his body. The hair on the back of his neck begins to bristle, and the battle-light is in his yellow eyes. She knows what this means, and lays her hand on the stick. The lower end of one of the partition slabs has a large crack on both sides. An evil pair of small, bright bead-like eyes glisten at one of these holes. The snake—a black one —comes slowly out, about a foot, and moves its head up and down. The dog lies still, and the woman sits as one fascinated. The snake comes out a foot further. She lifts her stick, and the reptile, as though suddenly aware of danger, sticks his head in through the crack on the other side of the slab, and hurries to get his tail round after him. Alligator springs, and his jaws come together with a snap. He misses, for his nose is large, and the snake's body close down in the angle formed by the slabs and the floor. He snaps again as the tail comes round. He has the snake now, and tugs it out eighteen inches. Thud, thud, comes the woman's club on the ground. Alligator pulls again. Thud, thud. Alligator gives another pull and he has the snake out—a black brute, five feet long. The head rises to dart about, but the dog has the enemy close to the neck. He is a big, heavy dog, but quick as a terrier. He shakes the snake as though he felt the original curse in common with mankind. The eldest boy wakes up, seizes his stick, and tries to get out of bed, but his mother forces him back with a grip of iron. Thud, thud—the snake's back is broken in several places. Thud, thud—its head is crushed, and Alligator's nose skinned again.

She lifts the mangled reptile on the point of her stick, carries it to the fire, and throws it in; then piles on the wood and watches the snake burn. The boy and dog watch too. She lays her hand on the dog's head, and all the fierce, angry light dies out of his yellow eyes. The younger children are quieted, and presently go to sleep. The dirty-legged boy stands for a moment in his shirt, watching the fire. Presently he looks up at her, sees the tears in her eyes, and, throwing his arms round her neck exclaims:

"Mother, I won't never go drovin'; blarst me if I do!"

And she hugs him to her worn-out breast and kisses him; and they sit thus together while the sickly daylight breaks over the bush.

THE BUSH UNDERTAKER

"Five Bob!"

The old man shaded his eyes and peered through the dazzling glow of that broiling Christmas Day. He stood just within the door of a slab-and-bark hut situated upon the bank of a barren creek; sheep-yards lay to the right, and a low line of bare, brown ridges formed a suitable background to the scene.

"Five Bob!" shouted he again; and a dusty sheep-dog rose wearily from the shaded side of the hut and looked inquiringly at his master, who pointed towards some sheep which were straggling from the flock.

"Fetch 'em back," he said confidently.

The dog went off, and his master returned to the interior of the hut.

"We'll yard 'em early," he said to himself; "the super won't know. We'll yard 'em early, and have the arternoon to ourselves."

"We'll get dinner," he added, glancing at some pots on the fire. "I cud do a bit of doughboy, an' that theer boggabri'll eat like tater-marrer along of the salt meat." He moved one of the black buckets from the blaze. "I likes to keep it just on the sizzle," he said in explanation to himself; "hard bilin' makes it tough—I'll keep it just a-simmerin'."

Here his soliloquy was interrupted by the return of the dog.

"All right, Five Bob," said the hatter, "dinner'll be ready dreckly. Jist keep yer eye on the sheep till I call yer; keep 'em well rounded up, an' we'll yard 'em afterwards and have a holiday."

This speech was accompanied by a gesture evidently intelligible, for the dog retired as though he understood English, and the cooking proceeded.

"I'll take a pick an' shovel with me an' root up that old blackfellow," mused the shepherd, evidently following up a recent train of thought; "I reckon it'll do now. I'll put in the spuds."

The last sentence referred to the cooking, the first to a blackfellow's grave about which he was curious.

"The sheep's a-campin'," said the soliloquizer, glancing through the door. "So me an' Five Bob'll be able to get our dinner in peace. I wish I had just enough fat to make the pan siss; I'd treat myself to a leatherjacket; but it took three weeks' skimmin' to get enough for them theer doughboys."

In due time the dinner was dished up; and the old man seated himself on a block, with the lid of a gin-case across his knees for a table. Five Bob squatted opposite with the liveliest interest and appreciation depicted on his intelligent countenance.

Dinner proceeded very quietly, except when the carver paused to ask the dog how some tasty morsel went with him, and Five Bob's tail declared that it went very well indeed.

"Here y'are, try this," cried the old man, tossing him a large piece of doughboy. A click of Five Bob's jaws and the dough was gone.

"Clean into his liver!" said the old man with a faint smile.

He washed up the tinware in the water the duff had been boiled in, and then, with the assistance of the dog, yarded the sheep.

This accomplished, he took a pick and shovel and an old sack, and started out over the ridge, followed, of course, by his four-legged mate. After tramping some three miles he reached a spur, running out from the main ridge. At the extreme end of this, under some gum-trees, was a little mound of earth, barely defined in the grass, and indented in the centre as all blackfellow's graves were.

He set to work to dig it up, and sure enough, in about half an hour he bottomed on payable dirt.

When he had raked up all the bones, he amused himself by putting them together on the grass and by speculating as to whether they had belonged to black or white, male or female. Failing, however, to arrive at any satisfactory conclusion, he dusted them with great care, put them in the bag, and started for home.

He took a short cut this time over the ridge and down a gully which was full of ring-barked trees and long white grass. He had nearly reached its mouth when a great greasy black goanna clambered up a sapling from under his feet and looked fightable.

"Dang the jumpt-up thing!" cried the old man. "It gin me a start!"

At the foot of the sapling he espied an object which he at first thought was the blackened carcass of a sheep, but on closer examination discovered to be the body of a man; it lay with its forehead resting on its hands, dried to a mummy by the intense heat of the western summer.

"Me luck's in for the day and no mistake!" said the shepherd, scratching the back of his head, while he took stock of the remains. He picked up a stick and tapped the body on the shoulder; the flesh sounded like leather. He turned it over on its side; it fell flat on its back like a board, and the shrivelled eyes seemed to peer up at him from under the blackened wrists.

He stepped back involuntarily, but, recovering himself, leant on his stick and took in all the ghastly details.

There was nothing in the blackened features to tell aught of name or face, but the dress proclaimed the remains to be those of a European. The old man caught sight of a black bottle in the grass, close beside the corpse. This set him thinking. Presently he knelt down and examined the soles of the dead man's blucher boots, and then, rising with an air of conviction, exclaimed: "Brummy! by gosh!—busted up at last!

"I tole yer so, Brummy," he said impressively, addressing the corpse. "I allers told yer as how it 'ud be—an' here y'are, you thundering jumpt-up cus-o'-God fool. Yer cud earn more'n any man in the colony, but yer'd lush it all away. I allers sed as how it 'ud end, an' now yer kin see fur y'self.

"I spect yer was a-comin' t' me t' get fixt up an' set straight agin; then yer

81

was a-goin' to swear off, same as yer allers did; an' here y'are, an' now I expect I'll have t' fix yer up for the last time an' make yer decent, for 'twon't do t' leave yer a-lyin' out here like a dead sheep."

He picked up the corked bottle and examined it. To his great surprise it was nearly full of rum.

"Well, this gits me," exclaimed the old man; "me luck's in, this Christmas, an' no mistake. He must 'a' got the jams early in his spree, or he wouldn't be a-making for me with near a bottleful left. Howsomenever, here goes."

Looking around, his eyes lit up with satisfaction as he saw some bits of bark which had been left by a party of strippers who had been getting bark there for the stations. He picked up two pieces, one about four and the other six feet long, and each about two feet wide, and brought them over to the body. He laid the longest strip by the side of the corpse, which he proceeded to lift on to it.

"Come on, Brummy," he said, in a softer tone than usual, "ye ain't as bad as yer might be, considerin' as it must be three good months since yer slipped yer wind. I spect it was the rum as preserved yer. It was the death of yer when yer was alive, an' now yer dead, it preserves yer like—like a mummy."

Then he placed the other strip on top, with the hollow side downwards— thus sandwiching the defunct between the two pieces—removed the saddle-strap, which he wore for a belt, and buckled it round one end, while he tried to think of something with which to tie up the other.

"I can't take any more strips off my shirt," he said, critically examining the skirts of the old blue overshirt he wore. "I might get a strip or two more off, but it's short enough already. Let's see; how long have I been a-wearin' of that shirt; oh, I remember, I bought it jist two days afore Five Bob was pupped. I can't afford a new shirt jist yet; howsomenever, seein' it's Brummy, I'll jist borrow a couple more strips and sew 'em on agen when I git home."

He up-ended Brummy, and placing his shoulder against the middle of the lower sheet of bark, lifted the corpse to a horizontal position; then, taking the bag of bones in his hand, he started for home.

"I ain't a-spendin' sech a dull Christmas arter all," he reflected, as he plodded on; but he had not walked above a hundred yards when he saw a black goanna sidling into the grass.

"That's another of them theer dang things!" he exclaimed. "That's two I've seed this mornin'."

Presently he remarked: "Yer don't smell none too sweet, Brummy. It must 'a' been jist about the middle of shearin' when yer pegged out. I wonder who got yer last cheque. Shoo! theer's another black goanner—theer must be a flock of 'em."

He rested Brummy on the ground while he had another pull at the bottle, and, before going on, packed the bag of bones on his shoulder under the body, but he soon stopped again.

"The thunderin' jumpt-up bones is all skew-whift," he said. " 'Ole on, Brummy, an' I'll fix 'em"—and he leaned the dead man against a tree while he settled the bones on his shoulder, and took another pull at the bottle.

About a mile further on he heard a rustling in the grass to the right, and, looking round, saw another goanna gliding off sideways, with its long snaky neck turned towards him.

This puzzled the shepherd considerably, the strangest part of it being that Five Bob wouldn't touch the reptile, but slunk off with its tail down when ordered to "sick 'em."

"Theer's sothin' comic about them theer goanners," said the old man at last. "I've seed swarms of grasshoppers an' big mobs of kangaroos, but dang me if ever I seed a flock of black goanners afore!"

On reaching the hut the old man dumped the corpse against the wall, wrong end up, and stood scratching his head while he endeavoured to collect his muddled thoughts; but he had not placed Brummy at the correct angle, and, consequently, that individual fell forward and struck him a violent blow on the shoulder with the iron toes of his blucher boots.

The shock sobered him. He sprang a good yard, instinctively hitching up his moleskins in preparation for flight; but a backward glance revealed to him the true cause of this supposed attack from the rear. Then he lifted the body, stood it on its feet against the chimney, and ruminated as to where he should lodge his mate for the night, not noticing that the shorter sheet of bark had slipped down on the boots and left the face exposed.

"I spect I'll have ter put yer into the chimney-trough for the night, Brummy," said he, turning round to confront the corpse. "Yer can't expect me to take yer into the hut, though I did it when yer was in a worse state than—Lord!"

The shepherd was not prepared for the awful scrutiny that gleamed on him from those empty sockets; his nerves received a shock, and it was some time before he recovered himself sufficiently to speak.

"Now, look a-here, Brummy," said he, shaking his finger severely at the delinquent, "I don't want to pick a row with yer; I'd do as much for yer an' more than any other man, an' well yer knows it; but if yer starts playin' any of yer jumpt-up pranktical jokes on me, and a-scarin' of me after a-humpin' of yer 'ome, by the 'only frost I'll kick yer to jim-rags, so I will."

This admonition delivered, he hoisted Brummy into the chimney-trough, and with a last glance towards the sheep-yards, he retired to his bunk to have, as he said, a snooze.

He had more than a snooze, however, for when he woke, it was dark, and the bushman's instinct told him it must be nearly nine o'clock.

He lit a slush-lamp and poured the remainder of the rum into a pannikin; but, just as he was about to lift the draught to his lips, he heard a peculiar rustling sound overhead, and put the pot down on the table with a slam that spilled some of the precious liquor.

Five Bob whimpered, and the old shepherd, though used to the weird and dismal, as one living alone in the bush must necessarily be, felt the icy breath of fear at his heart.

He reached hastily for his old shot-gun, and went out to investigate. He walked round the hut several times and examined the roof on all sides, but saw nothing. Brummy appeared to be in the same position.

At last, persuading himself that the noise was caused by possums or the wind, the old man went inside, boiled his billy, and, after composing his nerves somewhat with a light supper and a meditative smoke, retired for the night. He was aroused several times before midnight by the same mysterious sound overhead, but, though he rose and examined the roof on each occasion by the light of the rising moon, he discovered nothing.

At last he determined to sit up and watch until daybreak, and for this purpose took up a position on a log a short distance from the hut, with his gun laid in readiness across his knee.

After watching for about an hour, he saw a black object coming over the ridge-pole. He grabbed his gun and fired. The thing disappeared. He ran round to the other side of the hut, and there was a great black goanna in violent convulsions on the ground.

Then the old man saw it all. "The thunderin' jumpt-up thing has been a-havin' o' me," he exclaimed. "The same cus-o'-God wretch has a-follered me 'ome, an' has been a-havin' its Christmas dinner off of Brummy, an' a-hauntin' o' me into the bargain, the jumpt-up tinker!"

As there was no one by whom he could send a message to the station, and the old man dared not leave the sheep and go himself, he determined to bury the body the next afternoon, reflecting that the authorities could disinter it for inquest if they pleased.

So he brought the sheep home early and made arrangements for the burial by measuring the outer casing of Brummy and digging a hole according to those dimensions.

"That 'minds me," he said. "I never rightly knowed Brummy's religion, blest if ever I did. Howsomenever, there's one thing sartin—none o' them theer pianer-fingered parsons is a-goin' ter take the trouble ter travel out inter this God-fogotten part to hold sarvice over him, seein' as how his last cheque's blued. But, as I've got the fun'ral arrangements all in me own hands, I'll do jestice to it, and see that Brummy has a good comfortable buryin'—and more's unpossible."

"It's time yer turned in, Brum," he said, lifting the body down.

He carried it to the grave and dropped it into one corner like a post. He arranged the bark so as to cover the face, and, by means of a piece of clothes-line, lowered the body to a horizontal position. Then he threw in an armful of gum-leaves, and then, very reluctantly, took the shovel and dropped in a few shovelfuls of earth.

"An' this is the last of Brummy," he said, leaning on his spade and looking away over the tops of the ragged gums on the distant range.

This reflection seemed to engender a flood of memories, in which the old man became absorbed. He leaned heavily upon his spade and thought.

"Arter all," he murmured sadly, "arter all—it were Brummy."

"Brummy," he said at last. "It's all over now; nothin' matters now— nothin' didn't ever matter, nor—nor don't. You uster say as how it 'ud be all right termorrer" (pause); "termorrer's come, Brummy—come fur you—it ain't come fur me yet, but—it's a-comin'."

He threw in some more earth.

"Yer don't remember, Brummy, an' mebbe yer don't want to remember— I don't want to remember—but—well, but, yer see that's where yer got the pull on me."

He shovelled in some more earth and paused again.

The dog rose, with ears erect, and looked anxiously first at his master and then into the grave.

"Theer oughter be somethin' sed," muttered the old man; "'tain't right to put 'im under like a dog. Theer oughter be some sort o' sarmin."

He sighed heavily in the listening silence that followed this remark and proceeded with his work. He filled the grave to the brim this time, and fashioned the mound carefully with his spade. Once or twice he muttered the words, "I am the rassaraction." As he laid the tools quietly aside, and stood at the head of the grave, he was evidently trying to remember the something that ought to be said. He removed his hat, placed it carefully on the grass, held his hands out from his sides and a little to the front, drew a long deep breath, and said with a solemnity that greatly disturbed Five Bob: "Hashes ter hashes, dus ter dus, Brummy—an'—an' in hopes of a great an' gerlorious rassaraction!"

He sat down on a log near by, rested his elbows on his knees and passed his hand wearily over his forehead—but only as one who was tired and felt the heat; and presently he rose, took up the tools, and walked back to the hut.

And the sun sank again on the grand Australian bush—the nurse and tutor of eccentric minds, the home of the weird.

BRUMMY USEN

We caught up with an old swagman crossing the plain, and tramped along with him till we came to good shade to have a smoke in. We had got yarning about men getting lost in the bush or going away and being reported dead.

"Yes," said the old swagman, as he dropped his swag in the shade, sat down on it, and felt for his smoking tackle, "there's scarcely an old bushman alive—or dead, for the matter of it—who hasn't been dead a few times in his life—or reported dead, which amounts to the same thing for a while. In my time there was as many live men in the bush who was supposed to be dead as there was dead men who was supposed to be live—though it's the other way about now—what with so many jackeroos tramping about out back and getting lost in the dry country that they don't know anything about, and dying within a few yards of water sometimes. But even now, whenever I hear that an old bush mate of mine is dead, I don't fret about it or put a black band around my hat, because I know he'll be pretty sure to turn up sometime, pretty bad with the booze, and want to borrow half a crown.

"I've been dead a few times myself, and found out afterwards that my friends was so sorry about it, and that I was such a good sort of a chap after all, when I was dead that—that I was sorry I didn't stop dead. You see, I was one of them chaps that's better treated by their friends and better thought of when—when they're dead.

"Ah, well! Never mind. . . . Talking of killing bushmen before their time reminds me of some cases I knew. They mostly happened before the western spurs of the ranges. There was a bullock-driver named Billy Nowlett. He had a small selection, where he kept his family, and used to carry from the railway terminus to the stations up-country. One time he went up with a load and was not heard of for such a long time that his missus got mighty uneasy; and then she got a letter from a publican up Coonamble way to say that Billy was dead. Someone wrote, for the widow, to ask about the wagon and the bullocks, but the shanty-keeper wrote that Billy had drunk them before he died, and that he'd also to say that he'd drunk the money he got for the carrying; and the publican enclosed a five-pound note for the widow—which was considered very kind of him.

"Well, the widow struggled along and managed without her husband just the same as she had always struggled along and managed with him—a little better, perhaps. An old digger used to drop in of evenings and sit by the widow's fire, and yarn, and sympathize, and smoke, and think; and just as he began to yarn a lot less, and smoke and think a lot more, Billy Nowlett himself turned up with a load of rations for a sheep station. He'd been down by the other road, and the letter he'd wrote to his missus had gone astray. Billy wasn't surprised to hear that he was dead—he'd been killed before—but he was suprised about the five quid.

"You see, it must have been another bullock-driver that died. There was an old shanty-keeper up Coonamble way, so Billy said, that used to always mistake him for another bullocky and mistake the other bullocky for him—couldn't tell the one from the other no way—and he used to have bills against Billy that the other bullock-driver'd run up, and bills against the other that Billy'd run up, and generally got things mixed up in various ways, till Billy wished that one of 'em was dead. And the funniest part of the business was that Billy wasn't no more like the other man than chalk is like cheese. You'll often drop across some colour-blind old codger that can't tell the difference between two people that ain't got a bit of likeness between 'em.

"Then there was young Joe Swallow. He was found dead under a burned-down tree in Dead Man's Gully—'dead past all recognition,' they said—and he was buried there, and by and by his ghost began to haunt the gully: at least, all the school kids seen it, and there was scarcely a grown-up person who didn't know another person who'd seen the ghost— and the other person was always a sober chap that wouldn't bother about telling a lie. But just as the ghost was beginning to settle down to work in the gully, Joe himself turned up, and then the folks began to reckon that it was another man was killed there, and that the ghost belonged to the other man; and some of them began to recollect that they'd thought all along that the ghost wasn't Joe's ghost—even when they thought that it was really Joe that was killed there.

"Then again, there was the case of Brummy Usen—Hughison I think they spell it—the bushranger; he was shot by old Mr S——, of E——, while trying to stick the old gentleman up. There's something about it in a book called *Robbery Under Arms*, though the names is all altered—and some other time I'll tell you all about the digging of the body up for the inquest and burying it again. This Brummy used to work for a publican in a sawmill that the publican had; and this publican and his daughter identified the body by a woman holding up a branch tattooed on the right arm. I'll tell you all about that another time. This girl remembered how she used to watch this tatooed woman going up and down on Brummy's arm when he was working in the saw-pit—going up and down and up and down, like this, while Brummy was working his end of the saw. So the bushranger was inquested and justifiable-homicided as Brummy Usen, and buried again in his dust and blood stains and money-jacket.

"All the same it wasn't him; for the real Brummy turned up later on; but he couldn't make the people believe he wasn't dead. They were mostly English country people from Kent and Yorkshire and those places; and the most self-opinionated and obstinate people that ever lived when they got a thing into their heads; and they got it into their heads that Brummy Usen was shot while trying to bail up old Mr S—— and was dead and buried.

"But the wife of the publican that had the saw-pit knew him; he went to her, and she recognised him at once; she'd got it into her head from the first that it wasn't Brummy that was shot, and she stuck to it—she was just as self-opinionated as the neighbours, and many a barney she had with them about it. She would argue about it till the day she died, and then she said with her dying breath: 'It wasn't Brummy Usen.' No more it was—he was a different kind of man; he hadn't the spunk enough to be a bushranger, and it was a better man that was buried for him; it was a different kind of woman, holding up a different kind of branch, that was tatooed on Brummy's arm. But, you see, Brummy'd always kept himself pretty much to himself, and no one knew him very well; and, besides, most of them were pretty drunk at the inquest—except the girl, and she was too scared to know what she was saying—they had to be so because the corpse was in such a bad state.

"Well, Brummy hung around for a time, and tried to prove that he wasn't an imposter, but no one would believe him. He wanted to get some wages that was owing to him.

"He tried the police, but they were just as obstinate as the rest; and besides, they had their dignity to hold up. 'If I ain't Brummy,' he'd say, 'who are I?' But they answered that he knew best. So he did.

"At last he said that it didn't matter much, any road; and so he went away—Lord knows where—to begin life again, I s'pose."

The traveller smoked a while reflectively; then he quietly rolled up his right sleeve and scratched his arm.

And on that arm we saw the tattooed figure of a woman, holding up a branch.

We tramped on by his side again towards the station—thinking very hard and not feeling very comfortable.

He must have been an awful old liar, now we come to think of it.

THE UNION BURIES ITS DEAD

While out boating one Sunday afternoon on a billabong across the river, we saw a young man on horseback driving some horses along the bank. He said it was a fine day, and asked if the water was deep there. The joker of our party said it was deep enough to drown him, and he laughed and rode farther up. We didn't take much notice of him.

Next day a funeral gathered at a corner pub and asked each other in to have a drink while waiting for the hearse. They passed away some of the time dancing jigs to a piano in the bar parlour. They passed away the rest of the time skylarking and fighting.

The defunct was a young Union labourer, about twenty-five, who had been drowned the previous day while trying to swim some horses across a billabong of the Darling.

He was almost a stranger in town, and the fact of his having been a Union man accounted for the funeral. The police found some Union papers in his swag, and called at the General Labourers' Union Office for information about him. That's how we knew. The secretary had very little information to give. The departed was a "Roman," and the majority of the town were otherwise—but Unionism is stronger than creed. Liquor, however, is stronger than Unionism: and, when the hearse presently arrived, more than two-thirds of the funeral were unable to follow.

The procession numbered fifteen, fourteen souls following the broken shell of a soul. Perhaps not one of the fourteen possessed a soul any more than the corpse did—but that doesn't matter.

Four or five of the funeral, who were boarders at the pub, borrowed a trap which the landlord used to carry passengers to and from the railway station. They were strangers to us who were on foot, and we to them. We were all strangers to the corpse.

A horseman, who looked like a drover just returned from a big trip, dropped into our dusty wake and followed us a few hundred yards, dragging his packhorse behind him, but a friend made wild and demonstrative signals from an hotel veranda—hooking at the air in front with his right hand

89

and jobbing his left thumb over his shoulder in the direction of the bar—so the drover hauled off and didn't catch up to us any more. He was a stranger to the entire show.

We walked in twos. There were three twos. It was very hot and dusty; the heat rushed in fierce dazzling rays across every iron roof and light-coloured wall that was turned to the sun. One or two pubs closed respectfully until we got past. They closed their bar doors and the patrons went in and out through some side or back entrance for a few minutes. Bushmen seldom grumble at an inconvenience of this sort, when it is caused by a funeral. They have too much respect for the dead.

On the way to the cemetery we passed three shearers sitting on the shady side of a fence. One was drunk—very drunk. The other two covered their right ears with their hats, out of respect for the departed—whoever he might have been—and one of them kicked the drunk and muttered something to him.

He straightened himself up, stared, and reached helplessly for his hat, which he shoved half off and then on again. Then he made a great effort to pull himself together—and succeeded. He stood up, braced his back against the fence, knocked off his hat, and remorsefully placed his foot on it—to keep it off his head till the funeral passed.

A tall, sentimental drover, who walked by my side, cynically quoted Byronic verses suitable to the occasion—to death—and asked with pathetic humour whether we thought the dead man's ticket would be recognized "over yonder." It was a G.L.U. ticket, and the general opinion was that it would be recognized.

Presently my friend said:

"You remember when we were in the boat yesterday, we saw a man driving some horses along the bank?"

"Yes."

He nodded at the hearse and said:

"Well, that's him."

I thought a while.

"I didn't take any particular notice of him," I said. "He said something, didn't he?"

"Yes; said it was a fine day. You'd have taken more notice if you'd known that he was doomed to die in the hour, and that those were the last words he would say to any man in this world."

"To be sure," said a full voice from the rear. "If ye'd known that, ye'd have prolonged the conversation."

We plodded on across the railway line and along the hot, dusty road which ran to the cemetery, some of us talking about the accident, and lying about the narrow escapes we had had ourselves. Presently someone said:

"There's the Devil."

I looked up and saw a priest standing in the shade of the tree by the cemetery gate.

The hearse was drawn up and the tail-boards were opened. The funeral extinguished its right ear with its hat as four men lifted the coffin out and laid it over the grave. The priest—a pale, quiet young fellow—stood under the shade of a sapling which grew at thehead of the grave. He took off his hat, dropped it carelessly on the ground, and proceeded to business. I noticed that one or two heathens winced slightly when the holy water was sprinkled on the coffin. The drops quickly evaporated, and the little round black spots they left were soon dusted over; but the spots showed, by contrast, the cheapness and shabbiness of the cloth with which the coffin was covered. It seemed black before; now it looked a dusky grey.

Just here man's ignorance and vanity made a farce of the funeral. A big, bull-necked publican, with heavy, blotchy features, and a supremely ignorant expression, picked up the priest's straw hat and held it about two inches over the head of his reverence during the whole of the service. The father, be it remembered, was standing in the shade. a few shoved their hats on and off uneasily, struggling between their disgust for the living and their respect for the dead. The hat had a conical crown and a brim sloping down all round like a sunshade, and the publican held it with his great red claw spread over the crown. To do the priest justice, perhaps he didn't notice the incident. A sage priest or parson in the same position might have said, "Put the hat down, my friend; is not the memory of our departed brother worth more than my complexion?" A wattle-bark layman might have expressed himself in stronger language, none the less to the point. But my priest seemed unconscious of what was going on. Besides, the publican was a great and important pillar of the church. He couldn't, as an ignorant and conceited ass, lose such a good opportunity of asserting his faithfulness and importance to his church.

The grave looked very narrow under the coffin, and I drew a breath of relief when the box slid easily down. I saw a coffin get stuck once, at Rookwood, and it had to be yanked out with difficulty, and laid on the sods at the feet of the heart-broken relations, who howled dismally while the grave-diggers widened the hole. But they don't cut contracts so fine in the West. Our grave-digger was not altogether bowelless, and, out of respect for that human quality described as "feelin's," he scraped up some light and dusty soil and threw it down to deaden the fall of the clay lumps on the coffin. He also tried to steer the first few shovelfuls gently down against the end of the grave with the back of the shovel turned outwards, but the hard dry Darling River clods rebounded and knocked all the same. It didn't matter much—nothing does. The fall of lumps of clay on a stranger's coffin doesn't sound any different from the fall of the same things on an ordinary wooden box—at least I didn't notice anything awesome or unusual in the sound; but, perhaps, one of us—the most sensitive—might have been impressed by being reminded of a burial of long ago, when the thump of every sod jolted his heart.

I have left out the wattle—because it wasn't there. I have also neglected to mention the heart-broken old mate, with his grizzled head bowed and great pearly drops streaming down his rugged cheeks. He was absent—he was probably "out back." For similar reasons I have omitted reference to the suspicious moisture in the eyes of a bearded bush ruffian named Bill. Bill failed to turn up, and the only moisture was that which was induced by the heat. I have left out the "sad Australian sunset," because the sun was not going down at the time. The burial took place exactly at midday.

The dead bushman's name was Jim, apparently; but they found no portraits, nor locks of hair, nor any love letters, nor anything of that kind in his swag

Lawson is here scoffing at the stylistic literary clichés normally expected in short stories of the period. From this outburst it is obvious that he studied the technique and form of his medium much more closely than some of his critics have imagined.

—not even a reference to his mother; only some papers relating to Union matters. Most of us didn't know the name till we saw it on the coffin; we knew him as "that poor chap that got drowned yesterday."

"So his name's James Tyson," said my drover acquaintance, looking at the plate.

"Why! Didn't you know that before?" I asked.

"No; but I knew he was a Union man."

It turned out, afterwards, that J.T. wasn't his real name—only "the name he went by."

Anyhow he was buried by it, and most of the "Great Australian Dailies" have mentioned in their brevity columns that a young man named James John Tyson was drowned in a billabong of the Darling last Sunday.

We did hear, later on, what his real name was; but if we ever chance to read it in the "Missing Friends Column," we shall not be able to give any information to heart-broken mother or sister or wife, nor to anyone who could let him hear something to his advantage—for we have already forgotten the name.

Woolscour at Bourke, 1890. In 1892 Lawson's drinking and general behaviour was worrying his friends and at E. J. Brady's suggestion Archibald, editor of the *Bulletin,* sent Lawson to Bourke in quest of copy for his paper. At that time Bourke, over 500 miles from Sydney, on the banks of the Darling River, and the centre of a sheep-growing district, was a frontier town with less than 1,500 inhabitants. In fact, Thomas Livingstone Mitchell, then Surveyor-General of New South Wales, in 1835 had built a rough stockade about seven miles from the present site of the town, which he named Fort Bourke.

Lawson came to the town in the worst drought in memory and, to make it worse, it was also summertime. For the rest of his writing life his experiences in what he called the 'metropolis of the Great Scrubs' was to provide him with material for his creative writing. It was here that he saw the creed of mateship and unionism in full swing. Eurunderee had had nothing like this to show him. In short, Bourke was in the nature of a literary catalyst.

He walked in search of work from Bourke to Hungerford on the Queensland border, and back again and his mate, 'Jim Grahame' (J. W. Gordon), has written of Lawson's mateship during the rigours of the trip.

EUREKA

(A Fragment)

Roll up, Eureka's heroes, on that Grand Old Rush afar,
For Lalor's gone to join you in the big camp where you are;
Roll up and give him welcome such as only diggers can,
For well he battled for the rights of miner and of Man.
And there, in that bright, golden land that lies beyond our sight,
The record of his honest life shall be his Miner's Right;
But many a bearded mouth shall twitch, and many a tear be shed,
And many a grey old digger sigh to hear that Lalor's dead.
Yet wipe your eyes, old fossickers, o'er worked-out fields that roam,
You need not weep at parting from a digger going home.

Now from the strange wild seasons past, the days of golden strife,
Now from the Roaring Fifties comes a scene from Lalor's life:
All gleaming white amid the shafts o'er gully, hill, and flat
Again I see the tents that form the camp at Ballarat.
I hear the shovels and the picks, and all the air is rife
With the rattle of the cradles and the sounds of digger-life;
The clatter of the windlass-boles, as spinning round they go,
And then the signal to his mate, the digger's cry, "Below!"
From many a busy pointing-forge the sound of labour swells,
The tinkling at the anvils is as clear as silver bells.
I hear the broken English from the mouth, at least, of one
From every state and nation that is known beneath the sun;
The homely tongue of Scotland and the brogue of Ireland blend
With the dialects of England, right from Berwick to Land's End;
And to the busy concourse here the West has sent a part,
The land of gulches that has been immortalized by Harte;
The land where long from mining-camps the blue smoke upward curled;
The land that gave the "Partner" true and "Mliss" unto the world;
The men from all the nations in the New World and the Old,
All side by side, like brethren here, are delving after gold.
But suddenly the warning cries are heard on every side
As, closing in around the field, a ring of troopers ride.
Unlicensed diggers are the game—their class and want are sins,
And so, with all its shameful scenes, the digger-hunt begins.
The men are seized who are too poor the heavy tax to pay,
And they are chained, as convicts were, and dragged in gangs away.
Though in the eye of many a man the menace scarce was hid,
The diggers' blood was slow to boil, but scalded when it did.
But now another match is lit that soon must fire the charge,
A digger murdered in the camp; his murderer at large!

"Roll up! Roll up!" the pregnant cry awakes the evening air,
And angry faces surge like waves around the speakers there.
"What are our sins that we should be an outlawed class?" they say,
"Shall we stand by while mates are siezed and dragged like lags away?
Shall insult be on insult heaped? Shall we let these things go?"
And with a roar of voices comes the diggers' answer—"No!"
The day has vanished from the scene, but not the air of night
Can cool the blood that, ebbing back, leaves brows in anger white.
Lo, from the roof of Bentley's inn the flames are leaping high;
They write "Revenge!" in letters red across the smoke-dimmed sky.
"To arms! To arms!" the cry is out; "To arms and play your part;
For every pike upon a pole will find a tyrant's heart!"
Now Lalor comes to take the lead, the spirit does not lag,
And down the rough, wild diggers kneel beneath the Diggers' Flag;
Then, rising to their feet, they swear, while rugged hearts beat high,
To stand beside their leader and to conquer or to die!
Around Eureka's stockade now the shades of night close fast,
Three hundred sleep beside their arms, and thirty sleep their last.

About the streets of Melbourne town the sound of bells is borne
That call the citizens to prayer that fateful Sabbath morn;
But there, upon Eureka's hill, a hundred miles away,
The diggers' forms lie white and still above the blood-stained clay.
The bells that toll the diggers' death might also ring a knell
For those few gallant soldiers, dead, who did their duty well.
The sight of murdered heroes is to hero hearts a goad,
A thousand men are up in arms upon the Creswick road,
And wildest rumours in the air are flying up and down,
'Tis said the men of Ballarat will march on Melbourne town.
But not in vain those diggers died. Their comrades may rejoice,
For o'er the voice of tyranny is heard the people's voice;
It says: "Reform your rotten law, the diggers' wrongs make right,
Or else with them, our brothers now, we'll gather to the fight."

'Twas of such stuff the men were made who saw our nation born,
And such as Lalor were the men who led their footsteps on;
And of such men there'll many be, and of such leaders some,
In the roll-up of Australians on some dark day yet to come.

THE GLASS ON THE BAR

Three bushmen one morning rode up to an inn,
And one of them called for the drinks with a grin;
They'd only returned from a trip to the North,
And, eager to greet them, the landlord came forth.
He absently poured out a glass of Three Star,
And set down that drink with the rest on the bar.

"There, that is for Harry," he said, "and it's queer,
'Tis the very same glass that he drank from last year;
His name's on the glass, you can read it like print,
He scratched it himself with an old bit of flint;
I remember his drink—it was always Three Star"—
And the landlord looked out through the door of the bar.

He looked at the horses, and counted but three:
"You were always together—where's Harry?" cried he.
Oh, sadly they looked at the glass as they said,
"You may put it away, for our old mate is dead;"
But one, gazing out o'er the ridges afar,
Said, "We owe him a shout—leave the glass on the bar."

They thought of the far-away grave on the plain,
They thought of the comrade who came not again,
They lifted their glasses, and sadly they said:
"We drink to the name of the mate who is dead."
And the sunlight streamed in, and a light like a star
Seemed to glow in the depth of the glass on the bar.

And still in that shanty a tumbler is seen,
It stands by the clock, always polished and clean;
And often the strangers will read as they pass
The name of a bushman engraved on the glass;
And though on the shelf but a dozen there are,
That glass never stands with the rest on the bar.

MIDDLETON'S ROUSEABOUT

Tall and freckled and sandy,
  Face of a country lout;
This was the picture of Andy,
  Middleton's Rouseabout.

Type of a coming nation
  In the land of cattle and sheep;
Worked on Middleton's station,
  Pound a week and his keep;

On Middleton's wide dominions
  Plied the stockwhip and shears;
Hadn't any opinions,
  Hadn't any "idears".

Swiftly the years went over,
  Liquor and drought prevailed;
Middleton went as a drover
  After his station had failed.

Type of a careless nation,
  Men who are soon played out,
Middleton was:—and his station
  Was bought by the Rouseabout.

Flourishing beard and sandy,
  Tall and solid and stout;
This is the picture of Andy,
  Middleton's Rouseabout.

Now on his own dominions
  Works with his overseers;
Hasn't any opinions,
  Hasn't any idears.

MACQUARIE'S MATE

The chaps in the bar of Stiffner's shanty were talking about Macquarie, an absent shearer—who seemed, from their conversation, to be better known than liked by them.

"I ain't seen Macquarie for ever so long," remarked Box-o'-Tricks, after a pause. "Wonder where he could 'a' got to?"

"Jail, p'r'aps—or hell," growled Barcoo. "He ain't much loss, any road."

"My oath, yer right, Barcoo!" interposed "Sally" Thompson. "But, now I come to think of it, Old Awful Example there was a mate of his one time. Bless'd if the old soaker ain't comin' to life again!"

A shaky, rag-and-dirt-covered framework of a big man rose uncertainly from a corner of the room, and, staggering forward, brushed the staring thatch back from his forehead with one hand, reached blindly for the edge of the bar with the other, and drooped heavily.

"Well, Awful Example," demanded the shanty-keeper. "What's up with you now?"

The drunkard lifted his head and glared wildly round with bloodshot eyes.

"Don't you—don't you talk about him! *Drop it,* I say! Drop it!"

"What the devil's the matter with you now, anyway?" growled the barman. "Got 'em again? Hey?"

"Don't you—don't you talk about Macquarie! He's a mate of mine! Here! Gimme a drink!"

"Well, what if he is a mate of yours?" sneered Barcoo. "It don't reflec' much credit on you—nor him neither."

The logic contained in the last three words was unanswerable, and Awful Example was still fairly reasonable, even when rum oozed out of him at every pore. He gripped the edge of the bar with both hands, let his ruined head fall forward until it was on a level with his temporarily rigid arms, and stared blindly at the dirty floor; then he straightened himself up, still keeping his hold on the bar.

"Some of you chaps," he said huskily; "*one* of you chaps, in this bar to-day, called Macquarie a scoundrel, and a loafer, and a blackguard, and—and a sneak and a liar."

"Well, what if we did?" said Barcoo, defiantly. "He's all that, and a cheat into the bargain. And now, what are you going to do about it?"

The old man swung sideways to the bar, rested his elbow on it, and his head on his hand.

"Macquarie wasn't a sneak and he wasn't a liar," he said, in a quiet, tired tone; "and Macquarie wasn't a cheat!"

"Well, old man, you needn't get your rag out about it," said Sally Thompson, soothingly. "P'r'aps we was a bit too hard on him; and it isn't altogether right, chaps, considerin' he's not here. But then, you know, Awful, he might have acted straight to you that was his mate. The meanest blank—if he is a man at all—will do that."

"Oh, to blazes with the old sot!" shouted Barcoo. "I gave my opinion about Macquarie, and, what's more, I'll stand to it."

"I've got—I've got a point for the defence," the old man went on, without heeding the interruptions. "I've got a point or two for the defence."

"Well, let's have it," said Stiffner.

"In the first place—in the first place, Macquarie never talked about no man behind his back."

There was an uneasy movement, and a painful silence. Barcoo reached for his drink and drank slowly; he needed time to think—Box-o'-Tricks studied his boots—Sally Thompson looked out at the weather—the shanty-keeper wiped the top of the bar very hard—and the rest shifted round and "s'posed they'd try a game er cards."

Barcoo set his glass down very softly, pocketed his hands deeply and defiantly, and said:

"Well, what of that? Macquarie was as strong as a bull, and the greatest bully on the river into the bargain. He could call a man a liar to his face —and smash his face afterwards. And he did it often, too, and with smaller men than himself."

There was a breath of relief in the bar.

"Do you want to make out that I'm talking about a man behind his back?" continued Barcoo, threateningly, to Awful Example. "You'd best take care, old man."

"Macquarie wasn't a coward," remonstrated the drunkard, softly, but in an injured tone.

"What's up with you, anyway?" yelled the publican. "What yer growling at? D'ye want a row? Get out if yer can't be agreeable!"

The boozer swung his back to the bar, hooked himself on by his elbows, and looked vacantly out of the door.

"I've got—another point for the defence," he muttered. "It's always best —it's always best to keep the last point to—the last."

"Oh, Lord! Well, out with it! *Out with it!*"

"Macquarie's dead! That—that's what it is!"

Everyone moved uneasily: Sally Thompson turned the other side to the bar, crossed one leg behind the other, and looked down over his hip at the sole and heel of his elastic-side—the barman rinsed the glasses vigorously —Longbones shuffled and dealt on the top of a cask, and some of the others gathered round him and got interested—Barcoo thought he heard his horse breaking away, and went out to see to it, followed by Box-o'-Tricks and a couple more, who thought that it might be one of their horses.

Someone—a tall, gaunt, determined-looking bushman, with square features and haggard grey eyes—had ridden in unnoticed through the scrub to the back of the shanty and dismounted by the window.

When Barcoo and the others re-entered the bar it soon became evident that Sally Thompson had been thinking, for presently he came to the general rescue as follows:

"There's a blessed lot of tommy-rot about dead people in this world—a lot of damned old-woman nonsense. There's more sympathy wasted over dead and rotten skunks than there is justice done to straight, honest-livin' chaps. I don't b'lieve in this glory sentiment about the dead at the expense of the living. I b'lieve in justice for the livin'—and the dead too, for that matter—but justice for the livin'. Macquarie was a bad egg, and it don't alter the case if he was dead a thousand times."

There was another breath of relief in the bar, and presently somebody said: "Yer right, Sally!"

"Good for you, Sally, old man!" cried Box-o'-Tricks, taking it up. "An', besides, I don't b'lieve Macquarie is dead at all. He's always dyin', or being reported dead, and then turnin' up again. Where did you hear about it, Awful?"

The Example ruefully rubbed a corner of his roof with the palm of his hand.

"There's—there's a lot in what you say, Sally Thompson," he admitted slowly, totally ignoring Box-o'-Tricks. "But—but——"

"Oh, we've had enough of the old fool," yelled Barcoo. "Macquarie was a spieler, and any man that ud be his mate ain't much better."

"Here, take a drink and dry up, yer old hass!" said the man behind the bar, pushing a bottle and glass towards the drunkard. "D'ye want a row?"

The old man took the bottle and glass in his shaking hands and painfully poured out a drink.

"There's a lot in what Sally Thompson says," he went on, obstinately, "but—but," he added in a strained tone, "there's another point that I near forgot, and none of you seemed to think of it—not even Sally Thompson nor—nor Box-o'-Tricks there."

Stiffner turned his back, and Barcoo spat viciously and impatiently.

"Yes," drivelled the drunkard, "I've got another point for—for the defence —of my mate, Macquarie——"

"Oh, out with it! Spit it out, for God's sake, or you'll bust!" roared Stiffner. "What the blazes is it?"

"His mate's alive!" yelled the old man. "Macquarie's mate's alive! That's what it is!"

He reeled back from the bar, dashed his glass and hat to the boards, gave his pants a hitch by the waistband that almost lifted him off his feet, and tore at his shirt-sleeves.

"Make a ring boys," he shouted. "His mate's alive! Put up your hands, Barcoo! By God, his mate's alive!"

Someone had turned his horse loose at the rear and had been standing by the back door for the last five minutes. Now he slipped quietly in.

"Keep the old fool off, or he'll get hurt," snarled Barcoo.

Stiffner jumped the counter. There were loud, hurried words of remonstrance, then some stump-splitting oaths and a scuffle, consequent upon an attempt to chuck the old man out. Then a crash. Stiffner and Box-o'-Tricks were down, two others were holding Barcoo back, and someone had pinned Awful Example by the shoulders from behind.

"Let me go!" he yelled, too blind with passion to notice the movements of surprise among the men before him. "Let me go! I'll smash—any man—that—that says a word again' a mate of mine behind his back. Barcoo, I'll have your blood! Let me go! I'll, I'll, I'll—— Who's holdin' me? You—you——"

"It's Macquarie, old mate!" said a quiet voice.

Barcoo thought he heard his horse again, and went out in a hurry. Perhaps he thought that the horse would get impatient and break loose if he left it any longer, for he jumped into the saddle and rode off.

BILL, THE VENTRILOQUIAL ROOSTER

'Brammer' was the colloquial name for Brahmaputra poultry, particularly roosters, which had a reputation as game cocks.

"When we were up-country on the selection, we had a rooster at our place, named Bill," said Mitchell; "a big mongrel of no particular breed, though the old lady said he was a 'brammer'—and many an argument she had with the old man about it too; she was just as stubborn and obstinate in her opinion as the governor was in his. But, anyway, we called him Bill, and didn't take any particular notice of him till a cousin of some of us came from Sydney on a visit to the country, and stayed at our place because it was cheaper than stopping at a pub. Well, somehow this chap got interested in Bill, and studied him for two or three days, and at last he says:

"'Why, that rooster's a ventriloquist!'

"'A what?'

"'A ventriloquist!'

"'Go along with yer!'

"'But he is. I've heard of cases like this before; but this is the first I've come across. Bill's a ventriloquist right enough.'

"Then we remembered that there wasn't another rooster within five miles —our only neighbour, an Irishman named Page, didn't have one at the time —and we'd often heard another cock crow, but didn't think to take any notice of it. We watched Bill, and sure enough, he *was* a ventriloquist. The 'ka-cocka' would come all right, but the 'co-ka-koo-oi-oo' seemed to come from a distance. And sometimes the whole crow would go wrong, and come back like an echo that had been lost for a year. Bill would stand on tiptoe, and hold his elbows out, and curve his neck, and go two or three times as if he was swallowing nest-eggs, and nearly break his neck and burst his gizzard; and then there'd be no sound at all where he was—only a cock crowing in the distance.

"And pretty soon we could see that Bill was in great trouble about it himself. You see, he didn't know it was himself—thought it was another rooster challenging him, and he wanted badly to find that other bird. He would get up on the wood-heap, and crow and listen—crow and listen again—crow and listen, and then he'd go up to the top of the paddock, and get up on the stack, and crow and listen there. Then down to the other end of the paddock, and get up on a mullock-heap, and crow and listen there. Then across to the other side and up on a log among the saplings, and crow 'n' listen some more. He searched all over the place for that other rooster, but of course, couldn't find him. Sometimes he'd be out all day crowing and listening all over the country, and then come home dead tired, and rest and cool off in a hole that the hens had scratched for him in a damp place under the water-cask sledge.

"Well, one day Page brought home a big white rooster, and when he let it go it climbed up on Page's stack and crowed, to see if there was any more roosters round there. Bill had come home tired; it was a hot day, and he'd rooted out the hens, and was having a spell-oh under the cask when the white rooster crowed. Bill didn't lose any time getting out and on to the wood-heap, and then he waited till he heard the crow again; then he crowed, and the other rooster crowed again, and they crowed at each other for three days, and called each other all the wretches they could lay their tongues to, and after that they implored each other to come out and be made into chicken soup and feather pillows. But neither'd come. You see, there were *three* crows—there was Bill's crow, and the ventriloquist crow, and the white rooster's crow—and each rooster thought that there was *two* roosters in the opposition camp, and that he mightn't get fair play, and, consequently, both were afraid to put up their hands.

"But at last Bill couldn't stand it any longer. He made up his mind to go and have it out, even if there was a whole agricultural show of prize and honourable-mention fighting-cocks in Page's yard. He got down from the wood-heap and started off across the ploughed field, his head down, his elbows out, and his thick awkward legs prodding away at the furrows behind for all they were worth.

"I wanted to go down badly and see the fight, and barrack for Bill. But I daren't, because I'd been coming up the road late the night before with my brother Joe, and there was about three panels of turkeys roosting along on the top rail of Page's front fence; and we brushed 'em with a bough, and they got up such a blessed gobbling fuss about it that Page came out in his shirt and saw us running away; and I knew he was laying for us with a bullock-whip. Besides, there was friction between the two families on account of a thorough-bred bull that Page borrowed and wouldn't lend to us, and that got into our paddock on account of me mending a panel in the party fence, and carelessly leaving the top rail down after sundown while our cows was moving round there in the saplings.

"So there was too much friction for me to go down, but I climbed a tree as near the fence as I could and watched. Bill reckoned he'd found that rooster at last. The white rooster wouldn't come down from the stack, so Bill went up to him, and they fought there till they tumbled down the other side, and I couldn't see any more. Wasn't I wild? I'd have given my dog to have seen the rest of the fight. I went down to the far side of Page's fence and climbed a tree there, but, of course I couldn't see anything, so I came home the back way. Just as I got home Page came round to the front and sung out, 'Insoid there!' And me and Jim went under the house like snakes and looked out round a pile. But Page was all right—he had a broad grin on his face, and Bill safe under his arm. He put Bill down on the ground very carefully, and says he to the old folks:

" 'Yer rooster knocked the stuffin' out of my rooster, but I bear no malice. 'Twas a grand foight.'

"And then the old man and Page had a yarn, and got pretty friendly after that. And Bill didn't seem to bother about any more ventriloquism; but the white rooster spent a lot of time looking for that other rooster. Perhaps he thought he'd have better luck with him. But Page was on the look-out all the time to get a rooster that would lick ours. He did nothing else for a month but ride round and inquire about roosters: and at last he borrowed a game-bird in town, left five pounds deposit on him, and brought him home. And Page and the old man agreed to have a match—about the only thing they'd agreed about for five years. And they fixed it up for a Sunday when the old lady and the girls and kids were going on a visit to some relations, about fifteen miles away—to stop all night. The guv'nor made me go with them on horseback; but I knew what was up, and so my pony went lame about a mile along the road, and I had to come back and turn him out in the top paddock, and hide the saddle and bridle in a hollow log, and sneak home and climb up on the roof of the shed. It was an awful hot day, and I had to keep climbing backward and forward over the ridge-pole all the morning to keep out of sight of the old man, for he was moving about a good deal.

"Well, after dinner, the fellows from round about began to ride in and hang up their horses round the place till it looked as if there was going to be a funeral. Some of the chaps saw me, of course, but I tipped them the wink, and they gave me the office whenever the old man happened around.

"Well, Page came along with his game-rooster. Its name was Jim. It wasn't much to look at, and it seemed a good deal smaller and weaker than Bill. Some of the chaps were disgusted, and said it wasn't a game-rooster at all; Bill'd settle it in one lick, and they wouldn't have any fun.

"Well, they brought the game one out and put him down near the wood-heap, and routed Bill out from under his cask. He got interested at once. He looked at Jim, and got up on the wood-heap and crowed and looked at Jim again. He reckoned *this* at last was the fowl that had been humbugging him all along. Presently his trouble caught him, and then he'd crow and take a squint at the game 'un, and crow again, and have another squint at gamey, and try to crow and keep his eye on the game-rooster at the same time. But Jim never committed himself, until at last he happened to gape just after Bill's whole crow went wrong, and Bill spotted him. He reckoned he'd caught him this time, and he got down off that wood-heap and went for the foe. But Jim ran away—and Bill ran after him.

"Round and round the wood-heap they went, and round the shed, and round the house and under it, and back again, and round the wood-heap and over it and round the other way, and kept it up for close on an hour. Bill's bill was just within an inch or so of the game-rooster's tail feathers most of the time, but he couldn't get any nearer, do how he liked. And all the time the fellers kept chyackin' Page and singing out, 'What price yer game un, Page! Go it, Bill! Go it, old cock!' and all that sort of thing. Well, the game-rooster went as if it was a go-as-you-please, and he didn't care if it lasted a year. He didn't seem to take any interest in the business, but Bill got excited, and by and by he got mad. He held his head lower and lower and his wings further and further out from his sides, and prodded away harder and harder at the ground behind, but it wasn't any use. Jim seemed to keep ahead without trying. They stuck to the wood-heap towards the last. They went round first one way for a while, and then the other for a change, and now and then they'd go over the top to break the monotony; and the chaps got more interested in the race than they would have been in the fight—and bet on it, too. But Bill was handicapped with his weight. He was done up at last; he slowed down till he couldn't waddle, and then, when he was thoroughly knocked up, that game-rooster turned on him, and gave him the father of a hiding.

"And my father caught me when I'd got down in the excitement, and wasn't thinking, and *he* gave *me* the step-father of a hiding. But he had a lively time with the old lady afterwards, over the cock-fight.

"Bill was so disgusted with himself that he went under the cask and died."

STIFFNER AND JIM (THIRDLY, BILL)

We were tramping down in Canterbury, Maoriland, at the time, swagging it—me and Bill—looking for work on the new railway line. Well, one afternoon, after a long, hot tramp, we comes to Stiffner's Hotel—between Christchurch and that other place—I forget the name of it—with throats on us like sunstruck bones, and not the price of a stick of tobacco.

We had to have a drink, anyway, so we chanced it. We walked right into the bar, handed over our swags, put up four drinks, and tried to look as if we'd just drawn our cheques and didn't care a curse for any man. We looked solvent enough, as far as swagmen go. We were dirty and haggard and ragged and tired-looking, and that was all the more reason why we might have our cheques all right.

This Stiffner was a hard customer. He'd been a spieler, fighting man, bush parson, temperance preacher, and a policeman, and a commercial traveller, and everything else that was damnable; he'd been a journalist, and an editor; he'd been a lawyer, too. He was an ugly brute to look at, and uglier to have a row with—about six-foot-six, wide in proportion, and stronger than Donald Dinnie.

He was meaner than a goldfield Chinaman, and sharper than a sewer rat; he wouldn't give his own father a feed, nor lend him a sprat—unless some safe person backed the old man's I.O.U.

We knew that we needn't expect any mercy from Stiffner, but something had to be done, so I said to Bill:

"Something's got to be done, Bill! What do you think of it?"

Bill was mostly a quiet young chap, from Sydney, except when he got drunk—which was seldom—and then he was a lively customer from all round. He was cracked on the subject of spielers. He held that the population of the world was divided into two classes—one was spielers and the other was mugs. He reckoned that he wasn't a mug. At first I thought that he was a spieler, and afterwards I thought that he was a mug. He used to say that a man had to do it these times; that he was honest once and a fool, and was robbed and starved in consequence by his friends and relations; but now he intended to take all that he could get. He said that you either had to have or be had; that men were driven to be sharps, and there was no help for it.

Bill said:

"We'll have to sharpen our teeth, that's all, and chew somebody's lug."

"How?" I asked.

There was a lot of navvies at the pub, and I knew one or two by sight, so Bill says:

"You know one or two of these mugs. Bite one of their ears."

So I took aside a chap that I knowed and bit his ear for ten bob, and gave it to Bill to mind, for I thought it would be safer with him than with me.

"Hang on to that," I says, "and don't lose it for your natural life's sake, or Stiffner'll stiffen us."

We put up about nine bob's worth of drinks that night—me and Bill—and Stiffner didn't squeal: he was too sharp. He shouted once or twice.

By and by I left Bill and turned in, and in the morning when I woke up there was Bill sitting alongside of me, and looking about as lively as the fighting kangaroo in London in fog time. He had a black eye and eighteen pence. He'd been taking down some of the mugs.

"Well, what's to be done now?" I asked. "Stiffner can smash us both with one hand, and if we don't pay up he'll pound our swags and cripple us. He's just the man to do it. He loves a fight even more than he hates being had."

"There's only one thing to be done, Jim," says Bill, in a tired, disinterested tone that made me mad.

"Well, what's that?" I said.

"Smoke!"

"Smoke be damned," I snarled, losing my temper. "You know dashed well that our swags are in the bar, and we can't smoke without them."

"Well, then," says Bill, "I'll toss you to see who's to face the landlord."

"Well, I'll be blessed!" I says. "I'll see you further first. You have got a front. You mugged that stuff away, and you'll have to get us out of the mess."

It made him wild to be called a mug, and we swore and growled at each other for a while; but we daren't speak loud enough to have a fight, so at last I agreed to toss up for it, and I lost.

Bill started to give me some of his points, but I shut him up quick.

"You've had your turn, and made a mess of it," I said. "For God's sake give me a show. Now, I'll go into the bar and ask for the swags, and carry them out on to the veranda, and then go back to settle up. You keep him talking all the time. You dump the two swags together, and smoke like sheol. That's all you've got to do."

I went into the bar, got the swags from the missus, carried them out on to the veranda, and then went back.

Stiffner came in.

"Good morning!"

"Good morning, sir," says Stiffner.

"It'll be a nice day, I think?"

"Yes, I think so. I suppose you are going on?"

"Yes, we'll have to make a move to-day." Then I hooked carelessly on to the counter with one elbow, and looked dreary-like out across the clearing, and presently I gave a sort of sigh and said: "Ah, well! I think I'll have a beer."

"Right you are! Where's your mate?"

"Oh, he's round at the back. He'll be round directly; but he ain't drinking this morning."

Stiffner laughed that nasty empty laugh of his. He thought Bill was whipping the cat.

"What's your's, boss?" I said.

"Thankee . . . Here's luck!"

"Here's luck!"

The country was pretty open round there—the nearest timber was better than a mile away, and I wanted to give Bill a good start across the flat before the go-as-you-can commenced; so I talked for a while, and while we were talking I thought I might as well go the whole hog—I might as well die for a pound as a penny, if I had to die; and if I hadn't I'd have the pound to the good, anyway, so to speak. Anyhow, the risk would be about the same, or less, for I might have the spirit to run harder the more I had to run for—the more spirits I had to run for, in fact, as it turned out—so I says:

"I think I'll take one of them there flasks of whisky to last us on the road."

"Right y'are," says Stiffner. "What'll yer have—a small one or a big one?"

"Oh, a big one, I think—if I can get it into my pocket."

"It'll be a tight squeeze," he said, and he laughed.

"I'll try," I said. "Bet you two drinks I'll get it in."

"Done!" he says. "The top inside coat-pocket, and no tearing."

It was a big bottle, and all my pockets were small; but I got it into the pocket he'd betted against. It was a tight squeeze, but I got it in.

Then we both laughed, but his laugh was nastier than usual, because it was meant to be pleasant, and he'd lost two drinks; and my laugh wasn't easy—I was anxious as to which of us would laugh next.

Just then I noticed something, and an idea struck me—about the most up-to-date idea that ever struck me in my life. I noticed that Stiffner was limping on his right foot this morning, so I said to him:

"What's up with your foot?" putting my hand in my pocket.

"Oh, it's a crimson nail in my boot," he said. "I thought I got the blanky thing out this morning; but I didn't."

There just happened to be an old bag of shoemaker's tools in the bar, belonging to an old cobbler who was lying dead drunk on the veranda. So I said, taking my hand out of my pocket again:

"Lend us the boot, and I'll fix it in a minute. That's my old trade."

"Oh, so you're a shoemaker," he said. "I'd never have thought it."

He laughs one of his useless laughs that wasn't wanted, and slips off the boot—he hadn't laced it up—and hands it across the bar to me. It was an ugly brute—a great thick, iron-bound, boiler-plated navvy's boot. It made me feel sore when I looked at it.

I got the bag and pretended to fix the nail; but I didn't.

"There's a couple of nails gone from the sole," I said. "I'll put 'em in if I can find any hobnails, and it'll save the sole," and I rooted in the bag and found a good long nail, and shoved it right through the sole on the sly. He'd been a bit of a sprinter in his time, and I thought it might be better for me in the near future if the spikes of his running-shoes were inside.

"There, you'll find that better, I fancy," I said, standing the boot on the bar counter, but keeping my hand on it in an absent-minded kind of way. Presently I yawned and stretched myself, and said in a careless way:

"Ah, well! How's the slate?"

He scratched the back of his head and pretended to think.

"Oh, well, we'll call it thirty bob."

Perhaps he thought I'd slap down two quid.

"Well," I says, "and what will you do supposing we don't pay you?"

He looked blank for a moment. Then he fired up and gasped and choked once or twice; and then he cooled down suddenly and laughed his nastiest laugh—he was one of those men who always laugh when they're wild—and said in a nasty, quiet tone:

"You thundering, jumped-up crawlers! If you don't (something) well part up I'll take your swags and (something) well kick your gory pants so you won't be able to sit down for a month—or stand up either!"

"Well, the sooner you begin the better," I said; and I chucked the boot into a corner and bolted.

He jumped the bar counter, got his boot, and came after me. He paused to slip the boot on—but he only made one step, and then gave a howl and slung the boot off and rushed back. When I looked round again he'd got a slipper on, and was coming—and gaining on me, too. I shifted scenery pretty quick the next five minutes. But I was soon pumped. My heart began to beat against the ceiling of my head, and my lungs all choked up in my throat. When I guessed he was getting within kicking distance I glanced round so's to dodge the kick. He let out; but I shied just in time. He missed fire, and the slipper went about twenty feet up in the air and fell in a waterhole.

He was done then, for the ground was stubbly and stony. I seen Bill on ahead pegging out for the horizon, and I took after him and reached for the timber for all I was worth, for I'd seen Stiffner's missus coming with a shovel—to bury the remains, I suppose; and those two were a good match —Stiffner and his missus, I mean.

Bill looked round once, and melted into the bush pretty soon after that. When I caught up he was about done; but I grabbed my swag and we pushed on, for I told Bill that I'd seen Stiffner making for the stables when I'd last looked round; and Bill thought that we'd better get lost in the bush as soon as ever we could, and stay lost, too, for Stiffner was a man that couldn't stand being had.

The first thing that Bill said when we got safe into camp was: "I told you that we'd pull through all right. You need never be frightened when you're travelling with me. Just take my advice and leave things to me, and we'll hang out all right. Now——"

But I shut him up. He made me mad.

"Why, you ——! What the sheol did *you* do?"

"Do?" he says. "I got away with the swags, didn't I? Where'd they be now if it wasn't for me?"

Then I sat on him pretty hard for his pretensions, and paid him out for all the patronage he'd worked off on me, and called him a mug straight, and walked round him, so to speak, and blowed, and told him never to pretend to me again that he was a battler.

THE TEAMS

A cloud of dust on the long, white road,
  And the teams go creeping on
Inch by inch with the weary load;
And by the power of the green-hide goad
  The distant goal is won.

With eyes half-shut to the blinding dust,
  And necks to the yokes bent low,
The beasts are pulling as bullocks must;
And the shining tires might almost rust
  While the spokes are turning slow.

With face half-hid by a broad-brimmed hat,
  That shades from the heat's white waves,
And shouldered whip, with its green-hide plait,
The driver plods with a gait like that
  Of his weary, patient slaves.

He wipes his brow, for the day is hot,
  And spits to the left with spite;
He shouts at Bally, and flicks at Scot,
And raises dust from the back of Spot,
  And spits to the dusty right.

He'll sometimes pause as a thing of form
  In front of a settler's door,
And ask for a drink, and remark "It's warm",
Or say "There's signs of a thunderstorm";
  But he seldom utters more.

The rains are heavy on roads like these
  And, fronting his lonely home,
For days together the settler sees
The waggons bogged to the axletrees,
  Or ploughing the sodden loam.

And then, when the roads are at their worst,
  The bushman's children hear
The cruel blows of the whips reversed
While bullocks pull as their hearts would burst,
  And bellow with pain and fear.

And thus—with glimpses of home and rest—
  Are the long, long journeys done;
And thus—'tis a thankless life at the best—
Is distance fought in the mighty West,
  And the lonely battles won.

The sheer realism of this word-picture of the life of a teamster is outstanding. In forty short lines the poet blends man and environment into an unforgettable facet of a past way of life which he knew as the present.

SINCE THEN

I met Jack Ellis in town today—
   Jack Ellis—my old mate, Jack.
Ten years ago, from the Castlereagh,
We carried our swags together away
   To the Never-Again, Out Back.

But times have altered since those old days,
   And the times have changed the men.
Ah, well! there's little to blame or praise—
Jack Ellis and I have tramped long ways
   On different tracks since then.

His hat was battered, his coat was green,
   The toes of his boots were through,
But the pride was his! It was I felt mean—
I wished that my collar was not so clean,
   Nor the clothes I wore so new.

He saw me first, and he knew 'twas I—
   The holiday swell he met.
Why have we no faith in each other? Ah, why?—
He made as though he would pass me by,
   For he thought that I might forget.

He ought to have known me better than that,
   By the tracks we tramped far out—
The sweltering scrub and the blazing flat,
When the heat came down through each old felt hat
   In the hell-born western drought.

He took my hand in a distant way
  (I thought how we parted last),
And we seemed like men who have nought to say
And who meet—"Good-day," and who part—
    "Good-day,"
  Who never have shared the past.

I asked him in for a drink with me—
  Jack Ellis—my old mate, Jack—
But his manner no longer was careless and free,
He followed, but not with the grin that he
  Wore always in days Out Back.

I tried to live in the past once more—
  Or the present and past combine,
But the days between I could not ignore—
I couldn't but notice the clothes he wore,
  And he couldn't but notice mine.

He placed his glass on the polished bar,
  And he wouldn't fill up again;
For he is prouder than most men are—
Jack Ellis and I have tramped too far
  On different tracks since then.

He said that he had a mate to meet,
  And "I'll see you again", said he,
Then he hurried away through the crowded street,
And the rattle of 'buses and scrape of feet
  Seemed suddenly loud to me.

THE WATER-LILY

A lonely young wife
In her dreaming discerns
A lily-decked pool
With a border of ferns.
And a beautiful child,
With butterfly wings,
Trips down to the edge of the water and sings:
"Come, mamma! come!
Quick! follow me!
Step out on the leaves of the water-lily!"

And the lonely young wife,
Her heart beating wild,
Cries, "Wait till I come,
Till I reach you, my child!"
But the beautiful child
With butterfly wings
Steps out on the leaves of the lily and sings:
"Come, mamma! come!
Quick! follow me!
And step on the leaves of the water-lily!"

And the wife in her dreaming
Steps out on the stream,
But the lily leaves sink
And she wakes from her dream.
Ah, the waking is sad,
For the tears that it brings,
And she knows 'tis her dead baby's spirit that sings:
"Come, mamma! come!
Quick! follow me!
Step out on the leaves of the water-lily!"

THE CAPTAIN OF THE PUSH

As the night was falling slowly down on city, town, and bush,
From a slum in Jones's Alley sloped the Captain of the Push;
And he scowled towards the North, and he scowled towards the
    South,
As he hooked his little fingers in the corners of his mouth.
Then his whistle, loud and piercing, woke the echoes of "The
    Rocks",
And a dozen ghouls came sloping round the corners of the blocks.

There was nought to rouse their anger; yet the oath that each
    one swore
Seemed less fit for publication than the one that went before.
For they spoke the gutter language with the easy flow that comes
Only to the men whose childhood knew the gutters and the slums.
Then they spat in turn, and halted; and the one that came behind,
Spitting fiercely at the pavement, called on Heaven to strike him
    blind.

Let me first describe the captain, bottle-shouldered, pale and thin:
He was just the beau-ideal of a Sydney larrikin.
E'en his hat was most suggestive of the place where Pushes live,
With a gallows-tilt that no one, save a larrikin, can give;
And the coat, a little shorter than the fashion might require,
Showed a (more or less uncertain) lower part of his attire.

That which tailors know as "trousers"—known to him as "blooming
    bags"—
Hanging loosely from his person, swept, with tattered ends, the
    flags;
And he had a pointed sternpost to the boots that peeped below
(Which he laced up from the centre of the nail of his great toe),
And he wore his shirt uncollared, and the tie correctly wrong;
But I think his vest was shorter than should be on one so long.

It is likely that
this poem is based
on a set of verses
that belonged, in
a multitude of
variants, to
Australia's oral
tradition.

Then the captain crooked his finger at a stranger on the kerb,
Whom he qualified politely with an adjective and verb.
And he begged the Gory Bleeders that they wouldn't interrupt
Till he gave an introduction—it was painfully abrupt—
"Here's the bleedin' push, my covey—here's a (something) from
    the bush!
Strike me dead, he wants to join us!" said the captain of the push.

Said the stranger: "I am nothing but a bushy and a dunce;
But I read about the Bleeders in the *Weekly Gasbag* once:
Sitting lonely in the humpy when the wind began to woosh,
How I longed to share the dangers and the pleasures of the push!
Gosh! I hate the swells and good uns—I could burn 'em in their
    beds;
I am with you, if you'll have me, and I'll break their blazing heads."

"Now, look here," exclaimed the captain to the stranger from the bush,
"Now, look here—suppose a feller was to split upon the push,
Would you lay for him and down him, even if the traps were round?
Would you lay him out and kick him to a jelly on the ground?
Would you jump upon the nameless—kill, or cripple him, or both?
Speak? or else I'll—SPEAK!" The stranger answered, "My kerlonial
    oath!"

"Now, look here," exclaimed the captain to the stranger from the
    bush,
"Now, look here—suppose the Bleeders let you come and join the
    push,
Would you smash a bleedin' bobby if you got the blank alone?
Would you stoush a swell or Chinkie—split his garret with a stone?
Would you have a 'moll' to keep you—like to swear off work for
    good?"
"Yes, my oath!" replied the stranger. "My kerlonial oath! I would!"

"Now, look here," exclaimed the captain to that stranger from the bush,
"Now, look here—before the Bleeders let you come and join the
    push.
You must prove that you're a blazer—you must prove that you have
    grit
Worthy of a Gory Bleeder—you must show your form a bit—
Take a rock and smash that winder!" and the stranger, nothing loth,
Took the rock and—smash! The Bleeders muttered "My kerlonial
    oath!"

So they swore him in, and found him sure of aim and light of heel,
And his only fault, if any, lay in his excessive zeal.
He was good at throwing metal, but I chronicle with pain
That he jumped upon a victim, damaging the watch and chain
Ere the Bleeders had secured them; yet the captain of the push
Swore a dozen oaths in favour of the stranger from the bush.

Late next morn the captain, rising, hoarse and thirsty, from his lair,
Called the newly-feathered Bleeder; but the stranger wasn't there!
Quickly going through the pockets of his bloomin' bags, he learned
That the stranger had been through him for the stuff his moll had
    earned;
And the language that he uttered I should scarcely like to tell
(Stars! and notes of exclamation!! blank and dash will do as well).

That same night the captain's signal woke the echoes of The Rocks,
Brought the Gory Bleeders sloping through the shadows of the
    blocks;
And they swore the stranger's action was a blood-escaping shame,
While they waited for the nameless—but the nameless never came.
And the Bleeders soon forgot him; but the captain of the push
Still is laying round, in ballast, for the stranger "from the bush".

SAINT PETER

Now, I think there is a likeness
  'Twixt St Peter's life and mine,
For he did a lot of trampin'
  Long ago in Palestine.
He was "union" when the workers
  First began to organize,
And—I'm glad that old St Peter
  Keeps the gate of Paradise.

When the ancient agitator
  And his brothers carried swags,
I've no doubt he very often
  Tramped with empty tucker-bags;
And I'm glad he's Heaven's picket,
  For I hate explainin' things,
And he'll think a union ticket
  Just as good as Whitely King's.

When I reach the great head-station—
  Which is somewhere "off the track"—
I won't want to talk with angels
  Who have never been Out Back;
They might bother me with offers
  Of a banjo—meanin' well—
And a pair of wings to fly with,
  When I only want a spell.

I'll just ask for old St Peter,
  And I think, when he appears,
I shall only have to tell him
  That I carried swag for years.
"I've been on the track," I'll tell him
  "An' I done the best I could."
He will understand me better
  Than the other angels would.

He won't try to get a chorus
  Out of lungs that's worn to rags,
Or to graft the wings on shoulders
  Stiff with humpin' tucker-bags;
But I'll rest about the station,
  Where a work-bell never rings,
Till they blow the final trumpet
  And the Great Judge sees to things.

Tom Roberts (1856-1931) *Bourke Street, Melbourne* (1885-6)
49.53 x 74.61 cm   Canvas
Reproduced with the kind permission of the National Library Of Australia, Canberra

Tom Roberts (1856-1931)   *The Flowersellers*
38.1 x 53.4 cm   Oil on canvas
Reproduced with the kind permission of the Manly Art Gallery, Sydney

A WILD IRISHMAN

About seven years ago I drifted from out back in Australia to Wellington, the capital of New Zealand, and up-country to a little town called Pahiatua, which meaneth the "home of the gods," and is situated in the Wairarappa (rippling or sparkling water) district. They have a pretty little legend to the effect that the name of the district was not originally suggested by its rivers, streams, and lakes, but by the tears alleged to have been noticed, by a dusky squire, in the eyes of a warrior chief who was looking his first, or last—I don't remember which—upon the scene. He was the discoverer, I suppose, now I come to think of it, else the place would have been already named. Maybe the scene reminded the old cannibal of the home of his childhood.

Pahiatua was not the home of my god; and it rained for five weeks. While waiting for a remittance, from an Australian newspaper—which, I anxiously hoped, would arrive in time for enough of it to be left (after paying board) to take me away somewhere—I spent many hours in the little shop of a shoemaker who had been a digger; and he told me yarns of the old days on the West Coast of Middle Island. And, ever and anon, he returned to one, a hard case from the West Coast, called "The Flour of Wheat," and his cousin, and his mate, Dinny Murphy, dead. And ever and again the shoemaker (he was large, humorous, and good natured) made me promise that, when I dropped across an old West Coast digger—no matter who or what he was, or whether he was drunk or sober—I'd ask him if he knew the Flour of Wheat, and hear what he had to say.

I make no attempt to give any one shade of the Irish brogue—it can't be done in writing.

"There's the little red Irishman," said the shoemaker, who was Irish himself, "who always wants to fight when he has a glass in him; and there's the big sarcastic dark Irishman who makes more trouble and fights at a spree than half a dozen little red ones put together; and there's the cheerful easy-going Irishman. Now the Flour was a combination of all three and several other sorts. He was known from the first amongst the boys at Th' Canary as the Flour o' Wheat, but no one knew exactly why. Some said that the right name was the F-l-o-w-e-r, not F-l-o-u-r, and that he was called that because there was no flower on wheat. The name might have been a compliment paid to the man's character by someone who understood and appreciated it —or appreciated it without understanding it. Or it might have come of some chance saying of the Flour himself, or his mates—or an accident with bags of flour. He might have worked in a mill. but we've had enough of that. It's the man—not the name. He was just a big, dark, blue-eyed Irish digger. He worked hard, drank hard, fought hard—and didn't swear. No man had ever heard him swear (except once); all things were 'lovely' with him. He was always lucky. He got gold and threw it away.

"The Flour was sent out to Australia (by his friends) in connection with some trouble in Ireland in eighteen-something. The date doesn't matter; there was mostly trouble in Ireland in those days; and nobody that knew the man could have the slightest doubt that he helped the trouble—provided he was there at the time. I heard all this from a man who knew him in Australia. The relatives that he was sent out to were soon very anxious to see the end of him. He was as wild as they made them in Ireland. When he had a few drinks, he'd walk restlessly to and fro outside the shanty, swinging his right arm across in front of him with elbow bent and hand closed, as if he had a head in chancery, and muttering, as though in explanation to himself:

"'Oi must be walkin' or foightin'!—Oi must be walkin' or foightin'!— Oi must be walkin' or foightin'!'

"They say that he wanted to eat his Australian relatives before he was done; and the story goes that one night, while he was on the spree, they put their belongings into a cart and took to the bush.

"There's no Floury record for several years; then the Flour turned up on the West Coast of New Zealand and was never very far from a pub kept by a cousin (that he had tracked, unearthed, or discovered somehow) at a place called Th' Canary. I remember the first time I saw the Flour.

"I was on a bit of a spree myself, at Th' Canary, and one evening I was standing outside Brady's (the Flour's cousin's place) with Tom Lyons and Dinny Murphy, when I saw a big man coming across the flat with a swag on his back.

"'B' God, there's the Flour o' Wheat comin' this minute,' says Dinny Murphy to Tom, 'an' no one else.'

"'B' God, ye're right!' says Tom.

"There were a lot of new chums in the big room at the back, drinking and dancing and singing, and Tom says to Dinny:

"'Dinny, I'll bet you a quid an' the Flour'll run against some of those new chums before he's an hour on the spot.'

"But Dinny wouldn't take him up. He knew the Flour.

"'Good day, Tom! Good day, Dinny!'

"'Good day to you, Flour!'

I was introduced.

"'Well, boys, come along,' says the Flour.

"And so we went inside with him. The Flour had a few drinks, and then he went into the back room where the new chums were. One of them was dancing a jig, and so the Flour stood up in front of him and commenced to dance too. And presently the new chum made a step that didn't please the Flour, so he hit him between the eyes, and knocked him down—fair an' flat on his back.

"'Take that,' he says. 'Take that, me lovely whipper-snapper, an' lay there! You can't dance. How dare ye stand up in front of me face to dance when ye can't dance?'

"He shouted and drank, and gambled, and danced, and sang, and fought the new chums all night, and in the morning he said:

"'Well, boys, we had a grand time last night. Come and have a drink with me.'

"And of course they went in and had a drink with him.

"Next morning the Flour was walking along the street, when he met a drunken disreputable old hag, known among the boys as the 'Nipper.'

"'Good *morning,* me lovely Flour o' Wheat!' says she.

"'Good *morning,* me lovely Nipper!' says the Flour.

"And with that she outs with a bottle she had in her dress, and smashed him across the face with it. Broke the bottle to smithereens!

"A policeman saw her do it, and took her up; and they had the Flour as a witness, whether he liked it or not. And a lovely sight he looked, with his face all done up in bloody bandages, and only one damaged eye and a corner of his mouth on duty.

"'It's nothing at all, your Honour,' he said to the S.M.; 'only a pin-scratch —it's nothing at all. Let it pass. I had no right to speak to the lovely woman at all.'

"But they didn't let it pass—they fined her a quid.

"And the Flour paid the fine.

"But, alas for human nature! It was pretty much the same even in those days, and amongst those men, as it is now. A man couldn't do a woman a good turn without the dirty-minded blackguards taking it for granted there was something between them. It was a great joke amongst the boys who knew the Flour, and who also knew the Nipper; but as it was carried too far in some quarters, it got to be no joke to the Flour—nor to those who laughed too loud or grinned too long.

"The Flour's cousin thought he was a sharp man. The Flour got 'stiff.' He hadn't any money, and his credit had run out, so he went and got a blank summons from one of the police he knew. He pretended that he wanted to frighten a man who owed him some money. Then he filled it up and took it to his cousin.

"'What d'ye think of that?' he says, handing the summons across the bar. 'What d'ye think of me lovely Dinny Murphy now?'

"'Why, what's this all about?'

"'That's what I want to know. I borrowed a five-pound note off of him a fortnight ago when I was drunk, an' now he sends me that.'

"'Well, I never would have dream'd that of Dinny,' says the cousin, scratching his head and blinking. 'What's come over him at all?'

"'That's what I want to know.'

"'What have you been doing to the man?'

"'Divil a thing that I'm aware of.'

"The cousin rubbed his chin-tuft between his forefinger and thumb.

"'Well, what am I to do about it?' asked the Flour impatiently.

"'Do? Pay the man, of course.'

"'How can I pay the lovely man when I haven't got the price of a drink about me?'

"The cousin scratched his chin.

"'Well—here, I'll lend you a five-pound note for a month or two. Go and pay the man, and get back to work.'

"And the Flour went and found Dinny Murphy, and the pair of them had a howling spree together up at the opposition pub. And the cousin said he thought all the time he was being had.

"He was nasty sometimes, when he was about half-drunk. For instance, he'd come on the ground when the Orewell sports were in full swing and walk round, soliloquizing just loud enough for you to hear; and just when a big event was coming off he'd pass within earshot of some committee men—who had been bursting themselves for weeks to work the thing up and make it a success—saying to himself:

" 'Where's the Orewell sports that I hear so much about? I don't see them! Can anyone direct me to the Orewell sports?'

"Or he'd pass a raffle, lottery, lucky-bag, or golden-barrel business of some sort——

" 'No gamblin' for the Flour. I don't believe in their little shwindles. It ought to be shtopped. Leadin' young people ashtray.'

"Or he'd pass an Englishman he didn't like——

" 'Look at Jinneral Roberts! He's a man! He's an Irishman! England has to come to Ireland for its Jinnerals! Look at Jinneral Roberts in the marshes of Candyhar!'

"They always had sports at Orewell Creek on New Year's Day—except once—and old Duncan was always there—never missed it till the day he died. He was a digger, a humorous and good-hearted 'hard case.' They all knew 'old Duncan.'

"But one New Year's Eve he didn't turn up, and was missed at once. 'Where's old Duncan? Anyone seen old Duncan?' 'Oh, he'll turn up all right.' They inquired, and argued, and waited, but Duncan didn't come.

"Duncan was working at Duffers. The boys inquired of fellows who came from Duffers, but they hadn't seen him for two days. They had fully expected to find him at the creek. He wasn't at Aliaura nor Notown. They inquired of men who came from Nelson Creek, but Duncan wasn't there.

" 'There's something happened to the lovely man,' said the Flour of Wheat at last. 'Some of us had better see about it.'

"Pretty soon this was the general opinion, and so a party started out over the hills to Duffers before daylight in the morning, headed by the Flour.

"The door of Duncan's whare was closed—*but not padlocked*. The Flour noticed this, gave his head a jerk, opened the door, and went in. The hut was tidied up and swept out—even the fire-place. Duncan had 'lifted the boxes' and 'cleaned up,' and his little bag of gold stood on a shelf by his side—all ready for his spree. On the table lay a clean neckerchief folded ready to tie on. The blankets had been folded neatly and laid on the bunk, and on them was stretched old Duncan, with his arms lying crossed on his chest, and one foot—with a boot on—resting on the ground. He had his 'clean things' on, and was dressed except for one boot, the necktie, and his hat. Heart disease.

" 'Take your hats off and come in quietly, lads,' said the Flour. 'Here's the lovely man lying dead in his bunk.'

"There were no sports at Orewell that New Year. Someone said that the crowd from Nelson Creek might object to the sports being postponed on old Duncan's account, but the Flour said he'd see to that.

"One or two did object, but the Flour reasoned with them and there were no sports.

"And the Flour used to say, afterwards, 'Ah, but it was a grand time we had at the funeral when Duncan died at Duffers.'

"The Flour of Wheat carried his mate, Dinny Murphy, all the way in from Th' Canary to the hospital on his back. Dinny was very bad—the man was dying of the dysentery or something. The Flour laid him down on a spare bunk in the reception-room and hailed the staff.

"'Inside there—come out!'

"The doctor and some of the hospital people came to see what was the matter. The doctor was a heavy swell, with a big cigar held up in front of him between two fat, soft, yellow-white fingers, and a dandy little pair of gold-rimmed eye-glasses nipped on to his nose with a spring.

"'There's me lovely mate lying there dying of the dysentery,' says the Flour, 'and you've got to fix him up and bring him round.'

"Then he shook his fist in the doctor's face and said:

"'If you let that lovely man die—look out!'

"The doctor was startled. He backed off at first; then he took a puff at his cigar, stepped forward, had a careless look at Dinny, and gave some order to the attendants. The Flour went to the door, turned half round as he went out, and shook his fist at them again, and said:

"'If you let that lovely man die—mind!'

"In about twenty minutes he came back, wheeling a case of whisky in a barrow. He carried the case inside, and dumped it down on the floor.

"'There,' he said, 'pour that into the lovely man.'

"Then he shook his fist at such members of the staff as were visible, and said:

"'If you let that lovely man die—look out!'

"They were used to hard cases, and didn't take much notice of him, but he had the hospital in an awful mess; he was there all hours of the day and night; he would go down town, have a few drinks and a fight maybe, and then he'd say, 'Ah, well, I'll have to go up and see how me lovely mate's getting on.'

"And every time he'd go up he'd shake his fist at the hospital in general and threaten to murder 'em all if they let Dinny Murphy die.

"Well, Dinny Murphy died one night. The next morning the Flour met the doctor in the street, and hauled off and hit him between the eyes, and knocked him down before he had time to see who it was.

"'Stay there, ye little whipper-snapper,' said the flour of Wheat; 'you let that lovely man die!'

"The police happened to be out of town that day, and while they were waiting for them the Flour got a coffin and carried it up to the hospital, and stood it on end by the doorway.

"'I've come for me lovely mate!' he said to the scared staff—or as much of it as he bailed up and couldn't escape him. 'Hand him over. He's going back to be buried with his friends at Th' Canary. Now, don't be sneaking round and sidling off, you there; you needn't be frightened; I've settled with the doctor.'

"But they called in a man who had some influence with the Flour, and between them—and with the assistance of the prettiest nurse on the premises—they persuaded him to wait. Dinny wasn't ready yet; there were papers to sign; it wouldn't be decent to the dead; he had to be prayed over; he had to be washed and shaved, and fixed up decent and comfortable. Anyway, they'd have him ready in an hour, or take the consequences.

"The Flour objected on the ground that all this could be done equally as well and better by the boys at Th' Canary. 'However,' he said, 'I'll be round in an hour, and if you haven't got me lovely mate ready—look out!' Then he shook his fist sternly at them once more and said:

"'I know yer dirty tricks and dodges, and if there's e'er a pin-scratch on me mate's body—look out! If there's a parin' of Dinny's toe-nail missin' —look out!'

"Then he went out—taking the coffin with him.

"And when the police came to his lodgings to arrest him, they found the coffin on the floor by the side of the bed, and the Flour lying in it on his back, with his arms folded peacefully on his bosom. He was as dead drunk as any man could get to be and still be alive. They knocked air-holes in the coffin lid, screwed it on, and carried the coffin, the Flour, and all to the local lock-up. They laid their burden down on the bare, cold floor of the prison-cell, and then went out, locked the door, and departed several ways to put the 'boys' up to it. And about midnight the 'boys' gathered round with a supply of liquor, and waited, and somewhere along in the small hours there was a howl, as of a strong Irishman in Purgatory, and presently the voice of the Flour was heard to plead in changed and awful tones:

"'Pray for me soul, boys—pray for me soul! Let bygones be bygones between us, boys, and pray for me lovely soul! The lovely Flour's in Purgatory!'

"Then silence for a while; and then a sound like a dray-wheel passing over a packing-case . . . That was the only time on record that the Flour was heard to swear. And he swore then.

"They didn't pray for him—they gave him a month. And, when he came out, he went half-way across the road to meet the doctor, and he—to his credit, perhaps—came the other half. They had a drink together, and the Flour presented the doctor with a fine specimen of coarse gold for a pin.

"'It was the will o' God, after all, doctor,' said the Flour. 'It was the will o' God. Let bygones be bygones between us; gimme your hand, doctor . . . Good-bye.'

"Then he left for Th' Canary."

Mrs Bertha Lawson in the garden of her home at Northbridge, a Sydney suburb, in the 1930s.

In 1943 her reminiscences of her courtship, marriage, and life subsequent to the judicial separation in 1903, after six years, were published in *My Henry Lawson* (Sydney, Frank Johnson). The slender volume, in the compilation and writing of which she was assisted by Will Lawson, a New Zealand author and journalist, occasioned much comment at the time and threw little light on Lawson's biography.

After parting from her husband she worked for a time for Angus & Robertson, among others, before finally becoming an officer of the Children's Welfare Department in New South Wales. She continued to take a keen interest in the literary life of Sydney until her death in July, 1957.

Bertha Lawson, née Bredt, Henry Lawson's wife, as a young woman.

ACROSS THE STRAITS

We crossed Cook's Straits from Wellington in one of those rusty little iron tanks that go up and down and across there for twenty or thirty years and never get wrecked—for no other reason, apparently, than that they have every possible excuse to go ashore or go down on those stormy coasts. The age, construction, or condition of these boats, and the south-easters, and the construction of the coastline, are all decidedly in favour of their going down; the fares are high and the accommodation is small and dirty. It is always the same where there is no competition.

A year to two ago, when a company was running boats between Australia and New Zealand, without competition, the steerage fare was three pounds direct single, and two pounds ten shillings between Auckland and Wellington. The potatoes were black and green and soggy, the beef like bits scraped off the inside of a hide which had lain out for a day or so, the cabbage was cabbage leaves, the tea muddy. The whole business took away our appetite regularly three times a day, and there wasn't enough to go round, even if it had been good—enough tucker, we mean; there was enough appetite to go round three or four times, but it was driven away by disgust until after meals. If we had not, under cover of darkness, broached a deck cargo of oranges, lemons, and pineapples, and thereby run the risk of being run in on arrival, there would have been starvation, disease, and death on that boat before the end—perhaps mutiny.

You can go across now for one pound, and get something to eat on the road; but the travelling public will go on patronizing the latest reducer of fares until the poorer company gets starved out and fares go up again—then the travelling public will have to pay three of four times as much as they do now, and go hungry on the voyage; all of which ought to go to prove that the travelling public is as big a fool as the general public.

We can't help thinking that the captains and crews of our primitive little coastal steamers take the chances so often that they in time get used to it, and, being used to it, have no longer any misgivings or anxiety in rough weather concerning a watery grave, but feel as perfectly safe as if they were in church with their wives or sisters—only more comfortable—and go on feeling so until the worn-out machinery breaks down and lets the old tub run ashore, or knocks a hole in her side, or the side itself rusts through at last and lets

126

the water in, or the last straw in the shape of an extra ton of brine tumbles on board, and the *John Smith* (Newcastle) goes down with a swoosh before the cook has time to leave off peeling his potatoes and take to prayer.

These cheerful—and, maybe, unjust—reflections are perhaps in consequence of our having lost half a sovereign to start with. We arrived at the booking-office with two minutes to spare, two sticks of Juno tobacco, a spare wooden pipe—in case we lost the other—a letter to a friend's friend down south, a pound note (Bank of New Zealand), and two halfcrowns, with which to try our fortunes in the South Island. We also had a few things in a portmanteau and two blankets in a three-bushel bag, but they didn't amount to much. The clerk put down the ticket with the half-sovereign on top of it, and we wrapped the latter in the former and ran for the wharf. On the way we snatched the ticket out to see the name of the boat we were going by, in order to find it, and it was then, we suppose, that the semi-quid got lost.

Did you ever lose a sovereign or a half-sovereign under similar circumstances? You think of it casually and feel for it carelessly at first, to be sure that it's there all right; then, after going through your pockets three of four times with rapidly growing uneasiness, you lose your head a little and dredge for that coin hurriedly and with painful anxiety. Then you force yourself to be calm, and proceed to search yourself systematically, in a methodical manner. At this stage, if you have time, it's a good plan to sit down and think out when and where you last had that half-sovereign, and where you have been since, and which way you came from there, and what you took out of your pocket, and where, and whether you might have given it in mistake for sixpence at that pub where you rushed in to have a beer—and then you calculate the chances against getting it back again. The last of these reflections is apt to be painful, and the painfulness is complicated and increased when there happen to have been several pubs and a like number of hurried farewell beers in the recent past.

And for months after that you cannot get rid of the idea that the half-sov. might be about your clothes somewhere. It haunts you. You turn your pockets out, and feel the lining of your coat and vest inch by inch, and examine your letters, papers—everything you happen to have had in your pockets that day—over and over again, and by and by you peer into envelopes and unfold papers that you didn't have in your pocket at all, but might have had. And when the first search has worn off, and the fit takes you, you make another search. Even after many months have passed away, some day—or night—when you hard up for tobacco and a drink, you suddenly think of that late lamented half-sov., and are moved by adverse circumstances to look through your old clothes in a sort of forlorn hope, or to give good luck a sort of chance to surprise you—the only chance that you can give it.

By the way, seven-and-six of that half-quid should have gone to the landlord of the hotel where we stayed last, and somehow, in spite of this enlightened age, the loss of it seemed a judgement; and seeing that the boat was old and primitive, and there was every sign of a three days' sou'-easter, we sincerely hoped that judgment was complete—that supreme wrath had been appeased by the fine of ten bob without adding any Jonah business to it.

This reminds us that we once found a lost half-sovereign in the bowl of a spare pipe six months after it was lost. We wish it had stayed there and turned up to-night. But, although when you are in great danger—say, adrift in an open boat—tales of providential escapes and rescues may interest and comfort you, you can't get any comfort out of anecdotes concerning the turning up of lost quids when you have just lost one yourself. All you want is to find it.

It bothers you even not to be able to account for a bob. You always like to know that you have had something for your money, if only a long beer. You would sooner know that you fooled your money away on a spree, and made yourself sick, than lost it out of an extra hole in your pocket, and kept well.

We left Wellington with a feeling of pained regret, a fellow-wanderer by our side telling us how he had once lost a "fi-pun-note"—and about two-thirds of the city unemployed on the wharf looking for that half-sovereign.

A sailor said that the *Moa* was a good sea-boat, and, although she was small and old, *he* was never afraid of her. He'd sooner travel in her than in some of those big cheap ocean liners with more sand in them than iron or steel—you know the rest. Further on, in a conversation concerning the age of these coasters, he said that they'd last fully thirty years if well painted and looked after. He said that this one was seldom painted, and never painted properly; and then, seemingly in direct contradiction to his previously expressed confidence in the safety and seaworthiness of the *Moa*, he said that he could poke a stick through her anywhere. We asked him not to do it.

It came on to splash, and we went below to reflect, and search once more for that half-sovereign.

The cabin was small and close, and dimly lighted, and evil smelling, and shaped like the butt end of a coffin. It might not have smelt so bad if we hadn't lost that half-sovereign.

There was a party of those gipsy-like Assyrians—two families apparently —the women and children lying very sick about the lower bunks; and a big, good-humoured-looking young Maori propped between the end of the table and the wall, playing a concertina. The sick people were too sick, and the concertina seemed too much in sympathy with them, and the lost half-quid haunted us more than ever down there; so we started to climb out.

The first thing that struck us was the jagged top edge of that iron hood-like arrangement over the gangway. The top half only of the scuttle was open. There was nothing to be seen except a fog of spray and a Newfoundland dog sea-sick under the lee of something. The next thing that struck us was a tub of salt water, which came like a cannon ball and broke against the hood affair, and spattered on deck like a crockery shop. We climbed down again backwards, and sat on the floor with emphasis, in consequence of stepping down a last step that wasn't there, and cracked the back of our heads against the edge of the table. The Maori helped us up, and we had a drink with him at the expense of one of the half-casers mentioned in the beginning of this sketch. Then the Maori shouted, then we, then the Maori again, then we again; and then we thought, "Dash it, what's a half-sovereign? We'll fall on our feet all right."

We went up Queen Charlotte's sound, a long crooked arm of the sea between big, rugged, black-looking hills. There was a sort of lighthouse down near the entrance, and they said an old Maori woman kept it. there were some whitish things on the sides of the hills, which we at first took for cattle, and then for goats. They were sheep. Someone said that that country was only fit to carry sheep. It must have been bad, then, judging from some of the country in Australia which is only fit to carry sheep. Country that wouldn't carry goats would carry sheep, we think. Sheep are about the hardiest animals on the face of this planet—barring crocodiles.

You may rip a sheep open whilst watching for the boss's boots or yarning to a pen-mate, and then when you have stuffed the works back into the animal, and put a stitch in the slit, and poked it somewhere with a tar-stick (it doesn't matter much where) the jumbuck will be all right and just as lively as ever, and turn up next shearing without the ghost of a scratch on its skin.

We reached Picton, a small collection of twinkling lights in a dark pocket, apparently at the top of a sound. We climbed up on to the wharf, got through between two railway trucks, and asked a policeman where we were, and where the telegraph office was. There were several pretty girls in the office, laughing and chyacking the counter clerks, which jarred upon the feelings of this poor orphan wanderer in strange lands. We gloomily took a telegram form, and wired to a friend in North Island, using the following words: "Wire quid; stumped."

Then we crossed the street to a pub and asked for a room, and they told us to go up to No. 8. We went up, struck a match, lit the candle, put our bag in a corner, cleared the looking-glass off the toilet table, got some paper and a pencil out of our portmanteau, and sat down and wrote this sketch.

The candle is going out.

STEELMAN'S PUPIL

Steelman was a hard case, but some said that Smith was harder. Steelman was big and good-looking, and good-natured in his way; he was a spieler, pure and simple, but did things in humorous style. Smith was small and weedy, of the sneak variety; he had a whining tone and a cringing manner. He seemed to be always so afraid you were going to hit him that he would make you *want* to hit him on that account alone.

Steelman "had" you in a fashion that would make your friends laugh. Smith would "have" you in a way which made you feel mad at the bare recollection of having been taken in by so contemptible a little sneak.

They battled round together in the North Island of Maoriland for a couple of years.

One day Steelman said to Smith:

"Look here, Smithy, you don't know you're born yet. I'm going to take you in hand and teach you."

And he did. If Smith wouldn't do as Steelman told him, or wasn't successful in cadging, or mugged any game they had in hand, Steelman would threaten to stoush him; and, if the warning proved ineffectual after the second or third time, he *would* stoush him.

One day, on the track, they came to a place where an old Scottish couple kept a general store and shanty. They camped alongside the road, and Smith was just starting up to the house to beg supplies when Steelman cried:

"Here!—hold on. Now where do you think you're going to?"

"Why, I'm going to try and chew the old party's lug, of course. We'll be out of tucker in a couple of days," said Smith.

Steelman sat down on a stump in a hopeless, discouraged sort of way.

"It's no use," he said, regarding Smith with mingled reproach and disgust. "It's no use. I might as well give it best. I can see that it's only waste of time trying to learn you anything. Will I ever be able to knock some gumption into your thick skull? After all the time and trouble and pains I've took with your education, you hain't got any more sense than to go and mug a business like that! When will you learn sense? Hey? After all, I——Smith, you're a born mug!"

He always called Smith a "mug" when he was particularly wild at him, for it hurt Smith more than anything else.

"There's only two classes in the world, spielers and mugs—and you're a mug, Smith."

"What have I done, any way?" asked Smith helplessly. "That's all I want to know."

Steelman wearily rested his brow on his hand.

"That will do, Smith," he said listlessly; "don't say another word, old man; it'll only make my head worse; don't talk. You might, at the very least, have a little consideration for my feelings—even if you haven't for your own interests." He paused and regarded Smith sadly. "Well, I'll give you another show. I'll stage the business for you."

He made Smith doff his coat and get into his worst pair of trousers—and they were bad enough; they were hopelessly "gone" beyond the extreme limit of bush decency. He made Smith put on a rag of a felt hat and a pair of "'lastic-sides" which had fallen off a tramp and lain baking and rotting by turns on a rubbish heap; they had to be tied on Smith with bits of rag and string. He drew dark shadows round Smith's eyes, and burning spots on his cheek-bones with some grease-paints he used when they travelled as "The Great Steelman and Smith Combination Star Dramatic Co." He damped Smith's hair to make it dark and lank, and his face more corpse-like by comparison—in short, he made him up to look like a man who had long passed the very last stage of consumption, and had been artificially kept alive in the interests of science.

"Now, you're ready," said Steelman to Smith. "You left your whare the day before yesterday and started to walk to the hospital at Palmerston. An old mate picked you up dying on the road, brought you round, and carried you on his back most of the way here. You firmly believe that Providence had something to do with the sending of that old mate along at that time and place above all others. Your mate also was hard up; he was going to a job—the first show for work he'd had in nine months—but he gave it up to see you through; he'd give up his life rather than desert a mate in trouble. You only want a couple of shillings or a bit of tucker to help you on to Palmerston. You know you've got to die, and you only want to live long enough to get word to your poor old mother, and die on a bed.

"Remember, they're Scotch up at that house. You understand the Scotch barrack pretty well by now—if you don't it ain't my fault. You were born in Aberdeen, but came out too young to remember much about the town. Your father's dead. You ran away to sea and came out in the *Bobbie Burns* to Sydney. Your poor old mother's in Aberdeen now—Bruce or Wallace Wynd will do. Your mother might be dead now—poor old soul!—any way, you'll never see her again. You wish you'd never run away from home. You wish you'd been a better son to your poor old mother; you wish you'd written to her and answered her last letter. You only want to live long enough to write home and ask for forgiveness and a blessing before you die. If you had a drop of spirits of some sort to brace you up you might get along the road better. (Put this delicately.) Get the whine out of your voice and breathe with a wheeze—like this; get up the nearest approach to a death-rattle that you can. Move as if you were badly hurt in your wind —like this. (If you don't do it better'n that, I'll stoush you.) Make your face a bit longer and keep your lips dry—don't lick them, you damned fool!— *breathe* on them; make 'em dry as chips. That's the only decent pair of breeks you've got, and the only shoon. You're a Presbyterian—not a U.P., the Auld Kirk. Your mate would have come up to the house only—well, you'll have to use the stuffing in your head a bit; you can't expect me to do all the brain work. Remember it's consumption you've got—galloping consumption; you know all the symptoms—pain on top of your right lung, bad cough, and night sweats. Something tells you that you won't see the new year—it's a week off Christmas now. And if you come back without anything, I'll blessed soon put you out of your misery."

Smith came back with about four pounds of shortbread and as much various tucker as they could conveniently carry; a pretty good suit of cast-off tweeds; a new pair of 'lastic-sides from the store stock; two bottles of patent medicine and a black bottle half-full of home-made consumption-cure; also a letter to a hospital-committee man and three shillings to help him on his way to Palmerston. He also got about half a mile of sympathy, religious consolation, and medical advice which he didn't remember.

"*Now,*" he said, triumphantly, "am I a mug or not?"

Steelman kindly ignored the question. "I *did* have a better opinion of the Scotch," he said, contemptuously.

Steelman got on at an hotel as billiard-marker and decoy, and in six months he managed that pub. Smith, who'd been away on his own account, turned up in the town one day clean broke, and in a deplorable state. He heard of Steelman's luck, and thought he was "all right," so went to his old friend.

Cold type—or any other kind of type—couldn't do justice to Steelman's disgust. To think that this was the reward of all the time and trouble he'd spent on Smith's education! However, when he cooled down, he said:

"Smith, you're a young man yet, and it's never too late to mend. There is still time for reformation. I can't help you now; it would only demoralize you altogether. To think, after the way I trained you, you can't battle round any better'n this! I always thought you were an irreclaimable mug, but I expected better things of you towards the end. I thought I'd make *something* of you. It's enough to dishearten any man and disgust him with the world. Why! you ought to be a rich man now with the chances and training you had! To think—but I won't talk of that; it has made me ill. I suppose I'll have to give you something, if it's only to get rid of the sight of you. Here's a quid, and I'm a mug for giving it to you. It'll do you more harm than good; and it ain't a friendly thing nor the right thing for me—who always had your welfare at heart—to give it to you under the circumstances. Now, get away out of my sight, and don't come near me till you've reformed. If you do, I'll have to stoush you out of regard for my own health and feelings."

But Steelman came down in the world again and picked up Smith on the road, and they battled round together for another year or so; and at last they were in Wellington—Steelman "flush" and stopping at an hotel, and Smith stumped, as usual, and staying with a friend. One night they were drinking together at the hotel, at the expense of some mugs whom Steelman was "educating." It was raining hard. When Smith was going home, he said:

"Look here, Steely, old man. Listen to the rain! I'll get wringing wet going home. You might as well lend me your overcoat to-night. You won't want it, and I won't hurt it."

And, Steelman's heart being warmed by his successes, he lent the overcoat.

Smith went and pawned it, got glorious on the proceeds, and took the pawn-ticket to Steelman next day.

Smith had reformed.

HOW STEELMAN TOLD HIS STORY

It was Steelman's humour, in some of his moods, to take Smith into his confidence, as some old bushmen do their dogs.

"You're nearly as good as an intelligent sheep-dog to talk to, Smith—when a man gets tired of thinking to himself and wants a relief. You're a bit of a mug and a good deal of an idiot, and the chances are that you don't know what I'm driving at half the time—that's the main reason why I don't mind talking to you. You ought to consider yourself honoured; it ain't every man I take into my confidence, even that far."

Smith rubbed his head.

"I'd sooner talk to you—or a stump—any day than to one of those silent, suspicious, self-contained, wordly-wise chaps that listen to everything you say—sense and rubbish alike—as if you were trying to get them to take shares in a mine. I drop the man who listens to me all the time and doesn't seem to get bored. He isn't safe. He isn't to be trusted. He mostly wants to grind his axe against yours, and there's too little profit for me where there are two axes to grind, and no stone—though I'd manage it once, anyhow."

"How'd you do it?" asked Smith.

"There are several ways. Either you join forces, for instance, and find a grindstone—or make one of the other man's axe. But the last way is too slow, and, as I said, takes too much brain-work—besides, it doesn't pay. It might satisfy your vanity or pride, but I've got none. I had once, when I was younger, but it—well, it nearly killed me, so I dropped it.

"You can mostly trust the man who wants to talk more than you do; he'll make a safe mate—or a good grindstone."

Smith scratched the nape of his neck and sat blinking at the fire, with the puzzled expression of a woman pondering over a life-question or the trimming of a hat. Steelman took his chin in his hand and watched Smith thoughtfully.

"I—I say, Steely," exclaimed Smith, suddenly, sitting up and scratching his head and blinking harder than ever—"wha—what am I?"

"How do you mean?"

"Am I the axe or the grindstone?"

"Oh, your brain seems in extra good working order to-night, Smith. Well, you turn the grindstone and I grind." Smith settled. "If you could grind better than I, I'd turn the stone and let you grind. I'd never go against the interests of the firm—that's fair enough, isn't it?"

"Ye-es," admitted Smith; "I suppose so."

"So do I. Now, Smith, we've got along all right together for years, off and on, but you never know what might happen. I might stop breathing, for instance—and so might you."

Smith began to look alarmed.

"Poetical justice might overtake one or both of us—such things have happened before, though not often. Or, say, misfortune or death might mistake us for honest, hard-working mugs with big families to keep, and cut us off in the bloom of all our wisdom. You might get into trouble, and, in that case, I'd be bound to leave you there, on principle; or I might get into trouble, and you wouldn't have the brains to get me out—though I know you'd be mug

133

enough to try. I might make a rise and cut you, or you might be misled into showing some spirit, and clear out after I'd stoushed you for it. You might get tired of me calling you a mug, and bossing you and making a tool or convenience of you, you know. You might go in for honest graft (you were always a bit weak-minded) and then I'd have to wash my hands of you (unless you agreed to keep me) for an irreclaimable mug. Or it might suit me to become a respected and worthy fellow townsman, and then, if you came within ten miles of me or hinted that you ever knew me, I'd have you up for vagrancy, or soliciting alms, or attempting to levy blackmail. I'd have to fix you—so I give you fair warning. Or we might get into some desperate fix (and it needn't be very desperate, either) when I'd be obliged to sacrifice you for my own personal safety, comfort, and convenience. Hundreds of things might happen.

"Well, as I said, we've been at large together for some years, and I've found you sober, trustworthy, and honest; so, in case we do part—as we will sooner or later—and you survive, I'll give you some advice from my own experience.

"In the first place: If you ever happen to get born again—and it wouldn't do you much harm—get born with the strength of a bullock and the hide of one as well, and a swelled head, and no brains—at least no more brains than you've got now. I was born with a skin like tissue-paper, and brain; also a heart.

"Get born without relatives, if you can: if you can't help it, clear out on your own just as soon after you're born as you possibly can. I hung on.

"If you have relations, and feel inclined to help them any time when you're flush (and there's no telling what a weak-minded man like you might take it into his head to do)—don't do it. They'll get a down on you if you do. It only causes family troubles and bitterness. There's no dislike like that of a dependant. You'll get neither gratitude nor civility in the end, and be lucky if you escape with a character. (You've got *no* character, Smith; I'm only just supposing you have.) There's no hatred too bitter for, and nothing too bad to be said of, the mug who turns. The worst yarns about a man are generally started by his own tribe, and the world believes them at once on that very account. Well, the first thing to do in life is to escape from your friends.

"If you ever go to work—and miracles have happened before—no matter what your wages are, or how you are treated, you can take it for granted that you're sweated; act on that to the best of your ability, or you'll never rise in the world. If you go to see a show on the nod you'll be found a comfortable seat in a good place; but if you pay the chances are the ticket clerk will tell you a lie, and you'll have to hustle for standing room. The man that doesn't ante gets the best of this world; anything he'll stand is good enough for the man that pays. If you try to be too sharp you'll get into jail sooner or later; if you try to be too honest the chances are that the bailiff will get into your house—if you have one—and make a holy show of you before the neighbours. The honest softy is more often mistaken for a swindler, and accused of being one, than the out-and-out scamp; and the man that tells the truth too much is set down as an irreclaimable liar. But most of the time crow low and roost high, for it's a funny world, and you never know what might happen.

"And if you get married (and there's no accounting for a woman's taste) be as bad as you like, and then moderately good, and your wife will love you.

Walter Withers (1857-1914)   *Nearing the Township* (c. 1900)
Detail Only   109.2 x 183.2 cm   Oil on canvas
Reproduced with the kind permission of the Art Gallery Of New South Wales, Sydney

J. J. Hilder (1881-1916)   *Ploughing*
14.5 x 25 cm   Watercolour
Reproduced with the kind permission of Keith Wingrove, Adelaide

If you're bad all the time she can't stand it for ever, and if you're good all the time she'll naturally treat you with contempt. Never explain what you're going to do, and don't explain afterwards, if you can help it. If you find yourself between two stools, strike hard for your own self, Smith—strike hard, and you'll be respected more than if you fought for all the world. Generosity isn't understood nowadays, and what the people don't understand is either 'mad' or 'cronk.' Failure has no case, and you can't build one for it. . . . I started out in life very young—and very soft."

"I thought you were going to tell me your story, Steely," remarked Smith. Steelman smiled sadly.

THE GEOLOGICAL SPIELER

There's nothing so interesting as Geology, even to common and ignorant people, especially when you have a bank or the side of a cutting, studded with fossil fish and things and oysters that were stale when Adam was fresh to illustrate by. *(Remark made by Steelman, professional wanderer, to his pal and pupil, Smith.)*

The first man that Steelman and Smith came up to on the last embankment, where they struck the new railway line, was a heavy, gloomy, labouring man with bowyangs on and straps round his wrists. Steelman bade him the time of day and had a few words with him over the weather. The man of mullock gave it as his opinion that the fine weather wouldn't last, and seemed to take a gloomy kind of pleasure in that reflection; he said there was more rain down yonder, pointing to the south-east, than the moon could swallow up— the moon was in its first quarter, during which time it is popularly believed in some parts of Maoriland that the south-easter is most likely to be out on the wallaby and the weather bad. Steelman regarded that quarter of the sky with an expression of gentle remonstrance mingled as it were with a sort of fatherly indulgence, agreed mildly with the labouring man, and seemed lost for a moment in a reverie from which he roused himself to inquire cautiously after the boss. There was no boss, it was a co-operative party. That chap standing over there by the dray in the end of the cutting was their spokesman—their representative: they called him boss, but that was only his nickname in camp. Steelman expressed his thanks and moved on towards the cutting, followed respectfully by Smith.

Steelman wore a snuff-coloured sac suit, a wide-awake hat, a pair of professional-looking spectacles, and a scientific expression; there was a clerical atmosphere about him, strengthened, however, by an air as of unconscious

138

dignity and superiority, born of intellect and knowledge. He carried a black bag, which was an indispensable article in his profession in more senses than one. Smith was decently dressed in sober tweed and looked like a man of no account, who was mechanically devoted to his employer's interests, pleasures, or whims.

The boss was a decent-looking young fellow, with a good face—rather solemn—and a quiet manner.

"Good day, sir," said Steelman.

"Good day, sir," said the boss.

"Nice weather this."

"Yes, it is, but I'm afraid it won't last."

"I am afraid it will not by the look of the sky down there," ventured Steelman.

"No, I go mostly by the look of our weather prophet," said the boss with a quiet smile, indicating the gloomy man.

"I suppose bad weather would put you back in your work?"

"Yes, it will; we didn't want any bad weather just now."

Steelman got the weather question satisfactorily settled; then he said:

"You seem to be getting on with the railway."

"Oh yes, we are about over the worst of it."

"The worst of it?" echoed Steelman, with mild surprise: "I should have thought you were just coming into it," and he pointed to the ridge ahead.

"Oh, our section doesn't go any further than that pole you see sticking up yonder. We had the worst of it back there across the swamps—working up to our waists in water most of the time, in mid-winter too—and at eighteen-pence a yard."

"That was bad."

"Yes, rather rough. Did you come from the terminus?"

"Yes, I sent my baggage on in the brake."

"Commercial traveller, I suppose?" asked the boss, glancing at Smith, who stood a little to the rear of Steelman, seeming interested in the work.

"Oh no," said Steelman, smiling—"I am—well—I'm a geologist; this is my man here," indicating Smith. "(You may put down the bag, James, and have a smoke.) My name is Stoneleigh—you might have heard of it."

The boss said, "Oh," and then presently he added "indeed," in an undecided tone.

There was a pause—embarrassed on the part of the boss—he was silent not knowing what to say. Meanwhile Steelman studied his man and concluded that he would do.

"Having a look at the country, I suppose?" asked the boss presently.

"Yes," said Steelman; then after a moment's reflection: "I am travelling for my own amusement and improvement, and also in the interests of science, which amounts to the same thing. I am a member of the Royal Geological Society—vice-president in fact of a leading Australian branch;" and then, as if conscious that he had appeared guilty of egotism, he shifted the subject a bit. "Yes. Very interesting country this—very interesting indeed. I should like to make a stay here for a day or so. Your work opens right into my hands. I cannot remember seeing a geological formation which interested me so much. Look at the face of that cutting, for instance. Why! you can almost read the history of the geological world from yesterday—this morning as it were—beginning with the super-surface on top and going right down through the different layers and stratas—through the vanished ages—right down and back to the pre-historical—to the very primeval or fundamental geological formations!" And Steelman studied the face of the cutting as if he could read it like a book, with every layer or stratum a chapter, and every streak a note of explanation. The boss seemed to be getting interested, and Steelman gained confidence and proceeded to identify and classify the different "stratas and layers," and fix their ages, and describe the conditions and politics of man in their different times, for the boss's benefit.

"Now," continued Steelman, turning slowly from the cutting, removing his glasses, and letting his thoughtful eyes wander casually over the general scenery—"now the first impression that this country would leave on an ordinary intelligent mind—though maybe unconsciously, would be as of a new country—new in a geological sense; with patches of an older geological and vegetable formation cropping out here and there; as for instance that clump of dead trees on that clear alluvial slope there, that outcrop of limestone, or that timber yonder," and he indicated a dead forest which seemed alive and green because of the parasites. "But the country is old—old; perhaps the oldest geological formation in the world is to be seen here, the oldest vegetable formation in Australasia. I am not using the words old and new in an ordinary sense, you understand, but in a geological sense."

The boss said, "I understand," and that geology must be a very interesting study.

Steelman ran his eye meditatively over the cutting again, and turning to Smith said:

"Go up there, James, and fetch me a specimen of that slaty outcrop you see there—just above the coeval strata."

It was a stiff climb and slippery, but Smith had to do it, and he did it.

"This," said Steelman, breaking the rotten piece between his fingers, "belongs probably to an older geological period than its position would indicate—a primitive sandstone level perhaps. Its position on that layer is no doubt due to volcanic upheavals—such disturbances, or rather the results of such disturbances, have been and are the cause of the greatest trouble to geologists —endless errors and controversy. You see we must study the country, not as it appears now, but as it would appear had the natural geological growth been left to mature undisturbed; we must restore and reconstruct such disorganized portions of the mineral kingdom, if you understand me."

The boss said he understood.

Steelman found an opportunity to wink sharply and severely at Smith, who had been careless enough to allow his features to relapse into a vacant grin.

"It is generally known even amongst the ignorant that rock grows—grows from the outside—but the rock here, a specimen of which I hold in my hand, is now in the process of decomposition; to be plain it is rotting—in an advanced stage of decomposition—so much so that you are not able to identify it with any geological period or formation, even as you may not be able to identify any other extremely decomposed body."

The boss blinked and knitted his brow, but had the presence of mind to say: "Just so."

"Had the rock on that cutting been healthy—been alive, as it were—you would have had your work cut out; but it is dead and has been dead for ages perhaps. You find less trouble in working it than you would ordinary clay or sand, or even gravel, which formations together are really rock in embryo —before birth as it were."

The boss's brow cleared.

"The country round here is simply rotting down—simply rotting down."

He removed his spectacles, wiped them, and wiped his face; then his attention seemed to be attracted by some stones at his feet. He picked one up and examined it.

"I shouldn't wonder," he mused, absently, "I shouldn't wonder if there is alluvial gold in some of these creeks and gullies, perhaps tin or even silver, quite probably antimony."

The boss seemed interested.

"Can you tell me if there is any place in this neighbourhood where I could get accommodation for myself and my servant for a day or two?" asked Steelman presently. "I should very much like to break my journey here."

"Well, no," said the boss. "I can't say I do—I don't know of any place nearer than Pahiatua, and that's seven miles from here."

"I know that," said Steelman reflectively, "but I fully expected to have found a house of accommodation of some sort on the way, else I would have gone on in the van."

"Well," said the boss. "If you like to camp with us for to-night, at least, and don't mind roughing it, you'll be welcome, I'm sure."

"If I was sure that I would not be putting you to any trouble, or interfering in any way with your domestic economy——"

"No trouble at all," interrupted the boss. "The boys will be only too glad, and there's an empty whare where you can sleep. Better stay. It's going to be a rough night."

After tea Steelman entertained the boss and a few of the more thoughtful members of the party with short chatty lectures on geology and other subjects.

In the meantime Smith, in another part of the camp, gave selections on a tin whistle, sang a song or two, contributed, in his turn, to the sailor yarns, and ensured his popularity for several nights at least. After several draughts of something that was poured out of a demijohn into a pint-pot, his tongue became loosened, and he expressed an opinion that geology was all bosh, and said if he had half his employer's money he'd be dashed if he would go rooting round in the mud like a blessed old ant-eater; he also irreverently referred to his learned boss as "Old Rocks" over there. He had a pretty easy billet of it though, he said, taking it all round, when the weather was fine; he got a couple of notes a week and all expenses paid, and the money was sure; he was only required to look after the luggage and arrange for accommodation, grub out a chunk of rock now and then, and (what perhaps was the most irksome of his duties) he had to appear interested in old rocks and clay.

Towards midnight Steelman and Smith retired to the unoccupied whare which had been shown them, Smith carrying a bundle of bags, blankets, and rugs, which had been placed at their disposal by their good-natured hosts. Smith lit a candle and proceeded to make the beds. Steelman sat down, removed his specs and scientific expression, placed the glasses carefully on a ledge close at hand, took a book from his bag, and commenced to read. The volume was a cheap copy of Jules Verne's *Journey to the Centre of the Earth*. A little later there was a knock at the door. Steelman hastily resumed the spectacles, together with the scientific expression, took a note-book from his pocket, opened it on the table, and said, "Come in." One of the chaps appeared with a billy of hot coffee, two pint-pots, and some cake. He said he thought you chaps might like a drop of coffee before you turned in, and the boys had forgot to ask you to wait for it down in the camp. He also wanted to know whether Mr Stoneleigh and his man would be all right and quite comfortable for the night, and whether they had blankets enough. There was some wood at the back of the whare and they could light a fire if they liked.

Mr Stoneleigh expressed his thanks and his appreciation of the kindness shown him and his servant. He was extremely sorry to give them any trouble.

The navvy, a serious man, who respected genius or intellect in any shape or form, said that it was no trouble at all, the camp was very dull and the boys were always glad to have someone come round. Then, after a brief comparison of opinions concerning the probable duration of the weather which had arrived, they bade each other good night, and the darkness swallowed the serious man.

Steelman turned into the top bunk on one side and Smith took the lower on the other. Steelman had the candle by his bunk, as usual; he lit his pipe for a final puff before going to sleep, and held the light up for a moment so as to give Smith the full benefit of a solemn, uncompromising wink. The wink was silently applauded and dutifully returned by Smith. Then Steelman blew out the light, lay back, and puffed at his pipe for a while. Presently he chuckled, and the chuckle was echoed by Smith; by and by Steelman chuckled once more, and then Smith chuckled again. There was silence in the darkness, and after a bit Smith chuckled twice. Then Steelman said:

"For God's sake give her a rest, Smith, and give a man a show to get some sleep."

Then the silence in the darkness remained unbroken.

The invitation was extended next day, and Steelman sent Smith on to see that his baggage was safe. Smith stayed out of sight for two or three hours, and then returned and reported all well.

They stayed on for several days. After breakfast and when the men were going to work Steelman and Smith would go out along the line with the black bag and poke round amongst the "layers and stratas" in sight of the works for a while, as an evidence of good faith; then they'd drift off casually into the bush, camp in a retired and sheltered spot, and light a fire when the weather was cold, and Steelman would lie on the grass and read and smoke and lay plans for the future and improve Smith's mind until they reckoned it was about dinner-time. And in the evening they would come home with the black bag full of stones and bits of rock, and Steelman would lecture on those minerals after tea.

On about the fourth morning Steelman had a yarn with one of the men going to work. He was a lanky young fellow with a sandy complexion, and seemingly harmless grin. In Australia he might have been regarded as a "cove" rather than a "chap," but there was nothing of the "bloke" about him. Presently the cove said:

"What do you think of the boss, Mr Stoneleigh? He seems to have taken a great fancy for you, and he's fair gone on geology."

"I think he is a very decent fellow indeed, a very intelligent young man. He seems very well read and well informed."

"You wouldn't think he was a University man," said the cove.

"No, indeed! Is he?"

"Yes. I thought you knew!"

Steelman knitted his brows. He seemed slightly disturbed for the moment. He walked on a few paces in silence and thought hard.

"What might have been his special line?" he asked the cove.

"Why, something the same as yours. I thought you knew. He was reckoned the best—what do you call it?—the best minrologist in the country. He had a first-class billet in the Mines Department, but he lost it—you know—the booze."

"I think we will be making a move, Smith," said Steelman later on, when they were private. "There's a little too much intellect in this camp to suit me. But we haven't done so bad, anyway. We've had three days' good board and lodging with entertainments and refreshments thrown in." Then he said to himself: "We'll stay for another day anyway. If those beggars are having a lark with us, we're getting the worth of it anyway, and I'm not thin-skinned. They're the mugs and not us, anyhow it goes, and I can take them down before I leave."

But on the way home he had a talk with another man whom we might set down as a "chap."

"I wouldn't have thought the boss was a college man," said Steelman to the chap.

"A what?"

"A University man—University education."

"Why! Who's been telling you that?"

"One of your mates."

"Oh, he's been getting at you. Why, it's all the boss can do to write his own name. Now that lanky sandy cove with the birth-mark grin—it's him that's had the college education."

"I think we'll make a start to-morrow," said Steelman to Smith in the privacy of their whare. "There's too much humour and levity in this camp to suit a serious scientific gentleman like myself."

143

EURUNDEREE

There are scenes in the distance where beauty is not,
On the desolate flats where gaunt apple-trees rot.
Where the brooding old ridge rises up to the breeze
From his dark lonely gullies of stringy-bark trees,
There are voice-haunted gaps, ever sullen and strange;
But Eurunderee lies like a gem in the range.

Still I see in my fancy the dark-green and blue
Of the box-covered hills where the five-corners grew;
And the rugged old sheoaks that sighed in the bend
O'er the lily-decked pools where the dark ridges end,
And the scrub-covered spurs running down from the Peak
To the deep grassy banks of Eurunderee Creek.

On the knolls where the vineyards and fruit-gardens are
There's a beauty that even the drought cannot mar:
For it came to me oft, in the days that are lost,
As I strolled on the sidling where lingered the frost,
And, the shadows of night from the gullies withdrawn,
The hills in the background were flushed by the dawn.

I was there in late years, but there's many a change
Where the Cudgegong River flows down through the range;
For the curse of the town with the railroad has come,
And the goldfields are dead. And the girl, and the chum,
And the old home were gone; yet the oaks seemed to speak
Of the hazy old days on Eurunderee Creek.

And I stood by that creek, ere the sunset grew cold,
When the leaves of the sheoaks were traced on the gold,
And I thought of old days, and I thought of old folks,
Till I sighed in my heart to the sigh of the oaks;
For the years waste away like the waters that leak
Through the pebbles and sand of Eurunderee Creek.

TROOPER CAMPBELL

One day old Trooper Campbell
  Rode out to Blackman's Run;
His cap-peak and his sabre
  Were glancing in the sun.
'Twas New Year's Eve, and slowly
  Across the ridges low
The sad Old Year was drifting
  To where the old years go.

The trooper's mind was reading
  The love-page of his life—
His love for Mary Wylie
  Ere she was Blackman's wife;
He sorrowed for the sorrows
  Of the heart a rival won,
For he knew that there was trouble
  Out there on Blackman's Run.

The sapling shades had lengthened,
  The summer day was late,
When Blackman met the trooper
  Beyond the homestead gate;
And, if the hand of trouble
  Can leave a lasting trace,
The lines of care had come to stay
  On poor old Blackman's face.

"Not good day, Trooper Campbell,
  It's a bad, bad day for me—
You are of all the men on earth
  The one I wished to see.
The great black clouds of trouble
  Above our homestead hang;
That wild and reckless boy of mine
  Has joined M'Durmer's gang.

"Oh! save him, save him, Campbell,
  I beg in friendship's name!
For if they take and hang him,
  The wife would die of shame.
Could Mary and her sisters
  Hold up their heads again,
And face a woman's malice,
  Or claim the love of men?

"And if he does a murder
    We all were better dead.
Don't take him living, Trooper,
    If a price be on his head;
But shoot him! shoot him, Campbell,
    When you meet him face to face,
And save him from the gallows—
    And us from that disgrace."

"Now, Tom," cried Trooper Campbell,
    "You know your words are wild.
Though he is wild and reckless,
    Yet still he is your child;
So bear up in your trouble,
    Yes, meet it like a man,
And tell the wife and daughters
    I'll save him if I can."

.   .   .   .

The sad Australian sunset
    Had faded from the west;
But night brought darker shadows
    To hearts that could not rest;
And Blackman's wife sat rocking
    And moaning in her chair.
"I cannot bear disgrace," she moaned;
    "It's more than I can bear.

"In hardship and in trouble
    I struggle year by year
To make my children better
    Than other children here.
And if my son's a felon
    How can I show my face?
I cannot bear disgrace; my God,
    I cannot bear disgrace!

"Ah, God in Heaven pardon!
    I'm selfish in my woe—
My boy is better-hearted
    Than many that I know.
I'll face whatever happens,
    And, till his mother's dead,
My foolish child shall find a place
    To lay his outlawed head."

Sore-hearted, Trooper Campbell
   Rode out from Blackman's Run,
Nor noticed aught about him
   Till thirteen miles were done;
When, close beside a cutting,
   He heard the click of locks,
And saw the rifle-muzzles
   Trained on him from the rocks.

But suddenly a youth rode out,
   And, close by Campbell's side:
"Don't fire! don't fire, in Heaven's name!
   It's Campbell, boys!" he cried.
Then one by one in silence
   The levelled rifles fell,
For who'd shoot Trooper Campbell
   Of those who knew him well?

Oh, bravely sat old Campbell,
   No sign of fear showed he.
He slowly drew his carbine;
   It rested by his knee.
The outlaws guns were lifted,
   But none the silence broke.
Till steadfastly and firmly
   Old Trooper Campbell spoke,

"That boy that you would ruin
   Goes home with me, my men;
Or some of us shall never
   Ride through the Gap again.
You all know Trooper Campbell,
   And have you ever heard
That bluff or lead could turn him,
   That e'er he broke his word?

"That reckless lad is playing
   A heartless villain's part;
He knows that he is breaking
   His poor old mother's heart.
He's going straight to ruin;
   But 'tis not that alone,
He'll bring dishonour to a name
   That I'd be proud to own.

"I speak to you, M'Durmer—
  If your heart's not granite quite,
And if you'd seen the trouble
  At Blackman's home this night,
You'd help me now, M'Durmer—
  I speak as man to man—
I swore to save the foolish lad—
  I'll save him if I can."

"Oh, take him!" said M'Durmer,
  "He's got a horse to ride. . . ."
The youngster thought a moment,
  Then rode to Campbell's side. . . .
"Good-bye!" the outlaws shouted,
  As up the range they sped.
"A Merry New Year, Campbell,"
  Was all M'Durmer said.

Then fast along the ridges
  Two horsemen rode a race,
The moonlight lent a glory
  To Trooper Campbell's face.
And ere the new year's dawning
  They reached the homestead gate—
"I found him," said the Trooper,
  "And not, thank God, too late!"

Lawson's 'old home' at Eurunderee where he spent much of his childhood. It was erected by his father and was a typical settler's dwelling of the period. In his later years Lawson looked back to it as an unhappy home and it was here that Louisa's resentment at the trammels of life in the country made it no place for a woman. She left it in 1883.

In the 1930s, as Lawson's stature in Australian literature developed, a movement was initiated by various literary societies to have it restored as a literary shrine or memorial. The scheme was found to be impracticable owing to structural deterioration and it was ultimately demolished (see page 451).

MIDDLETON'S PETER

I
THE FIRST BORN

The struggling squatter is to be found in Australia as well as the "struggling farmer." The Australian squatter is not always the mighty wool king that English and American authors and other uninformed people apparently imagine him to be. Squatting, at the best, is but a game of chance. It depends mainly on the weather, and that, in New South Wales at least, depends on nothing.

Joe Middleton was a struggling squatter, with a station some distance to the westward of the furthest line reached by the ordinary new chum. His run, at the time of our story, was only about six miles square, and his stock was limited in proportion. The hands on Joe's run consisted of his brother Dave, a middle-aged man known only as "Middleton's Peter" (who had been in the service of the Middleton family ever since Joe Middleton could remember), and an old black shepherd, with his gin and two boys.

It was in the first year of Joe's marriage. He had married a very ordinary girl, as far as Australian girls go, but in his eyes she was an angel. He really worshipped her.

One sultry afternoon in midsummer all the station-hands, with the exception of Dave Middleton, were congregated about the homestead door, and it was evident from their solemn faces that something unusual was the matter. They appeared to be watching for something or someone across the flat, and the old black shepherd, who had been listening intently with bent head, suddenly straightened himself up and cried:

"I can hear the cart. I can see it!"

You must bear in mind that our blackfellows do not always talk the gibberish with which they are credited by story writers.

It was not until some time after Black Bill had spoken that the white—or, rather, the brown—portion of the party could see or even hear the approaching vehicle. At last, far out through the trunks of the native apple-trees, the cart was seen approaching; and as it came nearer it was evident that it was being driven at a breakneck pace, the horses cantering all the way, while the motion of the cart, at first one wheel and then the other sprang from a root or a rut, bore a striking resemblance to the Highland Fling. There were two persons in the cart. One was Mother Palmer, a stout, middle-aged party (who sometimes did the duties of a midwife), and the other was Dave Middleton, Joe's brother.

The cart was driven right up to the door with scarcely any abatement of speed, and was stopped so suddenly that Mrs Palmer was sent sprawling on to the horse's rump. She was quickly helped down, and, as soon as she had recovered sufficient breath, she followed Black Mary into the bedroom where young Mrs Middleton was lying, looking very pale and frightened. The horse which had been driven so cruelly had not done blowing before another cart appeared, also driven very fast. It contained old Mr and Mrs Middleton, who lived comfortably on a small farm not far from Palmer's place.

As soon as he had dumped Mrs Palmer, Dave Middleton left the cart and, mounting a fresh horse which stood ready saddled in the yard, galloped off through the scrub in a different direction.

Half an hour afterwards Joe Middleton came home on a horse that had been almost ridden to death. His mother came out at the sound of his arrival, and he anxiously asked her:

"How is she?"

"Did you find Doc. Wild?" asked the mother.

"No, confound him!" exclaimed Joe bitterly. "He promised me faithfully to come over on Wednesday and stay until Maggie was right again. Now he has left Dean's and gone—Lord knows where. I suppose he is drinking again. How is Maggie?"

"It's all over now—the child is born. It's a boy; but she is very weak. Dave got Mrs Palmer here just in time. I had better tell you at once that Mrs Palmer says if we don't get a doctor here to-night poor Maggie won't live."

"Good God! and what am I to do?" cried Joe desperately.

"Is there any other doctor within reach?"

"No; there is only the one at B——; that's forty miles away, and he is laid up with the broken leg he got in the buggy accident. Where's Dave?"

"Gone to Black's shanty. One of Mrs Palmer's sons thought he remembered someone saying that Doc. Wild was there last week. That's fifteen miles away."

"But it is our only hope," said Joe dejectedly. "I wish to God that I had taken Maggie to some civilized place a month ago."

Doc. Wild was a well-known character among the bushmen of New South Wales, and although the profession did not recognize him, and denounced him as an empiric, his skill was undoubted. Bushmen had great faith in him, and would often ride incredible distances in order to bring him to the bedside of a sick friend. He drank fearfully, but was seldom incapable of treating a patient; he would, however, sometimes be found in an obstinate mood and refuse to travel to the side of a sick person, and then the devil himself could not make the doctor budge. But for all this he was very generous—a fact that could, no doubt, be testified to by many a grateful sojourner in the lonely bush.

There doesn't seem to have been a back country district that didn't have at some time in its history a deregistered medical man whose skill was legendary. Drink, or some offence against medical ethics, was usually their downfall.

Lawson made very sparing use of the Aborigine in his work and by no means used them as figures of fun or derision. He seems to have accepted them as part of the world to which he belonged.

II
THE ONLY HOPE

Night came on, and still there was no change in the condition of the young wife, and no sign of the doctor. Several stockmen from the neighbouring stations, hearing that there was trouble at Joe Middleton's, had ridden over, and had galloped off on long, hopeless rides in search of a doctor. Being generally free from sickness themselves, these bushmen look upon it as a serious business even in its mildest form; what is more, their sympathy is always practical where it is possible for it to be so. One day, while out on the run after an "outlaw," Joe Middleton was badly thrown from his horse, and the breakneck riding that was done on that occasion from the time the horse came home with empty saddle until the rider was safe in bed and attended by a doctor was something extraordinary, even for the bush.

Before the time arrived when Dave Middleton might reasonably have been expected to return, the station people were anxiously watching for him, all except the old blackfellow and the two boys, who had gone to yard the sheep.

The party had been increased by Jimmy Nowlett, the bullocky, who had just arrived with a load of fencing wire and provisions for Middleton. Jimmy was standing in the moonlight, whip in hand, looking as anxious as the husband himself, and endeavouring to calculate by mental arithmetic the exact time it ought to take Dave to complete his double journey, taking into consideration the distance, the obstacles in the way, and the chances of horse-flesh.

But the time which Jimmy fixed for the arrival came without Dave.

Old Peter (as he was generally called, though he was not really old) stood aside in his usual sullen manner, his hat drawn down over his brow and eyes, and nothing visible but a thick and very horizontal black beard, from the depth of which emerged large clouds of very strong tobacco smoke, the product of a short, black, clay pipe.

They had almost given up all hope of seeing Dave return that night, when Peter slowly and deliberately removed his pipe and grunted:

"He's a-comin'."

He then replaced the pipe, and smoked on as before.

All listened, but not one of them could hear a sound.

"Yer ears must be pretty sharp for yer age, Peter. We can't hear him," remarked Jimmy Nowlett.

"His dog ken," said Peter.

The pipe was again removed and its abbreviated stem pointed in the direction of Dave's cattle-dog, who had risen beside his kennel with pointed ears, and was looking eagerly in the direction from which his master was expected to come.

Presently the sound of horse's hoofs was distinctly heard.

"I can hear two horses," cried Jimmy Nowlett excitedly.

"There's only one," said old Peter quietly.

A few moments passed, and a single horseman appeared on the far side of the flat.

"It's Doc. Wild on Dave's horse," cried Jimmy Nowlett. "Dave don't ride like that."

"It's Dave," said Peter, replacing his pipe and looking more unsociable than ever.

Dave rode up and, throwing himself wearily from the saddle, stood ominously silent by the side of his horse.

Joe Middleton said nothing, but stood aside with an expression of utter hopelessness on his face.

"Not there?" asked Jimmy Nowlett at last, addressing Dave.

"Yes, he's there," answered Dave, impatiently.

This was not the answer they expected, but nobody seemed surprised.

"Drunk?" asked Jimmy.

"Yes."

Here old Peter removed his pipe, and pronounced the one word "How?"

"What the hell do you mean by that?" muttered Dave, whose patience had evidently been severely tried by the clever but intemperate bush doctor.

"How drunk?" explained Peter, with great equanimity.

"Stubborn drunk, blind drunk, beastly drunk, dead drunk, and damned well drunk, if that's what you want to know!"

"What did Doc. say?" asked Jimmy.

"Said he was sick—had lumbago—wouldn't come for the Queen of England; said he wanted a course of treatment himself. Curse him! I have no patience to talk about him."

"I'd give him a course of treatment," muttered Jimmy viciously, trailing the long lash of his bullock-whip through the grass and spitting spitefully at the ground.

Dave turned away and joined Joe, who was talking earnestly to his mother by the kitchen door. He told them that he had spent an hour trying to persuade Doc. Wild to come, and, that before he had left the shanty, Black had promised him faithfully to bring the doctor over as soon as his obstinate mood wore off.

Just then a low moan was heard from the sick room, followed by the sound of Mother Palmer's voice calling old Mrs Middleton, who went inside immediately.

No one had noticed the disappearance of Peter, and when he presently returned from the stockyard, leading the only fresh horse that remained, Jimmy Nowlett began to regard him with some interest. Peter transferred the saddle from Dave's horse to the other, and then went into a small room off the kitchen, which served him as a bedroom; from it he soon returned with a formidable-looking revolver, the chambers of which he examined in the moonlight in full view of all the company. They thought for a moment the man had gone mad. Old Middleton leaped quickly behind Nowlett, and Black Mary, who had come out to the cask at the corner for a dipper of water, dropped the dipper and was inside like a shot. One of the black boys came softly up at that moment; as soon as his sharp eye "spotted" the weapon, he disappeared as though the earth had swallowed him.

"What the mischief are yer goin' ter do, Peter?" asked Jimmy.

"Goin' to fetch him," said Peter, and, after carefully emptying his pipe and replacing it in a leather pouch at his belt, he mounted and rode off at an easy canter.

Jimmy watched the horse until it disappeared at the edge of the flat, and then after coiling up the long lash of his bullock-whip in the dust until it looked like a sleeping snake, he prodded the small end of the long pine handle into the middle of the coil, as though driving home a point, and said in a tone of intense conviction:

"He'll fetch him."

III
DOC. WILD

Peter gradually increased his horse's speed along the rough bush track until he was riding at a good pace. It was ten miles to the main road, and five from there to the shanty kept by Black.

For some time before Peter started the atmosphere had been very close and oppressive. The great black edge of a storm-cloud had risen in the east, and everything indicated the approach of a thunderstorm. It was not long coming. Before Peter had completed six miles of his journey, the clouds rolled over, obscuring the moon, and an Australian thunderstorm came on with its mighty downpour, its blind lightning, and its earth-shaking thunder. Peter rode steadily on, only pausing now and then until a flash revealed the track in front of him.

Black's shanty—or, rather, as the sign had it, "Post Office and General Store"—was, as we have said, five miles along the main road from the point where Middleton's track joined it. The building was of the usual style of bush architecture. About two hundred yards nearer the creek, which crossed the road further on, stood a large bark-and-slab stable, large enough to have met the requirements of a legitimate bush "public."

The reader may doubt that a sly-grog shop could openly carry on business on a main government road along which mounted troopers were continually passing. But then, you see, mounted troopers get thirsty like other men; moreover, they could always get their thirst quenched gratis at these places; so the reader will be prepared to hear that on this very night two troopers' horses were stowed snugly away in the stable, and two troopers were stowed snugly away in the back room of the shanty, sleeping off the effects of their cheap but strong potations.

There were two rooms, of a sort, attached to the stables—one at each end. One was occupied by a man who was "generally useful," and the other was the surgery, office, and bedroom *pro tem.* of Doc. Wild.

Doc. Wild was a tall man, of spare proportions. He had a cadaverous face, black hair, bushy black eyebrows, eagle nose, and eagle eyes. He never slept while he was drinking. On this occasion he sat in front of the fire on a low three-legged stool. His knees were drawn up, his toes hooked round the front legs of the stool, one hand resting on one knee, and one elbow (the hand supporting the chin) resting on the other. He was staring intently into the fire, on which an old black saucepan was boiling and sending forth a pungent odour of herbs. There seemed something uncanny about the doctor as the red light of the fire fell on his hawk-like face and gleaming eyes. He might have been Mephistopheles watching some infernal brew.

He had sat there some time without stirring a finger, when the door suddenly burst open and Middleton's Peter stood within, dripping wet. The doctor turned his black, piercing eyes upon the intruder (who regarded him silently) for a moment, and then asked quietly:

"What the hell do you want?"

"I want you," said Peter.

"And what do you want me for?"

"I want you to come to Joe Middleton's wife. She's bad," said Peter calmly.

"I won't come," shouted the doctor. "I've brought enough horse-stealers into the world already. If any more want to come they can go to blazes for me. Now, you get out of this!"

"Don't get yer rag out," said Peter quietly. "The hoss-stealer's come, an' nearly killed his mother ter begin with; an' if yer don't get yer physic-box an' come wi' me, by the great God I'll——"

Here the revolver was produced and pointed at Doc. Wild's head. The sight of the weapon had a sobering effect upon the doctor. He rose, looked at Peter critically for a moment, knocked the weapon out of his hand, and said slowly and deliberately:

"Wall, ef the case es as serious as that, I (hic) reckon I'd better come."

Peter was still of the same opinion, so Doc. Wild proceeded to get his medicine-chest ready. He explained afterwards, in one of his softer moments, that the shooter didn't frighten him so much as it touched his memory— "sorter put him in mind of the old days in California, and made him think of the man he might have been," he'd say—"kinder touched his heart and slid the durned old panorama in front of him like a flash; made him think of the time when he slipped three leaden pills into 'Blue Shirt' for winking at a new chum behind his (the doc.'s) back when he was telling a truthful yarn, and charged the said 'Blue Shirt,' a hundred dollars for extracting the said pills."

Joe Middleton's wife is a grandmother now.

Peter passed after the manner of his sort; he was found dead in his bunk.

Poor Doc. Wild died in a shepherd's hut at the Dry Creeks. The shepherds (white men) found him, "naked as he was born and with the hide half burned off him with the sun," rounding up imaginary snakes on a dusty clearing one blazing hot day. The hut-keeper had some "quare" (queer) experiences with the doctor during the next three days and used, in after years, to tell of them, between the puffs of his pipe, calmly and solemnly and as if the story was rather to the doctor's credit than otherwise. The shepherds sent for the police and a doctor, and sent word to Joe Middleton. Doc. Wild was sensible towards the end. His interview with the other doctor was characteristic. "And, now you see how far I am," he said in conclusion—"have you brought the brandy?" The other doctor had. Joe Middleton came with his wagonette, and in it the softest mattress and pillows the station afforded. He also, in his innocence, brought a dozen of soda-water. Doc. Wild took Joe's hand feebly, and, a little later, he "passed out" (as he would have said) murmuring "something that sounded like poetry," in an unknown tongue. Joe took the body to the home station. "Who's the boss bringin'?" asked the shearers, seeing the wagonette coming very slowly and the boss walking by the horses' heads. "Doc. Wild," said a station-hand. "Take yer hats off."

They buried him with bush honours, and chiselled his name on a slab of blue-gum—a wood that lasts.

THE STORY OF THE ORACLE

"We young fellows," said "Sympathy Joe" to Mitchell, after tea, in their first camp west the river "—and you and I *are* young fellows, comparatively —think we know the world. There are plenty of young chaps knocking round in this country who reckon they've been through it all before they're thirty. I've met cynics and men-o'-the-world, aged twenty-one or thereabouts, who've never been further than a trip to Sydney. They talk about 'this world' as if they knocked around in half a dozen other worlds before they came across here—and they are just as off-hand about it as older Australians are when they talk about this colony as compared with the others. They say: 'My oath!—same here.' 'I've been there.' 'My oath!—you're right.' 'Take it from me!' and all that sort of thing. They understand women, and have a contempt for 'em; and chaps that don't talk as they talk, or do as they do, or see as they see, are either soft or ratty. A good many reckon that 'life ain't blanky well worth livin';' sometimes they feel so blanky somehow that they wouldn't give a blank whether they chucked it or not; but that sort never chuck it. It's mostly the quiet men that do that, and if they've got any complaints to make against the world they made 'em at the head station. Why, I've known healthy, single, young fellows under twenty-five who drank to drown their troubles—some because they reckoned the world didn't understand nor appreciate 'em—as if it *could*!"

"If the world don't understand or appreciate you," said Mitchell solemnly, as he reached for a burning stick to light his pipe—'*make* it!"

"To drown *their* troubles!" continued Joe, in a tone of impatient contempt. "The Oracle must be well on towards the sixties; he can take his glass with any man, but you never saw him drunk."

"What's the Oracle to do with it?"

"Did you ever hear his history?"

"No. Do you know it!"

"Yes, though I don't think he has any idea that I do. Now, we were talking about the Oracle a little while ago. We know he's an old ass; a good many outsiders consider that he's a bit soft or ratty, and, as we're likely to be mates together for some time on that fencing contract, if we get it, you might as well know what sort of a man he is and was, so's you won't get uneasy about him if he gets deaf for a while when you're talking, or does funny things with his pipe or pint-pot, or walks up and down by himself for an hour or so after tea, or sits on a log with his head in his hands, or leans on the fence in the gloaming and keeps looking in a blank sort of way, straight ahead, across the clearing. For he's gazing at something a thousand miles across country, south-east, and about twenty years back into the past, and no doubt he sees himself (as a young man), and a Gippsland girl, spooning under the stars along between the hop-gardens and the Mitchell River. And, if you get holt of a fiddle or a concertina, don't rasp or swank too much on old tunes, when he's around, for the Oracle can't stand it. Play something lively. He'll be down there at that suveyor's camp yarning till all hours, so we'll have plenty of time for the story—but don't you ever give him a hint that you know.

"My people knew him well; I got most of the story from them—mostly from Uncle Bob, who knew him better than any. The rest leaked out through the women—you know how things leak out amongst women?"

Mitchell dropped his head and scratched the back of it. *He* knew.

"It was on the Cudgegong River. My Uncle Bob was mates with him on one of those 'rushes' along there—the 'Pipeclay,' I think it was, or the 'Log Paddock.' The Oracle was a young man then, of course, and so was Uncle Bob (he was a match for most men). You see the Oracle now, and you can imagine what he was when he was a young man. Over six feet, and as straight as a sapling, Uncle Bob said, clean-limbed, and as fresh as they made men in those days; carried his hands behind him, as he does now, when he hasn't got the swag—but his shoulders were back in those days. Of course he wasn't the Oracle then; he was young Tom Marshall—but that doesn't matter. Everybody liked him—especially women and children. He was a bit happy-go-lucky and careless, but he didn't know anything about 'this world,' and didn't bother about it; he hadn't 'been there.' 'And his heart was as good as gold,' my aunt used to say. He didn't understand women as we young fellows do nowadays, and therefore he hadn't any contempt for 'em. Perhaps he understood, and understands them better than any of us, without knowing it. Anyway, you know, he's always gentle and kind where a woman or child is concerned, and doesn't like to hear us talk about women as we do sometimes.

"There was a girl on the goldfields—a fine lump of a blonde, and pretty gay. She came from Sydney, I think, with her people, who kept shanties on the fields. She had a splendid voice, and used to sing 'Madeline.' There might have been one or two bad women before that, in the Oracle's world, but no cold-blooded, designing ones. He calls the bad ones 'unfortunate.'

"Perhaps it was Tom's looks, or his freshness, or his innocence, or softness—or all together—that attracted her. Anyway, he got mixed up with her before the goldfield petered out.

"No doubt it took a long while for the facts to work into Tom's head that a girl might sing like she did and yet be thoroughly unprincipled. The Oracle was always slow at coming to a decision, but when he does it's generally the right one. Anyway, you can take that for granted, for you won't move him.

"I don't know whether he found out that she wasn't all that she pretended to be to him, or whether they quarrelled, or whether she chucked him over for a lucky digger. Tom never had any luck on the goldfields. Anyway, he left and went over to the Victorian side, where his people were, and went up Gippsland way. It was there for the first time in his life that he got what you would call 'properly gone on a girl'; he got hard hit—he met his fate.

"Her name was Bertha Bredt, I remember. Aunt Bob saw her afterwards. Aunt Bob used to say that she was 'a girl as God made her'—a good, true, womanly girl—one of the sort of girls that only love once. Tom got on with her father, who was packing horses through the ranges, to the new gold-fields—it was rough country, and there were no roads; they had to pack everything there in those days, and there was money in it. The girl's father took to Tom—as almost everybody else did—and, as far as the girl was concerned, I think it was a case of love at first sight. They only knew each other for about six months and were only 'courting' (as they called it then) for three or four months altogether; but she was that sort of girl that can love a man for six weeks and lose him for ever, and yet go on loving him to the end of her life—and die with his name on her lips.

"Well, things were brightening up every way for Tom, and he and his sweetheart were beginning to talk about their own little home in future, when there came a letter from the 'Madeline' girl in New South Wales.

"She was in terrible trouble. Her baby was to be born in a month. Her people had kicked her out, and she was in danger of starving. She begged and prayed of him to come back and marry her, if only for his child's sake. He could go then, and be free; she would never trouble him any more—only come and marry her for the child's sake.

"The Oracle doesn't know where he lost that letter, but I do. It was burnt afterwards by a woman, who was more than a mother to him in his trouble—Aunt Bob. She thought he might carry it round with the rest of his papers, in his swag, for years, and come across it unexpectedly when he was camped by himself in the bush and feeling dull. It wouldn't have done him any good then.

"He must have fought the hardest fight in his life when he got that letter. No doubt he walked to and fro, to and fro all night, with his hands behind him, and his eyes on the ground, as he does now sometimes. Walking up and down helps you to fight a thing out.

"No doubt he thought of things pretty well as he thinks now: the poor girl's shame on every tongue, and belled round the district by every hag in the township; and her looked upon by women as being as bad as any man who ever went to Bathurst in the old days, handcuffed between two troopers. There is sympathy, a pipe and tobacco, a cheering word, and, maybe a whisky now and then, for the criminal on his journey; but there is no mercy, at least as far as women are concerned, for the poor foolish girl, who has to sneak out the back way and round by back streets and lanes after dark, with a cloak on to hide her figure.

"Tom sent what money he thought he could spare, and next day he went to the girl he loved and who loved him, and told her the truth, and showed her the letter. She was only a girl—but the sort of girl you *could* go to in a crisis like that. He had made up his mind to do the right thing, and she loved him all the more for it. And so they parted.

"When Tom reached Pipeclay, the girl's relations, that she was stopping with, had a parson readied up, and they were married the same day."

"And what happened after that?" asked Mitchell.

"Nothing happened for three or four months; then the child was born. It wasn't his!"

Mitchell stood up with an oath.

"The girl was thoroughly bad. She'd been carrying on with God knows how many men, both before and after she trapped Tom."

"And what did he do then?"

"Well, you know how the Oracle argues over things, and I suppose he was as big an old fool then as he is now. He thinks that, as most men would deceive women if they could, when one man gets caught, he's got no call to squeal about it; he's bound, because of the sins of men in general against women, to make the best of it. What is one man's wrong counted against the wrongs of hundreds of unfortunate girls.

"It's an uncommon way of arguing—like most of the Oracle's ideas—but it seems to look all right at first sight.

"Perhaps he thought she'd go straight; perhaps she convinced him that he was the cause of her first fall; anyway he stuck to her for more than a year, and intended to take her away from that place as soon as he'd scraped enough money together. It might have gone on up till now, if the father of the child—a big black Irishman named Redmond—hadn't come sneaking back at the end of a year. He—well, he came hanging round Mrs Marshall while Tom was away at work—and she encouraged him. And Tom was forced to see it.

"Tom wanted to fight out his own battle without interference, but the chaps wouldn't let him—they reckoned that he'd stand very little show against Redmond, who was a very rough customer and a fighting man. My Uncle Bob, who was there still, fixed it up this way: the Oracle was to fight Redmond, and if the Oracle got licked Uncle Bob was to take Redmond on. If Redmond whipped Uncle Bob, that was to settle it; but if Uncle Bob thrashed Redmond, then he was also to fight Redmond's mate, another big rough Paddy named Duigan. Then the affair would be finished—no matter which way the last bout went. You see, Uncle Bob was reckoned more of a match for Redmond than the Oracle was, so the thing looked fair enough —at first sight.

"Redmond had his mate, Duigan, and one or two others of the rough gang that used to terrorize the fields round there in the roaring days of Gulgong. The Oracle had Uncle Bob, of course, and long Dave Regan, the drover—a good-hearted, sawny kind of chap that'd break the devil's own buckjumper, or smash him, or get smashed himself—and little Jimmy Nowlett, the bullocky, and one or two of the old, better-class diggers that were left on the field.

"There's a clear space among the saplings in Specimen gully, where they used to pitch circuses; and there, in the cool of a summer evening, the two men stood face to face. Redmond was a rough, roaring, foul-mouthed man; he stripped to his shirt, and roared like a bull, and swore, and sneered, and wanted to take the whole of Tom's crowd while he was at it, and make one clean job of 'em. Couldn't waste time fighting them all one after the other, because he wanted to get away to the new rush at Cattle Creek next day. The fool had been drinking shanty-whisky.

"Tom stood up in his clean, white moles and white flannel shirt—one of those sort with no sleeves, that give the arms play. He had a sort of set expression and a look in his eyes that Uncle Bob—nor none of them—had ever seen there before. 'Give us plenty of —— room!' roared Redmond; 'one of us is going to hell, now! This is going to be a fight to a finish, and a short one!' And it was!" Joe paused.

"Go on," said Mitchell—"go on."

Joe drew a long breath.

"The Oracle never got a mark! He was top-dog right from the start. Perhaps it was his strength that Redmond had underrated, or his want of science that puzzled him, or the awful silence of the man that frightened him (it made even Uncle Bob uneasy). Or, perhaps, it was Providence (it was a glorious chance for Providence), but anyway, as I say, the Oracle never got a mark, except on his knuckles. After a few rounds Redmond funked and wanted to give in, but the chaps wouldn't let him—not even his own mates—except Duigan. They made him take it as long as he could stand on his feet. He even shammed to be knocked out, and roared out something about having broken his —— ankle—but it was no use. And the Oracle! The chaps that knew him thought that he'd refuse to fight, and never hit a man that had given in. But he did. He just stood there with that quiet look in his eyes and waited, and, when he did hit, there wasn't any necessity for Redmond to *pretend* to be knocked down. You'll see a glint of that old light in the Oracle's eyes even now, once in a while; and when you do it's a sign that someone is going too far, and had better pull up, for it's a red light on the line, old as he is.

"Now, Jimmy Nowlett was a nuggety little fellow, hard as cast iron, good-hearted, but very excitable; and when the bashed Redmond was being carted off (poor Uncle Bob was always pretty high-strung, and was sitting on a log sobbing like a great child from the reaction), Duigan made some sneering remark that only Jimmy Nowlett caught, and in an instant he was up and at Duigan.

"Perhaps Duigan was demoralized by his mate's defeat, or by the suddenness of the attack; but, at all events, he got a hiding, too. Uncle Bob used to say that it was the funniest thing he ever saw in his life. Jimmy kept yelling: 'Let me get at him! By the Lord, let me get at him!' And nobody was attempting to stop him, he *was* getting at him all the time—and properly, too; and, when he'd knocked Duigan down, he'd dance round him and call on him to get up; and every time he jumped or bounced, he'd squeak like an india-rubber ball, Uncle Bob said, and he would nearly burst his boiler trying to lug the big man on to his feet so's he could knock him down again. It took two of Jimmy's mates all their time to lam him down into a comparatively reasonable state of mind after the fight was over.

"The Oracle left for Sydney next day, and Uncle Bob went with him. He stayed at Uncle Bob's place for some time. He got very quiet, they said, and gentle; he used to play with the children, and they got mighty fond of him. The old folks thought his heart was broken, but it went through a deeper sorrow still after that and it ain't broken yet. It takes a lot to break the heart of a man."

"And his wife," asked Mitchell—"what become of her?"

"I don't think he ever saw her again. She dropped down pretty low after "That's the worst part of it all, I think. The Oracle went up north he left her—I've heard she's living somewhere quietly. The Oracle's been sending someone money ever since I knew him, and I know it's a woman. I suppose it's she. He isn't the sort of a man to see a woman starve— especially a woman he had ever had anything to do with."

"And the Gippsland girl?" asked Mitchell.

"That's the worst part of it all, I think. The Oracle went up north somewhere. In the course of a year or two his affair got over Gippsland way through a mate of his who lived over there, and at last the story got to the ears of his girl, Bertha Bredt. She must have written a dozen letters to him, Aunt Bob said. She knew what was in 'em, but, of course, she'd never tell us. The Oracle only wrote one in reply. Then, what must the girl do but clear out from home and make her way over to Sydney—to Aunt Bob's place, looking for Tom. She never got any further. She took ill—brain-fever, or broken heart, or something of that sort. All the time she was down her cry was 'I want to see him! I want to find Tom! I only want to see Tom!'

"When they saw she was dying, Aunt Bob wired to the Oracle to come —and he came. When the girl saw it was Tom sitting by the bed, she just gave one long look in his face, put her arms round his neck, and laid her head on his shoulder—and died . . . Here comes the Oracle now."

Mitchell lifted the tea-billy on to the coals.

THE SHANTY-KEEPER'S WIFE

There were about a dozen of us jammed into the coach, on the box-seat and hanging on to the roof and tailboard as best we could. We were shearers, bagmen, agents, a squatter, a cockatoo, the usual joker—and one or two professional spielers, perhaps. We were tired and stiff and nearly frozen—too cold to talk and too irritable to risk the inevitable argument which an interchange of ideas would have led up to. We had been looking forward for hours, it seemed, to the pub where we were to change horses. For the last hour or two all that our united efforts had been able to get out of the driver was a grunt to the effect that it was "'bout a couple o' miles." Then he said, or grunted, "'Tain't fur now," a couple of times, and refused to commit himself any further; he seemed grumpy about having committed himself so far.

He was one of those men who take everything in dead earnest; who regard any expression of ideas outside their own sphere of life as trivial, or, indeed, if addressed directly to them, as offensive; who, in fact, are darkly suspicious of anything in the shape of a joke or laugh on the part of an outsider in their own particular dust-hole. He seemed to be always thinking, and thinking a lot; when his hands were not both engaged, he would tilt his hat forward and scratch the base of his skull with his little finger, and let his jaw hang. But his intellectual powers were mostly concentrated on a doubtful swingle-tree, a misfitting collar, or that there bay or piebald (on the off or near side) with the sore shoulder.

Casual letters or papers, to be delivered on the road, were matters which troubled him vaguely, but constantly—like the abstract ideas of his passengers.

The joker of our party was a humorist of the dry order, and had been slyly taking rises out of the driver for the last two or three stages. But the driver only brooded. He wasn't the one to tell you straight if you offended him, or if he fancied you offended him, and thus gain your respect, or prevent a misunderstanding which would result in life-long enmity. He might meet you in after years when you had forgotten all about your trepass—if indeed you had ever been conscious of it—and "stoush" you unexpectedly on the ear.

Also you might regard him as your friend, on occasion, and yet he would stand by and hear a perfect stranger tell you the most outrageous lies, to your hurt, and know that the stranger was telling lies, and never put you up to it. It would never enter his head to do so. It wouldn't be any affair of his—only an abstract question.

It grew darker and colder. The rain came as if the frozen south were spitting at our face and neck and hands, and our feet grew as big as camels', and went dead, and we might as well have stamped the footboards with wooden legs for all the feeling we got into our own. But they were more comfortable that way, for the toes didn't curl up and pain so much, nor did our corns stick out so hard against the leather, and shoot.

We looked out eagerly for some clearing, or fence, or light—some sign of the shanty where we were to change horses—but there was nothing save blackness all round. The long, straight, cleared road was no longer relieved by the ghostly patch of light, far ahead, where the bordering tree-walls came together in perspective and framed the ether. We were down in the bed of the bush.

We pictured a haven of rest with a suspended lamp burning in the frosty air outside and a big log fire in a cosy parlour off the bar, and a long table set for supper. But this is a land of contradictions; wayside shanties turn up unexpectedly, and in the most unreasonable places, and are, as likely as not, prepared for a banquet when you are not hungry and can't wait, and as cold and dark as a bushman's grave when you are and can.

Suddenly the driver said: "We're there now." He said this as if he had driven us to the scaffold to be hanged, and was firecely glad that he'd got us there safely at last. We looked but saw nothing; then a light appeared ahead and seemed to come towards us; and presently we saw that it was a lantern held up by a man in a slouch hat, with a dark bushy beard, and a three-bushel bag around his shoulders. He held up his other hand, and said something to the driver in a tone that might have been used by the leader of a search party who had just found the body. The driver stopped and then went on slowly.

"What's up?" we asked. "What's the trouble?"

"Oh, it's all right," said the driver.

"The publican's wife is sick," somebody said, "and he wants us to come quietly."

The usual little slab-and-bark shanty was suggested in the gloom, with a big bark stable looming in the background. We climbed down like so many cripples. As soon as we began to feel our legs and be sure we had the right ones and the proper allowance of feet, we helped, as quietly as possible, to take the horses out and round to the stable.

"Is she very bad?" we asked the publican, showing as much concern as we could.

"Yes," he said, in the subdued voice of a rough man who had spent several anxious, sleepless nights by the sick-bed of a dear one. "But, God willing, I think we'll pull her through."

Thus encouraged we said, sympathetically: "We're very sorry to trouble you, but I suppose we could manage to get a drink and a bit to eat?"

"Well, he said, "there's nothing to eat in the house, and I've only got rum and milk. You can have that if you like."

One of the pilgrims broke out here.

"Well, of all the pubs," he began, "that I've ever——"

"Hush-sh-sh!" said the publican.

The pilgrim scowled and retired to the rear. You can't express your feelings freely when there's a woman dying close handy.

"Well, who says rum and milk?" asked the joker in a low voice.

"Wait here," said the publican, and disappeared into the little front passage. Presently a light showed through a window with a scratched and fly-bitten

B and A on two panes, and a mutilated R on the third, which was broken. A door opened, and we sneaked into the bar. It was like having drinks after hours where the police are strict and independent.

When we came out the driver was scratching his head and looking at the harness on the veranda floor.

"You fellows'll have ter put in the time for an hour or so. The horses is out back somewheres," and he indicated the interior of Australia with a side jerk of his head, "and the boy ain't back with 'em yet."

"But dash it all," said the pilgrim, "me and my mate——"

"Hush!" said the publican.

"How long are the horses likely to be?" we asked the driver.

"Dunno," he grunted. "Might be three or four hours. It's all accordin'."

"Now, look here," said the pilgrim, "me and my mate wanter catch the train."

"Hush-sh-sh!" from the publican in a fierce whisper.

"Well, boss," said the joker, "can you let us have beds, then? I don't want to freeze here all night, anyway."

"Yes," said the landlord, "I can do that, but some of you will have to sleep double and some of you'll have to take it out of the sofas, and one or two'll have to make a shake-down on the floor. There's plenty of bags in the stable, and you've got rugs and coats with you. Fix it up amongst yourselves."

"But look here!" interrupted the pilgrim, desperately, "we can't afford to wait! We're only 'battlers,' me and my mate, pickin' up crumbs by the wayside. We've got to catch the——"

"Hush!" said the publican, savagely. "You fool, didn't I tell you my missus was bad? I won't have any noise."

"But look here," protested the pilgrim, "we must catch the train at Dead Camel——"

"You'll catch my boot presently," said the publican, with a savage oath, "and go further than Dead Camel. I won't have my missus disturbed for you or any other man! Just you shut up or get out, and take your blooming mate with you."

We lost patience with the pilgrim and sternly took him aside.

"Now, for God's sake, hold your jaw," we said. "Haven't you got any consideration at all? Can't you see the man's wife is ill—dying perhaps—and he nearly worried off his head?"

The pilgrim and his mate were scraggy little bipeds of the city push variety, so they were suppressed.

"Well," yawned the joker, "I'm not going to roost on a stump all night. I'm going to turn in."

"It'll be eighteenpence each," hinted the landlord. "You can settle now if you like to save time."

We took the hint, and had another drink. I don't know how we "fixed it up amongst ourselves," but we got settled down somehow. There was a lot of mysterious whispering and scuffling round by the light of a couple of dirty greasy bits of candle. Fortunately we dared not speak loud enough to have a row, though most of us were by this time in the humour to pick a quarrel with a long-lost brother.

The joker got the best bed, as good-humoured, good-natured chaps generally do, without seeming to try for it. The growler of the party got the floor and chaff-bags, as selfish men mostly do—without seeming to try for it either. I took it out of one of the "sofas," or rather that sofa took it out of me. It was short and narrow and down by the head, with a leaning to one corner on the outside, and had more nails and bits of gin-case than original sofa in it.

I had been asleep for three seconds, it seemed, when somebody shook me by the shoulder and said:

"Take yer seats."

When I got out, the driver was on the box, and the others were getting rum and milk inside themselves (and in bottles) before taking their seats.

It was colder and darker than ever and the South Pole seemed nearer; and pretty soon, but for the rum, we should have been in a worse fix than before.

There was a spell of grumbling. Presently someone said:

"I don't believe them horses was lost at all. I was round behind the stable before I went to bed, and seen horses there; and if they wasn't them same horses there, I'll eat 'em raw!"

"Would yer?" said the driver, in a disinterested tone.

"I would," said the passenger. Then, with a sudden ferocity, "and you too!"

The driver said nothing. It was an abstract question which didn't interest him.

We saw that we were on delicate ground, and changed the subject for a while. Then someone else said:

"I wonder where his missus was? I didn't see any signs of her about, or any other woman about the place, and we was pretty well all over it."

"Must have kept her in the stable," suggested the joker.

"No, she wasn't, for Scotty and that chap on the roof was there after bags."

"She might have been in the loft," reflected the joker.

"There was no loft," put in a voice from the top of the coach.

"I say, Mister—Mister man," said the joker suddenly to the driver, "Was his missus sick at all?"

"I dunno," replied the driver. "She might have been. He said so, anyway. I ain't got no call to call a man a liar."

"See here," said the cannibalistic individual to the driver, in the tone of a man who has made up his mind for a row, "has that shanty-keeper got a wife at all?"

"I believe he has."

"And is she living with him?"

"No, she ain't—if yer wanter know."

"Then where is she?"

"I dunno. How am I to know? She left him three or four years ago. She was in Sydney last time I heard of her. It ain't no affair of mine, anyways."

"And is there any woman about the place at all, driver?" inquired a professional wanderer reflectively.

"No—not that I knows of. There useter be an old black gin come pottering round sometimes, but I ain't seen her lately."

"And excuse me, driver, but is there anyone round there at all?" inquired the professional wanderer, with the air of a conscientious writer, collecting material for an Australian novel from life, and with an eye to detail.

"Naw," said the driver—and recollecting that he was expected to be civil and obliging to his employers' patrons, he added in surly apology, "Only the boss and the stableman, that I knows of." Then repenting of the apology, he asserted his manhood again, and asked, in a tone calculated to risk a breach of the peace, "Any more questions, gentlemen—while the shop's open?"

There was a long pause.

"Driver," asked the pilgrim appealingly, "was them horses lost at all?"

"I dunno," said the driver. "He said they was. He's got the looking after them. It was nothing to do with me."

"Twelve drinks at sixpence a drink"—said the joker, as if calculating to himself —"that's six bob, and, say on an average, four shouts—that's one pound four. Twelve beds at eighteenpence a bed—that's eighteen shillings; and say ten bob in various drinks and the stuff we brought with us, that's two pound twelve. That publican didn't do so bad out of us in two hours."

We wondered how much the driver got out of it, but thought it best not to ask him.

We didn't say much for the rest of the journey. There was the usual man who thought as much and knew all about it from the first, but he wasn't appreciated. We suppressed him. One or two wanted to go back and "stoush" that landlord, and the driver stopped the coach cheerfully at their request; but they said they'd come across him again, and allowed themselves to be persuaded out of it. It made us feel bad to think how we had allowed ourselves to be delayed, and robbed, and had sneaked round on tiptoe, and how we had sat on the inoffensive pilgrim and his mate, and all on account of a sick wife who didn't exist.

The coach arrived at Dead Camel in an atmosphere of mutual suspicion and distrust, and we spread ourselves over the train and departed.

UP THE COUNTRY

This was the opening poem in the verse controversy originally arranged by Lawson and A. B. Paterson and published in the *Bulletin* in 1893. Other writers joined in the wordy 'battle' and it finally became very heated.

I am back from up the country—very sorry that I went
Seeking out the Southern poets' land whereon to pitch my tent;
I have lost a lot of idols, which were broken on the track,
Burnt a lot of fancy verses, and I'm glad that I am back.
Farther out may be the pleasant scenes of which our poets boast,
But I think the country's rather more inviting round the coast.
Anyway, I'll stay at present at a boarding-house in town.
Drinking beer and lemon-squashes, taking baths and cooling down.

"Sunny plains!" Great Scott!—those burning wastes of barren soil
    and sand
With their everlasting fences stretching out across the land!
Desolation where the crow is! Desert where the eagle flies,
Paddocks where the luny bullock starts and stares with reddened
    eyes;
Where, in clouds of dust enveloped, roasted bullock-drivers creep
Slowly past the sun-dried shepherd dragged behind his crawling
    sheep.
Stunted peak of granite gleaming, glaring like a molten mass
Poured from some infernal furnace on a plain devoid of grass.

Miles and miles of thirsty gutters—strings of muddy waterholes
In the place of "shining rivers"—"walled by cliffs and forest boles".
Barren ridges, gullies, ridges! where the everlasting flies—
Fiercer than the plagues of Egypt—swarm about your blighted eyes!
Bush! where there is no horizon! where the buried bushman sees
Nothing—Nothing! but the sameness of the ragged, stunted trees!
Lonely hut mid drought eternal, suffocating atmosphere
Where the God-forgotten hatter dreams of city life and beer.

Treacherous tracks that trap the stranger, endless roads that gleam
    and glare,
Dark and evil-looking gullies, hiding secrets here and there!
Dull, dumb flats and stony rises, where the toiling bullocks bake,
And the sinister goanna joins the lizard and the snake!
Land of day and night—no morning freshness, and no afternoon,
When the great white sun in rising brings the summer heat in June.
Dismal country for the exile! Shades of sudden night that fall
From the sad heart-breaking sunset hurt the new chum worst of all.

Dreary land in sodden weather, where the endless cloud-banks drift
O'er the bushmen like a blanket that the Lord will never lift—
Dismal land when it is raining—growl of floods, and, oh! the woosh
Of the rain and wind together on the dark bed of the bush—
Ghastly fires in lonely humpies, where the granite rocks are piled
In the rain-swept wildernesses that are wildest of the wild.

Land where gaunt and haggard women live alone and work like
    men
Till their husbands, gone a-droving, will return to them again;
Homes of men; if home had ever such a God-forgotten place,
Where the wild selector's children fly before a stranger's face.
Home of tragedy applauded by the dingoes' dismal yell,
Heaven of the shanty-keeper—fitting fiend for such a hell—
Full of wallaroos and wombats, and, of course, the "curlew's call"—
And the lone sundowner tramping ever onward through it all!

I am back from up the country, up the country where I went
Seeking for the Southern poets' land whereon to pitch my tent;
I have shattered many idols out along the dusty track,
Burnt a lot of fancy verses—and I'm glad that I am back.
I believe the Southern poets' dream will not be realized
Till the plains are irrigated and the land is humanized.
I intend to stay at present, as I said before, in town,
Drinking beer and lemon-squashes, taking baths and cooling down.

THE CITY BUSHMAN

Lawson's reply to
Paterson's attack
on the sentiments
expressed in the
deliberately
controversial
'Up the Country'.

It was pleasant up the country, City Bushman, where you went,
For you sought the greener patches and you travelled like a gent;
And you curse the trams and buses and the turmoil and the push,
Though, you know, the squalid city needn't keep you from the
    bush;
But we lately heard you singing of the "plains where shade is not",
And you mentioned it was dusty—"all was dry and all was hot".

True, the bush "hath moods and changes"—and the bushman hath
    'em, too.
For he's not a poet's dummy—he's a man, the same as you;
But his back is growing rounder—slaving for the absentee—
And his toiling wife is thinner than a country wife should be.
For I noticed that the faces of the folks I chanced to meet
Should have made a greater contrast to the faces in the street;
And, in short, I think the bushman's being driven to the wall,
And it's doubtful if his spirit will be "loyal through it all".

Though the bush has been romantic and is nice to sing about,
There's a lot of patriot fervour that the land could do without—
Sort of *British Workman* nonsense that shall perish in the scorn
Of the drover who is driven and the shearer who is shorn—
Of the struggling western farmers who have little time to rest,
Facing ruin on selections in the sheep-infested West;
Droving songs are very pretty, but they call for little thanks
From the people of a country in possession of the Banks.

No, the "rise and fall of seasons" suits the rise and fall of rhyme,
But we know that western seasons do not run on schedule time;
For the drought will go on drying while there's anything to dry,
Then it rains until you'd fancy it would bleach the sunny sky,
Then it pelters out of reason, till the downpour day and night
Nearly sweeps the population to the Great Australian Bight.
It is up in Northern Queensland that the seasons do their best;
But it's doubtful if you ever saw a season in the West—
There are years without an autumn or a winter or a spring,
There are broiling Junes, and summers when it rains like anything.

In the bush my ears were opened to the singing of the bird,
But the "carol of the magpie" was a thing I never heard.
Once the beggar roused my slumbers in a shanty, it is true,
But I only heard him asking, "Who the blanky blank are you?"
And the bell-bird in the ranges—well, his "silver chime" is harsh
When it's heard beside the solo of the curlew in the marsh.

No, the bushman isn't always "trapping brumbies in the night",
Nor is he for ever riding when "the morn is fresh and bright",
And he isn't always singing in the humpies on the run,
And the camp-fire's "cheery blazes" are a trifle over-done.
We have grumbled with the bushman round the fire on rainy days
When the smoke would blind a bullock, and there wasn't any blaze
Save the blazes of our language, for we cursed the fire in turn
Till the atmosphere was heated and the wood began to burn.
Then we had to wring our blueys, which were rotting in the swags,
And we saw the sugar leaking through the bottoms of the bags,
And we couldn't raise a chorus for the toothache and the cramp,
While we spent the hours of darkness draining puddles round the
     camp.

Would you like to change with Clancy—go a-droving? tell us true,
For we rather think that Clancy would be glad to change with you,
And be something in the city; but 'twould give your muse a shock
To be losing time and money through the foot-rot in the flock;
And you wouldn't mind the beauties underneath the starry dome
If you had a wife and children and a lot of bills at home.

Did you ever guard the cattle when the night was inky-black,
And it rained, and icy water trickled gently down your back,
Till your saddle-weary backbone started aching at the roots
And you almost felt the croaking of the bull-frog in your boots?
Did you shiver in the saddle, curse the restless stock and cough
Till a squatter's blanky dummy cantered up to warn you off?
Did you fight the drought and pleuro when the "seasons" were
     asleep.
Felling sheoaks all the morning for a flock of starving sheep,
Drinking mud instead of water—climbing trees and lopping boughs
For the broken-hearted bullocks and the dry and dusty cows?

Do you think the bush was better in the "good old droving days",
When the squatter ruled supremely as the king of western ways,
When you got a slip of paper for the little you could earn—
But were forced to take provisions from the station in return—
When you couldn't keep a chicken at your humpy on the run.
For the squatter wouldn't let you, and your work was never done;
When you had to leave the missus in a lonely hut forlorn
While you "rose up Willy Riley"—in the days ere you were born?

Ah! we read about the drovers and the shearers and the like
Till we wonder why such happy and romantic fellows strike.
Don't you fancy that the poets ought to give the bush a rest
Ere they raise a just rebellion in the over-written West?
There the simple-minded bushman gets a meal and bed and rum
Just by riding round reporting phantom flocks that never come;
There the scalper—never troubled by the "war-whoop of the push"—
Has a quiet little billet, breeding rabbits in the bush;

There the shantykeeper never fails to make a draw,
And the dummy gets his tucker through provisions in the law;
There the labour-agitator—when the shearers rise in might—
Makes his money sacrificing all his substance for The Right;
There the squatter makes his fortune, and "the seasons rise and fall',
But the poor and honest bushman has to suffer for it all,
While the drovers and the shearers and the bushmen and the rest
Never reach that Eldorado of the poets of the West.

So you think the bush is purer, and that life is better there,
But it doesn't seem to pay you like the "squalid street and square".
Pray inform us, City Bushman, where you read, in prose or verse,
Of the awful "city urchin who would greet you with a curse".
There are golden hearts in gutters, though their owners lack the fat,
And I'll back a teamster's offspring to outswear a city brat.

Do you think we're never jolly where the trams and buses rage?
Did you hear the gods in chorus when "Ri-tooral" held the stage?
Did you catch a ring of sorrow in the city urchin's voice
When he yelled for Billy Elton, when he thumped the floor for
      Royce?
Do the bushmen, down on pleasure, miss the everlasting stars
When they drink and flirt, and so on, in the glow of private bars?

You've a down on "trams and buses", or the "roar" of 'em, you said,
And the "filthy, dirty attic", where you never toiled for bread.
(And about that selfsame attic—Lord!—wherever have you been?
For the struggling needlewoman mostly keeps her attic clean.)
But you'll find it very jolly with the cuff-and-collar push,
And the city seems to suit you, while you rave about the bush.

You'll admit that Up-the-Country, more especially in drought,
Isn't quite the Eldorado that the poets rave about,
Yet at times we long to gallop where the reckless bushman rides
In the wake of startled brumbies that are flying for their hides,
Long to feel the saddle tremble once again between our knees
And to hear the stockwhips rattle just like rifles in the trees,
Long to feel the bridle-leather tugging strongly in the hand—
Long to feel once more a little like a native of the land!
And the ring of bitter feeling in the jingling of our rhymes
Isn't suited to the country or the spirit of the times.
Let us go together droving, and returning, if we live,
Try to understand each other while we reckon up the div.

SWEENEY

It was somewhere in September, and the sun was going down,
When I came, in search of copy, to a Darling-River town;
"Come-and-Have-a-Drink" we'll call it—'tis a fitting name, I think—
And 'twas raining, for a wonder, up at Come-and-Have-a-Drink.

Underneath the pub veranda I was resting on a bunk
When a stranger rose before me, and he said that he was drunk;
He apologized for speaking; there was no offence, he swore;
But he somehow seemed to fancy that he'd seen my face before.

"No erfence," he said. I told him that he needn't mention it,
For I might have met him somewhere; I had travelled round a bit,
And I knew a lot of fellows in the Bush and in the streets—
But a fellow can't remember all the fellows that he meets.

Very old and thin and dirty were the garments that he wore,
Just a shirt and pair of trousers, and a boot, and nothing more;
He was wringing-wet and really in a sad and sinful plight,
And his hat was in his left hand, and a bottle in his right.

He agreed: You can't remember all the chaps you chance to meet,
And he said his name was Sweeney—people lived in Sussex-street.
He was camping in a stable, but he swore that he was right,
"Only for the blanky horses walkin' over him all night."

He'd apparently been fighting, for his face was black-and-blue,
And he looked as though the horses had been treading on him, too;
But an honest, genial twinkle in the eye that wasn't hurt
Seemed to hint of something better, spite of drink and rags and dirt.

It appeared that he mistook me for a long-lost mate of his—
One of whom I was the image, both in figure and in phiz—
(He'd have had a letter from him if the chap was livin' still,
For they'd carried swags together from the Gulf to Broken Hill).

Sweeney yarned awhile, and hinted that his folks were doing well,
And he told me that his father kept the Southern Cross Hotel;
And I wondered if his absence was regarded as a loss
When he left the elder Sweeney—landlord of the Southern Cross.

He was born in Parramatta, and he said, with humour grim,
That he'd like to see the city ere the liquor finished him,
But he couldn't raise the money. He was damned if he could think
What the Government was doing. Here he offered me a drink.

I declined—'twas self-denial—and I lectured him on booze,
Using all the hackneyed arguments that preachers mostly use;
Things I'd heard in temperance lectures (I was young and rather green),
And I ended by referring to the man he might have been.

Then a wise expression struggled with the bruises on his face,
Though his argument had scarcely any bearing on the case:
"What's the good o' keepin' sober? Fellers rise and fellers fall;
What I might have been and wasn't doesn't trouble me at all."

But he couldn't stay to argue, for his beer was nearly gone.
He was glad, he said, to meet me, and he'd see me later on,
But he guessed he'd have to go and get his bottle filled again;
And he gave a lurch and vanished in the darkness and the rain.

And of afternoons in cities, when the rain is on the land,
Visions come to me of Sweeney with his bottle in his hand,
With the stormy night behind him, and the pub veranda-post—
And I wonder why he haunts me more than any other ghost.

I suppose he's tramping somewhere where the bushmen carry swags,
Dragging round the western stations with his empty tucker-bags;
And I fancy that of evenings, when the track is growing dim,
What he "might have been and wasn't" comes along and troubles him.

MITCHELL ON MATRIMONY

"I suppose your wife will be glad to see you," said Mitchell to his mate in their camp by the dam at Hungerford. They were overhauling their swags, and throwing away the blankets, and calico, and old clothes, and rubbish they didn't want—everything, in fact, except their pocket-books and letters and portraits, things which men carry about with them always, that are found on them when they die, and sent to their relations if possible. Otherwise they are taken in charge by the constable who officiates at the inquest, and forwarded to the Minister of Justice along with the depositions.

It was the end of the shearing-season. Mitchell and his mate had been lucky enough to get two good sheds in succession, and were going to take the coach from Hungerford to Bourke on their way to Sydney. The morning stars were bright yet, and they sat down to a final billy of tea, two dusty johnny-cakes, and a scrag of salt mutton.

"Yes," said Mitchell's mate, "and I'll be glad to see her too."

"I suppose you will," said Mitchell. He placed his pint-pot between his feet, rested his arm against his knee, and stirred the tea meditatively with the handle of his pocket-knife. It was vaguely understood that Mitchell had been married at one period of his chequered career.

"I don't think we ever understood women properly," he said, as he took a cautious sip to see if his tea was cool and sweet enough, for his lips were sore; "I don't think we ever will—we never took the trouble to try, and if we did it would be only wasted brain power that might just as well be spent on the blackfellow's lingo; because by the time you've learnt it they'll be extinct, and woman'll be extinct before you've learnt her. . . . The morning star looks bright, doesn't it?

"Ah, well," said Mitchell after a while, "there's many little things we might try to understand women in. I read in a piece of newspaper the other day

174

about how a man changes after he's married; how he gets short, and impatient, and bored (which is only natural), and sticks up a wall of newspaper between himself and his wife when he's at home; and how it comes like a cold shock to her, and all her air-castles vanish, and in the end she often thinks about taking the baby and the clothes she stands in, and going home for sympathy and comfort to mother.

"Perhaps she never got a word of sympathy from her mother in her life, nor a day's comfort at home before she was married; but that doesn't make the slightest difference. It doesn't make any difference in your case either, if you haven't been acting like a dutiful son-in-law.

"Somebody wrote that a woman's love is her whole existence, while a man's love is only part of his—which is true, and only natural and reasonable, all things considered. But women never consider as a rule. A man can't go on talking lovey-dovey talk for ever, and listening to his young wife's prattle when he's got to think about making a living, and nursing her and answering her childish questions and telling her he loves his little ownest every minute in the day, while the bills are running up, and rent mornings begin to fly round and hustle and crowd him.

"He's got her and he's satisfied; and if the truth is known he loves her really more than he did when they were engaged, only she won't be satisfied about it unless he tells her so every hour in the day. At least that's how it is for the first few months.

"But a woman doesn't understand these things—she never will, she can't —and it would be just as well for us to try and understand that she doesn't and can't understand them."

Mitchell knocked the tea-leaves out of his pannikin against his boot, and reached for the billy.

"There's many little things we might do that seem mere trifles and nonsense to us, but mean a lot to her; that wouldn't be any trouble or sacrifice to us, but might help to make her life happy. It's just because we never think about these little things—don't think them worth thinking about, in fact— they never enter our intellectual foreheads.

"For instance, when you're going out in the morning you might put your arms round her and give her a hug and a kiss, without her having to remind you. You may forget about it and never think any more of it—but she will.

"It wouldn't be any trouble to you, and would only take a couple of seconds, and would give her something to be happy about when you're gone, and make her sing to herself for hours while she bustles about her work and thinks up what she'll get you for dinner."

Mitchell's mate sighed, and shifted the sugar-bag over towards Mitchell. He seemed touched and bothered over something.

"Then again," said Mitchell, "it mightn't be convenient for you to go home to dinner—something might turn up during the morning—you might have some important business to do, or meet some chaps and get invited to lunch and not be very well able to refuse, when it's too late, or you haven't a chance to send a message to your wife. But then again, chaps and business seem very big things to you, and only little things to the wife; just as lovey-dovey talk is important to her and nonsense to you. And when you come to analyse it, one is not so big, nor the other so small, after all; especially when you come to think that chaps can always wait, and business is only an inspiration in your mind, nine cases out of ten.

"Think of the trouble she takes to get you a good dinner, and how she keeps it hot between two plates in the oven, and waits hour after hour till the dinner gets dried up, and all her morning's work is wasted. Think how it hurts her, and how anxious she'll be (especially if you're inclined to booze) for fear that something has happened to you. You can't get it out of the heads of some young wives that you're liable to get run over, or knocked down, or assaulted, or robbed, or get into one of the fixes that a woman is likely to get into. But about the dinner waiting. Try and put yourself in her place. Wouldn't you get mad under the same circumstances? I know I would. I remember once, only just after I was married, I was invited unexpectedly to a kidney pudding and beans—which was my favourite grub at the time— and I didn't resist, especially as it was washing-day and I told the wife not to bother about anything for dinner. I got home an hour or so late, and had a good explanation thought out, when the wife met me with a smile as if we had just been left a thousand pounds. She'd got her washing finished without assistance, though I'd told her to get somebody to help her, and she had a kidney pudding and beans, with a lot of extras thrown in, as a pleasant surprise for me.

"Well, I kissed her, and sat down, and stuffed till I thought every mouthful would choke me. I got through with it somehow, but I've never cared for kidney pudding or beans since."

Mitchell felt for his pipe with a fatherly smile in his eyes.

"And then again," he continued, as he cut up his tobacco, "your wife might put on a new dress and fix herself up and look well, and you might think so and be satisfied with her appearance and be proud to take her out; but you want to tell her so, and tell her so as often as you think about it—and try to think a little oftener than men usually do, too."

"You should have made a good husband, Jack," said his mate, in a softened tone.

"Ah, well, perhaps I should," said Mitchell, rubbing up his tobacco; then he asked abstractedly: "What sort of a husband did you make, Joe?"

"I might have made a better one than I did," said Joe seriously, and rather bitterly, "but I know one thing, I'm going to try and make up for it when I go back this time."

"We all say that," said Mitchell reflectively, filling his pipe. "She loves you, Joe."

"I know she does," said Joe.

Mitchell lit up.

"And so would any man who knew her or had seen her letters to you," he said between the puffs. "She's happy and contented enough, I believe?"

"Yes," said Joe, "at least while I was there. She's never easy when I'm away. I might have made her a good deal more happy and contented without hurting myself much."

Mitchell smoked long, soft, measured puffs.

His mate shifted uneasily and glanced at him a couple of times, and seemed to become impatient, and to make up his mind about something; or perhaps he got an idea that Mitchell had been "having" him, and felt angry over being betrayed into maudlin confidences; for he asked abruptly:

"How is your wife now, Mitchell?"

"I don't know," said Mitchell calmly.

"Don't know?" echoed the mate. "Didn't you treat her well?"

Mitchell removed his pipe and drew a long breath.

"Ah, well, I tried to," he said wearily.

"Well, did you put your theory into practice?"

"I did," said Mitchell very deliberately.

Joe waited, but nothing came.

"Well?" he asked impatiently. "How did it act? Did it work well?"

"I don't know," said Mitchell (puff); "she left me."

"What!"

Mitchell jerked the half-smoked pipe from his mouth, and rapped the burning tobacco out against the toe of his boot.

"She left me," he said, standing up and stretching himself. Then, with a vicious jerk of his arm, "She left me for—another kind of a fellow!"

He looked east towards the public-house, where they were taking the coach-horses from the stable.

"Why don't you finish your tea, Joe? The billy's getting cold."

MITCHELL ON WOMEN

"All the same," said Mitchell's mate, continuing an argument by the camp-fire; "all the same, I think that a woman can stand cold water better than a man. Why, when I was staying in a boarding-house in Dunedin, one very cold winter, there was a lady lodger who went down to the shower-bath first thing every morning; never missed one; sometimes went in freezing weather when I wouldn't go into a cold bath for a fiver; and sometimes she'd stay under the shower for ten minutes at a time."

"How'd you know?"

"Why, my room was near the bathroom, and I could hear the shower and tap going, and her floundering about."

"Hear your grandmother!" exclaimed Mitchell, contemptuously. "You don't know women yet. Was this woman married? did she have a husband there?"

"No; she was a young widow."

"Ah, well, it would have been the same if she was a young girl—or an old one. Were there some passable men-boarders there?"

"*I* was there."

"Oh, yes! But I mean, were there any there beside you?"

"Oh, yes, there were three or four; there was—a clerk and a——"

"Never mind, as long as there was something with trousers on. Did it ever strike you that she never got into the bath at all?"

"Why, no! What would she want to go there at all for, in that case?"

"To make an impression on the men," replied Mitchell promptly. "She wanted to make out she was nice, and wholesome, and well-washed, and particular. Made an impression on *you*, it seems, or you wouldn't remember it."

"Well, yes, I suppose so; and, now I come to think of it, the bath didn't seem to injure her make-up or wet her hair; but I supposed she held her head from under the shower somehow."

"Did she make-up so early in the morning?" asked Mitchell.

"Yes—I'm sure."

"That's unusual; but it might have been so where there was a lot of boarders. And about the hair—that didn't count for anything, because washing the head ain't supposed to be always included in a lady's bath; it's only supposed to be washed once a fortnight, and some don't do it once

178

a month. The hair takes so long to dry; it don't matter so much if the woman's got short, scraggy hair; but if a girl's hair was down to her waist it would take hours to dry."

"Well, how do they manage it without wetting their heads?"

"Oh, that's easy enough. they have a little oilskin cap that fits tight over the forehead, and they put it on, and bunch their hair up in it when they go under the shower. Did you ever see a woman sit in a sunny place with her hair down after having a wash?"

"Yes, I used to see one do that regular where I was staying; but I thought she only did it to show off."

"Not at all—she was drying her hair; though perhaps she was showing off at the same time, for she wouldn't sit where you—or even a Chinaman—could see her, if she didn't think she had a good head of hair. Now, *I'll* tell you a yarn about a woman's bath. I was stopping at a shabby-genteel boarding-house in Melbourne once, and one very cold winter, too; and there was a rather good-looking woman there, looking for a husband. She used to go down to the bath every morning, no matter how cold it was, and flounder and splash about as if she enjoyed it, till you'd feel as though you'd like to go and catch hold of her and wrap her in a rug and carry her in to the fire and nurse her till she was warm again."

Mitchell's mate moved uneasily, and crossed the other leg; he seemed greatly interested.

"But she never went into the water at all!" continued Mitchell. "As soon as one or two of the men was up in the morning she'd come down from her room in a dressing-gown. It was a tony dressing-gown, too, and set her off properly. She knew how to dress, anyway; most of that sort of women do. The gown was a kind of green colour, with pink and white flowers all over it, and red lining, and a lot of coffee-coloured lace round the neck and down the front. Well, she'd come tripping downstairs and along the passage, holding up one side of the gown to show her little bare white foot in a slipper; and in th other hand she carried her tooth-brush and bath-brush, and soap—like this—so's we all could see 'em; trying to make out she was too particular to use soap after any one else. She could afford to buy her own soap, anyhow; it was hardly ever wet.

"Well, she'd go into the bathroom and turn on the tap and shower; when she got about three inches of water in the bath, she'd step in, holding up her gown out of the water, and go slithering and kicking up and down the bath, like this, making a tremendous splashing. Of course she'd turn off the shower first, and screw it off very tight—wouldn't do to let that leak, you know; she might get wet; but she'd leave the other tap on, so as to make all the more noise."

"But how did you come to know all about this?"

"Oh, the servant girl told me. One morning she twigged her through a corner of the bathroom window that the curtain didn't cover."

"You seem to have been pretty thick with servant girls."

"So do you with landladies! But never mind—let me finish the yarn. When she thought she'd splashed enough, she'd get out, wipe her feet, wash her face and hands, and carefully unbutton the two top buttons of her gown; then throw a towel over her head and shoulders, and listen at the door till

179

she thought she heard some of the men moving about. Then she'd start for her room, and, if she met one of the men-boarders in the passage or on the stairs, she'd drop her eyes, and pretend to see for the first time that the top of her dressing-gown wasn't buttoned—and she'd give a little start and grab the gown and scurry off to her room buttoning it up.

"And sometimes she'd come skipping into the breakfast-room late, looking awfully sweet in her dressing-gown; and if she saw any of us there, she'd pretend to be much startled, and say that she thought all the men had gone out, and make as though she was going to clear; and someone'd jump up and give her a chair, while someone else said, 'Come in, Miss Brown! come in! don't let us frighten you. Come right in, and have your breakfast before it gets cold.' So she'd flutter a bit in pretty confusion, and then make a sweet little girly-girly dive for her chair, and tuck her feet away under the table; and she'd blush, too, but I don't know how she managed that.

"I know another trick that women have; it's mostly played by private barmaids. That is, to leave a stocking by accident in the bathroom for the gentlemen to find. If the barmaid's got a nice foot and ankle, she uses one of her own stockings; but if she hasn't she gets hold of a stocking that belongs to a girl that has. Anyway, she'll have one readied up somehow. The stocking must be worn and nicely darned; one that's been worn will keep the shape of the leg and foot—at least till it's washed again. Well, the barmaid generally knows what time the gentlemen go to bath, and she'll make it a point of going down just as a gentleman's going. Of course he'll give her the preference—let her go first, you know—and she'll go in and accidentally leave the stocking in a place where he's sure to see it, and when she comes out he'll go in and find it; and very likely he'll be a jolly sort of fellow, and when they're all sitting down to breakfast he'll come in and ask them to guess what he's found, and then he'll hold up the stocking. The barmaid likes this sort of thing; but she'll hold down her head, and pretend to be confused, and keep her eyes on her plate, and there'll be much blushing and all that sort of thing, and perhaps she'll gammon to be mad at him, and the landlady'll say, 'Oh, Mr Smith! how can yer? At the breakfast-table, too!' and they'll all laugh and look at the barmaid, and she'll get more embarrassed than ever, and spill her tea, and make out as though the stocking didn't belong to her."

THE CATTLE-DOG'S DEATH

The plains lay bare on the homeward route,
And the march was heavy on man and brute;
For the Spirit of Drouth was on all the land,
And the white heat danced on the glowing sand.

The best of our cattle-dogs lagged at last;
His strength gave out ere the plains were passed;
And our hearts were sad as he crept and laid
His languid limbs in the nearest shade.

He saved our lives in the years gone by,
When no one dreamed of the danger nigh,
And treacherous blacks in the darkness crept
On the silent camp where the white men slept.

"Rover is dying," a stockman said,
As he knelt and lifted the shaggy head;
"'Tis a long day's march ere the run be near,
And he's going fast; shall we leave him here?"

But the super cried, "There's an answer there!"
As he raised a tuft of the dog's grey hair;
And, strangely vivid, each man descried
The old spear-mark on the shaggy hide.

We laid a bluey and coat across
A camp-pack strapped on the lightest horse,
Then raised the dog to his deathbed high,
And brought him far 'neath the burning sky.

At the kindly touch of the stockmen rude
His eyes grew human with gratitude;
And though we were parched, when his eyes grew dim
The last of our water was given to him.

The super's daughter we knew would chide
If we left the dog in the desert wide;
So we carried him home o'er the burning sand
For a parting stroke from her small white hand.

But long ere the station was seen ahead,
His pain was o'er, for Rover was dead;
And the folks all knew by our looks of gloom
'Twas a comrade's corpse that we carried home.

THE HERO OF REDCLAY

Originally conceived as a novel and advertised as such. The same story is told in the poem, 'Ruth'.

The boss-over-the-board was leaning with his back to the wall between two shoots, reading a reference handed to him by a green-hand applying for work as picker-up or wool-roller—a shed rouseabout. It was terribly hot. I was slipping past to the rolling-tables, carrying three fleeces to save a journey; we were only supposed to carry two. The boss stopped me:

"You've got three fleeces there, young man?"

"Yes."

Notwithstanding the fact that I had just slipped a light ragged fleece into the belly-wool and "bits" basket, I felt deeply injured, and righteously and fiercely indignant at being pulled up. It was a fearfully hot day.

"If I catch you carrying three fleeces again," said the boss quietly, "I'll give you the sack."

"I'll take it now if you like," I said.

He nodded. "You can go on picking-up in this man's place," he said to the jackeroo, whose reference showed him to be a non-union man—a "free-labourer," as the pastoralists had it, or, in plain shed terms, "a blanky scab." He was now in the comfortable position of a non-unionist in a union shed who had jumped into a sacked man's place.

Somehow the lurid sympathy of the men irritated me worse than the boss-over-the-board had done. It must have been on account of the heat, as Mitchell says. I was sick of the shed and the life. It was within a couple of days of cut-out, so I told Mitchell—who was shearing—that I'd camp up the Billabong and wait for him; got my cheque, rolled up my swag, got three days' tucker from the cook, said so-long to him, and tramped while the men were in the shed.

I camped at the head of the Billabong where the track branched, one branch running to Bourke, up the river, and the other out towards the Paroo—and hell.

About ten o'clock the third morning Mitchell came along with his cheque and his swag, and a new sheep-pup, and his quiet grin; and I wasn't too pleased to see that he had a shearer called "the Lachlan" with him.

The Lachlan wasn't popular at the shed. He was a brooding, unsociable sort of man, and it didn't make any difference to the chaps whether he had a union ticket or not. It was pretty well known in the shed—there were three or four chaps from the district he was reared in—that he'd done five years' hard for burglary. What surprised me was that Jack Mitchell seemed thick with him; often, when the Lachlan was sitting brooding and smoking by himself outside the hut after sunset, Mitchell would perch on his heels alongside him and yarn. But no one else took notice of anything Mitchell did out of the common.

"Better camp with us till the cool of the evening," said Mitchell to the Lachlan, as they slipped their swags. "Plenty time for you to start after sundown, if you're going to travel to-night."

So the Lachlan was going to travel all night and on a different track. I felt more comfortable, and put the billy on. I did not care so much what he'd been or had done, but I was green and soft yet, and his presence embarrassed me.

They talked shearing, sheds, tracks, and a little unionism—the Lachlan speaking in a quiet voice and with a lot of sound, common sense, it seemed to me. He was tall and gaunt, and might have been thirty, or even well on in the forties. His eyes were dark brown and deep set, and had something of the dead-earnest sad expression you saw in the eyes of union leaders and secretaries—the straight men of the strikes of ninety and ninety-one. I fancied once or twice I saw in his eyes the sudden furtive look of the "bad egg" when a mounted trooper is spotted near the shed; but perhaps this was prejudice. And with it all there was about the Lachlan something of the man who has lost all he had and the chances of all he was ever likely to have, and is past feeling or caring or flaring up—past getting mad about anything—something, all the same, that warned men not to make free with him.

He and Mitchell fished along the Billabong all the afternoon; I fished a little, and lay about the camp and read. I had an instinct that the Lachlan saw I didn't cotton on to his camping with us, though he wasn't the sort of man to show what he saw or felt. After tea, and a smoke at sunset, he shouldered his swag, nodded to me as if I was an accidental but respectful stranger at a funeral that belonged to him, and took the outside track. Mitchell walked along the track with him for a mile or so, while I poked round and got some boughs down for a bed, and fed and studied the collie-pup that Jack had bought from the shearers' cook.

I saw them stop and shake hands out on the dusty clearing, and they seemed to take a long time about it; then Mitchell started back, and the other began to dwindle down to a black peg and then to a dot on the sandy plain, that had just a hint of dusk and dreamy far away gloaming on it between the change from glaring day to hard, bare, broad moonlight.

I thought Mitchell was sulky, or had got the blues, when he came back; he lay on his elbow smoking, with his face turned from the camp towards the plain. After a bit I got wild—if Mitchell was going to go on like that he might as well have taken his swag and gone with the Lachlan. I don't know exactly what was the matter with me that day, but at last I made up my mind to bring the thing to a head.

"You seem mighty thick with the Lachlan," I said.

"Well, what's the matter with that?" asked Mitchell. "It ain't the first felon I've been on speaking terms with. I borrowed half a caser off a murderer once when I was in a hole and had no one else to go to, and the murderer hadn't served his time, neither. I've got nothing against the Lachlan, except that he's a white man and bears a faint family resemblance to a certain branch of my tribe."

I rolled out my swag on the boughs, got my pipe, tobacco, and matches handy in the crown of a spare hat, and lay down.

Mitchell got up, re-lit his pipe at the fire, and mooned round for a while, with his hands behind him, kicking sticks out of the road, looking out over the plain, down along the Billabong, and up through the mulga branches at the stars; then he comforted the pup a bit, shoved the fire together with his toe, stood the tea-billy on the coals, and came and squatted on the sand by my head.

"Joe! I'll tell you a yarn."

"All right; fire away! Has it got anything to do with the Lachlan?"

"No. It's got nothing to do with the Lachlan now; but it's about a chap he knew. Don't you ever breathe a word of this to the Lachlan or anyone, or he'll get on to me."

"All right. Go ahead."

"You know I've been a good many things in my time. I did a deal of house-painting at one time; I was a pretty smart brush hand, and made money at it. Well, I had a run of work at a place called Redclay, on the Lachlan side. You know the sort of town—two pubs, a general store, a post office, a blacksmith's shop, a police station, a branch bank, and a dozen private weather-board boxes on piles, with galvanized-iron tops, besides the humpies. There was a paper there, too, called the *Redclay Advertiser* (with which was incorporated the *Geebung Chronicle*), and a Roman Catholic church, a Church of England, and a Wesleyan chapel. Now, you see more of private life in the house-painting line than in any other—bar plumbing and gas fitting; but I'll tell you about my house-painting experiences some other time.

"There was a young chap named Jack Drew editing the *Advertiser* then. He belonged to the district, but had been sent to Sydney to a grammar school when he was a boy. He was between twenty-five and thirty; had knocked round a good deal, and gone the pace in Sydney. He got on as a boy reporter on one of the big dailies; he had brains, and could write rings round a good many, but he got in with a crowd that called themselves 'Bohemians,' and the drink got a hold on him. The paper stuck to him as long as it could (for the sake of his brains), but they had to sack him at last.

"He went out back, as most of them do, to try and work out their salvation, and knocked round amongst the sheds. He 'picked-up' in one shed where I was shearing, and we carried swags together for a couple of months. Then he went back to the Lachlan side, and prospected amongst the old fields round there with his elder brother Tom, who was all there was left of his family. Tom, by the way, broke his heart digging Jack out of a cave in a drive they were working, and died a few minutes after the rescue. But that's another yarn. Jack Drew had a bad spree after that; then he went to Sydney again, got on his old paper, went to the dogs, and a Parliamentary push that owned some city fly-blisters and country papers sent him up to edit the *Advertiser* at two quid a week. He drank again, and no wonder—you don't know what it is to run a *Geebung Advocate* or

Mudgee Budgee Chronicle, and live there. He was about the same build as the Lachlan, but stouter, and had something the same kind of eyes; but he was ordinarily as careless and devil-may-care as the Lachlan is grumpy and quiet.

"There was a doctor there, called Dr Lebinski. They said he was a Polish exile. He was fifty or sixty, a tall man, with the set of an old soldier when he stood straight; but he mostly walked with his hands behind him, studying the ground. Jack Drew caught that trick off him towards the end. They were chums in a gloomy way, and kept to themselves—they were the only two men with brains in that town. They drank and fought the drink together. The doctor was too gloomy and impatient over little things to be popular. Jack Drew talked too straight in the paper, and in spite of his proprietors —about pub spieling and such things—and was too sarcastic in his progress committee, town council, and toady reception reports. The doctor had a hawk's nose, pointed grizzled beard and moustache, and steely-grey eyes with a haunted look in them sometimes (especially when he glanced at you sideways), as if he loathed his fellow-men, and couldn't always hide it; or as if you were the spirit of morphia or opium, or a dead girl he'd wronged in his youth—or whatever his devil was, beside drink. He was clever, and drink had brought him down to Redclay.

"The bank manager was a heavy snob named Browne. He complained of being a bit dull of hearing in one ear—after you'd yelled at him three or four times; sometimes I've thought he was as deaf as a book-keeper in both. He had a wife and youngsters, but they were away on a visit while I was working in Redclay. His niece—or, rather, his wife's niece—a girl named Ruth Wilson, did the house-keeping. She was an orphan, adopted by her aunt, and was general slavey and scapegoat to the family—especially to the brats, as is often the case. She was rather pretty, and ladylike, and kept to herself. The women and girls called her Miss Wilson, and didn't like her. Most of the single men—and some of the married ones, perhaps— were gone on her, but hadn't the brains or the pluck to bear up and try their luck. I was gone worse than any, I think, but had too much experience or common sense. She was very good to me—used to hand me out cups of tea and plates of sandwiches, or bread and butter, or cake, mornings and afternoons the whole time I was painting the bank. The doctor had known her people, and was very kind to her. She was about the only woman—for she was more woman than girl—that he'd brighten up and talk for. Neither he nor Jack Drew were particularly friendly with Browne or his push.

"The banker, the storekeeper, one of the publicans, the butcher (a popular man with his hands in his pockets, his hat on the back of his head, and nothing in it), the postmaster, and his toady, the lightning squirter, were the scrub-aristocracy. The rest were crawlers, mostly pub spielers and bush larrikins, and the women were hags and larrikinesses. The town lived on cheque-men from the surrounding bush. It was a nice little place, taking it all round.

"I remember a ball at the local town hall, where the scrub aristocrats took one end of the room to dance in and the ordinary scum the other. It was a saving in music. Some day an Australian writer will come along who'll remind the critics and readers of Dickens, Carlyle, and Thackeray mixed, and he'll do justice to these little customs of ours in the little settled-district towns of Democratic Australia. This sort of thing came to a head one New Year's Night at Redclay, when there was a 'public' ball and peace on earth and goodwill towards all men—mostly on account of a railway to Redclay being surveyed. We were all there. They'd got the doc. out of his shell to act as M.C.

"One of the aristocrats was the daughter of the local storekeeper; she belonged to the lawn-tennis clique, and they *were* select. For some reason or other—because she looked upon Miss Wilson as a slavey, or on account of a fancied slight, or the heat working on ignorance, or on account of something that comes over girls and women that no son of sin can account for—this Miss Tea-'n'-sugar tossed her head and refused Miss Wilson's hand in the first set, and so broke the ladies' chain and the dance. Then there was a to-do. The doctor held up his hand to stop the music, and said, very quietly, that he must call upon Miss So-and-so to apologize to Miss Wilson or resign the chair. After a lot of fuss the girl did apologize in a snappy way that was another insult. Jack Drew gave Miss Wilson his arm and marched her off without a word—I saw she was almost crying. Someone said, 'Oh, let's go on with the dance.' The doctor flashed round on them, but they were too paltry for him, so he turned on his heel and went out without a word. But I was beneath them again in social standing, so there was nothing to prevent me from making a few well-chosen remarks on things in general—which I did; and broke up that ball, and broke some heads afterwards, and got myself a good deal of hatred and respect and two sweethearts; and lost all the jobs I was likely to get, except at the bank, the doctor's and the Royal.

"One day it was raining—general rain for a week. Rain, rain, rain, over ridge and scrub and galvanized iron and into the dismal creeks. I'd done all my inside work, except a bit under the doctor's veranda, where he'd been having some patching and altering done round the glass doors of his surgery, where he consulted his patients. I didn't want to lose time. It was a Monday and no day for the Royal, and there was no dust, so it was a good day for varnishing. I took a pot and brush and went along to give the doctor's doors a coat of varnish. The doctor and Drew were inside with a fire, drinking whisky and smoking, but I didn't know that when I started work. The rain roared on the iron roof like the sea. All of a sudden it held up for a minute, and I heard their voices. The doctor had been shouting on account of the rain, and forgot to lower his voice. 'Look here, Jack Drew,' he said, 'there are only two things for you to do if you have any regard for that girl; one is to stop this' (the liquor I suppose he meant) 'and pull yourself together; and I don't think you'll do that—I know men. The other is to throw up the *Advertiser*—it's doing you no good—and clear out.' 'I won't do that,' says Drew. 'Then shoot yourself,' said the doctor. '(There's another flask in the cupboard.) You know what this hole is like . . . She's a good true girl—a girl as God made her. I knew her father and mother, and I tell you, Jack, I'd sooner see her dead than . . .' The roof roared again. I felt a bit delicate about the business and didn't like to disturb them, so I knocked off for the day.

"About a week before that I was down in the bed of the Redclay Creek fishing for 'tailers.' I'd been getting on all right with the housemaid at the Royal—she used to have plates of pudding and hot pie for me on the big gridiron arrangement over the kitchen range; and after the third tuck-out I thought it was good enough to do a bit of a bear-up in that direction. She mentioned one day, yarning, that she liked a stroll by the creek sometimes in the cool of the evening. I thought she'd be off that day, so I said I'd go for a fish after I'd knocked off. I thought I might get a bite. Anyway, I didn't catch Lizzie—tell you about that some other time.

"It was Sunday. I'd been fishing for Lizzie about an hour, when I saw a skirt on the bank out of the tail of my eye—and thought I'd got a bite, sure. But I was had. It was Miss Wilson strolling along the bank in the sunset, all by her pretty self. She was a slight girl, not very tall, with reddish frizzled hair, grey eyes, and small, pretty features. She spoke as if she had more brains than the average, and had been better educated. Jack Drew was the only young man in Redclay she could talk to, or who could talk to a girl like her; and that was the whole trouble in a nutshell. The newspaper office was next to the bank, and I'd seen her hand cups of tea and cocoa over the fence to his office window more than once, and sometimes they yarned for a while.

"She said, 'Good afternoon, Mr Mitchell.'

"I said, 'Good afternoon, Miss.'

"There's some girls I can't talk to like I'd talk to other girls. She asked me if I'd caught any fish, and I said, 'No, miss.' She asked me if it wasn't me down there fishing with Mr Drew the other evening, and I said, 'Yes—it was me.' Then presently she asked me straight if he was fishing down the creek that afternoon. I guessed they'd been down fishing for each other before. I said, 'No, I thought he was out of town.' I knew he was pretty bad at the Royal. I asked her if she'd like to have a try with my line, but she said 'No, thanks,' she must be going; and she went off up the creek. I reckoned Jack Drew had got a bite and landed her. I felt a bit sorry for her, too.

"The next Saturday evening after the rainy Monday at the doctor's, I went down to fish for tailers—and Lizzie. I went down under the banks to where there was a big she-oak stump half in the water, going quietly, with an idea of not frightening the fish. I was just unwinding the line from my rod, when I noticed the end of another rod sticking out from the other side of the stump; and while I watched it was dropped into the water. Then I heard a murmur, and craned my neck round the back of the stump to see who it was. I saw the back view of Jack Drew and Miss Wilson; he had his arm round her waist, and her head was on his shoulder. She said, 'I *will* trust you, Jack—I know you'll give up the drink for my sake. And I'll help you, and we'll be so happy!' or words in that direction. A thunderstorm was coming on. The sky had darkened up with a great blue-black storm-cloud rushing over, and they hadn't noticed it. I didn't mind, and the fish bit best in a storm. But just as she said 'happy,' there came a blinding flash and a crash that shook the ridges, and the first drops came peltering down. They jumped up and climbed the bank, while I perched on the she-oak roots over the water to be out of sight as they passed. Half-way to the town I saw them standing in the shelter of an old stone chimney that stood

187

alone. He had his overcoat round her and was sheltering her from the wind . . .

"Smoke-ho, Joe. The tea's stewing."

Mitchell got up, stretched himself, and brought the billy and pint-pots to the head of my camp. The moon had grown misty. The plain horizon had closed in. A couple of boughs, hanging from the gnarled and blasted timber over the Billabong, were the perfect shapes of two men hanging side by side. Mitchell scratched the back of his neck and looked down at the pup curled like a glob of mud on the sand in the moonlight, and an idea struck him. He got a big old felt hat he had, lifted his pup, nose to tail, fitted it in the hat, shook it down, holding the hat by the brim, and stood the hat near the head of his doss, out of the moonlight. "He might get moonstruck," said Mitchell, "and I don't want that pup to be a genius." The pup seemed perfectly satisfied with this new arrangement.

"Have a smoke," said Mitchell. "You see," he added, with a sly grin, "I've got to make up the yarn as I go along, and it's hard work. It seems to begin to remind me of yarns your grandmother or aunt tells of things that happened when she was a girl—but those yarns are true. You won't have to listen long now; I'm well on into the second volume.

"After the storm I hurried home to the tent—I was batching with a carpenter. I changed my clothes, made a fire in the fire-bucket with shavings and ends of soft wood, boiled the billy, and had a cup of coffee. It was Saturday night. My mate was at the Royal; it was cold and dismal in the tent, and there was nothing to read, so I reckoned I might as well go up to the Royal, too, and put in the time.

"I had to pass the bank on the way. It was the usual weatherboard box with a galvanized-iron top—four rooms and a passage, and a detached kitchen and wash-house at the back; the front room to the right was the office, behind that was the family bedroom, the front room to the left was Miss Wilson's bedroom, and behind that was the living-room. The *Advertiser* office was next door. Jack Drew camped in a skillion room behind his printing-office, and had his meals at the Royal. I noticed the storm had taken a sheet of iron off the skillion, and supposed he'd sleep at the Royal that night. Next to the *Advertiser* office was the police station and the court-house. Next was the Imperial Hotel where the scrub aristocrats went. There was a vacant allotment on the other side of the bank, and I took a short cut across this to the Royal.

"They'd forgotten to pull down the blind of the dining-room window, and I happened to glance through and saw she had Jack Drew in there and was giving him a cup of tea. He had a bad cold, I remember, and I suppose his health had got precious to her, poor girl. As I glanced, she stepped to the window and pulled down the blind, which put me out of face a bit—though, of course, she hadn't seen me. I was rather surprised at her having Jack in there, till I heard that the banker, the postmaster, the constable, and some others were making a night of it at the Imperial, as they'd been doing pretty often lately—and went on doing till there was a blow-up about it, and the constable got transferred out back. I used to drink my share then. We smoked and played cards and yarned and filled 'em up again at the Royal till after one in the morning. Then I started home.

"I'd finished giving the bank a couple of coats of stone-colour that week, and was cutting in in dark colour round the spouting, doors, and window-frames that Saturday. My head was pretty clear going home, and as I passed the place it struck me that I'd left out the only varnish brush I had. I'd been using it to give the sashes a coat of varnish colour, and remembered that I'd left it on one of the window-sills—the sill of her bedroom window, as it happened. I knew I'd sleep in next day, Sunday, and guessed it would be hot, and I didn't want the varnish tool to get spoiled; so I reckoned I'd slip in through the side gate, get it, and take it home to camp and put it in oil. The window-sash was jammed, I remember, and I hadn't been able to get it up more than a couple of inches to paint the runs of the sash. the grass grew up close under the window, and I slipped in quietly. I noticed the sash was still up a couple of inches. Just as I grabbed the brush I heard low voices inside—Ruth Wilson's and Jack Drew's—in her room.

"The surprise sent about a pint of beer up into my throat in a lump. I tiptoed away out of there. Just as I got clear of the gate I saw the banker being helped home by a couple of cronies.

"I went home to the camp and turned in, but I couldn't sleep. I lay think —think—thinking, till I thought all the drink out of my head. I'd brought a bottle of ale home to last over Sunday, and I drank that. It only made matters worse. I didn't know how I felt—I—well, I felt as if I was as good a man as Jack Drew—I—you see I've—you might think it soft— but I loved that girl, not as I've been gone on other girls, but in the old-fashioned, soft, honest, hopeless, far-away sort of way; and now, to tell the straight truth, I thought I might have had her. You lose a thing through being too straight or sentimental, or not having enough cheek; and another man comes along with more brass in his blood and less sentimental rot, and takes it up—and the world respects him; and you feel in your heart that you're a weaker man than he is. Why, part of the time I must have felt like a man does when a better man runs away with his wife. But I'd drunk a lot, and was upset and lonely-feeling that night.

"Oh, but Redclay had a tremendous sensation next day! Jack Drew, of all the men in the world, had been caught in the act of robbing the bank. According to Browne's account in court and in the newspapers, he returned home that night at about twelve o'clock (which I knew was a lie, for I saw him being helped home nearer two), and immediately retired to rest (on top of the quilt, boots and all, I suppose). Sometime before daybreak he was roused by a fancied noise (I suppose it was his head swelling); he rose, turned up a night lamp (he hadn't lit it, I'll swear), and went through the dining-room passage and office to investigate (for whisky and water). He saw that the doors and windows were secure, returned to bed, and fell asleep again.

"There is something in a deaf person's being roused easily. I know the case of a deaf chap who'd start up at a step or movement in the house when no one else could hear or feel it; keen sense of vibration, I reckon. Well, just at daybreak (to shorten the yarn) the banker woke suddenly, he said, and heard a crack like a shot in the house. There was a loose flooring-board in the passage that went off like a pistol-shot sometimes when you trod on it; and I guess Jack Drew trod on it, sneaking out, and he weighed nearly twelve stone. If the truth were known, he probably heard Browne poking round, tried the window, found the sash jammed, and was slipping through the passage to the back door. Browne got his revolver, opened his door suddenly, and caught Drew standing between the girl's door (which was shut) and the office door, with his coat on his arm and his boots in his hands. Browne covered him with his revolver, swore he'd shoot if he moved, and yelled for help. Drew stood a moment like a man stunned; then he rushed Browne, and in the struggle the revolver went off, and Drew got hit in the arm. Two of the mounted troopers—who'd been up looking to the horses for an early start somewhere—rushed in then, and took Drew. He had nothing to say. What could he say? He couldn't say he was a blackguard who'd taken advantage of a poor unprotected girl because she loved him. They found the back door unlocked, by the way, which was put down to the burglar; of course Browne couldn't explain that he came home too muddled to lock doors after him.

"And the girl? She shrieked and fell when the row started, and they found her like a log on the floor of her room after it was over.

"They found in Jack's overcoat pocket a parcel containing a cold chisel, small screw-wrench, file, and one or two other things that he'd bought that evening to tinker up the old printing-press. I knew that, because I'd lent him a hand a few nights before, and he told me he'd have to get the tools. They found some scratches round the keyhole and knob of the office door That I'd made myself, scraping old splashes of paint off the brass and hand-plate so as to make a clean finish. Oh, it taught me the value of circumstantial evidence! If I was judge, I wouldn't give a man till the 'risin' av the coort' on it, any more than I would on the bare word of the noblest woman breathing.

"At the preliminary examination Jack Drew said he was guilty. But it seemed that, according to law, he couldn't be guilty until after he was committed. So he was committed for trial at the next Quarter Sessions. The excitement and gabble were worse than the Dean case, or Federation, and sickened me, for they were all on the wrong track. You lose a lot of life through being behind the scenes. But they cooled down presently to wait for the trial.

"They thought it best to take the girl away from the place where she'd got the shock; so the doctor took her to his house, where he had an old housekeeper who was as deaf as a post—a first-class recommendation for a housekeeper anywhere. He got a nurse from Sydney to attend on Ruth Wilson, and no one except he and the nurse were allowed to go near her. She lay like dead, they said, except when she had to be held down raving; brain-fever, they said, brought on by the shock of the attempted burglary and pistol shot. Dr Lebinski had another doctor up from Sydney at his own expense, but nothing could save her—and perhaps it was as well. She might have finished her life in a lunatic asylum. They were going to send her to Sydney, to a brain hospital; but she died a week before the sessions. She was right-headed for an hour, they said, and asking all the time for Jack. The doctor told her he was all right and was coming—and, waiting and listening for him, she died.

"The case was black enough against Drew now. I knew he wouldn't have the pluck to tell the truth now, even if he was that sort of man. I didn't know what to do, so I spoke to the doctor straight. I caught him coming out of the Royal, and walked along the road with him a bit. I suppose he thought I was going to show cause why his doors ought to have another coat of varnish.

"'Hallo, Mitchell!' he said, 'how's painting?'

"'Doctor!' I said, 'what am I going to do about this business?'

"'What business?'

"'Jack Drew's.'

"He looked at me sideways—the swift, haunted look. Then he walked on without a word, for half a dozen yards, hands behind, and studying the dust. Then he asked, quite quietly:

"'Do you know the truth?'

"'Yes!'

"About a dozen yards this time; then he said:

"'I'll see him in the morning, and see you afterwards,' and he shook hands and went on home.

"Next day he came to see me where I was doing a job on a step-ladder. He leaned his elbow against the steps for a moment, and rubbed his hand over his forehead, as if it ached and he was tired.

"'I've seen him, Mitchell,' he said.

"'Yes.'

"'You were mates with him, once, out back?'

"'I was.'

"'You know Drew's hand-writing?'

"'I should think so.'

"He laid a leaf from a pocket-book on top of the steps. I read the message written in pencil:

"*To Jack Mitchell—We were mates on the track. If you know anything of my affair, don't give it away.—J.D.*

"I tore the leaf and dropped the bits into the paint-pot.

"'That's all right, doctor,' I said; 'but is there no way?'

"'None.'

"He turned away, wearily. He'd knocked about so much over the world that he was past bothering about explaining things or being surprised at anything. But he seemed to get a new idea about me; he came back to the steps again, and watched my brush for a while, as if he was thinking, in a broody sort of way, of throwing up his practice and going in for house-painting. Then he said, slowly and deliberately:

"'If she—the girl—had lived, we might have tried to fix it up quietly. That's what I was hoping for. I don't see how we can help him now, even if he'd let us. He would never have spoken, anyway. We must let it go on, and after the trial I'll go to Sydney and see what I can do at headquarters. It's too late now. You understand, Mitchell?'

"'Yes. I've thought it out.'

"Then he went away towards the Royal.

"And what could Jack Drew or we do? Study it out whatever way you like. There was only one possible chance to help him, and that was to go to the judge; and the judge that happened to be on that circuit was a man who—even if he did listen to the story and believe it—would have felt inclined to give Jack all the more for what he was charged with. Browne was out of the question. The day before the trial I went for a long walk in the bush, but couldn't hit on anything that the doctor might have missed.

"I was in the court—I couldn't keep away. The doctor was there too. There wasn't so much of a change in Jack as I expected, only he had the jail white in his face already. He stood fingering the rail, as if it was the edge of a table on a platform and he was a tired and bored and sleepy chairman waiting to propose a vote of thanks."

The only well-known man in Australia who reminds me of Mitchell is Bland Holt, the comedian. Mitchell was about as good hearted as Bland Holt, too, under it all; but he was bigger and roughened by the bush. But he seemed to be taking a heavy part to-night, for, towards the end of his yarn, he got up and walked up and down the length of my bed, dropping the sentences as he turned towards me. He'd folded his arms high and tight, and his face in the moonlight was—well, it was very different from his careless tone of voice. He was like—like an actor acting tragedy and talking comedy. Mitchell went on, speaking quickly—his voice seeming to harden:

"The charge was read out—I forget how it went—it sounded like a long hymn being given out. Jack pleaded guilty. Then he straightened up for the first time and looked round the court, with a calm, disinterested look—as if we were all strangers, and he was noting the size of the meeting. And—it's a funny world, ain't it?—everyone of us shifted or dropped his eyes, just as if we were the felons and Jack the judge. Everyone except the doctor; he looked at Jack and Jack looked at him. Then the doctor smiled—I can't describe it—and Drew smiled back. It struck me afterwards that I should have been in that smile. Then the doctor did what looked like a strange thing—stood like a soldier with his hands to attention. I'd noticed that, whenever he'd made up his mind to do a thing, he dropped his hands to his sides: it was a sign that he couldn't be moved. Now he slowly lifted his hand to his forehead, palm out, saluted the prisoner, turned on his heel, and marched from the court-room. 'He's boozin' again,' someone whispered. 'He's got a touch of 'em.' 'My oath, he's ratty!' said someone else. One of the traps said:

"'Arder in the car-rt!'

"The judge gave it to Drew red-hot on account of the burglary being the cause of the girl's death and the sorrow in a respectable family; then he gave him five years' hard.

"It gave me a lot of confidence in myself to see the law of the land barking up the wrong tree, while only I and the doctor and the prisoner knew it. But I've found out since that the law is often the only one that knows it's barking up the wrong tree."

Mitchell prepared to turn in.

"And what about Drew?" I asked.

"Oh, he did his time, or most of it. The doctor went to headquarters, but either a drunken doctor from a geebung town wasn't of much account, or they weren't taking any romance just then at headquarters. So the doctor came back, drank heavily, and one frosty morning they found him on his back on the bank of the creek, with his face like note-paper where the blood hadn't dried on it, and an old pistol in his hand—that he'd used, they said, to shoot Cossacks from horseback when he was a young dude fighting in the bush in Poland."

Mitchell lay silent a good while; then he yawned.

"Ah, well! It's a lonely track the Lachlan's tramping to-night; but I s'pose he's got his ghosts with him."

I'd been puzzling for the last half-hour to think where I'd met or heard of Jack Drew; now it flashed on me that I'd been told that Jack Drew was the Lachlan's real name.

I lay awake thinking a long time, and wished Mitchell had kept his yarn for daytime. I felt—well, I felt as if the Lachlan's story should have been played in the biggest theatre in the world, by the greatest actors, with music for the intervals and situations—deep, strong music, such as thrills and lifts a man from his boot soles. And when I got to sleep I hadn't slept a moment, it seemed to me, when I started wide awake to see those infernal hanging boughs with a sort of nightmare idea that the Lachlan hadn't gone, or had come back, and he and Mitchell had hanged themselves sociably— Mitchell for sympathy and the sake of mateship.

But Mitchell was sleeping peacefully, in spite of a path of moonlight across his face—and so was the pup.

J. W. Gordon, better known as 'Jim Grahame', first met Lawson at Bourke and was his mate on the desperate walk from there to Hungerford during the scorching drought of 1892-3.

Twenty-five years later their friendship was renewed at Leeton where Jim Grahame had a small farm and enjoyed a reputation as a local poet, sealed when his volume of verse, *Under Wide Skies,* which included a poem 'When Lawson Walked with Me', was published in 1947 by a committee of 'The Citizens of Leeton'.

Lawson introduced Grahame into a number of the stories he wrote during and after his stay at Leeton and they would have often yarned about the old days in Bourke and laughed perhaps at Lawson's use of poetic licence in his poem on that town when he infers he was there in 1891-2, not 1893-4.

THE LOADED DOG

Dave Regan, Jim Bently, and Andy Page were sinking a shaft at Stony Creek in search of a rich gold quartz reef which was supposed to exist in the vicinity. There is always a rich reef supposed to exist in the vicinity; the only questions are whether it is ten feet or hundreds beneath the surface, and in which direction. They had struck some pretty solid rock, also water which kept them bailing. They used the old fashioned blasting-powder and time-fuse. They'd make a sausage or cartridge of blasting-powder in a skin of strong calico or canvas, the mouth sewn and bound round the end of the fuse; they'd dip the cartridge in melted tallow to make it watertight, get the drill-hole as dry as possible, drop in the cartridge with some dry dust, and wad and ram with stiff clay and broken brick. Then they'd light the fuse and get out of the hole and wait. The result was usually an ugly pot-hole in the bottom of the shaft and half a barrow-load of broken rock.

There was plenty of fish in the creek, fresh-water bream, cod, cat-fish, and tailers. The party were fond of fish, and Andy and Dave of fishing. Andy would fish for three hours at a stretch if encouraged by a "nibble" or a "bite" now and then—say once in twenty minutes. The butcher was always willing to give meat in exchange for fish when they caught more than they could eat; but now it was winter, and these fish wouldn't bite. However, the creek was low, just a chain of muddy waterholes, from the hole with a few bucketfuls in it to the sizeable pool with an average depth of six or seven feet, and they could get fish by bailing out the smaller holes or muddying up the water in the larger ones till the fish rose to the surface. There was the cat-fish, with spikes growing out of the sides of its head, and if you got pricked you'd know it, as Dave said. Andy took off his boots, tucked up his trousers, and went into a hole one day to stir up the mud with his feet, and he knew it. Dave scooped one out with his hand and got pricked, and he knew it too; his arm swelled, and the pain throbbed up into his shoulder, and down into his stomach, too, he said, like a toothache he had once, and kept him awake for two nights—only the toothache pain had a burred edge, Dave said.

Dave got an idea.

"Why not blow the fish up in the big waterhole with a cartridge?" he said. "I'll try it."

He thought the thing out and Andy Page worked it out. Andy usually put Dave's theories into practice if they were practicable, or bore the blame for the failure and the chaffing of his mates if they weren't.

He made a cartridge about three times the size of those they used in the rock. Jim Bently said it was big enough to blow the bottom out of the river. The inner skin was of stout calico; Andy stuck the end of a six-foot piece of fuse well down in the powder and bound the mouth of the bag firmly to it with whipcord. The idea was to sink the cartridge in the water with the open end of the fuse attached to a float on the surface, ready for lighting. Andy dipped the cartridge in melted bees-wax to make it watertight. "We'll have to leave it some time before we light it," said Dave, "to give the fish time to get over their scare when we put it in, and come nosing round again; so we'll want it well watertight."

Round the cartridge Andy, at Dave's suggestion, bound a strip of sail canvas—that they used for making water-bags—to increase the force of the explosion, and round that he pasted layers of stiff brown paper—on the plan of the sort of fireworks we called gun-crackers. He let the paper dry in the sun, then he sewed a covering of two thicknesses of canvas over it and bound the thing from end to end with stout fishing-line. Dave's schemes were elaborate, and he often worked his inventions out to nothing. The cartridge was rigid and solid enough now—a formidable bomb; but Andy and Dave wanted to be sure. Andy sewed on another layer of canvas, dipped the cartridge in melted tallow, twisted a length of fencing-wire round it as an afterthought, dipped it in tallow again, and stood it carefully against a tent-peg, where he'd know where to find it, and wound the fuse loosely round it. Then he went to the camp-fire to try some potatoes which were boiling in their jackets in a billy, and to see about frying some chops for dinner. Dave and Jim were at work in the claim that morning.

They had a big black young retriever dog—or rather an overgrown pup, a big, foolish, four-footed mate, who was always slobbering round them and lashing their legs with his heavy tail that swung round like a stock-whip. Most of his head was usually a red, idiotic slobbering grin of appreciation of his own silliness. He seemed to take life, the world, his two-legged mates, and his own instinct as a huge joke. He'd retrieve anything; he carted back most of the camp rubbish that Andy threw away. They had a cat that died in hot weather, and Andy threw it a good distance away in the scrub; and early one morning the dog found the cat, after it had been dead a week or so, and carried it back to camp, and laid it just inside the tent-flaps where it could best make its presence known when the mates should rise and begin to sniff suspiciously in the sickly smothering atmosphere of the summer sunrise. He used to retrieve them when they went in swimming; he'd jump in after them, and take their hands in his mouth, and try to swim out with them, and scratch their naked bodies with his paws. They loved him for his good-heartedness and his foolishness, but when they wished to enjoy a swim they had to tie him up in camp.

He watched Andy with great interest all the morning making the cartridge, and hindered him considerably, trying to help; but about noon he went off to the claim to see how Dave and Jim were getting on, and to come home to dinner with them. Andy saw them coming, and put a panful of mutton-chops on the fire. Andy was cook to-day; Dave and Jim stood with their backs to the fire, as bushmen do in all weathers, waiting till dinner should be ready. The retriever went nosing round after something he seemed to have missed.

Andy's brain still worked on the cartridge; his eye was caught by the glare of an empty kerosene-tin lying in the bushes, and it struck him that it wouldn't be a bad idea to sink the cartridge packed with clay, sand, or stones in the tin, to increase the force of the explosion. He may have been all out, from a scientific point of view, but the notion looked all right to him. Jim Bently, by the way, wasn't interested in their "damned silliness." Andy noticed an empty treacle-tin—the sort with the little tin neck or spout soldered on to the top for the convenience of pouring out the treacle— and it struck him that this would have made the best kind of cartridge-case: he would only have had to pour in the powder, stick the fuse in through the neck, and cork and seal it with bees-wax. He was turning to suggest this to Dave, when Dave glanced over his shoulder to see how the chops were doing— and bolted. He explained afterwards that he thought he heard the pan spluttering extra, and looked to see if the chops were burning. Jim Bently looked behind and bolted after Dave. Andy stood stock-still, staring after them.

"Run, Andy! Run!" they shouted back at him. "Run! Look behind you, you fool!" Andy turned slowly and looked, and there, close behind him, was the retriever with the cartridge in his mouth—wedged into his broadest and silliest grin. And that wasn't all. The dog had come round the fire to Andy, and the loose end of the fuse had trailed and waggled over the burning sticks into the blaze; Andy had slit and nicked the firing end of the fuse well, and now it was hissing and spitting properly.

Andy's legs started with a jolt; his legs started before his brain did, and he made for Dave and Jim. And the dog followed Andy.

Dave and Jim were good runners—Jim the best—for a short distance; Andy was slow and heavy, but he had the strength and the wind and could last. The dog capered round him, delighted as a dog could be to find his mates, as he thought, on for a frolic. Dave and Jim kept shouting back, "Don't foller us! Don't foller us, you coloured fool!" But Andy kept on, no matter how they dodged. They could never explain, any more than the dog, why they followed each other, but so they ran, Dave keeping in Jim's track in all its turnings, Andy after Dave, and the dog circling round Andy—the live fuse swishing in all directions and hissing and spluttering and stinking. Jim yelling to Dave not to follow him, Dave shouting to Andy to go in another direction—to "spread out," and Andy roaring at the dog to go home. Then Andy's brain began to work, stimulated by the crisis; he tried to get a running kick at the dog, but the dog dodged; he snatched up sticks and stones and threw them at the dog and ran on again. The retriever saw that he'd made a mistake about Andy, and left him and bounded after Dave. Dave who had the presence of mind to think that the fuse's time wasn't up yet, made a dive and a grab for the dog, caught him by the tail, and as he swung round snatched the cartridge out of his mouth and flung it as far as he could; the dog immediately bounded after it and retrieved it. Dave roared and cursed at the dog, who, seeing that Dave was offended, left him and went after Jim, who was well ahead. Jim swung to a sapling and went up it like a native bear; it was a young sapling, and Jim couldn't safely get more than ten or twelve feet from the ground. The dog laid the cartridge, as carefully as if it were a kitten, at the foot of the sapling, and capered and leaped and whooped joyously round under Jim. The big pup reckoned that this was part of the lark— he was all right now—it was Jim who was out for a spree. The fuse sounded as if it were going a mile a minute. Jim tried to climb higher and the sapling bent and cracked. Jim fell on his feet and ran. The dog swooped on the cartridge and followed. It all took but a very few moments. Jim ran to a digger's hole, about ten feet deep, and dropped down into it— landing on soft mud—and was safe. The dog grinned sardonically down on him, over the edge, for a moment, as if he thought it would be a good lark to drop the cartridge down on Jim.

"Go away, Tommy," said Jim feebly, "go away."

197

The dog bounded off after Dave, who was the only one in sight now; Andy had dropped behind a log, where he lay flat on his face, having suddenly remembered a picture of the Russo-Turkish war with a circle of Turks lying flat on their faces (as if they were ashamed) round a newly-arrived shell.

There was a small hotel or shanty on the creek, on the main road, not far from the claim. Dave was desperate, the time flew much faster in his stimulated imagination than it did in reality, so he made for the shanty. There were several casual bushmen on the veranda and in the bar; Dave rushed into the bar, banging the door to behind him. "My dog!" he gasped, in reply to the astonished stare of the publican, "the blanky retriever— he's got a live cartridge in his mouth——"

The retriever, finding the front door shut against him, had bounded round and in by the back way, and now stood smiling in the doorway leading from the passage, the cartridge still in his mouth and the fuse spluttering. They burst out of that bar, Tommy bounded first after one and then after another, for, being a young dog, he tried to make friends with everybody.

The bushmen ran round corners, and some shut themselves in the stable. There was a new weather-board and corrugated-iron kitchen and wash-house on piles in the backyard, with some women washing clothes inside. Dave and the publican bundled in there and shut the door—the publican cursing Dave and calling him a crimson fool, in hurried tones, and wanting to know what the hell he came here for.

The retriever went in under the kitchen, amongst the piles, but, luckily for those inside, there was a vicious yellow mongrel cattle-dog sulking and nursing his nastiness under there—a sneaking, fighting, thieving canine, whom neighbours had tried for years to shoot or poison. Tommy saw his danger—he'd had experience from this dog—and started out and across the yard, still sticking to the cartridge. Half-way across the yard the yellow dog caught him and nipped him. Tommy dropped the cartridge, gave one terrified yell, and took to the bush. The yellow dog followed him to the fence and then ran back to see what he had dropped. Nearly a dozen other dogs came from round all the corners and under the buildings—spidery, thievish, cold-blooded kangaroo dogs, mongrel sheep- and cattle-dogs, vicious black and yellow dogs—that slip after you in the dark, nip your heels, and vanish without explaining—and yapping, yelping small fry. They kept at a respectable distance round the nasty yellow dog, for it was dangerous to go near him when he thought he had found something which might be good for a dog or cat. He sniffed at the cartridge twice, and was just taking a third cautious sniff when——

It was very good blasting-powder—a new brand that Dave had recently got up from Sydney; and the cartridge had been excellently well made. Andy was very patient and painstaking in all he did, and nearly as handy as the average sailor with needles, twine, canvas and rope.

Bushmen say that kitchen jumped off its piles and on again. When the smoke and dust cleared away, the remains of the nasty yellow dog were lying against the paling fence of the yard looking as if he had been kicked into a fire by a horse and afterwards rolled in the dust under a barrow, and finally thrown against the fence from a distance. Several saddle-horses, which had been "hanging-up" round the veranda, were galloping wildly down the road in clouds of dust, with broken bridle-reins flying; and from a circle round the outskirts, from every point of the compass in the scrub, came the yelping of dogs. Two of them went home, to the place where they were born, thirty miles away, and reached it the same night and stayed there; it was not till towards evening that the rest came back cautiously to make inquiries. One was trying to walk on two legs, and most of 'em looked more or less singed; and a little, singed, stumpy-tailed dog, who had been in the habit of hopping the back half of him along on one leg, had reason to be glad that he'd saved up the other leg all those years, for he needed it now. There was one old one-eyed cattle-dog round that shanty for years afterwards, who couldn't stand the smell of a gun being cleaned. He it was who had taken an interest, only second to that of the yellow dog, in the cartridge. Bushmen said that it was amusing to slip up on his blind side and stick a dirty ramrod under his nose: he wouldn't wait to bring his solitary eye to bear—he'd take to the bush and stay out all night.

For half an hour or so after the explosion there were several bushmen round behind the stable who crouched, doubled up, against the wall, or rolled gently on the dust, trying to laugh without shrieking. There were two white women in hysterics at the house, and a half-caste rushing aimlessly round with a dipper of cold water. The publican was holding his wife tight and begging her between her squawks, to "hold up for my sake, Mary, or I'll lam the life out of ye."

Dave decided to apologize later on, "when things had settled a bit," and went back to camp. And the dog that had done it all, Tommy, the great, idiotic mongrel retriever, came slobbering round Dave and lashing his legs with his tail, and trotted home after him, smiling his broadest, longest, and reddest smile of amiability, and apparently satisfied for one afternoon with the fun he'd had.

Andy chained the dog up securely, and cooked some more chops, while Dave went to help Jim out of the hole.

And most of this is why, for years afterwards, lanky, easygoing bushmen, riding lazily past Dave's camp, would cry, in a lazy drawl and with just a hint of the nasal twang:

"'Ello, Da-a-ve! How's the fishin' getting on, Da-a-ve?"

199

WHEN THE WORLD WAS WIDE

The title of 'In the Days When the World was Wide', as it was called when first published, was shortened in 1917 by George Robertson for *Selected Poems*. It was written in New Zealand in 1894 and published in the *Bulletin*, on December 15 of the same year.

The world is narrow and ways are short, and our lives are dull
    and slow,
For little is new where the crowds resort, and less where the
    wanderers go;
Greater or smaller, the same old things we see by the dull roadside—
And tired of all is the spirit that sings of the days when the world
    was wide.

When the North was hale in the march of Time, and the South
    and the West were new,
And the gorgeous East was a pantomime, as it seemed in our
    boyhood's view;
When Spain was first on the waves of change, and proud in the
    ranks of pride,
And all was wonderful, new and strange in the days when the
    world was wide.

Then a man could fight if his heart were bold, and win if his
    faith were true—
Were it love, or honour, or power, or gold, or all that our hearts
    pursue;
Could live to the world for the family name, or die for the family
    pride,
Could flee from sorrow and wrong and shame in the days when
    the world was wide.

They roved away in the ships that sailed ere science controlled
    the main,
When the strong, brave heart of a man prevailed as 'twill never
    prevail again;
They knew not whither, nor much they cared—let Fate or the
    winds decide—
The worst of the Great Unknown they dared in the days when
    the world was wide.

They raised new stars on the silent sea that filled their hearts
    with awe;
They came to many a strange countree and marvellous sights they
    saw.
The villagers gaped at the tales they told, and old eyes glistened
    with pride—
When barbarous cities were paved with gold in the days when
    the world was wide.

Tom Roberts (1856-1931)   *The Breakaway*
135.9 x 166.4 cm   Oil on canvas
Reproduced with the kind permission of The Art Gallery Of South Australia

'Twas honest metal and honest wood, in the days of the Outward
    Bound,
When men were gallant and ships were good—roaming the wide
    world round.
The gods could envy a leader then when "Follow me, lads!" he
    cried—
They faced each other and fought like men in the days when
    the world was wide!

The good ship bound for the Southern Seas when the beacon
    was Ballarat,
With a "Ship ahoy!" on the freshening breeze, "Where bound?"
    and "What ship's that?"—
The emigrant train to New Mexico—the rush to the Lachlan-side—
Ah! faint is the echo of Westward Ho! from the days when the
    world was wide.

South, East, and West in advance of Time—and far in advance
    of Thought—
Brave men they were with a faith sublime—and is it for this
    they fought?
And is it for this damned life we praise the god-like spirit that died
At Eureka Stockade in the Roaring Days with the days when the
    world was wide?

With its dull, brown days of a-shilling-an-hour the dreary year
    drags round:
Is this the result of Old England's power?—the bourne of the
    Outward Bound?
Is this the sequel of Westward Ho!—of the days of Whate'er
    Betide?
The heart of the rebel makes answer "No! We'll fight till the world
    grows wide!"

The world shall yet be a wider world—for the tokens are manifest;
East and North shall the wrongs be hurled that followed us South
    and West.
The march of Freedom is North by the Dawn! Follow, whate'er
    betide!
Sons of the Exiles, march! March on! March till the world grows
    wide!

THE GOLDEN GRAVEYARD

Mother Middleton was an awful woman, an "old hand" (transported convict) some said. The prefix "mother" in Australia mostly means "old hag," and is applied in that sense. In early boyhood we understood, from old diggers, that Mother Middleton—in common with most other "old hands"—had been sent out for "knocking a donkey off a hen-roost." We had never seen a donkey. She drank like a fish and swore like a trooper when the spirit moved her; she went on periodical sprees, and swore on most occasions. There was a fearsome yarn, which impressed us greatly as boys, to the effect that once, in her best (or worst) days she had pulled a mounted policeman off his horse, and half-killed him with a heavy pick-handle, which she used for poking down clothes in her boiler. She said that he had insulted her.

She could still knock down a tree and cut a load of firewood with any bushman; she was square and muscular, with arms like a navvy's; she had often worked shifts, below and on top, with her husband, when he'd be putting down a prospecting shaft without a mate, as he often had to do—because of her mainly. Old diggers said that it was lovely to see how she'd spin up a heavy greenhide bucket full of clay and "tailings," and land and empty it with a twist of her wrist. Most men were afraid of her, and few diggers' wives were strong-minded enough to seek a second row with Mother Middleton. Her voice could be heard right across Golden Gully and Specimen Flat, whether raised in argument or in friendly greeting. She came to the old Pipeclay diggings with the "rough crowd" (mostly Irish), and when the old and new Pipeclays were worked out, she went with the rush to Gulgong (about the last of the great alluvial or "poor-man's" gold-fields) and came back to Pipeclay when the Log Paddock goldfield "broke out," adjacent to the old fields, and so helped prove the truth of the old diggers' saying, that no matter how thoroughly ground has been worked, there is always room for a new Ballarat.

Jimmy Middleton died at Log Paddock, and was buried, about the last, in the little old cemetery—appertaining to the old farming town on the river, about four miles away—which adjoined the district racecourse, in the bush, on the far edge of Specimen Flat. She conducted the funeral. Some said she made the coffin, and there were alleged jokes to the effect that her tongue had provided the corpse; but this, I think, was unfair and cruel, for she loved Jimmy Middleton in her awful way, and was, for all I ever heard to the contrary, a good wife to him. She then lived in a hut in Log Paddock, on a little money in the bank, and did sewing and washing for single diggers.

I remember hearing her one morning in neighbourly conversation, carried on across the gully, with a selector, Peter Olsen, who was hopelessly slaving to farm a dusty patch in the scrub.

"Why don't you chuck up that dust-hole and go up-country and settle on good land, Peter Olsen? You're only slaving your stomach out here." (She didn't say stomach.)

Peter Olsen (mild-whiskered little man, afraid of his wife): "But then

(1) Obviously a veiled reference to the author's parents. See also 'A Child in the Dark'.

you know my wife is so delicate, Mrs Middleton. I wouldn't like to take her out in the bush."

Mrs Middleton: "Delicate be damned! She's only shamming!" (at her loudest.) "Why don't you kick her off the bed and the book out of her hand, and make her go to work? She's as delicate as I am. Are you a man, Peter Olsen, or a——?"

This for the edification of the wife and of all within half a mile.

Log Paddock was "petering." There were a few claims still being worked down at the lowest end, where big, red-and-white wasteheaps of clay and gravel, rising above the blue-and-grey gum-bushes, advertised deep sinking; and little, yellow, clay-stained streams, running towards the creek over the drought-parched surface, told of trouble with the water below—time lost in bailing and extra expense in timbering. And diggers came up with their flannels and moleskins yellow and heavy, and dripping with wet "mullock."

Most of the diggers had gone to other fields, but there were a few prospecting, in parties and singly, out on the flats and amongst the ridges round Pipeclay. Sinking holes in search of a new Ballarat.

Dave Regan—lanky, easygoing bush native; Jim Bently—a bit of a "Flash Jack;" and Andy Page—a character like what Kit (in *The Old Curiosity Shop*) might have been after a voyage to Australia and some Colonial experience. These three were mates from habit and not necessity, for it was all shallow sinking where they worked. They were poking down pot-holes in the scrub in the vicinity of the racecourse, where the sinking was from ten to fifteen feet.

Dave had theories—"ideers" or "notions" he called them; Jim Bently laid claim to none—he ran by sight, not scent, like a kangaroo-dog. Andy Page —by the way, great admirer and faithful retainer of Dave Regan—was simple and trusting, but, on critical occasions, he was apt to be obstinately, uncomfortably, exasperatingly truthful, honest, and he had reverence for higher things.

Dave thought hard all one quiet drowsy Sunday afternoon, and next morning he, as head of the party, started to sink a hole as close to the cemetery fence as he dared. It was a nice quiet spot in the thick scrub, about three panels along the fence from the farthest corner post from the road. They bottomed here at nine feet, and found encouraging indications. They "drove" (tunnelled) inwards at right angles to the fence, and at a point immediately beneath it they were "making tucker"; a few feet farther and they were making wages. The old alluvial bottom sloped gently that way. The bottom here, by the way, was shelving, brownish, rotten rock.

Just inside the cemetery fence, and at right angles to Dave's drive lay the shell containing all that was left of the late fiercely lamented James Middleton, with older graves close at each end. A grave was supposed to be six feet deep, and local gravediggers had been conscientious. The old alluvial bottom sloped from nine to fifteen feet here.

Dave worked the ground all round from the bottom of his shaft, timbering —i.e., putting in a sapling prop—here and there where he worked wide; but the "payable dirt" ran in under the cemetery, and in no other direction.

Dave, Jim, and Andy held a consultation in camp over their pipes after tea, as a result of which Andy next morning rolled up his swag, sorrowfully but firmly shook hands with Dave and Jim, and started to tramp out back to look for work on a sheep station.

This was Dave's theory—drawn from a little experience and many long yarns with old diggers:—

He had bottomed on a slope to an old original watercourse, covered with clay and gravel from the hills by centuries of rains to the depth of from nine or ten to twenty feet; he had bottomed on a gutter running into the bed of the old buried creek, and carrying patches and streaks of "wash" or gold-bearing dirt. If he went on he might strike it rich at any stroke of his pick; he might strike the rich "lead" which was supposed to exist round there. (There was always supposed to be a rich lead round there somewhere. "There's gold in them ridges yet—if a man can only git at it," says the toothless old relic of the Roaring Days.)

Dave might strike a ledge, "pocket," or "pot-hole" holding wash rich with gold. He had prospected on the opposite side of the cemetery, found no gold, and the bottom sloping upwards towards the graveyard. He had prospected at the back of the cemetery, found a few "colours," and the bottom sloping downwards towards the point under the cemetery towards which all indications were now leading him. He had sunk shafts across the road opposite the cemetery frontage and found the sinking twenty feet and not a colour of gold. Probably the whole of the ground under the cemetery was rich—maybe the richest in the district. The old gravediggers had not been gold-diggers—besides, the graves, being six feet, would, none of them, have touched the alluvial bottom. There was nothing strange in the fact that none of the crowd of experienced diggers who rushed the district had thought of the cemetery and racecourse. Old brick chimneys and houses, the clay for the bricks of which had been taken from sites of subsequent goldfields, had been put through the crushing-mill in subsequent years and had yielded "payable gold." Fossicking Chinamen were said to have been the first to detect a case of this kind.

(2) 'A Golden Shanty' by Edward Dyson, is the classic Australian tale on this theme.

Dave reckoned to strike the "lead," or a shelf or ledge with a good streak of wash lying along it, at a point about forty feet within the cemetery. But a theory in alluvial gold-mining was much like a theory in gambling, in some respects. The theory might be right enough, but old volcanic disturbances—"the shrinkage of the earth's surface," and that sort of old thing—upset everything. You might follow good gold along a ledge, just under the grass, till it suddenly broke off and the continuation might be a hundred feet or so under your nose.

Had the "ground" in the cemetery been "open" Dave would have gone to the point under which he expected the gold to lie, sunk a shaft there, and worked the ground. It would have been the quickest and easiest way—it would have saved the labour and the time lost in dragging heavy buckets of dirt along a low lengthy drive to the shaft outside the fence. But it was very doubtful if the Government could have been moved to open the cemetery even on the strongest evidence of the existence of a rich goldfield under it, and backed by the influence of a number of diggers and their backers—which last was what Dave wished for least of all. He wanted, above all things, to keep the thing shady. Then, again, the old clannish local spirit of the old farming town, rooted in years way back of the goldfields, would have been too strong for the Government, or even a rush of wild diggers.

"We'll work this thing on the strict Q.T.," said Dave.

He and Jim had a consultation by the camp-fire outside their tent. Jim grumbled, in conclusion:

"Well, then, best go under Jimmy Middleton. It's the shortest and straightest, and Jimmy's the freshest, anyway."

Then there was another trouble. How were they to account for the size of the waste-heap of clay on the surface which would be the result of such an extraordinary length of drive or tunnel for shallow sinkings? Dave had an idea of carrying some of the dirt away by night and putting it down a deserted shaft close by; but that would double the labour, and might lead to detection sooner than anything else. There were boys possum-hunting on those flats every night. Then Dave got an idea.

There was supposed to exist—and it has since been proved—another, a second gold-bearing alluvial bottom on that field, and several had tried for it. One, the town watchmaker, had sunk all his money in "duffers," trying for the second bottom. It was supposed to exist at a depth of from eighty to a hundred feet—on solid rock, I suppose. This watchmaker, an Italian, would put men on to sink, and superintend in person, and whenever he came to a little "colour"-showing shelf, or false bottom, thirty or forty feet down—he'd go rooting round and spoil the shaft, and then start to sink another. It was extraordinary that he hadn't the sense to sink straight down, thoroughly test the second bottom, and if he found no gold there, to fill the shaft up to the other bottoms, or build platforms at the proper level and then explore them. He was living in a lunatic asylum the last time I heard of him. And the last time I heard from that field, they were boring the ground like a sieve, with the latest machinery, to find the best place to put down a deep shaft, and finding gold from the second bottom on the bore. But I'm right off the line again.

"Old Pinter," Ballarat digger—his theory on second and other bottoms ran as follows:—

"Ye see *this* here grass surface—this here surface with trees an' grass on it, that we're livin' on, has got nothin' to do with us. This here bottom in the shaller sinkin's that we're workin' on is the slope to the bed of the *new* crick that was on the surface about the time that men was missin'-links. The false bottoms, thirty or forty feet down, kin be said to have been on the surface about the time that men was monkeys. The *secon'* bottom—eighty or a hundred feet down—was on the surface about the time when men was frogs. Now——"

But it's with the missing-link surface we have to do, and had the friends of the local departed known what Dave and Jim were up to they would have regarded them as something lower than missing-links.

"We'll give out we're tryin' for the second bottom," said Dave Regan. "We'll have to rig a fan for air, anyhow, and you don't want air in shallow sinkings."

"And someone will come poking round, and look down the hole and see the bottom," said Jim Bently.

"We must keep 'em away," said Dave. "Tar the bottom, or cover it with tarred canvas, to make it black. Then they won't see it. There's not many diggers left, and the rest are going; they're chucking up the claims in Log Paddock. Besides, I could get drunk and pick rows with the rest and they wouldn't come near me. The farmers ain't in love with us diggers, so they won't bother us. No man has a right to come poking round another man's claim: it ain't ettykit—I'll root up that old ettykit and stand to it—it's rather worn out now, but that's no matter. We'll shift the tent down near the claim and see that no one comes nosing round on Sunday. They'll think we're only some more second-bottom lunatics, like Francea [the mining watchmaker]. We're going to get our fortune out from under that old graveyard, Jim. You leave it all to me till you're born again with brains."

Dave's schemes were always elaborate, and that was why they so often came to the ground. He logged up his windlass platform a little higher, bent about eighty feet of rope to the bole of the windlass, which was a new one, and thereafter, whenever a suspicious-looking party (that is to say, a digger) hove in sight, Dave would let down about forty feet of rope and then wind, with simulated exertion, until the slack was taken up and the rope lifted the bucket from the shallow bottom.

"It would look better to have a whip-pole and a horse, but we can't afford them just yet," said Dave.

But I'm a little behind. They drove straight in under the cemetery, finding good wash all the way. The edge of Jimmy Middleton's box appeared in the top corner of the "face" (the working end) of the drive. They went under the butt-end of the grave. They shoved up the end of the shell with a prop, to prevent the possibility of an accident which might disturb the mound above; they puddled, i.e. rammed—stiff clay up round the edges to keep the loose earth from dribbling down; and having given the bottom of the coffin a good coat of tar, they got over, or rather under, an unpleasant matter.

Jim Bently smoked and burnt paper during his shift below, and grumbled a good deal. "Blowed if I ever thought I'd be rooting for gold down among the blanky dead men," he said. But the dirt panned out better every dish they washed, and Dave worked the "wash" out right and left as they drove.

But, one fine morning, who should come along but the very last man whom Dave wished to see round there—"Old Pinter" (James Poynton), Californian and Victorian digger of the old school. He'd been prospecting down the creek, carried his pick over his shoulder—threaded through the eye in the heft of his big-bladed, short-handled shovel that hung behind—and his gold-dish under his arm.

" 'Ello, Dave!" said Pinter, after looking with mild surprise at the size of Dave's waste-heap. "Tryin' for the second bottom?"

"Yes," said Dave, guttural.

Pinter dropped his tools with a clatter at the foot of the waste-heap and scratched under his ear like an old cockatoo, which bird he resembled. Then he went to the windlass, and resting his hands on his knees, he peered down, while Dave stood by helpless and hopeless.

Pinter straightened himself, blinking like an owl, and looked carelessly over the graveyard.

"Tryin' for a secon' bottom," he reflected abently. "Eh, Dave?"

Dave only stood and looked black.

Pinter tilted back his head and scratched the roots of his chin-feathers, which stuck out all round like a dirty, ragged fan held horizontally.

"Kullers is safe," reflected Pinter.

"All right," snapped Dave. "I suppose we must let him into it."

"Kullers" was a big American buck nigger, and had been Pinter's mate for some time—Pinter was a man of odd mates: and what Pinter meant was that Kullers was safe to hold his tongue.

Next morning Pinter and his coloured mate appeared on the ground early, Pinter with some tools and the nigger with a windlass-bole on his shoulders. Pinter chose a spot about three panels or thirty feet along the other fence, the back fence of the cemetery, and started his hole. He lost no time for the sake of appearances; he sank his shaft and started to drive straight for the point under the cemetery for which Dave was making; he gave out that he had bottomed on good "indications" running in the other direction, and would work the ground outside the fence. Meanwhile Dave rigged a fan—partly for the sake of appearances, but mainly because his and Jim's lively imaginations made the air in the drive worse than it really was.

Dave was working the ground on each side as he went, when one morning a thought struck him that should have struck him the day Pinter went to work. He felt mad that it hadn't struck him sooner.

Pinter and Kullers had also shifted their tent down into a nice quiet place in the bush close handy; so, early next Sunday morning, while Pinter and Kullers were asleep, Dave posted Jim Bently to watch their tent, and whistle an alarm if they stirred, and then dropped down into Pinter's hole and saw at a glance what he was up to.

After that Dave lost no time: he drove straight on, encouraged by the thuds of Pinter's and Kullers's picks drawing nearer. They would strike his tunnel at right angles. Both parties worked long hours, only knocking off to fry a bit of steak in the pan, boil the billy, and throw themselves dressed on their bunks to get a few hours' sleep. Pinter had practical experience and a line clear of graves, and he made good time. The two parties now found it more comfortable to be not on speaking terms. Individually they grew furtive, and began to feel criminal like—at least Dave and Jim did. They'd start if a horse stumbled through the bush, and expected to see a mounted policeman ride up at any moment and hear him ask questions. They had driven about thirty-five feet when, one Saturday afternoon, the strain became too great, and Dave and Jim got drunk. The spree lasted over Sunday, and on Monday morning they felt too shaky to come to work, and had more to drink. On Monday afternoon, Kullers, whose shift it was below, stuck his pick through the "face" of his drive into the wall of Dave's, about four feet from the end of it: the clay flaked away, leaving a hole a big as a wash-hand basin. They knocked off for the day and decided to let the other party take the offensive.

Tuesday morning Dave and Jim came to work, still feeling shaky. Jim went below, crawled along the drive, lit his candle, and stuck it in the spiked iron socket and the spike in the wall of the drive, quite close to the hole, without noticing either the hole or the increased freshness of the air. He started picking away at the "face" and scraping the clay back from under his feet, and didn't hear Kullers come to work. Kullers came in softly and decided to try a bit of cheerful bluff. He stuck his great round black face through the hole, the whites of his eyes rolling horribly in the candle-light, and said, with a deep guffaw:

"'Ullo! you dar'?"

No bandicoot ever went into his hole with the dogs after him quicker than Jim came out of his. He scrambled up the shaft by the foot-holes, and sat on the edge of the waste-heap, looking very pale.

"What's the matter?" asked Dave. "Have you seen a ghost?"

"I've seen the—the devil!" gasped Jim. "I'm—I'm done with this here ghoul business."

The parties got on speaking terms again. Dave was very warm, but Jim's language was worse. Pinter scratched his chin-feathers reflectively till the other party cooled. There was no appealing to the commissioner for goldfields; they were outside all law, whether of the goldfields or otherwise—so they did the only thing possible and sensible, they joined forces and became "Poynton, Regan & Party." They agreed to work the ground from the separate shafts, and decided to go ahead, irrespective of appearances, and get as much dirt out and cradled as possible before the inevitable exposure came along. They found plenty of "payable dirt," and soon the drive ended in a cluster of roomy chambers. They timbered up many coffins of various ages, burnt tarred canvas and brown paper, and kept the fan going. Outside they paid the storekeeper with difficulty and talked of hard times.

But one fine sunny morning, after about a week of partnership, they got a bad scare. Jim and Kullers were below, getting out dirt for all they were worth, and Pinter and Dave at their windlasses, when who should march down from the cemetery gate but Mother Middleton herself. She was a hard woman to look at. She still wore the old-fashioned crinoline and her hair in a greasy net; and on this as on most other sober occasions, she wore the expression of a rough Irish navvy who has just enough drink to make him nasty, and is looking out for an excuse for a row. She had a stride like a grenadier. A digger had once measured her step by her footprints in the mud where she had stepped across a gutter; it measured three feet from toe to heel.

She marched to the grave of Jimmy Middleton, laid a dingy bunch of flowers thereon, with the gesture of an angry man banging his fist down on the table, turned on her heel, and marched out. The diggers were dirt beneath her feet. Presently they heard her drive on in her spring-cart on her way into town, and they drew breaths of relief.

It was afternoon. Dave and Pinter were feeling tired, and were just decided to knock off work for that day when they heard a scuffling in the direction of the different shafts, and both Jim and Kullers dropped down and bundled in in a great hurry. Jim chuckled in a silly way, as if there was something funny, and Kullers guffawed in sympathy.

"What's up now?" demanded Dave apprehensively.

"Mother Middleton," said Jim; "she's blind mad drunk, and she's got a bottle in one hand and a new pitchfork in the other, that she's bringing out for someone."

"How the hell did she drop to it?" exclaimed Pinter.

"Dunno," said Jim. "Anyway, she's coming for us. Listen to her!"

They didn't have to listen hard. The language which came down the

210

shaft—they weren't sure which one—and along the drives was enough to scare up the dead and make them take to the bush.

"Why didn't you fools make off into the bush and give us a chance, instead of giving her a lead here?" asked Dave.

Jim and Kullers began to wish they had done so.

Mrs Middleton began to throw stones down the shaft—it was Pinter's—and they, even the oldest and most anxious, began to grin in spite of themselves, for they knew she couldn't hurt them from the surface, and that, though she had been a working digger herself, she couldn't fill both shafts before the fumes of liquor overtook her.

"I wonder which shaf' she'll come down," asked Kullers in a tone befitting the place and occasion.

"You'd better go and watch your shaft, Pinter," said Dave, "and Jim and I'll watch mine."

"I—I won't," said Pinter hurriedly. "I'm—I'm a modest man."

Then they heard a clang in the direction of Pinter's shaft.

"She's thrown her bottle down," said Dave.

Jim crawled along the drive a piece, urged by curiosity, and returned hurriedly.

"She's broke the pitchfork off short, to use in the drive, and I believe she's coming down."

"Her crinoline'll handicap her," said Pinter vacantly, "that's a comfort."

"She's took it off!" said Dave excitedly; and peering along Pinter's drive, they saw first an elastic-sided boot, then a red-striped stocking, then a section of scarlet petticoat.

"Lemme out!" roared Pinter, lurching forward and making a swimming motion with his hands in the direction of Dave's drive. Kullers was already gone and Jim well on the way. Dave, lanky and awkward, scrambled up the shaft last. Mrs Middleton made good time, considering she had the darkness to face and didn't know the workings, and when Dave reached the top he had a tear in the leg of his moleskins, and the blood ran from a nasty scratch. But he didn't wait to argue over the price of a new pair of trousers. He made off through the bush in the direction of an encouraging whistle thrown back by Jim.

"She's too drunk to get her story listened to to-night," said Dave. "But to-morrow she'll bring the neighbourhood down on us."

"And she's enough, without the neighbourhood," reflected Pinter.

Some time after dark they returned cautiously, reconnoitred their camp, and after hiding in a hollow log such things as they couldn't carry, they rolled up their tents like the Arabs, and silently stole away.

Rylstone, a typical country township in central New South Wales, as it looked in the 1880s. Lawson would have seen it like this when, as a boy of fourteen, having just left school he worked there with his father on one of the latter's building contracts.

If Louisa, aware of the dangers of the nomadic life led by many bush workers, was apprehensive for her son's future welfare, we do know that Lawson enjoyed working beside his father for whom his sympathy and understanding stand out in the short story 'A Child in the Dark'.

A CHILD IN THE DARK

New Year's Eve! A hot night in midsummer in the drought. It was so dark
—with a smothering darkness—that even the low loom of the scrub-covered
ridges, close at hand across the creek, was not to be seen. The sky was not
clouded for rain, but with drought haze and the smoke of distant bushfires.

Down the hard road to the crossing at Pipeclay Creek sounded the footsteps
of a man. Not the crunching steps of an English labourer, clodhopping con-
tentedly home; these sounded more like the footsteps of one pacing steadily
to and fro, and thinking steadily and hopelessly—sorting out the past. Only
the steps went on. A glimmer of white moleskin trousers and a suggestion
of light-coloured tweed jacket, now and again, as if in the glimmer of a faint
ghost light in the darkness.

The road ran along by the foot of a line of low ridges, or spurs, and as he
passed the gullies or gaps he felt a breath of hotter air, like blasts from a
furnace in the suffocating atmosphere. He followed a two-railed fence for
a short distance, and turned in at a white batten gate. It seemed lighter now.
There was a house, or rather a hut, suggested, with whitewashed slab walls
and a bark roof. He walked quietly round to the door of a detached kitchen,
opened it softly, went in and struck a match. A candle stood, stuck in a blot
of its own grease, on one end of the dresser. He lit the candle and looked round.

The walls of the kitchen were of split slabs, the roof box-bark, the floor
clay, and there was a large clay-lined fireplace, the sides a dirty brown, and
the back black. It had evidently never been whitewashed. There was a bed
of about a week's ashes, and above it, suspended by a blackened hook and
chain from a grimy cross-bar, hung a black bucket full of warm water. The
man got a fork, explored the bucket, and found what he expected—a piece
of raw corned-beef in water which had gone off the boil before the meat had
been heated through.

The kitchen was furnished with a pine table, a well-made flour bin, and a
neat safe and sideboard, or dresser—evidently the work of a carpenter. The
top of the safe was dirty—covered with crumbs and grease and tea stains.
On one corner lay a school exercise book, with a stone ink-bottle and a pen
beside it. The book was open at a page written in the form of verse, in a
woman's hand, and headed: "Misunderstood". He took the edges of the book
between his fingers and thumbs, and made to tear it, but, the cover being
tough, and resisting the first savage tug, he altered his mind, and put the
book down. Then he turned to the table. There was a jumble of dirty crockery
on one end, and on the other, set on a sheet of stained newspaper, the
remains of a meal—a junk of badly-hacked bread, a basin of dripping (with
the fat over the edges), and a tin of treacle. The treacle had run down the
sides of the tin on to the paper. Knives, heavy with treacle, lay glued to the
paper. There was a dish with some water, a rag, and a cup or two in it—
evidently an attempt to wash-up.

The man took up a cup and pressed it hard between his palms, until it
broke. Then he felt relieved. He gathered the fragments in one hand, took

Although Lawson's
work is a suspect
source of auto-
biography, 'A Child
in the Dark and
a Foreign Father'
is considered a
valuable insight
into Lawson's
childhood.

213

the candle, and stumbled out to where there was a dust-heap. Kicking a hole in the ashes, he dropped in the bits of broken crockery, and covered them. Then his anger blazed again. He walked quickly to the back door of the house, thrust the door open, and flung in, but a child's voice said from the dark:

"Is that you, father? Don't tread on me, father."

The room was nearly as bare as the kitchen. There was a table, covered with cheap American oilcloth, and, on the other side, a sofa on which a straw mattress, a cloudy blanket, and a pillow without a slip had been thrown in a heap. On the floor, between the sofa and the table, lay a boy—child almost —on a similar mattress, with a cover of coarse sacking, and a bundle of dirty clothes for a pillow. A pale, thin-faced, dark-eyed boy.

"What are you doing here, sonny?" asked the father.

"Mother's bad again with her head. She says to tell you to come in quiet, and sleep on the sofa tonight. I started to wash up and clean up the kitchen, father, but I got sick."

"Why, what is the matter with you, sonny?" His voice quickened, and he held the candle down to the child's face.

"Oh, nothing much, father. I felt sick, but I feel better now."

"What have you been eating?"

"Nothing that I know of; I think it was the hot weather, father."

The father spread the mattress, blew out the candle, and lay down in his clothes. After a while the boy began to toss restlessly.

"Oh, it's too hot, father," he said. "I'm smothering."

The father got up, lit the candle, took a corner of the newspaper-covered "scrim" lining that screened the cracks of the slab wall, and tore it away; then he propped open the door with a chair.

"Oh, that's better already, father," said the boy.

The hut was three rooms long and one deep, with a veranda in front and a skillion, harness and tool room, about half the length, behind. The father opened the door of the next room softly, and propped that open, too. There was another boy on the sofa, younger than the first, but healthy and sturdy-looking. He had nothing on him but a very dirty shirt, a patchwork quilt was slipping from under him, and most of it was on the floor; the boy and the pillow were nearly off, too.

The father fixed him as comfortably as possible, and put some chairs by the sofa to keep him from rolling off. He noticed that somebody had started to scrub this room, and left it. He listened at the door of the third room for a few moments to the breathing within; then he opened it and gently walked in. There was an old-fashioned four-poster cedar bedstead, a chest of drawers, and a baby's cradle made out of a gin-case. The woman was fast asleep. She was a big, strong and healthy-looking woman, with dark hair and strong, square features. There was a plate, a knife and fork, and egg-shells, and a cup and saucer on the top of the chest of drawers; also two candles, one stuck in a mustard-tin, and one in a pickle-bottle, and a copy of *Ardath*.

He stepped out in the skillion, and lifted some harness on to its pegs from chaff-bags in the corner. Coming in again he nearly stumbled over a bucket half full of dirty water on the floor, with a scrubbing brush, some wet rags, and half a bar of yellow soap beside it. He put these things in the bucket, and carried it out. As he passed through the first room the sick boy said:

"I couldn't lift the saddle of the harness on to the peg, father. I had to leave the scrubbing to make some tea and cook some eggs for mother, and put baby to bed, and then I felt too bad to go on with the scrubbing—and I forgot about the bucket."

"Did the baby have any tea, sonny?"

"Yes. I made her bread and milk, and she ate a big plateful. The calves are in the pen all right, and I fixed the gate. And I brought a load of wood this morning, father, before mother took bad."

"You should not have done that. I told you not to. I could have done that on Sunday. Now, are you sure you didn't lift a log into the cart that was too heavy for you?"

"Quite sure, father. Oh, I'm plenty strong enough to put a load of wood on the cart."

The father lay on his back on the sofa, with his hands behind his head, for a few minutes.

"Aren't you tired, father?" asked the boy.

"No, sonny, not very tired; you must try and go to sleep now," and he reached across the table for the candle and blew it out.

Presently the baby cried, and in a moment the mother's voice was heard.

"Nils! Nils! Are you there, Nils?"

"Yes, Emma."

"Then for God's sake come and take this child away before she drives me mad! My head's splitting."

The father went in to the child and presently returned for a cup of water.

"She only wanted a drink," the boy heard him say to the mother.

"Well, didn't I tell you she wanted a drink? I've been calling for the last half-hour, with that child screaming, and not a soul to come near me, and me lying here helpless all day, and not a wink of sleep for two nights."

"But, Emma, you were asleep when I came in."

"How can you tell such infernal lies? I—. To think I'm chained to a man who can't say a word of truth! God help me! To have to lie night after night in the same bed with a liar!"

The child in the first room lay quaking with terror, dreading one of those cruel and shameful scenes which had made a hell of his childhood.

"Hush, Emma!" the man kept saying. "Do be reasonable. Think of the children. They'll hear us."

"I don't care if they do. They'll know soon enough, God knows! I wish I was under the turf!"

"Emma, do be reasonable."

"Reasonable! I—"

The child was crying again. The father came back to the first room, got something from his coat pocket, and took it in.

"Nils, are you quite mad, or do you want to drive me mad? Don't give the child that rattle! You must be either mad or a brute, and my nerves in this state. Haven't you got the slightest consideration for—"

"It's not a rattle, Emma; it's a doll.

"There you go again! Flinging your money away on rubbish that'll be on the dust-heap tomorrow, and your poor wife slaving her fingernails off for you in this wretched hole, and not a decent rag to her back. Me, your clever wife that ought to be—Light those candles and bring me a wet towel for my head. I must read now, and try and compose my nerves, if I can."

When the father returned to the first room, the boy was sitting up in bed, looking deathly white.

"Why, what's the matter, sonny?" said the father, bending over him, and putting a hand to his back.

"Nothing, father. I'll be all right directly. Don't you worry, father."

"Where do you feel bad, sonny?"

"In my head and stomach, father; but I'll be all right, d'rectly. I've often been that way."

In a minute or two he was worse.

"For God's sake, Nils, take that boy into the kitchen, or somewhere," cried the woman, "or I'll go mad. It's enough to kill a horse. Do you want to drive me into a lunatic asylum?"

"Do you feel better now, sonny?" asked the father.

"Yes, ever so much better, father," said the boy, white and weak. "I'll be all right in a minute, father."

"You had best sleep on the sofa tonight, sonny. It's cooler there."

"No, father, I'd rather stay here; it's much cooler now."

The father fixed the bed as comfortably as he could, and, despite the boy's protest, put his own pillow under his head. Then he made a fire in the kitchen, and hung the kettle and a big billy of water over it. He was haunted by recollections of convulsions amongst the children while they were teething. He took off his boots, and was about to lie down again when the mother called:

"Nils, Nils, have you made a fire?"

"Yes, Emma."

"Then for God's sake make me a cup of tea. I must have it after all this."

He hurried up the kettle—she calling every few minutes to know if "that kettle was boiling yet". He took her a cup of tea, and then a second. She said the tea was slush, and as sweet as syrup, and called for more, and hot water.

"How do you feel now, sonny?" he asked as he lay down on the sofa once more.

"Much better, father. You can put out the light now if you like."

The father blew out the candle, and settled back again, still dressed save for his coat, and presently the small, weak hand sought the hard, strong, horny, knotted one; and so they lay, as was customary with them. After a while the father leaned over a little and whispered:

"Asleep, sonny?"

"No, father."

"Feel bad again?"

"No, father."

Pause.

"What are you thinking about, sonny?"

"Nothing, father."

"But what is it? What are you worrying about? Tell me."

"Nothing, father, only—it'll be a good while yet before I grow up to be a man, won't it, father?"

The father lay silent and troubled for a few moments.

"Why do you ask me that question tonight, sonny? I thought you'd done with all that. You were always asking me that question when you were a child. You're getting too old for those foolish fancies now. Why have you always had such a horror of growing up to be a man?"

"I don't know, father. I always had funny thoughts—you know, father. I used to think that I'd been a child once before, and grew up to be a man, and grew old and died."

"You're not well tonight, sonny—that's what's the matter. You're queer, sonny; it's a touch of sun—that's all. Now, try to go to sleep. You'll grow up to be a man, in spite of laying awake worrying about it. If you do, you'll be a man all the sooner."

Suddenly the mother called out:

"Can't you be quiet? What do you mean by talking at this hour of the night? Am I never to get another wink of sleep? Shut those doors, Nils, for God's sake, if you don't want to drive me mad—and make that boy hold his tongue!"

The father closed the doors.

"Better try to go to sleep now, sonny," he whispered, as he lay down again.

The father waited for some time, then, moving very softly, he lit the candle at the kitchen fire, put it where it shouldn't light the boy's face, and watched him. And the child knew he was watching him, and pretended to sleep, and, so pretending, he slept. And the old year died as many old years had died.

The father was up about four o'clock—he worked at his trade in a farming town about five miles away, and was struggling to make a farm and a home between jobs. He cooked bacon for breakfast, washed-up the dishes and tidied the kitchen, gave the boys some bread and bacon fat, of which they were very fond, and told the eldest to take a cup of tea and some bread and milk to his mother and the baby when they woke.

The boy milked the three cows, set the milk, and heard his mother calling:
"Nils! Nils!"

"Yes, mother."

"Why didn't you answer when I called you? I've been calling here for the last three hours. Is your father gone out?"

"Yes, mother."

"Thank God! It's a relief to be rid of his everlasting growling. Bring me a cup of tea and the *Australian Journal,* and take this child out and dress her; she should have been up hours ago."

And so the New Year began.

THE STORM THAT IS TO COME

Another of Lawson's prophetic poems.

By our place in the midst of the farthest seas we are fated to stand
    alone—
When the nations fly at each other's throats let Australia look to
    her own;
Let her spend her gold on the barren West for the land and its
    manhood's sake;
For the South must look to the South for strength in the storm that
    is to come.

Now who shall gallop from cape to cape, and who shall defend
    our shores—
The crowd that stands on the kerb agape and glares at the cricket
    scores?
And who will hold the invader back when the shells tear up
    the ground—
The weeds that yelp by the cycling track while a nigger scorches
    round?

There may be many to man the forts in the big towns by the sea—
But the East will call to the West for scouts in the storm that is
    to be:
The West cries out to the East in drought, but the coastal towns
    are dumb;
And the East must look to the West for food in the war that is
    to come.

The rain comes down on the Western land and the rivers run
    to waste,
While the townsfolk rush for the special tram in their childish,
    senseless haste,
And never a pile of a lock we drive—but a few mean tanks we
    scratch—
For the fate of a nation is nought compared with the turn of
    a cricket match!

A. H. Fullwood (1863-1930) *The Station Boundary* (1891)
90.2 x 59.7 cm   Oil on canvas
Reproduced with the kind permission of the Art Gallery Of New South Wales, Sydney

Charles Conder (1868-1909) *Feeding the Chickens* (Richmond, NSW)
28.6 x 39.3 cm   Oil on wood
Reproduced with the kind permission of The Art Gallery Of South Australia

There's a gutter of mud where there spread a flood from the
    land-long western creeks,
There is dust and drought on the plains far out where the water
    lay for weeks,
There's a pitiful dam where a dyke should stretch and a tank
    where a lake should be,
And the rain goes down through the silt and sand and the floods
    waste into the sea.

I saw a vision in days gone by, and would dream that dream
    again,
Of the days when the Darling shall not back her billabongs up
    in vain.
There were reservoirs and grand canals where the sad, dry lands
    had been,
And a glorious network of aqueducts mid fields that were always
    green.

I have pictured long in the land I love what the land I love
    might be,
Where the Darling rises from Queensland rains and the floods
    rush out to the sea.
And is it our fate to wake too late to the truth that we have been
    blind,
With a foreign foe at our harbour-gate and a blazing drought
    behind?

TAKING HIS CHANCE

They stood by the door of the Inn on the Rise;
May Carney looked up in the bushranger's eyes:
"Oh! why did you come?—it was mad of you, Jack;
You know that the troopers are out on your track."
A laugh and a shake of his obstinate head—
"I wanted a dance, and I'll chance it," he said.

Some twenty-odd Bushmen had come to the ball,
But Jack from his youth had been known to them all,
And bushmen are soft where a woman is fair,
So the love of May Carney protected him there.
Through all the short evening—it seems like romance—
She danced with a bushranger taking his chance.

'Twas midnight—the dancers stood suddenly still,
For hoof-beats were heard on the side of the hill!
Ben Duggan, the drover, along the hillside
Came riding as only a bushman can ride.
He sprang from his horse, to the shanty he sped—
"The troopers are down in the gully!" he said.

Quite close to the shanty the troopers were seen.
"Clear out and ride hard for the ranges, Jack Dean!
Be quick!" said May Carney—her hand on her heart—
"We'll bluff them awhile, and 'twill give you a start."
He lingered a moment—to kiss her, of course—
Then ran to the trees where he'd hobbled his horse.

She ran to the gate, and the troopers were there—
The jingle of hobbles came faint on the air—
Then loudly she screamed: it was only to drown
The treacherous clatter of sliprails let down.
But troopers are sharp, and she saw at a glance
That someone was taking a desparate chance.

They chased, and they shouted, "Surrender, Jack Dean!"
They called him three times in the name of the Queen.
Then came from the darkness the clicking of locks;
The crack of a rifle was heard in the rocks!
A shriek, and a shout, and a rush of pale men—
And there lay the bushranger, chancing it then.

The sergeant dismounted and knelt on the sod—
"Your bushranging's over—make peace, Jack, with God!"
The dying man laughed—not a word he replied,
But turned to the girl who knelt down by his side.
He gazed in her eyes as she lifted his head:
"Just kiss me—my girl—and—I'll—chance it," he said.

222

Louisa Albury, at 18, became 'Peter Lawson's' wife at Eurunderee in 1865, not so very long before this photograph was taken. A first generation Australian of English parents, she was born at Guntawang, near Mudgee, in 1848. From her schooldays she gave evidence of literary interests and ambitions for which life in a small back country town provided no outlet and led to the frustrations with which her life was beset. The longed for escape into the world of action in the cities, which marriage seemed to promise, did not eventuate and was the main cause of the bitter quarrels between herself and her husband. The young Henry, torn between loyalties to mother and father, was never able to forget this period as one of torment and worry.

In 1883 Louisa's marriage came to an end and, with her children, she settled in Sydney, quickly throwing herself into the political maelstrom of the 1880s and 1890s. From 1887 she edited and published *Dawn*, under the pseudonym 'Dora Falconer'. The first journal was devoted to the cause of Women's Rights in Australia. Until the early 1900s she was a driving force behind her son's various literary activities, and in his success she seemed to have vicariously realized some of her own ambitions. In 1905 she published *The Lonely Crossing,* a book of her verses.

She died in 1920.

NO PLACE FOR A WOMAN

He had a selection on a long box-scrub sidling of the ridges, about half a mile back and up from the coach road. There were no neighbours that I ever heard of, and the nearest "town" was thirty miles away. He grew wheat among the stumps of his clearing, sold the crop standing to a cocky who lived ten miles away, and had some surplus sons; or, some seasons, he reaped it by hand, had it thrashed by travelling "steamer" (portable steam engine and machine), and carried the grain, a few bags at a time, into the mill on his rickety dray.

He had lived alone for upwards of fifteen years, and was known to those who knew him as "Ratty Howlett."

Trav'lers and strangers failed to see anything uncommonly ratty about him. It was known, or, at least, it was believed, without question, that while at work he kept his horse saddled and bridled, and hung up to the fence, or grazing about, with the saddle on—or, anyway, close handy for a moment's notice—and whenever he caught sight, over the scrub and through the quarter-mile break in it, of a traveller on the road, he would jump on his horse and make after him. If it was a horseman he usually pulled him up inside of a mile. Stories were told of unsuccessful chases, misunderstandings, and complications arising out of Howlett's mania for running down and bailing up travellers. Sometimes he caught one every day for a week, sometimes not one for weeks—it was a lonely track.

The explanation was simple, sufficient, and perfectly natural—from a bushman's point of view. Ratty only wanted to have a yarn. He and the traveller would camp in the shade for half an hour or so and yarn and smoke. The old man would find out where the traveller came from, and how long he'd been there, and where he was making for, and how long he reckoned he'd be away; and ask if there had been any rain along the traveller's back track, and how the country looked after the drought; and he'd get the traveller's ideas on abstract questions—if he had any. If it was a footman (swagman), and he was short of tobacco, old Howlett always had half a stick ready for him. Sometimes, but very rarely, he'd invite the swagman back to the hut for a pint of tea, or a bit of meat, flour, tea, or sugar, to carry him along the track.

And, after the yarn by the road, they said, the old man would ride back, refreshed, to his lonely selection, and work on into the night as long as he could see his solitary old plough-horse, or the scoop of his long-handled shovel.

And so it was that I came to make his acquaintance—or, rather, that he made mine. I was cantering easily along the track—I was making for

224

the north-west with a packhorse—when about a mile beyond the track to the selection I heard, "Hi, mister!" and saw a dust-cloud following me. I had heard of "Old Ratty Howlett" casually, and so was prepared for him.

A tall, gaunt man on a little horse. He was clean-shaven, except for a frill beard round under his chin, and his long wavy, dark hair was turning grey; a square, strong-faced man, and reminded me of one full-faced portrait of Gladstone more than any other face I had seen. He had large reddish-brown eyes, deep set under heavy eyebrows, and with something of the blackfellow in them—the sort of eyes that will peer at something on the horizon that no one else can see. He had a way of talking to the horizon, too—more than to his companion; and he had a deep vertical wrinkle in his forehead that no smile could lessen.

I got down and got out my pipe, and we sat on a log and yarned a while on bush subjects; and then, after a pause, he shifted uneasily, it seemed to me, and asked rather abruptly, and in an altered tone, if I was married. A queer question to ask a traveller; more especially in my case, as I was little more than a boy then.

He talked on again of old things and places where we had both been, and asked after men he knew, or had known—drovers and others—and whether they were living yet. Most of his inquiries went back before my time; but some of the drovers, one or two overlanders with whom he had been mates in his time, had grown old into mine, and I knew them. I notice now, though I didn't then—and if I had it would not have seemed strange from a bush point of view—that he didn't ask for news, nor seem interested in it.

Then after another uneasy pause, during which he scratched crosses in the dust with a stick, he asked me, in the same queer tone and without looking at me or looking up, if I happened to know anything about doctoring —if I'd ever studied it.

I asked him if any one was sick at his place. He hesitated and said "No." Then I wanted to know why he had asked me that question, and he was so long about answering that I began to think he was hard of hearing, when, at last, he muttered something about my face reminding him of a young fellow he knew of who'd gone to Sydney to "study for a doctor." That might have been, and looked natural enough; but why didn't he ask me straight out if I was the chap he "knowed of?" Travellers do not like beating about the bush in conversation.

He sat in silence for a good while, with his arms folded, and looking absently away over the dead level of the great scrubs that spread from the foot of the ridge we were on to where a blue peak or two of a distant range showed above the bush on the horizon.

I stood up and put my pipe away and stretched. Then he seemed to wake up. "Better come back to the hut and have a bit of dinner," he said. "The missus will about have it ready, and I'll spare you a handful of hay for the horses."

The hay decided it. It was a dry season. I was surprised to hear of a wife, for I thought he was a hatter—I had always heard so; but perhaps I had been mistaken, and he had married lately; or had got a housekeeper. The farm was an irregularly-shaped clearing in the scrub, with a good many stumps in it, with a broken-down two-rail fence along the frontage, and logs and "dog-leg" the rest. It was about as lonely-looking a place as I had seen, and I had seen some out-of-the-way, God-forgotten holes where men lived alone. The hut was in the top corner, a two-roomed slab hut, with a shingle roof, which must have been uncommon round there in the days when that hut was built. I was used to bush carpentering, and saw that the place had been put up by a man who had plenty of life and hope in front of him, and for someone else beside himself. But there were two unfinished skilling-rooms built on to the back of the hut; the posts, sleepers, and wall-plates had been well put up and fitted, and the slab walls were up, but the roof had never been put on. There was nothing but burrs and nettles inside those walls, and an old wooden bullock-plough and a couple of yokes were dry-rotting across the back doorway. The remains of a straw-stack, some hay under a bark humpy, a small iron plough, and an old stiff coffin-headed grey draught-horse, were all that I saw about the place.

But there was a bit of a surprise for me inside, in the shape of a clean white table-cloth on the rough slab table which stood on stakes driven into the ground. The cloth was coarse, but it was a table-cloth—not a spare sheet put on in honour of unexpected visitors—and perfectly clean. The tin plates, pannikins, and jam-tins that served as sugar-bowls and salt-cellars were polished brightly. The walls and fire-place were white-washed, the clay floor swept, and clean sheets of newspaper laid on the slab mantel-shelf under the row of biscuit-tins that held the groceries. I thought that his wife, or housekeeper, or whatever she was, was a clean and tidy woman about a house. I saw no woman; but on the sofa—a light, wooden, batten one, with runged arms at the ends—lay a woman's dress on a lot of sheets of old stained and faded newspapers. He looked at it in a puzzled way, knitting his forehead, then took it up absently and folded it. I saw then that it was a riding-skirt and jacket. He bundled them into the newspapers and took them into the bedroom.

"The wife was going on a visit down the creek this afternoon," he said rapidly and without looking at me, but stooping as if to have another look through the door at those distant peaks. "I suppose she got tired o' waitin', and went and took the daughter with her. But, never mind, the grub is ready." There was a camp-oven with a leg of mutton and potatoes sizzling in it on the hearth, and billies hanging over the fire. I noticed the billies had been scraped, and the lids polished.

There seemed to be something queer about the whole business, but then he and his wife might have had a "breeze" during the morning. I thought so during the meal, when the subject of women came up, and he said one never knew how to take a woman; but there was nothing in what he said that need necessarily have referred to his wife or to any woman in particular. For the rest he talked of old bush things, droving, digging, and old bush-ranging—but never about live things and living men, unless any of the old mates he talked about happened to be alive by accident. He was very restless in the house, and never took his hat off.

There was a dress and a woman's old hat hanging on the wall near the door, but they looked as if they might have been hanging there for a lifetime. There seemed something queer about the whole place—something wanting; but then all out-of-the-way bush homes are haunted by that some-thing wanting or, more likely, by the spirits of the things that should have been there, but never had been.

As I rode down the track to the road I looked back and saw old Howlett hard at work in a hole round a big stump with his long-handled shovel.

I'd noticed that he moved and walked with a slight list to port, and put his hand once or twice to the small of his back, and I set it down to lumbago, or something of that sort.

Up in the Never-Never I heard from a drover who had known Howlett that his wife had died in the first year, and so this mysterious woman, if she was his wife, was, of course, his second wife. The drover seemed surprised and rather amused at the thought of old Howlett going in for matrimony again.

I rode back that way five years later, from the Never-Never. It was early in the morning—I had ridden since midnight. I didn't think the old man would be up and about; and, besides, I wanted to get on home, and have a look at the old folk, and the mates I'd left behind—and the girl. But I hadn't got far past the point where Howlett's track joined the road, when I happened to look back, and saw him on horseback, stumbling down the track. I waited till he came up.

He was riding the old grey draught-horse this time, and it looked very much broken down. I thought it would have come down every step, and fallen like an old rotten humpy in a gust of wind. And the old man was not much better off. I saw at once that he was a very sick man. His face was drawn, and he bent forward as if he was hurt. He got down stiffly and awkwardly, like a hurt man, and as soon as his feet touched the ground he grabbed my arm, or he would have gone down like a man who steps off a train in motion. He hung towards the bank of the road, feeling blindly, as it were, for the ground, with his free hand, as I eased him down. I got my blanket and calico from the pack-saddle to make him comfortable.

"Help me with my back agen the tree," he said. "I must sit up—it's no use lyin' me down."

He sat with his hand gripping his side, and breathed painfully.

"Shall I run up to the hut and get the wife?" I asked.

"No." He spoke painfully. "No!" Then, as if the words were jerked out of him by a spasm: "She ain't there."

I took it that she had left him.

"How long have you been bad? How long has this been coming on?"

He took no notice of the question. I thought it was a touch of rheumatic fever, or something of that sort. "It's gone into my back and sides now—the pain's worse in me back," he said presently.

I had once been mates with a man who died suddenly of heart disease, while at work. he was washing a dish of dirt in the creek near a claim we were working; he let the dish slip into the water, fell back, crying, "Oh, my back!" and was gone. And now I felt by instinct that it was poor old Howlett's heart that was wrong. A man's heart is in his back as well as in his arms and hands.

The old man had turned pale with the pallor of a man who turns faint

227

in a heat wave, and his arms fell loosely, and his hands rocked helplessly with the knuckles in the dust. I felt myself turning white, too, and the sick, cold, empty feeling in my stomach, for I knew the signs. Bushmen stand in awe of sickness and death.

But after I'd fixed him comfortably and given him a drink from the water-bag the greyness left his face, and he pulled himself together a bit; he drew up his arms and folded them across his chest. He let his head rest back against the tree—his slouch hat had fallen off revealing a broad, white brow, much higher than I expected. He seemed to gaze on the azure fin of the range, showing above the dark blue-green bush on the horizon.

Then he commenced to speak—taking no notice of me when I asked him if he felt better now—to talk in that strange, absent, far-away tone that awes one. He told his story mechanically, monotonously—in set words, as I believe now, as he had often told it before; if not to others, then to the loneliness of the bush. And he used the names of people and places that I had never heard of—just as if I knew them as well as he did.

"I didn't want to bring her up the first year. It was no place for a woman. I wanted her to stay with her people and wait till I'd got the place a little more shipshape. The Phippses took a selection down the creek. I wanted her to wait and come up with them so's she'd have some company— a woman to talk to. They came afterwards, but they didn't stop. It was no place for a woman.

"But Mary would come. She wouldn't stop with her people down-country. She wanted to be with me, and look after me, and work and help me."

He repeated himself a great deal—said the same thing over and over again sometimes. He was only mad on one track. He'd tail off and sit silent for a while; then he'd become aware of me in a hurried, half-scared way, and apologize for putting me to all that trouble, and thank me. "I'll be all right d'reckly. Best take the horses up to the hut and have some breakfast; you'll find it by the fire. I'll foller you, d'reckly. The wife'll be waitin' and——" He would drop off, and be going again presently on the old track:

"Her mother was coming up to stay a while at the end of the year, but the old man hurt his leg. Then her married sister was coming, but one of the youngsters got sick and there was trouble at home. I saw the doctor in the town—thirty miles from here—and fixed it up with him. He was a boozer—I'd 'a' shot him afterwards. I fixed up with a woman in the town to come and stay. I thought Mary was wrong in her time. She must have been a month or six weeks out. But I listened to her. . . . Don't argue with a woman. Don't listen to a woman. Do the right thing. We should have had a mother woman to talk to us. But it was no place for a woman!"

He rocked his head, as if from some old agony of mind, against the tree-trunk.

"She was took bad suddenly one night, but it passed off. False alarm. I was going to ride somewhere, but she said to wait till daylight. Someone was sure to pass. She was a brave and sensible girl, but she had a terror of being left alone. It was no place for a woman!

"There was a black shepherd three or four miles away. I rode over while Mary was asleep, and started the black boy into town. I'd 'a' shot him afterwards if I'd 'a' caught him. The old black gin was dead the week before, or Mary would 'a' bin all right. She was tied up in a bunch with strips of blanket and greenhide, and put in a hole. So there wasn't even a gin near the place. It was no place for a woman!

"I was watchin' the road at daylight, and I was watchin' the road at dusk. I went down in the hollow and stooped down to get the gap agen the sky, so's I could see if any one was comin' over. . . . I'd get on the horse and gallop along towards the town for five miles, but something would drag me back, and then I'd race for fear she'd die before I got to the hut. I expected the doctor every five minutes.

"It come on about daylight next morning. I ran back'ards and for'ards between the hut and the road like a madman. And no one come. I was running amongst the logs and stumps, and fallin' over them, when I saw a cloud of dust agen sunrise. It was her mother and sister in the spring-cart, an' just catchin' up to them was the doctor in his buggy with the woman I'd arranged with in town. The mother and sister were staying at the town for the night, when they heard of the black boy. It took him a day to ride there. I'd 'a' shot him if I'd 'a' caught him ever after. The doctor'd been on the drunk. If I'd had the gun and known she was gone I'd have shot him in the buggy. They said she was dead. And the child was dead, too.

"They blamed me, but I didn't want her to come; it was no place for a woman. I never saw them again after the funeral. I didn't want to see them any more."

He moved his head wearily against the tree, and presently drifted on again in a softer tone—his eyes and voice were growing more absent and dreamy and far away.

"About a month after—or a year, I lost count of the time long ago—she came back to me. At first she'd come in the night, then sometimes when I was at work—and she had the baby—it was a girl—in her arms. And by and by she came to stay altogether. . . . I didn't blame her for going away that time—it was no place for a woman. . . . She was a good wife to me. She was a jolly girl when I married her. The little girl grew up like her. I was going to send her down-country to be educated—it was no place for a girl.

"But a month, or a year ago, Mary left me, and took the daughter, and never come back till last night—this morning, I think it was. I thought at first it was the girl with her hair done up, and her mother's skirt on, to surprise her old dad. But it was Mary, my wife—as she was when I married her. She said she couldn't stay, but she'd wait for me on the road; on—the road."

His arms fell, and his face went white. I got the water-bag. "Another turn like that and you'll be gone," I thought, as he came to again. Then I suddenly thought of a shanty that had been started, when I came that way last, ten or twelve miles along the road, towards the town. There was nothing for it but to leave him and ride on for help, and a cart of some kind.

"You wait here till I come back," I said. "I'm going for the doctor."

He roused himself a little. "Best come up to the hut and get some grub. The wife'll be waiting. . . ." He was off the track again.

"Will you wait while I take the horse down to the creek?"

"Yes—I'll wait by the road."

"Look!" I said, "I'll leave the water-bag handy. Don't move till I come back."

"I won't move—I'll wait by the road," he said.

I took the packhorse, which was the freshest and best, threw the pack-saddle and bags into a bush, left the other horse to take care of itself, and started for the shanty, leaving the old man with his back to the tree, his arms folded, and his eyes on the horizon.

One of the chaps at the shanty rode on for the doctor at once, while the other came back with me in a spring-cart. He told me that old Howlett's wife had died in child-birth the first year on the selection—"she was a fine girl he'd heerd!" He told me the story as the old man had told it, and in pretty well the same words, even to giving it as his opinion that it was no place for a woman. "And he 'hatted' and brooded over it till he went ratty."

I knew the rest. He not only thought that his wife, or the ghost of his wife, had been with him all those years, but that the child had lived and grown up, and that the wife did the housework; which, of course, he must have done himself.

When we reached him his knotted hands had fallen for the last time, and they were at rest. I only took one quick look at his face, but could have sworn that he was gazing at the blue fin of the range on the horizon of the bush.

Up at the hut the table was set as on the first day I saw it, and breakfast in the camp-oven by the fire.

THE BABIES IN THE BUSH

Oh, tell her a tale of the fairies bright—
   That only the Bushmen know—
Who guide the feet of the lost aright,
Or carry them up through the starry night,
   Where the Bush-lost babies go.

He was one of those men who seldom smile. There are many in the Australian bush, where drift wrecks and failures of all stations and professions (and of none) and from all the world. Or, if they do smile, the smile is either mechanical or bitter as a rule—cynical. They seldom talk. The sort of men who, as bosses, are set down by the majority—and without reason or evidence— as being proud, hard, and selfish—"too mean to live, and too big for their boots."

But when the boss did smile his expression was very, very gentle, and very sad. I have seen him smile down on a little child who persisted in sitting on his knee and prattling to him, in spite of his silence and gloom. He was tall and gaunt, with haggard grey eyes—haunted grey eyes sometimes —and hair and beard thick and strong, but grey. He was not above forty-five. He was of the type of men who die in harness, with their hair thick and strong, but grey or white when it should be brown. The opposite type, I fancy, would be the soft, dark-haired, blue-eyed men who grow bald sooner than they grow grey, and fat and contented, and die respectably in their beds.

His name was Head—Walter Head. He was a boss drover on the overland routes. I engaged with him at a place north of the Queensland border to travel down to Bathurst, on the Great Western Line in New South Wales, with something over a thousand head of store bullocks for the Sydney market. I am an Australian bushman (with city experience)—a rover, of course, and a ne'er-do-well, I suppose. I was born with brains and a thick skin—worse luck! It was in the days before I was married, and I went by the name of "Jack Ellis" this trip—not because the police were after me, but because I used to tell yarns about a man named Jack Ellis—and so the chaps nicknamed me.

The boss spoke little to the men: he'd sit at tucker or with his pipe by the camp-fire nearly as silently as he rode his night-watch round the big, restless, weird-looking mob of bullocks camped on the dusky star-lit plain. I believe that from the first he spoke oftener and more confidentially to me than to any other of the droving party. There was a something of sympathy between us—I can't explain what it was. It seemed as though it were an understood thing between us that we understood each other. He sometimes said things to me which would have needed a deal of explanation—so I thought—had he said them to any other of the party. He'd often, after

'The child lost in the bush' was a recurrent theme in the literature of Lawson's period and writers as far apart in style and temperament as Marcus Clarke and Joseph Furphy were attracted to i In this story Lawson saves the sympathy of his readers for the bereft mother.

Whether or not this tale is based on the report that *one* of the children of Walter Head, as he was known, had in fact been lost in the bush, 'Walter Head' (W. A. Wood) was one of his politico-journalist friends. 'Jack Ellis' is the reluctant mate he names in his poem 'Since Then'. This mixing of the names of real and imaginary characters gives an air of verisimilitude to his work.

231

brooding a long while, start a sentence, and break off with "You know, Jack." And somehow I understood, without being able to explain why. We had never met before I engaged with him for this trip. His men respected him, but he was not a popular boss: he was too gloomy, and never drank a glass nor "shouted" on the trip: he was reckoned a "mean boss," and rather a nigger-driver.

He was full of Adam Lindsay Gordon, the English-Australian poet who shot himself, and so was I. I lost an old copy of Gordon's poems on the route, and the boss overheard me inquiring about it; later on he asked me if I liked Gordon. We got to it rather sheepishly at first, but by and by we'd quote Gordon freely in turn when we were alone in camp. "Those are grand lines about Burke and Wills, the explorers, aren't they, Jack?" he'd say, after chewing his cud, or rather the stem of his briar, for a long while without a word. (He had his pipe in his mouth as often as any of us, but somehow I fancied he didn't enjoy it: an empty pipe or a stick would have suited him just as well, it seemed to me.) "Those are great lines," he'd say:

Refers to the memorial in Collins Street, Melbourne, erected to the memory of the explorers, Burke and Wills—another of Australia's tributes to failure.

"In Collins Street standeth a statue tall—
    A statue tall on a pillar of stone—
Telling its story to great and small
    Of the dust reclaimed from the sand-waste lone.

.   .   .   .   .   .

"Weary and wasted, worn and wan,
    Feeble and faint, and languid and low,
He lay on the desert a dying man,
    Who has gone, my friend, where we all must go.

"That's a grand thing, Jack. How does it go?—

"With a pistol clenched in his failing hand,
    And the film of death o'er his fading eyes,
He saw the sun go down on the sand,"—

The boss would straighten up with a sigh that might have been half a yawn—

"And he slept and never saw it rise,"

—speaking with a sort of quiet force all the time. Then maybe he'd stand with his back to the fire roasting his dusty leggings, with his hands behind his back and looking out over the dusky plain.

"What mattered the sand or the whit'ning chalk,
    The blighted herbage or blackened log,
The crooked beak of the eagle-hawk,
    Or the hot red tongue of the native dog?

"They don't matter much, do they, Jack?"
"Damned if I think they do, boss!" I'd say.

232

"The couch was rugged, those sextons rude,
But, in spite of a leaden shroud, we know
That the bravest and fairest are earth-worms' food
When once they have gone where we all must go."

Once he repeated the poem containing the lines:

"Love, when we wandered here together,
Hand in hand through the sparkling weather—
God surely loved us a little then.

"Beautiful lines those, Jack.

"Then skies were fairer and shores were firmer,
And the blue sea over the white sand rolled—
Babble and prattle, and prattle and murmur—

"How does it go, Jack?" He stood up and turned his face to the light, but not before I had a glimpse of it. I think that the saddest eyes on earth are mostly women's eyes, but I've seen few so sad as the boss's were just then.

It seemed strange that he, a bushman, preferred Gordon's sea poems to his horsey and bushy rhymes; but so he did. I fancy his favourite poem was that one of Gordon's with the lines:

I would that with sleepy embraces
The sea would fold me, would find me rest
In the luminous depths of its secret places,
Where the wealth of God's marvels is manifest!

He usually spoke quietly, in a tone as though death were in camp; but after we'd been on Gordon's poetry for a while he'd end it abruptly with, "Well, it's time to turn in," or, "It's time to turn out," or he'd give me an order in connection with the cattle. He had been a well-to-do squatter on the Lachlan river-side, in New South Wales, and had been ruined by the drought, they said. One night in camp, and after smoking in silence for nearly an hour, he asked:

"Do you know Fisher, Jack—the man that owns these bullocks?"

"I've heard of him," I said. Fisher was a big squatter, with stations both in New South Wales and in Queensland.

"Well, he came to my station on the Lachlan years ago without a penny in his pocket, or decent rag to his back, or a crust in his tucker-bag, and I gave him a job. He's my boss now. Ah, well! it's the way of Australia, you know, Jack."

The boss had one man who went on every droving trip with him; he was "bred" on the boss's station, they said, and had been with him practically all his life. His name was "Andy." I forget his other name, if he really had one. Andy had charge of the "droving-plant" (a tilted two-horse wagonette, in which we carried the rations and horse-feed), and he did the cooking and kept accounts. The boss had no head for figures. Andy might have been twenty-five or thirty-five, or anything in between. His hair stuck up like a well-made brush all round, and his big grey eyes also had an inquiring expression. His weakness was girls, or he theirs, I don't know which (half-castes not barred). He was, I think, the most innocent, good-natured, and open-hearted scamp I ever met. Towards the middle of the trip Andy spoke to me one night alone in camp about the boss.

"The boss seems to have taken to you, Jack, all right."

"Think so?" I said. I thought I smelt jealousy and detected a sneer.

"I'm sure of it. It's very seldom *he* takes to anyone."

I said nothing.

Then after a while Andy said suddenly:

"Look here, Jack, I'm glad of it. I'd like to see him make a chum of someone, if only for one trip. And don't you make any mistake about the boss. He's a white man. There's precious few that know him—precious few now; but I do, and it'll do him a lot of good to have someone to yarn with." And Andy said no more on the subject for that trip.

The long, hot, dusty miles dragged by across the blazing plains—big clearings rather—and through the sweltering hot scrubs, and we reached Bathurst at last; and then the hot dusty days and weeks and months that we'd left behind us to the Great North-West seemed as nothing—as I suppose life will seem when we come to the end of it.

The bullocks were going by rail from Bathurst to Sydney. We were all one long afternoon getting them into the trucks, and when we'd finished the boss said to me:

"Look here, Jack, you're going on to Sydney, aren't you?"

"Yes; I'm going down to have a fly round."

"Well, why not wait and go down with Andy in the morning? He's going down in charge of the cattle. The cattle-train starts about daylight. It won't be so comfortable as the passenger; but you'll save your fare, and you can give Andy a hand with the cattle. You've only got to have a look at 'em every other station, and poke up any that fall down in the trucks. You and Andy are mates, aren't you?"

I said it would just suit me. Somehow I fancied that the boss seemed anxious to have my company for one more evening, and, to tell the truth, I felt really sorry to part with him. I'd had to work as hard as any of the other chaps; but I liked him, and I believed he liked me. He'd struck me as a man who'd been quietened down by some heavy trouble, and I felt sorry for him without knowing what the trouble was.

"Come and have a drink, boss," I said. The agent had paid us off during the day.

He turned into an hotel with me.

"I don't drink, Jack," he said; "but I'll take a glass with you."

"I didn't know you were a teetotaller, boss," I said. I had not been surprised at his keeping so strictly from the drink on the trip; but now that it was over it was a different thing.

"I'm not a teetotaller, Jack," he said. "I can take a glass or leave it." And he called for a long beer, and we drank "Here's luck!" to each other.

"Well," I said, "I wish I could take a glass or leave it." And I meant it.

Then the boss spoke as I'd never heard him speak before. I thought for the moment that the one drink had affected him; but I understood before the night was over. He laid his hand on my shoulder with a grip like a man who has suddenly made up his mind to lend you five pounds. "Jack!" he said, "there's worse things than drinking, and there's worse things than heavy smoking. When a man who smokes gets such a load of trouble on him that he can find no comfort in his pipe, then it's a heavy load. And when a man who drinks gets so deep into trouble that he can find no comfort in liquor, then it's deep trouble. Take my tip for it, Jack."

He broke off, and half turned away with a jerk of his head, as if impatient with himself; then presently he spoke in his usual quiet tone:

"But you're only a boy yet, Jack. Never mind me. I won't ask you to take the second drink. You don't want it; and besides, I know the signs."

He paused, leaning with both hands on the edge of the counter, and looking down between his arms at the floor. He stood that way thinking for a while; then he suddenly straightened up like a man who'd made up his mind to something.

"I want you to come along home with me, Jack," he said; "we'll fix you a shake-down."

I forgot to tell you that he was married and lived in Bathurst.

"But won't it put Mrs Head about?"

"Not at all. She's expecting you. Come along; there's nothing to see in Bathurst, and you'll have plenty of knocking round in Sydney. Come on, we'll just be in time for tea."

He lived in a brick cottage on the outskirts of the town—an old-fashioned cottage, with ivy and climbing roses, like you see in some of those old settled districts. There was, I remember, the stump of a tree in front, covered with ivy till it looked like a giant's club with the thick end up.

When we got to the house the boss paused a minute with his hand on the gate. He'd been home a couple of days, having ridden in ahead of the bullocks.

"Jack," he said, "I must tell you that Mrs Head had a great trouble at one time. We—we lost our two children. It does her good to talk to a stranger now and again—she's always better afterwards; but there's very few I care to bring. You—you needn't notice anything strange. And agree with her, Jack. You know, Jack."

"That's all right, boss," I said. I'd knocked about the bush too long, and run against too many strange characters and things, to be surprised at anything much.

The door opened, and he took a little woman in his arms. I saw by the light of a lamp in the room behind that the woman's hair was grey, and I reckoned that he had his mother living with him. And—we do have odd thoughts at odd times in a flash—and I wondered how Mrs Head and her mother-in-law got on together. But the next minute I was in the room, and introduced to "My wife, Mrs Head," and staring at her with both eyes.

It was his wife. I don't think I can describe her. For the first minute or two, coming in out of the dark and before my eyes got used to the lamp-light, I had an impression as of a little old woman—one of those fresh-faced, well-preserved, little old ladies—who dressed young, wore false teeth, and aped the giddy girl. But this was because of Mrs Head's impulsive welcome of me, and her grey hair. The hair was not so grey as I thought at first, seeing it with the lamp-light behind it: it was like dull-brown hair lightly dusted with flour. She wore it short, and it became her that way. There was something aristocratic about her face—her nose and chin—I fancied, and something that you couldn't describe. She had big dark eyes—dark-brown, I thought, though they might have been hazel: they were a bit too big and bright for me, and now and again, when she got excited, the white showed all round the pupils—just a little, but a little was enough.

She seemed extra glad to see me. I thought at first that she was a bit of a gusher.

"Oh, I'm so glad you've come, Mr Ellis," she said, giving my hand a grip. "Walter—Mr Head—has been speaking to me about you. I've been expecting you. Sit down by the fire, Mr Ellis; tea will be ready presently. Don't you find it a bit chilly?" She shivered. It was a bit chilly now at night on the Bathurst plains. The table was set for tea, and set rather in swell style. The cottage was too well furnished even for a lucky boss drover's home; the furniture looked as if it had belonged to a toney home-stead at one time. I felt a bit strange at first, sitting down to tea, and almost wished that I was having a comfortable tuck-in at a restaurant or in a pub dining-room. But she knew a lot about the bush, and chatted away, and asked questions about the trip, and soon put me at my ease. You see, for the last year or two I'd taken my tucker in my hands—hunk of damper and meat and a clasp-knife mostly—sitting on my heel in the dust, or on a log or a tucker-box.

There was a hard, brown, wrinkled old woman that the Heads called "Auntie." She waited at the table; but Mrs Head kept bustling round herself most of the time, helping us. Andy came in to tea.

Mrs Head bustled round like a girl of twenty instead of a woman of thirty-seven, as Andy afterwards told me she was. She had the figure and movements of a girl, and the impulsiveness and expression too—a womanly girl; but sometimes I fancied there was something very childish about her face and talk. After tea she and the boss sat on one side of the fire and Andy and I on the other—Andy a little behind me at the corner of the table.

"Walter—Mr Head—tells me you've been out on the Lachlan River, Mr Ellis?" she said as soon as she'd settled down, and she leaned forward, as if eager to hear that I'd been there.

"Yes, Mrs Head. I've knocked round all about out there."

She sat up straight, and put the tips of her fingers to the side of her forehead and knitted her brows. This was a trick she had—she often did it during the evening. And when she did that she seemed to forget what she'd said last.

She smoothed her forehead, and clasped her hands in her lap.

"Oh, I'm so glad to meet somebody from the back country, Mr Ellis," she said. "Walter so seldom brings a stranger here, and I get tired of talking to the same people about the same things, and seeing the same faces. You don't know what a relief it is, Mr Ellis, to see a new face and talk to a stranger."

"I can quite understand that, Mrs Head," I said. And so I could. I never stayed more than three months in one place if I could help it.

She looked into the fire and seemed to try to think. The boss straightened up and stroked her head with his big sun-browned hand, and then put his arm round her shoulders. This brought her back.

"You know we had a station out on the Lachlan, Mr Ellis. Did Walter ever tell you about the time we lived there?"

"No," I said, glancing at the boss. "I know you had a station there; but, you know, the boss doesn't talk much."

"Tell Jack, Maggie," said the boss; "I don't mind."

She smiled. "You know Walter, Mr Ellis," she said. "You won't mind him. He doesn't like me to talk about the children; he thinks it upsets me, but that's foolish: it always relieves me to talk to a stranger." She leaned forward, eagerly it seemed, and went on quickly: "I've been wanting to tell you about the children ever since Walter spoke to me about you. I knew you would understand directly I saw your face. These town people don't understand. I like to talk to a bushman. You know we lost our children out on the station. The fairies took them. Did Walter ever tell you about the fairies taking the children away?"

This was a facer. "I—I beg pardon," I commenced, when Andy gave me a dig in the back. Then I saw it all.

"No, Mrs Head. The boss didn't tell me about that."

"You surely know about the Bush Fairies, Mr Ellis," she said, her big eyes fixed on my face—"the Bush Fairies that look after the little ones that are lost in the bush, and take them away from the bush if they are not found? You've surely heard of them, Mr Ellis? Most bushmen have that I've spoken to. Maybe you've seen them? Andy there has." Andy gave me another dig.

"Of course I've heard of them, Mrs Head," I said; "but I can't swear that I've seen one."

"Andy has. Haven't you, Andy?"

"Of course I have, Mrs Head. Didn't I tell you all about it the last time we were home?"

"And didn't you ever tell Mr Ellis, Andy?"

"Of course he did!" I said, coming to Andy's rescue; "I remember it now. You told me that night we camped on the Bogan River, Andy."

"Of course!" said Andy.

"Did he tell you about finding a lost child and the fairy with it?"

"Yes," said Andy; "I told him all about that."

"And the fairy was just going to take the child away when Andy found it, and when the fairy saw Andy she flew away."

"Yes," I said; "That's what Andy told me."

"And what did you say the fairy was like, Andy?" asked Mrs Head, fixing her eyes on his face.

"Like? It was like one of them angels you see in Bible pictures, Mrs Head," said Andy promptly, sitting bolt upright, and keeping his big innocent grey eyes fixed on hers lest she might think he was telling lies. "It was just like the angel in that Christ-in-the-stable picture we had at home on the station —the right-hand one in blue."

She smiled. You couldn't call it an idiotic smile, nor the foolish smile you see sometimes in melancholy mad people. It was more of a happy childish smile.

"I was so foolish at first, and gave poor Walter and the doctors a lot of trouble," she said. "Of course it never struck me, until afterwards, that the fairies had taken the children."

She pressed the tips of the fingers of both hands to her forehead, and sat so for a while; then she roused herself again——

"But what am I thinking about? I haven't started to tell you about the children at all yet. Auntie! bring the children's portraits, will you, please? You'll find them on my dressing-table."

The old woman seemed to hesitate.

"Go on, Auntie, and do what I ask you," said Mrs Head. "Don't be foolish. You know I'm all right now.

"You mustn't take any notice of Auntie, Mr Ellis," she said with a smile, while the old woman's back was turned. "Poor old body, she's a bit crotchety at times, as old women are. She doesn't like me to get talking about the children. She's got an idea that if I do I'll start talking nonsense, as I used to do the first year after the children were lost. I was very foolish then, wasn't I, Walter?"

"You were, Maggie," said the boss. "But that's all past. You mustn't think of that time any more."

"You see," said Mrs Head, in explanation to me, "at first nothing would drive it out of my head that the children had wandered about until they perished of hunger and thirst in the bush. As if the Bush Fairies would let them do that."

"You were very foolish, Maggie," said the boss; "but don't think about that."

The old woman brought the portraits, a little boy and a little girl: they must have been very pretty children.

"You see," said Mrs Head, taking the portraits eagerly, and giving them to me one by one, "we had these taken in Sydney some years before the children were lost; they were much younger then. Wally's is not a good portrait; he was teething then, and very thin. That's him standing on the chair. Isn't the pose good? See, he's got one hand and one little foot forward, and an eager look in his eyes. The portrait is very dark, and you've got to look close to see the foot. He wants a toy rabbit that the photographer is tossing up to make him laugh. In the next portrait he's sitting on the chair —he's just settled himself to enjoy the fun. But see how happy little Maggie looks! You can see my arm where I was holding her in the chair. She was six months old then, and little Wally had just turned two."

She put the portraits up on the mantelshelf.

"Let me see; Wally (that's little Walter, you know)—Wally was five and little Maggie three and a half when we lost them. Weren't they, Walter?"

"Yes, Maggie," said the boss.

"You were away, Walter, when it happened."

"Yes, Maggie," said the boss—cheerfully, it seemed to me—"I was away."

"And we couldn't find you, Walter. You see," she said to me, "Walter— Mr Head—was away in Sydney on business, and we couldn't find his address. It was a beautiful morning, though rather warm, and just after the break-up of the drought. The grass was knee-high all over the run. It was a lonely place; there wasn't much bush cleared round the homestead, just a hundred yards or so, and the great awful scrubs ran back from the edges of the clearing all round for miles and miles—fifty or a hundred miles in some directions without a break; didn't they, Walter?"

"Yes, Maggie."

"I was alone at the house except for Mary, a half-caste girl we had, who used to help me with the housework and the children. Andy was out on the run with the men, mustering sheep; weren't you, Andy?"

"Yes, Mrs Head."

"I used to watch the children close as they got to run about, because if they once got into the edge of the scrub they'd be lost; but this morning little Wally begged hard to be let take his little sister down under a clump of blue-gums in a corner of the home paddock to gather buttercups. You remember that clump of gums, Walter?"

"I remember, Maggie."

"'I won't go through the fence a step, mumma,' little Wally said. I could see Old Peter—an old shepherd and station-hand we had—I could see him working on a dam we were making across a creek that ran down there. You remember Old Peter, Walter?"

"Of course I do, Maggie."

"I knew that Old Peter would keep an eye to the children; so I told little Wally to keep tight hold of his sister's hand and go straight down to Old Peter and tell him I sent them."

She was leaning forward with her hands clasping her knee, and telling me all this with a strange sort of eagerness.

"The little ones toddled off hand in hand, with their other hands holding fast their straw hats. 'In case a bad wind blowed,' as little Maggie said. I saw them stoop under the first fence, and that was the last that anyone saw of them."

"Except the fairies, Maggie," said the boss quickly.

"Of course, Walter, except the fairies."

She pressed her fingers to her temples again for a minute.

"It seems that Old Peter was going to ride out to the musterers' camp that morning with bread for the men, and he left his work at the dam and started into the bush after his horse just as I turned back into the house, and before the children got near him. They either followed him for some distance or wandered into the bush after flowers and butterflies——" She broke off, and then suddenly asked me, "Do you think the Bush Fairies would entice children away, Mr Ellis?"

The boss caught my eye, and frowned and shook his head slightly.

"No. I'm sure they wouldn't, Mrs Head," I said—"at least not from what I know of them."

She thought, or tried to think, again for a while, in her helpless puzzled way. Then she went on, speaking rapidly, and rather mechanically, it seemed to me—

"The first I knew of it was when Peter came to the house about an hour afterwards, leading his horse, and without the children. I said—I said, 'O my God! where's the children?'" Her fingers fluttered up to her temples.

"Don't mind about that, Maggie," said the boss, hurriedly, stroking her head. "Tell Jack about the fairies."

"You were away at the time, Walter?"

"Yes, Maggie."

"And we couldn't find you, Walter?"

"No, Maggie," very gently. He rested his elbow on his knee and his chin on his hand, and looked into the fire.

"It wasn't your fault, Walter; but if you had been at home do you think the fairies would have taken the children?"

"Of course they would, Maggie. They had to: the children were lost."

"And they're bringing the children home next year?"

"Yes, Maggie—next year."

She lifted her hands to her head in a startled way, and it was some time before she went on again. There was no need to tell me about the lost children. I could see it all. She and the half-caste rushing towards where the children were seen last, with Old Peter after them. The hurried search in the nearer scrub. The mother calling all the time for Maggie and Wally, and growing wilder as the minutes flew past. Old Peter's ride to the musterers' camp. Horsemen seeming to turn up in no time and from nowhere, as they do in a case like this, and no matter how lonely the district. Bushmen galloping through the scrub in all directions. The hurried search the first day, and the mother mad with anxiety as night came on. Her long, hopeless, wild-eyed watch through the night; starting up at every sound of a horse's hoof, and reading the worst in one glance at the rider's face. The systematic work of the search-parties next day and the days following. How those days do fly past. The women from the next run or selection, and some from the town, driving from ten or twenty miles, perhaps, to stay with and try to comfort the mother. ("Put the horse to the cart, Jim: I must go to that poor woman!") Comforting her with improbable stories of children who had been lost for days, and were none the worse for it when they were found. The mounted policemen out with the black trackers. Search-parties cooeeing to each other about the bush, and lighting signal-fires. The reckless break-neck rides for news or more help. And the boss himself, wild-eyed and haggard, riding about the bush with Andy and one or two others perhaps, and searching hopelessly, days after the rest had given up all hope of finding the children alive. All this passed before me as Mrs Head talked, her voice sounding the while as if she were in another room; and when I roused myself to listen, she was on to the fairies again.

"It was very foolish of me, Mr Ellis. Weeks after—months after, I think— I'd insist on going out on the veranda at dusk and calling for the children. I'd stand there and call 'Maggie!' and 'Wally!' until Walter took me inside; sometimes he had to force me inside. Poor Walter! But of course I didn't know about the fairies then, Mr Ellis. I was really out of my mind for a time."

"No wonder you were, Mrs Head," I said. "It was terrible trouble."

"Yes, and I made it worse. I was so selfish in my trouble. But it's all right now, Walter," she said, rumpling the boss's hair. "I'll never be so foolish again."

"Of course you won't, Maggie."

"We're very happy now, aren't we, Walter?"

"Of course we are, Maggie."

"And the children are coming back next year."

"Next year, Maggie."

He leaned over the fire and stirred it up.

"You mustn't take any notice of us, Mr Ellis," she went on. "Poor Walter is away so much that I'm afraid I make a little too much of him when he does come home."

She paused and pressed her fingers to her temples again. Then she said quickly:

"They used to tell me that it was all nonsense about the fairies, but they were no friends of mine. I shouldn't have listened to them, Walter. You told me not to. But then I was really not in my right mind."

"Who used to tell you that, Mrs Head?" I asked.

"The Voices," she said; "you know about the Voices, Walter?"

"Yes, Maggie. But you don't hear the Voices now, Maggie?" he asked anxiously. "You haven't heard them since I've been away this time, have you, Maggie?"

"No, Walter. They've gone away a long time. I hear voices now sometimes, but they're the Bush Fairies' voices. I hear them calling Maggie and Wally to come with them." She paused again. "And sometimes I think I hear them call me. But of course I couldn't go away without you, Walter. But I'm foolish again. I was going to ask you about the other voices, Mr Ellis. They used to say that it was madness about the fairies; but then, if the fairies hadn't taken the children, Black Jimmy, or the black trackers with the police, could have tracked and found them at once."

"Of course they could, Mrs Head," I said.

"They said that the trackers couldn't track them because there was rain a few hours after the children were lost. But that was ridiculous. It was only a thunderstorm."

"Why!" I said, "I've known the blacks to track a man after a week's heavy rain."

She had her head between her fingers again, and when she looked up it was in a scared way.

"Oh, Walter!" she said, clutching the boss's arm; "whatever have I been talking about? What must Mr Ellis think of me? Oh! why did you let me talk like that?"

He put his arm round her. Andy nudged me and got up.

"Where are you going, Mr Ellis?" she asked hurriedly. "You're not going to-night. Auntie's made a bed for you in Andy's room. You mustn't mind me."

"Jack and Andy are going out for a little while," said the boss. "They'll be in to supper. We'll have a yarn, Maggie."

"Be sure you come back to supper, Mr Ellis," she said. "I really don't know what you must think of me—I've been talking all the time."

"Oh, I've enjoyed myself, Mrs Head," I said; and Andy hooked me out.

"She'll have a good cry and be better now," said Andy when we got away from the house. "She might be better for months. She has been fairly reasonable for over a year, but the boss found her pretty bad when he came back this time. It upset him a lot, I can tell you. She has turns now and again, and always ends up like she did just now. She gets a longing to talk about it to a bushman and a stranger; it seems to do her good. The doctor's against it, but doctors don't know everything."

"It's all true about the children, then?" I asked.

"It's cruel true," said Andy.

"And were the bodies never found?"

"Yes." Then, after a long pause, "I found them."

"You did!"

"Yes; in the scrub, and not so very far from home either—and in a fairly clear space. It's a wonder the search-parties missed it; but it often happens that way. Perhaps the little ones wandered a long way and came round in a circle. I found them about two months after they were lost. They had to be found, if only for the boss's sake. You see, in a case like this, and when the bodies aren't found, the parents never quite lose the idea that the little ones are wandering about the bush to-night (it might be years after) and perishing from hunger, thirst, or cold. That mad idea haunts 'em all their lives. It's the same, I believe, with friends drowned at sea. Friends ashore are haunted for a long while with the idea of the white sodden corpse tossing about and drifting round in the water."

"And you never told Mrs Head about the children being found?"

"Not for a long time. It wouldn't have done any good. She was raving mad for months. He took her to Sydney and then to Melbourne—to the best doctors he could find in Australia. They could do no good, so he sold the station—sacrificed everything, and took her to England."

"To England?"

"Yes; and then to Germany to a big German doctor there. He'd offer a thousand pounds where they only wanted fifty. It was no good. She got worse in England, and raved to go back to Australia and find the children. The doctors advised him to take her back, and he did. He spent all his money, travelling saloon, and with reserved cabins, and a nurse, and trying to get her cured; that's why he's droving now. She was restless in Sydney. She wanted to go back to the station and wait there till the fairies brought the children home. She'd been getting the fairy idea into her head slowly all the time. The boss encouraged it. But the station was sold, and he couldn't have lived there anyway without going mad himself. He'd married her from Bathurst. Both of them have got friends and relations here, so he thought best to bring her here. He persuaded her that the fairies were going to bring the children here. Everybody's very kind to them. I think it's a mistake to run away from a town where you're known, in a case like this, though most people do it. It was years before he gave up hope. I think he has hopes yet—after she's been fairly well for a longish time."

"And you never tried telling her that the children were found?"

"Yes; the boss did. The little ones were buried on the Lachlan River at first; but the boss got a horror of having them buried in the bush, so he had them brought to Sydney and buried in the Waverley Cemetery near the sea. He bought the ground, and room for himself and Maggie when they go out. It's all the ground he owns in wide Australia, and once he had thousands of acres. He took her to the grave one day. The doctors were against it; but he couldn't rest till he tried it. He took her out, and explained it all to her. She scarcely seemed interested. She read the names on the stone, and said it was a nice stone, and asked questions about how the children were found and brought here. She seemed quite sensible, and very cool about it. But when he got her home she was back on the fairy idea again. He tried another day, but it was no use; so then he let it be. I think it's better as it is. Now

242

and again, at her best, she seems to understand that the children were found dead, and buried, and she'll talk sensibly about it, and ask questions in a quiet way, and make him promise to take her to Sydney to see the grave next time he's down. But it doesn't last long, and she's always worse afterwards."

We turned into a bar and had a beer. It was a very quiet drink. Andy "shouted" in his turn, and while I was drinking the second beer a thought struck me.

"The boss was away when the children were lost?"

"Yes," said Andy.

"Strange you couldn't find him."

"Yes, it was strange; but *he'll* have to tell you about that. Very likely he will; it's either all or nothing with him."

"I feel damned sorry for the boss," I said.

"You'd be sorrier if you knew all," said Andy. "It's the worst trouble that can happen to a man. It's like living with the dead. It's—it's like a man living with his dead wife."

When we went home supper was ready. We found Mrs Head, bright and cheerful, bustling round. You'd have thought her one of the happiest and brightest little women in Australia. Not a word about children or the fairies. She knew the bush and asked me all about my trips. She told some good bush stories too. It was the pleasantest hour I'd spent for a long time.

"Good night, Mr Ellis," she said brightly, shaking hands with me when Andy and I were going to turn in. "And don't forget your pipe. Here it is! I know that bushmen like to have a whiff or two when they turn in. Walter smokes in bed. I don't mind. You can smoke all night if you like."

"She seems all right," I said to Andy when we were in our room.

He shook his head mournfully. We'd left the door ajar, and we could hear the boss talking to her quietly. Then we heard her speak; she had a very clear voice.

"Yes, I'll tell you the truth, Walter. I've been deceiving you, Walter, all the time, but I did it for the best. Don't be angry with me, Walter! The Voices did come back while you were away. Oh, how I longed for you to come back! They haven't come since you've been home, Walter. You must stay with me a while now. Those awful Voices kept calling me, and telling me lies about the children, Walter! They told me to kill myself; they told me it was all my own fault—that I killed the children. They said I was a drag on you, and they'd laugh—Ha! ha! ha!—like that. They'd say, 'Come on, Maggie; come on, Maggie.' They told me to come to the river, Walter."

Andy closed the door. His face was very miserable.

We turned in, and I can tell you I enjoyed a soft white bed after months and months of sleeping out at night, between watches, on the hard ground or the sand, or at best on a few boughs when I wasn't too tired to pull them down, and my saddle for a pillow.

But the story of the children haunted me for an hour or two. I've never since quite made up my mind as to why the boss took me home. Probably he really did think it would do his wife good to talk to a stranger; perhaps he wanted me to understand—maybe he was weakening as he grew older, and craved for a new word or hand-grip of sympathy now and then.

When I did get to sleep I could have slept for three or four days, but

Andy roused me out about four o'clock. The old woman that they called Auntie was up and had a good breakfast of eggs and bacon and coffee ready in the detached kitchen at the back. We moved about on tiptoe and had our breakfast quietly.

"The wife made me promise to wake her to see to our breakfast and say good-bye to you; but I want her to sleep this morning, Jack," said the boss. "I'm going to walk down as far as the station with you. She made up a parcel of fruit and sandwiches for you and Andy. Don't forget it."

Andy went on ahead. The boss and I walked down the wide silent street, which was also the main road; and wo walked two or three hundred yards without speaking. He didn't seem sociable this morning, or any way sentimental; when he did speak it was something about the cattle.

But I had to speak; I felt a swelling and rising up in my chest, and at last I made a swallow and blurted out:

"Look here, boss, old chap; I'm damned sorry!"

Our hands came together and gripped. The ghostly Australian daybreak was over the Bathurst plains.

We went on another hundred yards or so, and then the boss said quietly:

"I was away when the children were lost, Jack. I used to go on a howling spree every six or nine months. Maggie never knew. I'd tell her I had to go to Sydney on business, or out back to look after some stock. When the children were lost, and for nearly a fortnight after, I was beastly drunk in an out-of-the-way shanty in the bush—a sly-grog shop. The old brute that kept it was too true to me. He thought that the story of the lost children was a trick to get me home, and he swore that he hadn't seen me. He never told me. I could have found those children, Jack. They were mostly new chums and fools about the run, and not one of the three policeman was a bushman. I knew those scrubs better than any man in the country."

I reached for his hand again, and gave it a grip. That was all I could do for him.

"Good-bye, Jack!" he said at the door of the brake-van. "Good-bye, Andy! —keep those bullocks on their feet."

The cattle-train went on towards the Blue Mountains. Andy and I sat silent for a while, watching the guard fry three eggs on a plate over a coal-stove in the centre of the van.

"Does the boss never go to Sydney?" I asked.

"Very seldom," said Andy, "and then only when he has to, on business. When he finishes his business with the stock agents, he takes a run out to Waverley Cemetery perhaps, and comes home by the next train."

After a while I said, "He told me about the drink, Andy—about his being on the spree when the children were lost."

"Well, Jack," said Andy, "that's the thing that's been killing him ever since, and it happened over ten years ago."

TELLING MRS BAKER

Most bushmen who hadn't "known Bob Baker to speak to," had "heard tell of him." He'd been a squatter, not many years before, on the Macquarie River in New South Wales, and had made money in the good seasons, and had gone in for horse-racing and racehorse-breeding, and long trips to Sydney, where he put up at swell hotels and went the pace. So after a pretty severe drought, when the sheep died by thousands on his runs, Bob Baker went under, and the bank took over his station and put a manager in charge.

He'd been a jolly, open-handed, popular man, which means that he'd been a selfish man as far as his wife and children were concerned, for they had to suffer for it in the end. Such generosity is often born of vanity, or moral cowardice, or both mixed. It's very nice to hear the chaps sing "For he's a jolly good fellow," but you've mostly got to pay for it twice—first in company, and afterwards alone. I once heard the chaps singing that I was a jolly good fellow, when I was leaving a place and they were giving me a send-off. It thrilled me, and brought a warm gush to my eyes; but, all the same, I wished I had half the money I'd lent them, and spent on 'em, and I wished I'd used the time I'd wasted to be a jolly good fellow.

When I first met Bob Baker he was a boss drover on the great north-western route, and his wife lived at the township of Solong on the Sydney side. He was going north to new country round by the Gulf of Carpentaria with a big mob of cattle, on a two years' trip; and I and my mate, Andy M'Culloch, engaged to go with him. We wanted to have a look at the Gulf Country.

After we had crossed the Queensland border it seemed to me that the boss was too fond of going into wayside shanties and town pubs. Andy had been with him on another trip, and he told me that the boss was only going this way lately. Andy knew Mrs Baker well, and seemed to think a deal of her. "She's a good little woman," said Andy. "One of the right stuff. I worked on their station for a while when I was a nipper, and I know. She was always a damned sight too good for the boss, but she believed in him. When I was coming away this time she says to me, 'Look here, Andy, I am afraid Robert is drinking again. Now I want you to look after him for me, as much as you can—you seem to have as much influence with him as anyone. I want you to promise me that you'll never have a drink with him.'

"And I promised," said Andy, "and I'll keep my word." Andy was a chap who could keep his word, and nothing else. And, no matter how the boss persuaded, or sneered, or swore at him, Andy would never drink with him.

It got worse and worse; the boss would ride on ahead and get drunk at a shanty, and sometimes he'd be days behind us; and when he'd catch up to us his temper would be just about as much as we could stand. At last he went on a howling spree at Mulgatown, about a hundred and fifty miles north of the border, and, what was worse, he got in tow with a flash barmaid there —one of those girls who are engaged, by the publicans up-country, as baits for chequemen.

He went mad over that girl. He drew an advance cheque from the stock-owner's agent there, and knocked that down; then he raised some more money somehow, and spent that—mostly on the girl.

We did all we could. Andy got him along the track for a couple of stages, and just when we thought he was all right, he slipped us in the night and went back.

We had two other men with us, but had the devil's own bother on account of the cattle. It was a mixed-up job all round. You see it was all big runs round there, and we had to keep the bullocks moving along the route all the time, or else get into trouble for trespass. The agent wasn't going to go to the expense of putting the cattle in a paddock until the boss sobered up; there was very little grass on the route or the travelling-stock reserves or camps, so we had to keep travelling for grass.

The world might wobble and all the banks go bung, but the cattle have to go through—that's the law of the stock-routes. So the agent wired to the owners, and, when he got their reply, he sacked the boss and sent the cattle on in charge of another man. The new boss was a drover coming south after a trip; he had his two brothers with him, so he didn't want me and Andy; but anyway, we were full up of this trip, so we arranged, between the agent and the new boss, to get most of the wages due to us—the boss had drawn some of our stuff and spent it.

We could have started on the back track at once, but, drunk or sober, mad or sane, good or bad, it isn't bush religion to desert a mate in a hole; and the boss was a mate of ours; so we stuck to him.

We camped on the creek outside the town, and kept him in the camp with us as much as possible, and did all we could for him.

"How could I face his wife if I went home without him?" asked Andy, "or any of his old mates?"

The boss got himself turned out of the pub where the barmaid was, and then he'd hang round the other pubs, and get drink somehow, and fight, and get knocked about. He was an awful object by this time, wild-eyed and gaunt, and he hadn't washed or shaved for days.

Andy got the constable in charge of the police station to lock him up for a night, but it only made him worse: we took him back to the camp next morning, and while our eyes were off him for a few minutes he slipped away into the scrub, stripped himself naked, and started to hang himself to a leaning tree with a piece of clothes-line rope. We got to him just in time.

Then Andy wired to the boss's brother Ned, who was fighting the drought, the rabbit pest, and the banks, on a small station back on the border. Andy reckoned it was about time to do something.

Perhaps the boss hadn't been quite right in his head before he started drinking—he had acted queer sometimes, now we came to think of it; maybe he'd got a touch of sunstroke or got brooding over his troubles—anyway he died in the horrors within the week.

His brother Ned turned up on the last day, and Bob thought he was the devil, and grappled with him. It took the three of us to hold the boss down sometimes.

Sometimes, towards the end, he'd be sensible for a few minutes and talk about his "poor wife and children;" and immediately afterwards he'd fall a-cursing me, and Andy, and Ned, and calling us devils. He cursed everything; he cursed his wife and children, and yelled that they were dragging him down to hell. He died raving mad. It was the worst case of death in the horrors of drink that I ever saw or heard of in the bush.

Ned saw to the funeral: it was very hot weather, and men have to be buried quick who die out there in the hot weather—especially men who die in the state the boss was in. Then Ned went to the public-house where the barmaid was and called the landlord out. It was a desperate fight: the publican was a big man, and a bit of a fighting man; but Ned was one of those quiet, simple-minded chaps who will carry a thing through to death when they make up their minds. He gave that publican nearly as good a thrashing as he deserved. The constable in charge of the station backed Ned, while another policeman picked up the publican. Sounds queer to you city people, doesn't it?

Next morning we three started south. We stayed a couple of days at Ned Baker's station on the border, and then started on our three-hundred-mile ride down-country. The weather was still very hot, so we decided to travel at night for a while, and left Ned's place at dusk. He parted from us at the homestead gate. He gave Andy a small packet, done up in canvas, for Mrs Baker, which Andy told me contained Bob's pocket-book, letters, and papers. We looked back, after we'd gone a piece along the dusty road, and saw Ned still standing by the gate; and a very lonely figure he looked. Ned was a bachelor. "Poor old Ned," said Andy to me. "He was in love with Mrs Bob Baker before she got married, but she picked the wrong man—girls mostly do. Ned and Bob were together on the Macquarie, but Ned left when his brother married, and he's been up in these God-forsaken scrubs ever since. Look, I want to tell you something, Jack: Ned has written to Mrs Bob to tell her that Bob died of fever, and everything was done for him that could be done, and that he died easy—and all that sort of thing. Ned sent her some money, and she is to think it was the money due to Bob when he died. Now I'll have to go and see her when we get to Solong; there's no getting out of it, I'll have to face her—and you'll have to come with me."

"Damned if I will!" I said.

"But you'll have to," said Andy. "You'll have to stick to me; you're surely not crawler enough to desert a mate in a case like this? I'll have to lie like hell—I'll have to lie as I never lied to a woman before; and you'll have to back me and corroborate every lie."

I'd never seen Andy show so much emotion.

"There's plenty of time to fix up a good yarn," said Andy. He said no more about Mrs Baker, and we only mentioned the boss's name casually, until we were within about a day's ride of Solong; then Andy told me the yarn he'd made up about the boss's death.

"And I want you to listen, Jack," he said, "and remember every word—and if you can fix up a better yarn you can tell me afterwards. Now it was like this: the boss wasn't too well when he crossed the border. He complained of pains in his back and head and a stinging pain in the back of his neck, and he had dysentery bad—but that doesn't matter; it's lucky I ain't supposed to tell a woman all the symptoms. The boss stuck to the job as long as he could, but we managed the cattle and made it as easy as we could for him. He'd just take it easy, and ride on from camp to camp, and rest. One night I rode to a town off the route (or you did, if you like) and got some medicine for him; that made him better for a while, but at last, a day or two this side of Mulgatown, he had to give up. A squatter there drove him into town in his buggy and put him up at the best hotel. The publican knew the boss and did all he could for him—put him in the best room and wired for another doctor. We wired for Ned as soon as we saw how bad the boss was, and Ned rode night and day and got there three days before the boss died. The boss was a bit off his head some of the time with the fever, but was calm and quiet towards the end and died easy. He talked a lot about his wife and children, and told us to tell the wife not to fret but to cheer up for the children's sake. How does that sound?"

I'd been thinking while I listened, and an idea struck me.

"Why not let her know the truth?" I asked. "She's sure to hear of it sooner or later; and if she knew he was only a selfish, drunken blackguard she might get over it all the sooner."

"You don't know women, Jack," said Andy quietly. "And, anyway, even if she is a sensible woman, we've got a dead mate to consider as well as a living woman."

"But she's sure to hear the truth sooner or later," I said. "The boss was so well known."

"And that's just the reason why the truth might be kept from her," said Andy. "If he wasn't well known—and nobody could help liking him, after all, when he was straight—if he wasn't so well known the truth might leak out unawares. She won't know if I can help it, or at least not yet a while. If I see any chaps that come from the north, I'll put them up to it. I'll tell M'Grath, the publican at Solong, too: he's a straight man—he'll keep his ears open and warn chaps. One of Mrs Baker's sisters is staying with her, and I'll give her a hint so that she can warn off any woman that might get hold of a yarn. Besides, Mrs Baker is sure to go and live in Sydney, where all her people are—she was a Sydney girl; and she's not likely to meet anyone there that will tell her the truth. I can tell her that it was the last wish of the boss that she should shift to Sydney."

We smoked and thought a while, and by and by Andy had what he called a "happy thought." He went to his saddle-bags and got out the small canvas packet that Ned had given him: it was sewn up with packing-thread, and Andy ripped it open with his pocket-knife.

"What are you doing, Andy?" I asked.

"Ned's an innocent old fool, as far as sin is concerned," said Andy. "I guess he hasn't looked through the boss's letters, and I'm just going to see that there's nothing here that will make liars of us."

He looked through the letters and papers by the light of the fire. There were some letters from Mrs Baker to her husband, also a portrait of her and the children; these Andy put aside. But there were other letters from barmaids and women who were not fit to be seen in the same street with the boss's wife; and there were portraits—one or two flash ones. There were two letters from other men's wives too.

"And one of those men, at least, was an old mate of his!" said Andy, in a tone of disgust.

He threw the lot into the fire; then he went through the boss's pocket-book and tore out some leaves that had notes and addresses on them, and burnt them too. Then he sewed up the packet again and put it away in his saddle-bag.

"Such is life!" said Andy, with a yawn that might have been half a sigh.

We rode into Solong early in the day, turned our horses out in a paddock, and put up at M'Grath's pub until such time as we made up our minds as to what we'd do or where we'd go. We had an idea of waiting until the shearing season started and then making out back to the big sheds.

Neither of us was in a hurry to go and face Mrs Baker. "We'll go after dinner," said Andy at first; then after dinner we had a drink, and felt sleepy —we weren't used to big dinners of roast-beef and vegetables and pudding, and, besides, it was drowsy weather—so we decided to have a snooze and then go. When we woke up it was late in the afternoon, so we thought we'd put it off until after tea. "It wouldn't be manners to walk in while they're at tea," said Andy—"it would look as if we only came for some grub."

But while we were at tea a little girl came with a message that Mrs Baker wanted to see us, and would be very much obliged if we'd call up as soon as possible. You see, in those small towns you can't move without the thing getting round inside of half an hour.

"We'll have to face the music now!" said Andy, "and not get out of it." He seemed to hang back more than I did. There was another pub opposite where Mrs Baker lived, and when we got up the street a bit I said to Andy:

"Suppose we go and have another drink first, Andy? We might be kept in there an hour or two."

"You don't want another drink," said Andy, rather short. "Why, you seem to be going the same way as the boss!" But it was Andy who edged off towards the pub when we got near Mrs Baker's place. "All right!" he said. "Come on! We'll have this other drink, since you want it so bad."

We had the drink, then we buttoned up our coats and started across the road—we'd bought new shirts and collars, and spruced up a bit. Half-way across Andy grabbed my arm and asked:

"How do you feel now, Jack?"

"Oh, *I'm* all right," I said.

"For God's sake," said Andy, "don't put your foot in it and make a mess of it."

"I won't, if you don't."

Mrs Baker's cottage was a little weather-board box affair back in a garden.

When we went in through the gate Andy gripped my arm again and whispered:

"For God's sake, stick to me now, Jack!"

"I'll stick all right," I said—"you've been having too much beer, Andy."

I had seen Mrs Baker before, and remembered her as a cheerful, contented sort of woman, bustling about the house and getting the boss's shirts and things ready when we started north. Just the sort of woman that is contented with housework and the children, and with nothing particular about her in the way of brains. But now she sat by the fire looking like the ghost of herself. I wouldn't have recognized her at first. I never saw such a change in a woman, and it came like a shock to me.

Her sister let us in, and after a first glance at Mrs Baker I had eyes for the sister and no one else. She was a Sydney girl, about twenty-four or twenty-five, and fresh and fair—not like the sun-browned women we were used to see. She was a pretty, bright-eyed girl, and seemed quick to understand, and very sympathetic. She had been educated, Andy had told me, and wrote stories for the Sydney *Bulletin* and other Sydney papers. She had her hair done and was dressed in the city style, and that took us back a bit at first.

"It's very good of you to come," said Mrs Baker in a weak, weary voice, when we first went in. "I heard you were in town."

"We were just coming when we got your message," said Andy. "We'd have come before, only we had to see to the horses."

"It's very kind of you, I'm sure," said Mrs Baker.

They wanted us to have tea, but we said we'd just had it. Then Miss Standish (the sister) wanted us to have tea and cake; but we didn't feel as if we could handle cups and saucers and pieces of cake successfully just then.

There was something the matter with one of the children in a back room, and the sister went to see to it. Mrs Baker cried a little quietly.

"You mustn't mind me," she said. "I'll be all right presently, and then I want you to tell me all about poor Bob. It's seeing you, that saw the last of him, that set me off."

Andy and I sat stiff and straight, on two chairs against the wall, and held our hats tight, and stared at a picture of Wellington meeting Blücher on the opposite wall. I thought it was lucky that that picture was there.

The child was calling "mumma," and Mrs Baker went in to it, and her sister came out. "Best tell her all about it and get it over," she whispered to Andy. "She'll never be content until she hears all about poor Bob from someone who was with him when he died. Let me take your hats. Make yourselves comfortable."

She took the hats and put them on the sewing-machine. I wished she'd let us keep them, for now we had nothing to hold onto, and nothing to do with our hands; and as for being comfortable, we were just about as comfortable as two cats on wet bricks.

When Mrs Baker came into the room she brought little Bobby Baker, about four years old; he wanted to see Andy. He ran to Andy at once, and Andy took him up on his knee. He was a pretty child, but he reminded me too much of his father.

"I'm so glad you've come, Andy!" said Bobby.

"Are you, Bobby?"

"Yes. I wants to ask you about daddy. You saw him go away, didn't you?" and he fixed his great wondering eyes on Andy's face.

"Yes," said Andy.

"He went up among the stars, didn't he?"

"Yes," said Andy.

"And he isn't coming back to Bobby any more?"

"No," said Andy. "But Bobby's going to him by and by."

Mrs Baker had been leaning back in her chair, resting her head on her hand, tears glistening in her eyes; now she began to sob, and her sister took her out of the room.

Andy looked miserable. "I wish to God I was off this job!" he whispered to me.

"Is that the girl that writes the stories?" I asked.

"Yes," he said, staring at me in a hopeless sort of way, "and poems too."

"Is Bobby going up among the stars?" asked Bobby.

"Yes," said Andy—"if Bobby's good."

"And auntie?"

"Yes."

"And mumma?"

"Yes."

"Are you going, Andy?"

"Yes," said Andy, hopelessly.

"Did you see daddy go up among the stars, Andy?"

"Yes," said Andy, "I saw him go up."

"And he isn't coming down again any more?"

"No," said Andy.

"Why isn't he?"

"Because he's going to wait up there for you and mumma, Bobby."

There was a long pause, and then Bobby asked:

"Are you going to give me a shilling, Andy?" with the same expression of innocent wonder in his eyes.

Andy slipped half a crown into his hand. "Auntie" came in and told him he'd see Andy in the morning and took him away to bed, after he'd kissed us both solemnly; and presently she and Mrs Baker settled down to hear Andy's story.

"Brace up now, Jack, and keep your wits about you," whispered Andy to me just before they came in.

"Poor Bob's brother Ned wrote to me," said Mrs Baker, "but he scarcely told me anything. Ned's a good fellow, but he's very simple, and never thinks of anything."

Andy told her about the boss not being well after he crossed the border.

"I knew he was not well," said Mrs Baker, "before he left. I didn't want him to go. I tried to persuade him not to go this trip. I had a feeling that I oughtn't to let him go. But he'd never think of anything but me and the children. He promised he'd give up droving after this trip, and get something to do near home. The life was too much for him—riding in all weathers and camping out in the rain, and living like a dog. But he was never content at home. It was all for the sake of me and the children. He wanted to make money and start on a station again. I shouldn't have let him go. He only thought of me and the children! Oh! my poor, dear, kind, dead husband!" She broke down again and sobbed, and her sister comforted her, while Andy and I stared at Wellington meeting Blücher on the field at Waterloo. I thought the artist had heaped up the dead a bit extra, and I thought that I wouldn't like to be trod on by horses even if I was dead.

"Don't you mind," said Miss Standish, "she'll be all right presently," and she handed us the *Illustrated Sydney Journal*. This was a great relief—we bumped our heads over the pictures.

Mrs Baker made Andy go on again, and he told her how the boss broke down near Mulgatown. Mrs Baker was opposite him and Miss Standish opposite me. Both of them kept their eyes on Andy's face: he sat, with his hair straight up like a brush as usual, and kept his big innocent grey eyes fixed on Mrs Baker's face all the time he was speaking. I watched Miss Standish. I thought she was the prettiest girl I'd ever seen; it was a bad case of love at first sight, but she was far and away above me, and the case was hopeless. I began to feel pretty miserable, and to think back into the past; I just heard Andy droning away by my side.

"So we fixed him up comfortable in the wagonette with the blankets and coats and things," Andy was saying, "and the squatter started into Mulga-town. . . . It was about thirty miles, Jack, wasn't it?" he asked, turning suddenly to me. He always looked so innocent that there were times when I itched to knock him down.

"More like thirty-five," I said, waking up.

Miss Standish fixed her eyes on me, and I had another look at Wellington and Blücher.

"They were all very good and kind to the boss," said Andy. "They thought a lot of him up there. Everybody was fond of him."

"I know it," said Mrs Baker. "Nobody could help liking him. He was one of the kindest men that ever lived."

"Tanner, the publican, couldn't have been kinder to his own brother," said Andy. "The local doctor was a decent chap, but he was only a young fellow, and Tanner hadn't much faith in him, so he wired for an older doctor at Mackintyre, and he even sent out fresh horses to meet the doctor's buggy. Everything was done that could be done, I assure you, Mrs Baker."

"I believe it," said Mrs Baker. "And you don't know how it relieves me to hear it. And did the publican do all this at his own expense?"·

"He wouldn't take a penny, Mrs Baker."

"He must have been a good true man. I wish I could thank him."

"Oh, Ned thanked him for you," said Andy, though without meaning more than he said.

"I wouldn't have fancied that Ned would have thought of that," said Mrs Baker. "When I first heard of my poor husband's death, I thought perhaps he'd been drinking again—that worried me a bit."

"He never touched a drop after he left Solong, I can assure you, Mrs Baker," said Andy quickly.

Now I noticed that Miss Standish seemed surprised or puzzled, once or twice, while Andy was speaking, and leaned forward to listen to him; then she leaned back in her chair and clasped her hands behind her head and looked at him, with half-shut eyes, in a way I didn't like. Once or twice she looked at me as if she was going to ask me a question, but I always looked away quick and stared at Blücher and Wellington, or into the empty fire-place, till I felt her eyes were off me. Then she asked Andy a question or two, in all innocence I believe now, but it scared him, and at last he watched his chance and winked at her sharp. Then she gave a little gasp and shut up like a steel trap.

The sick child in the bedroom coughed and cried again. Mrs Baker went to it. We three sat like a deaf-and-dumb institution, Andy and I staring all over the place: presently Miss Standish excused herself, and went out of the room after her sister. She looked hard at Andy as she left the room, but he kept his eyes away.

"Brace up now, Jack," whispered Andy to me, "the worst is coming."

When they came in again Mrs Baker made Andy go on with his story.

"He—he died very quietly," said Andy, hitching round, and resting his elbows on his knees, and looking into the fire-place so as to have his face away from the light. Miss Standish put her arm round her sister. "He died very easy," said Andy. "He was a bit off his head at times, but that was while the fever was on him. He didn't suffer much towards the end—I don't think he suffered at all. . . . He talked a lot about you and the children." (Andy was speaking very softly now.) "He said that you were not to fret, but to cheer up for the children's sake. . . . It was the biggest funeral ever seen round there."

Mrs Baker was crying softly. Andy got the packet half-way of his pocket, but shoved it back again.

"The only thing that hurts me now," said Mrs Baker presently, "is to think of my poor husband buried out there in the lonely bush, so far from home. It's—cruel!" and she was sobbing again.

"Oh, that's all right, Mrs Baker," said Andy, losing his head a little. "Ned will see to that. Ned is going to arrange to have him brought down and buried in Sydney." Which was about the first thing Andy had told her that evening that wasn't a lie. Ned had said he would do it as soon as he sold his wool.

"It's very kind indeed of Ned," sobbed Mrs Baker. "I'd never have dreamed he was so kind-hearted and thoughtful. I misjudged him all along. And that is all you have to tell me about poor Robert?"

"Yes," said Andy—then one of his "happy thoughts" struck him. "Except that he hoped you'd shift to Sydney, Mrs Baker, where you've got friends and relations. He thought it would be better for you and the children. He told me to tell you that."

"He was thoughtful up to the end," said Mrs Baker. "It was just like poor Robert—always thinking of me and the children. We are going to Sydney next week."

Andy looked relieved. We talked a little more, and Miss Standish wanted to make coffee for us, but we had to go and see to our horses. We got up and bumped against each other, and got each other's hats, and promised Mrs Baker we'd come again.

"Thank you very much for coming," she said, shaking hands with us. "I feel much better now. You don't know how much you have relieved me.

Now, mind, you have promised to come and see me again for the last time."

Andy caught her sister's eye and jerked his head towards the door to let her know he wanted to speak to her outside.

"Good-bye, Mrs Baker," he said, holding on to her hand. "And don't you fret. You've—you've got the children yet. It's—it's all for the best; and, besides, the boss said you wasn't to fret." And he blundered out after me and Miss Standish.

She came out to the gate with us, and Andy gave her the packet.

"I want you to give that to her," he said: "it's his letters and papers. I hadn't the heart to give it to her, somehow."

"Tell me, Mr M'Culloch," she said. "You've kept something back—you haven't told her the truth. It would be better and safer for me to know. Was it an accident—or the drink?"

"It was the drink," said Andy. "I was going to tell you—I thought it would be best to tell you. I had made up my mind to do it, but, somehow, I couldn't have done it if you hadn't asked me."

"Tell me all," she said. "It would be better for me to know."

"Come a little farther away from the house," said Andy. She came along the fence a piece with us, and Andy told her as much of the truth as he could.

"I'll hurry her off to Sydney," she said. "We can get away this week as well as next." Then she stood for a minute before us, breathing quickly, her hands behind her back and her eyes shining in the moonlight. She looked splendid.

"I want to thank you for her sake," she said quickly. "You are good men! I like the bushmen! They are grand men—they are noble. I'll probably never see either of you again, so it doesn't matter," and she put her white hand on Andy's shoulder and kissed him fair and square on the mouth. "And you, too!" she said to me. I was taller than Andy, and had to stoop. "Good-bye!" she said, and ran to the gate and in, waving her hand to us. We lifted our hats again and turned down the road.

I don't think it did either of us any harm.

Mary Gilmore in 1934. She had become part of the 'Henry Lawson legend' when as Mary Cameron she came from the country to teach at the Public School at Neutral Bay, on Sydney's North Shore, in 1890. A serious romance between the two was quickly scotched by Henry's mother, Louisa, although they remained friends for life.

Over the years Mary Gilmore became a more than competent journalist, author and poet, was active in politics and various women's rights movements, and played a leading role in furthering Australian Literature for which she was created a Dame of the British Empire in 1938.

Her talents and her services to Australia were recognized on her death in 1962 with a State Funeral. She was then in her ninety-eighth year.

THE SONGS THEY USED TO SING

On the diggings up to twenty odd years ago—and as far back as I can remember —on Lambing Flat, Pipeclay, Gulgong, Home Rule, and so through the roaring list; in bark huts, tents, public houses, sly-grog shanties, and—well, the most glorious voice of all belonged to a bad girl. We were only children and didn't know why she was bad, but we weren't allowed to play near or go near the hut she lived in, and we were trained to believe firmly that something awful would happen to us if we stayed to answer a word, and didn't run away as fast as our legs could carry us, if she attempted to speak to us. We had before us the dread example of one urchin, who got an awful hiding and went on bread and water for twenty-four hours for allowing her to kiss him and give him lollies. She didn't look bad—she looked to us like a grand and beautiful lady-girl—but we got instilled into us the idea that she was an awful bad woman, something more terrible even than a drunken man, and one whose presence was to be feared and fled from. There were two other girls in the hut with her, also a pretty little girl, who called her "Auntie," and with whom we were not allowed to play—for they were all bad; which puzzled us as much as child-minds can be puzzled. We couldn't make out how everybody in one house could be bad. We used to wonder why these bad people weren't hunted away or put in jail if they were so bad. And another thing puzzled us. Slipping out after dark, when the bad girls happened to be singing in their house, we'd sometimes run against men hanging round the hut by ones and twos and threes, listening. They seemed mysterious. They were mostly good men, and we concluded they were listening and watching the bad women's house to see that they didn't kill anyone, or steal and run away with any bad little boys—ourselves, for instance —who ran out after dark; which, as we were informed, those bad people were always on the lookout for a chance to do.

We were told in after years that old Peter McKenzie (a respectable, married, hard-working digger) would sometimes steal up opposite the bad door in the dark, and throw in money done up in a piece of paper, and listen round until the bad girl had sung "The Bonnie Hills of Scotland" two or three times. Then he'd go and get drunk, and stay drunk two or three days at a time. And his wife caught him throwing the money in one night, and there was a terrible row, and she left him; and people always said it was all a mistake. But we couldn't see the mistake then.

But I can hear that girl's voice through the night, twenty years ago:

> Oh! the bloomin' heath, and the pale blue bell,
>   In my bonnet then I wore;
> And memory knows no brighter theme
>   Than those happy days of yore.
> Scotland! Land of chief and song!
> Oh, what charms to thee belong!

And I am old enough to understand why poor Peter McKenzie—who was married to a Saxon, and a Tartar—went and got drunk when the bad girl sang "The Bonnie Hills of Scotland."

> His anxious eye might look in vain
> For some loved form it knew!

And yet another thing puzzled us greatly at the time. Next door to the bad girl's house there lived a very respectable family—a family of good girls with whom we were allowed to play, and from whom we got lollies (those hard old red-and-white "fish lollies" that grocers sent home with parcels of groceries and receipted bills). Now one washing day, they being as glad to get rid of us at home as we were to get out, we went over to the good house and found no one at home except the grown-up daughter, who used to sing for us, and read *Robinson Crusoe* of nights, "out loud," and give us more lollies than any of the rest—and with whom we were passionately in love, notwithstanding the fact that she was engaged to a "grown-up man"—(we reckoned he'd be dead and out of the way by the time we were old enough to marry her). She was washing. She had carried the stool and tub over against the stick fence which separated her house from the bad house; and, to our astonishment and dismay, the bad girl had brought *her* tub over against her side of the fence. They stood and worked with their shoulders to the fence between them, and heads bent down close to it. The bad girl would sing a few words, and the good girl after her, over and over again. They sang very low, we thought. Presently the good grown-up girl turned her head and caught sight of us. She jumped, and her face went flaming red; she laid hold of the stool and carried it, tub and all, away from that fence in a hurry. And the bad grown-up girl took her tub back to her house. The good grown-up girl made us promise never to tell what we saw—that she'd been talking to a bad girl—else she would never, never marry us.

She told me, in after years, when she'd grown up to be a grandmother, that the bad girl was surreptitiously teaching her to sing "Madeline" that day.

I remember a dreadful story of a digger who went and shot himself one night after hearing that bad girl sing. We thought then what a frightfully bad woman she must be. The incident terrified us; and thereafter we kept carefully and fearfully out of reach of her voice, lest we should go and do what the digger did.

I have a dreamy recollection of a circus on Gulgong in the roaring days, more than twenty years ago, and a woman (to my child-fancy a being from another world) standing in the middle of the ring, singing:

> Out in the cold world—out in the street—
> Asking a penny from each one I meet;
> Cheerless I wander about all the day,
> Wearing my young life in sorrow away!

That last line haunted me for many years. I remember being frightened by women sobbing (and one or two great grown-up diggers also) that night in that circus.

"Father, Dear Father, Come Home with Me Now," was a sacred song then, not a peg for vulgar parodies and more vulgar "business" for fourth-rate clowns and corner-men. Then there was "The Prairie Flower." "Out on the prairie, in an early day"—I can hear the digger's wife yet: she was the prettiest girl on the field. They married on the sly and crept into camp after dark; but the diggers got wind of it and rolled up with gold dishes and shovels, and gave them a real good tin-kettling in the old-fashioned style, and a nugget or two to start housekeeping on. She had a very sweet voice.

> Fair as a lily, joyous and free,
> Light of the prairie home was she.

She's a "granny" now, no doubt—or dead.

And I remember a poor, brutally ill-used little wife, wearing a black eye mostly, and singing "Love Amongst the Roses" at her work. And they sang the "Blue Tail Fly," and all the first and best coon songs—in the days when old John Brown sank a duffer on the hill.

The great bark kitchen of Granny Mathews's "Redclay Inn." A fresh back-log thrown behind the fire, which lights the room fitfully. Company settled down to pipes, subdued yarning, and reverie.

Flash Jack—red sash, cabbage-tree hat on back of head with nothing in it, glossy black curls bunched up in front of brim. Flash Jack volunteers, without invitation, preparation, or warning, and through his nose:

> Hoh!
> There was a wild kerlonial youth,
>   John Dowlin was his name!
> He bountied on his parients,
>   Who lived in Castlemaine!

and so on to—

> He took a pistol from his breast
>   And waved that lit—tle toy—

"Little toy" with an enthusiastic flourish and great unction on Flash Jack's part:

> "I'll fight, but I won't surrender!" said
> The wild Kerlonial Boy.

Even this fails to rouse the company's enthusiasm. "Give us a song, Abe! Give us the 'Lowlands!'" Abe Mathews, bearded and grizzled, is lying on the broad of his back on a bench, with his hands clasped under his head—his favourite position for smoking, reverie, yarning, or singing. He had a strong, deep voice, which used to thrill me through and through, from hair to toenails, as a child.

They bother Abe till he takes his pipe out of his mouth and puts it behind his head on the end of the stool:

> The ship was built in Glasgow;
> 'Twas the "Golden Vanitee"—

Lines have dropped out of my memory during the thirty years gone between:

> And she ploughed in the Low Lands, Low!

The public-house people and more diggers drop into the kitchen, as all do within hearing, when Abe sings.

"Now then, boys:

and she ploughed in the Low Lands, Low!

"Now, all together!

The Low Lands! The Low Lands!
And she ploughed in the Low Lands, Low!

Toe and heel and flat of foot begin to stamp the clay floor, and horny hands to slap patched knees in accompaniment.

"Oh! save me, lads!" he cried,
"I'm drifting with the current,
And I'm drifting with the tide!
And I'm sinking in the Low Lands, Low!
The Low Lands! The Low Lands!"

The old bark kitchen is a-going now. Heels drumming on gin-cases under stools; hands, knuckles, pipe-bowls, and pannikins keeping time on the table.

And we sewed him in his hammock,
And we slipped him o'er the side,
And we sunk him in the Low Lands, Low!
The Low Lands! The Low Lands!
And we sunk him in the Low Lands, Low!

Old Boozer Smith—a dirty gin-sodden bundle of rags on the floor in the corner with its head on a candle box, and covered by a horse rug—old Boozer Smith is supposed to have been dead to the universe for hours past, but the chorus must have disturbed his torpor; for, with a suddenness and unexpectedness that makes the next man jump, there comes a bellow from under the horse rug:

Wot though!—I wear!—a rag!—ged coat!
I'll wear it like a man!

and ceases as suddenly as it commenced. He struggles to bring his ruined head and bloated face above the surface, glares round; then, no one questioning his manhood, he sinks back and dies to creation; and subsequent proceedings are only interrupted by a snore, as far as he is concerned.

Little Jimmy Nowlett, the bullock-driver, is inspired. "Go on, Jimmy! Give us a song!"

In the days when we were hard up
For want of wood and wire—

Jimmy always blunders; it should have been *"food and fire"*—

We used to tie our boots up
With lit—tle bits—er wire;

and—

I'm sitting in my lit—tle room,
It measures six by six;
The work-house wall is opposite,
I've counted all the bricks!

"Give us a chorus, Jimmy!"
Jimmy does, giving his head a short, jerky nod for nearly every word,
and describing a circle round his crown—as if he were stirring a pint of
hot tea—with his forefinger, at the end of every line:

Hall!—Round!—Me—Hat!
I wore a weepin' willer!

Jimmy is a Cockney.
"Now then, boys!"

Hall—round—me hat!

How many old diggers remember it?
And:

A butcher, and a baker, and a quiet-looking Quaker,
All a-courting pretty Jessie at the Railway Bar.

I used to wonder as a child what the "railway bar" meant.
And:

I would, I would, I would in vain
That I were single once again!
But ah, alas, that will not be
Till apples grow on the willow tree.

A drunken gambler's young wife used to sing that song—to herself.
A stir at the kitchen door, and a cry of "Pinter," and old Poynton, Ballarat
digger, appears and is shoved in; he has several drinks aboard, and they
proceed to "git Pinter on the singin' lay," and at last talk him round. He
has a good voice, but no "theory," and blunders worse than Jimmy Nowlett
with the words. He starts with a howl:

Hoh!
Way down in Covent Gar-ar-r-dings
A-strolling I did go,
To see the sweetest flow-ow-wers
That e'er in gardings grow.

260

He saw the rose and lily—the red and white and blue—and he saw the sweetest flow-ow-ers that e'er in gardings grew; for he saw two lovely maidens (Pinter calls 'em "virgings") underneath (he must have meant on top of) *"a garding chair,"* sings Pinter.

> And one was lovely Jessie,
> With the jet black eyes and hair,

roars Pinter,

> And the other was a vir-ir-ging,
> I solemn'lye declare!

"Maiden, Pinter!" interjects Mr Nowlett.
"Well, it's all the same," retorts Pinter. "A maiden *is* a virging, Jimmy. If you're singing, Jimmy, and not me, I'll leave off!" Chorus of "Order! Shut up, Jimmy!"

> I quicklye step-ped up to her,
>   And unto her did sa-a-y:
> Do you belong to any young man
>   Hoh, tell me that, I pra-a-y?

Her answer, according to Pinter, was surprisingly prompt and unconventional; also full and concise:

> No; I belong to no young man—
>   I solemnlye declare!
> I mean to live a virging
>   And still my laurels wear!

Jimmy Nowlett attempts to move an amendment in favour of "maiden," but is promptly suppressed. It seems that Pinter's suit has a happy termination, for he is supposed to sing in the character of a "Sailor Bold," and as he turns to pursue his stroll in "Covent Gar-ar-dings":

> "Oh, no! Oh, no! Oh, no!" she cried,
> "I love a Sailor Bold!"

"Hong-kore, Pinter! Give us the 'Golden Glove,' Pinter!"
Thus warmed up, Pinter starts with an explanatory "spoken" to the effect that the song he is about to sing illustrates some of the little ways of women, and how, no matter what you say or do, she is bound to have her own way in the end; also how, in one instance, she set about getting it.

> Hoh!
> Now, it's of a young squoire near Timworth did dwell,
> Who courted a nobleman's daughter so well—

The song has little or nothing to do with the "squire," except so far as "all friends and relations had given consent," and—

The troo-soo was ordered—appointed the day,
And a farmier were appointed for to give her away—

which last seemed a most unusual proceeding, considering the wedding was a toney affair; but perhaps there were personal interests—the nobleman might have been hard up, and the farmer backing him. But there was an extraordinary scene in the church, and things got mixed.

For as soon as this maiding this farmier espied:
"Hoh, my heart! Hoh, my heart!
Hoh, my heart!" then she cried.

Hysterics? Anyway, instead of being wed—

This maiden took sick and she went to her bed.

(N.B.—Pinter sticks to *virging*.)

Whereupon friends and relations and guests left the house in a body (a strange but perhaps a wise proceeding, after all—maybe they smelt a rat) and left her to recover alone, which she did promptly. And then:

Shirt, breeches, and waistcoat this maiding put on,
And a-hunting she went with her dog and her gun,
She hunted all round where this farmier did dwell,
Because in her own heart she love-ed him well.

The cat's out of the bag now:

And often she fired, but no game she killed—

which was not surprising—

Till at last the young farmier came into the field—

No wonder. She put it to him straight:

"Oh, why are you not at the wedding?" she cried,
"For to wait on the squoire, and to give him his bride."

He was as prompt and as delightfully unconventional in his reply as the young lady in Covent Gardings:

"Oh, no! and oh, no! For the truth I must sa-a-y,
I love her too well for to give her a-w-a-a-y!"

which was satisfactory to the disguised "virging."

". . . . and I'd take sword in hand,
And by honour I'd win her if she would command,"

Which was still more satisfactory.

Now this virging, being—

(Jimmy Nowlett: "Maiden, Pinter——" Jim is thrown on a stool and sat on by several diggers.)

Now this maiding, being please-ed to see him so bold,
She gave him her glove that was flowered with gold,

and explained that she found it in his field while hunting around with her dog and her gun. It is understood that he promised to look up the owner. Then she went home and put an advertisement in the local *Herald;* and that ad. must have caused considerable sensation. She stated that she had lost her golden glove, and

The young man that finds it and brings it to me,
Hoh! that very young man my husband shall be!

She had a saving clause in case the young farmer mislaid the glove before he saw the ad., and an *old* bloke got holt of it and fetched it along. But everything went all right. The young farmer turned up with the glove. He was a very respectable young farmer, and expressed his gratitude to her for having *"honour-ed him with her love."* They were married, and the song ends with a picture of the young farmeress milking the cow, and the young farmer going whistling to plough. The fact that they lived and grafted on the selection proves that I hit the right nail on the head when I guessed, in the first place, that the old nobleman was "stony."
In after years,

. . . she told him of the fun,
How she hunted him up with her dog and her gun.

But whether he was pleased or otherwise to hear it, after years of matrimonial experiences, the old song doesn't say, for it ends there.
Flash Jack is more successful with "Saint Patrick's Day."

I come to the river, I jumped it quite clever,
Me wife tumbled in, and I lost her for ever,
St Patrick's own day in the mornin'!

This is greatly appreciated by Jimmy Nowlett, who is suspected, especially by his wife, of being more cheerful when on the roads than when at home.

"Sam Holt" was a great favourite with Jimmy Nowlett in after years.

Oh, do you remember Black Alice, Sam Holt?
Black Alice so dirty and dark—
Who'd a nose on her face—I forget how it goes—
And teeth like a Moreton Bay shark.

Sam Holt must have been very hard up for tucker as well as beauty then, for

> Do you remember the 'possums and grubs
> She baked for you down by the creek?

Sam Holt was, apparently, a hardened Flash Jack.

> You were not quite the cleanly potato, Sam Holt.

Reference is made to his *"manner of holding a flush,"* and he is asked to remember several things which he, no doubt, would rather forget, including

> . . . the hiding you got from the boys.

The song is decidedly personal.

All the camps seem to be singing to-night:

> Ring the bell, watchman!
> Ring! Ring! Ring!
> Ring, for the good news
> Is now on the wing!

Good lines, the introduction:

> High on the belfry the old sexton stands,
> Grasping the rope with his thin bony hands! . . .
> Bon-fires are blazing throughout the land . . .
> Glorious and blessed tidings! Ring! Ring the bell!

Granny Mathews fails to coax her niece into the kitchen, but persuades her to sing inside. She is the girl who learnt *sub rosa* from the bad girl who sang "Madeline." Such as have them on instinctively take their hats off. Diggers, strolling past, halt at the first notes of the girl's voice, and stand like statues in the moonlight:

> Shall we gather at the river,
> Where bright angel feet have trod?
> The beautiful—the beautiful river
> That flows by the throne of God!

Diggers wanted to send that girl "Home," but Granny Mathews had the old-fashioned horror of any of her children becoming "public"—

> Gather with the saints at the river,
> That flows by the throne of God!

But it grows late, or rather, early. The "Eyetalians" go by in the frosty

264

moonlight, from their last shift in the claim (for it is Saturday night), singing a litany.

"Get up on one end, Abe!—stand up all!" Hands are clasped across the kitchen table. Redclay, one of the last of the alluvial fields has petered out, and the Roaring Days are dying. . . . The grand old song that is known all over the world; yet how many in ten thousand know more than one verse and the chorus? Let Peter McKenzie lead:

> Should auld acquaintance be forgot,
> And never brought to min'?

And hearts echo from far back in the past and across wide, wide seas:

> Should auld acquaintance be forgot,
> And days o' lang syne?

Now boys! all together!

> For auld lang syne, my dear,
>   For auld lang syne,
> We'll tak' a cup o' kindness yet,
>   For auld lang syne.
>
> We twa hae run about the braes,
>   And pu'd the gowans fine;
> But we've wandered mony a weary foot,
>   Sin' auld lang syne.

The world was wide then.

> We twa hae paidl't i' the burn,
>   Grae mornin' sun till dine:

the log fire seems to grow watery, for in wide, lonely Australia—

> But seas between us braid hae roar'd,
>   Sin' auld lang syne.

The kitchen grows dimmer, and the forms of the digger-singers seemed suddenly vague and insubstantial, fading back rapidly through a misty veil. But the words ring strong and defiant through hard years:

> And here's a hand, my trusty frien',
>   And gie's a grup o' thine;
> And we'll ta' a cup o' kindness yet,
>   For auld lang syne.

And the nettles have been growing for over twenty years on the spot where Granny Mathews's big bark kitchen stood.

But Sam Holt makes a pile and goes home, leaving many a better and worse man to pad the hoof out back. And—Jim Nowlett sang this with so much feeling as to make it appear a personal affair between him and the absent Holt—

> And, don't you remember the fiver, Sam Holt,
> You borrowed so careless and free?
> I reckon I'll whistle a good many tunes

(with increasing feeling)

> Ere you think of that fiver and me.

For the chances will be that Sam Holt's old mate

> Will be humping his drum on the Hughenden Road
> To the end of the chapter of fate.

An echo from "The Old Bark Hut," sung in the opposition camp across the gully:

> You may leave the door ajar, but if you keep it shut,
> There's no need of suffocation in the Ould Barrk Hut.

> The tucker's in the gin-case, but you'd better keep it shut—
> For the flies will canther round it in the Ould Barrk Hut.

However:

> What's out of sight is out of mind, in the Ould Barrk Hut.
> We washed our greasy moleskins
> On the banks of the Condamine.—

Somebody tackling the "Old Bullock Dray"; it must be over fifty verses now. I saw a bushman at a country dance start to sing that song; he'd get up to ten or fifteen verses, break down, and start afresh. At last he sat down on his heel to it, in the centre of the clear floor, resting his wrist on his knee, and keeping time with an index finger. It was very funny, but the thing was taken seriously all through.

Irreverent echo from the old Lambing Flat trouble, from camp across the gully:

> Rule Britannia! Britannia rules the waves!
> No more Chinamen will enter Noo South Wales!

and

> Yankee Doodle came to town
> On a little pony—
> Stick a feather in his cap,
> And call him Maccaroni!

REEDY RIVER

Ten miles down Reedy River
  A pool of water lies,
And all the year it mirrors
  The changes in the skies.
Within that pool's broad bosom
  Is room for all the stars;
Its bed of sand has drifted
  O'er countless rocky bars.

Around the lower edges
  There waves a bed of reeds,
Where water-rats are hidden
  And where the wild-duck breeds;
And grassy slopes rise gently
  To ridges long and low,
Where groves of wattle flourish
  And native bluebells grow.

Beneath the granite ridges
  The eye may just discern
Where Rocky Creek emerges
  From deep green banks of fern;
And standing tall between them,
  The drooping sheoaks cool
The hard, blue-tinted waters
  Before they reach the pool.

Ten miles down Reedy River
  One Sunday afternoon,
I rode with Mary Campbell
  To that broad, bright lagoon;
We left our horses grazing
  Till shadows climbed the peak,
And strolled beneath the sheoaks
  On the banks of Rocky Creek.

Then home along the river
  That night we rode a race,
And the moonlight lent a glory
  To Mary Campbell's face;
I pleaded for my future
  All through that moonlight ride,
Until our weary horses
  Drew closer side by side.

Ten miles from Ryan's Crossing
  And five below the peak,
I built a little homestead
  On the banks of Rocky Creek;
I cleared the land and fenced it
  And ploughed the rich red loam;
And my first crop was golden
  When I brought Mary home.

Now still down Reedy River
  The grassy sheoaks sigh;
The waterholes still mirror
  The pictures in the sky;
The golden sand is drifting
  Across the rocky bars;
And over all for ever
  Go sun and moon and stars.

But of the hut I builded
  There are no traces now,
And many rains have levelled
  The furrows of my plough.
The glad bright days have vanished;
  For sombre branches wave
Their wattle-blossom golden
  Above my Mary's grave.

Frank Mahony (1862-1916)   *Rounding Up A Straggler* (1889)
91.5 x 127.5 cm   Oil on canvas
Reproduced with the kind permission of the Art Gallery Of New South Wales, Sydney

J. Llewellyn Jones   *The Dry Season* (c. 1889)
76.5 x 45.5 cm   Oil on canvas
Reproduced with the kind permission of the Art Gallery Of New South Wales, Sydney

TO AN OLD MATE

Old Mate! In the gusty old weather,
When our hopes and our troubles were new,
In the years spent in wearing out leather,
I found you unselfish and true—
I have gathered these verses together
For the sake of our friendship and you.

You may think for awhile, and with reason,
Though still with a kindly regret,
That I've left it full late in the season
To prove I remember you yet;
But you'll never judge me by their treason
Who profit by friends—and forget.

I remember, Old Man, I remember—
The tracks that we followed are clear—
The jovial last nights of December,
The solemn first days of the year,
Long tramps through the clearings and timber,
Short partings on platform and pier.

I can still feel the spirit that bore us,
And often the old stars will shine—
I remember the last spree in chorus
For the sake of that other Lang Syne
When the tracks lay divided before us,
Your path through the future, and mine.

Through the frost-wind that cut like whip-lashes,
Through the ever-blind haze of the drought—
And in fancy at times by the flashes
Of light in the darkness of doubt—
I have followed the tent-poles and ashes
Of camps that we moved farther out.

You will find in these pages a trace of
That side of our past which was bright,
And recognize sometimes the face of
A friend who has dropped out of sight—
I send them along in the place of
The letters I promised to write.

THE STORY OF "GENTLEMAN ONCE"

They learn the world from black-sheep,
Who know it all too well.
                                    —*Out Back.*

Peter M'Laughlan, bush missionary, Joe Wilson and his mate, Jack
Barnes, shearers for the present, and a casual swagman named Jack Mitchell,
were camped at Cox's Crossing in a bend of Eurunderee Creek.

It was a grassy little flat with gum-trees standing clear and clean like
a park. At the back was the steep grassy siding of a ridge, and far away
across the creek to the south a spur from the Blue Mountain range ran
west, with a tall, blue granite peak showing clear in the broad moonlight,
yet dream-like and distant over the sweeps of dark green bush.

There was the jingle of hobble-chains and a crunching at the grass
where the horses moved in the soft shadows amongst the trees. Up the
creek on the other side was a surveyors' camp, and from there now and
again came the sound of a good voice singing verses of old songs; and later
on the sound of a violin and a cornet being played, sometimes together
and sometimes each on its own.

Wilson and Barnes were on their way home from shearing out back in
the great scrubs at Beenaway Shed. They had been rescued by Peter
M'Laughlan from a wayside shanty where they had fallen, in spite of
mutual oaths and past promises, sacred and profane, because they had got
wringing wet in a storm on the track and caught colds, and had been
tempted to take just one drink.

They were in a bad way, and were knocking down their cheques
beautifully when Peter M'Laughlan came along. He rescued them and some
of their cash from the soulless shanty-keeper, and was riding home with
them, on some pretence, because he had known them as boys, because Joe

Wilson had a vein of poetry in him—a something in sympathy with something in Peter; because Jack Barnes had a dear little girl-wife who was much too good for him, and who was now anxiously waiting for him in the pretty little farming town of Solong amongst the western spurs. Because, perhaps, of something in Peter's early past which was a mystery. Simply and plainly because Peter M'Laughlan was the kindest, straightest and truest man in the West—a "white man."

They all knew Mitchell and welcomed him heartily when he turned up in their camp, because he was a pathetic humorist and a kindly cynic—a "joker" or "hard case" as the bushmen say.

Peter was about fifty and the other three were young men.

There was another man in camp who didn't count and was supposed to be dead. Old Danny Quinn, champion "beer-chewer" of the district, was on his way out, after a spree, to one of Rouse's stations, where, for the sake of past services—long past—and because of old times, he was supposed to be working. He had spent his last penny a week before and had clung to his last-hope hotel until the landlord had taken him in one hand and his swag in the other and lifted them clear of the veranda. Danny had blundered on, this far, somehow; he was the last in the world who could have told how, and had managed to light a fire; then he lay with his head on his swag and enjoyed nips of whisky in judicious doses and at reasonable intervals, and later on a tot of mutton-broth, which he made in one of the billies.

It was after tea. Peter sat on a log by the fire with Joe and Jack Mitchell on one side and Jack Barnes on the other. Jack Mitchell sat on the grass with his back to the log, his knees drawn up, and his arms abroad on them: his most comfortable position and one which seemed to favour the flow of his philosophy. They talked of bush things or reflected, sometimes all three together, sometimes by turns.

From the surveyors' camp:

I remember, I remember,
  The house where I was born,
The little window where the sun
  Came peeping in at morn——

The breeze from the west strengthened and the voice was blown away.

"That chap seems a bit sentimental but he's got a good voice," said Mitchell. Then presently he remarked, round his pipe:

"I wonder if old Danny remembers?"

And presently Peter said quietly, as if the thought had just occurred to him:

"By the way, Mitchell, I forgot to ask after your old folk. I knew your father, you know."

"Oh, they're all right, Peter, thank you."

"Heard from them lately?" asked Peter, presently, in a lazy tone.

Mitchell straightened himself up. "N—no. To tell the truth, Peter, I haven't written for—I don't know how long."

Peter smoked reflectively.

"I remember your father well, Jack," he said. "He was a big hearted man."

Old Danny was heard remonstrating loudly with spirits from a warmer clime than Australia, and Peter stepped over to soothe him.

"I thought I'd get it, directly after I opened my mouth," said Mitchell. "I suppose it will be your turn next, Joe."

"I suppose so," said Joe, resignedly.

The wind fell.

> I remember, I remember,
>   And it gives me little joy,
> To think I'm further off from heaven,
>   Than when I was a boy!

When Peter came back another thought seemed to have occurred to him.

"How's your mother getting on, Joe?" he asked. "She shifted to Sydney after your father died, didn't she?"

"Oh, she's getting on all right!" said Joe, without elaboration.

"Keeping a boarding-house, isn't she?"

"Yes," said Joe.

"Hard to make ends meet, I suppose?" said Peter. "It's almost a harder life than it could have been on the old selection, and there's none of the old independence about it. A woman like your mother must feel it, Joe."

"Oh, she's all right," said Joe. "She's used to it by this time. I manage to send her a few pounds now and again. I send her all I can," he added resentfully.

Peter sat corrected for a few moments. Then he seemed to change the subject.

"It's some time since you were in Sydney last, isn't it, Joe?"

"Yes, Peter," said Joe. "I haven't been there for two years. I never did any good there. I'm far better knocking about out back."

There was a pause.

"Some men seem to get on better in one place, some in another," reflected Mitchell, lazily. "For my part, I seem to get on better in another."

Peter blinked, relit his pipe with a stick from the fire and reflected.

The surveyor's song had been encored:

> I remember, I remember——

Perhaps Peter remembered. Joe did, but there were no vines round the house where he was born, only drought and dust, and raspy voices raised in recrimination and hardship most times.

"I remember," said Peter, quietly, "I remember a young fellow at home in the old country. He had every advantage. He had a first-class education, a great deal more money than he needed—almost as much as he asked for, and nearly as much freedom as he wanted. His father was an English gentleman and his mother an English lady. They were titled people, if I remember rightly. The old man was proud, but fond of his son; he only asked him to pay a little duty or respect now and again. We don't understand these things in Australia—they seem formal and cold to us. The son paid his respects to his father occasionally—a week or so before he'd be

274

wanting money, as a rule. The mother was a dear lady. She idolized her son. She only asked for a little show of affection from him, a few days or a week of his society at home now and then—say once in three months. But he couldn't spare her even that—his time was taken up so much in fashionable London and Paris and other places. He would give the world to be able to take his proud, soft old father's hand now and look into his eyes as one man who understands another. He would be glad and eager to give his mother twelve months out of the year if he thought it would make her happier. It has been too late for more than twenty years."

Old Danny called for Peter.

Mitchell jerked his head approvingly and gave a sound like a sigh and chuckle conjoined, the one qualifying the other.

"I told you you'd get it, Joe," he said.

"I don't see how it hits me," said Joe.

"But it hit all the same, Joe."

"Well, I suppose it did," said Joe, after a short pause.

"He wouldn't have hit you so hard if you hadn't tried to parry," reflected Mitchell. "It's your turn now, Jack."

Jack Barnes said nothing.

"Now I know that Peter would do anything for a woman or child, or an honest, straight, hard-up chap," said Mitchell, straightening out his legs and folding his arms, "but I can't quite understand his being so partial to drunken scamps and vagabonds, black sheep and ne'er-do-wells. He's got a tremendous sympathy for drunks. He'd do anything to help a drunken man. Ain't it marvellous? It's my private opinion that Peter must have been an awful boozer and scamp in his time."

The other two only thought. Mitchell was privileged. He was a young man of freckled, sandy complexion, and quizzical grey eyes. "Sly Joker;" "Could take a rise out of anyone on the quiet;" "You could never tell when he was getting at you;" "Face of a born comedian," as bushmen said of Mitchell. But he would probably have been a dead and dismal failure on any other stage than that of wide Australia.

Peter came back and they sat and smoked, and maybe they reflected along four very different back-tracks for a while.

The surveyor started to sing again:

> I have heard the mavis singing
> Her love-song to the morn.
> I have seen the dew-drop clinging
> To the rose just newly born.

They smoked and listened in silence all through to the end. It was very still. The full moon was high. The long white slender branches of a box-tree stirred gently overhead; the she-oaks in the creek sighed as they are always sighing, and the southern peak seemed ever so far away.

> That has made me thine forever!
> Bonny Mary of Argyle.

"Blarst my pipe!" exclaimed Mitchell, suddenly. "I beg your pardon, Peter. My pipe's always getting stuffed up," and he proceeded to shell out and clear his pipe.

The breeze had changed and strengthened. They heard the violin playing "Annie Laurie."

"They must be having a Scotch night in that camp to-night," said Mitchell. The voice came again:

> Maxwelton Braes are bonny—
> Where early fa's the dew,
> For 'twas there that Annie Laurie
> Gie me her promise true———

Mitchell threw out his arm impatiently.

"I wish they wouldn't play and sing those old songs," he said. "They make you think of damned old things. I beg your pardon, Peter."

Peter sat leaning forward, his elbows resting on his knees and his hands fingering his cold pipe nervously. His sad eyes had grown haggard and haunted. It is in the hearts of exiles in new lands that the old songs are felt.

"Take no thought of the morrow, Mitchell," said Peter, abstractedly. "I beg your pardon, Mitchell. I mean———"

"That's all right, Peter," said Mitchell. "You're right; to-morrow is the past, as far as I'm concerned."

Peter blinked down at him as if he were a new species.

"You're an odd young man, Mitchell," he said. "You'll have to take care of that head of yours or you'll be found hanging by a saddle-strap to a leaning tree on a lonely track, or find yourself in a lunatic asylum before you're forty-five."

"Or else I'll be a great man," said Mitchell. "But—ah, well!"

Peter turned his eyes to the fire and smiled sadly.

"Not enjoyment and not sorrow, is our destined end or way," he repeated to the fire.

"But we get there just the same," said Mitchell, "destined or not."

> But to live, that each to-morrow,
> Finds us further than to-day!

"Why, that just fits my life, Peter," said Mitchell. "I might have to tramp two or three hundred miles before I get a cut* or a job, and if to-morrow didn't find me nearer than to-day I'd starve or die of thirst on a dry stretch."

"Why don't you get married and settle down, Mitchell?" asked Peter, a little tired. "You're a teetotaller."

"If I got married I couldn't settle down," said Mitchell. "I reckon I'd be the loneliest man in Australia." Peter gave him a swift glance. "I reckon I'd be single no matter how much married I might be. I couldn't get the girl I wanted, and—ah, well!"

Mitchell's expression was still quaintly humorous round the lower part

*Work as a shearer

of his face, but there was a sad light in his eyes. The strange light as of the old dead days, and he was still young.

The cornet had started in the surveyors' camp.

"Their blooming tunes seem to fit in just as if they knew what we were talking about," remarked Mitchell.

The cornet:

> You'll break my heart, you little bird,
> That sings upon the flowering thorn,—
> Thou mind'st me of departed joys,
> Departed never to return.

"Damn it all," said Mitchell, sitting up, "I'm getting sentimental." Then, as if voicing something that was troubling him, "Don't you think a woman pulls a man down as often as she lifts him up, Peter?"

"Some say so," said Peter.

"Some say so, and they write it, too," said Mitchell. "Sometimes it seems to me as if women were fated to drag a man down ever since Adam's time. If Adam hadn't taken his wife's advice—but there, perhaps he took her advice a good many times and found it good, and, just because she happened to be wrong this time, and to get him into a hole, the sons of Adam have never let the daughters of Eve hear the last of it. That's human nature."

Jack Barnes, the young husband, who was suffering a recovery, had been very silent all the evening. "I think a man's a fool to always listen to his wife's advice," he said, with the unreasonable impatience of a man who wants to think while others are talking. "She only messes him up, and drives him to the devil as likely as not, and gets a contempt for him in the end."

Peter gave him a surprised, reproachful look, and stood up. He paced backwards and forwards on the other side of the fire, with his hands behind his back for a while; then he came and settled himself on the log again and filled his pipe.

"Yes," he said, "a man can always find excuses for himself when his conscience stings him. He puts mud on the sting. Man at large is beginning all over the world to rake up excuses for himself; he disguises them as 'Psychological studies,' and thinks he is clean and clever and cultured, or he calls 'em problems—the sex problem, for instance, and thinks he is brave and fearless."

Danny was in trouble again, and Peter went to him. He complained that when he lay down he saw the faces worse, and he wanted to be propped up somehow, so Peter got a pack-saddle and propped the old man's shoulders up with that.

"I remember," Peter began, when he came back to the fire, "I remember a young man who got married——"

Mitchell hugged himself. He knew Jack Barnes. He knew that Jack had a girl-wife who was many times too good for him; that Jack had been wild, and had nearly broken her heart, and he had guessed at once that Jack had broken out again, and that Peter M'Laughlan was shepherding him home. Mitchell had worked as mates with Jack, and liked him because of the good heart that was in him in spite of all; and, because he liked him, he was glad that Jack was going to get a kicking, so to speak, which might do him good. Mitchell saw it coming, as he said afterwards, and filled his pipe, and settled himself comfortably to listen.

"I remember the case of a naturally selfish young man who got married," said Peter. "He didn't know he was selfish; in fact, he thought he was too much the other way—but that doesn't matter now. His name was—well, we'll call him—we'll call him, 'Gentleman Once.'"

"Do you mean Gentleman Once that we saw drinking back at Thomas's shanty?" asked Joe.

"No," said Peter, "not him. There have been more than one in the bush who went by the nickname of 'Gentleman Once.' I knew one or two. It's a big clan, the clan of Gentleman Once, and scattered all over the world."

"By the way," said Mitchell—"excuse me for interrupting, Peter—but wasn't old Danny, there, a gentleman once? I've heard chaps say he was."

"I know he was," said Peter.

"Gentleman Once! Who's talking about Gentleman Once?" said an awful voice, suddenly and quickly. "About twenty or thirty years ago I was called Gentleman Once or Gentleman Jack, I don't know which—Get out! *Get out,* I say! It's all lies, and you're the devil. There's four devils sitting by the fire. I see them."

Two of the four devils by the fire looked round, rather startled.

Danny was sitting up, his awful bloodshot eyes glaring in the firelight, and his ruined head looking like the bloated head of a hairy poodle that had been drowned and dried. Peter went to the old man and soothed him by waving off the snakes and devils with his hands, and telling them to go.

"I've heard Danny on the Gentleman Once racket before," remarked Mitchell. "Seems funny, doesn't it, for a man to be proud of the fact that he was called 'Gentleman Once' about twenty years ago?"

"Seems more awful than funny to me," said Joe.

"You're right, Joe," said Mitchell. "But the saddest things are often funny."

When Peter came back he went on with his story, and was only interrupted once or twice by Danny waking up and calling him to drive off the snakes, and green and crimson dogs with crocodile heads, and devils with flaming tails, and those unpleasant sorts of things that force their company on boozers and madmen.

"Gentleman Once," said Peter, "he came from the old country with a good education and no character. He disgraced himself and family once too often and came, or was sent, out to Australia to reform. It's a great mistake. If a man is too far gone, or hasn't the strength to live the past down and reform at home, he won't do it in a new country, unless a combination of circumstances compels him to it. A man rises by chance; just as often he falls by chance. Some men fall into the habit of keeping steady and stick to it, for the novelty of it, until they are on their feet and in their sane minds and can look at the past, present and future sensibly. I knew one case—— But that's got nothing to do with the story.

"Gentleman Once came out on the remittance system. That system is fatal in nine cases out of ten. The remittance system is an insult to any manhood that may be left in the black sheep, and an insult to the land he is sent to. The cursed quarterly allowance is a stone round his neck which will drag him down deeper in a new land than he would have fallen at home. You know that remittance men are regarded with such contempt in the bush that a man seldom admits he is one, save when he's drunk and reckless and wants money or credit. When a ne'er-do-well lands in Melbourne or Sydney without a penny he will probably buck-up and do something for himself. When he lands with money he will probably spend it all in the first few months and then straighten up, because he has to. But when he lands on the remittance system he drinks, first to drown homesickness. He decides that he'll wait till he gets his next quarter's allowance and then look round. He persuades himself that it's no use trying to do anything: that, in fact, he can't do anything until he gets his money. When he gets it he drifts into one 'last' night with chums he has picked up in second and third-rate hotels. He drinks from pure selfishness. No matter what precautions his friends at home take, he finds means of getting credit or drawing on his allowance before it is due—until he is two or three quarters behind. He drinks because he feels happy and jolly and clever and good-natured and brave and honest while he is drinking. Later on he drinks because he feels the reverse of all these things when he is sober. He drinks to drown the past and repentance. He doesn't know that a healthy-minded man doesn't waste time in repenting. He doesn't know how easy it is to reform, and is too weak-willed to try. He gets a muddled idea that the past can't be mended. He finds it easy to get drink and borrow money on the strength of his next quarter's allowance, so he soon gets a quarter or two behind, and sometimes gets into trouble connected with borrowed money. He drifts to the bush and drinks, to drown the past only. The past grows blacker and blacker until it is a hell without repentance; and often the black sheep gets to that state when a man dreads his sober hours. And the end? Well, you see old Danny there, and you saw old Awful Example back at Thomas's shanty—he's worse than Danny, if anything. Sometimes the end comes sooner. I saw a young new-land-new-leaf man dying in a cheap lodging-house in Sydney. He was a schoolmate of mine, by the way. For six weeks he lay on his back and suffered as I never saw a man suffer in this world; and I've seen some bad cases. They had to chloroform him every time they wanted to move him. He had affected to be hard and cynical, and I must say that he played it out to the end. It was a strong character, a strong mind sodden and diseased with drink. He never spoke of home and his people except when he was delirious. He never spoke, even to me, of his mental agony. That was English home training. You young Australians wouldn't understand it; most bushmen are poets and emotional.

"My old schoolmate was shifted to the Sydney Hospital at last, and consented to the amputation of one leg. But it was too late. He was gone from the hips down. Drink—third-rate hotel and bush shanty drink—and low debauchery."

Jack Barnes drew up his leg and rubbed it surreptitiously. He had "pins and needles." Mitchell noticed and turned a chuckle into a grunt.

"Gentleman Once was a remittance man," continued Peter. "But before he got very far he met an Australian girl in a boarding-house. Her mother was the landlady. They were bush people who had drifted to the city. The girl was pretty, intelligent and impulsive. She pitied him and nursed him. He wasn't known as Gentleman Once then, he hadn't got far enough to merit the nickname."

Peter paused. Presently he jerked his head, as if he felt a spasm of pain, and leaned forward to get a stick from the fire to light his pipe.

"Now, there's the girl who marries a man to reform him, and when she has reformed him never lets him hear the last of it. Sometimes, as a woman, she drives him back again. But this was not one of that sort of girls. I once held a theory that sometimes a girl who has married a man and reformed him misses in the reformed man the something which attracted her in the careless scamp, the something which made her love him—and so she ceases to love him, and their married life is a far more miserable one than it would have been had he continued drinking. I hold no theory of that kind now. Such theories ruin many married lives."

Peter jerked his head again as if impatient with a thought, and reached for a fire-stick.

"But that's got nothing to do with the story. When Gentleman Once reformed his natural selfishness came back. He saw that he had made a mistake. It's a terrible thing for a young man, a few months, perhaps a few weeks, after his marriage, to ask himself the question, 'Have I made a mistake?' But Gentleman Once wasn't to be pitied. He discovered that he had married beneath him in intellect and education. Home training again. He couldn't have discovered that he had married beneath him as far as birth was concerned, for his wife's father had been a younger son of an older and greater family than his own—But Gentleman Once wouldn't have been cad enough to bother about birth. I'll do him that much justice. He discovered, or thought he did, that he and his wife could never have one thought in common; that she couldn't possibly understand him. I'll tell you later on whether he was mistaken or not. He was gloomy most times, and she was a bright, sociable, busy little body. When she tried to draw him out of himself he grew irritable. Besides, having found that they couldn't have a thought in common he ceased to bother to talk to her. There are many men who don't bother talking to their wives; they don't think their wives feel it—because the wives cease to complain after a while; they grow tired of trying to make the man realize how they suffer. Gentleman Once tried his best—according to his lights—and weakness. Then he went in for self-pity and all the problems. He liked to brood, and his poor little wife's energy and cheerfulness were wearying to him. He wanted to be left alone. They were both high-spirited, in different ways; she was highly strung and so was he—because of his past life mostly. They quarrelled badly sometimes. Then he drank again and she stuck to him. Perhaps the only time he seemed cheerful and affectionate was when he had a few drinks in him. It was a miserable existence—a furnished room in a cheap lodging-house, and the use of the kitchen.

"He drank alone.

"Now a dipsomaniac mostly thinks he is in the right—except, perhaps, after he has been forced to be sober for a week. The noblest woman in the world couldn't save him—everything she does to reform him irritates him; but a strong friend can save him sometimes—a man who has been through it himself. The poor little wife of Gentleman Once went through it all. And she stuck to him. She went into low pubs after him."

Peter shuddered again.

"She went through it all. He swore promises. He'd come home sober and fill her with hope of future happiness, and swear that he'd never take another glass. 'And we'll be happy yet, my poor boy,' she'd say, 'we'll be happy yet. I believe you, I trust you' (she used to call him her 'bonny boy' when they were first married). And the next night he'd come home worse than ever. And one day he—he struck her!"

Peter shuddered, head and shoulders, like a man who had accidentally smashed his finger.

"And one day he struck her. He was sober when he did it—anyhow he had not taken drink for a week. A man is never sober who gets drunk more than once a week, though he might think he is. I don't know how it happened, but anyway he struck her, and that frightened him. He got a billet in the Civil Service up-country. No matter in what town it was. The little wife hoped for six months.

"I think it's a cruel thing that a carelessly selfish young man cannot realize how a sensitive young wife suffers for months after he has reformed. How she hopes and fears, how she dreads the moment he has to leave her, and frets every hour he is away from home—and suffers mental agony when he is late. How the horror of the wretched old past time grows upon her until she dares not think of it. How she listens to his step and voice and watches his face, when he comes home, for a sign of drink. A young man, a mate of mine, who drank hard and reformed, used to take a delight in pretending for a few minutes to be drunk when he came home. He was good-hearted, but dense. He said he only did it to give his wife a pleasant surprise afterwards. I thought it one of the most cruel things I had ever seen.

"Gentleman Once found that he could not stand the routine of office work and the dull life in that place. He commenced to drink again, and went on till he lost his billet. They had a little boy, a bright little boy, yet the father drank.

"The last spree was a terrible one. He was away from home a fortnight, and in that fortnight he got down as deep as a man could get. Then another man got hold of him and set him on his feet, and straightened him up. The other man was a ruined doctor, a wreck whose devil was morphia. I don't hold that a man's salvation is always in his own hands; I've seen mates pull mates out of hell too often to think that.

"Then Gentleman Once saw the past as he had never seen it before—he saw hope for the future with it. And he swore an oath that he felt he would keep.

"He suffered from reaction on his way home, and, as he neared the town, a sudden fear, born of his nervous state, no doubt, sent a cold, sick emptiness through him: 'Was it too late?'

"As he turned into the street where he lived, he noticed a little group

281

of bush larrikins standing at the corner. And they moved uneasily when they caught sight of him, and, as he passed, they touched and lifted their hats to him. Now he knew that he had lost the respect even of bush larrikins; and he knew enough of the bush to know that a bushman never lifts his hat to a man—only to death, and a woman sometimes. He hurried home and read the truth in his wife's eyes. His little boy was dead. He went down under the blow, and she held his head to her breast and kept saying, 'My poor boy, my poor boy!'

"It was he that she meant, not the boy she had lost. She knew him, she understood him better than he did himself, and, heart-broken as she was, she knew how he was going to suffer, and comforted him. 'My poor boy, my poor, foolish boy!'"

"LORD DOUGLAS"

They hold him true, who's true to one,
However false he be.
                    —*The Rouseabout of Rouseabouts.*

The Imperial Hotel was rather an unfortunate name for an out-back town pub, for out back is the stronghold of Australian democracy; it was the out-back vote and influence that brought about "One Man One Vote," "Payment of Members," and most of the democratic legislation of late years, and from out back came the overwhelming vote in favour of Australian as against Imperial Federation.

The name Royal Hotel is as familiar as that of the Railway Hotel, and passes unnoticed and ungrowled at, even by bush republicans. The Royal Hotel at Bourke was kept by an Irishman, one O'Donohoo, who was Union to the backbone, loudly in favour of "Australia for the Australians," and, of course, against even the democratic New South Wales Government of the time. He went round town all one St Patrick's morning with a bunch of green ribbon fastened to his coat-tail with a large fish-hook, and wasn't aware of the fact till he sat down on the point of it. But that's got nothing to do with it.

Some of the author's old-time radical friends thought they detected a weakening of his hitherto hard-line socialism when they first read this story.

The Imperial Hotel at Bourke was unpopular from the first. It was said that the very existence of the house was the result of a swindle. It had been built with money borrowed on certain allotments in the centre of the town and on the understanding that it should be built on the mortgaged land, whereas it was erected on a free allotment. Which fact was discovered, greatly to its surprise, by the building society when it came to foreclose on the allotments some years later. While the building was being erected the Bourke people understood, in a vague way, that it was to be a convent (perhaps the building society thought so, too), and when certain ornaments in brick and cement in the shape of a bishop's mitre were placed over the corners of the walls the question seemed decided. But when the place was finished a bar was fitted up, and up went the sign, to the disgust of the other publicans, who didn't know a licence had been taken out—for licensing didn't go by local option in those days. It was rumoured that the place belonged to, and the whole business was engineered by, a priest. And priests are men of the world.

The Imperial Hotel was patronized by the pastoralists, the civil servants, the bank manager and clerks—all the scrub aristocracy; it was the headquarters of the Pastoralists' Union in Bourke; a barracks for blacklegs brought up from Sydney to take the place of Union shearers on strike; and the new Governor, on his inevitable visit to Bourke, was banqueted at the Imperial Hotel. The editor of the local "capitalistic rag" stayed there; the pastoralists' member was elected mostly by dark ways and means devised at the Imperial Hotel, and one of its managers had stood as a dummy candidate to split the Labour vote; the management of the hotel was his reward. In short, it was there that most of the plots were hatched to circumvent Freedom, and put away or deliver into the clutches of law and order certain sons of Light and Liberty who believed in converting blacklegs into jellies by force of fists when bribes, gentle persuasion and pure Australian language failed to convert them to clean Unionism. The Imperial Hotel was called the "Squatters' Pub," the "Scabbery," and other and more expressive names.

The hotel became still more unpopular after Percy Douglas had managed

283

it for a while. He was an avowed enemy of Labour Unionists. He employed Chinese cooks, and that in the height of the anti-Chinese agitation in Australia, and he was known to have kindly feelings towards the Afghans who, with their camels, were running white carriers off the roads. If an excited Unionist called a man a "blackleg" or "scab" in the Imperial bar he was run out— sometimes with great difficulty, and occasionally as far as the lock-up.

Percy Douglas was a fine-looking man, "wid a chest on him an' well hung —a fine fee-*gure* of a man," as O'Donohoo pronounced it. He was tall and erect, he dressed well, wore small side-whiskers, had an eagle nose, and looked like an aristocrat. Like many of his type, who start sometimes as billiard-markers and suddenly become hotel managers in Australia, nothing was known of his past. Jack Mitchell reckoned, by the way he treated his employees and spoke to workmen, that he was the educated son of an English farmer—gone wrong and sent out to Australia. Someone called him "Lord Douglas," and the nickname caught on.

He made himself well hated. He got One-eyed Bogan "three months' hard" for taking a bottle of whisky off the Imperial bar counter because he (Bogan) was drunk and thirsty and had knocked down his cheque, and because there was no one minding the bar at the moment.

Lord Douglas dismissed the barmaid, and, as she was leaving, he had her boxes searched and gave her in charge for stealing certain articles belonging to the hotel. The chaps subscribed to defend the case, and subsequently put a few pounds together for the girl. She proved her gratitude by bringing a charge of a baby against one of the chaps—but that was only one of the little ways of the world, as Mitchell said. She joined a Chinese camp later on.

Lord Douglas employed a carpenter to do some work about the hotel, and because the carpenter left before the job was finished, Lord Douglas locked his tools in an outhouse and refused to give them up; and when the carpenter, with the spirit of an Australian workman, broke the padlock and removed his tool-chest, the landlord gave him in charge for breaking and entering. The chaps defended the case and won it, and hated Lord Douglas as much as if he were their elder brother. Mitchell was the only one to put in a word for him.

"I've been puzzling it out," said Mitchell, as he sat nursing his best leg in the Union Office, "and, as far as I can see, it all amounts to this—we're all mistaken in Lord Douglas. We don't know the man. He's all right. We don't understand him. He's really a sensitive, good-hearted man who's been shoved a bit off the track by the world. It's the world's fault—he's not to blame. You see, when he was a youngster he was the most good-natured kid in the school; he was always soft, and, consequently, he was always being imposed upon, and bullied, and knocked about. Whenever he got a penny to buy lollies he'd count 'em out carefully and divide 'em round amongst his school-mates and brothers and sisters. He was the only one that worked at home, and consequently they all hated him. His father respected him, but didn't love him, because he wasn't a younger son, and wasn't bringing his father's grey hairs down in sorrow to the grave. If it was in Australia, probably Lord Douglas was an elder son and had to do all the hard graft, and teach himself at night, and sleep in a bark skillion while his younger brothers benefited— they were born in the new brick house and went to boarding-schools. His mother had a contempt for him because he wasn't a black sheep and a prodigal, and, when the old man died, the rest of the family got all the stuff and Lord Douglas was kicked out because they could do without him now. And the family hated him like poison ever afterwards (especially his mother), and spread lies about him—because they had treated him shamefully and because his mouth was shut—they knew he wouldn't speak. Then probably he went in for Democracy and worked for Freedom, till Freedom trod on him once too often with her hob-nailed boots. Then the chances are, in the end, he was ruined by a girl or woman, and driven, against his will, to take refuge in pure individualism. He's all right, only we don't appreciate him. He's only fighting against his old ideals—his old self that comes up sometimes—and that's what makes him sweat his barmaids and servants, and hate us, and run us in; and perhaps when he cuts up extra rough it's because his conscience kicks him when he thinks of the damned soft fool he used to be. He's all right—take my word for it. It's all a mask. Why, he might be one of the kindest-hearted men in Bourke underneath."

Tom Hall rubbed his head and blinked, as if he was worried by an idea that there might be some facts in Mitchell's theories.

"You're allers findin' excuses for blacklegs an' scabs, Mitchell," said Barcoo-Rot, who took Mitchell seriously (and who would have taken a laughing jackass seriously). "Why, you'd find a white spot on a squatter. I wouldn't be surprised if you blacklegged yourself in the end."

This was an unpardonable insult, from a Union point of view, and the chaps half-unconsciously made room on the floor for Barcoo-Rot to fall after Jack Mitchell hit him. But Mitchell took the insult philosophically.

"Well, Barcoo-Rot," he said, nursing the other leg, "for the matter of that, I did find a white spot on a squatter once. He lent me a quid when I was hard up. There's white spots on the blackest characters if you only drop prejudice and look close enough. I suppose even Jack-the-Ripper's character was speckled. Why, I can even see spots on your character, sometimes, Barcoo-Rot. I've known white spots to spread on chaps' characters until they were little short of saints. Sometimes I even fancy I can feel my own wings sprouting. And as for turning blackleg—well, I suppose I've got a bit of the crawler in my composition (most of us have), and a man never knows what might happen to his principles."

"Well," said Barcoo-Rot, "I beg yer pardon—ain't that enough?"

"No," said Mitchell, "you ought to wear a three-bushel bag and ashes for three months, and drink water; but since the police would send you to an asylum if you did that, I think the best thing we can do is to go out and have a drink."

Lord Douglas married an Australian girl somewhere, somehow, and brought her to Bourke, and there were two little girls—regular little fairies. She was a gentle, kind-hearted little woman, but she didn't seem to improve him much, save that he was very good to her.

"It's mostly that way," commented Mitchell. "When a boss gets married and has children he thinks he's got a greater right to grind his fellowmen and rob their wives and children. I'd never work for a boss with a big family—it's hard enough to keep a single boss nowadays in this country."

After one stormy election, at the end of a long and bitter shearing strike, One-eyed Bogan, his trusty enemy, Barcoo-Rot, and one or two other enthusiastic reformers were charged with rioting, and got from one to three months' hard. And they had only smashed three windows of the Imperial Hotel and chased the Chinese cook into the river.

"I used to have some hopes for Democracy," commented Mitchell, "but I've got none now. How can you expect Liberty, Equality or Fraternity—how can you expect Freedom and Universal Brotherhood and Equal Rights in a country where Sons of Light get three months' hard for breaking windows and bashing a Chinaman? It almost makes me long to sail away in a gallant barque."

There were other cases in connection with the rotten-egging of Capitalistic candidates on the Imperial Hotel balcony, and it was partly on the evidence of Douglas and his friends that certain respectable Labour leaders got heavy terms of imprisonment for rioting and "sedition" and "inciting" in connection with organized attacks on blacklegs and their escorts.

Retribution, if it was retribution, came suddenly and in a most unexpected manner to Lord Douglas.

It seems he employed a second carpenter for six months to repair and make certain additions to the hotel, and put him off under various pretences until he owed him a hundred pounds or thereabout. At last, immediately after an exciting interview with Lord Douglas, the carpenter died suddenly of heart disease. The widow, a strong-minded bushwoman, put a bailiff in the hotel on very short notice—and against the advice of her lawyer, who thought the case hopeless—and the Lord Douglas bubble promptly burst. He had somehow come to be regarded as the proprietor of the hotel, but now the real proprietors or proprietor—he was still said to be a priest—turned Douglas out and put in a new manager. The old servants were paid after some trouble. The local storekeepers and one or two firms in Sydney, who had large accounts against the Imperial Hotel (and had trusted it, mainly because it was patronized by Capitalism and Fat), were never paid.

Lord Douglas cleared out to Sydney, leaving his wife and children, for the present, with her brother, a hay-and-corn storekeeper, who also had a large and hopeless account against the hotel; and when the brother went broke and left the district she rented a two-roomed cottage and took in dressmaking.

Dressmaking didn't pay so well in the bush then as it did in the old digging days when sewing-machines were scarce and the possession of one meant an independent living to any girl—when diggers paid ten shillings for a strip of "flannen" doubled over and sewn together, with holes for arms and head, and called a shirt. Mrs Douglas had a hard time, with her two little girls, who were still better and more prettily dressed than any other children in Bourke. One grocer still called on her for orders and pretended to be satisfied to wait "till Mr Douglas came back," and when she would no longer order what he considered sufficient provisions for her and the children, and commenced buying sugar, etc., by the pound, for cash, he one day sent a box of groceries round to her. He pretended it was a mistake.

"However," he said, "I'd be very much obliged if you could use 'em, Mrs Douglas. I'm overstocked now; haven't got room for another tin of sardines in the shop. Don't you worry about bills, Mrs Douglas; I can wait till Douglas comes home. I did well enough out of the Imperial Hotel when your husband

Julian Ashton (1851-1942)   *A Solitary Ramble* (1888)
35.6 x 25.7 cm   Watercolour
Reproduced with the kind permission of the Art Gallery Of New South Wales, Sydney

David Davies (1862-1939)   *From a distant land* (1899)
Detail Only   81.9 x 114.9 cm   Oil on canvas
Reproduced with the kind permission of the Art Gallery Of New South Wales, Sydney

had it, and a pound's worth of groceries won't hurt me now. I'm only too glad to get rid of some of the stock."

She cried a little, thought of the children, and kept the groceries.

"I suppose I'll be sold up soon meself if things don't git brighter," said that grocer to a friend, "so it doesn't matter much."

The same with Foley the butcher, who had a brogue with a sort of drawling groan in it, and was a cynic of the Mitchell school.

"You see," he said, "she's as proud as the devil, but when I send round a bit o' rawst, or porrk, or the undercut o' the blade-bawn, she thinks o' the little gur-r-rls before she thinks o' sendin' it back to me. That's where I've got the pull on her."

The Giraffe borrowed a horse and tip-dray one day at the beginning of winter and cut a load of firewood in the bush, and next morning, at daylight, Mrs Douglas was nearly startled out of her life by a crash at the end of the cottage, which made her think that the chimney had fallen in, or a tree fallen on the house; and when she slipped on a wrapper and looked out, she saw a load of short-cut wood by the chimney, and caught a glimpse of the back view of the Giraffe, who stood in the dray with his legs wide apart and was disappearing into the edge of the scrub; and soon the rapid clock-clock-clock of the wheels died away in the west, as if he were making for West Australia.

The next we heard of Lord Douglas he had got two years' hard for embezzlement in connection with some canvassing he had taken up. Mrs Douglas fell ill—a touch of brain-fever—and one of the labourers' wives took care of the children while two others took turns in nursing. While she was recovering, Bob Brothers sent round the hat, and, after a conclave in the Union Office—as mysterious as any meeting ever called with the object of downing bloated Capitalism—it was discovered that one of the chaps—who didn't wish his name to be mentioned—had borrowed just twenty-five pounds from Lord Douglas in the old days and now wished to return it to Mrs Douglas. So the thing was managed, and if she had any suspicions she kept them to herself. She started a little fancy goods shop and got along fairly comfortable.

Douglas, by the way, was publicly supposed, for her sake and because of the little girls, to be away in West Australia on the goldfields.

Time passes without much notice out back, and one hot day, when the sun hung behind the fierce sandstorms from the north-west as dully lurid as he ever showed in a London fog, Lord Douglas got out of the train that had just finished its five-hundred-miles' run, and not seeing a new chum porter, who started forward by force of habit to take his bag, he walked stiffly off the platform and down the main street towards his wife's cottage.

He was very gaunt, and his eyes, to those who passed him closely, seemed to have a furtive, hunted expression. He had let his beard grow, and it had grown grey.

It was within a few days of Christmas—the same Christmas that we lost the Pretty Girl in the Salvation Army. As a rule the big shearing-sheds within a fortnight of Bourke cut out in time for the shearers to reach the town and have their Christmas dinners and sprees—and for some of them to be locked up over Christmas Day—within sound of a church-going bell. Most of the chaps gathered in the Shearers' Union Office on New Year's Eve and discussed Douglas amongst other things.

"I vote we kick the cow out of the town!" snarled One-eyed Bogan, viciously.

"We can't do that," said Bob Brothers (the Giraffe), speaking more promptly than usual. "There's his wife and youngsters to consider, ye know."

"He something well deserted his wife," snarled Bogan, "an' now he comes crawlin' back to her to keep him."

"Well," said Mitchell, mildly, "but we ain't all got as much against him as you have, Bogan."

"He made a crimson jail-bird of me!" snapped Bogan.

"Well," said Mitchell, "that didn't hurt you much, anyway; it rather improved your character if anything. Besides, he made a jail-bird of himself afterwards, so you ought to have a fellow-feeling—a feathered feeling, so to speak. Now you needn't be offended, Bogan, we're all jail-birds at heart, only we haven't all got the pluck."

"I'm in favour of blanky well tarrin' an' featherin' him an' kickin' him out of the town!" shouted Bogan. "It would be a good turn to his wife, too; she'd be well rid of the ——."

"Perhaps she's fond of him," suggested Mitchell; "I've known such cases before. I saw them sitting together on the veranda last night when they thought no one was looking."

"He deserted her," said One-eyed Bogan, in a climbing-down tone, "and left her to starve."

"Perhaps the police were to blame for that," said Mitchell. "You know you deserted all your old mates once for three months, Bogan, and it wasn't your fault."

"He seems to be a crimson pet of yours, Jack Mitchell," said Bogan, firing up.

"Ah, well, all I know," said Mitchell, standing up and stretching himself wearily, "all I know is that he looked like a gentleman once, and treated us like a gentleman, and cheated us like a gentleman, and ran some of us in like a gentleman, and, as far as I can see, he's served his time like a gentleman and come back to face us and live himself down like a man. I always had a sneaking regard for a gentleman."

"Why, Mitchell, I'm beginning to think you are a gentleman yourself," said Jake Boreham.

"Well," said Mitchell, "I used to have a suspicion once that I had a drop of blue blood in me somewhere, and it worried me a lot; but I asked my old mother about it one day, and she scalded me—God bless her!—and father chased me with a stockwhip, so I gave up making inquiries."

"You'll join the bloomin' Capitalists next," sneered One-eyed Bogan.

"I wish I could, Bogan," said Mitchell. "I'd take a trip to Paris and see for myself whether the Frenchwomen are as bad as they're made out to be, or go to Japan. But what are we going to do about Douglas?"

"Kick the skunk out of town, or boycott him!" said one or two. "He ought to be tarred and feathered and hanged."

"Couldn't do worse than hang him," commented Jake Boreham, cheerfully.

"Oh, yes, we could," said Mitchell, sitting down, resting his elbows on his knees, and marking his points with one forefinger on the other. "For instance, we might boil him slow in tar. We might skin him alive. We might put him in a cage and poke him with sticks, with his wife and children in another cage to look on and enjoy the fun."

The chaps, who had been sitting quietly listening to Mitchell, and grinning, suddenly became serious and shifted their positions uneasily.

"But I can tell you what would hurt his feelings more than anything else we could do," said Mitchell.

"Well, what is it, Jack?" said Tom Hall, rather impatiently.

"Send round the hat and take up a collection for him," said Mitchell, "enough to let him get away with his wife and children and start life again in some less respectable town than Bourke. You needn't grin, I'm serious about it."

There was a thoughtful pause, and one or two scratched their heads.

"His wife seems pretty sick," Mitchell went on in a reflective tone. "I passed the place this morning and saw him scrubbing out the floor. He's been doing a bit of house-painting for old Heegard to-day. I suppose he learnt it in jail. I saw him at work and touched my hat to him."

"What!" cried Tom Hall, affecting to shrink from Mitchell in horror.

"Yes," said Mitchell, "I'm not sure that I didn't take my hat off. Now I know it's not bush religion for a man to touch his hat, except to a funeral, or a strange roof or woman sometimes; but when I meet a braver man than myself I salute him. I've only met two in my life."

"And who were they, Jack?" asked Jake Boreham.

"One," said Mitchell—"one is Douglas, and the other—well, the other was the man I used to be. But that's got nothing to do with it."

"But perhaps Douglas thought you were crowing over him when you took off your hat to him—sneerin' at him, like, Mitchell," reflected Jake Boreham.

"No, Jake," said Mitchell, growing serious suddenly. "There are ways of doing things that another man understands."

They all thought for a while.

"Well," said Tom Hall, "supposing we do take up a collection for him, he'd be too damned proud to take it."

"But that's where we've got the pull on him," said Mitchell, brightening up. "I heard Dr Morgan say that Mrs Douglas wouldn't live if she wasn't sent away to a cooler place, and Douglas knows it; and, besides, one of the little girls is sick. We've got him in a corner and he'll have to take the stuff. Besides, two years in jail takes a lot of the pride out of a man."

"Well, I'm damned if I'll give a sprat to help the man who tried his best to crush the Unions!" said One-eyed Bogan.

"Damned if I will either!" said Barcoo-Rot.

"Now, look here, One-eyed Bogan," said Mitchell, "I don't like to harp on old things, for I know they bore you, but when you returned to public life that time no one talked of kicking you out of the town. In fact, I heard that the chaps put a few pounds together to help you get away for a while till you got over your modesty."

No one spoke.

"I passed Douglas's place on my way here from my camp to-night," Mitchell went on musingly, "and I saw him walking up and down in the yard with his sick child in his arms. You remember that little girl, Bogan? I saw her run and pick up your hat and give it to you one day when you were trying to put it on with your feet. You remember, Bogan? The shock nearly sobered you."

There was a very awkward pause. The position had become too psychological altogether and had to be ended somehow. The awkward silence had to be broken, and Bogan broke it. He turned up Bob Brothers's hat, which was lying on the table, and chucked in a quid, qualifying the hat and the quid, and disguising his feelings with the national oath of the land.

"We've had enough of this gory, maudlin, sentimental tommy-rot," he said. "Here, Barcoo, stump up or I'll belt it out of your hide! I'll—I'll take yer to pieces!"

But Douglas didn't leave the town. He sent his wife and children to Sydney until the heat wave was past, built a new room on to the cottage, and started a book and newspaper shop, and a poultry farm in the back paddock, and flourished.

They called him Mr Douglas for a while, then Douglas, then Percy Douglas, and now he is well-known as Old Daddy Douglas, and the Sydney *Worker*, *Truth*, and *Bulletin*, and other democratic rags are on sale at his shop. He is big with schemes for locking the Darling River, and he gets his drink at O'Donohoo's. He is scarcely yet regarded as a straight-out democrat. He was a gentleman once, Mitchell said, and the old blood was not to be trusted. But, last elections, Douglas worked quietly for Unionism, and gave the leaders certain hints, and put them up to various electioneering dodges which enabled them to return, in the face of Monopoly, a Labour member who is as likely to go straight as long as any other Labour member.

292

THE GHOSTS OF MANY CHRISTMASES

Did you ever trace back your Christmas days?—right back to the days when you were innocent and Santa Claus was real. At times you thought you were very wicked, but you never realize how innocent you were until you've grown up and knocked about the world.

Let me think!

Christmas in an English village, with bare hedges and trees, and leaden skies that lie heavy on our souls as we walk, with overcoat and umbrella, sons of English exiles and exiles in England, and think of bright skies and suns overhead, and sweeps of country disappearing into the haze, and blue mountain ranges melting into the azure of distant lower skies, and curves of white and yellow sand beaches, and runs of shelving yellow sandstone sea-walls—and the glorious Pacific! Sydney Harbour at sunrise, and the girls we took to Manly Beach.

Christmas in a London flat. Gloom and slush and soot. It is not the cold that affects us Australians so much, but the horrible gloom. We get heart-sick for the sun.

Christmas at sea—three Christmases, in fact—one going saloon from Sydney to Westralia early in the Golden Nineties with funds; and one, the Christmas after next, coming back steerage with nothing but the clothes we'd slept in. All of which was bad judgment on our part—the order and manner of our going and coming should have been reversed.

Christmas in a hessian tent in "th' Westren," with so many old mates from the East that it was just old times over again. We had five pounds of corned beef and a kerosene-tin to boil it in; and while we were talking of old things the skeleton of a kangaroo-dog grabbed the beef out of the boiling water and disappeared into the scrub—which made it seem more like old times than ever.

Christmas going to New Zealand, with experience, by the s.s. *Tasmania*. We had plum duff, but it was too "soggy" for us to eat. We dropped it overboard, lest it should swamp the boat—and it sank to the ooze. The *Tasmania* was saved on that occasion, but she foundered next year outside Gisborne. Perhaps the cook had made more duff. There was a letter from a sweetheart of mine amongst her mails when she went down; but that's got nothing to do with it, though it made some difference in my life.

Christmas on a new telegraph line with a party of lining gangmen in New Zealand. There was no duff nor roast because there was no firewood within twenty miles. The cook used to pile armfuls of flax-sticks under the billies, and set light to them when the last man arrived in camp.

Christmas in Sydney, with a dozen invitations out to dinner. The one we accepted was to a sensible Australian Christmas dinner; a typical one, as it should be, and will be before the Commonwealth is many years old. Everything cold except the vegetables, the hose playing on the veranda and vines outside, the men dressed in sensible pyjama-like suits, and the women and girls fresh and cool and jolly, instead of being hot and cross and looking like boiled carrots, and feeling like boiled rags, and having headaches after dinner, as would have been the case had they broiled over the fire in a hot kitchen all the blazing forenoon to cook a scalding, indigestible dinner, as many Australian women do, and for no other reason than that it was the fashion in England. One of those girls was very pretty and—ah, well!——

Christmas dinner in a greasy Sydney sixpenny restaurant, that opened a few days before with brass band going at full blast at the door by way of advertisement. "Roast-beef, one! Cabbage and potatoes, one! Plum pudding, two!" (That was the first time I dined to music.) The Christmas dinner was a good one, but my appetite was spoilt by the expression of the restaurant keeper, a big man with a heavy jowl, who sat by the door with a cold eye on the sixpences, and didn't seem to have much confidence in human nature.

Christmas—no, that was New Year—on the Warrego River, out back (an alleged river with a sickly stream that looked like bad milk). We spent most of that night hunting round in the dark and feeling on the ground for camel and horse droppings with which to build fires and make smoke round our camp to keep off the mosquitoes. The mosquitoes started at sunset and left off at daybreak, when the flies got to work again.

Christmas dinner under a brush shearing-shed. Mutton and plum pudding —and fifty miles from beer!

An old bush friend of mine, one Jimmy Nowlett, who ranked as a bullock-driver, told me of a Christmas time he had. He was cut off by the floods with his team, and had nothing to eat for four days but potatoes and honey. He said potatoes dipped in honey weren't so bad; but he had to sleep on bullock yokes laid on the ground to keep him out of the water, and he got a toothache that paralysed him all down one side.

And speaking of plum pudding, I consider it one of the most barbarous institutions of the British. It is a childish, silly, savage superstition; it must have been a savage inspiration, looking at it all round—but then it isn't so long since the British were savages.

I got a letter last year from a mate of mine in Western Australia—prospecting the awful desert out beyond White Feather—telling me all about a "perish" he did on plum pudding. He and his mates were camped at the Boulder Soak with some three or four hundred miles—mostly sand and dust—between them and the nearest grocer's shop. They ordered a case of mixed canned provisions from Perth to reach them about Christmas. They didn't believe in plum pudding—there are a good many British institutions that bushmen don't believe in—but the cook was a new chum, and he said he'd go home to his mother if he didn't have plum pudding for Christmas, so they ordered a can for him. Meanwhile, they hung out on kangaroo and damper and the knowledge that it couldn't last for ever.

It was in a terrible drought, and the kangaroos used to come into the "Soak" for water, and they were too weak to run. Later on, when wells were dug, the kangaroos used to commit suicide in them—there was generally a kangaroo in the well in the morning.

The storekeeper packed the case of tinned dog, etc., but by some blunder he or his man put the label on the wrong box, and it went per rail, per coach, per camel, and the last stage per boot, and reached my friends' camp on Christmas Eve, to their great joy. My friend broke the case open by the light of the camp-fire.

"Here, Jack!" he said, tossing out a can, "here's your plum pudding."

He held the next can in his hand a moment longer and read the label twice.

"Why! he's sent two," he said, "and I'm sure I only ordered one. Never mind —Jack'll have a tuck-out."

He held the next can close to the fire and blinked at it hard.

"I'm damned if he hasn't sent three tins of plum pudding. Never mind, we'll manage to scoff some of it between us. You're in luck's way this trip, Jack, and no mistake."

He looked harder still at the fourth can; then he read the labels on the other tins again to see if he'd made a mistake.

He didn't tell me what he said then, but a milder mate suggested that the storekeeper had sent half a dozen tins by mistake. But when they reached the seventh can the language was not even fit to be written down on a piece of paper and handed up to the magistrate. The storekeeper had sent them an unbroken case of canned plum pudding, and probably by this time he was wondering what had become of that blanky case of duff.

The kangaroos disappeared about this time and my friend tells me that he and his mates had to live for a mortal fortnight on canned plum pudding. They tried it cold and they tried it boiled, they tried it baked, they tried it fried, and they had it toasted, they had it for breakfast, dinner and tea. They had nothing else to think, or talk, or argue and quarrel about; and they dreamed about it every night, my friend says. It wasn't a joke—it gave them the nightmare and day-horrors.

They tried it with salt. They picked as many of the raisins out as they could and boiled it with salt kangaroo. They tried to make Yorkshire pudding out of it; but it was too rich.

My friend was experimenting and trying to discover a simple process for separating the ingredients of plum pudding when a fresh supply of provisions came along. He says he was never so sick of anything in his life, and he has had occasion to be sick of a good many things.

The new chum jackeroo is still alive, but he won't ever eat plum pudding any more, he says. It cured him of homesickness. He wouldn't eat it even if his bride made it.

Christmas on the goldfields in the last of the roaring days, in the palmy days of Gulgong and those fields. Let's see! it must be nearly thirty years ago! Oh, how the time goes by!

Santa Claus, young, fresh-faced and eager; Santa Claus, blonde and flaxen; Santa Claus, dark; Santa Claus with a brogue and Santa Claus speaking broken English; Santa Claus as a Chinaman (Sun Tong Lee & Co., storekeepers), with strange, delicious sweets that melted in our mouths, and rum toys and Chinese dolls for the children.

Lucky diggers who were with difficulty restrained from putting pound notes and nuggets and expensive lockets and things into the little ones' stockings. Santa Claus in flannel shirt and clay-covered moleskins. Diggers who bought lollies by the pound and sent the little ones home with as much as they could carry.

Diggers who gave a guinea or more for a toy for a child that reminded them of some other child at home. Diggers who took as many children as they could gather on short notice into a store, slapped a five-pound note down on the counter and told the little ones to call for whatever they wanted. Who set a family of poor children side by side on the counter and called for a box of mixed children's boots—the best—and fitted them on with great care and anxiety and frequent inquiries as to whether they pinched. Who stood little girls and boys on the counter and called for the most expensive frocks, the latest and best in sailor suits, and the brightest ribbons; and things came long distances by bullock dray and were expensive in those days. Impressionable diggers—and most of them were—who threw nuggets to singers, and who, sometimes, slipped a parcel into the hands of a little boy or girl, with instructions to give it to an elder sister (or young mother, perhaps) whom the digger had never spoken to, only worshipped from afar off. And the elder sister or young mother, opening the parcel, would find a piece of jewellery or a costly article of dress, and wonder who sent it.

Ah, the wild generosity of luck-intoxicated diggers of those days! and the reckless generosity of the drinkers. "We thought it was going to last for ever!"

"If I don't spend it on the bairns I'll spend it on the drink," Sandy Burns used to say. "I ha' nane o' me own, an' the lass who was to gi' me bairns, she couldn't wait."

Sandy had kept steady and travelled from one end of the world to the other, and roughed it and toiled for five years, and the very day he bottomed his golden hole on the Brown Snake Lead at Happy Valley he got a letter from his girl in Scotland to say she had grown tired of waiting and was married. Then he drank, and drink and luck went together.

Gulgong on New Year's Eve! Rows and rows of lighted tents and camp-fires, with a clear glow over it all. Bonfires on the hills and diggers romping round them like big boys. Tin kettling—gold dishes and spoons, and fiddles, and hammers on pointing anvils, and sticks and empty kerosene-tins (*they* made a row); concertinas and cornets, shot-guns, pistols and crackers, all sorts of instruments, and "Auld Lang Syne" in one mighty chorus.

And now—a wretched little pastoral town; a collection of glaring corrugated-iron hip-roofs, and maybe a rotting propped-up bark or weather-board humpy or two—relics of the roaring days; a dried-up storekeeper and some withered hags; a waste of caved-in holes with rain-washed mullock heaps and quartz and gravel glaring in the sun; thistles and burrs where old bars were; drought, dryness, desolation and goats.

Lonely graves in the bush and grey old diggers here and there, anywhere in the world, doing anything for a living, lonely yet because of the girls who couldn't wait, but prospecting and fossicking here and there, and dreaming still.

They thought it was going to last for ever.

Christmas at Eurunderee Creek, amongst the old selection farms in the western spurs of the Blue Mountains. They used to call it "Th' Pipeclay" thirty years ago, but the old black names have been restored. They make

296

plum puddings yet, weeks beforehand, and boil them for hours and hang them in cloths to the rafters to petrify; then they take them down and boil them again. On Christmas Eve the boys cut boughs or young pines on the hills, and drag them home and lash them to the veranda-posts.

Ted has turned up with his wife and children from his selection out back. The wheat is in and shearing is over on the big stations. Tom—steady-going old Tom—clearing or fencing or dam-sinking up-country, hides his tools in the scrub and gets his horse and rides home. Aunt Emma (to every one's joy) has arrived from Sydney with presents (astonishing bargains in frocks, etc.) and marvellous descriptions of town life. ,

Joe, "poor" Mary's husband, who has been droving in Queensland since the Christmas before last—while poor Mary, who is afraid to live alone, shared a skillion and the family quarrels at home—Joe rides day and night and reaches home at sunrise on Christmas morning, tired and dusty, gaunt and haggard, but with his last cheque intact. He kisses his wife and child and throws himself on the bed to sleep till dinner-time, while Mary moves round softly, hushes the baby, dresses it and herself, lays out Joe's clean things, and bends over him now and then, and kisses him, perhaps, as he sleeps.

In the morning the boys and some of the men go down to the creek for a swim in the big shady pool under the she-oaks and take their Sunday clothes with them and dress there.

Some of them ride into town to church, and some of the women and children drive in in spring-carts—the children to go to Sunday school, leaving mother and the eldest daughter—usually a hard-worked, disappointed, short-tempered girl—at home to look after the cooking.

There is some anxiety (mostly on mother's part) about Jim, who is "wild," and is supposed to be somewhere out back. There was "a piece of blue paper" out for Jim on account of sweating (illegally using) a horse, but his mother or father has got a hint—given in a kindly way by the police-sergeant—that Jim is free to come home and stay at home if he behaves himself. (There is usually a horse missing when Jim goes out back.)

Jim turns up all right—save that he has no money—and is welcomed with tearful affection by his favourite sister Mary, shakes hands silently with his father, and has a long whispered conversation with his mother, which leaves him very subdued. His brothers forbear to sneer at him, partly because it is Christmas, partly on mother's account, and thirdly, because Jim can use his hands. Aunt Emma, who is fond of him, cheers him up wonderfully.

The family sit down to dinner. "An old mate of your father's"—a bearded old digger—has arrived and takes the place of honour. ("I knowed yer father, sonny, on the diggings long afore any of you was ever thought on.")

The family have only been a few hours together, yet there is an under-current of growling, that mysterious yet evident undercurrent of nastiness and resentment which goes on in all families and drags many a promising young life down. But Aunt Emma and the old mate make things brighter, and so the dinner—of hot roast and red-hot plum pudding—passes off fairly well.

The men sleep the afternoon away and wake up bathed in perspiration and helpless; some of the women have headaches. After tea they gather on the veranda in the cool of the evening, and that's the time when the best sides of their natures and the best parts of the past have a chance of coming uppermost, and perhaps they begin to feel a bit sorry that they are going to part again.

The local races or "sports" on Boxing Day. There is nothing to keep the boys home over New Year. Ted and his wife go back to their lonely life on their selection; Tom returns to his fencing or tank-sinking contract; Jim, who has borrowed "a couple of quid" from Tom, goes out back with strong resolutions for the New Year, and shears "stragglers," breaks in horses, cooks and clerks for survey parties, and gambles and drinks, and gets into trouble again. Maybe Joe "knocks about" the farm a bit before going into the Great North-West with another mob of cattle.

The last time I saw the Old Year out at Eurunderee the bush-fires were burning all over the ranges, and looked like great cities lighted up. No need for bonfires then.

Christmas in Bourke, the metropolis of the great pastoral scrubs and plains, five hundred miles west, with the thermometer one-hundred-and-something-scarey in the shade. The rough, careless shearers come in from stations many dusty miles out in the scrubs to have their Christmas sprees, to drink and "shout" and fight—and have the horrors some of them—and be run in and locked up with difficulty, within sound of a church-going bell.

The Bourke Christmas is a very beery and exciting one. The hotels shut up in front on Christmas Day to satisfy the law (or out of consideration for the feelings of the sergeant in charge of the police station), and open behind to satisfy the public, who are supposed to have made the law.

Sensible cold dinners are the fashion in Bourke, I think, with the hose going, and free-and-easy costumes.

The free males take their blankets and sleep in the "park"; the women sleep with doors and windows open, and the married men on mattresses on the verandas across the open doors—in case of accidents.

Christmas in Sydney, though Christmas holidays are not so popular as Easter, or even Anniversary Day, in the Queen city of the South. Buses, electric, cable and the old steam trams crowded with holiday-makers with baskets. Harbour boats loaded down to the water's edge with harbour picnic-parties. "A trip round the harbour and to the head of Middle Harbour one shilling return!" Strings of tourist trains running over the Blue Mountains and the Great Zigzag, and up the coast to Gosford and Brisbane Water, and down the south coast to beautiful Illawarra, until after New Year. Hundreds of young fellows going out with tents to fish in lonely bays or shoot in the mountains, and rough it properly like bushmen—not with deck chairs, crockery, a piano and servants. For you can camp in the grand and rugged solitude of the bush within a stone's throw of the city, so to speak.

Jolly camps and holiday parties all round the beautiful bays of the harbour, and up and down the coast, and all close to home. Camps in the moonlight on sandy beaches under great dark bluffs and headlands, where yellow, shelving, sandstone cliffs run, broken only by sandy-beached bays, and where the silver-white breakers leap and roar.

And Manly Beach on a holiday! Thousands of people in fresh summer dress, hundreds of bare-legged, happy children running where the "blue sea over the white sand rolls," racing in and out with the rollers, playing with the glorious Pacific. Manly—"Our Village"—Manly Beach, where we used to take our girls, with the most beautiful harbour in the world on one side, and the width of the grandest ocean on the other. Ferny gullies and "fairy dells" to north and south, and every shady nook its merry party or happy couple.

Manly Beach—I remember five years ago (oh, how the time goes by!)—and two names that were written together in the sand when the tide was coming in.

And the boat home in the moonlight, past the Heads, where we felt the roll of the ocean, and the moonlit harbour—and the harbour lights of Sydney—the grandest of them all.

THE SLIPRAILS AND THE SPUR

The colours of the setting sun
   Withdrew across the Western land—
He raised the sliprails, one by one,
   And shot them home with trembling hand;
Her brown hands clung—her face grew pale—
   Ah! quivering chin and eyes that brim!—
One quick, fierce kiss across the rail,
   And, "Good-bye, Mary!" "Good-bye, Jim!"

Oh, he rides hard to race the pain
   Who rides from love, who rides from home;
But he rides slowly home again,
   Whose heart has learnt to love and roam.

A hand upon the horse's mane,
   And one foot in the stirrup set,
And, stooping back to kiss again,
   With "Good-bye, Mary! don't you fret!
When I come back"—he laughed for her—
   "We do not know how soon 'twill be;
I'll whistle as I round the spur—
   You let the sliprails down for me."

She gasped for sudden loss of hope,
   As, with a backward wave to her,
He cantered down the grassy slope
   And swiftly round the darkening spur.
Black-pencilled panels standing high,
   And darkness fading into stars,
And, blurring fast against the sky,
   A faint white form beside the bars.

And often at the set of sun,
   In winter bleak and summer brown,
She'd steal across the little run,
   And shyly let the sliprails down,
And listen there when darkness shut
   The nearer spur in silence deep,
And when they called her from the hut
   Steal home and cry herself to sleep.

And he rides hard to dull the pain
   Who rides from one that loves him best...
And he rides slowly back again,
   Whose restless heart must rove for rest.

SEND ROUND THE HAT

Now this is the creed from the Book of the Bush—
Should be simple and plain to a dunce:
"If a man's in a hole you must pass round the hat—
Were he jail-bird or gentleman once."

"Is it any harm to wake yer?"

It was about nine o'clock in the morning, and, though it was Sunday morning, it was no harm to wake me; but the shearer had mistaken me for a deaf jackeroo, who was staying at the shanty and was something like me, and had good-naturedly shouted almost at the top of his voice, and he woke the whole shanty. Anyway he woke three or four others who were sleeping on beds and stretchers, and one on a shake-down on the floor, in the same room. It had been a wet night, and the shanty was full of shearers from Big Billabong Shed which had cut out the day before. My room mates had been drinking and gambling overnight, and they swore luridly at the intruder for disturbing them.

He was six-foot-three or thereabout. He was loosely built, bony, sandy-complexioned and grey-eyed. He wore a good-humoured grin at most times, as I noticed later on; he was of a type of bushman that I always liked—the sort that seem to get more good-natured the longer they grow, yet are hard-knuckled and would accommodate a man who wanted to fight, or thrash a bully in a good-natured way. The sort that like to carry somebody's baby round, and cut wood, carry water and do little things for overworked married bushwomen. He wore a saddle-tweed sac suit two sizes too small for him, and his face, neck, great hands and bony wrists were covered with sun-blotches and freckles.

"I hope I ain't disturbin' yer," he shouted, as he bent over my bunk, "but there's a cove——"

"You needn't shout!" I interrupted, "I'm not deaf."

"Oh—I beg your pardon!" he shouted. "I didn't know I was yellin'. I thought you was the deaf feller."

"Oh, that's all right," I said. "What's the trouble?"

"Wait till them other chaps is done swearin' and I'll tell yer," he said. He spoke with a quiet, good-natured drawl, with something of the nasal twang, but tone and drawl distinctly Australian—altogether apart from that of the Americans.

"Oh, spit it out for Christ's sake, Long-'un!" yelled One-eyed Bogan, who had been the worst swearer in a rough shed, and he fell back on his bunk as if his previous remarks had exhausted him.

"It's that there sick jackeroo that was pickin'-up at Big Billabong," said the Giraffe. "He had to knock off the first week, an' he's been here ever since. They're sendin' him away to the hospital in Sydney by the speeshall train. They're just goin' to take him up in the wagonette to the railway station, an' I thought I might as well go round with the hat an' get him a few bob. He's got a missus and kids in Sydney."

"Yer always goin' round with yer gory hat!" growled Bogan. "Yer'd blanky well take it round in hell!"

"That's what he's doing, Bogan," muttered Gentleman Once, on the shake-down, with his face to the wall.

The hat was a genuine "cabbage-tree," one of the sort that "last a lifetime." It was well coloured, almost black in fact with weather and age, and it had a new strap round the base of the crown. I looked into it and saw a dirty pound note and some silver. I dropped in half a crown, which was more than I could spare, for I had only been a green-hand at Big Billabong.

"Thank yer!" he said. "Now then, you fellers!"

"I wish you'd keep your hat on your head, and your money in your pockets and your sympathy somewhere else," growled Jack Moonlight as he raised himself painfully on his elbow and felt under his pillow for two half-crowns. "Here," he said, "here's two half-casers. Chuck 'em in and let me sleep for God's sake!"

Gentleman Once, the gambler, rolled round on his shake-down, bringing his good-looking, dissipated face from the wall. He had turned in in his clothes and, with considerable exertion he shoved his hand down into the pocket of his trousers, which were a tight fit. He brought up a roll of pound notes and could find no silver.

"Here," he said to the Giraffe, "I might as well lay a quid. I'll chance it anyhow. Chuck it in."

"You've got rats this mornin', Gentleman Once," growled the Bogan. "It ain't a blanky horse race."

"P'r'aps I have," said Gentleman Once, and he turned to the wall again with his head on his arm.

"Now, Bogan, yer might as well chuck in somethin'," said the Giraffe.

"What's the matter with the —— jackeroo?" asked the Bogan, tugging his trousers from under the mattress.

Moonlight said something in a low tone.

"The —— he has!" said Bogan. "Well, I pity the ——! Here, I'll chuck in half a —— quid!" and he dropped half a sovereign into the hat.

The fourth man, who was known to his face as "Barcoo-Rot," and behind his back as "The Mean Man," had been drinking all night, and not even Bogan's stump-splitting adjectives could rouse him. So Bogan got out of bed, and calling on us (as blanky female cattle) to witness what he was about to do, he rolled the drunkard over, prospected his pockets till he made up five shillings (or a "caser" in bush language), and "chucked" them into the hat.

And Barcoo-Rot is probably unconscious to this day that he was ever connected with an act of charity.

The Giraffe struck the deaf jackeroo in the next room. I heard the chaps cursing "Long-'un" for waking them, and "Deaf-'un" for being, as they thought at first, the indirect cause of the disturbance. I heard the Giraffe and his hat being condemned in other rooms and cursed along the veranda where more shearers were sleeping; and after a while I turned out.

The Giraffe was carefully fixing a mattress and pillows on the floor of a wagonette, and presently a man, who looked like a corpse, was carried out and lifted into the trap.

As the wagonette started, the shanty-keeper—a fat, soulless-looking man—put his hand in his pocket and dropped a quid into the hat which was still going round, in the hands of the Giraffe's mate, little Teddy Thompson, who was as far below medium height as the Giraffe was above it.

The Giraffe took the horse's head and led him along on the most level parts of the road towards the railway station, and two or three chaps went along to help get the sick man into the train.

The shearing-season was over in that district, but I got a job of house-painting, which was my trade, at the Great Western Hotel (a two-story brick place), and I stayed in Bourke for a couple of months.

The Giraffe was a Victorian native from Bendigo. He was well known in Bourke and to many shearers who came through the great dry scrubs from hundreds of miles round. He was stake-holder, drunkard's banker, peace-maker where possible, referee or second to oblige the chaps when a fight was on, big brother or uncle to most of the children in town, final court of appeal when the youngsters had a dispute over a foot-race at the school picnic, referee at their fights, and he was the stranger's friend.

"The feller as knows can battle around for himself," he'd say. "But I always like to do what I can for a hard-up stranger cove. I was a green-hand jackeroo once meself, and I know what it is."

"You're always bothering about other people, Giraffe," said Tom Hall, the shearers' union secretary, who was only a couple of inches shorter than the Giraffe. "There's nothing in it, you can take it from me—I ought to know."

"Well, what's a feller to do?" said the Giraffe. "I'm only hangin' round here till shearin' starts agen, an' a cove might as well be doin' something. Besides, it ain't as if I was like a cove that had old people or a wife an' kids to look after. I ain't got no responsibilities. A feller can't be doin' nothin'. Besides, I like to lend a helpin' hand when I can."

"Well, all I've got to say," said Tom, most of whose screw went in borrowed quids, etc. "All I've got to say is that you'll get no thanks, and you might blanky well starve in the end."

"There ain't no fear of me starvin' so long as I've got me hands about me; an' I ain't a cove as wants thanks," said the Giraffe.

He was always helping someone or something. Now it was a bit of a "darnce" that we was gettin' up for the girls; again it was Mrs Smith, the woman whose husban' was drowned in the flood in the Bogan River lars' Crismas, or that there poor woman down by the Billabong—her husband cleared out and left her with a lot o' kids. Or Bill Something, the bullocky, who was run over by his own wagon, while he was drunk, and got his leg broke.

Toward the end of his spree One-eyed Bogan broke loose and smashed nearly all the windows of the Carriers' Arms, and next morning he was fined heavily at the police court. About dinner-time I encountered the Giraffe and his hat, with two half-crowns in it for a start.

"I'm sorry to trouble yer," he said, "but One-eyed Bogan carn't pay his fine, an' I thought we might fix it up for him. He ain't half a bad sort of feller when he ain't drinkin'. It's only when he gets too much booze in him."

After shearing, the hat usually started round with the Giraffe's own dirty crumpled pound note in the bottom of it as a send-off, later on it was half a sovereign, and so on down to half a crown and a shilling, as he got short of stuff; till in the end he would borrow a "few bob"—which he always repaid after next shearing—"just to start the thing goin'."

There were several yarns about him and his hat. 'Twas said that the hat had belonged to his father, whom he resembled in every respect, and it had been going round for so many years that the crown was worn as thin as paper by the quids, half-quids, casers, half-casers, bobs and tanners or sprats—to say nothing of the scrums—that had been chucked into it in its time and shaken up.

They say that when a new governor visited Bourke the Giraffe happened to be standing on the platform close to the exit, grinning good-humouredly, and the local toady nudged him urgently and said in an awful whisper, "Take off your hat! Why don't you take off your hat?"

"Why?" drawled the Giraffe, "he ain't hard up, is he?"

And they fondly cherish an anecdote to the effect that, when the One-Man-One-Vote Bill was passed (or Payment of Members, or when the first Labour Party went in—I forget on which occasion they said it was) the Giraffe was carried away by the general enthusiasm, got a few beers in him, "chucked" a quid into his hat, and sent it round. The boys contributed by force of habit, and contributed largely, because of the victory and the beer. And when the hat came back to the Giraffe, he stood holding it in front of him with both hands and stared blankly into it for a while. Then it dawned on him.

"Blowed if I haven't bin an' gone an' took up a bloomin' collection for meself!" he said.

He was almost a teetotaller, but he stood his shout in reason. He mostly drank ginger beer.

"I ain't a feller that boozes, but I ain't got nothin' agen chaps enjoyin' themselves, so long as they don't go too far."

It was common for a man on the spree to say to him:

"Here! here's five quid. Look after it for me, Giraffe, will yer, till I get off the booze."

His real name was Bob Brothers, and his bush names, "Long-'un," "The Giraffe," "Send-round-the-hat," "Chuck-in-a-bob," and "Ginger-ale."

Some years before, camels and Afghan drivers had been imported to the Bourke district; the camels did very well in the dry country, they went right across country and carried everything from sardines to flooring-boards. And the teamsters loved the Afghans nearly as much as Sydney furniture makers love the cheap Chinese in the same line. They loved 'em even as union shearers on strike love blacklegs brought up-country to take their places.

Now the Giraffe was a good, straight unionist, but in cases of sickness or trouble he was as apt to forget his unionism, as all bushmen are, at all times (and for all time), to forget their creed. So, one evening, the Giraffe blundered into the Carriers' Arms—of all places in the world—when it was full of teamsters; he had his hat in his hand and some small silver and coppers in it.

"I say, you fellers, there's a poor, sick Afghan in the camp down there along the——"

A big, brawny bullock-driver took him firmly by the shoulders, or rather by the elbows, and ran him out before any damage was done. The Giraffe took it as he took most things, good-humouredly; but, about dusk, he was seen slipping down towards the Afghan camp with a billy of soup.

"I believe," remarked Tom Hall, "that when the Giraffe goes to heaven— and he's the only one of us, as far as I can see, that has a ghost of a show— I believe that when he goes to heaven, the first thing he'll do will be to take his infernal hat round amongst the angels—getting up a collection for this damned world that he left behind."

"Well, I don't think there's so much to his credit; after all," said Jack Mitchell, shearer. "You see, the Giraffe is ambitious; he likes public life, and that accounts for him shoving himself forward with his collections. As for bothering about people in trouble, that's only common curiosity; he's one of those chaps that are always shoving their noses into other people's troubles. And, as for looking after sick men—why! there's nothing the Giraffe likes better than pottering round a sick man, and watching him and studying him. He's awfully interested in sick men, and they're pretty scarce out here. I tell you there's nothing he likes better—except, maybe, it's pottering round a corpse. I believe he'd ride forty miles to help and sympathize and potter round a funeral. The fact of the matter is that the Giraffe is only enjoying himself with other people's troubles—that's all it is. It's only vulgar curiosity and selfishness. I set it down to his ignorance; the way he was brought up."

A few days after the Afghan incident the Giraffe and his hat had a run of luck. A German, one of a party who were building a new wooden bridge over the Big Billabong, was helping unload some girders from a truck at the railway station, when a big log slipped on the skids and his leg was smashed badly. They carried him to the Carriers' Arms, which was the nearest hotel, and into a bedroom behind the bar, and sent for the doctor. The Giraffe was in evidence as usual.

"It vas not that at all," said German Charlie, when they asked him if he was in much pain. "It vas not that at all. I don't cares a damn for der bain; but dis is der tird year—und I vas going home dis year—after der gontract— und der gontract yoost commence!"

That was the burden of his song all through, between his groans.

There were a good few chaps sitting quietly about the bar and veranda when the doctor arrived. The Giraffe was sitting at the end of the counter, on which he had laid his hat while he wiped his face, neck, and forehead with a big speckled "sweat-rag." It was a very hot day.

The doctor, a good-hearted young Australian, was heard saying something. Then German Charlie, in a voice that rung with pain:

"Make that leg right, doctor—quick! Dis is der tird pluddy year—und I must go home!"

The doctor asked him if he was in great pain.

"Neffer mind der pluddy bain, doctor! Neffer mind der pluddy bain! Dot vas nossing. Make dat leg vell quick, doctor. Dis vas der last contract, and

I vas going home dis year." Then the words jerked out of him by physical agony: "Der girl vas vaiting dree year, and—by Got! I must go home."

The publican—Watty Braithwaite, known as "Watty Broadweight," or, more familiarly, "Watty Bothways"—turned over the Giraffe's hat in a tired, bored sort of way, dropped a quid into it, and nodded resignedly at the Giraffe.

The Giraffe caught up the hint and the hat with alacrity. The hat went all round town, so to speak; and, as soon as his leg was firm enough not to come loose on the road German Charlie went home.

It was well known that I contributed to the Sydney *Bulletin* and several other papers. The Giraffe's bump of reverence was very large, and swelled especially for sick men and poets. He treated me with much more respect than is due from a bushman to a man, and with an odd sort of extra gentleness I sometimes fancied. But one day he rather surprised me.

"I'm sorry to trouble yer," he said in a shamefaced way. "I don't know as you go in for sportin', but One-eyed Bogan an' Barcoo-Rot is goin' to have a bit of a scrap down the Billybong this evenin', an'——"

"A bit of a what?" I asked.

"A bit of a fight to a finish," he said apologetically. "An' the chaps is tryin' to fix up a fiver to put some life into the thing. There's bad blood between One-eyed Bogan and Barcoo-Rot, an' it won't do them any harm to have it out."

It was a great fight, I remember. There must have been a couple of score blood-soaked handkerchiefs (or "sweat-rags") buried in a hole on the field of battle, and the Giraffe was busy the rest of the evening helping to patch up the principals. Later on he took up a small collection for the loser, who happened to be Barcoo-Rot in spite of the advantage of an eye.

The Salvation Army lassie, who went round with the *War Cry*, nearly always sold the Giraffe three copies.

A new-chum parson, who wanted a subscription to build or enlarge a chapel, or something, sought the assistance of the Giraffe's influence with his mates.

"Well," said the Giraffe, "I ain't a churchgoer meself. I ain't what you might call a religious cove, but I'll be glad to do what I can to help yer. I don't suppose I can do much. I ain't been to church since I was a kiddy."

The parson was shocked, but later on he learned to appreciate the Giraffe and his mates, and to love Australia for the bushman's sake, and it was he who told me the above anecdote.

The Giraffe helped fix some stalls for a Catholic Church bazaar, and some of the chaps chaffed him about it in the union office.

"You'll be taking up a collection for a joss-house down in the Chinamen's camp next," said Tom Hall in conclusion.

"Well, I ain't got nothin' agen the Roming Carflicks," said the Giraffe. "An' Father O'Donovan's a very decent sort of cove. He stuck up for the unions all right in the strike anyway." ("He wouldn't be Irish if he wasn't," someone commented.) "I carried swags once for six months with a feller that was a Carflick, an' he was a very straight feller. And a girl I knowed turned Carflick to marry a chap that had got her into trouble, an' she was always jes' the same to me after as she was before. Besides, I like to help everything that's goin' on."

Tom Hall and one or two others went out hurriedly to have a drink. But we all loved the Giraffe.

He was very innocent and very humorous, especially when he meant to be most serious and philosophical.

"Some of them bush girls is regular tomboys," he said to me solemnly one day. "Some of them is too cheeky altogether. I remember once I was stoppin' at a place—they was sort of relations o' mine—an' they put me to sleep in a room off the verander, where there was a glass door an' no blinds. An' the first mornin' the girls—they was sort o' cousins o' mine—they come gigglin' and foolin' round outside the door on the verander, an' kep' me in bed till nearly ten o'clock. I had to put me trowsis on under the bed-clothes in the end. But I got back on 'em the next night," he reflected.

"How did you do that, Bob?" I asked.

"Why, I went to bed in me trowsis!"

One day I was on a plank, painting the ceiling of the bar of the Great Western Hotel. I was anxious to get the job finished. The work had been kept back most of the day by chaps handing up long beers to me, and drawing my attention to the alleged fact that I was putting on the paint wrong side out. I was slapping it on over the last few boards when:

"I'm very sorry to trouble yer; I always seem to be troublin' yer; but there's that there woman and them girls——"

I looked down—about the first time I had looked down on him—and there was the Giraffe, with his hat brim up on the plank and two half-crowns in it.

"Oh, that's all right, Bob," I said, and I dropped in half a crown.

There were shearers in the bar, and presently there was some barracking. It appeared that that there woman and them girls were strange women, in the local as well as the Biblical sense of the word, who had come from Sydney at the end of the shearing-season, and had taken a cottage on the edge of the scrub on the outskirts of the town. There had been trouble this week in connection with a row at their establishment, and they had been fined, warned off by the police, and turned out by their landlord.

"This is a bit too red-hot, Giraffe," said one of the shearers. "Them ——s has made enough out of us coves. They've got plenty of stuff, don't you fret. Let 'em go to ——! I'm blanked if I give a sprat."

"They ain't got their fares to Sydney," said the Giraffe. "An', what's more, the little 'un is sick, an' two of them has kids in Sydney."

"How the —— do you know?"

"Why, one of 'em come to me an' told me all about it."

There was an involuntary guffaw.

"Look here, Bob," said Billy Woods, the rouseabouts' secretary, kindly. "Don't you make a fool of yourself. You'll have all the chaps laughing at you. Those girls are only working you for all you're worth. I suppose one of 'em came crying and whining to you. Don't you bother about 'em. *You* don't know 'em; they can pump water at a moment's notice. You haven't had any experience with women yet, Bob."

"She didn't come whinin' and cryin' to me," said the Giraffe, dropping his twanging drawl a little. "She looked me straight in the face an' told me all about it."

"I say, Giraffe," said Box-o'-Tricks, "what have you been doin'? You've bin

307

down there on the nod. I'm surprised at yer, Giraffe."

"An' he pretends to be so gory soft an' innocent, too," growled the Bogan. "We know all about you, Giraffe."

"Look here, Giraffe," said Mitchell the shearer. "I'd never have thought it of you. We all thought you were the only virgin youth west the river; I always thought you were a moral young man. You mustn't think that because your conscience is pricking you everyone else's is."

"I ain't had anythin' to do with them," said the Giraffe, drawling again. "I ain't a cove that goes in for that sort of thing. But other chaps has, and I think they might as well help 'em out of their fix."

"They're a rotten crowd," said Billy Woods. "You don't know them, Bob. Don't bother about them—they're not worth it. Put your money in your pocket. You'll find a better use for it before next shearing."

"Better shout, Giraffe," said Box-o'-Tricks.

Now in spite of the Giraffe's softness he was the hardest man in Bourke to move when he'd decided on what he thought was "the fair thing to do." Another peculiarity of his was that on occasion, such for instance as "sayin' a few words" at a strike meeting, he would straighten himself, drop the twang, and rope in his drawl, so to speak.

"Well, look here, you chaps," he said now. "I don't know anything about them women. I s'pose they're bad, but I don't suppose they're worse than men has made them. All I know is that there's four women turned out, without any stuff, and every woman in Bourke, an' the police, an' the law agen 'em. An' the fact that they is women is agenst 'em most of all. You don't expect 'em to hump their swags to Sydney! Why, only I ain't got the stuff I wouldn't trouble yer. I'd pay their fares meself. Look," he said, lowering his voice, "there they are now, an' one of the girls is cryin'. Don't let 'em see yer lookin'.'"

I dropped softly from the plank and peeped out with the rest.

They stood by the fence on the opposite side of the street, a bit up towards the railway station, with their portmanteaux and bundles at their feet. One girl leant with her arms on the fence rail and her face buried in them, another was trying to comfort her. The third girl and the woman stood facing our way. The woman was good-looking; she had a hard face, but it might have been made hard. The third girl seemed half defiant, half inclined to cry. Presently she went to the other side of the girl who was crying on the fence and put her arm round her shoulder. The woman suddenly turned her back on us and stood looking away over the paddocks.

The hat went round. Billy Woods was first, then Box-o'-Tricks, and then Mitchell.

Billy contributed with eloquent silence. "I was only jokin', Giraffe," said Box-o'-Tricks, dredging his pockets for a couple of shillings. It was some time after the shearing, and most of the chaps were hard up.

"Ah, well," sighed Mitchell. "There's no help for it. If the Giraffe would take up a collection to import some decent girls to this God-forgotten hole there might be some sense in it. . . . It's bad enough for the Giraffe to undermine our religious prejudices, and tempt us to take a morbid interest in sick Chows and Afghans, and blacklegs and widows; but when he starts mixing us up with strange women it's time to buck." And he prospected his pockets and contributed two shillings, some odd pennies, and a pinch of tobacco dust.

"I don't mind helping the girls, but I'm damned if I'll give a penny to help the old ——," said Tom Hall.

"Well, she was a girl once herself," drawled the Giraffe.

The Giraffe went round to the other pubs and to the union offices, and when he returned he seemed satisfied with the plate, but troubled about something else.

"I don't know what to do for them for to-night," he said. "None of the pubs or boardin'-houses will hear of them, an' there ain't no empty houses, an' the women is all agen 'em."

"Not all," said Alice, the big, handsome barmaid from Sydney. "Come here, Bob." She gave the Giraffe half a sovereign and a look for which some of us would have paid him ten pounds—had we had the money, and had the look been transferable.

"Wait a minute, Bob," she said, and she went in to speak to the landlord.

"There's an empty bedroom at the end of the store in the yard," she said when she came back. "They can camp there for to-night if they behave themselves. You'd better tell 'em, Bob."

"Thank yer, Alice," said the Giraffe.

Next day, after work, the Giraffe and I drifted together and down by the river in the cool of the evening, and sat on the edge of the steep, drought-parched bank.

"I heard you saw your lady friends off this morning, Bob," I said, and was sorry I said it, even before he answered.

"Oh, they ain't no friends of mine," he said. "Only four poor devils of women. I thought they mightn't like to stand waitin' with the crowd on the platform, so I jest offered to get their tickets an' told 'em to wait round at the back of the station till the bell rung. An' what do yer think they did, Harry?" he went on, with an exasperatingly unintelligent grin. "Why, they wanted to kiss me."

"Did they?"

"Yes. An' they would have done it, too, if I hadn't been so long. Why, I'm blessed if they didn't kiss me hands."

"You don't say so."

"God's truth. Somehow I didn't like to go on the platform with them after that; besides, they was cryin', and I can't stand women cryin'. But some of the chaps put them into an empty carriage." He thought a moment. Then:

"There's some terrible good-hearted fellers in the world," he reflected.

I thought so too.

"Bob," I said, "you're a single man. Why don't you get married and settle down?"

"Well," he said, "I ain't got no wife an' kids, that's a fact. But it ain't my fault."

He may have been right about the wife. But I thought of the look that Alice had given him, and——

"Girls seem to like me right enough," he said, "but it don't go no further than that. The trouble is that I'm so long, and I always seem to get shook after little girls. At least there was one little girl in Bendigo that I was properly gone on."

"And wouldn't she have you?"

"Well, it seems not."

"Did you ask her?"

"Oh, yes, I asked her right enough."

"Well, and what did she say?"

"She said it would be redicilus for her to be seen trottin' alongside of a chimbly like me."

"Perhaps she didn't mean that. There are any amount of little women who like tall men."

"I thought of that too—afterwards. P'r'aps she didn't mean it that way. I s'pose the fact of the matter was that she didn't cotton on to me, and wanted to let me down easy. She didn't want to hurt me feelin's, if yer understand—she was a very good-hearted little girl. There's some terrible tall fellers where I come from, and I know two as married little girls."

He seemed a hopeless case.

"Sometimes," he said, "sometimes I wish that I wasn't so blessed long."

"There's that there deaf jackeroo," he reflected presently. "He's something in the same fix about girls as I am. He's too deaf and I'm too long."

"How do you make that out?" I asked. "He's got three girls, to my knowledge, and, as for being deaf, why, he gasses more than any man in the town, and knows more of what's going on than old Mother Brindle the washerwoman."

"Well, look at that now!" said the Giraffe, slowly. "Who'd have thought it? He never told me he had three girls, an' as for hearin' news, I always tell him anything that's goin' on that I think he doesn't catch. He told me his trouble was that whenever he went out with a girl people could hear what they was sayin'—at least they could hear what she was sayin' to him, an' draw their own conclusions, he said. He said he went out one night with a girl, and some of the chaps foxed 'em an' heard her sayin' 'don't' to him, an' put it all round town."

"What did she say 'don't' for?" I asked.

"He didn't tell me that, but I s'pose he was kissin' her or huggin' her or something."

"Bob," I said presently, "didn't you try the little girl in Bendigo a second time?"

"No," he said. "What was the use. She was a good little girl, and I wasn't goin' to go botherin' her. I ain't the sort of cove that goes hangin' round where he isn't wanted. But somehow I couldn't stay about Bendigo after she gave me the hint, so I thought I'd come over an' have a knock round on this side for a year or two."

"And you never wrote to her?"

"No. What was the use of goin' pesterin' her with letters? I know what trouble letters give me when I have to answer one. She'd have only had to tell me the straight truth in a letter an' it wouldn't have done me any good. But I've pretty well got over it by this time."

A few days later I went to Sydney. The Giraffe was the last I shook hands with from the carriage window, and he slipped something in a piece of newspaper into my hand.

"I hope yer won't be offended," he drawled, "but some of the chaps thought you mightn't be too flush of stuff—you've been shoutin' a good deal; so they put a quid or two together. They thought it might help yer to have a bit of a fly round in Sydney."

I was back in Bourke before next shearing. On the evening of my arrival I ran against the Giraffe; he seemed strangely shaken over something, but he kept his hat on his head.

"Would yer mind takin' a stroll as fur as the Billerbong?" he said. "I got something I'd like to tell yer."

His big, brown, sunburnt hands trembled and shook as he took a letter from his pocket and opened it.

"I've just got a letter," he said. "A letter from that little girl at Bendigo. It seems it was all a mistake. I'd like yer to read it. Somehow I feel as if I want to talk to a feller, and I'd rather talk to you than any of them other chaps."

It was a good letter, from a big-hearted little girl. She had been breaking her heart for the great ass all these months. It seemed that he had left Bendigo without saying good-bye to her. "Somehow I couldn't bring meself to it," he said, when I taxed him with it. She had never been able to get his address until last week; then she got it from a Bourke man who had gone south. She called him "an awful long fool," which he was, without the slightest doubt, and she implored him to write, and come back to her.

"And will you go back, Bob?" I asked.

"My oath! I'd take the train to-morrow only I ain't got the stuff. But I've got a stand in Big Billerbong Shed an' I'll soon knock a few quid together. I'll go back as soon as ever shearin's over. I'm goin' to write away to her to-night."

The Giraffe was the "ringer" of Big Billabong Shed that season. His tallies averaged a hundred and twenty a day. He only sent his hat round once during shearing, and it was noticed that he hesitated at first and only contributed half a crown. But then it was a case of a man being taken from the shed by the police for wife desertion.

"It's always that way," commented Mitchell. "Those soft, good-hearted fellows always end by getting hard and selfish. The world makes 'em so. It's the thought of the soft fools they've been that finds out sooner or later and makes 'em repent. Like as not the Giraffe will be the meanest man out back before he's done."

When Big Billabong cut out, and we got back to Bourke with our dusty swags and dirty cheques, I spoke to Tom Hall:

"Look here, Tom," I said. "That long fool, the Giraffe, has been breaking his heart for a little girl in Bendigo ever since he's been out back, and she's been breaking her heart for him, and the ass didn't know it till he got a letter from her just before Big Billabong started. He's going to-morrow morning."

That evening Tom stole the Giraffe's hat. "I s'pose it'll turn up in the mornin'," said the Giraffe. "I don't mind a lark," he added, "but it does seem a bit red-hot for the chaps to collar a cove's hat and a feller goin' away for good, p'r'aps, in the mornin'."

Mitchell started the thing going with a quid.

"It's worth it," he said, "to get rid of him. We'll have some peace now. There won't be so many accidents or women in trouble when the Giraffe and his blessed hat are gone. Anyway, he's an eyesore in the town, and he's getting on my nerves for one. . . . Come on, you sinners! Chuck 'em in; we're only taking quids and half-quids."

About daylight next morning Tom Hall slipped into the Giraffe's room at the Carriers' Arms. The Giraffe was sleeping peacefully. Tom put the hat on a chair by his side. The collection had been a record one, and, besides the packet of money in the crown of the hat, there was a silver-mounted pipe with case—the best that could be bought in Bourke, a gold brooch, and several trifles—besides an ugly valentine of a long man in his shirt walking the room with a twin on each arm.

Tom was about to shake the Giraffe by the shoulder, when he noticed a great foot, with about half a yard of big-boned ankle and shank, sticking out at the bottom of the bed. The temptation was too great. Tom took up the hair-brush, and, with the back of it, he gave a smart rap on the point of an in-growing toe-nail, and slithered.

We heard the Giraffe swearing good-naturedly for a while, and then there was a pregnant silence. He was staring at the hat we supposed.

We were all up at the station to see him off. It was rather a long wait. The Giraffe edged me up to the other end of the platform.

He seemed overcome.

"There's—there's some terrible good-hearted fellers in this world," he said. "You mustn't forget 'em, Harry, when you make a big name writin'. I'm—well, I'm blessed if I don't feel as if I was just goin' to blubber!"

I was glad he didn't. The Giraffe blubberin' would have been a spectacle. I steered him back to his friends.

"Ain't you going to kiss me, Bob?" said the Great Western's big, handsome barmaid, as the bell rang.

"Well, I don't mind kissin' you, Alice," he said, wiping his mouth. "But I'm goin' to be married, yer know." And he kissed her fair on the mouth.

"There's nothin' like gettin' into practice," he said, grinning round.

We thought he was improving wonderfully; but at the last moment something troubled him.

"Look here, you chaps," he said, hesitatingly, with his hand in his pocket, "I don't know what I'm going to do with all this stuff. There's that poor washerwoman that scalded her legs liftin' the boiler of clothes off the fire——"

We shoved him into the carriage. He hung—about half of him—out the window, wildly waving his hat, till the train disappeared in the scrub.

Lawson's wish as expressed in the last paragraph, has been given effect by the citizens of Bendigo. Bob Brothers, 'The Giraffe', is the subject of a memorial there.

And, as I sit here writing by lamplight at midday, in the midst of a great city of shallow social sham, of hopeless, squalid poverty, of ignorant selfishness, cultured or brutish, and of noble and heroic endeavour frowned down or callously neglected, I am almost aware of a burst of sunshine in the room, and a long form leaning over my chair, and:

"Excuse me for troublin' yer; I'm always troublin' yer; but there's that there poor woman. . . ."

And I wish I could immortalize him!

312

This is 31 Euroka Street, North Sydney, where Lawson resided with Mrs Byers for some years. Standing at the gate is Tom Mutch, one time Minister for Education in the New South Wales State Parliament, who was Lawson's friend of many years. He recalled staying here with Lawson and Mrs Byers, whom he greatly admired for her dedication to the writer. In 1910 Mutch went with Lawson to Mallacoota and was the person the latter blamed for 'shanghaiing' him to such a place. In his last years Mr Mutch was a Trustee of the State Library Of New South Wales, then known as the Public Library, on the steps of which he would stand and talk about Lawson and his life for as long as he had a listener, invariably winding up with the remark, 'The truth must be told, the truth must be told, my boy, some day it must be published.' His papers are now at the State Library and are a valuable source of Lawson biographical material.

THE STAR OF AUSTRALASIA

We boast no more of our bloodless flag that rose from a nation's
    slime;
Better a shred of a deep-dyed rag from the storms of the olden
    time.
From grander clouds in our peaceful skies than ever were there
    before
I tell you the Star of the South shall rise—in the lurid clouds of
    war.
It ever must be while blood is warm and the sons of men increase;
For ever the nations rose in storm, to rot in a deadly peace.
There'll come a point that we will not yield, no matter if right or
    wrong;
And man will fight on the battle-field while passion and pride
    are strong—
So long as he will not kiss the rod, and his stubborn spirit sours—
For the scorn of Nature and curse of God are heavy on peace
    like ours.

There are boys out there by the western creeks, who hurry away
    from school
To climb the sides of the breezy peaks or dive in the shaded pool,
Who'll stick to their guns when the mountains quake to the tread
    of a mighty war,
And fight for Right or a Grand Mistake as men never fought
    before;
When the peaks are scarred and the sea-walls crack till the farthest
    hills vibrate,
And the world for a while goes rolling back in a storm of love
    and hate.

There are boys today in the city slum and the home of wealth
    and pride
Who'll have *one* home when the storm is come, and fight for it
    side by side,
Who'll hold the cliffs against armoured hells that batter a coastal
    town,
Or grimly die in a hail of shells when the walls come crashing
    down.
And many a pink-white baby girl, the queen of her home today,
Will see the wings of the tempest whirl the mist of our dawn
    away—
Will live to shudder and stop her ears to the thud of the distant
    gun,
And know the sorrow that has no tears when a battle is lost
    and won—
As a mother or wife in the years to come will kneel, wide-eyed
    and white,
And pray to God in her darkened home for the "men in the
    fort tonight".

But, oh! if the cavalry charge again as they did when the world
     was wide,
'Twill be grand in the ranks of a thousand men in that glorious
     race to ride,
And strike for all that is true and strong, for all that is grand
     and brave,
And all that ever shall be, so long as man has a soul to save.
He must lift the saddle, and close his "wings", and shut his
     angels out,
And steel his heart for the end of things, who'd ride with a
     stockman scout,
When the race they ride on the battle-track, and the waning
     distance hums,
When the shelled sky shrieks, and the rifles crack like stockwhips
     amongst the gums—
And the straight is reached and the field is gapped and the hoof-
     torn sward grows red
With the blood of those who are handicapped with iron and
     steel and lead;
And the gaps are filled, though unseen by eyes, with the spirit
     and with the shades
Of the world-wide rebel dead who'll rise and rush with the Bush
     Brigades.

All creeds and trades will have soldiers there—give every class
     its due—
And there'll be many a clerk to spare for the pride of the jackeroo.
They'll fight for honour and fight for love, and a few will fight
     for gold,
For the devil below and for God above, as our fathers fought
     of old;
And some half-blind with exultant tears, and some stiff-lipped,
     stern-eyed,
For the pride of a thousand after-years and the old eternal pride;
The soul of the world they will feel and see in the chase and the
     grim retreat—
They'll know the glory of victory—and the grandeur of defeat.
The South will wake to a mighty change ere a hundred years
     are done
With arsenals west of the mountain range and every spur its gun.
And many a rickety son of a gun, on the tides of the future
     tossed,
Will tell how battles were really won that History says were lost,
Will trace the field with his pipe, and shirk the facts that are
     hard to explain,
As grey old mates of the diggings work the old ground over again—
How "This was our centre, and this a redoubt, and that was a
     scrub in the rear,
And this was the point where the Guards held out, and the
     enemy's lines were here."

They'll tell the tales of the nights before and the tales of the ship
    and fort
Till the sons of Australia take to war as their fathers took to sport,
Till their breath comes deep and their eyes grow bright at the
    tales of our chivalry,
And every boy will want to fight, nor care what the cause may be—
When the children run to the doors and cry: "Oh, mother, the
    troops are come!"
And every heart in the town leaps high at the first loud thud
    of the drum.
They'll know, apart from its mystic charm, what music is at last,
When, proud as a boy with a broken arm, the regiment marches
    past.
And the veriest wreck in the drink-fiend's clutch, no matter how
    low or mean,
Will feel, when he hears that march, a touch of the man that he
    might have been.

And fools, when the fiends of war are out and the city skies aflame,
Will have something better to talk about than an absent woman's
    shame,
Will have something nobler to do by far than jest at a friend's
    expense.
Or blacken a name in a public bar or over a backyard fence.
And this we learn from the libelled past, though its methods were
    somewhat rude—
A Nation's born where the shells fall fast, or its lease of life
    renewed.
We in part atone for the ghoulish strife and the crimes of the
    peace we boast,
And the better part of a people's life in the storm comes uppermost.

The selfsame spirit that drives a man to the depths of drink and
    crime
Will do the deeds in the heroes' van that live till the end of time.
The living death in the lonely bush, the greed of the selfish town,
And even the creed of the outlawed push is chivalry—upside down.
'Twill be while ever our blood is hot, while ever the world goes
    wrong,
The nations rise in a war, to rot in a peace that lasts too long.
And southern Nation and southern State, aroused from their
    dream of ease,
Must sign in the Book of Eternal Fate their stormy histories.

THE VAGABOND

White handkerchiefs wave from the short black pier
  As we glide to the grand old sea—
But the song of my heart is for none to hear
  If none of them waves for me.
A careless roaming life is mine,
  Ever by field or flood—
For not far back in my father's line
  Was a dash of the Gipsy blood.

Flax and tussock and fern,
  Gum and mulga and sand,
Reef and palm—but my fancies turn
  Ever away from land;
Strange wild cities in ancient state,
  Range and river and tree,
Snow and ice. But my star of fate
  Is ever across the sea.

A god-like ride on a thundering sea
  When all but the stars are blind—
A desperate race from Eternity
  With a gale-and-a-half behind.
A jovial spree in the cabin at night,
  A song on the rolling deck,
A lark ashore with the ships in sight,
  Till—a wreck goes down with a wreck.

A smoke and a yarn on the deck by day,
  When life is a waking dream,
And care and trouble so far away
  That out of your life they seem.
A roving spirit in sympathy,
  Who has travelled the whole world o'er—
My heart forgets, in a week at sea,
  The trouble of years on shore.

A rolling stone—'tis a saw for slaves—
  Philosophy false as old—
Wear out or break 'neath the feet of knaves,
  Or rot in your bed of mould!
But I'd rather trust to the darkest skies
  And the wildest seas that roar,
Or die, where the stars of Nations rise,
  In the stormy clouds of war.

Cleave to your country, home and friends,
  Die in the sordid strife—
You can count your friends on your finger ends
  In the critical hours of life.
Sacrifice all for the family's sake,
  Bow to their selfish rule!
Slave till your big soft heart they break—
  The heart of the "family fool".

I've never a love that can sting my pride,
  Nor a friend to prove untrue;
For I leave my love ere the turning tide,
  And my friends are all too new.
The curse of the Powers on a peace like ours,
  With its greed and its treachery—
A stranger's hand, and a stranger-land,
  And the rest of the world for me!

But why be bitter? The world is cold
  To one with a frozen heart;
New friends are often so like the old,
  They seem of the Past a part—
As a better part of the past appears,
  When enemies, parted long,
Are come together in kinder years,
  With their better nature strong.

I had a friend, ere my first ship sailed,
  A friend I never deserved—
For the selfish strain in my blood prevailed
  As soon as my turn was served.
And the memory haunts my heart with shame—
  Or, rather, the pride that's there;
In different guises, but soul the same,
  I meet him everywhere.

I had a chum. When the times were tight
  We starved in Australian scrubs;
We froze together in parks at night,
  And laughed together in pubs.
And I often hear a laugh like his
  From a sense of humour keen,
And catch a glimpse in a passing phiz
  Of his broad, good-humoured grin.

And I had a love—'twas a love to prize—
  But I never went back again...
I have seen the light of her kind grey eyes
  In many a face since then.

.   .   .   .   .   .

The sailors say 'twill be rough tonight,
  As they fasten the hatches down;
The south is black, and the bar is white,
  And the drifting smoke is brown.
The gold has gone from the western haze,
  The sea-birds circle and swarm—
But we shall have plenty of sunny days,
  And little enough of storm.

The hill is hiding the short black pier,
  As the last white signal's seen;
The points run in, and the houses veer,
  And the great bluff stands between.
So darkness swallows each far white speck
  On many a wharf and quay;
The night comes down on a restless deck,—
  Grim cliffs—and—The Open Sea!

THE OLD BARK SCHOOL

It was built of bark and poles, and the roof was full of holes
   And each leak in rainy weather made a pool;
And the walls were mostly cracks lined with calico and sacks—
   There was little need for windows in the school.

Then we rode to school and back by the rugged gully-track,
   On the old grey horse that carried three or four;
And he looked so very wise that he lit the Master's eyes
   Every time he put his head in at the door.

He had run with Cobb and Co.—"That grey leader, let him go!"
   There were men "as knowed the brand upon his hide",
Some "as knowed him on the course"—Funeral service: "Good
     old horse!"
   When he burnt him in the gully where he died.

Kevin was the master's name, 'twas from Ireland that he came,
   Where the tanks are always full, and feed is grand;
And the joker then in vogue said his lessons wid a brogue—
   'Twas unconscious imitation, understand.

And we learnt the world in scraps from some ancient dingy maps
   Long discarded by the public-schools in town;
And as nearly every book dated back to Captain Cook
   Our geography was somewhat upside-down.

It was "in the book" and so—well, at that we'd let it go,
   For we never would believe that print could lie;
And we all learnt pretty soon that when school came out at noon
   "The sun is in the south part of the sky".

And Ireland!—*that* was known from the coast-line to Athlone,
　But little of the land that gave us birth;
Save that Captain Cook was killed (and was very likely grilled)
　And "our blacks are just the lowest race on earth".

And a woodcut, in its place, of the same degraded race,
　More like camels than the blackmen that we knew;
Jimmy Bullock, with the rest, scratched his head and gave it best;
　But he couldn't stick a bobtailed kangaroo!

Now the old bark school is gone, and the spot it stood upon
　Is a cattle-camp where curlews' cries are heard;
There's a brick school on the flat—an old school-mate teaches that—
　It was built when Mr Kevin was "transferred".

But the old school comes again with exchanges 'cross the plain—
　With the *Out-Back Press* my fancy roams at large
When I read of passing stock, of a western mob or flock,
　With James Bullock, Grey, or Henry Dale in charge.

When I think how Jimmy went from the old bark school content,
　"Eddicated", with his packhorse after him,
Well...perhaps, if I were back, I would follow in his track,
　And let Kevin "finish" me as he did Jim.

THE LIGHTS OF COBB AND CO.

Fire lighted; on the table a meal for sleepy men;
A lantern in the stable; a jingle now and then;
The mail-coach looming darkly by light of moon and star;
The growl of sleepy voices; a candle in the bar;
A stumble in the passage of folk with wits abroad;
A swear-word from a bedroom—the shout of "All aboard!"
"Tchk tchk! Git-up!" "Hold fast, there!" and down the range we go;
Five hundred miles of scattered camps will watch for Cobb and Co.

Old coaching towns already decaying for their sins;
Uncounted "Half-Way Houses", and scores of "Ten-Mile Inns";
The riders from the stations by lonely granite peaks;
The black-boy for the shepherds on sheep and cattle creeks;
The roaring camps of Gulgong, and many a "Digger's Rest";
The diggers on the Lachlan; the huts of Farthest West;
Some twenty thousand exiles who sailed for weal or woe—
The bravest hearts of twenty lands will wait for Cobb and Co.

The morning star has vanished, the frost and fog are gone,
In one of those grand mornings which but on mountains dawn;
A flask of friendly whisky—each other's hopes we share—
And throw our top-coats open to drink the mountain air.
The roads are rare to travel, and life seems all complete;
The grind of wheels on gravel, the trot of horses' feet,
The trot, trot, trot and canter, as down the spur we go—
The green sweeps to horizons blue that call for Cobb and Co.

We take a bright girl actress through western dusts and damps,
To bear the home-world message, and sing for sinful camps,
To stir our hearts and break them, wild hearts that hope and ache—
(Ah! when she thinks again of these her own must nearly break!)
Five miles this side the gold-field, a loud, triumphant shout:
Five hundred cheering diggers have snatched the horses out:
With "Auld Lang Syne" in chorus, through roaring camps they go
That cheer for her, and cheer for Home, and cheer for Cobb and Co.

Three lamps above the ridges and gorges dark and deep,
A flash on sandstone cuttings where sheer the sidlings sweep,
A flash on shrouded waggons, on water ghastly white;
Weird bush and scattered remnants of "rushes in the night";
Across the swollen river a flash beyond the ford:
Ride hard to warn the driver! He's drunk or mad, good Lord!
But on the bank to westward a broad and cheerful glow—
New camps extend across the plains new routes for Cobb and Co.

Swift scramble up the sidling where teams climb inch by inch;
Pause, bird-like, on the summit—then breakneck down the pinch;
By clear, ridge-country rivers, and gaps where tracks run high,
Where waits the lonely horseman, cut clear against the sky;
Past haunted half-way houses—where convicts made the bricks—
Scrub-yards and new bark shanties, we dash with five and six;
Through stringy-bark and blue-gum, and box and pine we go—
A hundred miles shall see tonight the lights of Cobb and Co.!

J. Le Gay Brereton,
a close friend of
Lawson's from
1894 when they were
introduced by
Mary Gilmore,
took exception to the
sentiments in
these verses.
Lawson wrote to him
from New Zealand
in an apologetic
mood, pointing to
Professor E. E.
Morris of Mel-
bourne University
as the target.

THE UNCULTURED RHYMER
TO HIS CULTURED CRITICS

Fight through ignorance, want, and care—
    Through the griefs that crush the spirit;
Push your way to a fortune fair,
    And the smiles of the world you'll merit.
Long, as a boy, for the chance to learn—
    For the chance that Fate denies you;
Win degrees where the Life-lights burn,
    And scores will teach and advise you.

My cultured friends! you have come too late
    With your bypath nicely graded;
I've fought thus far on my track of Fate,
    And I'll follow the rest unaided.
Must I be stopped by a college gate
    On the track of Life encroaching?
Be dumb to Love, and be dumb to Hate,
    For the lack of a college's coaching?

You grope for Truth in a language dead—
    In the dust 'neath tower and steeple!
What do you know of the tracks we tread,
    And what of the living people?
I "*must* read this, and that, and the rest",
    And write as the cult expects me?—
I'll read the book that may please me best,
    And write as my heart directs me!

You were quick to pick on a faulty line
    That I strove to put my soul in:
Your eyes were keen for a dash of mine
    In the place of a semi-colon—
And blind to the rest. And is it for such
    As you I must brook restriction?
"I was taught too little?" I learnt too much
    To care for a pedant's diction!

Must I turn aside from my destined way
    For a task your Joss would find me?
I come with strength of the living day,
    And with half the world behind me;
I leave you alone in your cultured halls
    To drivel and croak and cavil:
Till your voice goes farther than college walls,
    Keep out of the tracks we travel!

Cobb & Co.'s Coach at St George, Southern Queensland. When, in 1859, Freeman Cobb and his three partners sold out their respective interests in the coaching company which they had established six years previously in Victoria, the new proprietors saw no reason to change the name. The words had a ring about them that made the name somehow appropriate to its purpose, in much the same way that Wells Fargo, its American counterpart, had.

Freeman Cobb and his associates had come from America in quest of gold in the early 1850s but soon abandoned the digger's life for that of providing a needed and paying transport service to the mining fields and their inhabitants. Cobb and two of his friends returned to America where he became for a time a member of the American Senate. Coaching must have been in his blood for in 1873, the year of his death, he was running a company which transported men and merchandise from Port Elizabeth to the Kimberley diamond mines in South Africa.

He probably never knew how deeply his name was graven into the story of Australian transport where it became synonymous with the coaching days, a fact for which his successors in the company should take the credit.

Gradually the horse-drawn vehicles retreated before the competition of the railways, and later the motor coaches, and the last Cobb & Co. coach was taken off the road in the back country of Queensland in 1924.

"SHALL WE GATHER AT THE RIVER?"

God's preacher, of churches unheeded,
God's vineyard, though barren the sod,
Plain spokesman where spokesman is needed,
Rough link 'twixt the Bushman and God.

—The Christ of the Never.

TOLD BY JOE WILSON

I never told you about Peter M'Laughlan. He was a sort of bush missionary up-country and out back in Australia, and before he died he was known from Riverina down south in New South Wales to away up through the Never-Never country in western Queensland.

His past was a mystery, so, of course, there were all sorts of yarns about him. He was supposed to be a Scotchman from London, and some said that he had got into trouble in his young days and had had to clear out of the old country; or, at least, that he had been a ne'er-do-well and had been sent out to Australia on the remittance system. Some said he'd studied for the law, some said he'd studied for a doctor, while others believed that he was, or had been, an ordained minister. I remember one man who swore (when he was drinking) that he had known Peter M'Laughlan as a medical student in a big London hospital, and that he had started in practice for himself somewhere near Gray's Inn Road in London. Anyway, as I got to know him he struck me as being a man who had looked into the eyes of so much misery in his life that some of it had got into his own.

He was a tall man, straight and well built, and about forty or forty-five, when I first saw him. He had wavy dark hair, and a close, curly beard. I once heard a woman say that he had a beard like you see in some Bible pictures of Christ. Peter M'Laughlan seldom smiled; there was something in his big dark brown eyes that was scarcely misery, nor yet sadness—a sort of haunted sympathy.

He must have had money, or else he got remittances from home, for he paid his way and helped many a poor devil. They said that he gave away most of his money. Sometimes he worked for a while himself as bookkeeper at a shearing-shed, wool-sorter, shearer, even rouseabout; he'd work at anything a bushman could get to do. Then he'd go out back to God-forgotten districts and preach to bushmen in one place, and get a few children together in another and teach them to read. He could take his drink, and swear a little when he thought it necessary. On one occasion, at a rough shearing-shed, he called his beloved brethren "damned fools" for drinking their cheques.

Towards the end of his life if he went into a "rough" shed or shanty west of the Darling River—and some of them *were* rough—there would be a rest in the language and drinking, even a fight would be interrupted, and there would be more than one who would lift their hats to Peter M'Laughlan. A bushman very rarely lifts his hat to a man, yet the worst characters of the West have listened bareheaded to Peter when he preached.

It was said in our district that Peter only needed to hint to the squatter that he wanted fifty or a hundred pounds to help someone or something, and the squatter would give it to him without question or hesitation.

He'd nurse sick boundary-riders, shearers, and station-hands, often sitting in the desolate hut by the bedside of a sick man night after night. And, if he had time, he'd look up the local blacks and see how they were getting on. Once, on a far out back sheep station, he sat for three nights running, by the bedside of a young Englishman, a B.A. they said he was, who'd been employed as tutor at the homestead and who died a wreck, the result of five years of life in London and Paris. The poor fellow was only thirty. And the last few hours of his life he talked to Peter in French, nothing but French. Peter understood French and one or two other languages, besides English and Australian; but whether the young wreck was raving or telling the story of a love, or his life, none of us ever knew, for Peter never spoke of it. But they said that at the funeral Peter's eyes seemed haunted more than usual.

There's the yarn about Peter and the dying cattle at Piora Station one terrible drought, when the surface was as bare as your hand for hundreds of miles, and the heat like the breath of a furnace, and the sheep and cattle were perishing by thousands. Peter M'Laughlan was out on the run helping the station-hands to pull out cattle that had got bogged in the muddy water-holes and were too weak to drag themselves out, when, about dusk, a gentlemanly "piano-fingered" parson, who had come to the station from the next town, drove out in his buggy to see the men. He spoke to Peter M'Laughlan.

"Brother," he said, "do you not think we should offer up a prayer?"

"What for?" asked Peter, standing in his shirt sleeves, a rope in his hands and mud from head to foot.

"For? Why, for rain, brother," replied the parson, a bit surprised.

Peter held up his finger and said "Listen!"

Now, with a big mob of travelling stock camped on the plain at night, there is always a lowing, soughing or moaning sound, a sound like that of the sea on the shore at a little distance; and, altogether, it might be called the sigh or yawn of a big mob in camp. But the long, low moaning of cattle dying of hunger and thirst on the hot barren plain in a drought is altogether different, and, at night, there is something awful about it—you couldn't describe it. This is what Peter M'Laughlan heard.

"Do you hear that?" he asked the other preacher.

The little parson said he did. Perhaps *he* only heard the weak lowing of cattle.

"Do you think that God will hear us when He does not hear *that*?" asked Peter.

The parson stared at him for a moment and then got into his buggy and drove away, greatly shocked and deeply offended. But, later on, over tea at the homestead, he said that he felt sure that that "unfortunate man," Peter M'Laughlan, was not in his right mind; that his wandering, irregular life, or the heat, must have affected him.

I well remember the day when I first heard Peter M'Laughlan preach. I was about seventeen then. We used sometimes to attend service held on Sunday afternoon, about once a month, in a little slab-and-bark school-house in the scrub off the main road, three miles or so from our selection, in a barren hole amongst the western ridges of the Great Dividing Range. School was held in this hut for a few weeks or a few months now and again, when a teacher could be got to stay there and teach, and cook for himself, for a pound a week, more or less contributed by the parents. A parson from the farming town to the east, or the pastoral town over the ridges to the west, used to come in his buggy when it didn't rain and wasn't too hot to hold the service.

I remember this Sunday. It was a blazing hot day towards the end of a long and fearful drought which ruined many round there. The parson was expected, and a good few had come to "chapel" in spring-carts, on horseback, and on foot; farmers and their wives and sons and daughters. The children had been brought here to Sunday-school, taught by some of the girls, in the morning. I can see it all now quite plain. The one-roomed hut, for it was no more, with the stunted blue-grey gum scrub all round. The white, dusty road, so hot that you could cook eggs in the dust. The horses tied up, across the road, in the supposed shade under clumps of scraggy saplings along by the fence of a cattle-run. The little crowd outside the hut: selectors in washed and mended tweeds, some with paper collars, some wearing starched and ironed white coats, and in blucher boots, greased or blackened, or the young men wearing "larstins" (elastic-side boots). The women and girls in prints and cottons (or cheap "alpaca," etc.), and a bright

328

bit of ribbon here and there amongst the girls. The white heat blazed every-where, and "dazzled" across light-coloured surfaces—dead white trees, fence-posts, and sand-heaps, like an endless swarm of bees passing in the sun's glare. And over above the dry box-scrub-covered ridges, the great Granite Peak, glaring like a molten mass.

The people didn't like to go inside out of the heat and sit down before the minister came. The wretched hut was a rough school, sometimes with a clay fire-place where the teacher cooked, and a corner screened off with sacking where he had his bunk; it was a camp for tramps at other times, or lizards and possums, but to-day it was a house of God, and as such the people respected it.

The town parson didn't turn up. Perhaps he was unwell, or maybe the hot, dusty ten-mile drive was too much for him to face. One of the farmers, who had tried to conduct service on a previous occasion on which the ordained minister had failed us, had broken down in the middle of it, so he was out of the question. We waited for about an hour, and then who should happen to ride along but Peter M'Laughlan, and one or two of the elder men asked him to hold service. He was on his way to see a sick friend at a sheep station over the ridges, but he said that he could spare an hour or two. (Nearly every man who was sick, either in stomach or pocket, was a friend of Peter M'Laughlan.) Peter tied up his horse under a bush shed at the back of the hut, and we followed him in.

The "school" had been furnished with a rough deal table and a wooden chair for "the teacher," and with a few rickety desks and stools cadged from an old "provisional" school in town when the new public school was built; and the desks and stools had been fastened to the floor to strengthen them; they had been made for "infant" classes, and youth out our way ran to length. But when grown men over six feet high squeezed in behind the desks and sat down on the stools the effect struck me as being ridiculous. In fact, I am afraid that on the first occasion it rather took my attention from the sermon, and I remember being made very uncomfortable by a school chum, Jack Barnes, who took a delight in catching my eye and winking or grinning. He could wink without changing a solemn line in his face and grin without exploding, and I couldn't. The boys usually sat on seats, slabs on blocks of wood, along the wall at the far end of the room, which was comfortable, for they had a rest for their backs. One or two of the boys were nearing six feet high, so they could almost rest their chins on their knees as they sat. But I squatted with some of my tribe on a stool along the wall by the teacher's table, and so could see most of the congregation.

Above us bare tie-beams and the round sapling rafters (with the bark still on), and the inner sides of the sheets of stringy-bark that formed the roof. The slabs had been lined with sacking at one time, but most of it had fallen or dry-rotted away; there were wide cracks between the slabs and we could see the white glare of sunlight outside, with a strip of dark shade, like a deep trench in the white ground, by the back wall. Someone had brought a canvas water-bag and hung it to the beam on the other side of the minister's table, with a pint-pot over the tap, and the drip, drip from the bag made the whole place seem cooler.

I studied Peter M'Laughlan first. He was dressed in washed and mended tweed vest and trousers, and had on a long, light-coloured coat of a material which we called "Chinese silk." He wore a "soft" cotton shirt with collar attached, and blucher boots.

He gave out a hymn in his quiet, natural way, said a prayer, gave out another hymn, read a chapter from the Bible, and then gave out another hymn. They liked to sing, out in those places. The Southwicks used to bring a cranky little harmonium in the back of their old dog-cart, and Clara Southwick used to accompany the hymns. She was a very pretty girl, fair, and could play and sing well. I used to think she had the sweetest voice I ever heard. But—ah, well——

Peter didn't sing himself, at first. I got an idea that he couldn't. While they were singing he stood loosely, with one hand in his trouser-pocket, scratching his beard with his hymn-book, and looking as if he were thinking things over, and only rousing himself to give another verse. He forgot to give it once or twice, but we got through all right. I noticed the wife of one of the men who had asked Peter to preach looking rather black at her husband, and I reckoned that he'd get it hotter than the weather on the way home.

Then Peter stood up and commenced to preach. He stood with both hands in his pockets, at first, his coat ruffled back, and there was the stem of a clay pipe sticking out of his waistcoat-pocket. The pipe fascinated me for a while, but after that I forgot the pipe and was fascinated by the man. Peter's face was one that didn't strike you at first with its full strength, it grew on you; it grew on me, and before he had done preaching I thought it was the noblest face I had ever seen.

He didn't preach much of hope in this world. How could he? The drought had been blazing over these districts for nearly a year, with only a shower now and again, which was a mockery—scarcely darkening the baked ground. Wheat crops came up a few inches and were parched by the sun or mown for hay, or the cattle turned on them; and last year there had been rust and smut in the wheat. And, on top of it all, the dreadful cattle plague, pleuro-pneumonia, had somehow been introduced into the district. One big farmer had lost fifty milkers in a week.

Peter M'Laughlan didn't preach much of hope in this world; how could he? There were men there who had slaved for twenty, thirty, forty years; worked as farmers have to work in few other lands—first to clear the stubborn bush from the barren soil, then to fence the ground, and manure it, and force crops from it—and for what? There was Cox, the farmer, starved off his selection after thirty years and going out back with his drays to work at tank-sinking for a squatter. There was his eldest son going shearing or droving—anything he could get to do—a stoop-shouldered, young-old man of thirty. And behind them, in the end, would be a dusty patch in the scrub, a fence-post here and there, and a pile of chimneystones and a hardwood slab or two where the hut was—for thirty hard years of the father's life and twenty of the son's.

I forget Peter's text, if he had a text; but the gist of his sermon was that there was a God—there was a heaven! And there were men there listening who needed to believe these things. There was old Ross from across the creek, old, but not sixty, a hard man. Only last week he had broken down and fallen on his knees on the baked sods in the middle of his ploughed ground and prayed for rain. His frightened boys had taken him home, and later on, the same afternoon, when they brought news of four more cows down with "the pleuro" in an outer paddock, he had stood up outside his own door and shaken his fist at the brassy sky and cursed high heaven to the terror of his family, till his brave, sun-browned wife dragged him inside and soothed him. And Peter M'Laughlan knew all about this.

Ross's family had the doctor out to him, and persuaded him to come tc church this Sunday. The old man sat on the front seat, stooping forward, with his elbow resting on the desk and his chin on his hand, bunching up his beard over his mouth with his fingers and staring gloomily at Peter with dark, piercing eyes from under bushy eyebrows, just as I've since seen a Scotchman stare at Max O'Rell all through a humorous lecture called "A nicht wi' Sandy."

Ross's right hand resting on the desk was very eloquent: horny, scarred and knotted at every joint, with broken, twisted nails, and nearly closed, as though fitted to the handle of an axe or a spade. Ross was an educated man (he had a regular library of books at home), and perhaps that's why he suffered so much.

Peter preached as if he were speaking quietly to one person only, but every word was plain and every sentence went straight to someone. I believe he looked every soul in the eyes before he had done. Once he said something and caught my eye, and I felt a sudden lump in my throat. There was a boy there, a pale, thin, sensitive boy who was eating his heart out because of things he didn't understand. He was ambitious and longed for something different from this life; he'd written a story or two and some rhymes for the local paper; his companions considered him a "bit ratty" and the grown-up people thought him a "bit wrong in his head," idiotic, or at least "queer." And during his sermon Peter spoke of "unsatisfied longings," of the hope of something better, and said that one had to suffer much and for long years before he could preach or write; and then he looked at that boy. I knew the boy very well; he has risen in the world since then.

Peter spoke of the life we lived, of the things we knew, and used names and terms that we used. "I don't know whether it was a blanky sermon or a blanky lecture," said long swanky Jim Bullock afterwards, "but it was straight and hit some of us hard. It hit me once or twice, I can tell yer." Peter spoke of our lives: "And there is beauty—even in this life and in this place," he said. "Nothing is wasted—nothing is without reason. There is beauty even in this place——"

I noticed something like a hint of a hard smile on Ross's face; he moved the hand on the desk and tightened it.

"Yes," said Peter, as if in answer to Ross's expression and the movement of his hand, "there is beauty in this life here. After a good season, and when the bush is tall and dry, when the bush-fires threaten a man's crop of ripened wheat, there are tired men who run and ride from miles round to help that man, and who fight the fire all night to save his wheat—and some of them may have been wrangling with him for years. And in the morning, when the wheat is saved and the danger is past, when the fire

331

is beaten out or turned, there are blackened, grimy hands that come together and grip—hands that have not joined for many a long day."

Old Palmer, Ross's neighbour, moved uneasily. He had once helped Ross to put a fire out, but they had quarrelled again since. Ross still sat in the same position, looking the hard man he was. Peter glanced at Ross, looked down and thought a while, and then went on again:

"There is beauty even in this life and in this place. When a man loses his farm, or his stock, or his crop, through no fault of his own, there are poor men who put their hands into their pockets to help him."

Old Kurtz, over the ridge, had had his stacked crop of wheat in sheaf burned—some scoundrel had put a match to it at night—and the farmers round had collected nearly fifty pounds for him.

"There is beauty even in this life and in this place. In the blazing drought, when the cattle lie down and cannot rise from weakness, neighbours help neighbours to lift them. When one man has hay or chaff and no stock, he gives it or sells it cheaply to the poor man who has starving cattle and no fodder."

I only knew one or two instances of this kind; but Peter was preaching of what men should do as well as what they did.

"When a man meets with an accident, or dies, there are young men who go with their ploughs and horses and plough the ground for him or his widow and put in the crop."

Jim Bullock and one or two other young men squirmed. They had ploughed old Leonard's land for him when he met with an accident in the shape of a broken leg got by a kick from a horse. They had also ploughed the ground for Mrs Phipps when her husband died, working, by the way, all Saturday afternoon and Sunday, for they were very busy at home at that time.

"There is beauty even in this life and in this place. There are women who were friends in girlhood and who quarrelled bitterly over a careless word, an idle tale, or some paltry thing, who live within a mile of each other and have not spoken for years; yet let one fall ill, or lose husband or child, and the other will hurry across to her place and take off her bonnet and tuck up her sleeves, and set to work to help straighten things, and they will kiss, and cry in each other's arms, and be sisters again."

I saw tears in the eyes of two hard and hard-faced women I knew; but they were smiling to each other through their tears.

"And now," said Peter, "I want to talk to you about some other things. I am not preaching as a man who has been taught to preach comfortably, but as a man who has learned in the world's school. I know what trouble is. Men," he said, still speaking quietly, "and women too! I have been through trouble as deep as any of yours—perhaps deeper. I know how you toil and suffer, I know what battles you fight, I know. I too fought a battle, perhaps as hard as any you fight. I carry a load and am fighting a battle still." His eyes were very haggard just then. "But this is not what I wanted to talk to you about. I have nothing to say against a young man going away from this place to better himself, but there are young men who go out back shearing or droving, young men who are good-hearted but careless, who make cheques, and spend their money gambling or drinking and never think of the old folk at home until it is too late. They never think of the old people, alone perhaps, in a desolate hut on a worked-out farm in the scrub."

Jim Bullock squirmed again. He had gone out back last season and made a cheque, and lost most of it on horse-racing and cards.

"They never think—they cannot think how, perhaps, long years agone in the old days, the old father, as a young man, and his brave young wife, came out here and buried themselves in the lonely bush and toiled for many years, trying—it does not matter whether they failed or not—trying to make homes for their children; toiled till the young man was bowed and grey, and the young wife brown and wrinkled and worn out. Exiles they were in the early days—boy-husbands and girl-wives some of them, who left their native lands, who left all that was dear, that seemed beautiful, that seemed to make life worth living, and sacrificed their young lives in drought and utter loneliness to make homes for their children. I want you young men to think of this. Some of them came from England, Ireland, Bonnie Scotland." Ross straightened up and let his hands fall loosely on his knees. "Some from Europe—your foreign fathers—some from across the Rhine in Germany." We looked at old Kurtz. He seemed affected.

Then Peter paused for a moment and blinked thoughtfully at Ross, then he took a drink of water. I can see now that the whole thing was a battle between Peter M'Laughlan and Robert Ross—Scot met Scot. "It seemed to me," Jim Bullock said afterwards, "that Peter was only tryin' to make some of us blanky well blubber."

"And there are men," Peter went on, "who have struggled and suffered and failed, and who have fought and failed again till their tempers are spoiled, until they grow bitter. They go in for self-pity, and self-pity leads to moping and brooding and madness; self-pity is the most selfish and useless thing on the face of God's earth. It is cruel, it is deadly, both to the man and to those who love him, and whom he ought to love. His load grows heavier daily in his imagination, and he sinks down until it is in him to curse God and die. He ceases to care for or to think of his children who are working to help him." (Ross's sons were good, steady, hard-working boys.) "Or the brave wife who has been so true to him for many hard years, who left home and friends and country for his sake. Who bears up in the blackest of times, and persists in looking at the bright side of things for his sake; who has suffered more than he if he only knew it, and suffers now, through him and because of him, but who is patient and bright and cheerful while her heart is breaking. He thinks she does not suffer, that she cannot suffer as a man does. My God! he doesn't know. He has forgotten in her the bright, fresh-faced, loving lassie he loved and won long years agone—long years agone——"

There was a sob, like the sob of an over-ridden horse as it sinks down broken-hearted, and Ross's arms went out on the desk in front of him, and his head went down on them. He was beaten.

He was steered out gently with his wife on one side of him and his eldest son on the other.

"Don't be alarmed, my friends," said Peter, standing by the water-bag with one hand on the tap and the pannikin in the other. "Mr Ross has not

333

been well lately, and the heat has been too much for him." And he went out after Ross. They took him round under the bush shed behind the hut, where it was cooler.

When Peter came back to his place he seemed to have changed his whole manner and tone. "Our friend, Mr Ross, is much better," he said. "We will now sing"—he glanced at Clara Southwick at the harmonium—"we will now sing 'Shall We Gather at the River?'" We all knew that hymn; it was an old favourite round there, and Clara Southwick played it well in spite of the harmonium.

And Peter sang—the first and last time I ever heard him sing. I never had an ear for music; but I never before nor since heard a man's voice that stirred me as Peter M'Laughlan's. We stood like emus, listening to him all through one verse, then we pulled ourselves together.

> Shall we gather at the River,
>   Where bright angels' feet have trod—

The only rivers round there were barren creeks, the best of them only strings of muddy waterholes, and across the ridge, on the sheep-runs, the creeks were dry gutters, with baked banks and beds, and perhaps a mudhole every mile or so, and dead beasts rotting and stinking every few yards.

> Gather with the saints at the River,
>   That flows by the throne of God.

Peter's voice trembled and broke. He caught his breath, and his eyes filled. But he smiled then—he stood smiling at us through his tears.

> The beautiful, the beautiful River,
>   That flows by the throne of God.

Outside I saw women kiss each other who had been at daggers drawn ever since I could remember, and men shake hands silently who had hated each other for years. Every family wanted Peter to come home to tea, but he went across to Ross's, and afterwards down to Kurtz's place, and bled and inoculated six cows or so in a new way, and after tea he rode off over the gap to see his friend.

JOE WILSON'S COURTSHIP

There are many times in this world when a healthy boy is happy. When he is put into knickerbockers, for instance, and "comes a man to-day," as my little Jim used to say. When they're cooking something at home that he likes. When the "sandy blight" or measles breaks out amongst the children, or the teacher or his wife falls dangerously ill—or dies, it doesn't matter which—"and there ain't no school." When a boy is naked and in his natural state for a warm climate like Australia, with three or four of his schoolmates, under the shade of the creek-oaks in the bend where there's a good clear pool with a sandy bottom. When his father buys him a gun, and he starts out after kangaroos or possums. When he gets a horse, saddle, and bridle of his own. When he has his arms in splints or a stitch in his head—he's proud then, the proudest boy in the district.

I wasn't a healthy-minded, average boy; I reckon I was born for a poet by mistake, and grew up to be a bushman, and didn't know what was the matter with me—or the world—but that's got nothing to do with it.

There are times when a man is happy. When he finds out that the girl loves him. When he's just married. When he's a lawful father for the first time, and everything's going on all right: some men make fools of themselves then—I know I did. I'm happy to-night because I'm out of debt and can see clear ahead, and because I haven't been easy for a long time.

But I think that the happiest time in a man's life is when he's courting a girl, and finds out for sure that she loves him, and hasn't a thought for any one else. Make the most of your courting days, you young chaps, and keep them clean, for they're about the only days when there's a chance of poetry and beauty coming into this life. Make the best of them, and you'll never regret it the longest day you live. They're the days that the wife will look back to, anyway, in the brightest of times as well as in the blackest, and there shouldn't be anything in those days that might hurt her when she looks back. Make the most of your courting days, you young chaps, for they will never come again.

A married man knows all about it—after a while; he sees the woman world through the eyes of his wife; he knows what an extra moment's pressure of the hand means, and, if he has had a hard life, and is inclined to be cynical, the knowledge does him no good. It leads him into awful messes sometimes, for a married man, if he's inclined that way, has three times the chance with a woman that a single man has—because the married man knows. He is privileged; he can guess pretty closely what a woman means when she says something else; he knows just how far he can go; he can go farther in five minutes towards coming to the point with a woman than an innocent young man dares go in three weeks. Above all, the married man is more decided with women; he takes them and things for granted. In short he is—well, he is a married man. And, when he knows all this, how much better or happier is he for it? Mark Twain says that he lost all the beauty of the river when he saw it with a pilot's eye—and there you have it.

But it's all new to a young chap, provided he hasn't been a young blackguard. It's all wonderful, new, and strange to him. He's a different man. He finds that he never knew anything about women. He sees none of women's little ways and tricks in his girl. He is in heaven one day and down near the other place the next; and that's the sort of thing that makes life interesting.

'Joe Wilson' is regarded as a literary self-portrait of the author himself. There is a sense of continuity about them, broken though it may be, which indicate that Lawson hoped one day to weld them into a novel—a literary form that evaded him as much as did the drama. 'Joe Wilson's' world is certainly populated by many of Lawson's characters from other stories and perhaps from his real life too.

He takes his new world for granted. And, when she says she'll be his wife——!

Make the most of your courting days, you young chaps, for they've got a lot of influence on your married life afterwards—a lot more than you'd think. Make the best of them, for they'll never come any more, unless we do our courting over again in another world. If we do, I'll make the most of mine.

But, looking back, I didn't do so badly after all. I never told you about the days I courted Mary. The more I look back the more I come to think that I made the most of them, and if I had no more to regret in married life than I have in my courting days, I wouldn't walk to and fro in the room, or up and down the yard in the dark sometimes, or lie awake some nights thinking. . . . Ah, well!

I was between twenty-one and thirty then: birthdays had never been any use to me, and I'd left off counting them. You don't take much stock in birthdays in the bush. I'd knocked about the country for a few years, shearing and fencing and droving a little, and wasting my life without getting anything for it. I drank now and then, and made a fool of myself. I was reckoned "wild;" but I only drank because I felt less sensitive, and the world seemed a lot saner and better and kinder when I had a few drinks: I loved my fellow-man then and felt nearer to him. It's better to be thought "wild" than to be considered eccentric or ratty. Now, my old mate, Jack Barnes, drank—as far as I could see—first because he'd inherited the gambling habit from his father along with his father's luck; he'd the habit of being cheated and losing very bad, and when he lost he drank. Till drink got a hold of him. Jack was sentimental too, but in a different way. I was sentimental about other people—more fool I!—whereas Jack was sentimental about himself. Before he was married, and when he was recovering from a spree, he'd write rhymes about "Only a boy, drunk by the roadside," and that sort of thing; and he'd call 'em poetry, and talk about signing them and sending them to the *Town and Country Journal*. But he generally tore them up when he got better. The bush is breeding a race of poets, and I don't know what the country will come to in the end.

Well. It was after Jack and I had been out shearing at Beenaway Shed in the big scrubs. Jack was living in the little farming town of Solong, and I was hanging round. Black, the squatter, wanted some fencing done, and a new stable built, or buggy and harness-house, at his place at Haviland, a few miles out of Solong. Jack and I were good bush carpenters, so we took the job to keep us going till something else turned up. "Better than doing nothing," said Jack.

"There's a nice little girl in service at Black's," he said. "She's more like an adopted daughter, in fact, than a servant. She's a real good little girl, and good-looking into the bargain. I hear that young Black is sweet on her, but they say she won't have anything to do with him. I know a lot of chaps that have tried for her, but they've never had any luck. She's a regular little dumpling, and I like dumplings. They call her Possum. You ought to try a bear up in that direction, Joe."

I was always shy with women—except perhaps some that I should have fought shy of; but Jack wasn't—he was afraid of no woman, good, bad, or indifferent. I haven't time to explain why, but somehow, whenever a girl took any notice of me I took if for granted that she was only playing with me, and felt nasty about it. I made one or two mistakes, but—ah well!

"My wife knows little Possum," said Jack. "I'll get her to ask her out to our place, and let you know."

I reckoned that he wouldn't get me there then, and made a note to be on the watch for tricks. I had a hopeless little love-story behind me, of course. I suppose most married men can look back to their lost love; few marry the first flame. Many a married man looks back and thinks it was damned lucky that he didn't get the girl he couldn't have. Jack had been my successful rival, only he didn't know it—I don't think his wife knew it either. I used to think her the prettiest and sweetest little girl in the district.

But Jack was mighty keen on fixing me up with the little girl at Haviland. He seemed to take it for granted that I was going to fall in love with her at first sight. He took too many things for granted as far as I was concerned, and got me into awful tangles sometimes.

"You let me alone, and I'll fix you up, Joe," he said, as we rode up to the station. "I'll make it all right with the girl. You're rather a good-looking chap. You've got the sort of eyes that take with girls, only you don't know it; you haven't got the go. If I had your eyes along with my other attractions, I'd be in trouble on account of a woman about once a week."

"For God's sake shut up, Jack," I said.

Do you remember the first glimpse you got of your wife? Perhaps not in England, where so many couples grow up together from childhood; but it's different in Australia, where you may hail from two thousand miles away from where your wife was born, and yet she may be a countrywoman of yours, and a countrywoman in ideas and politics too. I remember the first glimpse I got of Mary.

It was a two-story brick house with wide balconies and verandas all round, and a double row of pines down to the front gate. Parallel at the back was an old slab-and-shingle place, one room deep and about eight rooms long, with a row of skillions at the back: the place was used for kitchen, laundry and servants' rooms. This was the old homestead before the new house was built. There was a wide, old-fashioned brick-floored veranda in front, with an open end; there was ivy climbing up the veranda-post on one side and a baby-rose on the other, and a grape-vine near the chimney. We rode up to the end of the veranda, and Jack called to see if there was anyone at home, and Mary came trotting out; so it was in the frame of vines that I first saw her.

More than once since then I've had a fancy to wonder whether the rose-bush killed the grape-vine or the ivy smothered 'em both in the end. I used to have a vague idea of riding that way some day to see. You do get strange fancies at odd times.

Jack asked her if the boss was in. He did all the talking. I saw a little girl, rather plump, with a complexion like a New England or Blue Mountain girl, or a girl from Tasmania, or from Gippsland in Victoria. Red and white girls were very scarce in the Solong district. She had the biggest and brightest eyes I'd seen round there, dark hazel eyes, as I found out afterwards, and bright as a possum's. No wonder they called her "Possum." I forgot at once that Mrs Jack Barnes was the prettiest girl in the district. I felt a sort of comfortable satisfaction in the fact that I was on horseback; most bushmen look better on

337

horseback. It was a black filly, a fresh young thing, and she seemed as shy of girls as I was myself. I noticed Mary glanced in my direction once or twice to see if she knew me; but, when she looked, the filly took all my attention. Mary trotted in to tell old Black he was wanted, and after Jack had seen him and arranged to start work next day, we started back to Solong.

I expected Jack to ask me what I thought of Mary—but he didn't. He squinted at me sideways once or twice, and didn't say anything for a long time, and then he started talking of other things. I began to feel wild at him. He seemed so damnably satisfied with the way things were going. He seemed to reckon that I was a gone case now; but as he didn't say so, I had no way of getting at him. I felt sure he'd go home and tell his wife that Joe Wilson was properly gone on little Possum at Haviland. That was all Jack's way.

Next morning we started to work. We were to build the buggy-house at the back near the end of the old house, but first we had to take down a rotten old place that might have been the original hut in the bush before the old house was built. There was a window in it, opposite the laundry window in the old place, and the first thing I did was to take out the sash. I'd noticed Jack yarning with Possum before he started work. While I was at work at the window he called me round to the other end of the hut to help him lift a grindstone out of the way; and when we'd done it, he took the tip of my ear between his fingers and thumb and stretched it and whispered into it:

"Don't hurry with that window, Joe; the strips are hardwood and hard to get off—you'll have to take the sash out very carefully so as not to break the glass." Then he stretched my ear a little more and put his mouth closer:

"Make a looking-glass of that window, Joe," he said.

I was used to Jack, and when I went back to the window I started to puzzle out what he meant, and presently I saw it by chance.

That window reflected the laundry window: the room was dark inside, and there was a good clear reflection; and presently I saw Mary come to the laundry window and stand with her hands behind her back, thoughtfully watching me. The laundry window had an old-fashioned hinged sash, and I like that sort of window—there's more romance about it, I think. There was a thick dark-green ivy all round the window, and Mary looked prettier than a picture. I squared up my shoulders and put my heels together, and put as much style as I could into my work. I couldn't have turned round to save my life.

Presently Jack came round, and Mary disappeared.

"Well?" he whispered.

"You're a fool, Jack," I said. "She's only interested in the old house being pulled down."

"That's all right," he said. "I've been keeping an eye on the business round the corner, and she ain't interested when *I'm* round this end."

"You seem mightly interested in the business," I said.

"Yes," said Jack. "This sort of thing just suits a man of my rank in times of peace."

"What made you think of the window?" I asked.

"Oh, that's as simple as striking matches. I'm up to all those dodges.

Why, where there wasn't a window, I've fixed up a piece of looking-glass to see if a girl was taking any notice of me when she thought I wasn't looking."

He went away and presently Mary was at the window again, and this time she had a tray with cups of tea and a plate of cake and bread-and-butter. I was prizing off the strips that held the sash, very carefully, and my heart suddenly commenced to gallop, without any reference to me. I'd never felt like that before, except once or twice. It was just as if I'd swallowed some clock-work arrangement, unconsciously, and it had started to go, without warning. I reckon it was all on account of that blarsted Jack working me up. He had a quiet way of working you up to a thing, that made you want to hit him sometimes—after you'd made an ass of yourself.

I didn't hear Mary at first. I hoped Jack would come round and help me out of the fix, but he didn't.

"Mr—Mr Wilson!" said Mary. She had a sweet voice.

I turned round.

"I thought you and Mr Barnes might like a cup of tea."

"Oh, thank you!" I said, and I made a dive for the window, as if hurry would help it. I trod on an old cask-hoop; it sprang up and dinted my shin and I stumbled—and that didn't help matters much.

"Oh! did you hurt yourself, Mr Wilson?" cried Mary.

"Hurt myself! Oh no, not at all, thank you," I blurted out. "It takes more than that to hurt me."

I was about the reddest shy lanky fool of a bushman that ever was taken at a disadvantage on foot, and when I took the tray my hands shook so that a lot of the tea was spilt into the saucers. I embarrassed her too, like the damned fool I was, till she must have been as red as I was, and it's a wonder we didn't spill the whole lot between us. I got away from the window in as much of a hurry as if Jack had cut his leg with a chisel and fainted, and I was running with whisky for him. I blundered round to where he was, feeling like a man feels when he has just made an ass of himself in public. The memory of that sort of thing hurts you worse and makes you jerk your head more impatiently than the thought of a past crime would, I think.

I pulled myself together when I got to where Jack was.

"Here, Jack!" I said. "I've struck something all right; here's some tea and brownie—we'll hang out here all right."

Jack took a cup of tea and a piece of cake and sat down to enjoy it, just as if he'd paid for it and ordered it to be sent out about that time.

He was silent for a while, with the sort of silence that always made me wild at him. Presently he said, as if he'd just thought of it:

"That's a very pretty little girl, Possum, isn't she, Joe? Do you notice how she dresses?—always fresh and trim. But she's got on her best bib-and-tucker to-day, and a pinafore with frills to it. And it's ironing-day, too. It can't be on your account. If it was Saturday or Sunday afternoon, or some holiday, I could understand it. But perhaps one of her admirers is going to take her to the church bazaar in Solong to-night. That's what it is."

He gave me time to think over that.

"But yet she seems interested in you, Joe," he said. "Why didn't you offer to take her to the bazaar instead of letting another chap get in ahead of you? You miss all your chances, Joe."

Then a thought struck me. I ought to have known Jack well enough to have thought of it before.

"Look here, Jack," I said. "What have you been saying to that girl about me?"

"Oh, not much," said Jack. "There isn't much to say about you."

"What did you tell her?"

"Oh, nothing in particular. She'd heard all about you before."

"She hadn't heard much good, I suppose," I said.

"Well, that's true, as far as I could make out. But you've only got yourself to blame. I didn't have the breeding and rearing of you. I smoothed over matters with her as much as I could."

"What did you tell her?" I said. "That's what I want to know."

"Well, to tell the truth, I didn't tell her anything much. I only answered questions."

"And what questions did she ask?"

"Well, in the first place, she asked if your name wasn't Joe Wilson; and I said it was, as far as I knew. Then she said she heard that you wrote poetry, and I had to admit that that was true."

"Look here, Jack," I said, "I've two minds to punch your head."

"And she asked me if it was true that you were wild," said Jack, "and I said you was, a bit. She said it seemed a pity. She asked me if it was true that you drank, and I drew a long face and said that I was sorry to say it was true. She asked me if you had any friends, and I said none that I knew of, except me. I said that you'd lost all your friends; they stuck to you as long as they could, but they had to give you best, one after the other."

"What next?"

"She asked me if you were delicate, and I said no, you were tough as fencing-wire. She said you looked rather pale and thin, and asked me if you had an illness lately. And I said no—it was all on account of the wild dissipated life you'd led. She said it was a pity you hadn't had a mother or a sister to look after you—it was a pity that something couldn't be done for you, and I said it was, but I was afraid that nothing could be done. I told her that I was doing all I could to keep you straight."

I knew enough of Jack to know that most of this was true. And so she only pitied me after all. I felt as if I'd been courting her for six months and she'd thrown me over—but I didn't know anything about women yet.

"Did you tell her I was in jail?" I growled.

"No, by gum! I forgot that. But never mind, I'll fix that up all right. I'll tell her that you got two years' hard for horse-stealing. That ought to make her interested in you, if she isn't already."

We smoked a while.

"And was that all she said?" I asked.

"Who?—oh! Possum," said Jack, rousing himself. "Well—no; let me think—we got chatting of other things—you know a married man's privileged, and can say a lot more to a girl than a single man can. I got talking nonsense about sweethearts, and one thing led to another till at last she said, "I suppose Mr Wilson's got a sweetheart, Mr Barnes?"

"And what did you say?" I growled.

"Oh, I told her that you were a holy terror amongst the girls," said Jack. "You'd better take back that tray, Joe, and let us get to work."

I wouldn't take the tray back—but that didn't mend matters, for Jack took it back himself.

I didn't see Mary's reflection in the window again, so I took the window out. I reckoned that she was just a big-hearted, impulsive little thing, as many Australian girls are, and I reckoned that I was a fool for thinking for a moment that she might give me a second thought, except by way of kindness. Why! young Black and half a dozen better men than me were sweet on her, and young Black was to get his father's station and the money—or rather his mother's money, for she held the stuff (she kept it close, too, by all accounts). Young Black was away at the time, and his mother was dead against him about Mary, but that didn't make any difference, as far as I could see. I reckoned that it was only just going to be a hopeless, heart-breaking, stand-far-off-and-worship affair, as far as I was concerned—like my first love affair, that I haven't told you about yet. I was tired of being pitied by good girls. You see, I didn't know women then. If I had known, I think I might have made more than one mess of my life.

Jack rode home to Solong every night. I was staying at a pub some distance out of town, between Solong and Haviland. There were three or four wet days, and we didn't get on with the work. I fought shy of Mary till one day she was hanging out clothes and the line broke. It was the old-style sixpenny clothes-line. The clothes were all down, but it was clean grass, so it didn't matter much. I looked at Jack.

"Go and help her, you capital idiot!" he said, and I made the plunge.

"Oh, thank you, Mr Wilson!" said Mary, when I came to help. She had the broken end of the line, and was trying to hold some of the clothes off the ground, as if she could pull it an inch with the heavy wet sheets and table-cloths and things on it, or as if it would do any good if she did. But that's the way with some women—especially little women—some of 'em would try to pull a store bullock if they got the end of the rope on the right side of the fence. I took the line from Mary and accidentally touched her soft, plump little hand as I did so: it sent a thrill right through me. She seemed a lot cooler than I was.

Now, in cases like this, especially if you lose your head a bit, you get hold of the loose end of the rope that's hanging from the post with one hand, and the end of the line with the clothes on with the other, and try to pull 'em far enough together to make a knot. And that's about all you do for the present, except look like a fool. Then I took off the post end, spliced the line, took it over the fork, and pulled, while Mary helped me with the prop. I thought Jack might have come and taken the prop from her, but he didn't; he just went on with his work as if nothing was happening inside the horizon.

She'd got the line about two-thirds full of clothes, it was a bit short now, so she had to jump and catch it with one hand and hold it down while she pegged a sheet she'd thrown over. I'd made the plunge now, so I volunteered to help her. I held down the line while she threw the things over and pegged out. As we got near the post and higher I straightened out some ends and pegged myself. Bushmen are handy at most things. We laughed, and now and again Mary would say, "No, that's not the way, Mr Wilson; that's not right; the sheet isn't far enough over; wait till I fix it." I'd a reckless idea once of holding her up while she pegged, and I was glad afterwards that I hadn't made such a fool of myself.

"There's only a few more things in the basket, Miss Brand," I said. "You can't reach—I'll fix 'em up."

She seemed to give a little gasp.

"Oh, those things are not ready yet," she said, "they're not rinsed," and she grabbed the basket and held it away from me. The things looked the same to me as the rest on the line; they looked rinsed enough and blued too. I reckoned that she didn't want me to take the trouble, or thought that I mightn't like to be seen hanging out clothes, and was only doing it out of kindness.

"Oh, it's no trouble," I said, "let me hang 'em out. I like it. I've hung out clothes at home on a windy day," and I made a reach into the basket. But she flushed red, with temper, I thought, and snatched the basket away.

"Excuse me, Mr Wilson," she said, "but those things are not ready yet!" and she marched into the wash-house.

"Ah, well! you've got a little temper of your own," I thought to myself.

When I told Jack, he said that I'd made another fool of myself. He said I'd both disappointed and offended her. He said that my line was to stand off a bit and be serious and melancholy in the background.

That evening when we'd started home, we stopped some time yarning with a chap we met at the gate; and I happened to look back and saw Mary hanging out the rest of the things—she thought that we were out of sight. Then I understood why those things weren't ready while we were round.

For the next day or two Mary didn't take the slightest notice of me, and I kept out of her way. Jack said I'd disillusioned her—and hurt her dignity—which was a thousand times worse. He said I'd spoilt the thing altogether. He said that she'd got an idea that I was shy and poetic, and I'd only shown myself the usual sort of bush-whacker.

I noticed her talking and chatting with other fellows once or twice, and it made me miserable. I got drunk two evenings running, and then, as it appeared afterwards, Mary consulted Jack, and at last said to him, when we were together:

"Do you play draughts, Mr Barnes?"

"No," said Jack.

"Do you, Mr Wilson?" she asked, suddenly turning her big bright eyes on me, and speaking to me for the first time since last washing-day.

"Yes," I said, "I do a little." Then there was a silence, and I had to say something else.

"Do you play draughts, Miss Brand?" I asked.

"Yes," she said, "but I can't get anyone to play with me here of an evening, the men are generally playing cards or reading." Then she said,

"It's very dull these long winter evenings when you've got nothing to do. Young Mr Black used to play draughts, but he's away."

I saw Jack winking at me urgently.

"I'll play a game with you, if you like," I said, "but I ain't much of a player."

"Oh, thank you Mr Wilson! When shall you have an evening to spare?"

We fixed it for that same evening. We got chummy over the draughts. I had a suspicion even then that it was a put-up job to keep me away from the pub.

Perhaps she found a way of giving a hint to old Black without committing herself. Women have ways—or perhaps Jack did it. Anyway, next day the boss came round and said to me:

"Look here, Joe, you've got no occasion to stay at the pub. Bring along your blankets and camp in one of the spare rooms of the old house. You can have your tucker here."

He was a good sort, was Black the squatter: a squatter of the old school, who'd shared the early hardships with his men, and couldn't see why he should not shake hands and have a smoke and a yarn over old times with any of his old station hands that happened to come along. But he'd married an Englishwoman after the hardships were over, and she'd never got any Australian notions.

Next day I found one of the skillion rooms scrubbed out and a bed fixed up for me. I'm not sure to this day who did it, but I suppose that good-natured old Black had given one of the women a hint. After tea I had a yarn with Mary, sitting on a log of the wood-heap. I don't remember exactly how we came to be there, or who sat down first. There was about two feet between us. We got very chummy and confidential. She told me about her childhood and her father.

He'd had been an old mate of Black's, a younger son of a well-to-do English family (with blue blood in it, I believe), and sent out to Australia with a thousand pounds to make his way, as many younger sons are, with more or less. They think they're hard done by; they blue their thousand pounds in Melbourne or Sydney, and they don't make any more nowadays, for the Roarin' Days have been dead these thirty years. I wish I'd had a thousand pounds to start on!

Mary's mother was the daughter of a German immigrant, who selected up there in the old days. She had a will of her own as far as I could understand, and bossed the home till the day of her death. Mary's father made money, and lost it, and drank—and died. Mary remembered him sitting on the veranda one evening with his hand on her head, and singing a German song (the "Lorelei," I think it was) softly, as if to himself. Next day he stayed in bed, and the children were kept out of the room: and, when he died, the children were adopted round (there was a little money coming from England).

Mary told me all about her girlhood. She went first to live with a sort of cousin in town, in a house where they took cards in on a tray, and then she came to live with Mrs Black, who took a fancy to her at first. I'd had no boyhood to speak of, so I gave her some of my ideas on what the world ought to be, and she seemed interested.

Next day there were sheets on my bed, and I felt pretty cocky until I remembered that I'd told her I had no one to care for me; then I suspected pity again.

But next evening we remembered that both our fathers and mothers were dead, and discovered that we had no friends except Jack and old Black, and things went on very satisfactorily.

And next day there was a little table in my room with a crocheted cover and a looking-glass.

I noticed the other girls began to act mysterious and giggle when I was round, but Mary didn't seem aware of it.

We got very chummy. Mary wasn't comfortable at Haviland. Old Black was very fond of her and always took her part, but she wanted to be independent. She had a great idea of going to Sydney and getting into the hospital as a nurse. She had friends in Sydney, but she had no money. There was a little money coming to her when she was twenty-one—a few pounds—and she was going to try and get it before that time.

"Look here, Miss Brand," I said, after we'd watched the moon rise. "I'll lend you the money. I've got plenty—more than I know what to do with."

But I saw I'd hurt her. She sat up very straight for a while, looking before her; then she said it was time to go in, and said, "Good night, Mr Wilson."

I reckoned I'd done it that time; but Mary told me afterwards that she was only hurt because it struck her that what she said about money might have been taken for a hint. She didn't understand me yet, and I didn't know human nature. I didn't say anything to Jack—in fact about this time I left off telling him about things. He didn't seem hurt; he worked hard and seemed happy.

I really meant what I said to Mary about the money. It was pure good nature. I'd be a happier man now, I think, and a richer man perhaps, if I'd never grown more selfish than I was that night on the wood-heap with Mary. I felt a great sympathy for her—but I got to love her. I went through all the ups and downs of it. One day I was having tea in the kitchen and Mary and another girl, named Sarah, reached me a clean plate at the same time: I took Sarah's because she was first, and Mary seemed very nasty about it, and that gave me great hopes. But all next evening she played draughts with a drover that she'd chummed up with. I pretended to be interested in Sarah's talk, but it didn't seem to work.

A few days later a Sydney jackeroo visited the station. He had a good pea-rifle, and one afternoon he started to teach Mary to shoot at a target. They seemed to get very chummy. I had a nice time for three or four days, I can tell you. I was worse than a wall-eyed bullock with the pleuro. The other chaps had a shot out of the rifle. Mary called "Mr Wilson" to have a shot, and I made a worse fool of myself by sulking. If it hadn't been a blooming jackeroo I wouldn't have minded so much.

Next evening the jackeroo and one or two other chaps and the girls went out possum shooting. Mary went. I could have gone, but I didn't. I mooched round all the evening like an orphan bandicoot on a burnt ridge, and then I went up to the pub and filled myself up with beer, and damned

344

the world, and came home and went to bed. I think that evening was the only time I ever wrote poetry down on a piece of paper. I got so miserable that I enjoyed it.

I felt better next morning, and reckoned I was cured. I ran against Mary accidentally, and had to say something.

"How did you enjoy yourself yesterday evening, Miss Brand?" I asked.

"Oh, very well, thank you, Mr Wilson," she said. Then she asked, "How did you enjoy yourself, Mr Wilson?"

I puzzled over that afterwards, but couldn't make anything out of it. Perhaps she only said it for the sake of saying it. But about this time my handkerchiefs and collars disappeared from the room and turned up washed and ironed, and laid tidily on my table. I used to keep an eye out, but could never catch anybody near my room. I straightened up, and kept my room a bit tidy, and when my handkerchief got too dirty, and I was ashamed of letting it go to the wash, I'd slip down to the river after dark and wash it out, and dry it next day, and rub it up to look as if it hadn't been washed, and leave it on my table. I felt so full of hope and joy that I worked twice as hard as Jack, till one morning he remarked casually:

"I see you've made a new mash, Joe. I saw the half-caste cook tidying up your room this morning and taking your collars and things to the wash-house."

I felt very much off colour all the rest of the day, and I had such a bad night of it that I made up my mind next morning to look the hopelessness square in the face and live things down.

It was the evening before Anniversary Day. Jack and I had put in a good day's work to get the job finished, and Jack was having a smoke and a yarn with the chaps before he started home. We sat on an old log along by the fence at the back of the house. There was Jimmy Nowlett the bullock-driver, and Long Dave Regan the drover, and Jim Bullock the fencer, and one or two others. Mary and the station girls and one or two visitors were sitting under the old veranda. The jackeroo was there too, so I felt happy. It was the girls who used to bring the chaps hanging round. They were getting up a dance party for Anniversary night. Along in the evening another chap came riding up to the station: he was a big shearer, a dark, handsome fellow, who looked like a gipsy; it was reckoned that there was foreign blood in him. He went by the name of Romany. He was supposed to be shook after Mary too. He had the nastiest temper and the best violin in the district, and the chaps put up with him a lot because they wanted him to play at bush dances. The moon had risen over Pine Ridge, but it was dusky where we were. We saw Romany loom up, riding in from the gate; he rode round the end of the coach-house and across towards where we were—I suppose he was going to tie up his horse at the fence; but about half-way across the grass he disappeared. It struck me that there was something peculiar about the way he got down, and I heard a sound like a horse stumbling.

"What the hell's Romany trying to do?" said Jimmy Nowlett. "He couldn't have fell off his horse—or else he's drunk."

A couple of chaps got up and went to see. Then there was that waiting, mysterious silence that comes when something happens in the dark, and nobody knows what it is. I went over, and the thing dawned on me. I'd stretched a wire clothes-line across there during the day and had forgotten all about it for the moment. Romany had no idea of the line and, as he rode up, it caught him on a level with his elbows, and scraped him off his horse. He was sitting on the grass, swearing in a surprised voice, and the horse looked surprised too. Romany wasn't hurt, but the sudden shock had spoilt his temper. He wanted to know who'd put up that bloody line. He came over and sat on the log. The chaps smoked for a while.

"What did you git down so sudden for, Romany?" asked Jim Bullock, presently. "Did you hurt yerself on the pommel?"

"Why didn't you ask the horse to go round?" asked Dave Regan.

"I'd only like to know who put up that bleeding wire!" growled Romany.

"Well," said Jimmy Nowlett, "if we'd put up a sign to beware of the line you couldn't have seen it in the dark."

"Unless it was a transparency with a candle behind it," said Dave Regan. "But why didn't you get down on one end, Romany, instead of all along? It wouldn't have jolted yer so much."

All this with the bush drawl, and between the puffs of their pipes. But I didn't take any interest in it. I was brooding over Mary and the jackeroo.

"I've heard of men getting down over their horse's head," said Dave presently, in a reflective sort of way—"In fact, I've done it myself—but I never saw a man get off backwards over his horse's rump."

But they saw that Romany was getting nasty, and they wanted him to play the fiddle next night, so they dropped it.

Mary was singing an old song. I always thought she had a sweet voice, and I'd have enjoyed it if that damned jackeroo hadn't been listening too. We listened in silence until she'd finished.

"That gal's got a nice voice," said Jimmy Nowlett.

"Nice voice!" snarled Romany, who'd been waiting for a chance to be nasty. "Why, I've heard a tom-cat sing better."

I moved and Jack, he was sitting next me, nudged me to keep quiet. The chaps didn't like Romany's talk about Possum at all. They were all fond of her: she wasn't a pet or tomboy, for she wasn't built that way, but they were fond of her in such a way that they didn't like to hear anything said about her. They said nothing for a while, but it meant a lot. Perhaps the single men didn't care to speak for fear that it would be said that they were gone on Mary. But presently Jimmy Nowlett gave a big puff at his pipe and spoke:

"I suppose you got bit, too, in that quarter, Romany?"

"Oh, she tried it on, but it didn't go," said Romany. "I've met her sort before. She's setting her cap at that jackeroo now. Some girls will run after anything with trousers on," and he stood up.

Jack Barnes must have felt what was coming, for he grabbed my arm, and whispered, "Sit still, Joe, damn you! He's too good for you!" But I was on my feet and facing Romany as if a giant hand had reached down and wrenched me off the log and set me there.

"You're a damned crawler, Romany!" I said.

Little Jimmy Nowlett was between us, and the other fellows round us before a blow got home. "Hold on, you damned fools!" they said. "Keep quiet till we get away from the house!" There was a little clear flat down by the river, and plenty of light there, so we decided to go down there and have it out.

Now I never was a fighting man; I'd never learnt to use my hands. I scarcely knew how to put them up. Jack often wanted to teach me, but I wouldn't bother about it. He'd say, "You'll get into a fight some day, Joe, or out of one, and shame me"; but I hadn't the patience to learn. He'd wanted me to take lessons at the station after work, but he used to get excited, and I didn't want Mary to see him knocking me about. Before he was married, Jack was always getting into fights—he generally tackled a better man and got a hiding; but he didn't seem to care so long as he made a good show—though he used to explain the thing away from a scientific point of view for weeks after. To tell the truth, I had a horror of fighting; I had a horror of being marked about the face; I think I'd sooner stand off and fight a man with revolvers than fight him with fists; and then I think I would say, last thing, "don't shoot me in the face!" Then again I hated the idea of hitting a man. It seemed brutal to me. I was too sensitive and sentimental, and that was what the matter was. Jack seemed very serious on it as we walked down to the river, and he couldn't help hanging out blue lights.

"Why didn't you let me teach you to use your hands?" he said. "The only chance now is that Romany can't fight after all. If you'd waited a minute I'd have been at him." We were a bit behind the rest, and Jack started giving me points about lefts and rights, and "half-arms," and that sort of thing. "He's left-handed, and that's the worst of it," said Jack. "You must only make as good a show as you can, and one of us will take him on afterwards."

But I just heard him and that was all. It was to be my first fight since I was a boy, but somehow I felt cool about it—sort of dulled. If the chaps had known all they would have set me down as a cur. I thought of that, but it didn't make any difference with me then; I knew it was a thing they couldn't understand. I knew I was reckoned pretty soft. But I knew one thing that they didn't know. I knew that it was going to be a fight to a finish, one way or the other. I had more brains and imagination than the rest put together, and I suppose that that was the real cause of most of my trouble. I kept saying to myself, "You'll have to go through with it now, Joe, old man! It's the turning point of your life." If I won the fight, I'd set to work and win Mary; if I lost, I'd leave the district for ever. A man thinks a lot in a flash sometimes; I used to get excited over little things, because of the very paltriness of them, but I was mostly cool in a crisis—Jack was the reverse. I looked ahead: I wouldn't be able to marry a girl who could look back and remember when her husband was beaten by another man—no matter what sort of brute the other man was.

I never in my life felt so cool about a thing. Jack kept whispering instructions, and showing with his hands, up to the last moment, but it was all lost on me.

Looking back, I think there was a bit of romance about it: Mary singing under the vines to amuse a jackeroo dude, and a coward going down to the river in the moonlight to fight for her.

It was very quiet in the little moonlit flat by the river. We took off our coats and were ready. There was no swearing or barracking. It seemed an understood thing with the men that if I went out first round Jack would fight Romany; and if Jack knocked him out somebody else would fight Jack to square matters. Jim Bullock wouldn't mind obliging for one; he was a mate of Jack's, but he didn't mind who he fought so long as it was for the sake of fair play—or "peace and quietness," as he said. Jim was very good-natured. He backed Romany, and of course, Jack backed me.

As far as I could see, all Romany knew about fighting was to jerk one arm up in front of his face and duck his head by way of a feint, and then rush and lunge out. But he had the weight and strength and length of reach, and my first lesson was a very short one. I went down early in the round. But it did me good; the blow and the look I'd seen in Romany's eyes knocked all the sentiment out of me. Jack said nothing—he seemed to regard it as a hopeless job from the first. Next round I tried to remember some things Jack had told me, and made a better show, but I went down in the end.

I felt Jack breathing quick and trembling as he lifted me up.

"How are you, Joe?" he whispered.

"I'm all right," I said.

"It's all right," whispered Jack in a voice as if I was going to be hanged, but it would soon be all over. "He can't use his hands much more than you can—take your time, Joe—try to remember something I told you, for God's sake!"

When two men fight who don't know how to use their hands, they stand a show of knocking each other about a lot. I got some awful thumps, but mostly on the body. Jimmy Nowlett began to get excited and jump round—he was an excitable little fellow.

"Fight! you ——!" he yelled. "Why don't you fight? That ain't fightin'. Fight, and don't try to murder each other. Use your crimson hands, or, by God, I'll chip you! Fight, or I'll blanky well bullock-whip the pair of you;" then his language got awful. They said we went like windmills, and that nearly every one of the blows we made was enough to kill a bullock if it had got home. Jimmy stopped us once, but they held him back.

Presently I went down pretty flat, but the blow was well up on the head, and didn't matter much—I had a good thick skull. And I had one good eye yet.

"For God's sake, hit him!" whispered Jack—he was trembling like a leaf. "don't mind what I told you. I wish I was fighting him myself! Get a blow home, for God's sake! Make a good show this round and I'll stop the fight."

That showed how little even Jack, my old mate, understood me.

I had the bushman up in me now, and wasn't going to be beaten while I could think. I was wonderfully cool, and learning to fight. There's nothing like a fight to teach a man. I was thinking fast, and learning more in three seconds than Jack's sparring could have taught me in three weeks. People think that blows hurt in a fight, but they don't—not till afterwards. I fancy that a fighting man, if he isn't altogether an animal, suffers more mentally than he does physically.

While I was getting my wind I could hear through the moonlight and still air the sound of Mary's voice singing up at the house. I thought hard into the future, even as I fought. The fight only seemed something that was passing.

I was on my feet again and at it, and presently I lunged out and felt such a jar on my arm that I thought it was telescoped. I thought I'd put out my wrist and elbow. And Romany was lying on the broad of his back.

I heard Jack draw three breaths of relief in one. He said nothing as he straightened me up, but I could feel his heart beating. He said afterwards that he didn't speak because he thought a word might spoil it.

I went down again, but Jack told me afterwards that he *felt* I was all right when he lifted me.

Then Romany went down, then we fell together and the chaps separated us. I got another knock-down blow in, and was beginning to enjoy the novelty of it, when Romany staggered and limped.

"I've done," he said. "I've twisted my ankle." He'd caught his heel against a tuft of grass.

"Shake hands," yelled Jimmy Nowlett.

I stepped forward, but Romany took his coat, and limped to his horse.

"If yer don't shake hands with Wilson, I'll lam yer," howled Jimmy; but Jack told him to let the man alone, and Romany got on his horse somehow and rode off.

I saw Jim Bullock stoop and pick up something from the grass, and heard him swear in surprise. There was some whispering, and presently Jim said:

"If I thought that, I'd kill him."

"What is it?" asked Jack.

Jim held up a butcher's knife. It was common for a man to carry a butcher's knife in a sheath fastened to his belt.

"Why did you let your man fight with a butcher's knife in his belt?" asked Jimmy Knowlett.

But the knife could easily have fallen out when Romany fell, and we decided it that way.

"Any way," said Jimmy Nowlett, "if he'd stuck Joe in hot blood before us all it wouldn't be so bad as if he sneaked up and stuck him in the back in the dark. But you'd best keep an eye over your shoulder for a year or two, Joe. That chap's got Eye-talian blood in him somewhere. And now the best thing that you chaps can do is to keep your mouth shut and keep all this dark from the gals."

Jack hurried me on ahead. He seemed to act queer, and when I glanced at him I could have sworn that there was water in his eyes. I said that Jack had no sentiment except for himself, but I forgot, and I'm sorry I said it.

"What's up, Jack?" I asked.

"Nothing," said Jack.

"What's up, you old fool?" I said.

"Nothing," said Jack, "except that I'm damned proud of you, Joe, you old ass!" and he put his arm round my shoulders and gave me a shake. "I didn't know it was in you, Joe—I wouldn't have said it before, or listened to any other man say it, but I didn't think you had the pluck—God's truth, I didn't. Come along and get your face fixed up."

We got into my room quietly, and Jack got a dish of water, and told one of the chaps to sneak a piece of fresh beef from somewhere.

Jack was as proud as a dog with a tin tail as he fussed round me. He fixed up my face in the best style he knew, and he knew a good many—he'd been mended himself so often.

While he was at work we heard a sudden hush and a scraping of feet amongst the chaps that Jack had kicked out of the room, and a girl's voice whispered. "Is he hurt? Tell me. I want to know—I might be able to help."

It made my heart jump, I can tell you. Jack went out at once, and there was some whispering. When he came back he seemed wild.

"What is it Jack?" I asked.

"Oh, nothing," he said, "only that damned slut of a half-caste cook overheard some of those blanky fools arguing as to how Romany's knife got out of the sheath, and she's put a nice yarn round amongst the girls. There's a regular bobbery, but it's all right now, Jimmy Nowlett's telling 'em lies at a great rate."

Presently there was another hush outside, and a saucer with vinegar and brown paper was handed in.

One of the chaps brought some beer and whisky from the pub, and we had a quiet little time in my room. Jack wanted to stay all night, but I reminded him that his little wife was waiting for him in Solong, so he said he'd be round early in the morning, and went home.

I felt the reaction pretty bad. I didn't feel proud of the affair at all. I thought it was a low brutal business all round. Romany was a quiet chap after all, and the chaps had no right to chyack him. Perhaps he'd had a hard life, and carried a big swag of trouble that we didn't know anything about. He seemed a lonely man. I'd gone through enough myself to teach me not to judge men. I made up my mind to tell him how I felt about the matter next time we met. Perhaps I made my usual mistake of bothering about "feelings" in another party that hadn't any feelings at all—perhaps I didn't; but it's generally best to chance it on the kind side in a case like this. Altogether I felt as if I'd made another fool of myself, and been a weak coward. I drank the rest of the beer and went to sleep.

About daylight I woke and heard Jack's horse on the gravel. He came round the back of the buggy-shed and up to my door, and then, suddenly a girl screamed out. I pulled on my trousers and 'lastic-side boots and hurried out. It was Mary herself, dressed and sitting on an old stone step at the back of the kitchen with her face in her hands, and Jack was off his horse and stooping by her side with his hand on her shoulder. She kept saying, "I thought you were——! I thought you were——!" I didn't catch the name. An old single-barrel muzzle-loader shot-gun was lying in the grass at her feet. It was the gun they used to keep loaded and hanging in straps in a room off the kitchen ready for a shot at a cunning old hawk that they called "'Tarnal Death," and that used to be always after the chickens.

When Mary lifted her face it was as white as notepaper and her eyes seemed to grow wilder when she caught sight of me.

"Oh, you did frighten me, Mr Barnes," she gasped. Then gave a little ghost of a laugh and stood up, and some colour came back.

"Oh, I'm a little fool!" she said quietly. "I thought I heard old 'Tarnal Death at the chickens, and I thought it would be a great thing if I got the gun and brought him down; so I got up and dressed quietly so as not to wake Sarah. And then you came round the corner and frightened me. I don't know what you must think of me, Mr Barnes."

"Never mind," said Jack. "You go and have a sleep, or you won't be able to dance to-night. Never mind the gun—I'll put that away." And he steered her round to the door of her room off the brick veranda where she slept with one of the other girls.

"Well, that's a rum start!" I said.

"Yes, it is," said Jack; "it's very funny. Well, how's your face this morning, Joe?"

He seemed a lot more serious than usual.

We were hard at work all the morning cleaning out the big wool-shed and getting it ready for the dance, hanging hoops for the candles, and making seats. I kept out of sight of the girls as much as I could. One side of my face was a sight, and the other wasn't too classical. I felt as if I had been stung by a swarm of bees.

"You're a fresh, sweet-scented beauty now, and no mistake, Joe," said Jimmy Nowlett—he was going to play the accordian that night.

"You ought to fetch the girls now, Joe. But never mind, your face'll go down in about three weeks. My lower jaw is crooked yet; but that fight straightened my nose, that had been knocked crooked when I was a boy—so I didn't lose much beauty by it.

When we'd done in the shed, Jack took me aside and said:

"Look here, Joe; if you won't come to the dance to-night—and I can't say you'd ornament it—I tell you what you'll do. You get little Mary away on the quiet and take her out for a stroll—and act like a man. The job's finished now, and you won't get another chance like this."

"But how am I to get her out?" I said.

"Never you mind. You be mooching round by the big peppermint-tree near the river-gate, say about half-past ten."

"What good'll that do?"

"Never you mind. You just do as you're told, that's all you've got to do," said Jack, and he went home to get dressed and bring his wife.

After the dancing started that night I had a peep in once or twice. The first time I saw Mary dancing with Jack, and looking serious; and the second time she was dancing with the blarsted jackeroo dude, and looking excited and happy. I noticed that some of the girls, that I could see sitting on a stool along the opposite wall, whispered, and gave Mary black looks as the jackeroo swung her past. It struck me pretty forcibly that I should have taken fighting lessons from him instead of from poor Romany. I went away and walked about four miles down the river road, getting out of the way into the bush whenever I saw any chap riding by. I thought of poor Romany and wondered where he was, and thought that there wasn't much to choose between us as far as happiness was concerned. Perhaps he was walking by himself in the bush, and feeling like I did. I wished I could shake hands with him.

But somehow, about half-past ten, I drifted back to the river sliprails, and leant over them in the shadow of the peppermint-tree, looking at the rows of river-willows in the moonlight. I didn't expect anything, in spite of what Jack said.

I didn't like the idea of hanging myself: I'd been with a party who found a man hanging in the bush, and it was no place for a woman round where he was. And I'd helped drag two bodies out of the Cudgegong River in a flood, and they weren't sleeping beauties. I thought it was a pity that a chap couldn't lie down on a grassy bank in a graceful position in the moonlight, and die just by thinking of it—and die with his eyes and mouth shut. But then I remembered that I wouldn't make a beautiful corpse anyway it went, with the face I had on me.

I was just getting comfortably miserable when I heard a step behind me, and my heart gave a jump. And I gave a start, too.

"Oh, is that you, Mr Wilson?" said a timid little voice.

"Yes," I said. "Is that you, Mary?"

And she said yes. It was the first time I called her Mary, but she did not seem to notice it.

"Did I frighten you?" I asked.

"No—yes—just a little," she said. "I didn't know there was any one——" then she stopped.

"Why aren't you dancing?" I asked her.

"Oh, I'm tired," she said. "It was too hot in the wool-shed. I thought I'd like to come out, and get my head cool, and be quiet a little while."

"Yes," I said. "It must be hot in the wool-shed."

She stood looking out over the willows. Presently she said: "It must be very dull for you, Mr Wilson—you must feel lonely. Mr Barnes said——" Then she gave a little gasp and stopped—as if she was just going to put her foot in it.

"How beautiful the moonlight looks on the willows!" she said.

"Yes," I said, "doesn't it? Supposing we have a stroll by the river."

"Oh, thank you, Mr Wilson. I'd like it very much."

I didn't notice it then, but, now I come to think of it, it was a beautiful scene: there was a horse-shoe of high blue hills round behind the house, with the river running round under the slopes, and in front was a rounded hill covered with pines, and pine ridges, and a soft blue peak away over the ridges, ever so far in the distance.

I had a handkerchief over the worst of my face, and kept the best side turned to her. We walked down by the river, and didn't say anything for a good while. I was thinking hard. We came to a white smooth log in a quiet place out of sight of the house.

"Suppose we sit down for a while, Mary," I said.

"If you like, Mr Wilson," she said.

There was about a foot of log between us.

"What a beautiful night!" she said.

"Yes," I said, "isn't it!"

Presently she said, "I suppose you know I'm going away next month, Mr Wilson?"

I felt suddenly empty. "No," I said, "I didn't know that."

"Yes," she said, "I thought you knew. I'm going to try to get into the hospital to be trained for a nurse, and if that doesn't come off I'll get a place as assistant public-school teacher."

We didn't say anything for a while.

Sydney Long (1871-1955) *By Tranquil Waters* (1894)
Detail Only   111.1 x 183.7 cm   Oil on canvas
Reproduced with the kind permission of the Art Gallery Of New South Wales, Sydney

Tom Roberts (1856-1931) *Shearing the Rams*
119.4 x 180.3 cm   Oil on canvas on board   Felton Bequest 1932
Reproduced with the kind permission of the National Gallery Of Victoria, Melbourne

"I suppose you won't be sorry to go, Miss Brand?" I said.

"I—I don't know," she said. "Everyone's been so kind to me here."

She sat looking straight before her, and I fancied her eyes glistened. I put my arm round her shoulders, but she didn't seem to notice it. In fact I scarcely noticed it myself at the time.

"So you think you'll be sorry to go away?" I said.

"Yes, Mr Wilson. I suppose I'll fret for a while. It's been my home, you know.

I pressed my hand on her shoulder, just a little, so she couldn't pretend not to know it was there. But she didn't seem to notice.

"Ah, well," I said, "I suppose I'll be on the wallaby again next week."

"Will you, Mr Wilson?" she said. Her voice seemed very soft.

I slipped my arm round her waist, under her arm. My heart was going like clockwork now.

Presently she said:

"Don't you think it's time to go back now, Mr Wilson?"

"Oh, there's plenty of time!" I said. I shifted up, and put my arm further round, and held her closer. She sat straight up, looking right in front of her, but she began to breathe hard.

"Mary," I said.

"Yes," she said.

"Call me Joe," I said.

"I—I don't like to," she said. "I don't think it would be right."

So I just turned her face round and kissed her. She clung to me and cried.

"What is it Mary?" I said.

She only held me tighter and cried.

"What is it, Mary?" I said. "Ain't you well? Ain't you happy?"

"Yes Joe," she said, "I'm very happy." Then she said, "Oh, your poor face! Can't I do anything for it?"

"No," I said. "That's all right. My face doesn't hurt me a bit now."

But she didn't seem right.

"What is it Mary?" I said. "are you tired? You didn't sleep last night——" Then I got an inspiration.

"Mary," I said, "what were you doing out with the gun this morning?"

And after some coaxing it all came out, a bit hysterical.

"I couldn't sleep—I was frightened. Oh! I had such a bad dream about you, Joe! I thought Romany came back and got into your room and stabbed you with his knife. I got up and dressed, and about daybreak I heard a horse at the gate; then I got the gun down from the wall—and—and Mr Barnes came round the corner and frightened me. He's something like Romany, you know."

Then I got as much of her as I could into my arms.

And, oh, but wasn't I happy walking home with Mary that night! She was too little for me to put my arm round her waist, so I put it round her shoulder, and that felt just as good. I remember I asked her who'd cleaned up my room and washed my things, but she wouldn't tell.

She wouldn't go back to the dance yet; she said she'd go into her room and rest awhile. There was no one near the old veranda; and when she stood on the end of the floor she was just on a level with my shoulder.

"Mary," I whispered, "put your arms round my neck and kiss me."

She put her arms round my neck, but she didn't kiss me; she only hid her face.

"Kiss me, Mary!" I said.

"I—I don't like to," she whispered.

"Why not, Mary?"

Then I felt her crying or laughing, or half-crying and half-laughing. I'm not sure to this day which it was.

"Why won't you kiss me, Mary? Don't you love me?"

"Because," she said, "because—because I—I don't—I don't think it's right for—for a girl to—to kiss a man unless she's going to be his wife."

Then it dawned on me! I'd forgot all about proposing.

"Mary," I said, "would you marry a chap like me?"

And that was all right.

Next morning Mary cleared out my room and sorted out my things, and didn't take the slightest notice of the other girls' astonishment.

But she made me promise to speak to old Black, and I did the same evening. I found him sitting on the log by the fence, having a yarn on the quiet with an old bushman; and when the old bushman got up and went away, I sat down.

"Well, Joe," said Black, "I see somebody's been spoiling your face for the dance." And after a bit he said, "Well, Joe, what is it? Do you want another job? If you do, you'll have to ask Mrs Black, or Bob" (Bob was his eldest son); "they're managing the station for me now, you know." He could be bitter sometimes in his quiet way.

"No," I said; "it's not that, boss."

"Well, what is it, Joe?"

"I—well, the fact is, I want little Mary."

He puffed at his pipe for a long time, then I thought he spoke.

"What did you say, boss?" I said.

"Nothing, Joe," he said. "I was going to say a lot, but it wouldn't be any use. My father used to say a lot to me before I was married."

I waited a good while for him to speak.

"Well, boss," I said, "what about Mary?"

"Oh! I suppose that's all right, Joe," he said. "I—I beg your pardon. I got thinking of the days when I was courting Mrs Black."

BRIGHTEN'S SISTER-IN-LAW

Jim was born on Gulgong, New South Wales. We used to say "on" Gulgong—and old diggers still talked of being "on th' Gulgong"—though the goldfield there had been worked out for years, and the place was only a dusty little pastoral town in the scrubs. Gulgong was about the last of the great alluvial "rushes" of the "roaring days"—and dreary and dismal enough it looked when I was there. The expression "on" came from being on the "diggins" or goldfield —the workings or the goldfield was all underneath, of course, so we lived (or starved) on them—not in nor at 'em.

Mary and I had been married about two years when Jim came—his name wasn't "Jim," by the way, it was "John Henry," after an uncle godfather; but we called him Jim from the first—(and before it)—because Jim was a popular bush name, and most of my old mates were Jims. The bush is full of good-hearted scamps called Jim.

We lived in an old weather-board shanty that had been a sly-grog shop, and the Lord knows what else! in the palmy days of Gulgong; and I did a bit of digging ("fossicking," rather), a bit of shearing, a bit of fencing, a bit of bush-carpentering, tank-sinking—anything, just to keep the billy boiling.

We had a lot of trouble with Jim with his teeth. He was bad with every one of them, and we had most of them lanced—couldn't pull him through without. I remember we got one lanced and the gum healed over before the tooth came through, and we had to get it cut again. He was a plucky little chap, and after the first time he never whimpered when the doctor was lancing his gum: he used to say "tar" afterwards, and want to bring the lance home with him.

The first turn we got with Jim was the worst. I had had the wife and Jim camping with me in a tent at a dam I was making at Cattle Creek; I had two men working for me, and a boy to drive one of the tip-drays, and I took Mary out to cook for us. And it was lucky for us that the contract was finished and we got back to Gulgong, and within reach of a doctor, the day we did. We were just camping in the house, with our goods and chattels anyhow, for the night; and we were hardly back home an hour when Jim took convulsions for the first time.

Did you ever see a child in convulsions? You wouldn't want to see it again: it plays the devil with a man's nerves. I'd got the beds fixed up on the floor and the billies on the fire—I was going to make some tea, and put a piece of corned beef on to boil overnight—when Jim (he'd been queer all day, and his mother was trying to hush him to sleep)—Jim, he screamed out twice. He'd been crying a good deal, and I was dog-tired and worried (over some money a man owed me) or I'd have noticed at once that there was something unusual in the way the child cried out: as it was I didn't turn round till Mary screamed "Joe! Joe!" You know how a woman cries out when her child is in danger or dying—short, and sharp, and terrible. "Joe! Look! Look! Oh, my God, our child! Get the bath, quick! quick! it's convulsions!"

Jim was bent back like a bow, stiff as a bullock-yoke, in his mother's arms, and his eyeballs were turned up and fixed—a thing I saw twice afterwards and don't want ever to see again.

I was falling over things getting the tub and the hot water, when the woman who lived next door rushed in. She called to her husband to run for the doctor, and before the doctor came she and Mary had got Jim into a hot bath and pulled him through.

The neighbour woman made me up a shake-down in another room and stayed with Mary that night; but it was a long while before I got Jim and Mary's screams out of my head and fell asleep.

You may depend I kept the fire in, and a bucket of water hot over it for a good many nights after that; but (it always happens like this) there came a night, when the fright had worn off, when I was too tired to bother about the fire, and that night Jim took us by surprise. Our wood-heap was done, and I broke up a new chair to get a fire, and had to run a quarter of a mile for water; but this turn wasn't so bad as the first, and we pulled him through.

You never saw a child in convulsions? Well, you don't want to. It must be only a matter of seconds, but it seems long minutes; and half an hour afterwards the child might be laughing and playing with you, or stretched out dead. It shook me up a lot. I was always pretty high-strung and sensitive. After Jim took the first fit, every time he cried, or turned over, or stretched out in the night, I'd jump: I was always feeling his forehead in the dark to see if he was feverish, or feeling his limbs to see if he was "limp" yet. Mary and I often laughed about it—afterwards. I tried sleeping in another room, but for nights after Jim's first attack I'd just be dozing off into a sound sleep, when I'd hear him scream, as plain as could be, and I'd hear Mary cry, "Joe!—Joe!"—short, sharp, and terrible—and I'd be up and into their room like a shot, only to find them sleeping peacefully. The I'd feel Jim's head and his breathing for signs of convulsions, see to the fire and water, and go back to bed and try to sleep. For the first few nights I was like that all night, and I'd feel relieved when daylight came. I'd be in first thing to see if they were all right; then I'd sleep till dinner-time if it was Sunday or I had no work. But then I was run down about that time: I was worried about some money for a woolshed I put up and never got paid for; and besides, I'd been pretty wild before I met Mary.

I was fighting hard then—struggling for something better. Both Mary and I were born to better things, and that's what made the life so hard for us.

Jim got on all right for a while: we used to watch him well, and have his teeth lanced in time.

It used to hurt and worry me to see how—just as he was getting fat and rosy and like a natural happy child, and I'd feel proud to take him out—a tooth would come along, and he'd get thin and white and pale and bigger-eyed and old-fashioned. We'd say, "He'll be safe when he gets his eye-teeth"; but he didn't get them till he was two; then, "He'll be safe when he gets his two-year-old teeth", they didn't come till he was going on for three.

He was a wonderful little chap—yes, I know all about parents thinking that their child is the best in the world. If your boy is small for his age, friends will say that small children make big men; that he's a very bright, intelligent child, and that it's better to have a bright, intelligent child than a big, sleepy lump of fat. And if your boy is dull and sleepy, they say that the dullest boys make the cleverest men—and all the rest of it. I never took any notice of that sort of chatter—took it for what it was worth; but, all the same, I don't think I ever saw such a child as Jim was when he turned two. He was everybody's favourite. They spoilt him rather. I had my own ideas about bringing up a child. I reckoned Mary was too soft with Jim. She'd say, "Put that" (whatever it was) "out of Jim's reach, will you, Joe?" and I'd say, "No! leave it there, and make him understand he's not to have it. Make him have his meals without any nonsense and go to bed at a regular hour," I'd say. Mary and I had many a breeze over Jim. She'd say that I forgot he was only a baby: but I held that a baby could be trained from the first week; and I believe I was right.

But, after all, what are you to do? You'll see a boy that was brought up strict turn out a scamp; and another that was dragged up anyhow (by the hair of the head, as the saying is) turn out well. Then, again, when a child is delicate—and you might lose him any day—you don't like to spank him, though he might be turning out a little fiend, as delicate children often do. Suppose you gave a child a hammering, and the same night he took convulsions, or something, and died—how'd you feel about it? You never know what a child is going to take, any more than you can tell what some women are going to say or do.

I was very fond of Jim, and we were great chums. Sometimes I'd sit and wonder, what the deuce he was thinking about, and often, the way he talked, he'd make me uneasy. When he was two he wanted a pipe above all things, and I'd get him a clean new clay and he'd sit by my side, on the edge of the veranda, or on a log of the wood-heap, in the cool of the evening, and suck away at his pipe, and try to spit when he saw me do it. He seemed to understand that a cold empty pipe wasn't quite the thing, yet to have the sense to know that he couldn't smoke tobacco yet: he made the best he could of things. And if he broke a clay pipe he wouldn't have a new one, and there'd be a row; the old one had to be mended up, somehow, with string or wire. If I got my hair cut, he'd want his cut too; and it always troubled him to see me shave—as if he thought there must be something wrong somewhere, else he ought to have to be shaved too. I lathered him one day, and pretended to shave him: he sat through it as solemn as an owl, but didn't seem to appreciate it—perhaps he had sense enough to know that it couldn't possibly be the real thing. He felt his face, looked very hard at the lather I scraped off, and whimpered, "No blood, daddy!"

I used to cut myself a good deal: I was always impatient over shaving.

Then he went in to interview his mother about it. She understood his lingo better than I did.

But I wasn't always at ease with him. Sometimes he'd sit looking into the fire, with his head on one side, and I'd watch him and wonder what he was thinking about (I might as well have wondered what a Chinaman was thinking about) till he seemed at least twenty years older than me: sometimes, when I moved or spoke, he'd glance round just as if to see what that old fool of a dadda of his was doing now.

I used to have a fancy that there was something Eastern, or Asiatic— something older than our civilization or religion—about old-fashioned children. Once I started to explain my idea to a woman I thought would understand— and as it happened she had an old-fashioned child, with very slant eyes— a little tartar he was too. I suppose it was the sight of him that unconsciously reminded me of my infernal theory, and set me off on it, without warning me. Anyhow it got me mixed up in an awful row with the woman and her husband —and all their tribe. It wasn't an easy thing to explain myself out of it, and the row hasn't been fixed up yet. There were some Chinamen in the district.

I took a good-sized fencing contract, the frontage of a ten-mile paddock, near Gulgong, and did well out of it. The railway had got as far as the Cudgegong River—some twenty miles from Gulgong and two hundred from the coast—and "carrying" was good then. I had a couple of draught horses, that I worked in the tip-drays when I was tank-sinking, and one or two others running in the bush. I bought a broken-down wagon cheap, tinkered it up myself—christened it "The Same Old Thing"—and started carrying from the railway terminus through Gulgong and along the bush roads and tracks that branch out fanlike through the scrubs to the one-pub towns and sheep and cattle stations out there in the howling wilderness. It wasn't much of a team. There were the two heavy horses for "shafters", a stunted colt, that I'd bought out of the pound for thirty shillings; a light, spring-cart horse; an old grey mare, with points like a big red-and-white Australian store bullock, and with the grit of an old washerwoman to work; and a horse that had spanked along in Cobb & Co's mail-coach in his time. I had a couple there that didn't belong to me: I worked them for the feeding of them in the dry weather. And I had all sorts of harness, that I mended and fixed up myself. It was a mixed team, but I took light stuff, got through pretty quick, and freight rates were high. So I got along.

Before this, whenever I made a few pounds I'd sink a shaft somewhere, prospecting for gold; but Mary never let me rest till she had talked me out of that.

I made up my mind to take on a small selection farm—that an old mate of mine had fenced in and cleared, and afterwards chucked up—about thirty miles out west of Gulgong, at a place called Lahey's Creek. (The places were all called Lahey's Creek, or Spicer's Flat, or Murphy's Flat, or Ryan's Crossing, or some such name—round there.) I reckoned I'd have a run for the horses and be able to grow a bit of feed. I always had a dread of taking Mary and the children too far away from a doctor—or a good woman neighbour; but there were some people came to live on Lahey's Creek, and besides, there was a young brother of Mary's—a young scamp (his name was Jim, too, and we called him "Jimmy" at first to make room for our Jim—he hated the name "Jimmy"—or James). He came to live with us—without asking—and I thought he'd find enough work at Lahey's Creek to keep him out of mischief. He wasn't to be depended on much—he thought nothing of riding off, five hundred miles or so, "to have a look at the country"—but he was fond of Mary, and he'd stay by her till I got someone else to keep her company while I was on the road. He would be a protection against "sundowners" or any

360

shearers who happened to wander that way in the "d.t's" after a spree. Mary had a married sister come to live at Gulgong just before we left, and nothing would suit her and her husband but we must leave little Jim with them for a month or so—till we got settled down at Lahey's Creek. They were newly married.

Mary was to have driven into Gulgong, in the spring-cart, at the end of the month, and taken Jim home; but when the time came she wasn't too well —and besides, the tyres of the cart were loose, and I hadn't time to get them cut, so we let Jim's time run on a week or so longer, till I happened to come out through Gulgong from the river with a small load of flour for Lahey's Creek way. The roads were good, the weather grand—no chance of it raining, and I had a spare tarpaulin if it did—I would only camp out one night; so I decided to take Jim home with me.

Jim was turning three then, and he was a cure. He was so old-fashioned that he used to frighten me sometimes—I'd almost think that there was something supernatural about him; though, of course, I never took any notice of that rot about some children being too old-fashioned to live. There's always the ghoulish old hag (and some not so old nor haggish either) who'll come round and shake up young parents with such croaks as, "You'll never rear that child—he's too bright for his age." To the devil with them! I say.

But I really thought that Jim was too intelligent for his age, and I often told Mary that he ought to be kept back, and not let talk too much to old diggers and long lanky jokers of bushmen who rode in and hung their horses outside my place on Sunday afternoons.

I don't believe in parents talking about their own children everlastingly— you get sick of hearing them; and their kids are generally little devils, and turn out larrikins as likely as not.

But, for all that, I really think that Jim, when he was three years old, was the most wonderful little chap, in every way, that I ever saw.

For the first hour or so, along the road, he was telling me all about his adventures at his auntie's.

"But they spoilt me too much, dad," he said, as solemn as a native bear. "An' besides, a boy ought to stick to his parrans!"

I was taking out a cattle-pup for a drover I knew, and the pup took up a good deal of Jim's time.

Sometimes he'd jolt me the way he talked; and other times I'd have to turn away my head and cough, or shout at the horses, to keep from laughing outright. And once, when I was taken that way, he said:

"What are you jerking your shoulders and coughing, and grunting, and going on that way for, dad? Why don't you tell me something?"

"Tell you what, Jim?"

"Tell me some talk."

So I told him all the talk I could think of. And I had to brighten up, I can tell you, and not draw too much on my imagination—for Jim was a terror at cross-examination when the fit took him; and he didn't think twice about telling you when he thought you were talking nonsense. Once he said:

"I'm glad you took me home with you, dad. You'll get to know Jim."

"What!" I said.

"You'll get to know Jim."

"But don't I know you already?"

"No, you don't. You never has time to know Jim at home."

And, looking back, I saw that it was cruel true. I had known in my heart all along that this was the truth; but it came to me like a blow from Jim. You see, it had been a hard struggle for the last year or so; and when I was home for a day or two I was generally too busy, or too tired and worried, or full of schemes for the future to take much notice of Jim. Mary used to speak to me about it, sometimes. "You never take notice of the child," she'd say. "You could surely find a few minutes of an evening. What's the use of always worrying and brooding? Your brain will go with a snap some day, and, if you get over it, it will teach you a lesson. You'll be an old man, and Jim a young one, before you realize that you had a child once. Then it will be too late."

This sort of talk from Mary always bored me and made me impatient with her, because I knew it all too well. I never worried for myself—only for Mary and the children. And often, as the days went by, I said to myself, "I'll take more notice of Jim and give Mary more of my time, just as soon as I can see things clear ahead a bit." And the hard days went on, and the weeks, and the months, and the years——Ah, well!

Mary used to say, when things would get worse, "Why don't you talk to me, Joe? Why don't you tell me your thoughts, instead of shutting yourself up in yourself and brooding—eating your heart out? It's hard for me: I get to think you're tired of me, and selfish. I might be cross and speak sharp to you when you are in trouble. How am I to know, if you don't tell me?"

But I didn't think she'd understand.

And so, getting acquainted, and chumming and dozing, with the gums closing over our heads here and there, and the ragged patches of sunlight and shade passing up, over the horses, over us, on the front of the load, over the load, and down on to the white, dusty road again—Jim and I got along the lonely bush road and over the ridges some fifteen miles before sunset, and camped at Ryan's Crossing on Sandy Creek for the night. I got the horses out and took the harness off. Jim wanted badly to help me, but I made him stay on the load; for one of the horses—a vicious, red-eyed chestnut—was a kicker; he'd broken a man's leg. I got the feed-bags stretched across the shafts, and the chaff and corn into them; and there stood the horses all round with their rumps north, south, and west, and their heads between the shafts, munching and switching their tails. We use double shafts, you know, for horse-teams— two pairs side by side—and prop them up, and stretch bags between them, letting the bags sag to serve as feed boxes. I threw the spare tarpaulin over the wheels on one side, letting about half of it lie on the ground in case of damp, and so making a floor and a breakwind. I threw down bags and the blankets and possum rug against the wheel to make a camp for Jim and the cattle-pup, and got a gin-case we used for a tucker-box, the frying-pan and billy down, and made a good fire at a log close handy, and soon everything was comfortable. Ryan's Crossing was a grand camp. I stood with my pipe in my mouth, my hands behind my back, and my back to the fire, and took the country in.

Sandy Creek came down along a western spur of the range: the banks here were deep and green, and the water ran clear over the granite bars, boulders, and gravel. Behind us was a dreary flat covered with those gnarled, grey-barked, dry-rotted "native apple-trees" (about as much like apple-trees as the native bear is like any other), and a nasty bit of sand-dusty road that I was always glad to get over in wet weather. To the left on our side of the creek were reedy marshes, with frogs croaking, and across the creek the dark box-scrub-covered ridges ended in steep "sidings" coming down to the creek-bank, and to the main road that skirted them, running on west up over a "saddle" in the ridges and on towards Dubbo. The road by Lahey's Creek to a place called Cobborah branched off, through dreary apple-tree and stringy-bark flats to the left, just beyond the crossing: all these fanlike branch tracks from the Cudgegong were inside a big horse-shoe in the Great Western Line, and so they gave small carriers a chance, now that Cobb & Co's coaches and the big teams and vans had shifted out of the main western terminus. There were tall she-oaks all along the creek and a clump of big ones over a deep waterhole just above the crossing. The creek oaks have rough barked trunks, like English elms, but are much taller and higher to the branches—and the leaves are reedy; Kendall, the Australian poet, calls them the "she-oak harps Aeolian." Those trees are always sigh-sigh-sighing—more of a sigh than a sough or the "whoosh" of gum-trees in the wind. You always hear them sighing, even when you can't feel any wind. It's the same with telegraph wires: put your head against a telegraph-post on a dead, still day, and you'll hear and feel the far-away roar of the wires. But then the oaks are not connected with the distance, where there might be wind; and they don't *roar* in a gale, only sigh louder and softer according to the wind, and never seem to go above or below a certain pitch—like a big harp with all the strings the same. I used to have a theory that those creek oaks got the wind's voice telephoned to them, so to speak, through the ground.

I happened to look round and there was Jim (I thought he was on the tarpaulin playing with the pup): he was standing close beside me with his legs wide apart, his hands behind his back, and his back to the fire.

He held his head a little on one side, and there was such an old, old, wise expression in his big brown eyes—just as if he'd been a child for a hundred years or so, or as though he were listening to those oaks, and understanding them in a fatherly sort of way.

"Dad!" he said presently—"Dad! do you think I'll ever grow up to be a man?"

"Wh—why, Jim?" I gasped.

"Because I don't want to."

I couldn't think of anything against this. It made me uneasy. But I remember *I* used to have a childish dread of growing up to be a man.

"Jim," I said, to break the silence, "do you hear what the she-oaks say?"

"No, I don't. Is they talking?"

"Yes," I said, without thinking.

Kendall's grave at Waverley Cemetery was one of the first places to which Mrs Lawson took her son when he came to reside in Sydney in 1883.

"What is they saying?" he asked.

I took the bucket and went down to the creek for some water for tea. I thought Jim would follow with a little tin billy he had, but he didn't: when I got back to the fire he was again on the possum rug, comforting the pup. I fried some bacon and eggs that I'd brought out with me. Jim sang out from the wagon:

"Don't cook too much, dad—I mightn't be hungry."

I got the tin plates, and pint-pots and things out on a clean new flour-bag, in honour of Jim, and dished up. He was leaning back on the rug looking at the pup in a listless sort of way. I reckoned he was tired out, and pulled the gin-case up close to him for a table and put his plate on it. But he only tried a mouthful or two, and then he said:

"I ain't hungry, dad! You'll have to eat it all."

It made me uneasy—I never liked to see a child of mine turn from his food. They had given him some tinned salmon in Gulgong and I was afraid that that was upsetting him. I was always against tinned muck.

"Sick, Jim?" I asked.

"No, dad, I ain't sick; I don't know what's the matter with me."

"Have some tea, sonny?"

"Yes, dad."

I gave him some tea, with some milk in it that I'd brought in a bottle from his aunt's for him. He took a sip or two and then put the pint-pot on the gin-case.

"Jim's tired, dad," he said.

I made him lie down while I fixed up a camp for the night. It had turned a bit chilly, so I let the big tarpaulin down all round—it was made to cover a high load, the flour in the wagon didn't come above the rail, so the tarpaulin came down well on to the ground. I fixed Jim up a comfortable bed under the tail-end of the wagon: when I went to lift him in he was lying back, looking up at the stars in a half-dreamy, half-fascinated way that I didn't like. Whenever Jim was extra old-fashioned, or affectionate, there was danger.

"How do you feel now, sonny?"

It seemed a minute before he heard me and turned from the stars.

"Jim's better, dad." Then he said something like, "The stars are looking at me." I thought he was half asleep. I took off his jacket and boots and carried him in under the wagon and made him comfortable for the night.

"Kiss me 'night-night, daddy," he said.

I'd rather he hadn't asked me—it was a bad sign. As I was going to the fire he called me back.

"What is it, Jim?"

"Get me my things and the cattle-pup, please, daddy."

I was scared now. His things were some toys and rubbish he'd brought from Gulgong, and I remembered, the last time he had convulsions, he took all his toys and a kitten to bed with him. And "night-night" and "daddy" were two-year-old language to Jim. I'd thought he'd forgotten those words— he seemed to be going back.

"Are you quite warm enough, Jim?"

"Yes, dad."

I started to walk up and down—I always did this when I was extra worried.

I was frightened now about Jim, though I tried to hide the fact from myself. Presently he called again. "What is it, Jim?"

"Take the blankets off me, fahver—Jim's sick!" (They'd been teaching him to say father.)

I was scared now. I remembered a neighbour of ours had a little girl die (she swallowed a pin), and when she was going she said:

"Take the blankets off me, muvver—I'm dying."

And I couldn't get that out of my head.

I threw back a fold of the possum rug, and felt Jim's head—he seemed cool enough.

"Where do you feel bad, sonny?"

No answer for a while; then he said suddenly, but in a voice as if he were talking in his sleep:

"Put my boots on, please, daddy. I want to go home to muvver!"

I held his hand, and comforted him for a while; then he slept—in a restless, feverish sort of way.

I got the bucket I used for water for the horses and stood it over the fire; I ran to the creek with the big kerosene-tin bucket and got it full of cold water and stood it handy. I got the spade (we always carried one to dig wheels out of bogs in wet weather) and turned a corner of the tarpaulin back, dug a hole, and trod the tarpaulin down into the hole to serve for a bath, in case of the worst. I had a tin of mustard, and meant to fight a good round for Jim, if death came along.

I stooped in under the tail-board of the wagon and felt Jim. His head was burning hot, and his skin parched and dry as a bone.

Then I lost nerve and started blundering backward and forward between the wagon and the fire, and repeating what I'd heard Mary say the last time we fought for Jim: "God! don't take my child! God! don't take my boy!" I'd never had much faith in doctors, but, my God! I wanted one then. The nearest was fifteen miles away.

I threw back my head and stared up at the branches in desperation; and —well, I don't ask you to take much stock in this, though most old bushmen will believe anything of the bush by night; and—now, it might have been that I was unstrung, or it might have been a patch of the sky outlined in the gently moving branches, or the blue smoke rising up. But I saw the figure of a woman, all white, come down, down, nearly to the limbs of the trees, point on up the main road, and then float up and up and vanish, still pointing. I thought Mary was dead! Then it flashed on me——

Four or five miles up the road, over the "saddle," was an old shanty that had been a half-way inn before the Great Western Line got round as far as Dubbo, and took the coach traffic off those old bush roads. A man named Brighten lived there. He was a selector; did a little farming, and as much sly-grog selling as he could. He was married—but it wasn't that: I'd thought of them, but she was a childish, worn-out, spiritless woman, and both were pretty "ratty" from hardship and loneliness—they weren't likely to be of any use to me. But it was this: I'd heard talk, among some women in Gulgong, of a sister of Brighten's wife who'd gone out to live with them lately; she'd been a hospital matron in the city, they said; and there were yarns about her. Some said she got the sack for exposing the doctors—or carrying on with them—

I didn't remember which. The fact of a city woman going out to live in such a place, with such people, was enough to make talk among women in a town twenty miles away, but then there must have been something extra about her, else bushmen wouldn't have talked and carried her name so far; and I wanted a woman out of the ordinary now. I even reasoned this way, thinking like lightning, as I knelt over Jim between the big back wheels of the wagon.

I had an old racing mare that I used as a riding hack, following the team. In a minute I had her saddled and bridled; I tied the end of a half-full chaff-bag, shook the chaff into each end and dumped it on to the pommel as a cushion or buffer for Jim; I wrapped him in a blanket, and scrambled into the saddle with him.

The next minute we were stumbling down the steep bank, clattering and splashing over the crossing, and struggling up the opposite bank to the level. The mare, as I told you, was an old racer, but broken-winded—she must have run without wind after the first half-mile. She had the old racing instinct in her strong, and whenever I rode in company I'd have to pull her hard else she'd race the other horse or burst. She ran low fore and aft, and was the easiest horse I ever rode. She ran like wheels on rails, with a bit of a tremble now and then—like a railway carriage—when she settled down to it.

The chaff-bag had slipped off, in the creek I suppose, and I let the bridle-rein go and held Jim up to me like a baby the whole way. Let the strongest man, who isn't used to it, hold a baby in one position for five minutes—and Jim was fairly heavy. But I never felt the ache in my arms that night—it must have gone before I was in a fit state of mind to feel it. And at home I'd often growled about being asked to hold the baby for a few minutes. I could never brood comfortably and nurse a baby at the same time. It was a ghostly moonlight night. There's no timber in the world so ghostly as the Australian bush in moonlight—or just about daybreak. The all-shaped patches of moonlight falling between ragged, twisted boughs; the ghostly blue-white bark of the "white-fox" trees; a dead, naked white ring-barked tree, or dead white stump starting out here and there, and the ragged patches of shade and light on the road that made anything, from the shape of a spotted bullock to a naked corpse laid out stark. Roads and tracks through the bush made by moonlight—every one seeming straighter and clearer than the real one; you have to trust to your horse then. Sometimes the naked white trunk of a red stringy-bark tree, where a sheet of bark had been taken off, would start out like a ghost from the dark bush. And dew or frost glistening on these things according to the season. Now and again a great grey kangaroo, that had been feeding on a green patch down by the road, would start with a "thump-thump," and away up the siding.

The bush seemed full of ghosts that night—all going my way—and being left behind by the mare. Once I stopped to look at Jim: I just sat back and the mare "propped"—she'd been a stock-horse, and was used to "cutting-out." I felt Jim's hands and forehead; he was in a burning fever. I bent forward, and the old mare settled down to it again. I kept saying out loud—and Mary and me often laughed about it (afterwards): "He's limp yet!—Jim's limp yet!" (the words seemed jerked out of me by sheer fright)—"He's limp yet!" till the mare's feet took it up. Then, just when I thought she was doing her best and racing her hardest, she suddenly started forward, like a cable tram

366

gliding along on its own and the grip put on suddenly. It was just what she'd do when I'd be riding alone and a strange horse drew up from behind —the old racing instinct. I *felt* the thing too! I felt as if a strange horse *was* there! And then—the words just jerked out of me by sheer funk—I started saying, "Death is riding to-night! . . . Death is racing to-night! . . . Death is riding to-night!" till the hoof-beats took that up. And I believe the old mare felt the black horse at her side and was going to beat him or break her heart.

I was mad with anxiety and fright: I remember I kept saying, "I'll be kinder to Mary after this! I'll take more notice of Jim!" and the rest of it.

I don't know how the old mare got up the last "pinch." She must have slackened pace, but I never noticed it: I just held Jim up to me and gripped the saddle with my knees—I remember the saddle jerked from the desperate jumps of her till I thought the girth would go. We topped the gap and were going down into a gully they called Dead Man's Hollow, and there, at the back of a ghostly clearing that opened from the road where there were some black-soil springs, was a long, low, oblong weather-board-and-shingle building, with blind, broken windows in the gable-ends, and a wide steep veranda roof slanting down almost to the level of the window-sills—there was something sinister about it, I thought—like the hat of a jail-bird slouched over his eyes. The place looked both deserted and haunted. I saw no light, but that was because of the moonlight outside. The mare turned in at the corner of the clearing to take a short cut to the shanty, and, as she struggled across some marshy ground, my heart kept jerking out the words, "It's deserted! They've gone away! It's deserted!" The mare went round to the back and pulled up between the back door and a big bark-and-slab kitchen. Someone shouted from inside:

"Who's there?"

"It's me. Joe Wilson. I want your sister-in-law—I've got the boy—he's sick and dying!"

Brighten came out, pulling up his moleskins. "What boy?" he asked.

"Here, take him," I shouted, "and let me get down."

"What's the matter with him?" asked Brighten, and he seemed to hang back. And just as I made to get my leg over the saddle, Jim's head went back over my arm, he stiffened, and I saw his eyeballs turned up and glistening in the moonlight.

I felt cold all over then and sick in the stomach—but *clear-headed* in a way: strange, wasn't it? I don't know why I didn't get down and rush into the kitchen to get a bath ready. I only felt as if the worst had come, and I wished it were over and gone. I even thought of Mary and the funeral.

Then a woman ran out of the house—a big, hard-looking woman. She had on a wrapper of some sort, and her feet were bare. She laid her hand on Jim, looked at his face, and then snatched him from me and ran into the kitchen—and me down and after her. As great good luck would have it they had some dirty clothes on to boil in a kerosene-tin—dish-cloths or something.

Brighten's sister-in-law dragged a tub out from under the table, wrenched the bucket off the hook, and dumped in the water, dish-cloths and all, snatched a can of cold water from a corner, dashed that in, and felt the

367

water with her hand—holding Jim up to her hip all the time—and I won't say how he looked. She stood him in the tub and started dashing water over him, tearing off his clothes between the splashes.

"Here, that tin of mustard—there on the shelf!" she shouted to me.

She knocked the lid off the tin on the edge of the tub, and went on splashing and spanking Jim.

It seemed an eternity. And I? Why, I never thought clearer in my life. I felt cold-blooded—I felt as if I'd like an excuse to go outside till it was all over. I thought of Mary and the funeral—and wished that that was past. All this in a flash, as it were. I felt that it would be a great relief, and only wished the funeral was months past. I felt—well, altogether selfish. I only thought of myself.

Brighten's sister-in-law splashed and spanked him hard—hard enough to break his back I thought, and—after about half an hour it seemed—the end came; Jim's limbs relaxed, he slipped down into the tub, and the pupils of his eyes came down. They seemed dull and expressionless, like the eyes of a new baby, but he was back for the world again.

I dropped on the stool by the table.

"It's all right," she said. "It's all over now. I wasn't going to let him die." I was only thinking, "Well it's over now, but it will come on again. I wish it was over for good. I'm tired of it."

She called to her sister, Mrs Brighten, a washed-out, helpless little fool of a woman, who'd been running in and out and whimpering all the time:

"Here, Jessie! bring the new white blanket off my bed. And you, Brighten, take some of that wood off the fire, and stuff something in that hole there to stop the draught."

Brighten—he was a nuggety little hairy man with no expression to be seen for whiskers—had been running in with sticks and back logs from the wood-heap. He took the wood out, stuffed up the crack, and went inside and brought out a black bottle—got a cup from the shelf, and put both down near my elbow.

Mrs Brighten started to get some supper or breakfast, or whatever it was, ready. She had a clean cloth, and set the table tidily. I noticed that all the tins were polished bright (old coffee and mustard-tins and the like, that they used instead of sugar-basins and tea-caddies and salt-cellars), and the kitchen was kept as clean as possible. She was all right at little things. I knew a haggard, worked-out bushwoman who put her whole soul—or all she'd got left—into polishing old tins till they dazzled your eyes.

I didn't feel inclined for corned beef and damper, and post-and-rail tea. So I sat and squinted, when I thought she wasn't looking, at Brighten's sister-in-law. She was a big woman, her hands and feet were big, but well-shaped and all in proportion—they fitted her. She was a handsome woman—about forty I should think. She had a square chin, and a straight thin-lipped mouth—straight save for a hint of a turn down at the corners, which I fancied (and I have strange fancies) had been a sign of weakness in the days before she grew hard. There was no sign of weakness now. She had hard grey eyes and blue-black hair. She hadn't spoken yet. She didn't ask me how the boy took ill or how I got there, or who or what I was—at least not until the next evening at tea-time.

She sat upright with Jim wrapped in the blankehand laid across her knees, with one hand under his neck and the other laid lightly on him, and she just rocked him gently.

She sat looking hard and straight before her, just as I've seen a tired needlewoman sit with her work in her lap, and look away back into the past. And Jim might have been the work in her lap, for all she seemed to think of him. Now and then she knitted her forehead and blinked.

Suddenly she glanced round and said—in a tone as if I was her husband and she didn't think much of me:

"Why don't you eat something?"

"Beg pardon?"

"Eat something!"

I drank some tea, and sneaked another look at her. I was beginning to feel more natural, and wanted Jim again, now that the colour was coming back into his face, and he didn't look like an unnaturally stiff and staring corpse. I felt a lump rising, and wanted to thank her. I sneaked another look at her.

She was staring straight before her—I never saw a woman's face change so suddenly—I never saw a woman's eyes so haggard and hopeless. Then her great chest heaved twice, I heard her draw a long shuddering breath, like a knocked-out horse, and two great tears dropped from her wide open eyes down her cheeks like rain-drops on a face of stone. And in the firelight they seemed tinged with blood.

I looked away quick, feeling full up myself. And presently (I hadn't seen her look round) she said:

"Go to bed."

"Beg pardon?" (Her face was the same as before the tears.)

"Go to bed. There's a bed made for you inside on the sofa."

"But—the team—I must——"

"What?"

"The team. I left it at the camp. I must look at it."

"Oh! Well, Brighten will ride down and bring it up in the morning—or send the half-caste. Now you go to bed, and get a good rest. The boy will be all right. I'll see to that."

I went out—it was a relief to get out—and looked to the mare. Brighten had got her some corn and chaff in a candle-box, but she couldn't eat yet. She just stood or hung resting one hind leg and then the other, with her nose over the box—and she sobbed. I put my arms round her neck and my face down on her ragged mane, and cried for the second time since I was a boy.

As I started to go in I heard Brighten's sister-in-law say, suddenly and sharply:

"Take *that* away, Jessie."

And presently I saw Mrs Brighten go into the house with the black bottle.

The moon had gone behind the range. I stood for a minute between the house and the kitchen and peeped in through the kitchen window.

She had moved away from the fire and sat near the table. She bent over Jim and held him up close to her and rocked herself to and fro.

I went to bed and slept till the next afternoon. I woke just in time to hear the tail-end of a conversation between Jim and Brighten's sister-in-law. He was asking her out to our place, and she promising to come.

"And now," says Jim, "I want to go home to 'muffer' in 'The Same Ol' Fling.'"

"What?"

Jim repeated.

"Oh! 'The Same Old Thing'—the wagon."

The rest of the afternoon I poked round the gullies with old Brighten, looking at some "indications" (of the existence of gold) he had found. It was no use trying to "pump" him concerning his sister-in-law; Brighten was an "old hand," and had learned in the old bushranging and cattle-stealing days to know nothing about other people's business. And, by the way, I noticed then that the more you talk and listen to a bad character, the more you lose your dislike for him.

I never saw such a change in a woman as in Brighten's sister-in-law that evening. She was bright and jolly, and seemed at least ten years younger. She bustled round and helped her sister to get tea ready. She rooted out some old china that Mrs Brighten had stowed away somewhere, and set the table as I seldom saw it set out there. She propped Jim up with pillows, and laughed and played with him like a great girl. She described Sydney and Sydney life as I'd never heard it described before; and she knew as much about the bush and old digging days as I did. She kept old Brighten and me listening and laughing till nearly midnight. And she seemed quick to understand everything when I talked. If she wanted to explain anything that we hadn't seen, she wouldn't say that it was "like a—like a"—and hesitate (you know what I mean); she'd hit the right thing on the head at once. A squatter with a very round, flaming red face and a white cork hat had gone by in the afternoon; she said it was "like a mushroom on the rising moon." She gave me a lot of good hints about children.

But she was quiet again next morning. I harnessed up, and she dressed Jim and gave him his breakfast, and made a comfortable place for him on the load with a possum rug and a spare pillow. She got up on the wheel to do it herself. Then was the awkward time. I'd half start to speak to her, and then turn away and go fixing up round the horses, and then make another false start to say good-bye. At last she took Jim up in her arms and kissed him, and lifted him on the wheel; but he put his arms tight round her neck, and kissed her—a thing Jim seldom did with anybody, except his mother, for he wasn't what you'd call an affectionate child—he'd never more than offer his cheek to me, in his old-fashioned way. I'd got up the other side of the load to take him from her.

"Here, take him," she said.

I saw his mouth twitching as I lifted him. Jim seldom cried nowadays—no matter how much he was hurt. I gained some time fixing Jim comfortable.

"You'd better make a start," she said. "You want to get home early with that boy."

I got down and went round to where she stood. I held out my hand and tried to speak, but my voice went like an ungreased wagon-wheel, and I gave it up, and only squeezed her hand.

George W. Lambert (1873-1930) *Across the Black Soil Plains* (1899)
91.6 x 305.5 cm   Oil on canvas
Reproduced with the kind permission of the Art Gallery Of New South Wales, Sydney

Sir Hans Heysen, O.B.E. (1877-1968)   *Approaching Storm with Bush Fire Haze* (1912)
61 x 81.3 cm   Oil on canvas
Reproduced with the kind permission of The Art Gallery Of South Australia

"That's all right," she said; then tears came into her eyes, and she suddenly put her hand on my shoulder and kissed me on the cheek. "You be off—you're only a boy yourself. Take care of that boy; be kind to your wife, and take care of yourself."

"Will you come to see us?"

"Some day," she said.

I started the horses, and looked round once more. She was looking up at Jim, who was waving his hand to her from the top of the load. And I saw that haggard, hungry, hopeless look come into her eyes in spite of the tears.

I smoothed over that story and shortened it a lot when I told it to Mary—I didn't want to upset her. But, some time after I brought Jim home from Gulgong, and while I was at home with the team for a few days, nothing would suit Mary but she must go over to Brighten's shanty and see Brighten's sister-in-law. So James drove her over one morning in the spring-cart: it was a long way, and they stayed at Brighten's overnight and didn't get back till late the next afternoon. I'd got the place in a pig-muck, as Mary said, "doing for" myself, and I was having a snooze on the sofa when they got back. The first thing I remember was someone stroking my head and kissing me, and I heard Mary saying "My poor boy! My poor old boy!"

I sat up with a jerk. I thought that Jim had gone off again. But it seems that Mary was only referring to me. Then she started to pull grey hairs out of my head and put 'em in an empty match-box—to see how many she'd get. She used to do this when she felt a bit soft. I don't know what she said to Brighten's sister-in-law or what Brighten's sister-in-law said to her, but Mary was extra gentle for the next few days.

"WATER THEM GERANIUMS"

I

A LONELY TRACK

The time Mary and I shifted out into the bush from Gulgong to "settle on the land" at Lahey's Creek.

I'd sold the two tip-drays that I used for tank-sinking and dam-making and I took the traps out in the wagon on top of a small load of rations and horse-feed that I was taking to a sheep station out that way. Mary drove out in the spring-cart. You remember we left little Jim with his aunt in Gulgong till we got settled down. I'd sent James (Mary's brother) out the day before, on horseback, with two or three cows and some heifers and steers and calves we had, and I'd told him to clean up a bit, and make the hut as bright and cheerful as possible before Mary came.

We hadn't much in the way of furniture. There was the four-poster cedar bedstead that I bought before we were married, and Mary was rather proud of it: it had "turned" posts and joints that bolted together. There was a plain hardwood table, that Mary called her "ironing-table," upside down on top of the load, with the bedding and blankets between the legs; there were four of those common black kitchen-chairs—with apples painted on the hard board backs—that we used for the parlour; there was a cheap batten sofa with arms at the ends and turned rails between the uprights of the arms (we were a little proud of the turned rails); and there was the camp-oven, and the three-legged pot, and pans and buckets, stuck about the load and hanging under the tail-board of the wagon.

There was the little Wilcox & Gibb's sewing-machine—my present to Mary when we were married (and what a present, looking back to it!). There was a cheap little rocking-chair, and a looking glass and some pictures that were presents from Mary's friends and sister. She had her mantleshelf ornaments and crockery and nick-nacks packed away, in the linen and old clothes, in a big tub made of half a cask, and a box that had been Jim's cradle. The live stock was a cat in one box, and in another an old rooster, and three hens that formed cliques, two against one, turn about, as three of the same sex will do all over the world. I had my old cattle-dog, and of course a pup on the load—I always had a pup that I gave away, or sold and didn't get paid for, or had "touched" (stolen) as soon as it was old enough. James had his three spidery, sneaking, thieving, cold-blooded kangaroo-dogs with him. I was taking out three months' provisions in the way of ration-sugar, tea, flour, and potatoes.

I started early, and Mary caught up to me at Ryan's Crossing on Sandy Creek, where we boiled the billy and had some dinner.

Mary bustled about the camp and admired the scenery and talked too much, for her, and was extra cheerful, and kept her face turned from me as much as possible. I saw what was the matter. She'd been crying to herself coming along the road. I thought it was on account of leaving little Jim behind for the first time. She told me that she couldn't make up her mind till the last moment to leave him. And that, a mile or two along the road, she'd have turned back for him, only that she knew her sister would laugh at her. She was always terribly anxious about the children.

We cheered each other up, and Mary drove with me the rest of the way to the creek, along the lonely branch track, across native apple-tree flats. It was a dreary, hopeless track. There was no horizon, nothing but the rough ashen trunks of the gnarled and stunted trees in all directions, little or no undergrowth, and the ground, save for the coarse, brownish tufts of dead grass, as bare as the road, for it was a dry season: there had been no rain for months, and I wondered what I should do with the cattle if there wasn't more grass on the creek.

In this sort of country a stranger might travel for miles without seeming to have moved, for all the difference there is in the scenery. The new tracks were "blazed"—that is, slices of bark cut from both sides of the trees, within sight of each other, in a line, to mark the track until the horses and wheel marks made it plain. A smart bushman, with a sharp tomahawk, can blaze a track as he rides. But a bushman a little used to the country soon picks out differences amongst the trees, half unconsciously as it were, and so finds his way about.

Mary and I didn't talk much along this track—we couldn't have heard each other very well, anyway, for the "clock-clock" of the wagon and the rattle of the cart over the hard lumpy ground. And I suppose we both began to feel pretty dismal as the shadows lengthened. I'd noticed lately that Mary and I had got out of the habit of talking to each other—noticed it in a vague sort of way that irritated me (as vague things will irritate one) when I thought of it. But then I thought, "It won't last long—I'll make life brighter for her by and by."

As we went along—and the track seemed endless—I got brooding, of course, back into the past. And I feel now, when it's too late, that Mary must have been thinking that way too. I thought of my early boyhood, of the hard life of "grubbin'" and "milkin'" and "fencin'" and "ploughin'" and "ring-barkin'" and all for nothing. The few months at the little bark school, with a teacher who couldn't spell. The cursed ambition or craving that tortured my soul as a boy—ambition or craving for—I didn't know what for! For something better and brighter, anyhow. And I made the life harder by reading at night.

It all passed before me as I followed on in the wagon, behind Mary in the spring-cart. I thought of these old things more than I thought of her. She had tried to help me to better things. And I tried too—I had the energy of half a dozen men when I saw the road clear before me, but shied at the first check. Then I brooded, or dreamed of making a home—that one might call a home—for Mary—some day. Ah, well!——

And what was Mary thinking about, along the lonely, changeless miles? I never thought of that. Of her kind, careless, gentleman father, perhaps. Of her girlhood. Of her homes—not the huts and camps she lived in with me. Of our future?—she used to plan a lot, and talk a good deal of our future—but not lately. These things didn't strike me at the time—I was so deep in my own brooding. Did she think now—did she begin to feel now that she had made a great mistake and thrown away her life, but must make the best of it? This might have roused me, had I thought of it. But whenever I thought Mary was getting indifferent towards me, I'd think, "I'll soon win her back. We'll be sweethearts again—when things brighten up a bit."

It's an awful thing to me, now I look back to it, to think how far apart we had grown, what strangers we were to each other. It seems, now, as though we had been sweethearts long years before, and had parted, and had never really met since.

The sun was going down when Mary called out:

"There's our place, Joe!"

She hadn't seen it before, and somehow it came new and with a shock to me, who had been out here several times. Ahead, through the trees to the right, was a dark green clump of she-oaks standing out of the creek, darker for the dead grey grass and blue-grey bush on the barren ridge in the background. Across the creek (it was only a deep, narrow gutter—a watercourse with a chain of waterholes after rain), across on the other bank, stood the hut, on a narrow flat between the spur and the creek, and a little higher than this side. The land was much better than on our old selection, and there was good soil along the creek on both sides: I expected a rush of selectors out here soon. A few acres round the hut were cleared and fenced in by a light two-rail fence of timber split from logs and saplings. The man who took up this selection left it because his wife died here.

It was a small oblong hut built of split slabs, and he had roofed it with shingles which he split in spare times. There was no veranda, but I built one later on. At the end of the house was a big slab-and-bark shed, bigger than the hut itself, with a kitchen, a skillion for tools, harness, and horse-feed, and a spare bedroom partitioned off with sheets of bark and old chaff-bags. The house itself was floored roughly, with cracks between the boards; there were cracks between the slabs all round—though he'd nailed strips of tin, from old kerosene tins, over some of them; the partitioned-off bedroom was lined with old chaff-bags with newspapers pasted over them for wall-paper. There was no ceiling, calico or otherwise, and we could see the round pine rafters and battens, and the under ends of the shingles. But ceilings make a hut hot and harbour insects and reptiles—snakes sometimes. There was one small glass window in the "dining-room" with three panes and a sheet of greased paper, and the rest were rough wooden shutters. There was a pretty good cow-yard and calf-pen, and—that was about all. There was no dam or tank (I made one later on); there was a water-cask, with the hoops falling off and the staves gaping, at the corner of the house, and spouting, made of lengths of bent tin, ran round the eaves. Water from a new shingle roof is wine-red for a year or two, and water from a stringy-bark roof is like tan-water for years. In dry weather the selector had got his house water from a cask sunk in the gravel at the bottom of the deepest waterhole in the creek, and the longer the drought lasted, the farther he had to go down the creek for his water, with a cask on a cart, and take his cows to drink, if he had any. Four, five, six or seven miles—even ten miles to water is nothing in some places.

James hadn't found himself called upon to do more that milk old "Spot" (the grandmother cow of our mob), pen the calf at night, make a fire in the kitchen, and sweep out the house with a bough. He helped me unharness and water and feed the horses, and then started to get the furniture off the wagon and into the house. James wasn't lazy, so long as one thing didn't last too long; but he was too uncomfortably practical and matter-of-fact for me. Mary and I had some tea in the kitchen. The kitchen was permanently furnished with a table of split slabs, adzed smooth on top, and supported by four stakes driven into the ground, a three-legged stool and a block of wood, and two long stools made of half-round slabs (saplings trunks split in halves) with auger-holes bored in the round side and sticks stuck into them for legs. The floor was of clay; the chimney of slabs and tin; the fire-place was about eight feet wide, lined with clay, and with a blackened pole across, with sooty chains and wire hooks on it for the pots.

Mary didn't seem able to eat. She sat on the three-legged stool near the fire, though it was warm weather, and kept her face turned from me. Mary was still pretty, but not the little dumpling she had been: she was thinner now. She had big dark hazel eyes that shone a little too much when she was pleased or excited. I thought at times that there was something very German about her expression; also sometimes aristocratic about the turn of her nose, which nipped in at the nostrils when she spoke. There was nothing aristocratic about me. Mary was German in figure and walk. I used sometimes to call her "Little Dutchy" and "Pigeon Toes." She had a will of her own, as shown sometimes by the obstinate knit in her forehead between the eyes.

Mary sat still by the fire, and presently I saw her chin tremble.

"What is it, Mary?"

She turned her face farther from me. I felt tired, disappointed, and irritated—suffering from a reaction.

"Now, what is it, Mary?" I asked; "I'm sick of this sort of thing. Haven't you got everything you wanted? You've had your own way. What's the matter with you now?"

"You know very well, Joe."

"But I *don't* know," I said. I knew too well.

She said nothing.

"Look here, Mary," I said, putting my hand on her shoulder, "don't go on like that; tell me what's the matter."

"It's only this," she said suddenly, "I can't stand this life here, it will kill me!"

I had a pannikin of tea in my hand, and I banged it down on the table.

"This is more than a man can stand!" I shouted. "You know very well that it was you that dragged me out here. You run me on to this. Why weren't you content to stay in Gulgong?"

"And what sort of a place was Gulgong, Joe?" asked Mary quietly.

(I thought even then in a flash what sort of a place Gulgong was. A wretched remnant of a town on an abandoned goldfield. One street, each side of the dusty main road three or four one story square brick cottages with hip-roofs of galvanised iron that glared in the heat—four rooms and a passage—the police station, bank-manager's and schoolmaster's cottages. Half a dozen tumble-down weather-board shanties—the three pubs, the two stores, and the post office. The town tailing off into weather-board boxes with tin tops, and old bark huts—relics of the digging days—propped up by many rotting poles. The men, when at home, mostly asleep or droning over their pipes or hanging about the veranda-posts of the pubs, saying "'Ullo, Bill!" or "'Ullo, Jim!"—or sometimes drunk. The women mostly hags, who blackened each other's and girls' characters with their tongues, and criticized the aristocracy's washing hung on the line: "And the colour of the clothes! Does that woman wash her clothes at all? or only soak 'em and hang 'em out?"—that was Gulgong.)

"Well, why didn't you come to Sydney, as I wanted you to?" I asked Mary.

"You know very well, Joe," said Mary quietly.

(I knew very well, but the knowledge only maddened me. I had had an idea of getting a billet in one of the big wool-stores—I was a fair wool expert—but Mary was afraid of the drink. I could keep well away from it so long as I worked hard in the bush. I had gone to Sydney twice since I met Mary, once before we were married, and she forgave me when I came back; and once afterwards. I got a billet there then, and was going to send for her in a month. After eight weeks she raised the money somehow and came to Sydney and brought me home. I got pretty down that time.)

"But Mary," I said, "it would be different this time. You would have been with me. I can take a glass now or leave it alone."

"As long as you take a glass there is danger," she said.

"Well, what did you want to advise me to come out here for, if you can't stand it? Why didn't you stay where you were?" I asked.

"Well," she said, "why weren't you more decided?"

I'd sat down, but I jumped to my feet then.

"Good God!" I shouted, "this is more than a man can stand. I'll chuck it all up! I'm damned well sick and tired of the whole thing."

"So am I, Joe," said Mary wearily.

We quarrelled badly then—that first hour in our new home. I know now whose fault it was.

I got my hat and went out and started to walk down the creek. I didn't feel bitter against Mary—I had spoken too cruelly to her to feel that way. Looking back, I could see plainly that if I had taken her advice all through instead of now and again, things would have been all right with me. I had come away and left her crying in the hut, and James telling her, in a brotherly way, that it was all her fault. The trouble was that I never liked to "give in" or go half-way to make it up—not half-way—it was all the way or nothing with our natures.

"If I don't make a stand now," I'd say, "I'll never be master. I gave up the reins when I got married, and I'll have to get them back again."

What women some men are! But the time came, and not too many years after, when I stood by the bed where Mary lay, white and still; and, amongst other things, I kept saying, "I'll give in, Mary—I'll give in," and then I'd laugh. They thought I was raving mad, and took me from the room. But that time was to come.

As I walked down the creek track in the moonlight the question rang in my ears again, as it had done when I first caught sight of the house that evening:

"Why did I bring her here?"

I was not fit to "go on the land." The place was only fit for some stolid German, or Scotsman, or even Englishman and his wife, who had no ambition but to bullock and make a farm of the place. I had only drifted here through carelessness, brooding and discontent.

I walked on and on till I was more than half-way to the only neigh-bours—a wretched selector's family, about four miles down the creek—and I thought I'd go on to the house and see if they had any fresh meat.

A mile or two farther I saw the loom of the bark hut they lived in, on a patchy clearing in the scrub, and heard the voice of the selector's wife—I had seen her several times: she was a gaunt, haggard bushwoman, and I supposed the reason why she hadn't gone mad through hardship and loneliness was that she hadn't either the brains or the memory to go further than she could see through the trunks of the "apple-trees."

"You, An-nay!" (Annie.)

"Ye-es" (from somewhere in the gloom).

"Didn't I tell yer to water them geraniums!"

"Well, didn't I?"

"Don't tell lies or I'll break your young back!"

"I did, I tell yer—the water won't soak inter the ashes."

Geraniums were the only flowers I saw grow in the drought out there. I remembered this woman had a few dirty-grey-green leaves behind some sticks against the bark wall near the door; and in spite of the sticks the fowls used to get in and scratch beds under the geraniums and scratch dust over them, and ashes were thrown there—with an idea of helping the flowers, I suppose; and greasy dish-water, when fresh water was scarce—till you might as well try to water a dish of fat.

Then the woman's voice again:

"You, Tom-may!" (Tommy.)

Silence, save for an echo on the ridge.

"Y-o-u T-o-m-*may!*"

"Y-e-s!" shrill shriek from across the creek.

"Didn't I tell you to ride up to them new people and see if they want any meat or anythink?" in one long reach.

"Well—I karn't find the horse."

"Well - find - it - first - thing - in - the - morning - and - don't - forgit - to - tell - Mrs - Wi'son - that - mother'll - be - up - as - soon - as - she - can."

I didn't feel like going to the woman's house that night. I felt—and the thought came like a whipstroke on my heart—that this was what Mary would come to if I left her here.

I turned and started to walk home, fast. I'd made up my mind. I'd take Mary straight back to Gulgong in the morning—I forgot about the load I had to take to the sheep station. I'd say, "Look here, Girlie" (that's what I used to call her), "we'll leave this wretched life; we'll leave the bush for ever. We'll go to Sydney, and I'll be a man! and work my way up." And I'd sell wagon, horses, and all, and go.

When I got to the hut it was lighted up. Mary had the only kerosene lamp, a slush-lamp, and two tallow candles going. She had got both rooms washed out—to James's disgust, for he had to move the furniture and boxes out. She had a lot of things unpacked on the table; and she had laid clean newspapers on the mantleshelf—a slab on two pegs over the fire-place—and put the little wooden clock in the centre and some of the ornaments on each side, and was tacking a strip of vandyked American oilcloth round the rough edge of the slab.

"How does that look, Joe? We'll soon get things shipshape."

I kissed her, but she had her mouth full of tacks. I went out in the kitchen, drank a pint of cold tea, and sat down.

Somehow I didn't feel satisfied with the way things had gone.

II
"PAST CARIN'"

Next morning things looked a lot brighter. Things always look brighter in the morning—more so in the Australian bush, I should think, than in most other places. It is when the sun goes down on the dark bed of the lonely bush, and the sunset flashes like a sea of fire and then fades, and then glows out again, like a bank of coals, and then burns away to ashes—it is then that old things come home to one. And strange, new-old things too, that haunt and depress you terribly, and that you can't understand. I often think how, at sunset, the past must come home to a new-chum black sheep, sent out to Australia and drifted into the bush. I used to think that they couldn't have much brains, or the loneliness would drive them mad.

I'd decided to let James take the team for a trip or two. He could drive all right; he was a better business man, and no doubt would manage better than me—as long as the novelty lasted; and I'd stay at home for a week or so, till Mary got used to the place, or I could get a girl from somewhere to come and stay with her. The first weeks or few months of loneliness are the worst, as a rule, I believe, as they say the first weeks in jail are—I was never there. I know it's so with tramping or hard graft: the first day or two are twice as hard as any of the rest. But, for my part, I could never get used to loneliness and dullness; the last days used to be the worst with me: then I'd have to make a move, or drink. When you've been too much and too long alone in a lonely place, you begin to do queer things, and think queer thoughts—provided that you have any imagination at all. You'll sometimes sit of an evening and watch the lonely track, by the hour, for a horseman or a cart or someone that's never likely to come that way—someone, or a stranger, that you can't and don't really expect to see. I think that most men who have been alone in the bush for any length of time—and married couples too—are more or less mad. With married couples it is generally the husband who is painfully shy and awkward when strangers come. The woman seems to stand the loneliness better, and can hold her own with strangers, as a rule. It's only afterwards, and looking back, that you see how queer you got. Shepherds and boundary-riders, who are alone for months, *must* have their periodical spree, at the nearest shanty, else they'd go raving mad. Drink is the only break in the awful monotony, and the yearly or half-yearly spree is the only thing they've got to look forward to: it keeps their minds fixed on something definite ahead.

But Mary kept her head pretty well through the first months of loneliness. *Weeks* rather, I should say, for it wasn't as bad as it might have been farther up-country: there was generally someone came of a Sunday afternoon—a spring-cart with a couple of women, or maybe a family—or a lanky shy bush native or two on lanky shy horses. On a quiet Sunday, after I'd brought Jim home, Mary would dress him and herself—just the same as if we were in town—and make me get up on one end and put on a collar and take her and Jim for a walk along the creek. She said she wanted to keep me civilized. She tried to make a gentleman of me for years, but gave it up gradually.

Well. It was the first morning on the creek: I was greasing the wagon-wheels, and James out after a horse, and Mary hanging out clothes, in an old print dress and a big ugly white hood, when I heard her being hailed as "Hi missus!" from the front sliprails.

It was a boy on horseback. He was a light-haired, very much freckled boy of fourteen or fifteen, with a small head, but with limbs, especially his bare sun-blotched shanks, that might have belonged to a grown man. He had a good face and frank grey eyes. An old, nearly black cabbage-tree hat rested on the butts of his ears, turning them out at right angles from his head, and rather dirty sprouts they were. He wore a dirty torn Crimean shirt; and a pair of men's moleskin trousers rolled up above the knees, with a wide waistband gathered under a greenhide belt. I noticed, later on, that even when he wore trousers short enough for him, he always rolled 'em up above the knees when on horseback, for some reason of his own: to suggest leggings, perhaps, for he had them rolled up in all weathers, and he wouldn't have bothered to save them from the sweat of the horse, even if that horse ever sweated.

He was seated astride a three-bushel bag thrown across the ridge-pole of a big grey horse, with a coffin-shaped head, and built astern something after the style of a roughly put up hip-roofed box-bark humpy. His colour was like old box-bark, too, a dirty bluish-grey; and, one time, when I saw his rump looming out of the scrub, I really thought it was some old shepherd's hut that I hadn't noticed there before. When he cantered it was like the humpy starting off on its corner-posts.

"Are you Mrs Wilson?" asked the boy.

"Yes," said Mary.

"Well, mother told me to ride acrost and see if you wanted anythink. We killed lars' night, and I fetched a piece er cow."

"Piece of *what*?" asked Mary.

He grinned and handed a sugar-bag across the rail with something heavy in the bottom of it, that nearly jerked Mary's arm out when she took it. It was a piece of beef, that looked as if it had been cut off with a wood-axe, but it was fresh and clean.

"Oh, I'm so glad!" cried Mary. She was always impulsive, save to me sometimes. "I was just wondering where we were going to get any fresh meat. How kind of your mother! Tell her I'm very much obliged to her indeed." And she felt behind her for a poor purse she had. "And now—how much did your mother say it would be?"

The boy blinked at her, and scratched his head.

"How much will it be," he repeated, puzzled. "Oh—how much does it weigh I-s'pose-yer-mean. Well, it ain't been weighed at all—we ain't got no scales. A butcher does all that sort of thing. We just kills it, and cooks it, and eats it—and goes by guess. What won't keep we salts down in the cask. I reckon it weighs about a ton by the weight of it if yer wanter know. Mother thought that if she sent any more it would go bad before you could scoff it. I can't see——"

"Yes, yes," said Mary, getting confused. "But what I want to know is, how do you manage when you sell it?"

He glared at her, and scratched his head. "Sell it? Why, we only goes halves in a steer with someone, or sell steers to the butcher—or maybe some meat to a party of fencers or surveyors, or tank-sinkers, or them sorter people——"

"Yes, yes; but what I want to know is, how much am I to send your mother for this?"

"How much what?"

"Money, of course, you stupid boy," said Mary. "You seem a very stupid boy."

Then he saw what she was driving at. He began to fling his heels convulsively against the sides of his horse, jerking his body backward and forward at the same time, as if to wind up and start some clockwork machinery inside the horse, that made it go, and seemed to need repairing or oiling.

"We ain't that sorter people, missus," he said. "We don't sell meat to new people that come to settle here." Then, jerking his thumb contemptuosly towards the ridges, "Go over ter Wall's if yer wanter buy meat; they sell meat to strangers." (Wall was the big squatter over the ridges.)

"Oh!" said Mary, "I'm *so* sorry. Thank your mother for me. She *is* kind."

"Oh, that's nothink. She said to tell yer she'll be up as soon as she can. She'd have come up yisterday evening—she thought yer'd feel lonely comin' new to a place like this—but she couldn't git up."

The machinery inside the old horse showed signs of starting. You almost heard the wooden joints *creak* as he lurched forward, like an old propped-up humpy when the rotting props give way; but at the sound of Mary's voice he settled back on his foundations again. It must have been a very poor selection that couldn't afford a better spare horse than that.

"Reach me up that lump er wood, will yer, missus?" said the boy, and he pointed to one of my "spreads" (for the team-chains) that lay inside the fence. "I'll fling it back again over the fence when I git this ole cow started."

"But wait a minute—I've forgotten your mother's name," said Mary.

He grabbed at his thatch impatiently. "Me mother—oh!—the old woman's name's Mrs Spicer. (Git up, karn't yer!)" He twisted himself round, and brought the stretcher down on one of the horse's "points" (and he had many) with a crack that must have jarred his wrist.

"Do you go to school?" asked Mary. There was a three-days-a-week school over the ridges at Wall's station.

"No!" he jerked out, keeping his legs going. "Me—why I'm going on fur fifteen. The last teacher at Wall's finished me. I'm going to Queensland next month drovin'." (Queensland border was over three hundred miles away.)

"Finished you? How?" asked Mary.

"Me edgercation, of course! How do yer expect me to start this horse when yer keep talkin'?"

He split the "spread" over the horse's point, threw the pieces over the fence, and was off, his elbows and legs flying wildly, and the old saw-stool lumbering along the road like an old working bullock trying a canter. That horse wasn't a trotter.

And next month he *did* start for Queensland. He was a younger son and a surplus boy on a wretched, poverty-stricken selection; and as there was "northin' doin'" in the district, his father (in a burst of fatherly kindness, I suppose) made him a present of the old horse and a new pair of blucher boots, and I gave him an old saddle and a coat, and he started for the Never-Never country.

And I'll bet he got there. But I'm doubtful if the old horse did.

Mary gave the boy five shillings, and I don't think he had anything more except a clean shirt and an extra pair of white cotton socks.

"Spicer's farm" was a big bark humpy on a patchy clearing in the native apple-tree scrub. The clearing was fenced in by a light "dog-legged" fence (a fence of sapling poles resting on forks and X-shaped uprights), and the dusty ground round the house was almost entirely covered with cattle-dung. There was no attempt at cultivation when I came to live on the creek; but there were old furrow-marks amongst the stumps of another shapeless patch in the scrub near the hut. There was a wretched sapling cow-yard and calf-pen, and a cow-bail with one sheet of bark over it for shelter. There was no dairy to be seen, and I suppose the milk was set in one of the two skillion rooms, or lean-to's behind the hut—the other was "the boys' bedroom." The Spicers kept a few cows and steers, and had thirty or forty sheep. Mrs Spicer used to drive down the creek once a week, in her rickety old spring-cart, to Cobborah, with butter and eggs. The hut was nearly as bare inside as it was out—just a frame of "round-timber" (sapling poles) covered with bark. The furniture was permanent (unless you rooted it up), like in our kitchen: a rough slab table on stakes driven into the ground, and seats made the same way. Mary told me afterwards that the beds in the bag-and-bark partitioned-off room ("mother's bedroom") were simply poles laid side by side on cross-pieces supported by stakes driven into the ground, with straw mattresses and some worn-out bed-clothes. Mrs Spicer had an old patchwork quilt, in rags, and the remains of a white one, and Mary said it was pitiful to see how these things would be spread over the beds—to hide them as much as possible—when she went down there. A packing-case, with something like an old print skirt draped round it, and a cracked looking-glass (without a frame) on top, was the dressing-table. There were a couple of gin-cases for a wardrobe. The boys' beds were three bushel bags stretched between poles fastened to uprights. The floor was the original surface, tramped hard, worn uneven with much sweeping, and with puddles in rainy weather where the roof leaked. Mrs Spicer used to stand old tins, dishes and buckets under as many of the leaks as she could. The saucepans, kettles and boilers were old kerosene-tins and billies. They used kerosene-tins, too, cut longways in halves, for setting the milk in. The plates and cups were of tin; there were two or three cups without saucers, and a crockery plate or two—also two mugs, cracked and without handles, one with "For a Good Boy" and the other with "For a Good Girl" on it; but all these were kept on the mantleshelf for ornament and for company. They were the only ornaments in the house, save a little wooden clock that hadn't gone for years. Mrs Spicer had a superstition that she had "some things packed away for the children."

The pictures were cut from old copies of the *Illustrated Sydney News* and pasted on to the bark. I remember this, because I remembered, long ago, the Spencers, who were our neighbours when I was a boy, had the walls of their bedroom covered with illustrations of the American Civil War, cut from illustrated London papers, and I used to "sneak" into "mother's bedroom" with Fred Spencer whenever we got a chance, and gloat over the prints. I gave him the blade of a pocket-knife once, for taking me in there.

I saw very little of Spicer. He was a big, dark, dark-haired and bewhiskered man. I had an idea that he wasn't a selector at all, only a "dummy" for the squatter of the Cobborah run. You see, selectors were allowed to take up land on runs or pastoral leases. The squatters kept them off as much as possible, by all manner of dodges and paltry persecution. The squatter would get as much freehold as he could afford, "select" as much land as the law allowed one man to take up, and then employ dummies (dummy selectors) to take up bits of land that he fancied about his run, and hold them for him.

Spicer seemed gloomy and unsociable. He was seldom at home. He was generally supposed to be away shearin', or fencin', or workin' on somebody's station. It turned out that the last six months he was away it was on the evidence of a cask of beef and a hide with the brand cut out, found in his camp on a fencing contract up-country, and which he and his mates couldn't account for satisfactorily, while the squatter could. Then the family lived mostly on bread and honey, or bread and treacle, or bread and dripping, and tea. Every ounce of butter and every egg was needed for the market, to keep them in flour, tea, and sugar. Mary found that out, but couldn't help them much—except by "stuffing" the children with bread and meat or bread and jam whenever they came to our place—for Mrs Spicer was proud with the pride that lies down in the end and turns its face to the wall and dies.

Once, when Mary asked Annie, the oldest girl at home, if she was hungry, she denied it—but she looked it. A ragged mite she had with her explained things. The little fellow said:

"Mother told Annie not to say we was hungry if yer asked; but if yer give us anythink to eat, we was to take it an' say thenk yer, Mrs Wilson."

"I wouldn't 'a' told yer a lie; but I thought Jimmy would split on me, Mrs Wilson," said Annie. "Thenk yer, Mrs Wilson."

She was not a big woman. She was gaunt and flat chested, and her face was "burnt to a brick", as they say out here. She had brown eyes, nearly red, and a little wild-looking at times, and a sharp face—ground sharp by hardship—the cheeks drawn in. She had an expression like—well, like a woman who had been very curious and suspicious at one time, and wanted to know everybody's business and hear everything, and had lost all her curiosity, without losing the expression or the quick suspicious movements of the head. I don't suppose you understand. I can't explain it any other way. She was no more than forty.

I remembered the first morning I saw her. I was going up the creek to look at the selection for the first time, and called at the hut to see if she had a bit of fresh mutton, as I had none and was sick of "corned beef."

"Yes—of—course," she said, in a sharp nasty tone, as if to say, "Is there anything more you want while the shop's open?" I'd met just the same sort of woman years before while I was carrying swag between the shearing-sheds in the awful scrubs out west of the Darling River, so I didn't turn on my heels and walk away. I waited for her to speak again.

"Come—inside," she said, "and sit down. I see you've got the wagon outside. I s'pose your name's Wilson, ain't it? You're thinkin' about takin' on Harry Marshfield's selection up the creek, so I heard. Wait till I fry you a chop, and boil the billy."

Her voice sounded, more than anything else, like a voice coming out of a phonograph—I heard one in Sydney the other day—and not like a voice coming out of her. But sometimes when she got outside her everyday life on this selection she spoke in a sort of—in a sort of lost groping-in-the-dark kind of voice.

She didn't talk much this time—just spoke in a mechanical way of the drought, and the hard times, "an butter 'n' eggs down, an' her husband an' eldest son bein' away, an' that makin' it so hard for her."

I don't know how many children she had. I never got a chance to count them, for they were nearly all small, and shy as piccaninnies, and used to run and hide when anybody came. They were mostly nearly black as piccaninnies too. She must have averaged a baby a year for years—and God only knows how she got over her confinements! Once they said she only had a black gin with her. She had an elder boy and girl, but she seldom spoke of them. The girl, "Liza," was "in service in Sydney." I'm afraid I knew what that meant. The elder son was "away." He had been a bit of a favourite round there, it seemed.

Someone might ask her, "How's your son Jack, Mrs Spicer?" or, "Heard of Jack lately? and where is he now?"

"Oh, he's somewheres up-country," she'd say in the "groping" voice, or "He's drovin' in Queensland," or "Shearin' on the Darlin' the last time I heerd from him. We ain't had a line from him since—le's see—since Chris'mas 'fore last."

And she'd turn her haggard eyes in a helpless, hopeful sort of way towards the west—towards "up-country" and "out back."

The eldest girl at home was nine or ten, with a little old face and lines across her forehead: she had an older expression than her mother. Tommy went to Queensland, as I told you. The oldest son at home, Bill (older than Tommy), was "a bit wild."

I've passed the place in smothering hot mornings in December, when the droppings about the cow-yard had crumpled to dust that rose in the warm, sickly, sunrise wind, and seen that woman at work in the cow-yard, "bailing up" and leg-roping cows, milking, or hauling at a rope round the neck of a half-grown calf that was too strong for her (and she was tough as fencing-wire), or humping great buckets of sour cream to the pigs or the "poddies" (hand-fed calves) in the pen. I'd get off the horse and give her a hand sometimes with a young steer, or a cranky old cow that wouldn't "bail-up" and threatened her with her horns. She'd say:

"Thenk yer, Mr Wilson. Do you think we're ever goin' to have any rain?"

I've ridden past the place on bitter black rainy mornings in June or July, and seen her trudging about the yard—that was ankle deep in black liquid filth—with an old pair of blucher boots in, and an old coat of her husband's, or maybe a three-bushel bag over her shoulders. I've seen her climbing on the roof by means of the water-cask at the corner, and trying to stop a leak by shoving a piece of tin under the bark. And when I'd fixed the leak:

"Thenk yer, Mr Wilson. This drop of rain's a blessin'! Come in and have a dry at the fire and I'll make yer a cup of tea." And, if I was in a hurry, "Come in, man alive! Come in! and dry yerself a bit till the rain holds up. Yer can't go home like this! Yer'll git yer death o' cold."

I've even seen her, in the terrible drought, climbing she-oaks and apple-trees by a makeshift ladder, and awkwardly lopping off boughs to feed the starving cattle.

"Jist tryin' ter keep the milkers alive till the rain comes."

They said that when the pleuro-pneumonia was in the district and amongst her cattle she bled and physicked them herself, and fed those that were down with slices of half-ripe pumpkins (from a crop that had failed).

"An' one day," she told Mary, "There was a big barren heifer (that we called Queen Elizabeth) that was down with the ploorer. She'd been down for four days and hadn't moved, when one mornin' I dumped some wheaten chaff—we had a few bags that Spicer brought home—I dumped it in front of her nose, an'—would yer b'lieve me, Mrs Wilson?—she stumbled onter her feet an' chased me all the way to the house! I had to pick up me skirts an' run! Wasn't it redic'lus?"

They had a sense of the ridiculous, most of those poor sun-dried bush-women. I fancy that that helped save them from madness.

"We lost nearly all our milkers," she told Mary. "I remember one day Tommy came running to the house and screamed: 'Marther! [mother] there's another milker down with the ploorer!' Jist as if it was great news. Well, Mrs Wilson, I was dead-beat, an' I giv' in. I jist sat down to have a good cry, and felt for my han'kerchief—it *was* a rag of a han'kerchief, full of holes (all me others was in the wash). Without seein' what I was doin' I put my finger through the hole in the han'kerchief an' me thumb through the other, and poked me fingers into me eyes, instead of wipin' them. Then I had to laugh."

There's a story that once, when the bush, or rather grass, fires were out all along the creek on Spicer's side, Wall's station-hands were up above our place, trying to keep the fire back from the boundary, and towards the evening one of the men happened to think of the Spicers: they saw smoke down that way. Spicer was away from home, and they had a small crop of wheat, nearly ripe, on the selection.

"My God! that poor devil of a woman will be burnt out, if she ain't already!" shouted young Bill Wall. "Come along, three or four of you chaps"—it was shearing-time, and there were plenty of men on the station.

They raced down the creek to Spicer's, and were just in time to save the wheat. She had her sleeves tucked up, and was beating out the burning grass with a bough. She'd been at it for an hour, and was as black as a gin, they said. She only said when they'd turned the fire: "Thenk yer! Wait an' I'll make some tea."

After tea the first Sunday she came to see us, Mary asked:

"Don't you feel lonely, Mrs Spicer, when your husband goes away?"

"Well—no, Mrs Wilson," she said in the groping sort of voice. "I uster, once. I remember, when we lived on the Cudgegong River—we lived in a brick house then—the first time Spicer had to go away from home I nearly fretted my eyes out. And he was only goin' shearin' for a month. I muster bin a fool; but then we were only jist married a little while. He's been away drovin' in Queensland as long as eighteen months at a time since then. But" (her voice seemed to grope in the dark more than ever) "I don't mind —I somehow seem to have got past carin'. Besides—besides, Spicer was a very different man then to what he is now. He's got so moody and gloomy at home, he hardly ever speaks."

Mary sat silent for a minute thinking. Then Mrs Spicer roused herself:

"Oh, I don't know what I'm talkin' about! You mustn't take any notice of me, Mrs Wilson—I don't often go on like this. I do believe I'm gittin' a bit ratty at times. It must be the heat and the dullness."

But once or twice afterwards she referred to a time "when Spicer was a different man to what he was now."

I walked home with her a piece along the creek. She said nothing for a long time, and seemed to be thinking in a puzzled way. Then she said suddenly:

"What-did-you-bring-her-here-for? She's only a girl."

"I beg pardon, Mrs Spicer."

"Oh, I don't know what I'm talkin' about! I b'lieve I'm gettin' ratty. You mustn't take any notice of me, Mr Wilson."

She wasn't much company for Mary; and often, when she had a child with her, she'd start taking notice of the baby while Mary was talking, which used to exasperate Mary. But poor Mrs Spicer couldn't help it, and she seemed to hear all the same.

Her great trouble was that she "couldn't git no reg-lar schoolin' for the children."

"I learns 'em at home as much as I can. But I don't git a minute to call me own; an' I'm ginerally that dead-beat at night that I'm fit for nothink."

Mary had some of the children up now and then later on, and taught them a little. When she first offered to do so, Mrs Spicer laid hold of the handiest youngster and said:

"There—do you hear that? Mrs Wilson is goin' to teach yer, an' it's more

387

than yer deserve!" (the youngster had been "cryin'" over something). "Now, go up an' say 'thenk yer, Mrs Wilson.' And if yer ain't good, and don't do as she tells yer, I'll break every bone in yer young body!"

The poor little devil stammered something, and escaped.

The children were sent by turns over to Wall's to Sunday-school. When Tommy was at home he had a new pair of elastic-side boots, and there was no end of rows about them in the family—for the mother made him lend them to his sister Annie, to go to Sunday-school in her turn. There were only about three pairs of anyway decent boots in the family, and these were saved for great occasions. The children were always clean and tidy as possible when they came to our place.

And I think the saddest and most pathetic sight on the face of God's earth is the children of very poor people made to appear well: the broken worn-out boots polished or greased, the blackened (inked) pieces of string for laces; the clean patched pinafores over the wretched threadbare frocks. Behind the little row of children hand-in-hand—and no matter where they are—I always see the worn face of the mother.

Towards the end of the first year on the selection our little girl came. I'd sent Mary to Gulgong for four months that time, and when she came back with the baby Mrs Spicer used to come up pretty often. She came up several times when Mary was ill, to lend a hand. She wouldn't sit down and condole with Mary, or waste her time asking questions, or talking about the time when she was ill herself. She'd take off her hat—a shapeless little lump of black straw she wore for visiting—give her hair a quick brush back with the palms of her hands, roll up her sleeves, and set to work to "tidy up." She seemed to take most pleasure in sorting out our children's clothes, and dressing them. Perhaps she used to dress her own like that in the days when Spicer was a different man from what he was now. She seemed interested in the fashion-plates of some women's journals we had, and used to study them with an interest that puzzled me, for she was not likely to go in for fashion. She never talked of her early girlhood; but Mary, from some things she noticed, was inclined to think that Mrs Spicer had been fairly well brought up. For instance, Dr Balanfantie, from Cudgegong, came out to see Wall's wife, and drove up the creek to our place on his way back to see how Mary and the baby were getting on. Mary got out some crockery and some table-napkins that she had packed away for occasions like this; and she said that the way Mrs Spicer handled the things, and helped set the table (though she did it in a mechanical sort of way) convinced her that she had been used to table-napkins at one time in her life.

Sometimes, after a long pause in the conversation, Mrs Spicer would say suddenly:

"Oh, I don't think I'll come up next week, Mrs Wilson."

"Why, Mrs Spicer?"

"Because the visits doesn't do me any good. I git the dismals afterwards."

"Why, Mrs Spicer? What on earth do you mean?"

"Oh, I-don't-know-what-I'm-talkin'-about. You mustn't take any notice of me." And she'd put on her hat, kiss the children—and Mary too, sometimes, as if she mistook her for a child—and go.

Mary thought her a little mad at times. But I seemed to understand.

Once, when Mrs Spicer was sick, Mary went down to her, and down again next day. As she was coming away the second time Mrs Spicer said:

"I wish you wouldn't come down any more till I'm on my feet, Mrs Wilson. The children can do for me."

"Why, Mrs Spicer?"

"Well, the place is in such a muck, and it hurts me."

We were the aristocrats of Lahey's Creek. Whenever we drove down on Sunday afternoon to see Mrs Spicer, and as soon as we got near enough for them to hear the rattle of the cart, we'd see the children running to the house as fast as they could split, and hear them screaming:

"Oh, marther! Here comes Mr and Mrs Wilson in their spring-cart."

And we'd see her bustle round, and two or three fowls fly out the front door, and she'd lay hold of a broom (made of a bound bunch of "broom-stuff"—coarse reedy grass or bush from the ridges—with a stick stuck in it) and flick out the floor, with a flick or two round in front of the door perhaps. The floor nearly always needed at least one flick of the broom on account of the fowls. Or she'd catch a youngster and scrub his face with a wet end of a cloudy towel or twist the towel round her finger and dig out his ears—as if she was anxious to have him hear every word that was going to be said.

No matter what state the house would be in she'd always say, "I was jist expectin' yer, Mrs Wilson." And she was original in that, anyway.

She had an old patched and darned white table-cloth that she used to spread on the table when we were there, as a matter of course ("The others is in the wash, so you must excuse this, Mrs Wilson"), but I saw by the eyes of the children that the cloth was rather a wonderful thing for them. "I must really git some more knives and forks next time I'm in Cobborah," she'd say. "The children will break an' lose 'em till I'm ashamed ter ask Christians ter sit down ter the table."

She had many bush yarns, some of them very funny, some of them rather ghastly, but all interesting, and with a grim sort of humour about them. But the effect was often spoilt by her screaming at the children to "Drive out them fowls, karn't yer," or "Take yer maulies [hands] outer the sugar," or "Don't touch Mrs Wilson's baby with them dirty maulies," or "Don't stand starin' at Mrs Wilson with yer mouth an' ears in that vulgar way."

Poor woman! she seemed everlastingly nagging at the children. It was a habit, but they didn't seem to mind. Most bushwomen get the nagging habit. I remember one, who had the prettiest, dearest, sweetest, most willing, and affectionate little girl I think I ever saw, and she nagged that child from daylight till dark—and after it. Taking it all round, I think that the nagging habit in a mother is often worse on ordinary children, and more deadly on sensitive youngsters, than the drinking habit in a father.

One of the yarns Mrs Spicer told us was about a squatter she knew who used to go wrong in his head every now and again, and try to commit suicide. Once, when the station-hand, who was watching him, had his eye off him for a minute, he hanged himself to a beam in the stable. The men ran in and found him hanging and kicking. "They let him hang for a while," said Mrs Spicer, "till he went black in the face and stopped kicking. Then they cut him down and threw a bucket of water over him."

"Why! what on earth did they let the man hang for?" asked Mary.

"To give him a good bellyful of it: they thought it would cure him of tryin' to hang himself again."

"Well, that's the coolest thing I ever heard of," said Mary.

"That's jist what the magistrate said, Mrs Wilson," said Mrs Spicer.

"One morning," said Mrs Spicer, "Spicer had gone off on his horse somewhere, and I was alone with the children, when a man came to the door and said:

"'For God's sake, woman, give me a drink!'

"Lord only knows where he came from! He was dressed like a new chum, his clothes was good, but he looked as if he'd been sleepin' in them in the bush for a month. He was very shaky. I had some coffee that mornin' so I gave him some in a pint-pot; he drank it, and then he stood on his head till he tumbled over, and then he stood up on his feet and said, 'thenk yer, mum.'

"I was so surprised that I didn't know what to say, so I jist said, 'Would you like some more coffee?'

"'Yes, thenk yer,' he said—about two quarts.'

"I nearly filled the pint-pot, and he drank it and stood on his head as long as he could, and when he got right end up he said, 'thenk yer, mum—it's a fine day,' and then he walked off. He had two saddle-straps in his hands."

"Why, what did he stand on his head for?" asked Mary.

"To wash it up and down, I suppose, to get twice as much taste of the coffee. He had no hat. I sent Tommy across to Wall's to tell them that there was a man wanderin' about the bush in the horrors of drink, and to get someone to ride for the police. But they were too late, for he hanged himself that night."

"O Lord!" cried Mary.

"Yes, right close to here, jist down the creek where the track to Wall's branches off. Tommy found him while he was out after the cows. Hangin' to the branch of a tree with two saddle-straps."

Mary stared at her, speechless.

"Tommy came home yellin' with fright. I sent him over to Wall's at once. After breakfast, the minute my eyes was off them, the children slipped away and went down there. They came back screamin' at the tops of their voices. I did give it to them. I reckon they won't want ter see a dead body again in a hurry. Every time I'd mention it they'd huddle together, or ketch hold of me skirts and howl.

"'Yer'll go agen when I tell yer not to,' I'd say.

"'Oh, no, mother,' they'd howl.

"'Yer wanted ter see a man hangin',' I said.

"'Oh, don't, mother! Don't talk about it.'

"'Yer wouldn't be satisfied till yer see it,' I'd say; 'yer had to see it or burst. Yer satisfied now, ain't yer?'

"'Oh, don't, mother!'

"'Yer run all the way there, I s'pose?'

"'Don't, mother!'

"'But yer run faster back, didn't yer?'

" 'Oh, don't, mother.'

"But," said Mrs Spicer, in conclusion, "I'd been down to see it myself before they was up."

"And ain't you afraid to live alone here, after all these horrible things?" asked Mary.

"Well, no; I don't mind. I seem to have got past carin' for anythink now. I felt it a little when Tommy went away—the first time I felt anythink for years. But I'm over that now."

"Haven't you got any friends in the district, Mrs Spicer?"

"Oh yes. There's me married sister near Cobborah, and a married brother near Dubbo; he's got a station. They wanted to take me an' the children between them, or take some of the younger children. But I couldn't bring my mind to break up the home. I want to keep the children together as much as possible. There's enough of them gone, God knows. But it's a comfort to know that there's someone to see to them if anythink happens me."

One day—I was on my way home with the team that day—Annie Spicer came running up the creek in terrible trouble.

"Oh, Mrs Wilson! something terrible's happened at home. A trooper" (mounted policeman—they called them "mounted troopers" out there), "a trooper's come and took Billy!" Billy was the eldest son at home.

"What?"

"It's true, Mrs Wilson."

"What for? What did the policeman say?"

"He—he—he said, 'I—I'm very sorry, Mrs Spicer; but—I—I want William.'"

It turned out that William was wanted on account of a horse missed from Wall's station and sold down-country.

"An' mother took on awful," sobbed Annie; "an' now she'll only sit stock-still an' stare in front of her, and won't take no notice of any of us. Oh! it's awful, Mrs Wilson. The policeman said he'd tell Aunt Emma" (Mrs Spicer's sister at Cobborah), "and send her out. But I had to come to you, an' I've run all the way."

James put the horse to the cart and drove Mary down.

Mary told me all about it when I came home.

"I found her just as Annie said; but she broke down and cried in my arms. Oh, Joe! it was awful. She didn't cry like a woman. I heard a man at Haviland cry at his brother's funeral, and it was just like that. She came round a bit after a while. Her sister's with her now. . . . Oh, Joe! you must take me away from the bush."

Later on Mary said:

"How the oaks are sighing to-night, Joe!"

Next morning I rode across to Wall's station and tackled the old man; but he was a hard man, and wouldn't listen to me—in fact, he ordered me off his station. I was a selector and that was enough for him. But young Billy Wall rode after me.

"Look here, Joe!" he said, "it's a blanky shame. All for the sake of a horse! As if that poor devil of a woman hasn't got enough to put up with already! I wouldn't do it for twenty horses. *I'll* tackle the boss, and if he won't listen to me, I'll walk off the run for the last time, if I have to carry my swag."

Billy Wall managed it. The charge was withdrawn, and we got young Billy Spicer off up-country.

But poor Mrs Spicer was never the same after that. She seldom came up to our place unless Mary dragged her, so to speak; and then she would talk of nothing but her last trouble, till her visits were painful to look forward to.

"If it only could have been kep' quiet—for the sake of the other children; they are all I think of now. I tried to bring 'em all up decent, but I s'pose it was my fault, somehow. It's the disgrace that's killin' me—I can't bear it."

I was at home one Sunday with Mary, and a jolly bush-girl named Maggie Charlsworth, who rode over sometimes from Wall's station (I must tell you about her some other time; James was "shook after her"), and we got talkin' about Mrs Spicer. Maggie was very warm about old Wall.

"I expected Mrs Spicer up to-day," said Mary. "She seems better lately."

"Why!" cried Maggie Charlsworth, "if that ain't Annie coming running up along the creek. Something's the matter!"

We all jumped up and ran out.

"What is it, Annie?" cried Mary.

"Oh, Mrs Wilson! Mother's asleep, and we can't wake her!"

"What?"

"It's—it's the truth, Mrs Wilson."

"How long has she been asleep?"

"Since lars' night."

"My God!" cried Mary, *since last night?*"

"No, Mrs Wilson, not all the time; she woke wonst, about daylight this mornin'. She called me and said she didn't feel well, and I'd have to manage the milkin'."

"Was that all she said?"

"No. She said not to go for you; and she said to feed the pigs and calves; and she said to be sure and water them geraniums."

Mary wanted to go, but I wouldn't let her. James and I saddled our horses and rode down the creek.

Mrs Spicer looked very little different from what she did when I last saw her alive. It was some time before we could believe that she was dead. But she was "past carin'" right enough.

A DOUBLE BUGGY AT LAHEY'S CREEK

I

SPUDS, AND A WOMAN'S OBSTINACY

Ever since we were married it had been Mary's great ambition to have a buggy. The house or furniture didn't matter so much—out there in the bush where we were—but, where there were no railways or coaches, and the roads were long and mostly hot and dusty, a buggy was the great thing. I had a few pounds when we were married, and was going to get one then; but new buggies went high, and another party got hold of a second-hand one that I'd had my eye on, so Mary thought it over and at last she said, "Never mind the buggy, Joe; get a sewing-machine and I'll be satisfied. I'll want the machine more than the buggy, for a while. Wait till we're better off."

After that, whenever I took a contract—to put up a fence or wool-shed, or sink a dam or something—Mary would say, "You ought to knock a buggy out of this job, Joe;" but something always turned up—bad weather or sickness. Once I cut my foot with the adze and was laid up; and, another time, a dam I was making was washed away by a flood before I finished it. Then Mary would say, "Ah, well—never mind, Joe. Wait till we are better off." But she felt it hard the time I built a wool-shed and didn't get paid for it, for we'd as good as settled about another second-hand buggy then.

I always had a fancy for carpentering, and was handy with tools. I made a spring-cart—body and wheels—in spare time, out of colonial hardwood, and got Little the blacksmith to do the ironwork: I painted the cart myself. It wasn't much lighter than one of the tip-drays I had, but it *was* a spring-cart, and Mary pretended to be satisfied with it: anyway, I didn't hear any more of the buggy for a while.

I sold that cart for fourteen pounds, to a Chinese gardener who wanted a strong cart to carry his vegetables round through the bush. It was just before our first youngster came: I told Mary that I wanted the money in case of extra expense—and she didn't fret much at losing the cart. But the fact was that I was going to make another try for a buggy, as a present for Mary when the child was born. I thought of getting the turn-out while she was laid up, keeping it dark from her till she was on her feet again, and then showing her the buggy standing in the shed. But she had a bad time, and I had to have the doctor regularly, and get a proper nurse, and a lot of things extra; so the buggy idea was knocked on the head. I was set on it, too; I'd thought of how, when Mary was up and getting strong, I'd say one morning, "Go round and have a look in the shed, Mary; I've got a few fowls for you," or something like that—and follow her round to watch her eyes when she saw the buggy. I never told Mary about that—it wouldn't have done any good.

Later on I got some good timber—mostly scraps that were given to me—and made a light body for a spring-cart. Galletly, the coach-builder at Cudgegong, had got a dozen pairs of American hickory wheels up from Sydney, for light spring-carts, and he let me have a pair for cost price and carriage. I got him to iron the cart, and he put it through the paintshop for nothing. He sent it out, too, at the tail of Tom Tarrant's big van—to increase the surprise. We were swells then for a while; I heard no more of a buggy until after we'd been settled at Lahey's Creek for a couple of years.

I told you how I went into the carrying line, and took up a selection at Lahey's Creek—for a run for the horses and to grow a bit of feed—and shifted

Mary and little Jim out there from Gulgong, with Mary's young scamp of a brother James to keep them company while I was on the road. The first year I did well enough carrying, but I never cared for it—it was too slow; and, besides, I was always anxious when I was away from home. The game was right enough for a single man—or a married one whose wife had got the nagging habit (as many bushwomen have—God help 'em), and who wanted peace and quietness sometimes. Besides, other small carriers started (seeing me getting on); Tom Tarrant, the coach-builder at Cudgegong, had another heavy spring-van built, and put it on the road, and he took a lot of the light stuff.

The second year I made a rise—out of "spuds," of all the things in the world. It was Mary's idea. Down at the lower end of our selection—Mary called it "the run"—was a shallow watercourse called Snake's Creek, dry most of the year, except for a muddy waterhole or two; and, just above the junction, where it ran into Lahey's Creek, was a low piece of good black-soil flat, on our side—about three acres. The flat was fairly clear when I came to the selection —save for a few logs that had been washed up there in some big "old man" flood, way back in blackfellows' times: and one day when I had a spell at home, I got the horses and trace-chains and dragged the logs together— those that wouldn't split for fencing timber—and burnt them off. I had a notion to get the flat ploughed and make a lucerne-paddock of it. There was a good waterhole, under a clump of she-oak in the bend, and Mary used to take her stools and tubs and boiler down there in the spring-cart in hot weather, and wash the clothes under the shade of the trees—it was cooler, and saved carrying water to the house. And one evening after she'd done the washing she said to me:

"Look here, Joe; the farmers out here never seem to get a new idea: they don't seem to me ever to try and find out beforehand what the market is going to be like—they just go on farming the same old way, and putting in the same old crops year after year. They sow wheat, and if it comes on anything like the thing, they reap and thresh it; if it doesn't they mow it for hay— and some of 'em don't have the brains to do that in time. Now I was looking at that bit of flat you cleared, and it struck me that it wouldn't be a half-bad idea to get a bag of seed potatoes, and have the land ploughed—old Corny George would do it cheap—and get them put in at once. Potatoes have been dear all round for the last couple of years."

I told her she was talking nonsense, that the ground was no good for potatoes, and the whole district was too dry. "Everybody I know has tried it, one time or another, and made nothing of it," I said.

"All the more reason why you should try it, Joe," said Mary. "Just try one crop. It might rain for weeks, and then you'll be sorry you didn't take my advice."

"But I tell you the ground is not potato-ground," I said.

"How do you know? You haven't sown any there yet."

"But I've turned up the surface and looked at it. It's not rich enough, and too dry, I tell you. You need swampy, boggy ground for potatoes. Do you think I don't know land when I see it?"

"But you haven't tried to grow potatoes there yet, Joe. How do you know—"

I didn't listen to any more. Mary was obstinate when she got an idea into her head. It was no use arguing with her. All the time I'd be talking she'd just knit her forehead and go on thinking straight ahead, on the track she'd started—just as if I wasn't there—and it used to make me mad. She'd keep driving at me till I took her advice or lost my temper—I did both at the same time, mostly.

I took my pipe and went out to smoke and cool down.

A couple of days after the potato breeze, I started with the team down to Cudgegong for a load of fencing-wire I had to bring out; and after I'd kissed Mary good-bye, she said:

"Look here, Joe, if you bring out a bag of seed potatoes, James and I will slice them, and old Corny George down the creek would bring his plough up in the dray, and plough the ground for very little. We could put the potatoes in ourselves if the ground were only ploughed."

I thought she'd forgotten all about it. There was no time to argue—I'd be sure to lose my temper, and then I'd either have to waste an hour comforting Mary, or go off in a "huff," as the women call it, and be miserable for the trip. So I said I'd see about it. She gave me another hug and a kiss. "Don't forget, Joe," she said as I started. "Think it over on the road." I reckon she had the best of it that time.

About five miles along, just as I turned into the main road, I heard someone galloping after me, and I saw young James on his hack. I got a start, for I thought that something had gone wrong at home. I remember the first day I left Mary on the creek, for the first five or six miles I was half a dozen times on the point of turning back—only I thought she'd laugh at me.

"What is it, James?" I shouted, before he came up—but I saw he was grinning.

"Mary says to tell you not to forget to bring a hoe out with you."

"You clear off home!" I said, "or I'll lay the whip about your young hide; and don't come riding after me again as if the run was on fire."

"Well, you needn't get shirty with me!" he said. "*I* don't want to have anything to do with a hoe." And he rode off.

I *did* get thinking about those potatoes, though I hadn't meant to. I knew of an independent man in that district who'd made his money out of a crop of potatoes; but that was away back in the roaring fifties—fifty-four—when spuds went up to twenty-eight shillings a hundredweight (in Sydney), on account of the gold rush. We might get good rain now, and, anyway, it wouldn't cost much to put the potatoes in. If they came on well, it would be a few pounds in my pocket; if the crop was a failure, I'd have a better show with Mary next time she was struck by an idea outside housekeeping, and have something to grumble about when I felt grumpy.

I got a couple of bags of potatoes—we could use those that were left over; and I got a small iron plough and harrow that Little the blacksmith had lying in his yard and let me have cheap—only about a pound more than I told Mary I gave for them. When I took advice I generally made the mistake of taking more than was offered, or adding notions of my own. It was vanity, I suppose. If the crop came on well I could claim the plough-and-harrow part of the idea, anyway. (It didn't strike me that if the crop failed Mary would have the plough and harrow against me, for old Corny would plough the ground for ten or fifteen shillings.) Anyway, I'd want a plough and harrow later on, and I might as well get it now; it would give James something to do.

I came out by the western road, by Guntawang, and up the creek home; and the first thing I saw was old Corny George ploughing the flat. And Mary was down on the bank superintending. She'd got James with the trace-chains and the spare horses, and had made him clear off every stick and bush where another furrow might be squeezed in. Old Corny looked pretty grumpy on it—he'd broken all his ploughshares but one, in the roots; and James didn't look much brighter. Mary had an old felt hat and a new pair of 'lastic-side boots of mine on, and the boots were covered with clay, for she'd been down hustling James to get a rotten old stump out of the way by the time old Corny came round with his next furrow.

"I thought I'd make the boots easy for you, Joe," said Mary.

"It's all right, Mary," I said, "I'm not going to growl." Those boots were a bone of contention between us; but she generally got them off before I got home.

Her face fell when she saw the plough and harrow in the wagon, but I said that would be all right—we'd want a plough anyway.

"I thought you wanted old Corny to plough the ground," she said.

"I never said so."

"But when I sent Jim after you about the hoe to put the spuds in, you didn't say you wouldn't bring it," she said.

I had a few days at home, and entered into the spirit of the thing. When Corny was done, James and I cross-ploughed the land, and got a stump or two, a big log, and some scrub out of the way at the upper end and added nearly an acre, and ploughed that. James was all right at most bushwork: he'd bullock so long as the novelty lasted; he liked ploughing or fencing, or any graft he could make a show at. He didn't care for grubbing out stumps, or splitting posts and rails. We sliced the potatoes of an evening—and there was trouble between Mary and James over cutting through the "eyes." There was no time for the hoe—and besides it wasn't a novelty to James—so I just ran furrows and they dropped the spuds in behind me, and I turned another furrow over them, and ran the harrow over the ground. I think I hilled those spuds, too, with furrows—or a crop of Indian corn I put in later on.

It rained heavens-hard for over a week: we had regular showers all through, and it was the finest crop of potatoes ever seen in the district. I believe at first Mary used to slip down at daybreak to see if the potatoes were up; and she'd write to me about them, on the road. I forget how many bags I got but the few who had grown potatoes in the district sent theirs to Sydney, and spuds went up to twelve and fifteen shillings a hundredweight in that district. I made a few quid out of mine—and saved carriage too, for I could take them out on the wagon. Then Mary began to hear (through James) of a buggy that someone had for sale cheap, or a dogcart that somebody else wanted to get rid of—and let me know about it, in an off-hand way.

II
JOE WILSON'S LUCK

There was good grass on the selection all the year. I'd picked up a small lot—about twenty head—of half-starved steers for next to nothing, and turned them on the run; they came on wonderfully, and my brother-in-law

(Mary's sister's husband), who was running a butchery at Gulgong, gave me a good price for them. His carts ran out twenty or thirty miles, to little bits of gold rushes that were going on at th' Home Rule, Happy Valley, Guntawang, Tallawang, and Cooyal, and those places round there, and he was doing well.

Mary had heard of a light American wagonette, when the steers went—a tray-body arrangement, and she thought she'd do with that. "It would be better than the buggy, Joe," she said. "There'd be more room for the children, and, besides, I could take butter and eggs to Gulgong, or Cobborah, when we get a few more cows." Then James heard of a small flock of sheep that a selector—who was about starved off his selection out Talbragar way—wanted to get rid of. James reckoned he could get them for less than half a crown a head. We'd had a heavy shower of rain, that came over the ranges and didn't seem to go beyond our boundaries. Mary said, "It's a pity to see all that grass going to waste, Joe. Better get those sheep and try your luck with them. Leave some money with me, and I'll send James over for them. Never mind about the buggy—we'll get that when we're on our feet."

So James rode across to Talbragar and drove a hard bargain with that unfortunate selector, and brought the sheep home. There were about two hundred, wethers and ewes, and they were young and looked a good breed too, but so poor they could scarcely travel; they soon picked up, though. The drought was blazing all round and out back, and I think that my corner of the ridges was the only place where there was any grass to speak of. We had another shower or two, and the grass held out. Chaps began to talk of "Joe Wilson's luck."

I would have liked to shear those sheep; but I hadn't time to get a shed or anything ready—along towards Christmas there was a bit of a boom in the carrying line. Wethers in wool were going as high as thirteen to fifteen shillings at the Homebush yards at Sydney, so I arranged to truck the sheep down from the river by rail, with another small lot that was going, and I started James off with them. He took the west road, and down Guntawang way a big farmer who saw James with the sheep (and who was speculating, or adding to his stock, or took a fancy to the wool) offered James as much for them as he reckoned I'd get in Sydney, after paying the carriage and the agents and the auctioneer. James put the sheep in a paddock and rode back to me. He was all there where riding was concerned. I told him to let the sheep go. James made a Greener shot-gun, and got his saddle done up, out of that job.

I took up a couple more forty-acre blocks—one in James's name, to encourage him with the fencing. There was a good slice of land in an angle between the range and the creek, farther down, which everybody thought belonged to Wall, the squatter, but Mary got an idea, and went to the local land office, and found out that it was unoccupied Crown land, and so I took it up on pastoral lease, and got a few more sheep—I'd saved some of the best-looking ewes from the last lot.

One evening—I was going down next day for a load of fencing-wire for myself—Mary said:

"Joe! do you know that the Matthews have got a new double buggy?"

The Matthews were a big family of cockatoos, along up the main road, and I didn't think much of them. The sons were all "bad-eggs," though the old woman and girls were right enough.

"Well, what of that?" I said. "They're up to their neck in debt, and camping like blackfellows in a big bark humpy. They do well to go flashing round in a double buggy."

"But that isn't what I was going to say," said Mary. "They want to sell their old single buggy, James says. I'm sure you could get it for six or seven pounds; and you could have it done up."

"I wish James to the devil!" I said. "Can't he find anything better to do than ride round after cock-and-bull yarns about buggies?"

"Well," said Mary, "it was James who got the steers and the sheep."

Well, one word led to another, and we said things we didn't mean—but couldn't forget in a hurry. I remember I said something about Mary always dragging me back just when I was getting my head above water and struggling to make a home for her and the children; and that hurt her, and she spoke of the "homes" she'd had since she was married. And that cut me deep.

It was about the worst quarrel we had. When she began to cry I got my hat and went out and walked up and down by the creek. I hated anything that looked like injustice—I was so sensitive about it that it made me unjust sometimes. I tried to think I was right, but I couldn't—it wouldn't have made me feel any better if I could have thought so. I got thinking of Mary's first year on the selection and the life she'd had since we were married.

When I went in she'd cried herself to sleep. I bent over and, "Mary," I whispered.

She seemed to wake up.

"Joe—Joe!" she said.

"What is it, Mary?" I said.

"I'm pretty sure that old Spot's calf isn't in the pen. Make James go at once!"

Old Spot's last calf was two years old now; so Mary was talking in her sleep, and dreaming she was back in her first year.

We both laughed when I told her about it afterwards; but I didn't feel like laughing just then.

Later on in the night she called out in her sleep:

"Joe—Joe! Put that buggy in the shed, or the sun will blister the varnish!"

I wish I could say that that was the last time I ever spoke unkindly to Mary.

Next morning I got up early and fried the bacon and made the tea, and took Mary's breakfast in to her—like I used to do, sometimes, when we were first married. She didn't say anything—just pulled my head down and kissed me.

When I was ready to start, Mary said:

"You'd better take the spring-cart in behind the dray, and get the tyres cut and set. They're ready to drop off, and James has been wedging them up till he's tired of it. The last time I was out with the children I had to knock one of them back with a stone: there'll be an accident yet."

So I lashed the shafts of the cart under the tail of the wagon and mean and ridiculous enough the cart looked, going along that way. It suggested a man stooping along handcuffed, with his arms held out and down in front of him.

It was dull weather, and the scrubs looked extra dreary and endless—and I got thinking of old things. Everything was going all right with me, but that didn't keep me from brooding sometimes—trying to hatch out stones, like an old hen we had at home. I think, taking it all round, I used to be happier when I was mostly hard up—and more generous. When I had ten pounds I was more likely to listen to a chap who said, "Lend me a pound note, Joe" than when I had fifty; *then* I fought shy of careless chaps—and lost mates that I wanted afterwards—and got the name of being mean. When I got a good cheque I'd be as miserable as a miser over the first ten pounds I spent; but when I got down to the last I'd buy things for the house. And now that I was getting on, I hated to spend a pound on anything. But then, the farther I got away from poverty the greater the fear I had of it—and, besides, there was always before us all the thought of the terrible drought, with blazing runs as bare and dusty as the road, and dead stock rotting every yard, all along the barren creeks.

I had a long yarn with Mary's sister and her husband that night in Gulgong, and it brightened me up. I had a fancy that that sort of a brother-in-law made a better mate than a nearer one; Tom Tarrant had one, and he said it was sympathy. But while we were yarning I couldn't help thinking of Mary, out there in the hut on the creek, with no one to talk to but the children, or James, who was sulky at home, or Black Mary or Black Jimmy (our black boy's father and mother), who weren't over-sentimental. Or, maybe, a selector's wife (the nearest was five miles away) who could talk only of two or three things—"lambin'" and "shearin'" and "cookin' for the men," and what she said to her old man, and what he said to her—and her own ailments over and over again.

It's a wonder it didn't drive Mary mad!—I know I could never listen to that woman more than an hour. Mary's sister said:

"Now if Mary had a comfortable buggy, she could drive in with the children oftener. Then she wouldn't feel the loneliness so much."

I said "Good night" then and turned in. There was no getting away from that buggy. Whenever Mary's sister started hinting about a buggy, I reckoned it was a put-up job between them.

III
THE GHOST OF MARY'S SACRIFICE

When I got to Cudgegong I stopped at Galletly's coach-shop to leave the cart. The Galletlys were good fellows: there were two brothers—one was a saddler and harness-maker. Big brown-bearded men—the biggest men in the district, 'twas said.

Their old man had died lately and left them some money; they had men, and only worked in their shops when they felt inclined, or there was a special work to do; they were both first-class tradesmen. I went into the painter's shop to have a look at a double buggy that Galletly had built for a man who couldn't pay cash for it when it was finished—and Galletly wouldn't trust him.

There it stood, behind a calico screen that the coach-painters used to keep out the dust when they were varnishing. It was a first-class piece of work— pole, shafts, cushions, whip, lamps and all complete. If you only wanted to drive one horse you could take out the pole and put in the shafts, and there you were. There was a tilt over the front seat; if you only wanted the buggy to carry two, you could fold down the back seat, and there you had a handsome, roomy, single buggy. It would go near fifty pounds.

While I was looking at it, Bill Galletly came in and slapped me on the back.

"Now, there's a chance for you, Joe!" he said. "I saw you rubbing your head round that buggy the last time you were in. You wouldn't get a better one in the colonies, and you won't see another like it in the district again in a hurry —for it doesn't pay to build 'em. Now you're a full-blown squatter, and it's time you took little Mary for a fly round in her own buggy now and then, instead of having her stuck out there in the scrub, or jolting through the dust in a cart like some old Mother Flourbag."

He called her "Little Mary" because the Galletly family had known her when she was a girl.

I rubbed my head and looked at the buggy again. It was a great temptation.

"Look here, Joe," said Bill Galletly in a quieter tone. "I'll tell you what I'll do. I'll let *you* have the buggy. You can take it out and send along a bit of a cheque when you feel you can manage it, and the rest later on—a year will do, or even two years. You've had a hard pull, and I'm not likely to be hard up for money in a hurry."

They were good fellows the Galletlys, but they knew their men. I happened to know that Bill Galletly wouldn't let the man he built the buggy for take it out of the shop without cash down, though he was a big-bug round there. But that didn't make it easier for me.

Just then Robert Galletly came into the shop. He was rather quieter than his brother, but the two were very much alike.

"Look here, Bob," said Bill; "here's a chance for you to get rid of your harness. Joe Wilson's going to take that buggy off my hands."

Bob Galletly put his foot up on a saw-stool, took one hand out of his pocket, rested his elbow on his knee and his chin on the palm of his hand, and bunched up his big beard with his fingers, as he always did when he was thinking. Presently he took his foot down, put his hand back in his pocket, and said to me, "Well, Joe, I've got a double set of harness made for the man who ordered that damned buggy, and if you like I'll let you have it. I suppose when Bill there has squeezed all he can out of you I'll stand a show of getting something. He's a regular Shylock, he is."

I pushed my hat forward and rubbed the back of my head and stared at the buggy.

"Come across to the Royal, Joe," said Bob.

But I knew that a beer would settle the business, so I said I'd get the wool up to the station first and think it over, and have a drink when I came back.

I thought it over on the way to the station, but it didn't seem good enough. I wanted to get some more sheep, and there was the new run to be fenced in, and the instalments on the selections. I wanted lots of things that I couldn't well do without. Then, again, the farther I got away from debt and hard-upedness the greater the horror I had of it. I had two horses that would do; but I'd have to get another later on, and altogether the buggy would run me nearer a hundred than fifty pounds. Supposing a dry season threw me back with that buggy on my hands. Besides, I wanted a spell. If I got the buggy it would only mean an extra turn of hard graft for me. No, I'd take Mary for a trip to Sydney, and she'd have to be satisfied with that.

I'd got it settled, and was just turning in through the big white gates to the goods-shed when young Black, the squatter, dashed past to the station in his big new wagonette, with his wife and a driver and a lot of portmanteaux and rugs and things. They were going to do the grand in Sydney over Christmas. Now it was young Black who was so shook after Mary when she was in service with the Blacks before the old man died, and if I hadn't come along—and if girls never cared for vagabonds—Mary would have been mistress of Haviland homestead, with servants to wait on her; and she was far better fitted for it than the one that was there. She would have been going to Sydney every holiday and putting up at the old Royal, with every comfort that a woman could ask for, and seeing a play every night. And I'd have been knocking around amongst the big stations out back, or maybe drinking myself to death at the shanties.

The Blacks didn't see me as I went by, ragged and dusty, and with an old, nearly black, cabbage-tree hat drawn over my eyes. I didn't care a damn for them, or any one else, at most times, but I had moods when I felt things.

One of Black's big wool-teams was just coming away from the shed, and the driver, a big, dark, rough fellow, with some foreign blood in him, didn't seem inclined to wheel his team an inch out of the middle of the road. I stopped my horses and waited. He looked at me and I looked at him—hard. Then he wheeled off, scowling, and swearing at his horses. I'd given him a hiding, six or seven years before, and he hadn't forgotten it. And I felt then as if I wouldn't mind trying to give someone a hiding.

The goods clerk must have thought that Joe Wilson was pretty grumpy that day. I was thinking of Mary, out there in the lonely hut on a barren creek in the bush—for it was little better—with no one to speak to except a haggard, worn-out bushwoman or two, that came to see her on Sunday. I thought of the hardships she went through in the first year—that I haven't told you about yet; of the time she was ill, and I away, and no one to understand; of the time she was alone with James and Jim sick; and of the loneliness she fought through out there. I thought of Mary, outside in the blazing heat, with an old print dress and a felt hat, and a pair of 'lastic-siders of mine on, doing the work of a station manager as well as that of a housewife and mother. And her cheeks were getting thin, and the colour was going: I thought of the gaunt, brick-brown saw-file voiced, hopeless and spiritless bushwomen I knew—and some of them not much older than Mary.

When I went back into the town, I had a drink with Bill Galletly at the Royal, and that settled the buggy; then Bob shouted, and I took the harness. Then I shouted, to wet the bargain. When I was going, Bob said, "Send in that young scamp of a brother of Mary's with the horses: if the collars don't fit I'll fix up a pair of makeshifts, and alter the others." I thought they both gripped my hand harder than usual, but that might have been the beer.

IV
THE BUGGY COMES HOME

I "whipped the cat" a bit, the first twenty miles or so, but then, I thought, what did it matter? What was the use of grinding to save money until we were too old to enjoy it. If we had to go down in the world again, we might as well fall out of a buggy as out of a dray—there'd be some talk about it, anyway, and perhaps a little sympathy. When Mary had the buggy she wouldn't be tied down so much to that wretched hole in the bush; and the Sydney trips needn't be off either. I could drive down to Wallerawang on the main line, where Mary had some people, and leave the buggy and horses there, and take the train to Sydney, or go right on, by the old coach road, over the Blue Mountains: it would be a grand drive. I thought best to tell Mary's sister at Gulgong about the buggy; I told her I'd keep it dark from Mary till the buggy came home. She entered into the spirit of the thing, and said she'd give the world to be able to go out with the buggy, if only to see Mary open her eyes when she saw it; but she couldn't go, on account of a new baby she had. I was rather glad she couldn't, for it would spoil the surprise a little, I thought. I wanted that all to myself.

I got home about sunset next day, and, after tea, when I'd finished telling Mary all the news, and a few lies as to why I didn't bring the cart back, and one or two other things, I sat with James, out on a log of the wood-heap, where we generally had our smokes and interviews, and told him all about the buggy. He whistled, then he said:

"But what do you want to make it such a bushranging business for? Why can't you tell Mary now? It will cheer her up. She's been pretty miserable since you've been away this trip."

"I want it to be a surprise," I said.

"Well, I've got nothing to say against a surprise, out in a hole like this; but it 'ud take a lot to surprise me. What am I to say to Mary about taking the two horses in? I'll only want one to bring the cart out, and she's sure to ask."

"Tell her you're going to get yours shod."

"But he had a set of slippers only the other day. She knows as much about horses as we do. I don't mind telling a lie so long as a chap has only got to tell a straight lie and be done with it. But Mary asks so many questions."

"Well, drive the other horse up the creek early, and pick him up as you go."

"Yes. And she'll want to know what I want with two bridles. But I'll fix her—*you* needn't worry."

"And, James," I said, "get a chamois leather and sponge—we'll want 'em anyway—and you might give the buggy a wash down in the creek, coming home. It's sure to be covered with dust."

"Oh!—orlright."

"And if you can, time yourself to get here in the cool of the evening, or just about sunset."

"What for?"

I'd thought it would be better to have the buggy there in the cool of the evening, when Mary would have time to get excited and get over it—better than in the blazing hot morning, when the sun rose as hot as at noon, and we'd have the long broiling day before us.

"What do you want me to come at sunset for?" asked James. "Do you want me to camp out in the scrub and turn up like a blooming sundowner?"

"Oh well," I said, "get here at midnight if you like."

We didn't say anything for a while—just sat and puffed at our pipes. Then I said:

"Well, what are you thinking about?"

"I'm thinking it's time you got a new hat, the sun seems to get in through your old one too much," and he got out of my reach and went to see about penning the calves. Before we turned in he said:

"Well, what am I to get out of the job, Joe?"

He had his eye on a double-barrel gun that Franca the gunsmith in Cudgegong had—one barrel shot, and the other rifle; so I said:

"How much does Franca want for that gun?"

"Five-ten; but I think he'd take my single barrel off it. Anyway, I can squeeze a couple of quid out of Phil Lambert for the single barrel." (Phil was his bosom chum.)

"All right," I said. "Make the best bargain you can."

He got his own breakfast and made an early start next morning, to get clear of any instructions or messages that Mary might have forgotten to give him overnight. He took his gun with him.

I'd always thought that a man was a fool who couldn't keep a secret from his wife—that there was something womanish about him. I found out. Those three days waiting for the buggy were about the longest I ever spent in my life. It made me scotty with everyone and everything; and poor Mary had to suffer for it. I put in the time patching up the harness and mending the stockyard and the roof, and, the third morning, I rode up the ridges to look for trees for fencing timber. I remember I hurried home that afternoon because I thought the buggy might get there before me.

At tea-time I got Mary on to the buggy business.

"What's the good of a single buggy to you, Mary?" I asked. "There's only room for two, and what are you going to do with the children when we go out together?"

"We can put them on the floor at our feet, like other people do. I can always fold up a blanket or possum rug for them to sit on."

But she didn't take half so much interest in buggy talk as she would have taken at any other time, when I didn't want her to. Women are aggravating that way. But the poor girl was tired and not very well, and both the children were cross. She did look knocked up.

"We'll give the buggy a rest, Joe," she said. (I thought I heard it coming then.) "It seems as far off as ever. I don't know why you want to harp on it to-day. Now, don't look so cross, Joe—I didn't mean to hurt you. We'll wait until we can get a double buggy, since you're so set on it. There'll be plenty of time when we're better off."

After tea, when the youngsters were in bed, and she'd washed up, we sat on the edge of the veranda floor, Mary sewing, and I smoking and watching the track up the creek.

"Why don't you talk, Joe?" asked Mary. "You scarcely ever speak to me now: it's like drawing blood out of a stone to get a word from you. What makes you so cross, Joe?"

"Well, I've got nothing to say."

"But you should find something. Think of me—it's very miserable for me. Have you anything on your mind? Is there any new trouble? Better tell me, no matter what it is, and not go worrying and brooding and making both our lives miserable. If you never tell me anything, how can you expect me to understand?"

I said there was nothing the matter.

"But there must be, to make you so unbearable. Have you been drinking, Joe—or gambling?"

I asked her what she'd accuse me of next.

"And another thing I want to speak to you about," she went on. "Now, don't knit up your forehead like that, Joe, and get impatient——"

"Well, what is it?"

"I wish you wouldn't swear in the hearing of the children. Now, little Jim to-day, he was trying to fix his little go-cart, and it wouldn't run right, and—and——"

"Well, what did he say?"

"He—he" (she seemed a little hysterical, trying not to laugh)—"he said, 'Damn it!'"

I had to laugh. Mary tried to keep serious but it was no use.

"Never mind, old woman," I said, putting an arm round her, for her mouth was trembling, and she was crying more than laughing. "It won't be always like this. Just wait till we're a bit better off."

Just then a black boy we had (I must tell you about him some other time) came sidling along by the wall, as if he were afraid somebody was going to hit him—poor little devil! I never did.

"What is it, Harry?" said Mary.

"Buggy comin', I bin thinkit."

"Where?"

He pointed up the creek.

"Sure it's a buggy?"

"Yes, missus."

"How many horses?"

"One—two."

We knew that he could hear and see things long before we could. Mary went and perched on the wood-heap, and shaded her eyes—though the sun had gone—and peered through between the eternal grey trunks of the stunted trees on the flat across the creek. Presently she jumped down and came running in.

"There's someone coming in a buggy, Joe!" she cried, excitedly. "And both my white table-cloths are rough dry. Harry! put two flat-irons down to the fire, quick, and put on some more wood. It's lucky I kept those new sheets packed away. Get up out of that, Joe? What are you sitting grinning like that for? Go and get on another shirt. Hurry—Why, it's only James—by himself."

She stared at me, and I sat there, grinning like a fool.

"Joe!" she said. "Whose buggy is that?"

"Well, I suppose it's yours," I said.

She caught her breath, and stared at the buggy, and then at me again.

James drove down out of sight into the crossing, and came up close to the house.

"Oh, Joe! what have you done?" cried Mary. "Why, it's a new double buggy." Then she rushed at me and hugged my head. "Why didn't you tell me, Joe? You poor old boy!—and I've been nagging at you all day!" And she hugged me again.

James got down and started taking the horses out—as if it was an everyday occurrence. I saw the double-barrel gun sticking out from under the seat. He'd stopped to wash the buggy, and I suppose that's what made him grumpy. Mary stood on the veranda, with her eyes twice as big as usual, and breathing hard—taking the buggy in.

James skimmed the harness off, and the horses shook themselves and went down to the dam for a drink. "You'd better look under the seats," growled James, as he took his gun out with great care.

Mary dived for the buggy. There was a dozen of lemonade and ginger-beer in a candle-box from Galletly—James said that Galletly's men had a gallon of beer, and they cheered him, James (I suppose he meant they cheered the buggy), as he drove off; there was a "little bit of a ham" from Pat Murphy, the storekeeper at Home Rule, that he'd "cured himself" —it was the biggest I ever saw; there were three loaves of baker's bread, a cake, and a dozen yards of something "to make up for the children," from Aunt Gertrude at Gulgong; there was a fresh-water cod, that long Dave Regan had caught the night before in the Macquarie River, and sent out packed in salt in a box; there was a holland suit for the black boy, with red braid to trim it; and there was a jar of preserved ginger, and some lollies (sweets) ("for the lil' boy"), and a rum-looking Chinese doll and a rattle ("for lil' girl") from Sun Tong Lee, our storekeeper at Gulgong— James was chummy with Sun Tong Lee, and got his powder and shot and caps there on tick when he was short of money. And James said that the people would have loaded the buggy with "rubbish" if he'd waited. They all seemed glad to see Joe Wilson getting on—and these things did me good.

We got the things inside, and I don't think either of us knew what we were saying or doing for the next half-hour. Then James put his head in and said, in a very injured tone:

"What about my tea? I ain't had anything to speak of since I left Cudgegong. I want some grub."

Then Mary pulled herself together.

"You'll have your tea directly," she said. "Pick up that harness at once, and hang it on the pegs in the skillion; and you, Joe, back that buggy under the end of the veranda, the dew will be on it presently—and we'll put wet bags up in front of it to-morrow, to keep the sun off. And James will have to go back to Cudgegong for the cart—we can't have that buggy to knock about in."

"All right," said James—"anything! Only get me some grub."

Mary fried the fish, in case it wouldn't keep till the morning, and rubbed over the table-cloths, now the irons were hot—James growling all the time—and got out some crockery she had packed away that had belonged to her mother, and set the table in a style that made James uncomfortable.

"I want some grub—not a blooming banquet!" he said. And he growled a lot because Mary wanted him to eat his fish without a knife, "and that sort of tommy-rot." When he'd finished he took his gun, and the black boy, and the dogs, and went out possum-shooting.

When we were alone Mary climbed into the buggy to try the seat, and made me get up alongside her. We hadn't had such a comfortable seat for years; but we soon got down, in case anyone came by, for we began to feel like a pair of fools up there.

Then we sat, side by side, on the edge of the veranda, and talked more than we'd done for years—and there was a good deal of "Do you remember?" in it—and I think we got to understand each other better that night.

And at last Mary said, "Do you know, Joe, why, I feel to-night just—just like I did the day we were married."

And somehow I had that strange, shy sort of feeling too.

THE WRITER WANTS TO SAY A WORD

In writing the first sketch of the Joe Wilson series, which happened to be "Brighten's Sister-in-Law," I had an idea of making Joe Wilson a strong character. Whether he is or not, the reader must judge. It seems to me that the man's natural sentimental selfishness, good-nature, "softness," or weakness—call it what you like—developed as I wrote on.

I know Joe Wilson very well. He has been through deep trouble since the day he brought the double buggy to Lahey's Creek. I met him in Sydney the other day. Tall and straight yet—rather straighter than he had been—dressed in a comfortable, serviceable sac suit of "saddle-tweed," and wearing a new sugar-loaf, cabbage-tree hat, he looked over the hurrying street people calmly as though they were sheep of which he was not in charge, and which were not likely to get "boxed" with his. Not the worst way in which to regard the world.

He talked deliberately and quietly in all that roar and rush. He is a young man yet, comparatively speaking, but it would take little Mary a long while now to pick the grey hairs out of his head, and the process would leave him pretty bald.

In two or three short sketches in another book I hope to complete the story of his life.

Writing of his holiday at Mallacoota with his old friend of *Bulletin* days, E. J. Brady, Lawson said that he was 'shanghaied' there by Tom Mutch, one of his most sincere mates.

E. J. ('Ted') Brady (1869-1952) was born at Carcoar, NSW, and as a young man played a vigorous part as a journalist in the radicalism of the late nineteenth and early twentieth centuries. In 1914 he finally settled at Mallacoota and remained there, except for brief periods, until his death. He was married four times and had a family of six children.

His first book, *The Ways of Many Waters* (1899), a collection of sea songs and shanties was praised by John Masefield. He continued to write from his retreat at Mallacoota for many Australian periodicals and had a number of books published. At all times championing the cause of Australian literature and the dignity of authorship his long essay on 'The Truth about Henry Lawson' is a clear statement of his attitudes, tinged, as may be, with emotion. He also contributed 'Mallacoota Days and Other Things' to *Henry Lawson by His Mates*, Angus & Robertson, 1931, edited by Lawson's daughter, Bertha, and J. Le Gay Brereton. It was re-issued in 1973.

DAYS WHEN WE WENT SWIMMING

The breezes waved the silver grass
   Waist-high along the siding,
And to the creek we ne'er could pass,
   Three boys, on bare back riding;
Beneath the sheoaks in the bend
   The waterhole was brimming—
Do you remember yet, old friend,
   The times we went in swimming?

The days we played the wag from school—
   Joys shared—but paid for singly—
The air was hot, the water cool—
   And naked boys are kingly!
With mud for soap, the sun to dry—
   A well-planned lie to stay us,
And dust well rubbed on neck and face
   Lest cleanliness betray us.

And you'll remember farmer Kutz—
   Though scarcely for his bounty—
He'd leased a forty-acre block,
   And thought he owned the county;
A farmer of the old-world school,
   That men grew hard and grim in,
He drew his water from the pool
   That we preferred to swim in.

And do you mind when down the creek
   His angry way he wended,
A green-hide cartwhip in his hand
   For our young backs intended?
Three naked boys upon the sand—
   Half-buried and half-sunning—
Three startled boys without their clothes
   Across the paddocks running.

We'd had some scares, but we looked blank
   When, resting there and chumming,
We glanced by chance along the bank
   And saw the farmer coming!
Some home impressions linger yet
   Of cups of sorrow brimming;
I hardly think that we'll forget
   The last day we went swimming.

PROFESSIONAL WANDERERS

When you've knocked about the country—been away from home
    for years;
When the past, by distance softened, nearly fills your eyes with
    tears—
You are haunted oft, wherever or however, you may roam,
By a fancy that you ought to go and see the folks at home,
You forget the ancient quarrels—little things that used to jar—
And you think of how they'll worry—how they wonder where you
    are:
You will think you served them badly, and your own part you'll
    condemn,
And it strikes you that you'll surely be a novelty to them,
For your voice has somewhat altered, and your face has somewhat
    changed,
And your views of men and matters over wider fields have ranged;
Then it's time to save your money, or to watch it (how it goes!);
Then it's time to get a Gladstone and a decent suit of clothes;
Then it's time to practise daily with a hair-brush and a comb,
Till you drop in unexpected on the folks and friends at home.

When you've been at home for some time, and the novelty's
    worn off,
And old chums no longer court you, and your friends begin to
    scoff;
When the girls no longer kiss you, crying "Jack! how you have
    changed!"
When you're stale to your relations, and their manner seems
    estranged;

When the old domestic quarrels round the table, thrice a day,
Make it too much like the old times—make you wish you'd stayed
    away;
When, in short, you've spent your money in the fullness of your
    heart,
And your clothes are getting shabby ... then it's high time to
    depart.

WRITTEN AFTERWARDS
(To J. Le Gay Brereton)

So the days of my riding are over,
   The days of my tramping are done—
I'm about as content as a rover
   Will ever be under the sun;
I write, after reading your letter—
   My mind with old memories rife—
And I feel in a mood that had better
     Not meet the true eyes of the wife.

You must never admit a suggestion
   That old things are good to recall;
You must never consider the question:
   "Was I happier then, after all?"
You must banish the old hope and sorrow
   That make the sad pleasures of life;
You must live for Today and Tomorrow
   If you want to be just to the wife.

I have changed since the first day I kissed her,
   Which is due—Heaven bless her!—to her;
I'm respected and trusted—I'm "Mister",
   Addressed by the children as "Sir".
I feel the respect without feigning,
   And you'd laugh the great laugh of your life
If you only saw me entertaining
   An old lady friend of the wife.

By the way, when you're writing, remember
  You never went drinking with me,
And forget our Last Nights of December,
  Lest our several accounts disagree.
And, for my sake, old man, you had better
  Avoid the old language of strife,
For the technical terms of your letter
  Will be misconstrued by the wife.

Never hint of the girls appertaining
  To the past, when you're writing again,
For they take such a lot of explaining—
  And you know how I hate to explain.
There are some things, we know to our sorrow,
  That cut to the heart like a knife,
And your past is Today and Tomorrow
  If you want to be true to the wife.

No doubt you are dreaming as I did
  And going the careless old pace,
But my future grows dull and decided,
  And the world narrows down to the Place.
Let it be. If my reason's resented,
  You may do worse, old man, in your life;
Let me dream, too, that I am contented—
  For the sake of a true little wife.

FAREWELL TO THE BUSHMEN

Some carry their swags in the Great North-west,
    Where the bravest battle and die,
And a few have gone to their last long rest,
    And a few have said "Good-bye!"
The coast grows dim, and it may be long
    Ere the Gums again I see;
So I put my soul in a farewell song
    To the chaps who barracked for me.

Their days are hard at the best of times,
    And their dreams are dreams of care—
God bless them all for their big soft hearts,
    And the brave, brave grins they wear!
God keep me straight as a man can go,
    And true as a man may be,
For the sake of the hearts that were always so,
    Of the men who had faith in me!

And a ship-side word I would say, you chaps
    Of the blood of the Don't-give-in!
The world will call it a boast, perhaps—
    But I'll win, if a man can win!
And not for gold or the world's applause—
    Though ways to an end they be—
I'll win, if a man might win, because
    Of the men who believe in me.

DRIFTING APART

I told you how we took up a selection at Lahey's Creek, and how little Jim had convulsions on the road out, and Brighten's sister-in-law saved him; and about the hard struggle we had for years; and poor Mrs Spicer, who was "past carin'", and died like a broken-down horse; and how I was lucky, got to be a squatter, and bought a brand-new, first-class double buggy for Mary—and how her brother James brought it as a surprise to Lahey's Creek. And before that I told you all about how I first met Mary at Haviland Station, and how we fell in love, courted, and got married. Ah, well! How the time goes by!

I had luck, and did well for three or four seasons running. I was always going to build a new brick-and-shingle house for Mary—bricks and shingles are cooler than slabs and iron—but that was one of the houses I never built —except in the air. I've lived on the bank of the creek, and the place looked about the same as ever—and about as dreary and lonely and God-forsaken. I didn't even get any more furniture, in a good many of 'em.

So we still lived in the old slab-and-bark house and Mary got tired of bothering me about it. I'd always say, "Wait till the new house is built." It was no home for a woman. I can see that now.

You remember how I was always talking about making a nice home for Mary, and giving her more of my time, and trying to make her life a little brighter when things brightened up. I tried to do it by taking her trips to Sydney whenever I could get her to go, leaving her brother James to look after the station. At first I'd send the black boy ahead with fresh horses, and we'd flash down in the buggy the hundred miles or so of glorious mountain and valley road to Wallerawang, leave the buggy and two horses there, and take the train over the Blue Mountains to the Big Smoke. Then again, when wool was up, I'd take berths in a sleeping-carriage from Dubbo, and put up at the Royal in Sydney, and do the thing in great style. But Mary thought the sleeping-carriage was unnecessary expense, and she didn't like stopping at an hotel. She was always anxious about me and the drink. She preferred some "cheap, quiet place". "A run of bad seasons might come along at any time, Joe," she said, "and then you'll be sorry for the money you throw away now."

I thought it was very unjust of her to talk of throwing away money when I was only trying to give her pleasure—but then women were always unjust and unreasonable.

"If we don't enjoy ourselves when we've got the chance, we never will," I said.

"We could do that just as well at home, Joe," said Mary, "if you only knew—if you'd listen to me, and go the right way to work about it. Why can't you settle down in your own home, and make it bright, and be contented?"

"Well, what's the use of furniture, or a new house for that matter, when there's no one but bushies to look at it?" I said. "We might just as well live in a tent. What's the use of burying ourselves in the blasted bush altogether? We've got two pretty children, and you're good-looking yet, Mary, and it isn't as if we were an old man and woman."

"I'm nearly twenty-seven," said Mary. "I only thought of it today, and it came like a shock to me. I feel like an old woman."

I'd learnt enough of women not to argue with Mary while she was in that mood. The fact of the matter was that after the first trip or two she didn't seem to enjoy herself in the city. You see, she always insisted on taking the children with her. She couldn't bring herself to trust them at home with the girl, and I knew that if she did she'd be worrying all the time, and spoil her pleasure and mine, and so we always took them with us. But they were an awful drag in the city. Mary wouldn't trust 'em with a strange woman or girl, except perhaps for a few hours when they were in bed, and we went to one of the theatres. So we always carted them round the town with us. I soon got tired of humping one or the other of 'em. But crossing the streets was the worst. It was bad enough with Mary when we were out alone. She would hang back when the crossing was clear, and suddenly make a start when there was a rush of traffic, and balk as often as not, and sometimes turn and run back to the kerb from the middle of the street—me trying to hang on to her all the time—till I'd get rippin' wild, and go for her.

"Damn it all!" I said, "why can't you trust to me and come when I tell you? One would think I came out with the fixed intention of getting you run over, and getting rid of you."

And Mary would lose her temper and say, "Ah, well, Joe, I sometimes think you do want to get rid of me, the way you go on," or something like that, and our pleasure would be spoilt for the day.

But with the children! What with one or the other of them always whimpering or crying, and Jim always yelling when we got into a tram, or bus, or boat, or into some place that he didn't trust, or when we reckoned we were lost, which was about every twenty minutes—and, what with Mary losing her temper every time I lost mine, there were times when I really wished in my heart I was on my own....Ah, well, there came a day when I had my wish.

I forgot about the hard life in huts and camps in the bush, and the bitter, heart-breaking struggle she'd shared with me since we were married, and how she'd slaved and fought through the blazing drought on that wretched, lonely selection, in the first year, while I was away with the team most of the time—how she'd stuck to me through thick and thin. I only thought she was very irritable and selfish and unreasonable, and that she ought to be able to keep the children in better order. I believed that she had spoilt them. And I was wild to think how our holiday was being wasted.

After the first time or two Mary didn't seem to enjoy the theatre. She told me one night, when we got a bit confidential, that the play had depressed her, and made her sad.

"How's that?" I asked.

"Well, Joe," she said, "I don't want to hurt you, Joe, but, if you must know, I was thinking all the time of the past—of our own lives."

That hurt me and made me wild. I'd been thinking, too, all the time I was watching the play, of life as it was, and my own dull, sordid, hopeless, monotonous life in particular. But I hadn't been thinking of hers. The truth seemed that we were getting on each other's nerves—we'd been too long together alone in the bush; and it isn't good for a man and his wife to be too much alone. I at least had come to think that when Mary said unpleasant things she only did it to irritate me.

"What are you always raking up the past for?" I said. "Can't you have done with it? Ain't I doing my best to make you happy? What more do you want?"

"I want a good many little things, Joe," said Mary.

We quarrelled then, but in the hard, cold, quiet, sarcastic way we'd got into lately—not the old short, fierce quarrel of other days, when we'd make it up and love each other all the more afterwards. I don't know how much I hurt her, but I knew she cut me to the heart sometimes, as a woman can cut a man.

Next evening I went out alone, and didn't get back to the hotel till after twelve. Mary was up, waiting; but she didn't say much, only that she had been afraid to go to bed. Next morning she asked me to stay and watch the children while she went shopping and bought the things she wanted to take home, and I did, and we made it up, and got along smoothly until after tea; then I wanted to go out, and Mary didn't want me to—she wanted me to sit on the balcony with her.

I remember she was very earnest about me staying in with her that evening, and if I hadn't been drinking the night before I would have stayed. I waited a while, and then I got restless, and found I was out of tobacco.

"I will send out for it, Joe," said Mary.

"What nonsense," I said. "I'll run out and get it myself. I'm all right. I'll get some fruit, too, and chocolates, for the children. I'll only be a few minutes."

"Well, if you must go, you must," she said, in the hard tone again.

"I'll only be a few minutes, I tell you," I said. "Don't start the thing again, for God's sake."

"Well, promise me you won't be more than a quarter of an hour," said Mary, "and I'll wait here for you. I don't like being left alone in a place full of strange men."

"That's all right, Mary," I said, and I stepped out for half an hour. I was restless as a hen that didn't know where to lay. I wanted to walk, and was fond of the noise and bustle of the streets. They fascinated me, and dragged me out.

I didn't get back to the hotel till daylight.

I hoped to find Mary asleep, and I went into the bedroom very softly. She was in bed, but she was awake. She took the thing so quietly that it made me uneasy. When an impulsive, determined little woman begins to take things very quietly it's time for the man to straighten up and look out. She didn't even ask me where I'd been, and that made me more uneasy (I had a good yarn readied up), and when she spoke of a murder case in the *Herald,* and asked me if I'd read the divorce case where a wife sued her husband for drunkenness and adultery, I began to get scared. I wished she'd go for me, and have done with it, but she didn't. At last, at breakfast, she said:

"I think we'll go home today, Joe; we'll take the evening train from Redfern. You can get any business done that you want to do by that time."

And I thought so, too.

It was a miserable journey—one of the most dreary and miserable I ever made in my life. Both the children were peevish all the way. While there were other passengers in the carriage I couldn't talk to Mary, and when we were alone she wouldn't talk to me—except to answer yes and no.

The worst of it was that I didn't know what she thought, or how much she suspected. I wondered whether she believed that I had deceived her, and that worried me a lot. I hadn't been drinking much, and I came home sober that morning, so drink was no excuse for me being out all night. I thought once or twice that it would have been much better if I'd come home drunk, with a muddled yarn about meeting an old chum and having a glorious auld-lang-syne night at some club.

I was very attentive all the way. I got tea and cake and sandwiches at every refreshment-room, and whatever fruit I could lay hands on, and nursed the children to sleep by turns; but it didn't soften Mary. She wasn't a child any longer. She only said, "Thank you, Joe," and as I watched her face it seemed to grow harder and more set and obstinate.

"Mary," I said at last, when we were going down the Great Zigzag, "suppose we get out at Wallerawang, and go up through Cudgegong? We can rest there for a day, and then go to Gulgong, and see your sister and Dick, and stay there for a night perhaps."

"If you like, Joe," said Mary.

"You'd like to see Hilda, Mary, wouldn't you?"

"Yes, Joe," she said, in the same cold, disinterested tone, "I would like to see her."

The case seemed hopeless. I had first-class tickets through to Dubbo, and would have to get others for the Cudgegong (Mudgee) line; besides, the coach fares would be extra, and I thought Mary would rouse herself, and buck at the waste of money, but she didn't seem to mind that a bit. But Haviland cattle-station was on the Cudgegong line, and it was at Haviland where I first met Mary. She was brought up there from a child, and I thought that the sight of the place would break her down, if anything would.

We changed trains at Wallerawang Junction at midnight, and passed the great Capertee Valley and Macdonald's Hole in the moonlight—a great basin in the mountains, where "Starlight" and the Marsdens used to ride, and hide sometimes for months together, in *Robbery Under Arms,* and where thousands of tourists will go some day. All along the Western Line I saw old roads and tracks where I came droving as a boy, and old camps where I camped; and the ruins of one old half-way house, dismal and haunted, in the heavy scrub, where my old chum Jack Barnes and I had a glorious spree one time; and Gerty—but never mind that; and lonely, deserted old roads, where I "carried" when I grew up, and often tramped beside the bullocks or horses, and spouted Gordon's poetry till it lifted me, and wished to God that I could write like that, or do something, or break away from the life that was driving me mad. And it all made me feel very dismal now and hopeless, and I hated the bush worse than ever, and made up my mind to take Mary and the children out of it just as soon as I could get rid of the station. I'd take the first reasonable offer that came.

Mary slept, or pretended to sleep, most of the time, and I kept the children quiet. I watched her face a good deal, and tried to persuade myself that she hadn't changed much since the days when I had courted her at Haviland; but, somehow, Mary and the girl I got to love me years ago seemed very different. It seemed to me as if—well, as if I'd courted a girl and married a woman. But perhaps it was time and distance—or I might have changed most. I began to feel myself getting old (forty was very near), but it had never struck me that Mary would feel that way too.

We had breakfast at Rylstone. After that Mary talked a little, but still in

416

a hard, cold way. She wondered how things were at home, and hoped it would rain soon. She said the weather looked and smelt like the beginning of a drought. Hanging out blue lights, I thought. Then she'd be silent for miles, except to speak to the children; and then I got a suspicion that she was talking at me through them, and it made me wild, and I had a job to keep from breaking out. It was during that journey that I first began to wonder what my wife was thinking about, and to worry over it—to distrust her silence. I wished she'd cry, and then it struck me that I hadn't seen tears in Mary's eyes for God knows how long—and the thought of it hurt me a lot.

We had the carriage to ourselves after Dungaree, and Haviland was the next station. I wished we could have passed Haviland by moonlight, or in the evening, instead of the garish morning. I thought it would have been more likely to soften Mary. I'd rehearsed the business, half unconsciously, humbugging myself, as men will. I was going to be very silent, and look extra sad, and keep gazing out of the window, and never look at Mary, and try, if possible, to squeeze some suspicious moisture into my eyes, as we passed the place. But I felt by instinct that my barneying and pleading and bluffing and acting and humbugging days were past—also my bullying days. I couldn't work on Mary's feelings now like I used to. I knew, or thought I knew, that she saw through me, and felt that she knew I knew it. Most men's wives see through their husbands sooner or later, and when a wife does it's time for a husband to drop his nonsense, and go straight. She'll know when he's sincere and when he's not—he needn't be afraid of that.

And so, the nearer we got to Haviland, the more helpless and unprepared I felt. But when the train swung round the horn of the crescent of hills in which Haviland lay there wasn't any need for acting. There was the old homestead, little changed, and as fair as it seemed in those faraway days, nearly eight years ago, when that lanky scamp, Joe Wilson, came hanging round after "Little Possum", who was far too good for the likes of him. There was the stable and buggy-house that Jack Barnes and I built between shearings. There was the wide, brick-floored, vine-covered veranda where I first saw Mary; and there was the little green flat by the river where I stood up, that moonlight night, like a man, and thrashed big Romany, the station-hand, because he'd said something nasty about little Mary Brand—all the time she was sitting singing with the other girls under the veranda to amuse a new chum jackeroo. And there, near the willows by the river, was the same old white, hardwood log where Mary and I sat in the moonlight next night, while all the rest were dancing in the big woolshed—when I made her understand how awfully fond of her I was. And there—

There was no need for humbugging now. The trouble was to swallow the lumps in my throat, and keep back the warm gush of suspicious moisture that came to my eyes. Mary sat opposite, and I stole a glance at her. She was staring out with wide-opened eyes, and there were tears in them—and a scared look, I fancied for the moment. Then suddenly she turned from the window and looked at me, her eyes wide and brimming, and—well, it was the same little Mary, my sweetheart, after our first quarrel years ago.

I jumped up and sat down by her side, and put my arm round her; and she just put her arms round my neck and her head down on my chest, and cried till the children cried too, and little Jim interfered—he thought I was hurting his mother. Then Mary looked up and smiled. She comforted the children, and told them to kiss their father, and for the rest of the journey we talked of those old days, and at last Mary put her arms round my neck, and said:

"You never did deceive me, Joe, did you? I want you to swear that to me."

"No, Mary," I said, "I never did. I swear to God I never did!"

And God knew whether I had done so or not.

"You've got the scar on the bridge of your nose still," said Mary, kissing it, "and"—as if she'd just noticed it for the first time—"why your hair is greyer than ever!" and she pulled down my head, and her fingers began to go through my hair as in the days of old. And when we got to the hotel at Cudgegong she made me have a bath and lie down on the bed and go to sleep. And when I awoke, late in the afternoon, she was sitting by my side, smoothing my hair.

A VOICE FROM THE CITY

On western plain and eastern hill,
  Where once my fancy ranged,
The station hands are riding still
  And they are little changed.
But I have lost in London gloom
  The glory of the day—
The old, sweet scent of wattle-bloom
  Is faint and far away.

I warp my life on pavement stones
  That drag me ever down,
A paltry slave to little things,
  By custom chained to town.
I've lost the strength to strike alone,
  The heart to do and dare—
When swag and will were still my own
  I'd tramp to God-knows-where.

I mind the time when I was shy
  To meet the brown Bush girls—
I've lunched with lords since then, and I
  Have been at home with earls:
I learned to smile and learned to bow
  And lie to ladies gay—
But to a gaunt Bushwoman now
  What should I have to say?

And if I sought her home out west
  From scenes of show and sham,
The hard bare place would grimly test
  The poor weak thing I am.
I could not meet her hopeless eyes
  That look one through and through,
The haggard woman, hardship-wise,
  Who once thought I was true.

But nought on earth can last for aye,
  And, wild with care and pain,
Some day by chance I'll break away
  And seek the Bush again.
And find awhile from bitter years
  The rest the Bush can bring,
And hear, perhaps, with truer ears,
  The songs it has to sing.

BOURKE

The poet's memory played him false in this poem. He was at Bourke in 1892 and 1893.

I've followed all my tracks and ways, from old bark school to
    Leicester Square;
I've been right back to boyhood's days, and found no light or
    pleasure there.
But every dream and every track—and there were many that I
    knew—
They all lead on, or they lead back, to Bourke in Ninety-one
    and two.

No sign that green grass ever grew in scrubs that blazed beneath
    the sun;
The plains were dust in Ninety-two, and hard as bricks in
    Ninety-one.
On glaring iron-roofs of Bourke the scorching, blinding sandstorms
    blew,
No hint of beauty lingered there in Ninety-one and Ninety-two.

Save grit and pulse of generous hearts—great hearts that broke and
    healed again—
The hottest drought that ever blazed could never parch the souls
    of men;
And they were men in spite of all, and they were straight, and
    they were true;
The hat went round at trouble's call in Ninety-one and Ninety-two.

They drank—when all is said and done—they gambled, and their
    speech was rough;
You'd only need to say of one "He was my mate!" That was enough.
But hint a bushman was not white, nor to his Union straight and
    true—
'Twould mean a long and bloody fight in Ninety-one and Ninety-
    two.

The yard behind the Shearers' Arms was reckoned best of battle-
    grounds,
And there in peace and quietness they fought their ten or fifteen
    rounds;
And then they wiped the blood away, and then shook hands—
    as strong men do—
And washed away the bitterness, in Ninety-one and Ninety-two.

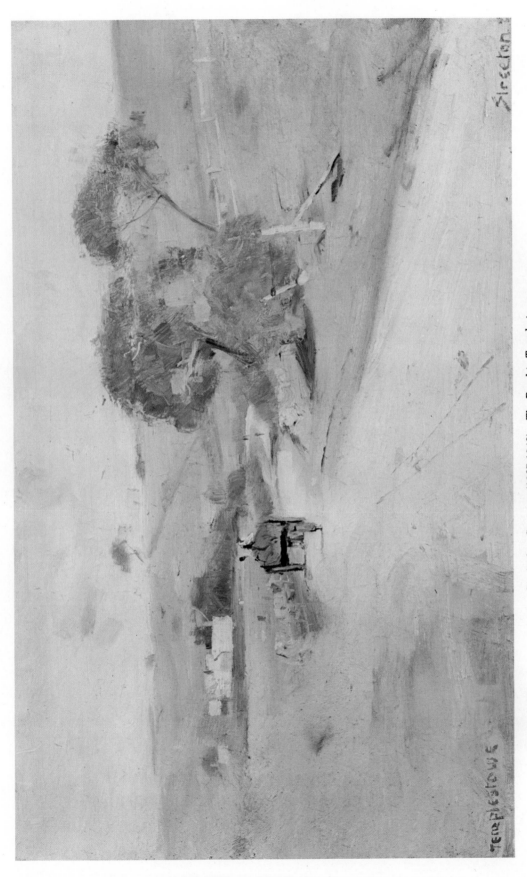

Sir Arthur Streeton (1867-1943)   *The Road to Templestowe*
25.4 x 40.6 cm   Oil on canvas
Reproduced with the kind permission of The Art Gallery Of South Australia

Frederick McCubbin (1855-1917)   *On the Wallaby Track* (1896)
122 x 223.5 cm   Oil on canvas
Reproduced with the kind permission of the Art Gallery Of New South Wales, Sydney

The "Army" on the grand old creek was mighty in those days
      gone by,
For they had sisters who could shriek, and brothers who could
      testify;
And by the muddy waterholes they tackled sin till all was blue—
They took our bobs and damned our souls in Ninety-one and
      Ninety-two.

By shanty-bar and shearing-shed they took their toll and did their
      work;
But now and then they lost their heads, and raved of hotter hells
      than Bourke:
The only message from the dead that ever came distinctly through
Was "Send my overcoat to hell"; it came to Bourke in Ninety-two.

They're scattered wide and scattered far—by fan-like tracks, north,
      east, and west—
The cruel New Australia star drew off the bravest and the best.
The Cape and Klondyke claim their bones, the streets of London
      damned a few,
And jingo-cursed Australia mourns for Ninety-one and Ninety-two.

They say the world has changed out there, and western towns
      have altered quite:
They don't know how to drink and swear—they've half forgotten
      how to fight;
They've almost lost the strength to trust, they leave their mate to
      battle through—
Their hearts beat true in drought and dust in Ninety-one and
      Ninety-two.

And could I roll the summers back, or bring the dead time here
      again,
Or from the grave or world-wide track recall to Bourke the vanished
      men,
With mind content I'd go to sleep, and leave those mates to judge
      me true,
And leave my name to Bourke to keep—the Bourke of Ninety-one
      and two.

Miles Franklin, pictured here, aged 17, owed a great deal to Lawson whose personal interest led to her first book being published in England by William Blackwood & Sons in 1901. His preface, which is an interesting document in view of Lawson's unhappy stay in London, reads:
    'A few months before I left Australia I got a letter from the Bush signed "Miles Franklin", saying that the writer had written a novel, but knew nothing of editors and publishers and asking me to read and advise. Something about the letter, which was written in a strong original hand, attracted me, so I sent for the MS, and one dull afternoon started to read it. I hadn't read three pages when I saw what you will no doubt see at once — that the story had been written by a girl. And as I went on I saw that the work was Australian — born of the Bush. I don't know about the girlishly emotional parts of the book — I leave that to the girl readers to judge; but the descriptions of Bush life and scenery came startlingly, painfully real to me, and I know that, as far as they are concerned, the book is true to Australia — truest I ever read.
    I wrote to Miles Franklin, and she confessed that she was a girl. I saw her before leaving Sydney. She is just a little Bush girl, barely twenty-one yet, and has scarcely even been out of the Bush in her life.
    She has lived her book, and I feel proud of it for the sake of the country I came from, where people toil and bake and suffer and are kind; where every second sun-burnt Bushman is a sympathetic humorist, with the sadness of the Bush deep in his eyes and a brave grin for the worst of times, and where every third Bushman is a poet, with a big heart that keeps his pockets empty. England, April, 1901.'

HIS BROTHER'S KEEPER

By his paths through the parched desolation,
  Hot rides and the terrible tramps;
By the hunger, the thirst, the privation
  Of his work in the furthermost camps;

— By his worth in the light that shall search men
  And prove—ay! and justify each—
I place him in front of all Churchmen
  Who feel not, who *know* not—but preach!
                                    —*The Christ of the Never.*

I told you about Peter M'Laughlan, the bush missionary, and how he preached in the little slab-and-bark school-house, in the scrub on Ross's Creek that blazing hot Sunday afternoon long ago, when the drought was ruining the brave farmers all round there and breaking their hearts. And how hard old Ross, the selector, broke down at the end of the sermon, and blubbered, and had to be taken out of church.

I left home and drifted to Sydney, and "back into the Great North-West where all the rovers go," and knocked about the country for six or seven years before I met Peter M'Laughlan again. I was young yet, but felt old at times, and there were times, in the hot, rough, greasy shearing-shed on blazing days, or in the bare "men's hut" by the flicker of the stinking slush-lamp at night, or the wretched wayside shanty with its drink-madness and blasphemy, or tramping along the dusty, endless track—there were times when I wished I could fall back with all the experience I'd got, and sit once more in the little slab-and-bark "chapel" on Ross's Creek and hear Peter M'Laughlan and the poor, struggling selectors sing "Shall We Gather at the River?" and then go out and start life afresh.

My old school chum and bush mate, Jack Barnes, had married pretty little Clara Southwick, who used to play the portable harmonium in chapel. I nearly broke my heart when they were married, but then I was a young fool. Clara was a year or so older than I, and I could never get away from a boyish feeling of reverence for her, as if she was something above and out of my world. And so, while I was worshipping her in chapel once a month, and at picnics and parties in between, and always at a distance, Jack used to ride up to Southwick's place on Saturday and Sunday afternoons, and on other days, and hang his horse up outside, or turn it in the paddock, and argue with old Southwick, and agree with the old woman, and court Clara on the sly. And he got her.

It was at their wedding that I first got the worse for drink.

Jack was a blue-eyed, curly black-haired, careless, popular young scamp; as good-hearted as he was careless. He could ride like a circus monkey, do all kinds of bush work, add two columns of figures at once, and write like copper-plate.

Jack was given to drinking, gambling and roving. He steadied up when he got married and started on a small selection of his own; but within the year Clara was living in a back skillion of her father's house and Jack was up-country shearing. He was "ringer" of the shed at Piora Station one season and made a decent cheque; and within a fortnight after the shed "cut out" he turned up at home in a very bad state from drink and with about thirty shillings in his pockets. He had fallen from his horse in the creek near Southwick's, and altogether he was a nice sort of young husband to go home to poor, heart-broken Clara.

I remember that time well. She stopped me one day as I was riding past to ask me if I'd seen Jack, and I got off my horse. Her chin and mouth began to twitch and tremble and I saw her eyes filling with tears. She laid her hand on my arm and asked me to promise not to drink with Jack if I met him, but to try and persuade him to come home. And—well, have you, as a man, ever, with the one woman that you can't have, and no matter at what time or place, felt a sudden mad longing to take her in your arms and kiss her—and damn the world? I got on my horse again. She must have thought me an ignorant brute, but I felt safer there. And when I thought how I had nearly made a fool of myself, and been a cowardly brute, and a rotten mate to my mate, I rode ten miles to find Jack and get him home.

He straightened up again after a bit and went out and got another shed, and they say that Peter M'Laughlan got hold of him there. I don't know what Peter did to him then—Jack never spoke of it, even to me, his old mate; but, anyway, at the end of the shearing season Jack's cheque came home to Clara in a registered envelope, addressed in Peter's handwriting, and about a week later Jack turned up a changed man.

He got work as a temporary clerk in the branch government lands office at Solong, a pretty little farming town in a circle of blue hills on the banks of a clear, willow-fringed river, where there were rich, black-soil, river-flat farms, and vineyards on the red-soil slopes, and blue peaks in the distance. It was a great contrast to Ross's Creek. Jack paid a deposit on an allotment of land, a bit out of town, on the river bank, and built a little weather-board box of a cottage in spare times, and planted roses and grape-vines to hide its ugliness by and by. It wasn't much of a place, but Clara was mighty proud of it because it was "our house." They were very happy, and she was beginning to feel sure of Jack. She seemed to believe that the miserable old time was all past and gone.

When the work at the lands office gave out, Jack did all sorts of jobs about town, and at last, one shearing season, when there was a heavy clip of wool, and shearers were getting £1 a hundred, he decided to go out back. I know that Clara was against it, but he argued that it was the only chance for him, and she persuaded herself that she could trust him. I was knocking about Solong at the time, and Jack and I decided to go out together and share his packhorse between us. He wrote to Beenaway Shed, about three hundred miles north-west in the Great Scrubs, and got pens for both of us.

It was a fine fresh morning when we started; it was in a good season and the country looked grand. When I rode up to Jack's place I saw his horse and packhorse tied up outside the gate. He had wanted me to come up the evening before and have tea with them and camp at his place for the night. "Come up! man alive!" he said. "We'll make you a shake-down!" But I wouldn't; I said I had to meet a chap. Jack wouldn't have understood. I had been up before, but when I saw him and Clara so happy and comfortable, and thought of the past and my secret, and thought of myself, a useless, purposeless, restless, homeless sort of fellow, hanging out at a boarding-house, it nearly broke me up, and I had to have a drink or two afterwards. I often wonder if Clara guessed and understood. You never know how much a woman knows; but—ah, well!

Jack had taken my things home with him and he and Clara had packed them. I found afterwards that she had washed, dried and ironed some collars and handkerchiefs of mine during the night. Clara and Jack came out to the gate, and as I wouldn't go in to have a cup of tea there was nothing for it but to say good-bye. She was dressed in a fresh-looking print blouse and dark skirt, and wore a white hood that fell back from her head; she was a little girl, with sweet, small, freckled features, and red-gold hair, and kind, sympathetic grey eyes. I thought her the freshest, and fairest, and daintiest little woman in the district.

I was Jack's mate, so she always treated me as a sort of brother-in-law, and called me by my Christian name. Mates are closer than brothers in the bush.

I turned my back and pretended to tighten the straps and girths on the packhorse while she said good-bye to Jack. I heard her speaking earnestly to him, and once I heard her mention Peter M'Laughlan's name. I thought Jack answered rather impatiently. "Oh, that's all right, Clara," he said, "that's all over—past and gone. I wish you would believe it. You promised never to speak of that any more."

I know how it was. Jack never cared to hear about Peter; he was too ashamed of the past, perhaps; besides, deep down, we feel a sort of resentment towards any reference to a man who has helped or saved us in the past. It's human nature.

Then they spoke in low tones for a while, and then Jack laughed, and

427

kissed her, and said, "Oh, I'll be back before the time's up." Then he ran into the house to say good-bye to Mary's sister, who was staying with her, and who was laid up with a sprained ankle.

Then Clara stepped up to me and laid her fingers on my shoulder. I trembled from head to foot and hoped she didn't notice it.

"Joe," she said, looking at me with her big, searching grey eyes, "I believe I can trust you. I want you to look after Jack. You know why. Never let him have one drink if you can help it. One drink—the first drink will do it. I want you to promise me that you will never have a drink with Jack, no matter what happens or what he says."

"I never will," I said, and I meant it.

"It's the first time he's been away from me since he gave up drinking, and if he comes back all right this time I will be sure of him and contented. But, Joe, if he comes back wrong it will kill me; it will break my heart. I want you to promise that if anything happens you will ride or wire for Peter M'Laughlan. I hear he's wool-sorting this year at Beenaway Station. Promise me that if anything happens you will ride for Peter M'Laughlan and tell him, no matter what Jack says."

"I promise," I said.

She half-held out her hand to me, but I kept both mine behind my back. I suppose she thought I didn't notice that she wanted to shake hands on the bargain; but the truth was that my hands shook so, and I didn't want her to notice *that.*

I got on my horse and felt steadier. Then, "Good-bye, Clara"—"Good-bye, Jack." She bore up bravely, but I saw her eyes brimming. Jack got on his horse, and I bent over and shook hands with her. Jack bent down and kissed her while she stood on tip-toe. "Good-bye, little woman," he said. "Cheer up, and I'll be back before you know where you are! You mustn't fret—you know why."

"Good-bye, Jack!"—she was breaking down.

"Come on, Jack!" I said, and we rode off, turning and waving our hats to her as she stood by the gate, looking a desolate little thing, I thought, till we turned down a bend of the road into the river.

As we jogged along with the packhorse trotting behind us, and the quart-pots and hobble-chains jingling on the pack-saddle, I pictured Clara running inside, to cry a while in her sister's arms, and then to bustle round and cheer up, for Jack's sake—and for the sake of something else.

"I'll christen him after you, Joe," said Jack, later on, when we'd got confidential over our pipes after tea in our first camp. It never seemed to enter his head that there was the ghost of a chance that it might be a girl. "I'm glad he didn't come along when I was drinking," he said.

And as we lay rolled in our blankets under the stars I swore a big oath to myself.

We got along comfortably and reached Beenaway Station in about a week, the day before the shearers' roll-call. Jack never showed the slightest inclination to go into a shanty; and several times we talked about old times and what damned fools we'd been throwing away our money over shanty bars shouting for loafers and cadgers. "Isn't this ever so much better, Joe?" said Jack, as we lay on our blankets smoking one moonlight night. "There's nothing in boozing, Joe, you can take it from me. Just you sling it for a year and then look back; you won't want to touch it again. You've been straight for a couple of months. Sling it for good, Joe, before it gets a hold on you, like it did on me."

It was the morning after cut-out at Beenaway Shed, and we were glad. We were tired of the rush and roar and rattle and heat and grease and blasphemy of the big, hot, iron machine shed in that dusty patch in the barren scrubs. Swags were rolled up, saddle-bags packed, horses had been rounded up and driven in, the shearers' cook and his mate had had their fight, and about a hundred men—shearers, rouseabouts, and wool-washers— were waiting round the little iron office to get their cheques.

We were about half through when one bushman said to another: "Stop your damned swearin', Jim. Here's Peter M'Laughlan!" Peter walked up and the men made way for him and he went into the office. There was always considerably less swearing for a few feet round about where Peter M'Laughlan happened to be working in a shearing-shed. It seemed to be an understood thing with the men. He took no advantages, never volunteered to preach at a shed where he was working, and only spoke on union subjects when the men asked him to. He was "rep." (Shearers' Union representative) at this shed, but squatters and station managers respected him as much as the men did.

He seemed much greyer now, but still stood square and straight. And his eyes still looked one through.

When Peter came out and the crowd had cleared away he took Jack aside and spoke to him in a low voice for a few minutes. I heard Jack say, "Oh, that's all right, Peter! You have my word for it," and he got on his horse. I heard Peter say the one word, "Remember!" "Oh, that's all right," said Jack, and he shook hands with Peter, shouted, "Come on, Joe!" and started off with the packhorse after him.

"I wish I were going down with you, Joe," said Peter to me, "but I can't get away till to-morrow. I've got that sick rouseabout on my hands, and I'll have to see him fixed up somehow and started off to the hospital" (the nearest was a hundred miles away). "And, by the way, I've taken up a collection for him; I want a few shillings from you, Joe. I nearly forgot you. The poor fellow only got in about a fortnight's work, and there's a wife and youngsters in Sydney. I'll be down after you to-morrow. I promised to go to Comesomehow* and get the people together and start an agitation for a half-time school there. Anyway, I'll be there by the end of the week. Good-bye, Joe. I must get some more money for the rouser from some of those chaps before they start."

*There is a postal town in New South Wales called "Come-by-Chance."

Comesomehow was a wretched cockatoo settlement, a bit off the track, about one hundred and fifty miles on our road home, where the settlers lived like savages and the children ran wild. I reckoned that Peter would have his work cut out to start a craving for education in that place.

By saying he'd be there I think he intended to give me a hint, in case anything happened. I believe now that Jack's wife had got anxious and had written to him.

We jogged along comfortably and happily for three or four days, and as we passed shanty after shanty, and town after town, without Jack showing the slightest inclination to pull up at any of them, I began to feel safe about him.

Then it happened, in the simplest way, as most things of this sort happen if you don't watch close.

The third night it rained, rained heavens-hard, and rainy nights can be mighty cold out on those plains, even in mid-summer. Jack and I rigged up a strip of waterproof stuff we had to cover the swags on the packhorse, but the rain drove in, almost horizontally, and we got wet through, blankets, clothes and all. Jack got a bad cold and coughed fit to break himself; so about daylight, when the rain held up a bit, we packed up and rode on to the next pub, a wretched little weather-board place in the scrub.

Jack reckoned he'd get some stuff for his cold there. I didn't like to speak, but before we reached the place I said, "You won't touch a drink, Jack."

"Do you think I'm a blanky fool?" said Jack, and I shut up.

The shanty was kept by a man who went by the name of Thomas, a notorious lamber-down,† as I found out afterwards. He was a big, awkward bullock of a man, a selfish, ignorant brute, as anyone might have seen by his face; but he had a loud voice, and adopted a careless, rollicking, hail-fellow-well-met! come-in-and-sit-down-man-alive! clap-you-on-the-back-style, which deceived a good many, or which a good many pretended to believe in. His "missus" was an animal of his own species, but she was duller and didn't bellow.

He had a rather good-looking girl there—I don't know whether she was his daughter or not. They said that when he saw the shearers coming, he'd say, "Run and titivate yourself, Mary; here comes the shearers!"

But what surprised me was that Jack Barnes didn't seem able to see through Thomas; he thought that he was all right, "a bit of a rough diamond." There are any amount of scoundrels and swindlers knocking about the world disguised as rough diamonds.

Jack had a fit of coughing when we came in.

"Why, Jack!" bellowed Thomas, "that's a regular church-yarder you've got. Go in to the kitchen fire and I'll mix you a stiff toddy."

"No, thank you, Thomas," said Jack, glancing at me rather sheepishly, I thought. "I'll have a hot cup of coffee presently, that'll do me more good."

"Why, man alive, one drink won't hurt you!" said Thomas. "I know you're on the straight, and you know I'm the last man that 'ud try to get you off it. But you want something for that cold. You don't want to die on the track, do you? What would your missus say? That cough of yours is enough to bust a bullock."

† "Lamber-down," a shanty-keeper who entices cheque-men to drink.

"Jack isn't drinking, Thomas," I said rather shortly, "and neither am I."

"I'll have a cup of coffee at breakfast," said Jack; "thank you all the same, Thomas."

"Right you are, Jack!" said Thomas. "Mary!" he roared at the girl, "chuck yourself about and get breakfast, and make a strong cup of coffee; and I say, missus" (to his wife), "git some honey and vinegar in a cup, will yer? or see if there's any of that cough stuff left in the bottle. Go into the kitchen, you chaps, and dry yourselves at the fire, you're wringing wet." Jack went through into the kitchen.

I stepped out to see if the horses were all right, and as I came in again through the bar, Thomas, who had slipped behind the counter, crooked his finger at me and poured out a stiff whisky. "I thought you might like to have it on the quiet," he whispered, with a wink.

Now, there was this difference between Jack and me. When I was on the track, and healthy and contented, I could take a drink, or two drinks, and then leave it; or at other times I could drink all day, or all night, and be as happy as a lord, and be mighty sick and repentant all next day, and then not touch drink for a week; but if Jack once started, he was a lost man for days, for weeks, for months—as long as his cash or credit lasted. I felt a cold coming on me this morning, and wanted a whisky, so I had a drink with Thomas. Then, of course, I shouted in my turn, keeping an eye out in case Jack should come in. I went into the kitchen and steamed with Jack for a while in front of a big log fire, taking care to keep my breath away from him. Then we went in to breakfast. Those two drinks were all I meant to have, and we were going right on after breakfast.

It was a good breakfast, ham and eggs, and we enjoyed it. The two whiskies had got to work. I hadn't touched drink for a long time. I shouldn't like to say that Thomas put anything in the drink he gave me. Before we started breakfast he put a glass down in front of me and said:

"There's a good ginger-ale, it will warm you up."

I tasted it; it was rum, hot. I said nothing. What could I say?

There was some joke about Jack being married and settled and steadied down, and me, his old mate, still on the wallaby; and Mrs Thomas said that I ought to follow Jack's example. And just then I felt a touch of that loneliness that some men feel when an old drinking mate turns teetotaller.

Jack started coughing again, like an old cow with the pleuro.

"That cough will kill you, Jack," said Thomas. "Let's put a drop of brandy in your coffee, that won't start you, anyhow; it's real 'Three Star.'" And he reached a bottle from the side-table.

I should have stood up then, for my manhood, for my mate, and for little Clara, but I half rose from my chair, and Jack laughed and said, "Sit down, Joe, you old fool, you're tanked. I know all about your seeing about the horses and your ginger-ales. It's all right, old man. Do you think I'm going on the booze? Why, I'll have to hold you on the horse all day." I sat down and took up my glass.

"Here's luck, Joe!" said Jack, laughing, and lifting up his cup of coffee with the brandy in it. "Here's luck, Joe."

Then suddenly, and as clearly as I ever heard it, came Clara's voice to my ear: "Promise me, whatever you do, that you will never have a drink with Jack." And I felt cold and sick to the stomach.

I got up and went out. They thought that the drink had made me sick, but if I'd stayed there another minute I would have tackled Thomas; and I knew that I needed a clear head to tackle a bullock like him. I walked about a bit, and when I came in again Jack and Thomas were in the bar, and Jack had a glass before him.

"Come on, Joe, you old bounder," said Jack, "come and have a whisky-and-soda; it will straighten you up."

"What's that you're drinking, Jack?" I asked.

"Oh, don't be a fool!" said Jack. "One drink won't hurt me. Do you think I'm going on the booze? Have a soda and straighten up; we must make a start directly."

I remember we had two or three whiskies, and then suddenly I tackled Thomas, and Jack was holding me back, and laughing and swearing at me at the same time, and I had a tussle with him; and then I was suddenly calmer and sensible, and we were shaking hands all round, and Jack was talking about just one more spree for the sake of old times.

"A bit of a booze won't hurt me, Joe, you old fool," he said. "We'll have one more night of it, for the sake of Auld Lang Syne, and start at daylight in the morning. You go and see to the horses, it will straighten you up. Take the saddles off and hobble 'em out."

But I insisted on starting at once, and Jack promised he would. We were gloriously happy for an hour or so, and then I went to sleep.

When I woke it was late in the afternoon. I was very giddy and shaky; the girl brought me a whisky-and-soda, and that steadied me. Some more shearers had arrived, and Jack was playing cards with two of them on top of a cask in the bar. Thomas was dead drunk on the floor, or pretending to be so, and his wife was behind the bar. I went out to see to the horses; I found them in a bush yard at the back. The packhorse was rolling in the mud with the pack-saddle and saddle-bags on. One of the chaps helped me take off the saddles and put them in the harness-room behind the kitchen.

I'll pass over that night. It wouldn't be very edifying to the great, steady-living, sober majority, and the others, the ne'er-do-wells, the rovers, wrecks and failures, will understand only too well without being told—only too well, God help them!

When I woke in the morning I couldn't have touched a drink to save my life. I was fearfully shaky, and swimming about the head, but I put my head over a tub under the pump and got the girl to pump for a while, and then I drank a pint of tea and managed to keep it down, and felt better.

All through the last half of the night I'd kept saying, in a sort of drink nightmare, "I'll go for Peter M'Laughlan in the morning. I'll go for Peter as soon as I can stand!" and repeating Clara Barnes's words, "Ride for Peter if anything happens. Ride for Peter M'Laughlan."

There were drunken shearers, horsemen and swagmen sleeping all over the place, and in all sorts of odd positions; some on the veranda with their heads on their swags, one sitting back against the wall, and one on the broad of his back with his head on the bare boards and his mouth open.

There was another horse rolling in its saddle, and I took the saddle off. The horse belonged to an English University man.

I went in to see how Jack was. He was lying in the parlour on a little, worn-out, horse-hair sofa, that might have seen better days in some clean home in the woman-and-girl world. He had been drinking and playing cards till early that morning, and he looked awful—he looked as if he'd been boozing for a month.

"See what you've done!" he said, sitting up and glaring at me; then he said, "Bring me a whisky-and-soda, Joe, for God's sake!"

I got a whisky-and-soda from the girl and took it to him.

I talked to him for a while, and at last he said, "Well, go and get the horses and we'll start."

I got the horses ready and brought them round to the front, but by that time he'd had more drink, and he said he wanted to sleep before he started. Next he was playing cards with one of the chaps, and asked me to wait till he'd finished that game. I knew he'd keep promising and humbugging me till there was a row, so at last I got him aside and said:

"Look here, Jack, I'm going for Peter M'Laughlan——"

"Go to hell!" said Jack.

I put the other horses back in the yard, the saddles in the skillion, got on my horse and rode off. Thomas and the others asked me no questions, they took no notice. In a place like that a man could almost do anything, short of hanging himself, without anyone interfering or being surprised. And probably, if he did hang himself, they'd let him swing for a while to get a taste of it.

Comesomehow was about fifteen miles back on a track off the main road. I reckoned that I could find Peter and bring him on by the afternoon, and I rode hard, sick as I was. I was too sick to smoke.

As it happened, Peter had started early from his last camp and I caught him just as he was turning off into Comesomehow track.

"What's up, Joe?" he asked as I rode up to him—but he could see.

"Jack Barnes is on the booze at Thomas's," I said.

Peter just looked right through me. Then he turned his horse's head without a word, and rode back with me. And, after a while, he said, as if to himself:

"Poor Clara! Poor little lassie!"

By the time we reached the shanty it was well on in the afternoon. A fight was stopped in the first round and voices lowered when the chaps caught sight of us. As Peter walked into the bar one or two drunks straightened themselves and took off their hats with drunken sentiment.

"Where is Jack Barnes, Thomas?" asked Peter, quietly.

"He's in there if you want to see him," said Thomas, jerking his head towards the parlour.

We went in, and when Peter saw Jack lying there I noticed that swift, haunted look came into his eyes, as if he'd seen a ghost of the past.

He sat down by the sofa to wait until Jack woke. I thought as he sat there that his eyes were like a woman's for sympathy and like a dog's for faithfulness. I was very shaky.

Presently Thomas looked in. "Is there anything I can do for you,

M'Laughlan?" he asked in as civil a tone as he could get to.

"Yes," said Peter, "bring me a flask of your best whisky—your own, mind—and a glass."

"We shall need the whisky for him on the track, Joe," said Peter, when the flask came. "Get another glass and a bottle of soda; you want a nip." He poured out a drink for himself.

"The first thing we've got to do is to get him away; then I'll soon put him on his feet. But we'll let him sleep a while longer. I find I've got business near Solong, and I'm going down with you."

By and by Jack woke up and glared round, and when he caught sight of Peter he just reached for his hands and said, "Peter! Thank God you've come!" Then he said, "But I must have a drink first, Peter."

"All right, Jack, you shall have a drink," said Peter; and he gave him a stiff nobbler. It steadied Jack a bit.

"Now listen to me, Jack," said Peter. "How much money have you got left?"

"I—I can't think," said Jack. "I've got a cheque for twenty pounds here, sewn inside my shirt."

"Yes; but you drew thirty-six in three cheques. Where's the rest?"

"Thomas has ten," said Jack, "and the six—well, the six is gone. I was playing cards last night."

Peter stepped out into the bar.

"Look here, Thomas," he said quietly, "you've got a ten-pound cheque from Barnes."

"I know I have."

"Well, how much of it does he owe you?"

"The whole, and more."

"Do you mean to tell me that? He has only been here since yesterday morning."

"Yes; but he's been shoutin' all round. Look at all these chaps here."

"They only came yesterday afternoon," said Peter. "Here, you had best take this and give me the cheque;" and Peter laid a five-pound note on the bar. Thomas bucked at first, but in the end he handed over the cheque—he had had several warnings from the police. Then he suddenly lost all control over himself; he came round from behind the bar and faced Peter.

"Now, look here, you mongrel parson!" he said. "What the —— do you mean by coming into my bar and interfering with me. Who the —— are you anyway? A ——!" He used the worst oaths that were used in the bush. "Take off your —— coat!" he roared at last, shaping up to Peter.

Peter stepped back a pace and buttoned his coat and threw back his head.

"No need to take off my coat, Thomas," he said, "I am ready." He said it very quietly, but there was a danger-signal—a red light in his eyes. He was quiet-voiced but hard-knuckled, as some had reason to know.

Thomas balked like a bull at a spread umbrella. Jack lurched past me as I stood in the parlour door, but I caught him and held him back; and almost at the same moment a wretched old boozer that we called "Awful Example," who had been sitting huddled, a dirty bundle of rags and beard and hair, in the corner of the bar, struggled to his feet, staggered forward

434

and faced Thomas, looking once again like something that might have been a man. He snatched a thick glass bottle from the counter and held it by the neck in his right hand.

"Stand back, Thomas!" he shouted. "Lay a hand—lay a finger on Peter M'Laughlan, and I'll smash your head, as sure as there's a God above us and I'm a ruined man!"

Peter took "Awful" gently by the shoulders and sat him down. "You keep quiet, old man," he said; "nothing is going to happen." Thomas went round behind the bar muttering something about it not being worth his while to, etc.

"You go and get the horses ready, Joe," said Peter to me; "and you sit down, Jack, and keep quiet."

"He can get the horses," growled Thomas, from behind the bar, "but I'm damned if he gets the saddles. I've got them locked up, and I'll some-thing well keep them till Barnes is sober enough to pay me what he owes me."

Just then a tall, good-looking chap, with dark-blue eyes and a long, light-coloured moustache, stepped into the bar from the crowd on the veranda.

"What's all this, Thomas?" he asked.

"What's that got to do with you, Gentleman Once?" shouted Thomas.

"I think it's got something to do with me," said Gentleman Once. "Now, look here, Thomas; you can do pretty well what you like with us poor devils, and you know it, but we draw the line at Peter M'Laughlan. If you really itch for the thrashing you deserve you must tempt someone else to give it to you."

"What the —— are you talking about?" snorted Thomas. "You're drunk or ratty!"

"What's the trouble, M'Laughlan?" asked Gentleman Once, turning to Peter.

"No trouble at all, Gentleman Once," said Peter; "thank you all the same. I've managed worse men than our friend Thomas. Now, Thomas, don't you think it would pay you best to hand over the key of the harness-room and have done with this nonsense? I'm a patient man—a very patient man—but I've not always been so, and the old blood comes up sometimes, you know."

Thomas couldn't stand this sort of language, because he couldn't under-stand it. He threw the key on the bar and told us to clear out.

We were all three very quiet riding along the track that evening. Peter gave Jack a nip now and again from the flask, and before we turned in in camp he gave him what he called a soothing draught from a little medicine chest that he carried in his saddle-bag. Jack seemed to have got rid of his cough; he slept all night, and in the morning, after he'd drunk a pint of mutton-broth that Peter had made in one of the billies, he was all right—except that he was quiet and ashamed. I had never known him to be so quiet, and for such a length of time, since we were boys together. He had learned his own weakness; he'd lost all his cocksureness. I know now just exactly how he felt. He felt as if his sober year had been lost and he would have to live it all over again.

Peter didn't preach. He just jogged along and camped with us as if he were an ordinary, every-day mate. He yarned about all sorts of things. He could tell good yarns, and when he was fairly on you could listen to him all night. He seemed to have been nearly all over the world. Peter never preached except when he was asked to hold service in some bush pub, station-homestead or bush church. But in a case like ours he had a way of telling a little life story, with something in it that hit the young man he wanted to reform, and hit him hard. He'd generally begin quietly, when we were comfortable with our pipes in camp after tea, with "I once knew a young man——" or "That reminds me of a young fellow I knew——" and so on. You never knew when he was going to begin, or when he was going to hit you. In our last camp, before we reached Solong, he told two of his time-fuse yarns. I haven't time to tell them now, but one stuffed up my pipe for a while, and made Jack's hand tremble when he tried to light his. I'm glad it was too dark to see our faces. We lay a good while afterwards, rolled in our blankets, and couldn't get to sleep for thinking; but Peter seemed to fall asleep as soon as he turned in.

Next day he told Jack not to tell Clara that he'd come down with us. He said he wouldn't go right into Solong with us; he was going back along another road to stay a day or two with an old friend of his.

When we reached Solong we stopped on the river-bank just out of sight of Jack's house. Peter took the ten-pound cheque from his pocket and gave it to Jack. Jack hadn't seen Peter give the shanty-keeper the five-pound note.

"But I owed Thomas something," said Jack, staring. "However did you manage to get the cheque out of him?"

"Never mind, Jack, I managed," said Peter.

Jack sat silent for a while, then he began to breathe hard.

"I don't know what to say, Peter."

"Say nothing, Jack. Only promise me that you will give Clara the cheques as soon as you go home, and let her take care of the cash for a while."

"I will," said Jack.

Jack looked down at the ground for a while, then he lifted his head and looked Peter in the eyes.

"Peter," he said, "I can't speak. I'm ashamed to make a promise; I've broken so many. I'll try to thank you in a year's time from now."

"I ask for no promises," said Peter, and he held out his hand. Jack gripped it.

"Aren't you coming home with me, Joe?" he asked.

"No," I said; "I'll go into town. See you in the morning."

Jack rode on. When he got along a piece Peter left his horse and moved up to the head of the lane to watch Jack, and I followed. As Jack neared the cottage we saw a little figure in a cloak run out to the front gate. She had heard the horses and the jingle of the camp-ware on the pack-saddle. We saw Jack jump down and take her in his arms. I looked at Peter, and as he watched them, something, that might have been a strange look of the old days, came into his eyes.

He shook hands with me. "Good-bye, Joe."

He rode across the river again. He took the track that ran along the foot of the spurs by the river, and up over a gap in the curve of blue hills, and down and out west towards the Big Scrubs. And as he rounded the last spur, with his packhorse trotting after him, I thought he must have felt very lonely. And I felt lonely too.

"BUCKOLTS' GATE"

PROLOGUE

Old Abel Albury had a genius for getting the bull by the tail with a tight grip and holding on with both hands, and an obstinacy born of ignorance—and not necessarily for the sake of self-preservation or selfishness—while all the time the bull might be, so to speak, rooting up life-long friendships and neighbourly relations, and upsetting domestic customs and traditions with his horns.

Yes, Uncle Abel was always grasping the wrong end of things, and sticking to it with that human mulishness which is often stronger, and more often wearies and breaks down the opposition than an intelligent man's arguments. He was—or professed to be, the family said—unable for a long time to distinguish between his two grand-nephews, one of whom was short and fat, while the other was tall and thin, the only points of resemblance between them being that each possessed the old family nose and eyes. When they were boys he used to lay the strap about one in mistake for the other. They had a saying that Uncle Abel saw with ten squinting eyes.

Also, he could never—or would not, as the family said—remember names. He referred to Mrs Porter, a thin, haggard selector's wife, as "Mrs Stout" and he balanced matters by calling Mrs Southwick "Mrs Porterwicket"—when he didn't address her as "Mrs What's-the-woman's-name"—and he succeeded in deeply offending both ladies.

Uncle Abel was Mrs Carey's uncle. Down at the lower end of Carey's selection at Rocky Rises, in the extreme corner of the lower or outer paddock, were sliprails opening into the main road, which ran down along the sidling, round the foot of a spur from ridge, and out west. These sliprails were called "The Lower Sliprails" by the family, and it occurred to Uncle Abel to refer to them as "Buckolts' Gate," for no other reason apparently than that Buckolts' farm lay in that direction. The farm was about a mile farther on, on the other side of the creek, and the gate leading to it from the main road was round the spur, out of sight of Carey's selection. It is quite possible that Uncle Abel reasoned the thing out for days, for of such material are some human brains. Sliprails, or a slip-panel, is a panel of fencing of which the rails are made to be slipped out of the mortise holes in the posts so as to give passage to horses, vehicles and cattle. I suppose Abel called it a gate, because he was always going to hang a proper gate there some day. The family were unaware of his new name for the Lower Sliprails, and after he had, on one or two occasions, informed the boys that they would find a missing cow or horse at the Buckolts' Gate, and they had found it calmly camped at the Lower Sliprails, and after he had made several appointments to meet parties at Buckolts' Gate, and had been found leaning obstinately on the fence by the Lower Sliprails with no explanation to offer other than that he *was* waiting at Buckolts' Gate, they began to fear that he was becoming weak in his mind.

Frederick McCubbin (1855-1917) *The Lost Child*
114.3 x 72.4 cm   Oil on canvas   Felton Bequest 1940
Reproduced with the kind permission of the National Gallery Of Victoria, Melbourne

Frederick McCubbin (1855-1917)   *Down on His Luck* (1889)
114.3 x 152.4 cm   Canvas
Reproduced with the kind permission of The Western Australian Art Gallery

ACT I

It was New Year's Eve at Rocky Rises. There was no need for fireworks nor bonfires, for the bush-fires were out all along the ranges to the east, and, as night came on, lines and curves of lights—clear lights, white lights, and, in the near distance, red lights and smoky lights—marked the sidlings and ridges of a western spur of the Blue Mountain Range, and seemed suspended against a dark sky, for the stars and the loom of the hills were hidden by smoke and drought haze.

There was a dance at Careys'. Old Carey was a cheerful, broad-minded bushman, haunted at times by the memories of old days, when he was the beau of the bush balls, and so when he built his new slab-and-bark barn he had it properly floored with hard-wood, and the floor well-faced "to give the young people a show when they wanted a dance," he said. The floor had a spring in it, and bush boys and girls often rode twenty miles and more to dance on that floor. The girls said it was a lovely floor.

On this occasion Carey had stacked his wheat outside until after the New Year. Spring-carts, and men and girls on horseback came in from miles round. "Sperm" candles had been cut up and thrown on the floor during the afternoon, and rubbed over by feet cased tightly in 'lastic-sides; and hoops were hung horizontally from the tie-beams, with candles stuck round them. There were fresh-faced girls, and sweet, freckled-faced girls, and jolly girls, and shy girls —all sorts of girls except sulky, "toney" girls—and lanky chaps, most of them sawney, and weird, whiskered agriculturists, who watched the dancers with old, old time-worn smiles, or stood, or sat on their heels yarning, with their pipes, outside, where two boilers were slung over a log-fire to boil water for tea; and there were leathery women, with complexions like dried apples, who gossiped—for the first time in months perhaps—and watched the young people, and thought at times, no doubt, of other days—of other days when they were girls. (And not so far distant either, in some cases, for women dry quickly in the bush.)

And there were one or two old soldiers and their wives, whose eyes glistened when Jim Bullock played "The Girl I Left Behind Me."

Jim Bullock was there with his concertina. He sat on a stool in front of a bench, on which was a beer-keg, piles of teacups and saucers, several big tin teapots, and plates of sandwiches, sponge-cakes, and tarts. Jim sat in his shirt-sleeves, with his flat-brimmed, wire-bound, "hard-hitter" hat on, slanting over his weaker eye. He held one leg loosely and the other rigid, with the concertina on his knee, and swanked away at the instrument by the hour, staring straight in front of him with the expression of a cod-fish, and never moving a muscle except the muscles of his great hairy arms and big chapped and sun-blotched hands; while chaps in tight "larstins" (elastic-side boots), slop suits of black, bound with braid, and with coats too short in the neck and arms, and trousers bell-mouthed at the bottoms, and some with paper collars, narrow red ribbon ties, or scarfs through walnut shells, held their partners rigidly, and went round the room with their eyes—most of them—cocked at the rafters in semi-idiotic ecstasy.

But there was tall, graceful, pink-and-white Bertha Buckolt, blue-eyed and blue-and-black haired, and little Mary Carey with the kind, grey eyes and red-gold hair; there was Mary's wild brother Jim, with curly black hair and blue eyes and dimples of innocence; and there was Harry Dale, the drover,

441

Jim's shearing and droving mate, a tall, good-looking, brown-eyed and brown-haired young fellow, a "better-class" bushman and the best dancer in the district. Uncle Abel usurped the position of M.C., and roared "Now then! take yer partners!" and bawled instructions and interrupted and tangled up the dancers, until they got used to taking no notice of his bull voice. Mary Carey was too shy—because she loved him, and secretly and fondly hoped and doubted that he cared for her—to be seen dancing more than once with Harry Dale, so he shared Bertha Buckolt, the best girl dancer there, with Jim Carey, who danced with his sister when Harry was dancing with Bertha Buckolt, and who seemed, for some reason best known to himself, to be perfectly satisfied with the arrangement. Poor little Mary began to fret presently, and feel a little jealous of Bertha, her old schoolmate. She was little and couldn't dance like Bertha, and she couldn't help noticing how well Bertha looked to-night, and what a well-matched pair she and Harry made; and so, when twelve o'clock came and they all went outside to watch the Old Year out and the New Year in—with a big bonfire on the distant ridge where the grass fires had reached a stretch of dry scrub—and to join hands all round and sing "Auld Lang Syne," little Mary was not to be found, for she was sitting on a log round behind the cow-yard, crying softly to herself.

And when about three o'clock they all started home, Mary gave Bertha her cheek to kiss instead of her mouth, and that hurt Bertha, who had *her* cry riding home, to the astonishment and irritation of her brother Jack, who rode home with her.

But when they were all gone Mary was missing again and when her mother called her, and, after a pause, the voice of Harry Dale said, respectfully, in the darkness, "She's here, Mrs Carey, she's all right," the two were discovered sitting on a convenient log of the wood-heap, with an awkward and over-acted interval of log between them.

Old Carey liked Harry Dale, and seemed very well satisfied with the way things appeared to be going. He pressed Harry to stay at the selection over-night. "The missus will make you a shake-down on the floor," he said. Harry had no appointments, and stayed cheerfully, and old Carey, having had a whisky or two, insisted on Mary making the shake-down, and the old folks winked at each other behind the young folks' backs to see how poor little Mary spread a spare mattress, with red-hot, averted face, and found an extra pillow and a spare pair of ironed sheets for the shake-down.

At sunrise she stole out to milk the cows, which was her regular duty; there was no other way out from her room than through the dining-room, where Harry lay on his back, with his arms folded, resting peacefully. He seemed sound asleep and safe for a good two hours, so she ventured. As she passed out she paused a moment looking down on him with all the lovelight in her eyes, and, obeying a sudden impulse, she stooped softly and touched his forehead with her lips, then she slipped out. Harry stretched, opened his eyes, winked solemnly at the ceiling, and then, after a decent interval, he got up, dressed, and went out to help her to milk.

Harry Dale and Jim Carey were going out to take charge of a mob of bullocks going north-west, away up in Queensland, and as they had lost a day and night to be at the dance, they decided to start in the cool of the evening and travel all night. Mary walked from the homestead to the Lower Sliprails between her brother, who rode—because he was her brother—and led a packhorse on the other side, and Harry, who walked and led his horse— because he was her sweetheart, avowed only since last night.

There were thunderstorms about, and Mary had repented sufficiently with regard to Bertha Buckolt to wear on her shoulders a cape which Bertha had left behind her last night.

When they reached the Lower Sliprails Jim said he'd go on and that Harry needn't hurry: he stooped over his horse's neck, kissed his sister, promised to keep away from the drink, not to touch a card, and to leave off fighting, and rode on. And when he rounded the Spur he saw a tall, graceful figure slipping through the trees from the creek towards Buckolts' Gate.

Then came the critical time at the Lower Sliprails. The shadows from the setting sun lengthened quickly on the sidling, and then the sun slipped out of sight over a "saddle" in the ridges, and all was soon dusk save the sunlit peaks of the Blue Mountains away to the east over the sweeps of blue-grey bush.

"Ah, well! Mary," said Harry, "I must make a start now."

"You'll—you'll look after Jim, won't you, Harry?" said Mary.

"I will, Mary, for your sake."

Her mouth began to twitch, her chin to tremble, and her eyes brimmed suddenly.

"You must cheer up, Mary," he said with her in his arms. "I'll be back before you know where you are, and then we'll be married right off at once and settle down for life."

She smiled bravely.

"Good-bye, Mary!"

"Good-bye, Harry!"

He led his horse through the rails and lifted them, with trembling hands, and shot them home. Another kiss across the top rail and he got on his horse. She mounted the lower rail, and he brought his horse close alongside the fence and stooped to kiss her again.

"Cheer up, Mary!" he said. "I'll tell you what I'll do—when I come back I'll whistle when I reach the Spur and you be here to let the sliprails down for me. I'll time myself to get here about sundown. I'll whistle 'Willie Riley,' so you'll know it's me. Good-bye, little girl! I must go now. Don't fret—the time will soon go by."

He turned, swung his horse, and rode slowly down the track, turning now and again to wave his hand to her, with a farewell flourish of his hat as he rounded the Spur. His track, five hundred miles, or perhaps, a thousand, into the great north-west; his time, six months, or perhaps a year. Hers a hundred yards or so back to the dusty, dreary drudgery of selection life.

The daylight faded into starlight, the sidlings grew very dim, and a faint white figure blurred against the bars of the slip-panel.

ACT II

It was the last day of the threshing—shortly after New Year—at Rocky Rises. The green boughs, which had been lashed to the veranda-posts on Christmas Eve, had withered and been used for firewood. The travelling steamer had gone with its gang of men, and the family sat down to tea, the men tired with hard work and heat, and with prickly heat and irritating wheaten chaff and dust under their clothes—and with smut (for the crop had been a smutty one) "up their brains" as Uncle Abel said—the women worn out with cooking for a big gang of shearers.

Good-humoured Aunt Emma—who was Uncle Abel's niece—recovered first, and started the conversation. There were one or two neighbours' wives who had lent crockery and had come over to help with the cooking in their turns. Jim Carey's name came up incidentally, but was quickly dropped, for ill reports of Jim had come home. Then Aunt Emma mentioned Harry Dale, and glanced meaningly at Mary, whose face flamed as she bent over her plate.

"Never mind, Mary," said Aunt Emma, "it's nothing to be ashamed of. We were all girls once. There's many a girl would jump at Harry."

"Who says I'm ashamed?" said Mary, straightening up indignantly.

"Don't tease her, Emma," said Mrs Carey, mildly.

"I'll tell yer what," said young Tom Carey, frankly, "Mary got a letter from him to-day. I seen her reading it behind the house."

Mary's face flamed again and went down over her plate.

"Mary," said her mother, with sudden interest, "did Harry say anything of Jim?"

"No, mother," said Mary. "And that's why I didn't tell you about the letter."

There was a pause. Then Tommy said, with that delightful tact which usually characterizes young Tommies:

"Well, Mary needn't be so cocky about Harry Dale, anyhow. I seen him New Year's Eve when we had the dance. I seen him after the dance liftin' Bertha Buckolt onter her horse in the dark—as if she couldn't get on herself —she's big enough. I seen him lift her on, an' he took her right up an' lifted her right inter the saddle, 'stead of holdin' his hand for her to tread on like that new-chum jackeroo we had. An', what's more, I seen him hug her an' give her a kiss before he lifted her on. He told her he was as good as her brother."

"What did he mean by that, Tommy?" asked Mrs Porter, to break an awkward pause.

"How'm I ter know what he means?" said Tommy, politely.

"And, Tommy, I seen Harry Dale give young Tommy Carey, a lick with a strap the day before New Year's Eve for throwing his sister's cat into the dam," said Aunt Emma, coming to poor Mary's rescue. "Never mind, Mary, my dear, he said good-bye to you last."

"No, *he didn't!*" roared Uncle Abel.

They were used to Uncle Abel's sudden bellowing, but it startled them this time.

"Why, Uncle Abel," cried both Aunt Emma and Mrs Carey, "whatever do you mean?"

"What I means is that I ain't a-goin' to have the feelin's of a niece of mine trifled with. What I means is that I seen Harry Dale with Bertha Buckolt on New Year's night after he left here. That's what I means——"

"Don't speak so loud, Abel, we're not deaf," interrupted Carey, as Mary started up white-faced. "What do you want to always shout for?"

"I speak loud because I want people to hear me!" roared Uncle Abel, turning on him.

"Go on, Uncle Abel," said Mary, "tell me what you mean."

"I mean," said Uncle Abel, lowering his voice a little, "that I seen Harry Dale and Bertha Buckolt at Buckolts' Gate that night—I seen it all——"

"*At Buckolts'* Gate!" cried Mary.

"*Yes!* at Buckolts' Gate! Ain't I speakin' loud enough?"

"And where were you?"

"Never mind wheers I was. I was comin' home along the ridges, and I seen them. I seen them say good-bye; I seen them hug an' kiss——"

"Uncle Abel!" exclaimed Aunt Emma.

"It's no use Uncle Abelin' me. What I sez I sez. I ain't a-goin' to have a niece of mine bungfoodled——"

"Uncle Abel," cried Mary, staring at him wild-eyed, "do be careful what you say. You must have made a mistake. Are you sure it was Bertha and Harry?"

"Am I sure my head's on me neck?" roared Uncle Abel. "Would I see 'em if I didn't see 'em? I tell you——"

"Now wait a moment, Uncle Abel," interrupted Mary, with dangerous calmness. "Listen to me. Harry Dale and I are engaged to be married, and——"

"Have you got the writin's!" shouted Uncle Abel.

"The what?" said Mary.

"The writin's."

"No, of course not."

"Then that's where you are," said Uncle Abel, triumphantly. "If you had the writin's you could sue him for breach of contract."

Uncle Abel, who couldn't read, had no faith whatever in verbal agreements (he wouldn't sign one, he said), all others he referred to as "writings."

"Now, listen to me, Uncle Abel," said Mary, trembling now, "Are you sure you saw Harry Dale and Bertha Buckolt at Buckolts' Gate after he left here that night?"

"Yes. An' what's more, I seen young Tommy there ridin' on his pony along by the Spur a little while after, an' he muster seen them too, if he's got a tongue."

Mary turned quickly to her brother.

"Well, all I can say," said Tommy, quietened now, "is that I seen *her* at Buckolts' Gate that night. I was comin' home from Two-Mile Flat, and I met Jim with his packhorse about a mile the other side of Buckolts', and while we was talkin' Harry Dale caught up, so I jist said 'So-long' an' left 'em. And when I got to Buckolts' Gate I seen Bertha Buckolt. She was standin' under a tree, and she looked as if she was cryin'——"

But Mary got her bonnet and started out.

"Where are you going to, Mary?" asked her mother, starting up nervously.

"I'm going across to Buckolts' to find out the truth," said Mary, and she went out.

"Better let her go, Lizzie," said Aunt Emma, detaining her sister. "You've done it now, Uncle Abel."

"Well, why didn't she get the writin's?" retorted Uncle Abel.

Half-way to Buckolts' Mary met Bertha Buckolt herself, coming over to the selection for the first time since the night of the party. Bertha started forward to kiss Mary, but stopped short as Mary stood stock-still and faced her, with her hands behind her back.

"Why! whatever is the matter, Mary?" exclaimed Bertha.

"You know very well, Bertha."

"Why! Whatever do you mean? What have I done?"

"What haven't you done? You've—you've broken my heart."

"Good gracious me! Whatever are you talking about? Tell me what it is Mary?"

"You met him at your gate that night?"

"I know I did."

"Oh, Bertha! How could you be so mean and deceitful?"

"Mean and deceitful! What do you mean by that? Whatever are you talking about? I suppose I've got as good a right to meet him as anyone else."

"No, you haven't," retorted Mary, "you're only stringing him on. You only did it to spite me. You helped him to deceive me. You ought to be ashamed to look me in the face."

"Good gracious! Whatever are you talking about? Ain't I good enough for him? I ought to be, God knows! I suppose he can marry who he likes, and if I'm poor fool enough to love him and marry him, what then? Mary, you ought to be the last to speak—speak to—to me like that."

"Yes. He can marry all the girls in the country for all I care. I never want to see either him or you any more. You're a cruel, deceitful, brazen-faced hussy, and he's a heartless, deceiving blackguard."

"Mary! I believe you're mad," said Bertha, firmly. "How dare you speak to me like that! And as for him being a blackguard. Why, you ought to be the last in the world to say such a thing; you ought to be the last to say a word against him. Why, I don't believe you ever cared a rap for him in spite of all your pretence. He could go to the devil for all you cared."

"That's enough, Bertha Buckolt!" cried Mary. "*You*—you! Why, you're a barefaced girl, that's what you are! I don't want to see your brazen face again." With that she turned and stumbled blindly in the direction of home.

"Send back my cape," cried Bertha as she too turned away.

Mary walked wildly home and fled to her room and locked the door. Bertha did likewise.

Mary let Aunt Emma in after a while, ceased sobbing and allowed herself to be comforted a little. Next morning she was out milking at the usual time, but there were dark hollows under her eyes, and her little face was white and set. After breakfast she rolled the cape up very tight in a brown-paper parcel, addressed it severely to—

MISS BERTHA BUCKOLT,
Eurunderee Creek

and sent it home by one of the school-children.

She wrote to Harry Dale and told him that she knew all about it (not stating what), but she forgave him and hoped he'd be happy. She never wanted to see his face again, and enclosed his portrait.

Harry, who was as true and straight as a bushman could be, puzzled it out and decided that some one of his old love affairs must have come to Mary's ears, and wrote demanding an explanation.

She never answered that letter.

ACT III

It was Christmas Day at Rocky Rises. The plum puddings had been made, as usual, weeks beforehand, and hung in rags to the tie-beams and taken down and boiled again. Poultry had been killed and plucked and cooked, and all the toil had been gone through, and every preparation made for a red-hot dinner on a blazing hot day—and for no other reason than that our great-grandmothers used to do it in a cold climate at Christmas-times that came in mid-winter. Merry men hadn't gone forth to the wood to gather in the mistletoe (if they ever did in England, in the olden days, instead of sending shivering, wretched vassals in rags to do it); but Uncle Abel had gone gloomily up the ridge on Christmas Eve, with an axe on his shoulder (and Tommy unwillingly in tow, scowling and making faces behind his back), and had cut young pines and dragged them home and lashed them firmly to the veranda-posts, which was the custom out there.

There was little goodwill or peace between the three or four farms round Rocky Rises that Christmas Day, and Uncle Abel had been the cause of most of the ill-feeling, though they didn't know, and he was least aware of it of any.

It all came about in this way.

Shortly after last New Year Ryan's bull had broken loose and gone astray for two days and nights, breaking into neighbours' paddocks and filling himself with hay and damaging other bulls, and making love by night and hiding in the scrub all day. On the second night he broke through and jumped over Reid's fences, and destroyed about an acre of grape-vines and adulterated Reid's stock, besides interfering with certain heifers which were not of a marriageable age. There was a £5 penalty on a stray bull. Reid impounded the bull and claimed heavy damages. Ryan, a small selector of little account, was always pulling some neighbour to court when he wasn't being "pulled" himself, so he went to court over this case.

Now, it appears that the bull, on his holiday, had spent a part of the first night in Carey's lower paddock, and Uncle Abel (who was out mooching about the bush at all hours, "havin' a look at some timber" or some "indercations" [of gold], or on some mysterious business or fad, the mystery of which was of his own making)—Uncle Abel saw the bull in the paddock at daylight and turned it out the sliprails, and talked about it afterwards, referring to the sliprails as "Buckolts' Gate," of course, and spoke mysteriously of the case, and put on an appearance of great importance, and allowed people to get an idea that he knew a lot if he only liked to speak; and finally he got himself "brought up" as a witness for Ryan.

He had a lot of beer in town before he went to the courthouse. All he knew would have been of no use to either party, but he swore that he had seen Ryan's bull inside Buckolts' Gate at daylight (on the day which wasn't in question) and had turned him out. Uncle Abel mixed up the court a good deal, and roared like the bull, and became more obstinate the more

447

he was cross-examined, and narrowly escaped being committed for contempt of court.

Ryan, who had a high opinion of the breed of his bull, got an idea that the Buckolts had enticed or driven the bull into their paddock for stock-raising purposes, instead of borrowing it honestly or offering to pay for the use of it. Then Ryan wanted to know why Abel had driven his bull out of Buckolts' Gate, and the Buckolts wanted to know what business Abel Albury had to drive Ryan's bull out of their paddock, if the bull had really ever been there. And so it went on till Rocky Rises was ripe for a tragedy.

The breach between the Careys and the Buckolts was widened, the quarrel between Ryan and Reid intensified. Ryan got a down on the Careys because he reckoned that Uncle Abel had deliberately spoilt his case with his evidence; and the Reids and Careys were no longer on speaking terms, because nothing would convince old Reid that Abel hadn't tried to prove that Ryan's bull had never been in Reid's paddock at all.

Well, it was Christmas Day, and the Carey family and Aunt Emma sat down to dinner. Jim was present, having arrived overnight, with no money, as usual, and suffering a recovery. The elder brother, Bob (who had a selection up-country), and his wife were there. Mrs Carey moved round with watchful eyes and jealous ears, lest there should be a word or a look which might hurt the feelings of her wild son—for of such are mothers.

Dinner went on very moodily, in spite of Aunt Emma, until at last Jim spoke—almost for the first time, save for a long-whispered and, on his part, repentant conversation with his mother.

"Look here, Mary!" said Jim. "What did you throw Harry Dale over for?"

"Don't ask me, Jim."

"Rot! What did he do to you? I'm your brother" (with a glance at Bob), "and I ought to know."

"Well, then, ask Bertha Buckolt. She saw him last."

"What!" cried Jim.

"Hold your tongue, Jim! You'll make her cry," said Aunt Emma.

"Well, what's it all about, anyway?" demanded Jim. "All I know is that Mary wrote to Harry and threw him over, and he ain't been the same man since. He swears he'll never come near the district again."

"Tell Jim, Aunt Emma," said Mary. And Aunt Emma started to tell the story as far as she knew.

"Saw her at Buckolts' sliprails!" cried Jim, starting up. "Well, he couldn't have had time to more than say good-bye to her, for I was with her there myself, and Harry caught up to me within a mile of the gate—and I rode pretty fast."

"He had a jolly long good-bye with her," shouted Uncle Abel. "Look here, Jim! I ain't goin' to stand by and see a nephew of mine bungfoodled by no girl; an', I tell you I seen 'em huggin' and kissin' and canoodlin' for half an hour at Buckolts' Gate!"

"It's a—a—— Look here, Uncle Abel, be careful what you say. You've got the bull by the tail again, that's what it is!" Jim's face grew whiter—

and it had been white enough on account of the drink. "How did you know it was them? You're always mistaking people. It might have been someone else."

"I know Harry Dale on horseback two miles off!" roared Uncle Abel. "And I knowed her by her cape."

It was Mary's turn to gasp and stare at Uncle Abel.

"Uncle Abel," she managed to say, "Uncle Abel! Wasn't it at our Lower Sliprails you saw them and not Buckolts' Gate?"

"Well!" bellowed Uncle Abel. "You might call 'em the 'Lower Sliprails,' but I calls 'em Buckolts' Gate! They lead to'rds Buckolts', don't they? Hey? Them other sliprails"—jerking his arms in the direction of the upper paddock—"them theer other sliprails that leads outer Reid's lane I calls Reid's Sliprails. I don't know nothing about no upper or lower, or easter or wester, or any other la-di-dah names you like to call 'em."

"Oh, uncle," cried Mary, trembling like a leaf, "why didn't you explain this before? Why didn't you tell us?"

"What cause have I got to tell any of you everything I sez or does or thinks? It 'ud take me all me time. Ain't you got any more brains than Ryan's bull, any of you? Hey!—You've got heads, but so has cabbages. Explain! Why, if the world wasn't stuffed so full of jumped-up fools there'd be never no need for explainin'."

Mary left the table.

"What is it, Mary?" cried Aunt Emma.

"I'm going across to Bertha," said Mary, putting on her hat with trembling hands. "It was me Uncle Abel saw. I had Bertha's cape on that night."

"Oh, Uncle Abel," cried Aunt Emma, "whatever have you done?"

"Well," said Uncle Abel, "why didn't she get the writin's as I told her? It's to be hoped she won't make such a fool of herself next time."

Half an hour later, or thereabouts, Mary sat on Bertha Buckolt's bed, with Bertha beside her and Bertha's arm round her, and they were crying and laughing by turns.

"But—but—why didn't you *tell* me it was Jim?" said Mary.

"Why didn't you tell me it was Harry, Mary?" asked Bertha. "It would have saved all this year of misery.

"I didn't see Harry Dale at all that night," said Bertha. "I was—I was crying when Jim left me, and when Harry came along I slipped behind a tree until he was past. And now, look here, Mary, I can't marry Jim until he steadies down, but I'll give him another chance. But, Mary, I'd sooner lose him than you."

Bertha walked home with Mary, and during the afternoon she took Jim aside and said:

"Look here, Jim, I'll give you another chance—for a year. Now I want you to ride into town and send a telegram to Harry Dale. How long would it take him to get here?"

"He couldn't get here before New Year," said Jim.

"That will do," said Bertha, and Jim went to catch his horse.

Next day Harry's reply came: "Coming."

ACT IV

New Year's Eve. The dance was at Buckolts' this year, but Bertha didn't dance much; she was down by the gate most of the time with little Mary Carey, waiting, and watching the long, white road, and listening for horses' feet, and disappointed often as other horsemen rode by or turned up to the farm.

And in the hot sunrise that morning, within a hundred miles of Rocky Rises, a tired, dusty drover camped in the edge of a scrub, boiled his quart-pot, broiled a piece of mutton on the coals, and lay down on the sand to rest an hour or so before pushing on to a cattle station he knew to try and borrow fresh horses. He had ridden all night.

Old Buckbolt and Carey and Reid smoked socially under the grape-vines, with bottles of whisky and glasses, and nudged each other and coughed when they wanted to laugh at Old Abel Albury, who was, for about the first time in his life, condescending to explain. He was explaining to them what thund'rin' fools they had been.

Later on they sent a boy on horseback with a bottle of whisky and a message to Ryan, who turned up in time to see the New Year in with them and contradict certain slanders concerning the breed of his bull.

Meanwhile Bertha comforted Mary, and at last persuaded her to go home. "He's sure to be here to-morrow, Mary," she said, "and you need to look fresh and happy."

But Mary didn't sleep that night; she was up before daylight, had the kettle on and some chops ready to fry, and at daybreak she was down by the sliprails again. She was turning away for the second time when she heard a clear whistle round the Spur—then the tune of "Willie Riley," and the hobble-chains and camp-ware on the packhorse jingling to the tune.

She pulled out the rails with eager, trembling hands and leaned against the tree.

An hour later a tired drover lay on his back, in his ragged, track-worn clothes and dusty leggings, on Mary's own little bed in the skillion off the living-room, and rested. Mary bustled round getting breakfast ready, and singing softly to herself; once she slipped in, bent over Harry and kissed him gently on the lips, and ran out as he stirred.

"Why, who's that?" exclaimed Uncle Abel, poking round early and catching a glimpse of Harry through the open door.

"It's only Harry, Uncle Abel," said Mary.

Uncle Abel peered in again to make sure.

"Well, be sure you git the writin's this time," he said.

The Henry Lawson Memorial at Eurunderee — on the site of the 'old home' (see page 451) — which was unveiled by the poet's widow, Bertha Lawson, in 1949. Incorporated into the memorial are the stone chimney and fireplace, which are all that remained of the original building. It is possible that round the fireplace in the kitchen the family listened to the tales told by members of the family about one another — a story such as 'Buckholt's Gate' may well have been first heard here.

THE LAST REVIEW

Turn the light down, nurse, and leave me, while I hold my
    last review,
For the Bush is slipping from me, and the town is going too.
Draw the blinds. The streets are lighted, and I hear the tramp
    of feet—
And I'm weary, very weary, of the Faces in the Street.

In the dens of Grind and Heartbreak, in the streets of Never-Rest,
I have lost the scent and colour and the music of the West:
I would fain recall old faces with the memories they bring—
Where are Bill and Jim and Mary and the Songs They Used
    to Sing?

They are coming! They are coming! they are passing through the
    room
With the smell of gum-leaves burning, and the scent of wattle-bloom!
And behind them in the timber, after dust and heat and toil,
Others sit beside the camp-fire yarning While the Billies Boil.

In the Gap above the ridges there's a flash and there's a glow—
Swiftly down the scrub-clad sidling come the Lights of Cobb
    and Co.,
Red face from the box-seat beaming—oh, how plain those faces come!
From his Golden Hole 'tis Peter McIntosh who's going home.

Dusty patch in desolation, bare slab walls and earthen floor,
And a blinding drought that blazes from horizon to the door:
Milkless tea and ration sugar, damper, junk, and pumpkin mash—
And a Day on our Selection passes by me in a flash.

Rush of big, wild-eyed, store bullocks while the sheep crawl
    hopelessly,
And the loaded wool-teams rolling, lurching on like ships at sea—
With his whip across his shoulder (and the wind just now abeam)
There goes Jimmy Nowlett, ploughing through the dust beside
    his team!

Sunrise on the olden diggings! (Oh, what life and hopes are here.)
From a hundred pointing-forges comes a tinkle, tinkle, clear—
Strings of drays with wash to puddle, clack of countless windlass-
    boles,
Here and there the red flag flying, flying over golden holes.

Picturesque, unspoiled, romantic, chivalrous, and brave and free,
Clean in living, true in mateship—reckless generosity—
Mates are buried here as comrades who on fields of battle fall;
And the dreams—the aching, hoping lover-hearts beneath it all!

Rough-built theatres and stages where the world's best actors trod;
Singers bringing reckless rovers nearer boyhood, home, and God;
Paid in laughter, tears, and nuggets in the drama fortune plays—
'Tis the palmy days of Gulgong—Gulgong in the Roaring Days.

Pass the same old scenes before me—and again my heart will ache—
There the Drover's Wife sits watching (not as Eve did) for a snake.
And I see the drear deserted goldfields when the night is late,
And the stony face of Mason, watching by his Father's Mate.

And I see my Haggard Women plainly as they were in life;
'Tis the form of Mrs Spicer and her friend, Joe Wilson's wife,
Sitting hand in hand, Past Carin'—not a sigh and not a moan—
Staring steadily before them, while the slow tears trickle down.

It was No Place for a Woman where the women worked like men;
From the Bush and Jones's Alley come their haunting forms again.
Let this also be recorded when I've answered to the roll,
That I pitied haggard women—wrote for them with all my soul.

Narrow bedroom in the city in the hard days that are dead,
An alarm clock on the table, and a pale boy on the bed:
Arvie Aspinall's Alarm Clock with its harsh and startling call
Never more shall break his slumbers—*I* was Arvie Aspinall.

Maoriland and cynic Steelman, stiff-lipped spieler, battler-through
(Kept a wife and child in comfort, but of course they never knew—
Thought he was an honest bagman). Well, old man, you needn't
    hug—
Sentimental? you of all men!—Steelman, oh! I *was* a mug!

Ghostly lines of scrub at daybreak—dusty daybreak in the drought—
See a lonely swagman tramping on the track to Further Out:
Like a shade the form of Mitchell, nose-bag full and bluey up,
And between the swag and shoulders lolls his foolish cattle-pup.

Kindly cynic, sad comedian! Mitchell, when you've left the Track,
And have shed your load of sorrow as we slipped our swags Out
    Back,
We shall have a yarn together in the land of Rest Awhile—
And across his ragged shoulder Mitchell smiles his quiet smile.

Shearing-sheds, and tracks, and shanties—girls that wait at home-
    stead gates—
Camps and stern-eyed Union leaders, and Joe Wilson and his Mates,
True and straight; and to my fancy, each one as he passes through
Deftly down upon the table slips a dusty "note" or two.

So at last the end has found me (end of all the human push),
And again in silence round me come my Children of the Bush!
Listen, who are young, and let them—if in late and bitter days
Reckless lines I wrote—forget them; there is little there to praise.

I was human, very human; and if in the days misspent
I have injured man or woman, it was done without intent.
If at times I blundered blindly—bitter heart and aching brow—
If I wrote a line unkindly—I am sorry for it now.

Days in London like a nightmare—dreams of foreign lands and sea—
Dreams—for far Australia only is a real land to me.
Tell the Bushmen to Australia and each other to be true—
Tell the boys to stick together! I have held my Last Review.

THE BUSH FIRE

On the runs to the west of the Dingo Scrub there was drought,
    and ruin, and death,
And the sandstorm came from the dread north-east with the blast
    of a furnace-breath;
Till at last one day, at the fierce sunrise, a boundary-rider woke,
And saw in the place of the distant haze a curtain of light-blue
    smoke.

There is saddling-up by the cocky's hut, and out in the station yard,
And away to the north, north-east, north-west, the bushmen are
    riding hard.
The pickets are out, and many a scout, and many a mulga wire,
While Bill and Jim, their faces grim, are riding to meet the fire.

It roars for days in the trackless scrub, and across, where the
    ground seems clear,
With a crackle and rush, like the hissing of snakes, the fire draws
    near and near;
Till at last, exhausted by sleeplessness, and the terrible toil and heat,
The squatter is crying, "My God! the wool!" and the farmer, "My
    God! the wheat!"

But there comes a drunkard (who reels as he rides) with news
    from the roadside pub:—
"Pat Murphy—the cocky—cut off by the fire!—way back in the
    Dingo Scrub!
Let the wheat and the woolshed go to ——" Well, they do as
    each great heart bids;
They are riding a race for the Dingo Scrub—for Pat and his
    wife and kids.

And who are leading the race with Death? An ill-matched three,
    you'll allow;
Flash Jim, the Breaker, and Boozing Bill (who is riding steadily now),
And Constable Dunn, of the Mounted Police, on the grey between
    the two
(He wants Flash Jim, but that job can wait till they get the
    Murphys through).

As they strike the track through the blazing scrub, the trooper
    is heard to shout:
"We'll take them on to the Two-mile Tank, if we cannot bring
    them out!"
A half-mile more, and the rest rein back, retreating, half-choked,
    half-blind;
And the three are gone from the sight of men, and the bush fire
    roars behind.

The Bushmen wiped the smoke-made tears, and like Bushmen
laughed and swore
"Poor Bill will be wanting his drink tonight as never he did before."
"And Dunn was the best in the whole damned force!" says a client
of Dunn's, with pride;
"I reckon he'll serve his summons on Jim—when they get to the
other side."

.   .   .   .   .   .

It is daylight again, and the fire is past, and the black scrub silent
and grim
Except for the blaze in an old dead tree, or the crash of a falling
limb;
And the Bushmen are riding across the waste, with hearts and
with eyes that fill,
To look at the bodies of Constable Dunn, Flash Jim, and Boozing
Bill.

They are found in the mud of the Two-mile Tank, where a fiend
might scarce survive,
But the Bushmen gather from words they hear that the bodies
are much alive.
There is Swearing Pat, with his grey beard singed, and language
of lurid hue,
And his tough old wife, and his half-baked kids, and the three
who dragged them through.

Old Pat is deploring his burnt-out home, and his wife the climate
warm;
And Jim the loss of his favourite horse and Dunn of his uniform;
And Boozing Bill, with a raging thirst, is cursing the Dingo Scrub,
But all he'll ask is the loan of a flask and a lift to the nearest pub.

Flash Jim the Breaker is lying low—blue-paper is after Jim,
But Dunn, the trooper, is riding his rounds with a blind eye out
for him;
And Boozing Bill is fighting D.Ts. in the township of Sudden Jerk—
When they're wanted again in the Dingo Scrub, they'll be there
to do the work.

TO HANNAH

Spirit girl, to whom 'twas given
    To revisit scenes of pain,
From the hell I thought was heaven
    You have lifted me again;
Through the world that I inherit,
    Where I loved you ere you died,
I am walking with the spirit
    Of a dead girl by my side.

Through my old possessions only
    For a very little while;
And they say that I am lonely,
    And they pity—but I smile:
For the brighter side has won me
    By the calmness that it brings,
And the peace that is upon me
    Does not come of earthly things.

Spirit girl, the good is in me,
    But the flesh, we know, is weak,
And with no pure soul to win me
    I might miss the path I seek;
Lead me by the love you bore me
    When you trod the earth with me,
Till the light is clear before me
    And my spirit, too, is free.

News of Hannah
Thornburn's tragic
death at Melbourne
in 1902 reached
Lawson at a critical
time in his relation-
ship with his wife.
Her real part in
Lawson's love-life
seems to me to be
highly conjectural.
See Introduction to
this volume.

ONE-HUNDRED-AND-THREE

With the frame of a man and the face of a boy, and a manner
strangely wild,
And the great, wide, wondering, innocent eyes of a silent-suffering
child;
With his hideous dress and his heavy boots, he drags to Eternity—
And the Warder says, in a softened tone: "Catch step, One-
Hundred-and-Three."

Written in 1908
from the bitterness
of first-hand
experience, hardly
'recollected in
tranquillity', this
poem is a major
contribution to
'gaol' literature.

'Tis a ghastly parody of drill—or a travesty of work—
But One-Hundred-and-Three he catches step with a start, a shuffle
and jerk.
He is silenced and starved and "drilled" in gaol—and a waster's
son was he:
His sins were written before he was born—(Keep step! One-
Hundred-and-Three.)

They shut a man in the four-by-eight, with a six-inch slit for air,
Twenty-three hours of the twenty-four, to brood on his virtues there.
The dead stone walls and the iron door close in like iron bands
On eyes that had followed the distant haze out there on the Level
Lands.

Bread and water and hominy, and a scrag of meat and a spud,
A Bible and thin flat Book of Rules, to cool a strong man's blood;
They take the spoon from the cell at night—and a stranger would
think it odd;
But a man might sharpen it on the floor, and go to his own Great
God.

One-Hundred-and-Three, it is hard to believe that you saddled your
horse at dawn,
And strolled through the bush with a girl at eve, or lolled with her
on the lawn.
There were picnic parties in sunny bays, and ships on the shining
sea;
There were foreign ports in the glorious days—(Hold up, One-
Hundred-and-Three!)

A man came out at exercise time from one of the cells today:
'Twas the ghastly spectre of one I knew, and I thought he was
far away;
We dared not speak, but he signed "Farewell—fare—well," and
I knew by this
And the number stamped on his clothes (not sewn) that a heavy
sentence was his.

Where five men do the work of a boy, with warders *not* to see—
It is sad and bad and uselessly mad, it is ugly as it can be,
From the flower-beds shaped to fit the gaol, in circle and line
    absurd,
To the gilded weathercock on the church, agape like a strangled
    bird—

Agape like a strangled bird in the sun, and I wonder what he
    can see—
The Fleet come in, and the Fleet go out? (Hold-up, One-Hundred-
    and-Three!)
The glorious sea, and the bays and Bush, and the distant mountains
    blue—
(Keep step, keep step, One-Hundred-and-Three, for my heart is
    halting too).

The great, round church with its volume of sound, where we dare
    not turn our eyes—
They take us there from our separate hells to sing of Paradise;
The High Church service swells and swells where the tinted Christs
    look down—
It is easy to see who is weary and faint and weareth the thorny
    crown.

Though every creed hath its Certain Hope, yet here, in hopeless
    doubt,
Despairing prisoners faint in church, and the warders carry them out.
There are swift-made signs that are not to God as they march
    us hellward then;
It is hard to believe that we knelt as boys to "For ever and ever,
    Amen".

They double-lock at four o'clock; the warders leave their keys,
And the Governor strolls with a friend at eve through his stone
    conservatories;
Their window-slits are like idiot mouths, with square stone chins
    adrop,
And the weatherstains for the dribble, and the dead flat foreheads
    atop.

Rules, regulations—Red Tape and rules; all and alike they bind:
Under separate treatment place the deaf; in the dark cell shut
    the blind!
And somewhere down in his sandstone tomb, with never a word
    to save,
One-Hundred-and-Three is keeping step, as he'll keep it to his grave.

The press is printing its smug, smug lies, and paying its shameful
    debt—
It speaks of the comforts that prisoners have, and "holidays" prisoners
    get.
The visitors come with their smug, smug smiles through the gaol
    on a working day,
And the public hears with its large, large ears what "Authorities"
    have to say.

They lay their fingers on well-hosed walls, and they tread on the
    polished floors;
They peep in the generous, shining cans with their Ration Number
    Four.
And the visitors go with their smug, smug smiles; and the reporters'
    work is done;
*Stand up! my men, who have done your time on Ration Number
    One!*

He shall be buried alive without meat, for a day and a night
    unheard,
If he speak a word to his fellow-corpse—who died for want of a
    word.
He shall be punished, and he shall be starved, and he shall in
    darkness rot.
He shall be murdered, body and soul—and God saith: "Thou shalt
    not."

I've seen the remand-yard men go forth by the subway out of the
    yard—
And I've seen them come in with a foolish grin and a sentence
    of Three Years Hard.
They send a half-starved man to the Court, where the hearts of
    men they carve—
Then feed him up in the hospital to give him the strength to starve.

You get the gaol-dust into your throat, your skin goes the dead
    gaol-white;
You get the gaol-whine in your voice and in every letter you write.
And into your eyes comes the bright gaol-light—not the glare
    of the world's distraught,
Not the hunted look, nor the guilty look, but the awful look
    of the Caught.

The brute is a brute, and a kind man's kind, and the strong heart
    does not fail—
A crawler's a crawler everywhere, but a man is a man in gaol;
For the kindness of man to man is great when penned in a sand-
    stone pen—
The public call us the "criminal class", but the warders call us
    "the men".

460

We crave for sunlight, we crave for meat, we crave for the Might-
        have-Been,
But the cruellest thing in the walls of a gaol is the craving for
        nicotine.
Yet the spirit of Christ is in every place where the soul of a man
        can dwell—
It comes like tobacco in prison, or like news to the separate cell.

The champagne lady comes home from the course in charge of
        the criminal swell—
They carry her in from the motor-car to the lift in the Grand
        Hotel;
But armed with the savage Habituals Act they are waiting for
        you and me—
And drunkards in judgment on drunkards sit (Keep step, One-
        Hundred-and-Three!).

WARATAH AND WATTLE

Though poor and in trouble I wander alone,
  With a rebel cockade in my hat;
Though friends may desert me, and kindred disown,
  My country will never do that!
You may sing of the Shamrock, the Thistle, the Rose,
  Or the three in a bunch, if you will;
But I know of a country that gathered all those,
And I love the great land where the Waratah grows,
  And the Wattle-bough blooms on the hill.

Australia! Australia! so fair to behold—
  While the blue sky is arching above;
The stranger should never have need to be told,
That the Wattle-bloom means that her heart is of gold,
  And the Waratah's red with her love.

Australia! Australia! most beautiful name,
  Most kindly and bountiful land;
I would die every death that might save her from shame,
  If a black cloud should rise on the strand;
But whatever the quarrel, whoever her foes,
  Let them come! Let them come when they will!
Though the struggle be grim, 'tis Australia that knows
That her children shall fight while the Waratah grows,
  And the Wattle blooms out on the hill.

THE BUSH GIRL

So you rode from the range where your brothers "select",
   Through the ghostly grey bush in the dawn—
You rode slowly at first, lest her heart should suspect
   That you were so glad to be gone;
You had scarcely the courage to glance back at her
   By the homestead receding from view,
And you breathed with relief as you rounded the spur,
   For the world was a wide world to you.

Grey eyes that grow sadder than sunset or rain,
   Fond heart that is ever more true,
Firm faith that grows firmer for watching in vain—
   She'll wait by the sliprails for you.

Ah! the world is a new and a wide one to you,
   But the world to your sweetheart is shut,
For a change never comes to the lonely Bush girl
   From the stockyard, the bush, and the hut;
And the only relief from its dullness she feels
   Is when ridges grow softened and dim,
And away in the dusk to the sliprails she steals
   To dream of past meetings "with him".

Do you think, where, in place of bare fences, dry creeks,
   Clear streams and green hedges are seen—
Where the girls have the lily and rose in their cheeks,
   And the grass in midsummer is green—
Do you think now and then, now or then, in the whirl
   Of the city, while London is new,
Of the hut in the Bush, and the freckled-faced girl
   Who is eating her heart out for you?

Grey eyes that are sadder than sunset or rain,
   Bruised heart that is ever more true,
Fond faith that is firmer for trusting in vain—
   She waits by the sliprails for you.

DO YOU THINK THAT I DO NOT KNOW?

They say that I never have written of love,
  As a writer of songs should do;
They say that I never could touch the strings
  With a touch that is firm and true;
They say I know nothing of women and men
  In the fields where Love's roses grow,
I must write, they say, with a halting pen—
  Do you think that I do not know?

My love-burst came, like an English Spring,
  In the days when our hair was brown,
And the hem of her skirt was a sacred thing,
  And her hair was an angel's crown.
The shock when another man touched her arm,
  Where the dancers sat in a row,
The hope, the despair, and the false alarm—
  Do you think that I do not know?

By the arbour lights on the western farms,
  You remember the question put,
While you held her warm in your quivering arms
  And you trembled from head to foot.
The electric shock from her finger-tips,
  And the murmuring answer low,
The soft, shy yielding of warm red lips—
  Do you think that I do not know?

She was buried at Brighton, where Gordon sleeps,
  When I was a world away;
And the sad old garden its secret keeps,
  For nobody knows today.
She left a message for me to read,
  Where the wild, wide oceans flow;
Do you know how the heart of a man can bleed?—
  Do you think that I do not know?

I stood by the grave where the dead girl lies,
  When the sunlit scene was fair,
'Neath white clouds high in the autumn skies
  I answered the message there.
But the haunting words of the dead to me
  Shall go wherever I go.
She lives in the Marriage that Might Have Been—
  Do you think that I do not know?

464

AH SOON

I don't know whether a story about a Chinaman would be popular or acceptable here and now; and, for the matter of that, I don't care. I am anti-Chinese as far as Australia is concerned; in fact, I am all for a White Australia. But one may dislike, or even hate, a nation without hating or disliking an individual of that nation. One may be on friendly terms; even pals in a way. I had a good deal of experience with the Chinese in the old years; and I never knew or heard of a Chinaman who neglected to pay his debts, who did a dishonest action, or who forgot a kindness to him or his, or was not charitable when he had the opportunity.

I want to tell the story of one Chinaman I knew; a vegetable John who had a white heart. He was an old and extremely plain Chinaman, with a very fat and flabby face; or rather, withered, lined and wrinkled like one of his own turnips that had lain out on the roof during a drought—and about the same colour. If he had any expression at all it was one of agonized anxiety—perhaps for fear his old horse should fall down. He and his countrymen had gardens on Lawson's Creek (not named after the writer), near Mudgee, N.S.W. He drove a long, bony horse, in a long, rickety cart, with a slip of tin on the side of it, whereon was written in white letters on a black ground, the name AH SOON. It looked like a sigh.

Looking out of the front door of a house, or rather hut—say, on a blazing Monday or Friday that made the shadow of the house nearly black—you'd see the hammer-head of Ah Soon's old horse slowly come into focus; then the shoulders, the reins above jerk, jerk, jerking incessantly; then the rest of him up to the step-board of the cart; then the tin plate with its sad "Ah Soon", and above it, well in front, old Ah Soon himself, a withered, drooping image of the Patience of the Ages, jogging the reins unceasingly. I never saw him hit that horse—never saw a whip or stick. How he "got there" the Lord only knows; but he did, for he always turned up to time on his next round—and his was a long weary round through the dusty hot scrubs, too, and back to the Creek. He bought another cart from my father, when his own went to pieces; but he never bought another horse. I remember that he, a younger partner, and a son, or nephew, or something (lately from China), had dinner with us on the conclusion of the bargain, and very decent and unembarrassed Chinamen they proved themselves to be. Let it be understood that this was in the Dry Districts many years ago, when saints and sinners, Christian and heathen, European and Asiatic were fighting a long and cruel drought side by side; through blazing days that seemed black to their blighted eyes. If men couldn't be brothers, or at least charitable and kind and courteous to each other and forgetful of nationality and creed under such conditions—when could they?

Ah Soon used to assure his clients that all his melons were "wi' 'art" (white heart), which, of course, none of them should have been. He knew that that was a good thing about a cabbage, and he applied the phrase to all his goods to indicate their perfect condition. His melons were red-hearted enough, so long as the drought left enough liquid in Lawson's Creek to feed his water-wheel (of a fashion some ten thousand years old), working day and night to water his garden.

His days were Mondays and Fridays, and we called him "Next-time-Friday"; because if he didn't have a vegetable wanted when he came on Monday he'd always say "All li'! Nexy-time-Fliday."

We got to like the old man, and when the Great Drought was coming to a climax he told us that we could come and cart off his hopeless crop of young pumpkins to feed our starving and pleuro-stricken milkers.

At the garden, with the cart, I made the acquaintance of a young Chinaman named Ah See, or something like that. He was a very bright, good-natured, good-humoured, half-childishly shy young fellow—they generally are. He was a son, or nephew, of Ah Soon. He could both speak and write a little English, and was learning something about weights and measures and figures, for business purposes, and I, being a bush schoolboy, used to help him a bit with lbs., cwts., and other things that I've forgotten now; also with his writing —he called it "delightum".

Well, to make a short story shorter, they were one day passing near our place with a cartload of stringybark poles (not the old vegetable horse this time) when the cart went over on a steep siding—this main road hadn't been graded or "made" then. The two other Chinamen on the cart were thrown clear, but poor Ah Soon got the most of the load on top of him. My father was on hand—he generally was in times of sickness, trouble or danger—and, with the help of the other two Chinamen, he got Ah Soon clear. He seemed hurt about the ribs or chest. Mother came running from the house, dragging the best mattress, and carrying a dipper of water. (She was a strong bush-woman in those days.) We fixed up Ah Soon as well as we could, got the cart righted, and the mattress in it, with the addition of some pillows, and got Ah Soon on to them; and father started off with them for the hospital and the doctor at Mudgee. Ah Soon was conscious all the time, and very "thank you". He said that he was "All li'." Ah See told us "All li'—lospital", when he came out next day for the poles; but Ah Soon never came back "Nexy-time-Fliday", nor the Friday after. He never came back any more, and I have no doubt, from what I saw of Ah See, that Ah Soon's old bones have been peacefully mouldering in China this many a long year.

We left the district shortly after the accident, and drifted to the city, as many a bush family did. And the years went past. And my father went from his earthly toil to his fathers—the same way as Ah Soon went to his. And I went up in the world, and round the world, as the years rolled on, and came down in the world, and at length anchored for a while in a little cottage in a dirty little street in a mean Sydney suburb. And there the bailiff visited me. Or, rather, the landlady put him in. We got friendly, the bailiff and I; but when I sent him out for beer one night while I was trying to write him out in verses he got drunk and was run in; so I had to bail him out and bring him home— but that has got nothing to do with the yarn.

A Chinaman used to come round there with vegetables. There was no white greengrocer handy, and, anyhow, the white fruit and vegetable hawkers in those days were spiteful weeds of the larrikin variety, with the cigarette dribbling out of the corner of their mouths. They'd stick a foot in the doorway and insult the wife, likely as not, if they thought there was no man about. A Chinaman would never do that. This John was flat-faced and deeply wrinkled and anxious-looking. Perhaps he'd gone up in the world, and come down in the world, and had had a bailiff amongst his cabbages, so to speak. He'd come to the front garden gate and call out "Vegerbuls!" before setting down his baskets, only stooping so that they just rested on the ground—the stick still heavy on the shoulders. Then, if no one appeared within a reasonable time, he'd call out "Vegerbuls!" again, louder and more gruffly, and with more than a touch of impatience, gripping his stick firmer fore and aft, and stiffening his knees, preparatory to straightening up, after giving his pants a hitch with one hand. Then, if no one came, he'd bark out "Vegerbuls!" like a very gruff watchdog, in one short bark, straighten up, give his baskets a hoist, and depart.

One morning I got into conversation with "Vegerbuls" when he happened to be at the gate. I asked him how he was getting on (I always called him "Asia" to his face), and he said "All li'," with that rare smile of his that redeemed his ugliness and made it pleasing. And then, a tantalizing half-memory recurring to me, I asked him, involuntarily as it were, if he'd ever been up the country. And he said: "Long time ago."

And then it came out that he knew "Log Pladdock", and had worked in a Chinese garden at Lawson's Creek. But even then, of course, I didn't connect him with old Ah Soon.

When, at our next meeting, "Vegerbuls" addressed me by name, I wasn't surprised. I suppose he'd ascertained it from one of the neighbours. But when he asked me if my "sissister" was alive I was rather puzzled and indignant. I suppose now he meant my mother, whose kindness he remembered as a young man. She was only between eighteen and nineteen years older than I. But how he knew later on that I had the bailiff in, the Lord only knows, unless some unknown spiteful neighbour had told him. He brought us the usual jar of preserved ginger a few days earlier this year; also a box of delicious preserved turnip.

A few days before the bailiff was due to sell, "Vegerbuls" told me that he had sold out his garden to a cousin of his, and he was going to China, but he didn't know whether he was coming back. He said his cousin would "come lound". "Never mind vegerbuls," he said; meaning that the "cledit" would go on as usual.

The last day he came was the last day but one of the bailiff—the day before the sale, when the few poor sticks, so hardly got together, would go for half their value—perhaps less. And I felt pretty miserable about it, I can tell you.

We owed "Vegerbuls" money. He said nothing; he lifted out a clean new basket that fitted into the top of one of his big ones. They were nearly empty, and he was on his way home. It was piled with assorted vegetables, and he placed it inside the gate-post.

"Me go 'way next week," he said.

"I can't pay you, Asia," I said, hopelessly.

"Never mind. Pay my cousin. He send it." He took a long clean deal box from under where the basket had been, and handed it to me.

"Chillun," he said simply.

I supposed it was a box of Chinese sweets or toys for the children. Then he shot this at me: "Bellailiff man here yet?"

I was too dull to be surprised or indignant; but I roused myself just a little bit.

"What do you mean, Asia?" I said.

"Log Pladdock," said Asia, with that innocent centuries-old smile that baffles and disarms one. "My fader."

"Yes, he's here yet," I said, weary of it all—referring to the "bellailiff" man. I couldn't see the connection between Log Pladdock and his "fader" (presumably in China with a long white horse-tail beard and in an outlandish dress) and a miserable, sordid little "selling-up" in a mean, miserable suburb of Sydney. "Sell off tomorrow," I said. "But I'll see your cousin paid. Thank you very much for the things, Asia. Good luck, a pleasant voyage!"

He felt in the pocket of his shabby coat and handed me a flaming red envelope.

"You take that. Open by and by. Give bellailiff man," he said, speaking with fearful rapidity, and fixing his tackle and hoisting his baskets with a lightning dexterity that I'd never seen equalled by a Chinaman. "You teach me delightum!—Ah See! Good-bye!" And with an outward throw of his free arm and hand he trotted round the corner towards the market gardens and departed—for Asia, I suppose, as I never saw or heard of him again.

I had a vague notion that the red envelope contained lottery tickets for the bailiff, and that "Vegerbuls" had thought it fitting and proper to make presents to my entire household. I couldn't make out what he meant by my teaching him "delightum"—unless I had taught him the "luxury of doing good"—and "Ah See?" seemed strange in the mouth of a Chinaman, as I took him to mean "D' yer see?"

When I opened the red envelope I found that it contained a half-sheet of common ruled writing paper, folded over a five-pound note and a one-pound note; and five pounds was just within a shilling or so of the amount my bailiff was in for! And on both sides of the half-sheet of notepaper was written, or rather printed, the words—AH SOON.

Then it slowly dawned on me—and I saw: "Vegerbuls" was Ah See, the son of the old Ah Soon, and I was the son of my father and my mother; and my father and my mother had been good to Ah Soon, the father of Ah See; and Ah See had remembered. Besides, I used to teach him "delightum" in those dim, half-forgotten days. "You cannot fathom the Oriental mind," they say. It seems very simple to me.

GRANDFATHER'S COURTSHIP

It was Christmas time and a younger brother, a younger uncle and I had come with a couple of doubtful shotguns and the fisherman's faith to spend the holidays with grandfather at Mount Victoria. He was caretaker in an old mountain residence at the head of a ragged gully and we had spent the day before Christmas in helping him to bring the timber he had split up from the head of the gully. In the evening he and I decided to rest and smoke while the other two went in to the township.

Described by Cecil Mann as 'fiction disguised as actuality', this tale has all the marks of straight biography.

Grandfather sat against the wall smoking his pipe, which he had cleared and filled with the deliberate care of an old bushman. I was trying to smoke, too, being over twenty-one and allowed that privilege by grandfather. We were both gazing into the broad moonlight across the old orchard to the cliffs on the other side of the gully and the blue peaks beyond. After a spell of silence I had asked grandfather to sing, and he had sung "The Golden Glove" and "The Mistletoe Bough". Then we were quiet again for a while and the silence was broken by grandfather.

"Henery, did I ever tell you how I courted your grandmother?"

I had heard the story, but I kept that dark, and then grandfather told me all about it.

"I was a young man then, Henery," said grandfather, "about your age—but they did say I was something to look at." Grandfather paused with his quizzical, sidelong glance at me, but I didn't take the matter up, so grandfather went on, evidently disappointed. "An' I didn't wear la-di-dah clothes an' write poetry for papers, an' walk like a 'en to make meself look like what I wasn't."

I let that pass, too, considering it weak and unworthy of grandfather.

"Howsomever, we was all livin' at a place between Windsor and Penrith on the upper Hawkesbury—on the Nepean—nearabouts where we were all born and brought up, at a place called Never Mind—at least that's what we called it. It would be called Kick-up-a-Fuss in these la-di-dah days. We had a sawpit and timber-trucks—they're all gone now, tyres and all, and the saw-pit's gone, too, an' so's the timber. They're makin' new forests, I've heerd, but they won't be like the old 'uns. The last time I took a holiday trip down there to see the place there was nothing but a heap of stones with tangle growin' over 'em, an' a frill-lizard thinkin' in the sun; he must have been a old 'un, fer he seemed to remember me and didn't make to go away. But there was a dint in the ground yit where the sawpit was; and dirty water; an' some tadpoles an' maybe a crawfish or two—the water was too muddy for me to see; an' some ducks holdin' a mothers' meetin', about me comin', I s'pose!"

"Go on, grandfather."

"Howsomever, it was Saturday, and we knocked off at one o'clock and I went home dog-tired. I had a sloosh and went in and sat down to dinner. Mother was away, monthly nursin', at the minister's house—the parsonage near Penrith; an' my sister Margaret was keepin' house. You never saw your great-aunt Margaret, Henery?" (I had seen the old lady since, and she recognized me and said she'd know one of our tribe if she saw the skins spread out on a gooseberry bush. Then I recognized her.)

"Howsomever, father—that's your great-grandfather—was at home, growlin' round, which was about all he did nowadays. You see, he had crotchety Old Country ideas. Howsomever, we wanted a growler in the family to make

469

the home complete. It was a big family, but poor old father filled the job right down to the ground and up to the roof.

"After dinner I stretched out on the broad of me back on the big home-made sofa and smoked an' rested. It was good. After a while Margaret (yer great-aunt) said:

"'I want you to take the clean clothes to mother at the minister's place this afternoon, Harry, if you will.' You see she was washing for the parsonage.

"'Oh, confound it!' I said. 'You're allers a worrit-worrit-worriting the life out of a man; ain't a man to get no rest at all? Let some of the others do it.'

"Margaret didn't say anything, but went on foldin' and ironin' an' fillin' the basket. She always knew what she was about. Bimeby I felt rested and got restless and oneasy and sat up.

"'You wimmin is always worrit-worrit-worriting a man,' I said; 'he don't git no peace at all.'

"'What's the matter with you now, Harry?' she says. 'Who's aworriting you?'

"'Have you got those clothes ready?' I shouted.

"'Presently,' she said, 'you needn't howl about it.'

"I went out and tidied up a bit and put on my boots. We didn't wear our boots every day in the week then. And then I histed the basket on to my shoulder an' started up the river to the minister's place.

"When I got there I went round to the back and knocked at the kitchen door; it was shut, being a windy day. It was opened and I seen the prettiest girl east of the mountains. She was short and slight and had blue eyes and hair like new straw—(but all you rascals are dark, like me). I was taken aback, not expectin' her, though I had heern that there was a young English servant-girl at the parsonage, but I took no notice on it. I was flustered and took up the basket agen, like a big fool, to have somethin' to hold on to, and was offerin' it to her as if it had been a bookay. But she wasn't no more flustered at seein' me there than if I'd been the cat come home—or she'd been one. Wimmin are like cats in some ways. I recollected myself presently and put the basket down an' scraped off me hat.

"'If you please, miss,' I said, 'I'd like to hascertain if mother is in. Missis Albury, miss,' I says.

"'Oh, you're Harry,' she said; 'I beg your pardon—Mr Albury. Come in and sit down. Put the basket down anywheres and I'll go and tell your mother you're here.'

"I went in and put down the basket in the middle of the big brick floor where it 'ud be in everyone's road. It was one of them old-style kitchens, with everything big and scrubbed, and white and bright and yellow and red. She started to drag a big old-fashioned cane chair out, with legs spread out like a kangaroo-dog runnin', an' a dished back all string-bound. I put me hat down very carefully in a corner on the brick floor, where it couldn't fall off.

"Then I went to help her with the chair, an' accedently touched her hand, and it took all the presence of mind out of me that was left in me, it was so small and cool and soft. I said, 'Beg yer pardon, miss,' for nothing, and sat down suddenly, an' the chair set down, too—the legs went all ways for Sunday; and that didn't improve matters."

"What did you do then, grandfather?"

"Got up, o' course, you ass. Do you think I was going to sit there all day?"

"She'd have thought it rather strange, grandfather, if you had. But what did she say? Did she laugh?"

"No, she didn't; she wasn't a lot of thundrin' jumptup laughin' jackhasses, like my grandchildren. She looked—she looked—well—"

"Demure, grandfather?"

"Now, I don't want none of your la-di-dah words! She looked, well—"

"Concerned?" I ventured.

"Consarn you! She looked—hanxious—she wanted to hascertain if I was hurt."

"To what?"

"Well, to know, if you must know. I said I wasn't. I was concerned, as you call it, about the chair. I wanted to take it out an' mend it right away, but she wouldn't hear of it. She said it was all her fault; the cook ought to have had it put in the lumber-room long ago; the minister, Mr Kinghorn, had told them to; but how it could be all her fault and the cook's, too, I didn't think at the time. 'An' would you carry it into the shed for me, please, Mr er-er-Harry?' And Mr Harry pleased. When I came back she was dragging out a big old grandfather chair from a nook—the cook's special, I s'pose— and I reckoned she must be a big woman. I took the chair from her and put it near the door and sat down, it seemed safer there, and she started for the foot of the stairs; but mother called over the rail:

"'What's that noise, Harriet? Who's there?' I s'pose she knowed all the time.

"'It's Mr—Mr Harry, ma'am,' said Harriet. 'The chair broke!'

"'The what?' says mother.

"'The chair, ma'am,' said Harriet. 'It broke.'

"'Well, you ain't been losin' much time,' says mother, 'I must say—Well, keep him there till I come down, an' don't let him fall inter the fire.'

"I wanted to get up and smother mother—about the chair, I mean, but I don't think Harriet guessed what mother was driving at. Anyways, Harriet said afterwards that she didn't.

"Well, I sat still, and Harriet said nothing. She was the quietest little house-maid I ever see. Mousemaid rather. It was the cook's afternoon out, I s'pose. Harriet moved round like a mouse, polishin' an' brightenin' up already, an' we went on sayin' nothin' to each other as fast as ever we could.

"Arter about two years hard, I think, I heerd mother comin' downstairs, pat, pat, pat, pat, with a basket of dirty clothes—at least I wouldn't 'a' called 'em dirty—"

"Soiled linen, grandfather?"

"All right! Some of yer la-di-dahdy. Howsomever, when mother got to the foot of the stairs and turns round like a stopper in a bottle . . . (She was short and stout like a Yorkshire dumpling, like yer granny was when you knew her—a bundle as long as she was broad. Strange how all our mothers and wives are so short and dumpy, an' we so long, an' sometimes lanky, like you.) Howsomever, mother squinted at me an' then at Harriet.

"'Well, you are making a lot o' noise between you, you two,' says she, 'for sich new acquaintances. Leastways, when I was a gal we waited till we was

471

introduced at least. Well, how are they all at home, Harry?'

"That's the first time that I ever see Harriet—that's your grandmother—redden up. She flushed to the roots of her hair, as the sayin' is (an half-way down her back, perhaps, though I didn't see it). She went crimson, the more so that she was fair, and it become her wonderfully. I wanted to smother mother agen, but had to kiss her instead.

"Harriet went inside, arter some business of her own, while mother heerd the news an' give me some messages for Margaret. Mother wanted me to stay an' have a cup o' tea; but I wouldn't. I'd had enough, an' besides I didn't know how I'd manage a cup an' sarser; especially if Harriet was in the kitchen —though the parson's kitchen crockery was big an' homely enough, it skeered me to think o' tryin'. You see, we used mugs or pannikins at home. So I said I was going somewheres that arternoon and wanted to get home.

"'Very well, then,' says mother, tyin' a cloth over the basket, 'but ain't you goin' to wait an' say good-bye to Harriet? Where's yer manners?'

"'Is her name Harriet, mother?' I says.

"'Yes of course it is,' said mother; 'Henrietta—Harriet. Didn't yer hear me call her so half a dozen times?'

"'Well, that's funny,' I says, scratchin' my head.

"'What's funny? You great galoot!' says mother.

"'Why, my name's Henery—an' Harry, too,' I said.

"'But it ain't Henrietta, nor yet Harrieta,' says mother; 'though you've been lookin' and actin' more like than she has all the arternoon. Or like a Mary Ann rather. Why can't yer hold yer own an' be a man when yer meet a good-lookin' gal? Your father could, worse luck, an' so can your brothers.'

"Jist then Harriet came back an' see me standing by the basket ready.

"'Why, isn't Mr Albury going to stay an' have some tea, Mrs Albury?' she said. 'I'll get it ready in a minute.'

"'No thank you, miss,' I said, 'I've got to go somewheres; an' besides, I'm full as a new straw-bed tick.'

"I could 'a' bitten me tongue out for makin' such a hole in me manners; but it was too late now an' I dived for the basket.

"'Well!—say goodbye to Harriet,' says mother.

"So I blundered up to Harriet, an' nearly over her; an' she held out her little hand a little way. Gosh, it gave me a skeer. It was so soft an' cool an' small—I never thought a girl could have such a small hand. It seemed alive an' knowin', too, like a tame white rat in your hand. It startled me an' I must have gripped it in my nervousness, for she gave a little sound, like a small 'Oh,' an' put both her hands behind her. Then she recollected herself an' put 'em in front, under her apron, where she was rubbin' the numbness off the one she gave me with the other, I s'pose. It was all just like as if she'd given me a tame frog, unexpected, to take home and take keer of for her— that little hand was. I seen I'd hurt her, so I dived for the basket, histed it on me shoulder, and kissed mother on the nose—or chin, I didn't know which; they both stuck out like yours will when you lose a few more teeth; and then I collared the parson's garden hat that was hangin' on a peg on the wall an' bolted."

I waited, expectant, while grandfather saw to his pipe and then studied the moonlight reflectively.

472

"Talkin' o' teeth," said grandfather, "I wonder how you young 'uns all seem to lose your teeth so early. I s'pose it's the la-di-dah tucker an' soft slush you get in Sydney. It wasn't so in my time, when we had to gnaw raw pumpkin an' cob corn when the floods cut the teams off."

"Confound it, grandfather, why don't you go on with the story!"

"How kin I when yer always keep int'ruptin' me?" said grandfather. "Will you hold your tongue?" (Pause for reply, but I didn't fall in.) "Howsomever, I'd gone about a mile along the road before I recollected that I hadn't said good-bye to Harriet after all. That will show you how a—"

"Grandfather," I said severely, "what did you take the minister's hat for?"

"How was I to know?" said grandfather in a suspiciously mild and injured tone, "an' how in thunder am I to know now, five and forty years afterwards?"

"I beg your pardon, grandfather."

"Well, don't do it again. You're allers breakin' a thread in me dishcloth, as old Betty Campney uster say. Howsomenever—I didn't know I had the parson's hat on till I got home. I thought it strange, afterwards, in a funny sort o' way, that a parson should have the same size head as I had. But then agen, come to think of it, why shouldn't he? Howsomenever, some of 'em I passed agoin' into Penrith in carts an' on horseback did look unusual hard at me. I noticed, an' I wondered what devilment I'd been up to in town the last Saturday. One or two on horseback called out to ask if Harry Albury was ordained yet; if I'd taken 'Oly Horders; and I couldn't make out what they were drivin' at, unless they guessed I'd come from the minister's place. They'd soon 'a' found out what they was drivin' at if I hadn't 'a' bin afoot; for we wasn't scoffers, whatever else we might 'a' been. An' don't you go in for none of that," (he referred to scoffing), "Henery, because if you ain't sorry arterwards you'll be ashamed. Yer grandmother was strick in those matters, you remember; bein' a poor minister's darter afore she immigrated. She might have been more comfortable for all on us," grandfather went on reflectively, "if she hadn't had such strick convictions about shirt sleeves on Sundays, and little things like that. But I forgit. You see that 'at was well, a parson's 'at; it was of a—a—"

"A clerical cut, grandfather?"

"A whatter?"

"Clerical cut."

"Clerical," said grandfather, trying it on himself, "sounds like the name of a bantam rooster, it seems to me. Well, all right, it will do for the present, you can tell me the meaning of it arterwards."

So I had at last got at least one la-di-dah word accepted conditionally.

"What's dimure?" said grandfather suddenly, and somewhat aggressively, it seemed to me. I could see that he had been turning it over, all unsuspected, in his second mind, part of the time. Like many keenly intelligent and totally uneducated men he would be attracted by the sound of a word—the shorter the better. I explained "demure" as well as I could, and handed it over to grandfather. So I saw that I had a second la-di-dah word accepted, unconditionally this time; and was sure of meeting it again, later on, in grandfather's possession.

"Howsomenever, when I got home I went into the kitchen an' put the basket down. 'There yer are,' I says to Margaret, 'now it's to be hoped you'll stop worritin' an' let me have a little rest.'

"Margaret looked at the basket an' then at me; an' then she looked at my head—and then she looked harder at it. It was brushed back on the back of me head by the arm I used steadyin' the basket, overarm; I must have wore it home most of the way that way, an' no wonder Margaret looked, to see me with a gamecock-clarrickle hat on the back of me head.

"'Well, you'll know me presently,' I said; 'better look at me feet to make sure.'

"'Why, Harry,' she said, 'whatever have you got on?'

"'Me clothes,' I said, thinkin' she was referrin' to me comin' so early and wonderin' what devilment I was up to, fer we never hung about the sawpits on Saturday afternoon. They was monotonous enough all the week. I took off me hat to throw it on the kitchen sofa, and when I felt and caught sight of it I stared at it harder than Margaret did. I thought at first someone must have played a trick on me. It couldn't have bin the parson, for I didn't see him.

"'Well, I'm bewitched!' I said.

"Margaret thought a second—she was the quickest-thinkin' woman I ever saw, was your great-aunt Margaret, Henery. Then she said, 'I think you are, Harry.'

"'It must be the parson's hat,' I said.

"'It must be', says Margaret.

"'I muster wore it home by mistake,' I says.

"'You must have,' says Margaret.

"I hung the hat up and took out me pipe, and set down on the kitchen sofa to bluff Margaret. You see, I was suspicious of her. I knew her. I think it's a cowardly thing to take your hat an' walk away from a woman's tongue, no matter how soft it is, an' she thinks so, too. You see, it generally hurts her—her pride or something; an', if she happens to be a wife naggin' it's worse, an' sometimes more dangerous, than sittin' silent, or whistlin' 'The Last Rose of Summer.' She might go, too—home to her mother.

"Margaret was ironin' out our Sunday things; she was ironin' one o' father's big white shirts, with frills like a jew-lizard all down the front of it, like they wore in them days, for father to go to chapel in on Sunday. She ironed a couple of frills down very carefully" (I suppose grandfather meant "tucks" or "pleats"), "and then she says:

"'Did you bring anything else home from the minister's, Harry?'

"'I brought the dirty clothes. There's the basket under yer nose. Can't yer see it? What in thunder else would I bring?'

"Then I thought. 'I brought a message from mother,' I said, 'but your jackhassin' put it clean out o' me head.' An' I give the message to head her off from whatever she had comin'.

"She ironed down another frill.

"'Did you leave anything at the minister's except your hat, Harry?' she asked.

"'I left the clean clothes,' I said. 'What in thunder else would I leave?' I said. 'What in thunder are yer drivin' at, at all?'

"That was a slip; it's allers a mistake to swear—it spoils the rest of what you say. An' it's a bigger mistake to ask a woman what she means.

"Margaret ironed down another frill very carefully; lookin' what you'd call 'dimure', only not just that way. Presently she says:

"'See anyone at the minister's, Harry?'

"'I see mother,' I said; 'who else did yer think I'd see? The parson was out. Did yer expect me to go up to Mrs Parson's bedroom and ask her how many teeth the baby had? It was only born last week.'

"She ironed down another frill, a middle one, very carefully, from top to bottom, looking more dimurer in another sort of way—a sisterly sort of way—than ever. She said nothin' when she'd finished it, but started on another frill, one of the shorter ones; and I got oneasy. She was like the cattle stringin' off in the dark. At last I thought I'd ride ahead of where I thought their lead was, and have done with it one way or the other.

"'I seen the job-man there,' I said, 'an' he wasn't much to look at; an' a gal—a nursemaid or something, they call Mary-Ann or some such name; an' I seen some fowls an' the pig. Now are you satisfied?'

"'Oh! That was Harriet Wynn,' says Margaret.

"'Harriet what?'

"'Wynn,' says Margaret, 'that's her name, Harriet Wynn. Didn't mother tell you?'

"'Oh! the gal!' I said. 'I thought you meant the pig. I didn't know the parson had taken to christenin' pigs as well as kids. Well, I've had enough o' naggin' fer one day,' I said. 'I'm goin' out to have some peace and quietness.' And I got me old workin' hat and went out."

Short pause, and then grandfather gave me one of his quizzical glances to see what I thought of his address and strategy in the matter. And I nodded my head emphatically at the still moonlit path with all the worldly wisdom of twenty-one.

"But I kept the girl's name in me mind for 'future reference', as you'd call it.

"I went out an' lay down on a bank on the grass, with my hands under me head. The sun was low down over the poplars, and the willers and the mountains. They was purple, mostly o' mornin's, but was dark green, an' deep blue, an' light blue now, and lighter the farther away you got till they went into the sky; and I got thinkin'—which reminds me," said grandfather, "that I want to think a bit now while I fill me pipe."

I was thinking, too. Thinking of great-aunt Margaret on Berry's Estate, North Sydney, old and withered but wiry and bright-eyed; dressed in a gaunt, prim, old-fashioned early Victorian style that was the fashion when she was a girl and considered neither gaunt nor prim then.

Thinking of granny as I last saw her, taking off the old black bonnet and putting on the little old lace cap; chin and nose coming closer together, crotchety, rather, and too unpleasantly truthful (or "tactless") for these "la-di-dah" days; and with a growing tendency to get hold of the wrong end of little things with those little old hands and hold on tight. What work those hands had done in their time! With stronger views than ever on the subject of shirt sleeves on Sundays; and with a most uncomfortable and unconquerable distrust of clocks and watches on those days when she donned her black silk —or lustre, or cashmere, or whatever it was—and black Sunday bonnet and gloves that all looked as good as if they were bought last week.

Thinking of her I could see the black bonnet go bobbing up past the railings to church. Brave old eyes that had seen more of the wildest of the early days —more of drought, flood, wilderness, hardship, and danger, by track and tent and hut, than would fill volumes. Brave old eyes that had looked at the downcast ones of Syd Lardner, Frank Wall, and "Bunny" Hughison, whilst she lectured those foolish haunted men on the evil of their ways and gave them honest advice, what time the bushrangers fumbled with their cabbage-tree hats; or sat in a row on a bench like scolded schoolboys; what time the brave old hands, not withered then, set forth damper and junk on the rough slab table and made hot coffee. Their bowed heads were grace enough. Granny *could* make coffee.

And here was grandfather, unbent with age—he kept himself straight carrying timber; but with hair and frill beard getting dusty very fast. Square and strong of face, with chin, mouth, and cheeks clean-shaven to the world. His razor had wakened me that morning, like an early-style stripping machine going through a heavy crop of wheat.

And, *hey presto!* the river above Windsor; a hint of willows down in the bend and the long-unconquerable mountains above; back to the left, up-river, a row of poplars against the skyline in a mile-distant by-lane. Homes in English style and dress, with old red brick gable-ends, and ivy; and one with the great long motherly roof coming close down to the ground on each side like the wings of a good old hen with a big clutch of chickens. Margaret, a handsome, buxom young woman, elder sister—sister mother in charge; wise and witty, with an instinctive knowledge of the world and its ways. Away behind the poplars the minister's place, with the nursemaid, young Harriet Wynn, a minister's daughter herself at home—pretty, winsome, and demure. And grandfather, tall, straight, strong, with thick, wavy black hair. He might have said, in all seriousness, that he was something to look at then. Aunt Bess used to tell me as a boy that he "looked like a Greek god" in his young days; and I wondered where she had seen a Greek god, for Uncle-by-marriage Mack wasn't one (going by what I'd seen in some old book decorations) —unless Greek gods were short and sandy, and bow-legged from much riding, and walked like a hen, and had the "drought-peer", and had their hair blown off in many 'nor' western duststorms on the overland route. No, Uncle Mack was a grand chap and a king of drovers; but I'd seen him in swimming, and Uncle Mack wasn't a Greek god....

"Howsomenever," said grandfather—"wheer was I? You're always interruptin'."

I hadn't interrupted unless it was by thinking, but I said nothing, fearing a trap.

"Howsomenever, next Saturday I come home from the sawpit as tired an' happy, an' proud as two dogs that had followed their master ridin' home all day, and chased every kangaroo-rat a mile off the track, and caught a native cat in a holler log at last an' spoilt the skin by pullin' the cat in halves. We'd put in a good week's work, Abel was out with the timber trucks, and I'd been in the pit all mornin' with a bag over me head to keep the sawdust off, fer Bill was top-sawyer and he had a touch of sandy-blight an' couldn't take his shift below.

"I went home and got towel and soap and some clean things, an' had a dip in the swimmin' hole, way down amongst the willers. All the young fellers round used to swim an' scrub themselves an' dress there on Sunday mornin's for chapel—or some other devilment among the girls. When I went into dinner, Margaret says:

"'Someone's cleanin' up early this week, I notice, Harry.'

"'You mind yer own P's and Q's, Margaret,' I said. (She was shellin' peas for Sunday.) 'I'm goin' into Penrith this afternoon to see what's on. There's a kick-up of some sort there. D'yer expect a young feller to be allers slave-slavin' an' worritin', an' listenin' to wimmin's clack an' father's growlin'? Ain't a man to have any pleasure at all?'

"Margaret said nothin', but got me my dinner an' went on shellin' peas. After dinner I took a turn out of the sofa, and had a grand rest and smoke, expectin' Margaret to say somethin' about them clothes—but she didn't. She could take her time, could your great-aunt Margaret when she wanted to get at somethin', or do somethin'.

"Presently I got up an' went to finish tidyin' meself. 'Margaret!' I shouted from the skillion.

"'Yes, Harry,' she said, as meek as mild.

"'If you've got anything to take to mother, you'd better get it ready quick. I don't want to waste the whole afternoon.' I'd twigged the basket of clothes ready on the big kitchen dresser.

"'O-o-h! Will you take them, Harry?' she said. 'I didn't like to ask you after doin' it last Saturday.'

"'Oh, come, I'll take 'em!' I said. 'Haven't I told you so half a dozen times. How many more times do you want me to tell yer?'

"'But, you know, Harry,' she says (see how a woman hangs on to a thing); 'but, you know, Harry,' she says, 'you spoilt your last Saturday half-holiday.'

"'Hang last Saturday!' I shouted. 'It hain't this Saturday, is it? Haven't I yelled at yer a hundred times that I'm goin' to Penrith, an' it's only a step up a lane outer me way!'

"'But Abel's goin' to ride in on his mare just as soon as he comes down from the mountain—an' Bill's goin' in, too, later on, on the colt,' said Margaret, still hangin' on, womanlike, 'an' either of 'em could take the basket in easy on the horse in front of 'em and save you the trouble.'

"'Hang Abel!' I shouted. 'He'll be tireder than me, an' the mare, too. Haven't I told you a dozen times I gotter get me 'at an' take back the parson's.'

"'Bill or Abel could do that,' said Margaret, quiet like.

"'An' me go in me old un!' I yelled. 'An' them at the parson's thinkin' I was too shamefaced to face 'em. Get them clothes ready quick or I won't take 'em at all.'

"'They're all ready, Harry,' says Margaret, soft and meek like, 'an' the minister's hat, too.'

"Then I squinted through a crack and seen me sister Margaret laughin' on the quiet to herself over the peas. Yes, she was awfully tickled about somethin'; and I knowed I was bein' had all the time.

"No: I wasn't jealous of me own brothers already," says grandfather, looking at me narrowly out of the corners of his eyes, "as you're thinkin', Henery." (I didn't protest.) "Only I knowed Bill and Abel.

"Besides, they'd been pokin' it at me all the week about the parson's hat; and I heern 'em talkin' about the pretty girl at the minister's, and Harry, in their skillion one night; so they wanted a lesson. I didn't want 'em hangin' round the parson's place when I wasn't there to take keer on 'em—or any other time jist now, for that matter, interruptin' me. At first I thought of lettin' Bill's colt out of the yard by accident—it was hard to ketch—an' so save him the trouble of goin' to Penrith at all. He wanted rest, anyways, an' besides the night air was bad for his eyes. But we three brothers didn't play no tricks like that on each other; so I went into their skillion and borrowed Abel's best hat, because it suited me better'n Bill's. Bill's was a bit tight. I seen Abel comin' down the mount'in with the bullocks, an' expected Bill at any minute: so I histed the basket an' started to start. The parson's hat was on top, well brushed an' done up in brown paper—and brown paper was skeerce round our place in them days.

"Jist as I was goin', Margaret says, 'Harry,' says she, 'if you do happen to see Harriet, remind her of her promise to come over. Tell her I've been expectin' her ever since I was there last.'

"'There yer go agen!' I says. 'Expectin' me to go carryin' messages and clack-clackin' round amongst a parsil o' girls! All right! Now are yer satisfied?' an' off I goes.

"I seemed to get to the parson's long before I was ready," said grandfather. "But I wasn't the first," he reflected, looking at the fire, "an' I mightn't be the last," he continued, with a side squint at me. "I seemed to get there before I started—in a dream like. (Some goes in a nightmare.) Howsomenever, I put the basket down very quietly inside the gate an' looked round for somethin' to mend, an' presently I seen a back gate wanted attendin' to; and then I was satisfied. So I took up the basket an' went to the kitchen door, an' there was Harriet. She seemed half expectin' to see me—p'raps she saw me comin' along the road through the side window; it was open, now I come to think of it. They was hinged windows they had in them days; that opened sideways and outwards; with vines and roses round 'em," reflected grandfather; "not the la-di-dah, bare-faced, go-up-an'-down windows they have nowadays. Howsomenever, she seemed to have her best bib-an'-tucker on, now I come to look at her; an' that's sayin' a lot. Fresh as the flowers o' May, as mother used to say. She seemed a bit flushed and flustered, too, an' that give me more strength, so to speak. I was all on a sudden a lot more stiddy on me pins than I was last time.

"'Oh, Mr Albury!' says Harriet, 'I'm so glad you come—mother was expectin' you.' (She didn't say *she* was.) 'Come in an' put the basket down, anywheres. An' sit down. You must be tired after your day's work and walk.'

"'Thank you, miss,' I said; 'but I ain't a bit tired. I bin only loafin' round all the mornin'.' An' I put the basket down in one corner steady an' took off me hat. I took the parson's hat off the top of the clothes an' handed it to her without droppin' it or makin' a bungle between the two. It was quite a bit of sleight o' hand.

"'I had to call an' bring Mr Kinghorn's hat,' I said, 'seein' that none of the others had the sense to send it, or bring it. An' apologize,' I said, 'an' hassertain if Mr Kinghorn was anyways annoyed or inconvenienced.' Kinghorn was the parson's name—an' he was a man, by the way.

"'No, not at all,' she said. 'Mr Kinghorn only laughed when your mother told him. But I'm sorry you forgot your hat, Mr Albury. But sit down, Mr

Albury.' Then she looks at my hat—or rather Abel's. 'Your mother's busy just now. She'll be down in a few minutes.'

"So I sits down, while Harriet goes on, rather quick and glad like. 'But I'm so glad you're got another good hat. It might have been inconvenient.'

"So she bustled round, very busy doin' nothin' as a woman can be.

"'Yes, miss,' I said, 'it would be of. But I generally have two or three handy, in case of the wind and floods. I lost a good one in the river last flood time.' So I had; but I didn't tell her that the other two I had handy belonged to Abel and Bill.

"'Oh! I'm so sorry you lost that hat,' she said; 'but I'm glad you've got more, Mr Albury.'

"I looked at her, but couldn't see anything. But I didn't know how much mother'd been tellin' her about me, an' I wanted to have done with the hat subject. She looked too dimure, as you'd put it.

"Presently I gets up agen.

"'Oh! You're not goin', Mr Albury', she says, all in a flutter. 'Mother'd be down in a minit.'

"'O' course I'm not goin', miss,' I said. 'What made you think that? But I seen a back gate that wants lookin' to and I might as well do it while I'm waitin', if so you'd be kind enough to show me where the tool-box is kept. I ain't in no particular hurry this arternoon.'

"'I'm so glad,' she began, an' then she caught herself an' gasped an' blushed, an' showed me where the tools was.

"While I was mendin' that gate she took courage to come out an' said it would be just lovely; an' it was allers a nuisance, an' Mr Kinghorn tried to mend it himself, an' I must be very clever. An' while I was talkin' to her about gates an' things, and showin' her how they ought to be made an' fitted, I seen Abel ridin' past at the foot of the lane. He had on what looked like Bill's hat in the distance; so I s'pose'd he'd borrered Bill's, an' Bill got a rest for his eyes. Then we both saw Mr Kinghorn comin' up the lane in his gig and Harriet run inside.

"Mr Kinghorn had a new kind of duck that interested me vastly. They was called Muscovies; and they hadn't been long imported, I think—leastways, I hadn't seen any before anywheres. They was about twice as big as an ordinary quack, only they didn't quack; only just gibber and whisper. I christened 'em the Gibberers. No, they couldn't talk, not even old Mrs Muscovy; they was the only females I'd seen as couldn't speak.

"I said I'd like to come and potter round a bit next Saturday and fix up things for him; and maybe run up a new fowl-shed; and he said, 'Well, Harry, it will keep you out of mischief, anyhow, an' I'll be very thankful.' (You see he knew me.) He said he'd give me a pair of young Gibberers to breed from as soon as they was ready, an' that suited me down to a T.

"'An' now, Harry,' says Mr Kinghorn, 'run in an' see if Harriet can't knock you up a snack. You must be hungry; young fellows mostly are. I think I see your mother wavin' from the back door.'

"Mother showed me where to sit down. I never seen a table set so well as that before, an' I was a bit shy of it. There was some white stuff rolled up in two rings on the table, and I asked mother what them things was.

"'They're napkins,' she says.

"Presently Harriet comes down, an' I noticed she seemed to have titivated her hair up a different way; but it only made her prettier. She redded a bit when mother looked at her—I saw that. I watched mother drinkin' her tea, an' managin' her bread and butter, an' did accordin', an' finished my cup at the same time. Then Harriet put her left hand on mother's shoulder an' says, 'Will you have another cup o' tea, Mrs Albury?' An' mother says, 'Thank you, Harriet,' an' handed up her cup. Then Harriet put her right hand on my shoulder an' she says: 'Will *you* have another cup, Mr Harry?'

"By gosh! It rattled me," said grandfather. "It rattled the crockery, too, for I upset the cup in the sarcer handin' up to her, an' spilt the tea that was left. But she caught 'em from me all right an' quick, or I'd have dropped both over my shoulder. You see she had—she had—."

"Tact, grandfather?" I ventured.

"No! Nor tacks neither!" said grandfather. "She had—the way about her. Mother said, 'Why, wheer's your manners, Harry?' And that's what I wanted to know. They'd bolted like a flock of kangaroos at the sight of a kangaroo-dog. You see, Henery, that was the first time your grandmother ever touched me with her hand and voice.

"She touched me more than once with both—arterwards," grandfather mused presently; "but only when I deserved it. I—I wish she could do it now. But—never mind. Wheer was I?

"'If you please, miss,' I said over me shoulder, as soon as I got me wits together a bit; 'but only half a cup.' So she pours out about three-quarters of a cup an' puts it down keerfully alongside me plate. I couldn't see her face; an' mother was very intent on her tea. She seemed to be enjoying it.

"Presently I got up an' said, 'Ah, well, mother, I must be goin'; and when she's finished givin' me a message to Margaret I turned round an' Harriet was standin' there waitin' with her hands behind her back. She looked very—dimure," said grandfather, with a quick glance at me. "I thought at first she was frightened I'd hurt her agen; but she brings one hand round an' there was my own hat in it—brushed an' the veil fixed up as I seen arterwards. We wore sort o' puggeree veils in those days.

"'Thank you very much, miss,' I said, takin' it from her. An' then I give her Margaret's message in a hurry, without bunglin' much; whilst holdin' me hat very tight in both hands and lookin' round for it everywheres.

"Then I heern mother gulpin' over her third cup o' tea, an' I looked an' seen what I was a-doin' of. Then she laughed out an' said, 'What are you lookin' for, Harry?' An' then Harriet laughed a little and pointed to the hat in me hand, an' then I laughs an' we was all comfortable again. And I shook hands with her without hurtin' her this time; and said good-bye to mother; an' got out 'n' started for home.

"Down near the foot of the lane I seen Abel's mare, Gipsy, comin' home alone along the road from Penrith with the bridle hangin' loose. She'd lost Abel somewheres, or got disgusted with the way he started carryin' on. She wasn't goin' to stay with him on the spree all night, so she come home, as she'd done once or twice before. She stopped at the bottom of the lane when she seen me, and waited for me to get on; but I didn't feel like ridin'; I wanted a walk, an' a long 'un to think happy; so I fixed up her bridle for her an' went on ahead.

"So I walks on an' on an' on, thinkin' and thinkin' as happy as Larry. *You'll* know what I was thinkin' about some day—I suppose it was the touch of that there gal's hand on me shoulder an' the sound of her voice half-callin' me by my Christian name. I didn't feel the ground beneath me feet. I was— I was——."

"Elated, grandfather," I suggested.

"All right!" said grandfather. "E-lated (I didn't pay fer yer edgication). I was b-lated, too, by the way, for it was broad moonlight, an' I didn't feel the ground, as I said—it was like a light treadmill, but I was goin' up all the time. I walks right past the house in a dream, and about half a mile beyond when I thought I heers somethin' behind me an' pulls up sudden.

"It was just about where Fisher's Ghost was last seen; and I thought all on a sudden of other ghosts that harnted round there. There was the ghost of a man leanin' against the fence in the moonlight with his back tords yer; and the ghost of the lamed horse with the trailin' bridle, whose master was murdered with a fence-rail. I peered back, but couldn't see anythin' in the black moonlight shadders o' the big trees by the roadside; but presently I hears a haltin' step right enough, an' me own legs took me on into the next stretch o' moonlight in double-quick time—with no haltin' steps, I can tell you, Henery. An' sure enough a limpin' horse did come out of the shadders. But afore I threw up me heart quite, or me stommick quite froze, I seen it was Gipsy.

"She'd followed me all the way at leisure and watched me carryin's on— I might a' been wavin' me arms an' singin' or recitin' a bit, part o' the way —or maybe practisin' a step-dance; howsomenever, she'd seen me go past home, an' got anxious, an' hurried on, jerked her bridle loose in her hurry an' that was what was trippin' her. So I waited till the old gal come up, an' took her nose under me arm, an' told her I was all right. An' then I got on an' she swung round contented and took me home.

"When I got home, Margaret was still up, finishin' up ready to begin agen on Sunday. She ain't done yet, your great-aunt Margaret. She said nothin', but I was ready for her an' said nothin' too; but stood by the fire.

"Presently she said:

"'Well, Harry?'

"And I said, 'Well, Margaret?' an' went to bed.

"An' it was not till then that it struck me, somehow, that I'd forgotten Abel's hat. It was wonderful how much mischief an innercent-lookin' parson's hat could do. It nearly bust up a lifelong friendship between three livin' brothers in the mornin'. Bill had growled round a bit about his hat and then gone fishin' in the cool.

"Next Saturday I had no bother at home. Abel got home first an' went to Windsor in my hat, an' Bill got home next an' went somewheres else in his; but that didn't matter—I was workin' at the parson's now, an' only wanted clean an' decent workin' clothes. So I borrered a clean pair o' cords that Abel had ready to take timber down to Sydney on Monday in, an' Bill's goin'-to-work coat that was better'n mine—it was summer weather, so that was all right. An' I borrered father's work-day waistcoat that he never went to work in at all, so it was pretty clean, an' nearly as good as new. But I didn't ask him, for he was asleep—resting after a hard week's growlin'. Besides, father was always very touchy an' particular about his workin' clothes, an' always wanted them clean an' ready to go to work in on Monday.

"On the way to the parson's I felt like I was bein' roped in, like a two-year-old, for brandin' and breakin'; but I was very happy an' contented about it, and I didn't let the rope slacken all the way to the parson's this time.

"I was branded all right by an' by, too," grandfather mused, looking at the fire. He might have said that the letters were on his heart still.

"Howsomenever, we all had a comfortable arternoon. I got the frame of the fowlhouse agenst the fence in a couple of hours, and put the roof on an' roosts in, for I was a good bush carpenter in them days. But I left the rest till next Saturday, in case things didn't hurry up, for I had some sense—even in them days.

"I didn't see Harriet about when I came in for some tea, an' I got awfully disappointed and anxious. I thought perhaps it was her comin' out an' she'd gone somewheres; but I wouldn't risk asking mother for the world.

"Well, jist as I was givin' it up an' feelin' sinkin', mother said, as if she'd just remembered it, 'Oh, by the way, Harry, it's Harriet's day out tomorrow, an' she was thinkin' o' spendin' the day with Margaret; so I told her she must be a bit tired o' the house—she ain't had a Sunday out since the baby came—so if she liked, you'd take her along tonight, an' she'd have a chance of a longer chat with Margaret, an' Margaret 'ud fix her up in the spare room for the night.'

"'Well, mother,' I said, arter a while, 'what did she say to that?'

"'She didn't say much,' said mother. 'She's upstairs gettin' ready now. So you'll have to bring her back in good time tomorrow evenin', mind—that's if you've got nothin' else on. Anyways, in that case,' says mother, 'I dare say one of the others would do it; so that'll be all right.'

"'All right, mother,' I says.

"Presently Harriet comes down all flustered up and dressed, I don't know how, in some dark stuff an' a bonnet like you see in old portraits, an' the big crinoline they wore to keep off intruders. Young fellers couldn't get so clost to their girls in them days, an' it was quite right. So I took the dirty clothes—they wasn't much—an' Harriet came along with me with mother's messages to Margaret, and Abel's hat in brown paper. I wished she hadn't taken that trouble—it would have done in the basket.

"An' so we went along down the lane an' into the road, an' it was moonlight agen."

Grandfather sat silent for a while—I knew he was looking back along those roads and lanes.

"An' what did you talk about, grandfather?" I asked, after a decent pause.

"Hens," said grandfather, reflectively, without changing his attitude. "'I see, Miss Wynn,' I said, 'that hen they call yours has got all her chickens out all right,' an' that started us.

"You see, Henry," said grandfather, "no two hens ever acts or lays or sits or brings up their chickens exactly alike. It's the same with the animals an' things, I think; an' maybe with fishes and snakes. Male, female, or neuter (it's the same with trees and plants), no two things o' the same kind an' gender ever acts prezactly alike. There's as much—as much——."

"Individuality, grandfather."

"Difference!" said grandfather decidedly; and I saw that another la-di-dah word had missed fire. "There's so much difference between 'em as there is between human bein's. Miss Harriet had noticed it with hens; but the parson hadn't. He seemed more interested in me noticin' it when I spoke to him about it."

"And what did Harriet have to say to all this?"

"She wasn't Harriet yet," said grandfather, reprovingly. "She might 'a' been, though, in these—howsomenever, she said, 'Yes, Mr Albury,' an' 'No, Mr Albury,' an' she noticed that herself, and she seemed to listen very respectfully to all I said. She was about the first that did.

"Then we got talkin' of the timber and the birds, and things round there, just like a new brother an' sister talkin' contented an' interested of the things that was round us. I hurried her on, for the wrong clouds were comin' up an' I knowed Hawkesbury weather. The first drops fell afore we got home; an' Margaret took charge of Harriet an' her bonnet just as if she was a big child; an' so she was, come to think of it.

"We all got cosy and comfortable around the fire, the more so because it rained heavens hard, and it was a cold rain. Even father lost his growl an' told some yarns, as he could tell 'em; and when I went to bed I felt more happy and contented an' satisfied than I'd ever been in my life afore. An', bein' abed," reflected grandfather, after a think, "did you ever hear how I come to swear at your grandmother for the first time? I s'pose you have— I never heerd the last on it.

"Howsomenever, next mornin' it fined up, and Margaret packed us off to chapel in Windsor (and father found his growl about his workin' weskit, an' went in the gig somewheers); but Harriet would stay an' help Margaret with the dinner. She seemed happy there, an' freer, an' seemed to like some of our happy-go-lucky ways.

"At dinner-time I noticed one or two more young fellers than usual hangin' round our place. They stayed to dinner, of course—there was allers plenty for everybody. Arter dinner I kept 'em away from about the kitchen with my yarns.

"'I see yer doin' some work for the parson, Harry?' one of 'em remarks to the Blue Mountains, scratching behind his ear like a cross between a donkey an' a cockatoo.

"The Blue Mountains said nothin' an' neither did I.

"'Is that so?' said another. 'How much are yer gettin' the arternoon, Harry —five bob?'

"'More'n that,' I said.

"'Ten?'

"'More'n that!' I said. He shied then. Thought I was leadin' him on to a slippery bridge.

"'An' that was all. Abel had said to nobody at all at breakfast that morning that he'd heard the parson's housemaid was a judge o' gates, and that it was unusual in a newchum. But the girl was in the house now; an' there was no jokin' about her. That's the sort of young fellers there was in them days.

"Arter dinner we had a row on the river in the two boats; but Harriet kept close to Margaret, while Abel and Bill and the others did the pullin'

483

an' I fished and saw to things generally; an' arter tea Margaret said, 'You'd better take Harriet away along home now, or mother'll be gettin' anxious.'

"While Harriet was gettin' ready, Joe Buckman—Margaret's boy—come ridin' past from Penrith, an' stopped to say somethin' to Margaret, an' I heerd Margaret say that she was glad father had took the gig, and that big galoot would have to help her over the crick now; but I didn't know what she meant till Harriet an' me got to a little cross crick about half-way to the parson's. Last night's rain had swelled it, and the steppin'-stones was awash even now. I don't know how it happened, but we got no time to argy. I jus' ketched her up round the waist and splashed right through with her, and my heart thumpin' by the time I got acrost as if I'd carried a bullock over; an' she was as light as a feather to me. An' she was pantin', too, when I set her down, as if she'd carried me over. There was a big dry white log on the bank in the moonlight.

"'Oh, Mr Albury,' she said, 'I do feel so giddy! Do let us sit down on that log for a minute, I feel quite faint.'

"'I'm afraid yer muster been frightened, Miss Wynn,' I said, sitting down an' puttin' my arm round her shoulders to steady her in case she fainted off the log. 'I'm afraid I was too sudden.'

"'Oh, no! Not at all,' she said, though she didn't mean it that way. 'I'll be right directly, Mr Albury—I don't know what come over me.'

"I kept stiddyin' her.

"After a while she gave a sort of sigh, an' she said, 'I'm all right now, Mr Albury, thank you. I don't know what could have come over me. I think we'd best go on now. Your mother'll be waitin' up.'

"So I helped her up and took her along the road."

"Still steadyin' her, grandfather?" I said.

"Never you mind," said grandfather. "I had to keep her out of the puddles in the shadders. Presently, when we got in sight of the house, I said:

"'Ah, well! It's a lonely world, Miss Wynn.'

"'It is, Mr Albury,' she said.

"I waited, and presently she asked:

"'Do you feel lonely, Mr Albury?'

"'I do, Miss Wynn,' I said, an' presently I said, 'Do you ever feel lonely, Miss Wynn?'

"'Yes,' she says, 'I do, very much, sometimes.'

"Then I said, 'Well! Are yer satisfied, then?' And she said, 'Perfectly, Mr Albury.' And that settled it.

"An' now, Henery," said grandfather, sitting up and stretching himself, "it's about time those young shavers turned up; an', besides, we've been maggin' enough, Lord knows, for one night. Jist put the billy on the coals, will you."

"Grandfather," I said sternly, "d'ye mean to say the story's finished?"

"Yes; what else?"

"Do you mean to tell me that's how you proposed?"

"Proposed what?"

"Marriage, of course—to Harriet!"

"Marriage yer grandmother!" said grandfather. "We didn't go a-courtin' in that way in my time. Courtin' came a-courtin'-us. I tell you I only proposed keepin' company with Harriet, an' I hassertained if she was willin'."

"But didn't you kiss her, grandfather?"

"No, I did not! We didn't go huggin' and muggin' on sight in them days."

"And you had your arm round her waist all the time, 'steadying her,' as you call it!"

"You thundrin' jumpt-up fool, how could I? You saw your grandmother, an' she hadn't grow'd since. I tell yer I had me arm round her shoulders! Put the billy on the coals."

But presently grandfather relented.

"Listen here, Henery—is it your courtship or mine?"

"Yours, of course, grandfather."

"Did you ever court your granny except for lolly money, or to be let stay at her place?"

"Well, maybe. I beg pardon, grandfather."

"Then don't interrupt agen, an' don't hurry me. I'm gittin' old—though I'll see close on the hundred, an' that's more'n some of you will.

"Howsomenever, we went on to the parson's gate; but I wouldn't go in. I seen a light in the kitchen winder an' knowed mother was up and about; but I said good-bye, an' Harriet run inside quick an' I started back home. But I hadn't gone a dozen yards down the lane when I heers mother callin':

"'Harry! You Harry!'

"So I goes back.

"'What are yer runnin' off like that for?' said mother. 'Been misbehavin' yerself?'

"'I thought you was in bed, mother,' I said.

"'Then thought's your master agen,' she says. 'Come in an' dry yer feet.'

"So I slips off my boots on the veranda and went in. There was a good fire. Harriet had gone up to take off some of her armour.

"Presently Mr Kinghorn comes into the passage. He must have overheerd something.

"'Better give Harry a dry pair o' socks o' mine, Mrs Albury,' he says, 'an' a spare pair o' dry boots of any o' mine that'll fit him. They might since me hat does.'

"Next minute Harriet comes down, all practical, with socks, an' went to hunt up a pair of boots while I changed 'em. It's allers that way. When a girl gets a man's heart she starts to look arter the rest o' him straight away. I noticed her clingin' an' hoverin' round mother a good deal more than usual. Now, I wonder," reflected grandfather, "if them two was in collision all the time?"

"I think they all were, grandfather," I said (he meant collusion). "I could have betted on great-aunt Margaret, anyhow."

"Anyways," concluded grandfather, "when I was goin', mother said:

"'You'd best see that big galoot out the gate, Harriet, or he'll forget to shut it; and Harriet did as she was told."

"And then it happened, grandfather?"

"Well, I s'pose it did. You ought to know," in a loud voice. "I know all about you and the baker's daughter down by the gatehouse night afore last."

I was dumb with surprise. It was such a very close guess.

MY ARMY, O MY ARMY!

My army, O my army! The time I dreamed of comes!
I want to see your colours; I long to hear your drums!
I heard them in my boyhood when all men's hearts seemed cold;
I heard them through the Years of Life—and now I'm growing old!
My army, O my army! The signs are manifold!

My army, O my army! My army and my Queen!
I sang your Southern battle-songs when I was seventeen!
They echoed down the Ages, they came from far and near;
They came to me from Paris, they came to me from Here!—
They came while I was marching with the Army of the Rear.

My Queen's dark eyes were flashing (oh, she was younger then!)
My Queen's Red Cap was redder than the reddest blood of men!
My Queen marched like an Amazon, with anger manifest—
Her wild hair darkly matted from a knife-gash in her breast
(For blood will flow where milk will not—her sisters knew the rest).

My legions ne'er were listed, they had no need to be;
My army ne'er was trained to arms—'twas trained to misery!
It took long years to mould it, but war could never drown
The shuffling of my army's feet at drill in Hunger Town—
A little child was murdered, and so Tyranny went down.

My army kept no order, my army kept no time;
My army dug no trenches, yet died in dust and slime;
Its troops were fiercely ignorant, as to the manner born;
Its clothes were rags and tatters—patched rags, the patches torn—
Ah me! It wore a uniform that I have often worn.

The faces of my army were ghastly as the dead;
My army's cause was Hunger, my Army's cry was "Bread!"
It called on God and Mary and Christ of Nazareth;
It cried to kings and courtesans that fainted at its breath—
Its women beat their poor, flat breasts where babes had starved to
    death.

   .   .   .   .   .   .

My army! O my army—I hear the sound of drums
Above the roar of battle—and, lo, my army comes!
Nor creed of man may stay it—nor war, nor nations' law
The pikes go through the firing-lines as pitchforks go through
    straw—
Like pitchforks through the litter—while empires stand in awe.

BLACK BONNET

A day of seeming innocence,
　A glorious sun and sky,
And, just above my picket fence,
　Black Bonnet passing by.
In knitted gloves and quaint old dress,
　Without a spot or smirch,
Her worn face lit with peacefulness,
　Old Granny goes to church.

Her hair is richly white, like milk,
　That long ago was fair—
And glossy still the old black silk
　She keeps for "chapel wear";

Her bonnet, of a bygone style
　That long has passed away,
She must have kept a weary while
　Just as it is today.

The parasol of days gone by—
　Old days that seemed the best—
The hymn and prayer books carried high
　Against her warm, thin breast;
As she had clasped—come smiles come tears
　Come hardship, ay, and worse—
On market days, through faded years,
　The slender household purse.

Although the road is rough and steep,
　She takes it with a will,
For, since she hushed her first to sleep
　Her way has been uphill.
Instinctively I bare my head
　(A sinful one, alas!)
Whene'er I see, by church bells led,
　Brave Old Black Bonnet pass.

For she has known the cold and heat
   And dangers of the Track:
Has fought bush-fires to save the wheat
   And little home Out Back.
By barren creeks the Bushman loves,
   In stockyard, hut, and pen,
The withered hands in those old gloves
   Have done the work of men.

.   .   .   .   .   .

They called it "Service" long ago,
   When Granny yet was young,
And in the chapel, sweet and low,
   As girls her daughters sung.
And when in church she bends her head
   (But not as others do)
She sees her loved ones, and her dead,
   And hears their voices too.

Fair as the Saxons in her youth,
   Not forward, and not shy;
And strong in healthy life and truth
   As after years went by;
She often laughed with sinners vain,
   Yet passed from faith to sight—
God gave her beauty back again
   The more her hair grew white.

She came out in the Early Days,
   (Green seas, and blue—and grey)—
The village fair, and English ways,
   Seemed worlds and worlds away.
She fought the haunting loneliness
   Where brooding gum-trees stood;
And won through sickness and distress
   As Englishwomen could.

   .   .   .   .   .   .

By verdant swath and ivied wall
   The congregation's seen—
White nothings where the shadows fall,
   Black blots against the green.
The dull, suburban people meet
   And buzz in little groups,
While down the white steps to the street
   A quaint old figure stoops.

And then along my picket fence
   Where staring wallflowers grow—
World-wise Old Age, and Common-sense!—
   Black Bonnet, nodding slow.
But not alone; for on each side
   A little dot attends
In snowy frock and sash of pride,
   And these are Granny's friends.

To them her mind is clear and bright,
  Her old ideas are new;
They know her "real talk" is right,
  Her "fairy talk" is true.
And they converse as grown-ups may,
  When all the news is told;
The one so wisely young today,
  The two so wisely old.

At home, with dinner waiting there,
  She smooths her hair and face,
And puts her bonnet by with care
  And dons a cap of lace.
The table minds it p's and q's
  Lest one perchance be hit
By some rare dart, which is a part
  Of her old-fashioned wit.

    .   .   .   .   .

Her son and son's wife are asleep;
  She puts her apron on—
The quiet house is hers to keep,
  With all the youngsters gone.
There's scarce a sound of dish on dish
  Or cup slipped into cup,
When, left alone, as is her wish,
  Black Bonnet "washes up".

Lawson outside his cottage at Leeton in 1917. It was provided for him as part of his agreement with the State Government of New South Wales when he was appointed as a roving publicist for the Murrumbidgee Irrigation Area.

A considerable part of his time was spent in this cottage editing a revised edition of his poems at the request of George Robertson. In reasonably good health, he wrote letters defending his lines, objecting or agreeing to changes only after much argument.

He nevertheless found time to absorb the atmosphere of the Area, as his short story 'The Green Lady' shows.

THE GREEN LADY

I have used the editing by the late Cecil Mann, which he justified in a note: '(It) first appeared as two separate sketches, here linked together, following the lead of Henry Lawson's similar linking of related sketches to make that fine character study 'A Wild Irishman'.' I recall agreeing with Cecil Mann on this point at the time he was preparing the typescript for publication by Angus & Robertson in the 1960s.

Previous Convictions' little, dumpy, sawn-off swag was standing on end right in the middle of the garden path opposite my front veranda steps, like the daylight ghost of a little, furred, grey-white stump; but Previous himself was nowhere to be detected. However, he faded in presently, round the big grey front gate-post and on to the lower step; and glancing along the bank of the irrigation channel, in the direction from which he had come, I was aware of a turned-down brim of a hat and a pair of drawn-up knees just showing behind a tree.

After a while the voice of Previous was vague in the hot, heavy air.

"I left Dotty along there behind the ornamental tree," he said, "but I lost sight of his hat for a minute when I got here, so I went back to see if he was goin' in for a swim—or tryin' to thieve the canal. But he was only down in the reeds fishing for yabbies with a bit of meat on a string."

(I might mention that yabbies are little things of the crayfish kind that undermine the banks of the irrigation channels and help let the water soak on and waste, while the reeds do their best to choke the channels, and have to be cut every year.)

"I promised once to tell you why I brought Dotty from the river," Previous went on, "after old S'Sam gave us permission to camp an' fish an' shoot there, and after he'd thieved the cow that chased me into the water—I mean Dotty did, not old S'Sam. The fish leave off biting after Easter, and it was the last of the soft nights. You know the rain that come last week? Well, it started next night and we was out in it all. We was miserable—drenched an' wet an' cold, in spite of a fire we had under the lee of the log. Dotty rigged a sort of a fly between the log and two saplings that stood near it—did it with one of his blankets and pieces of clothes-line he'd thieved from somewhere. Thieved 'em for me to hang meself with, I suppose, if I felt that way. But the blanket sagged and leaked worse than the sky did, so I had to take it down to keep us from bein' drowned as well as froze.

"The weather held up a bit to let in the daybreak, and Dotty built the fire and I had a sleep, crouched up against the log. When I woke, Dotty was gone

492

and the rain coming on again, and I didn't know how long I'd been unconscious. I sploshed through it all to the station, but Dotty wasn't there, and they didn't seem like as if old S'Sam or anything else was missin'. They wanted me to stay and have breakfast and dry meself at the big old fire-place; but I told 'em I had to go and look after my mate, and they understood that. One of the stationhands looked up the best part of an old oilcoat that had belonged to him, and an old canvas raincoat that had belonged to a horse, and made me take them. When I got back to the camp Dotty wasn't there again, and just when I was going to give it up I seen him comin' across a creek from the old Hay road. He had a real waterproof tent-fly that he'd borrowed from some civilized blacks—the last of the Hay tribe, that lived in a corrugated-iron camp across the road, towards Yanco railway station. He said they'd lent it to him, and I believed him. You see, Dotty doesn't lie; he either tells the truth or smiles that vacant, idiot smile of his, and says nothing. I wondered what the blacks thought of Dotty; and, to have done with that, when we returned the fly on our way here Dotty and the old king and queen grinned at each other a treat. Perhaps he could talk some of their lingo and sing the songs of their childhood—songs he'd learnt in his first childhood.

"Well, Dotty fixed the fly and cooked breakfast between showers. He built up a roaring fire that held its own in spite of the rain that got at it, and what with the wind and the fire he got the blankets dry. Next he kept throwing hot coals and ashes under the fly, and sweeping 'em off. Then he pulled down a lot of boughs, when it held up a bit, and beat the wet out of 'em against a tree, and dried 'em out against the fire; and we spread the old horse-rug and oilcoat on them and made a good camp-bed. We'd kept the bread and flour and things dry in the burnt-out hollow at the bottom of an old tree, an' we drank hot tea and lay on our backs on a dry bed and under dry blankets, and didn't care for nothing nor nobody—at least, I didn't; I had a book to read. And, if he didn't feel it, Dotty looked as happy as if he'd thieved Heaven.

"Dotty had got some wire-fence posts from a pile up the river-bank and stacked them to the side of me, away from the fire, to make it warmer and keep the wind off. And to make us feel more happy and comfortable the rain and the wind came on like they did the night before. But we were all right so long as the wind stayed in that quarter. A stationhand rode up, between the rainstorms, in a big oilskin overcoat, with the tail of it spread out on his horse's rump, and bent down on his horse's neck and said, 'Day, mates. It's a wet day.' Dotty pointed to the billy of tea on the coals and jerked his thumb up to where there was a pint-pot upside-down on the log. The stationhand said 'Thank yer,' and got down from his horse, and Dotty reached him the sugar-bag and he had some tea. The stationhand's wet sheep-dog came up, too, and shook himself on the other side of the fire; then he dodged round closer to us, and laughed at us in a friendly way. The stationhand stood by the fire for a while; then he scratched the back of his head with his little finger, and said 'So-long,' and got on his horse and rode off, and his dog went after him.

"Nobody else come to see us except an old magpie. Dotty threw it a bit of meat and so startled it that it jumped away—it'd thought Dotty was asleep. It swore at Dotty; and then it snatched up the meat and flew off with it. By and by it come back and cursed Dotty some more an' woke me; so Dotty threw it another bit of meat, and it swore its thanks and flew away with that too. I suppose it wanted that bit for its wife and kids. Anyway, it come back again and had a last piece comfortably by itself on the dry ground by the fire after cursing Dotty and all his family, good and hard, for about two minutes. It said Dotty was a foundling, or something such—like any other real bushman does when he meets an old mate unexpected after some years.

"I heard that all the wild magpies were half tame round Leeton until young civil-servant gawps came round bangin' off guns at 'em. I've seen one of them fancy fishermen la-di-dahs down there by the river shoot a bird like a curlew and break its leg. There was a strong barb-wire and netted fence between 'em, so he couldn't get at what he'd shot. But the bird kept hopping round on one leg, with his face towards us all the time, screamin' out, for all the world, 'Now-see-what-yer-done!' 'Now-see-what-yer-done!' 'Now-see-what-yer-done!' till his mates come an' got him away.

"Well, to get on with it. The rain and wind come on with the night, worse 'n' the first night; but the wind still held in the right quarter for us—as if all the winds in the Southern World lived there an' was goin' up to blow all the Japs outer the North o' Queensland. But we was as snug as two rugs in a bug—what yer grinnin' at?—an' I slept well. Till something woke me. Yer know how something wakes yer—anywhere in Australia; whether in the bosom of your family, when a child gets sick in the night, or in the bush, or in quod. The rain had cleared at midnight, as it does at midday in Sydney mostly, and it was broad moonlight, and all was still. But Dotty was gone agen. I reckoned maybe he mighter gone with that old magpie of his, to look after his red cow an' calf, 'n' inquire how they was gettin' on, an' whether they'd found a warm gully outer the wind to sleep in. So I give it best, an' stood up an' stretched meself, an' put some more limbs on the fire, an' turned round an' took in the scenery.

"The tourists never see the Murrumbidgee as it is; they never see it even in the mountains above Burrinjuck, nor below it, either—except perhaps at Gundagai or Narrandera or Hay. Where they do see it it's like pictures of the Upper Darling at Bourke, except for the river timber, and that grows tall and straight and sound mostly. But down here it's the oldest river in the world, in the oldest bush. Them knotted an' gnarled an' stunted an' twisted old trees have been burnt out in a hundred bushfires, an' rotted in a hundred floods: but they won't die—except where the fire has burnt 'em down, or the floods have undermined 'em an' the river drowned 'em an' poisoned 'em with slime an' mud. But you've been there, an' you know.

"Well, right opposite to that camp we had there on the Murrumbidgee, but a bit lower down," said Previous, "there's a sort of island with a tree right in the middle of the river. It's greener than anything anywhere around. It doesn't seem to belong to Australia at all. The tree and the little island seem all one; the island must be matted roots an' moss mostly, and it's bin through an' under God knows how many floods. The whole thing looks like a lady, dressed just as yer mother used to dress in the seventies or the eighties—bonnet and bustle, full-back skirt an' all, just leanin' forward an' glidin' up the river. They call her the Green Lady, and she's always glidin' up the stream. The faster the current runs the faster the Green Lady seems to glide. While all other trees are dark, with black shadders, there she is green in the moonlight, gliding up the river, and seeming more anxious than ever to get there, as if she had a son in trouble up somewhere at the head of it.

"I'd turned in agen, but just as it seemed I was droppin' off there was sounds —or, rather, one great sound. It seemed to me at first as if it was the Sydney Town Hall organ playin' an' all the kids round Darling Harbour singin'. I thought, for the moment, that my mate Dotty had thieved the Heavenly Choir, or the other one, or both, an' brought 'em to entertain me. I sat up quick, and the sound went. I crawled from under the tent-fly and knelt up and looked over the log that was protectin' us from the weather, but there was nothing there, except the everlasting old haunting of the bush in the moonlight. So I stood up. The wind had changed to another quarter, an' it was blowin' quite warm. The moon went under some of the bluey-white clouds that was flyin' home—like kids that had frightened 'emselves tellin' ghost yarns. An' I heard a man's voice—it seemed like a mad preacher's voice. I jumped round like a party politician that smells dissolution. The moon popped out from behind the flying kiddy-clouds, an' I looked along the steep clay bank. There was Dotty, standin' half-way down near the water, on the steep clay bank, on a sort of ledge we'd dug to fish from, clear in ther moonlight."

Previous Convictions paused a while, and seemed to think of it as if in a vague way he didn't approve of it.

"It was Dotty, all right," he continued—"Dotty standing there on that clay ledge above the river that was full of black snags in the moonlight. But the voice wasn't Dotty's, an' the man, to look at him, wasn't Dotty. Either he was—well, he was another man and was raving; an' the worst of it was it was sane ravin'. He was standin' up straight, facing across the river to the Green Lady, and wavin' his arms and ravin' to her. He was ravin' about his ruined life and his wrongs and woman's devilment and lies—most of the things I knew about him and a good many I didn't. He raved about his life before he was married, and his family, and his wife, and the other man. He raved about relations who spread lies, and he cursed all neighbours who listen to them, and all smug, comfortable magistrates who listen to them, and who send innocent men to jail and starvation and disgrace, and drive them to drink and madness. And he cursed all soft, good-natured fools of husbands; though I don't know what he did that for.

"And the Green Lady didn't say anything, but kept gliding up the river as if she was in a hurry to get past; but all the other crooked old witch trees up on the level seemed to wave their broken, blackened arms and ragged fingers an' sing an' curse an' rave too.

"I sat down on a broken limb of the log, about knocked up, an' took me head in me hands. If that was Dotty sane, I'd rather have him dotty. It was a lot worse than the nights when he pinched the garden-chair and the mat and the stained-glass angel for me to furnish a stable with.

"What with worry and want of rest and sleep, with sheer funk, there were so many sounds and voices in my head that I didn't notice, for a minute or two, that Dotty's new mad voice had stopped. As soon as I noticed it I jumped up, and couldn't see Dotty anywhere. I thought he'd gone into the river and down with it. And then there came to me a new, cold, sudden terror—swift as they say things come to a drownin' man. You know what it would look like to come away from a place like that in the bush without yer mate!

"Perhaps it was the worry an' want of rest, and the guilty knowledge of

495

me old criminal tendencies; but it was worse than all me old previous con-wictions put together, with a charge of housebreakin an' manslaughter thrown in, and detectives standin' across the street lookin' as innercent as fourteen chinamen outside a fan-tan an' opium joint. An' here, of all times, them lines of 'Gilrooney', the outback poet, come ringin' in me ears:

'Twas Murderin' Mick who killed his mate between the dawn an' day;
He cut his throat from ear to ear, and left him where he lay.
'Twas Murderin' Mick that came to wear a queer white cap at morn,
An' ne'er before in Goulburn Gaol was cap so lightly worn.

"I had a mad thought that I saw that cap, an' wondered how it would fit me. I even felt it over me ears, with an elastic-band under 'em—an' the band seemed to hurt more than the rope did. No, I don't want to wear a queer white cap at morn, or any other time, for that matter; and I don't think I'd wear it lightly, neither, for Dotty nor no one else—no matter how much he deserves it.

"But just as I was sliding down the steep bank to the river—whether with an idea of savin' Dotty from drownin' an' me from ther gallows, or, failin' that, drownin' meself for the same reason, I don't know—but just then I seen a bunyip or something heave itself onter the mud, an' Dotty comes climbin' up the bank on three legs, with a fish in the other. He'd been down attending to the lines, and got a fish off one of 'em. Either his mad-sane fit had passed or it was all a dream.

"Dotty put the fish in an old kerosene-tin half-full of water that he kept for the purpose. He reckoned it was cruel to string 'em through the gills and mouth on a reed or string or piece of wire, and hang 'em from a branch or let 'em die slow in the dust and dirt. No—he kept 'em alive an' as happy as they could be till he was ready to clean 'em. Poor Dotty never knew how he got me in the gills sometimes.

"I turned in an' slept till the sun was up amongst the tree-trunks, bright an' white an' hot; but Dotty had rigged boughs to keep it off my face. He was cookin' breakfast when I woke; it was the smell of it that woke me. (Did yer ever smell bacon or chops cookin' at the camp-fire in the mornin' when you was hungry?) Dotty had fish and ham, and last night's bread from the stationhand cook. Mine was fried ham, and Dotty brought breakfast to me in bed in an old tin-plate that he'd found and straightened and polished with ashes. He was just his same old good-natured idiotic self again. His old red cow and calf came to the edge of the bank and looked down at us—looked at Dotty in a mild, anxious, motherly sort of way, as if she thought he might have been a twin-calf that she'd forgot. Me she gave a last look of disgust and went away."

Previous Convictions thought a while. Then he said: "That last night on the river was enough for me, and I'd made up my mind to bring Dotty away from it, whether he was stained angel or a stained devil or a moon-struck lunatic—whatever he was. We went to the station to say good-bye to the ratty cook and the good-natured stationhand, and take back the old raincoats they'd lent us; but they wouldn't have 'em, and I'm glad they wouldn't, though they're a bit more load; for we'll want 'em on the Hay track this winter.

"I forgot to tell yer that the men's quarters at Yanco are in the old homestead, behind the Mansion, an' the pint-pots and bread and meat and sugar are slid out fer 'travellers' in the same old hospitable way on the big old cedar dinin'-room table, in the long old dinin'-room with its high panelled ceilin' an' wall and deep panelled doorways and winders, an' the cook standin' with his legs wide apart, an' his back to the big old-fashioned fireplace, presidin' an' beamin' like a prodigal father. He was short and stout, with a big apron, an' looked like a sea-cook, an' he was ratty—like all station and shearers' cooks I'd ever seen. He gave me some poetry he'd wrote about old S'Sam and got printed, and some he'd made up about himself; and as much tucker as we'd like to carry; and so we went back to camp to roll up our swags.

"A lot of magpies come round and cursed us till Dotty threw out the rest of the meat for 'em, and they sung 'For He's a Jolly Good Feller' as we took the track.

"Before we struck the road Dotty called at a little old slab-and-iron cottage standin' by itself in a garden 'longside McCaughey's old main-irrigation canal —all full of tall reeds now except for a narrow channel of clear water, and looking wonderfully fresh and green. An old Irish couple lived there, private and independent. They were old retainers, I suppose. They seemed to have seen Dotty before this trip—perhaps in one of his private peregrinations—and knew he was afflicted, for the old woman crossed herself, and the old man took off his hat. It looked as if he only took it off at other times when he went to bed, 'n' perhaps not then. And they told us of a short cut across the paddocks, an' pointed where to strike it. After we left them Dotty's old magpie caught us and come with us, and nagged at us from the top of every wire-fence post for about a mile; but he took us the short cut all right, and gave us a good, hearty, affectionate cursing at the end."

ON THE NIGHT TRAIN

Have you seen the Bush by moonlight, from the train, go
    running by,
Here a patch of glassy water, there a glimpse of mystic sky?
Have you heard the still voice calling, yet so warm, and yet so cold:
"I'm the Mother-Bush that bore you! Come to me when you are
    old?"

Did you see the Bush below you sweeping darkly to the range,
All unchanged and all unchanging, yet so very old and strange!
Did you hear the Bush a-calling, when your heart was young
    and bold:
"I'm the Mother-Bush that nursed you! Come to me when you
    are old?"

Through the long, vociferous cutting as the night train swiftly sped,
Did you hear the grey Bush calling from the pine-ridge overhead:
"You have seen the seas and cities; all seems done, and all seems
    told;
I'm the Mother-Bush that loves you! Come to me, now you are old?"

Lucy Cassidy (née Sullivan) delighted to tell how her old friend, Henry Lawson, transcribed 'On the Night Train' into her autograph album in 1922. In 1920 some of his friends banded together, as they usually did when he needed help most, and arranged for him to be sent on a holiday to the country. R. J. Cassidy ('Gilrooney'), a staff journalist on the *Worker* and poet and novelist, arranged all details and on the day that Lawson was to leave for Coolac a watchful eye was kept on him. As Mrs Cassidy told the story '... Henry was shepherded on to the train, quite sober...'. As the train started to leave the platform she, her husband, and Rod Quinn, were quite relieved. Suddenly Lawson leant out of carriage window and showed them a bottle of whisky he'd kept hidden all day.

He did not remain long at Coolac and on his return to Sydney began drinking heavily again.

In February 1922, a few months before his death, he copied 'On the Night Train', in a remarkably steady hand considering his health, and told Mrs Cassidy that it had been inspired by the train trip to Coolac.

SHORT STORIES—INDEX OF TITLES

POEMS—INDEX OF TITLES

POEMS—INDEX OF FIRST LINES

A CHECK-LIST OF THE FIRST EDITIONS OF BOOKS BY HENRY LAWSON

Because of certain complexities that marked Lawson's dealings with both printers and publishers, it is not possible to do more, within this volume, than list the first editions and ignore the variant editions which delight, and sometimes confuse, the devout collectors of Lawsoniana. I have purposely omitted poems first published on single sheets, foreign translations, and the many local and overseas anthologies in which his work has appeared. Details of these minor publications may be found in *An Annotated Bibliography of Henry Lawson* by George Mackaness (Sydney, Angus & Robertson, 1951).

Short Stories in Prose & Verse, 1894

In the Days When the World was Wide, 1896

While the Billy Boils, 1896

On the Track and Over the Sliprails, 1900 (*On the Track* and *Over the Sliprails* issued as separate titles in the same year)

Verses Popular and Humorous, 1900

The Country I Come From, 1901 (Published in England)

Joe Wilson and his Mates, 1901 (Published in England)

Children of the Bush, 1902 (Published in England)

When I was King and Other Verses, 1905 (Later published in two parts as separate titles: *When I was King* and *The Elder Son*)

The Rising of the Court and Other Sketches in Prose and Verse, 1910

The Skyline Riders and Other Verses, 1910

A Coronation Ode and Retrospect, 1911

Mateship A Discursive Yarn, 1911

The Stranger's Friend, 1911

Triangles of Life, 1913

For Australia and Other Poems, 1913

My Army, O, My Army! and Other Songs, 1915 (Published in England as *Songs of the Dardanelles*, 1916, with contents re-arranged)

Selected Poems, 1918

Joseph's Dreams, 1923

The Auld Shop and the New, 1923 (This, and the preceding volume, appeared after Lawson's death in editions limited to 75 copies 'for private distribution')

Life@Work

The Essentials

LIFE@WORK GROUPZINE™
Volume 2: The Essentials

Published by Nelson Impact, a Division of Thomas Nelson, Inc.,
P.O. Box 141000, Nashville, Tennessee 37214.

Creative Design: Rebecca Corrales, Allysa Luttrell, Atlanta, Georgia (**www.corralesindustries.com**)

Life@Work would like to thank:
Bob Gordon, Rebecca Corrales, Wayne Kinde, Lori Jones, Neil Rogers, Beth Nelson, Amanda Hindson, Hudson Phillips, Mark Cole, Reggie Goodin, Cindy Gould, Anne Alexander, Steve Graves, and all our contributors.

For more information on Life@Work or to order additional copies of the *Life@Work GroupZine™*, call INJOY customer service at 1-800-333-6506 or visit **www.lifeatworkgroupzine.com**.

To learn more about sponsorship opportunities or exhibiting at a Life@Work event, contact Stacy Coleman (stacy.coleman@injoy.com).

ISBN-10: 1-4185-0322-3
ISBN-13: 978-1-4185-0322-2

Printed in the United States of America.

06 07 08 09 CJK 9 8 7 6 5 4 3 2 1

HOW TO USE A GROUPZINE

A Note for Small Group Leaders

Welcome to The Essentials — the next volume in the **Life@Work GroupZine**™ series from **INJOY.** As with any new tool, it's helpful to read the directions... so here are some ideas on how best to use this GroupZine in your small group.

The Process

As you browse through this GroupZine you'll notice four overarching themes—Skill, Calling, Serving, & Character—which represent the essential qualities of a Life@Work leader. There are two study sessions per theme, or eight total sessions. Each study session contains a primary curriculum article (the Life@Work Study), feature articles & book excerpts, practical toolbox application articles, and profiles of workplace leaders.

At the end of each session there are **"Journal Entry"** pages with questions for group study. These allow the reader to reflect and respond to the ideas found in the entire session.

And finally, wrapping up each theme you'll find the **"In Focus"** pages which recap the main ideas and offer suggestions for creating an action plan or "next steps".

It would be beneficial for your group to tackle these sessions within a focused timeframe, but feel free to create your own schedule. Some groups might take one week per session, while others might spend one month per theme. Choose a meeting and study schedule that works best for the specific needs of your group.

The Conversation

As a small group leader, you are often expected to have all the answers ... and let's be honest—you don't have all the answers! However, as the leader, you should have the most questions and the confidence to share them.

That's really the best way to lead through this GroupZine: bring your questions and comments to the group and find the answers together. Conversation is the starting point to form true community, and through these discussions, your group will naturally grow closer.

Discussion points are provided throughout the GroupZine, but you'll notice there is also plenty of white space to doodle, dream, create your own questions, or ponder what you have just read.

Online Leader's Guide

For those of you who need a little more structure for your group setting, you can download a more detailed leader's guide from the Life@Work GroupZine website at **www.lifeatworkgroupzine.com**.

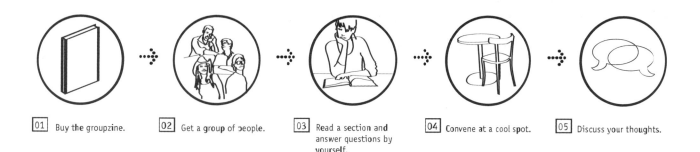

01 Buy the groupzine. 02 Get a group of people. 03 Read a section and answer questions by yourself. 04 Convene at a cool spot. 05 Discuss your thoughts.

Inside the LIFE@WORK GROUPZINE™: The Essentials

Every once in a great while, hunger in our culture
aligns with an imperative from Scripture.

Never before (*at least in our lifetimes*) has there been such a
great window of opportunity to take our faith to work.

That window of opportunity currently exists regarding
the need for work to provide meaning, satisfaction,
and a sense of eternal significance.

THE LIFE@WORK STORY

The Life@Work Company began with a supernatural push from God and His people as a response to society's desperate search for answers that will make sense and bring relevancy to the world of work and how it relates to the other aspects of our lives. From 1998-2002 Life@Work produced a very successful magazine called the *Life@Work Journal*. Over the last nine years, Life@Work has built a leading brand in the emerging faith/work category and developed a significant network of faith professionals.

In 2004, Life@Work was acquired by the INJOY Group, an organization based in Atlanta, Georgia and founded by Dr. John C. Maxwell. Recognized as a thought leader in this field, Life@Work continues to answer the question, *"How do you resource and equip the men and women who attend church on Sunday... and then go to work on Monday?"* by providing fresh thinking, biblical perspective, and ongoing solutions for men and women of faith in the workplace,

We are dedicated to serving workplace leaders through innovative resources, events, and training; providing local churches, pastors, and workplace leaders with effective and engaging "inreach" and "outreach" ministry opportunities; and equipping them to understand, embrace, and live out a biblical view of work and faith. For more information, visit **www.lifeatwork.com**.

OUR VISION
Churches transforming workplace leaders

OUR PURPOSE
To help the local church prepare and unleash its workplace leaders to glorify God in their work

OUR MISSION
To provide the local church with an integrated faith and work solution through high-profile personality events, curriculum, and networking

LETTER FROM THE EDITOR

Welcome to The Essentials, Volume 2 of the Life@Work GroupZine. With The Essentials, we're focusing on four fundamentals that we all need to hone if we're committed to honoring God with our Life@Work:

- Skill
- Calling
- Serving
- Character

I was excited when INJOY called and asked me to again serve as the editor of this project. After all, I have some experience and awareness in these areas:

Skill: Having played soccer in college, I thought I had some skill ... until I covered the World Cup as a sportswriter. I was in awe watching the skill of world's best players: the Italians, the Germans, and the Brazilians — especially the Brazilians! That's when I discovered what true skill looks like.

Calling: I also like to fancy myself as a writer ... until I read a play by Shakespeare, a short story by Flannery O'Connor, or a children's book by Dr. Seuss. After enjoying one of these gifted writers, I inherently find myself wrestling with my calling.

Serving: Since becoming a follower of Christ, I have actively engaged in serving. Or at least that's what I call it ... until I read a biography of Mother Theresa or Marin Luther King Jr. Talk about true servanthood!

Character: Of course, when it comes to character, let's just say I've been called that enough to know a thing or two about it!

Thankfully, we've been able to connect with gifted thinkers, practitioners, and everyday people in the workplace who understand the importance of our daily intersection of faith and career.

I hope these stories and studies will help you think deeply, and will challenge you to move more proactively toward honoring God with your skill, calling, serving, and character: The Essentials of Life@Work.

As you've seen, I sure can use the help!

In this together,

Bob

Bob Gordon

Volume 2: The Essentials

Life@Work
PO Box 7700
Atlanta, GA 30357
www.lifeatwork.com

Executive Editor
Brad Lomenick

Editor
Bob Gordon

Managing Editor
Kerry Priest

Design and Art Director
Rebecca Corrales

Contributing Writers:

Amy Baker	Kenneth Boa
Andy Stanley	Kerry Priest
Ben Carson	Marcus Buckingham
Bill Hybels	Margaret Feinberg
Bill Strickland	Mark Sanborn
Bob Coy	Matthew Barnett
Bob Gordon	Os Guinness
Brad Lomenick	Os Hillman
Christine Willard	Phil Hodges
Dale Bronner	Randy Kilgore
Dave Ramsey	Regi Campbell
David Roth	Rick Packer
Dennis Bakke	Stephen R. Graves
Dianna Booher	Stephen Caldwell
John Brandon	Ted Haggard
John C. Maxwell	Thomas G. Addington
John Ortberg	Todd Duncan
John Wooden	Tom Mullins
Justin Pinkerman	Valorie Burton
Ken Blanchard	

If you have a story idea, questions, feedback, or would like to submit a person or company to be profiled in the next *Life@Work GroupZine™*, email us **info@lifeatworkgroupzine.com**. To purchase other INJOY or Life@Work resources call 1-800-333-6506.

SKILL@WORK

Skill: Understanding something completely and transforming that knowledge into creations of wonder and excellence

Life@Work Study

The Wonder of Skill

Awe-Inspiring Excellence Provides a Glimpse of Divine Essence

BY STEPHEN R. GRAVES

SESSION ONE

With just seconds remaining in the game, the little point guard eludes two towering defenders and hits a twenty-foot fade-away jumper from the baseline. The buzzer sounds. The crowd goes wild. But consider the moment just before the celebration begins — that split-second of awed silence after the ball swishes through the net ... but before the pandemonium breaks loose.

We are designed to celebrate skill; we are also designed to marvel at it. There's something genuinely awe-inspiring about seeing skill in action. It doesn't matter which side you're cheering for. It's quite independent of the thrill of victory and the agony of defeat. When you are witness to excellence — innate, God-given skill honed to a sharp edge and expressing itself under incredible pressure — you can't help but feel awe.

Human beings are amazing creatures. Thomas Edison said, "If we all did the things we are capable of doing, we would literally astound ourselves." Just think of all the incredible things that the human mind has thought up and what human hands have achieved: the pyramids of Giza, the Great Wall of China, the Faberge eggs of czarist Russia, the athletic feats of the Olympics, the moon landings ... the list is nearly endless. God has made us with incredible capability.

> What is it about human excellence that inspires us so? Perhaps it has something to do with the fact that skill expresses the divine essence that still resides in each of us.

Skill, however, is not the limited domain of extraordinary genius. As Booker T. Washington observed, "Excellence is to do a common thing in an uncommon way." We know skill when we see it:

- A mechanic who finds and fixes a problem that no one else could locate or solve.

- An entrepreneur who creates a successful business from nothing.

- A professional truck driver who deftly maneuvers a 55-foot 18-wheeler into a hard-to-get-to freight dock with only inches of leeway on either side.

- A tenacious salesman who negotiates through almost insurmountable obstacles to close a tough deal.

- An artist who brings living color out of a blank white canvas.

Our work is a kind of art. There is beauty in it. What we do is the pinnacle achievement of creation. The simplest of human tasks are unmatched in the animal world. Computers and machines struggle to do things that even a child takes for granted.

When we watch someone accomplish a task with real skill, we are simply amazed. Eugene Ionesco observed, "The end of childhood is when things cease to astonish us." There is a child in each of us that is amazed by how things work. We think, Wow! That was really something! How did she do that?

The Divine Essence

Why is that? What is it about human excellence that inspires us so? Perhaps it has something to do with the fact that skill expresses the divine essence that still resides in each of us. It's a little reminder that we are all made in the image of the One who "doeth all things well."

It's strange that contemporary Christian writers have had so little to say about the value of skill in our workaday world. Maybe it's because we've bought into the world's notion of what skill is and what it's good for, forgetting what God thinks about it. In the world's eyes, skill is a weapon. You sharpen your skills in order to get an advantage in a Darwinistic dog-eat-dog fight for survival. Skill is a means of keeping score, of demonstrating that you're better than everybody else. It's all about winning — or, more to the point, making sure everybody else loses.

If that's what skill is about, no wonder Christians shy away from the subject. But that's not a biblical view of skill and excellence. God values human talent because it's one of the most important ways He builds His kingdom. From a biblical perspective, skill is a mastery of your work that is creative and constructive, not domineering or self-aggrandizing. We define it this way: **Skill is understanding something completely, and transforming that knowledge into creations of wonder and excellence.**

Goliath used his tremendous skill to destroy nations. David used his to build a nation. Goliath exalted himself and intimidated his rivals. David affirmed the goodness of God in his work, and he created things of lasting value. As he built the kingdom of Israel, he was helping to build the kingdom of God.

When people use the phrase, "the Lord's work," they're usually talking about such "spiritual" pursuits as evangelizing and preaching, counseling and baptizing. But the wonder of skill in action is a reminder that all honest work can be "the Lord's work."

> God expects — and deserves — a return on His investment in you. True humility motivates you to get down to the business of being excellent for God's glory.

God is the Creator and the Sustainer. To work skillfully is to join God in the work He's been doing all along.

Adam and Eve, remember, had work to do even before the Fall. They tended the Garden, cooperating with God as stewards and vicegerents over His created order. Sure, in this fallen world, work is often difficult and less than fulfilling. "In the sweat of your face you shall eat bread till you return to the ground" (Genesis 3:19 NKJV). But that's not all there is to work. There is still purpose and pleasure and fulfillment to be had from honest work done well. To work, to join in with "the Lord's work," has always been part of what it means to be fully human — even before Adam and Eve's sin complicated matters.

Your work is an arena where you can shape and give expression to the skills and excellencies that God hard-wired into you. Your work is a place where you can become what God made you to be. Which is to say, God is concerned with a lot more than your "spiritual life." The Holy Spirit is just as involved helping believers on the job as He is when they contribute at church. God didn't just give each of us a set of skills and leave us to our own devices. Instead, for those in the family of faith, He wants to come alongside us at the office or on the jobsite and infuse our skills with His empowering presence.

Skill is Important to God

Consider God's instructions to Moses regarding the building of the tabernacle. After He gave Moses the Ten Commandments, God kept the prophet up on Mount Sinai for some additional and rather lengthy instruction. He was very specific; this was to be an ISO-certified project. "Make the tabernacle with ten curtains of finely twisted linen and blue, purple and scarlet yarn, with cherubim worked into them by a *skilled craftsman* (Exodus 26:1, NKJV, emphasis added). A couple of chapters later: "Tell all the *skilled men to whom I have given wisdom in such matters* that they are to make garments for Aaron, for his consecration, so he may serve me as priest" (Exodus 28:3, NKJV, emphasis added).

The skill that God is looking for is a skill that He gave. It comes from Him. He asks that we use the gifts that He originally gave us *for Him*. But the most fascinating reference is the one in which God specifically identifies the craftsmen He has in mind for the project:

"Then the Lord said to Moses, 'See, I have chosen Bezalel son of Uri, the son of Hur, of the tribe of Judah, and I have *filled him with the Spirit of God, with skill, ability and knowledge in all kinds of crafts* — to make artistic designs for work in gold, silver and bronze, to cut and set stones, to work in wood, and to engage in all kinds of craftsmanship. Moreover, I have appointed Oholiab son of Ahisamach, of the tribe of Dan, to help him. Also *I have given skill to all the craftsmen* to make everything I have commanded you: the Tent of Meeting, the ark of the Testimony with the atonement cover on it, and all the other furnishings of the tent'" (Exodus 31:1-7, NKJV, emphasis added).

According to this Scripture, Bezalel was personally appointed by God. Then he was filled with the Holy Spirit — specifically as a supplement to his skill as a craftsman — for the purpose of his work. Not only does God order the best skill, not only was He the one from whom it came, but His Spirit continues to supernaturally enable it.

Witnessing Skill in Action Takes You Inward

When you see skill in another person, it has a way of making you take a closer look at yourself. It's only human to compare your skills to another person's — to calculate how you stack up. But that's not really the point. The point is to allow another person's excellence to inspire your own excellence in those areas where God has given you skills.

It's a matter of stewardship — managing the talents and abilities that God has entrusted to you and earning a return on God's investment. The tug you feel when you see skill in action may be more than mere envy or competitive spirit. It may be the call of God, urging you to make the most of the gifts He has given you.

So much for the sight of excellence in other people. What of your own excellence? What does it do for you when you witness your own skills in action? Do you ever consider the fact that you yourself are a marvel? Don't worry: it's not vanity to think so — not if you give credit where credit is due. David marveled, "I am fearfully and wonderfully made; marvelous are Your works, and that my soul knows very well" (Psalm 139:14 NKJV). You are a piece of incredible craftsmanship — you and everybody else you've ever met. There's no need for false humility when it comes to the skills and talents that God put into your make-up. It brings no glory to God for you to disparage His workmanship.

True humility has nothing to do with manufacturing a low image of your abilities. Rather, it means having a true view of who you are in relation to God. You are not your own. Your skills aren't yours either — neither yours to boast about nor yours to waste. They belong to God. God expects — and deserves — a return on His investment in you. True humility motivates you to get down to the business of being excellent for God's glory. That's how the kingdom of God expands, not just to encompass more individuals, but all of life.

> Your work is an arena where you can shape and give expression to the skills and excellencies that God hard-wired into you. Your work is a place where you can become what God made you to be.

God wants our skill to be a divinely choreographed ballet, us doing our best, following God as the lead dancer. He wants it to be a thing of beauty, not of stress. He meant for it to work for good, not just work for results. He gave us our skill to be used for His glory, not ours.

Skill matters to God. It should matter to us too. Excellence in our skills is an extension of our spiritual relationship with our Creator. We cannot be satisfied with mediocrity and still work wholeheartedly as unto God. We cannot "just get by" and still glorify God in all we do. Skill is not a business necessity, but a spiritual imperative.

L@W

Stephen R. Graves, Ph. D., is a highly sought business coach and life guide for entrepreneurs and leaders desiring to successfully make it to the finish line of life. In 1991, he co-founded the Cornerstone Group, a company built to integrate biblical wisdom and business excellence (**www.cornerstoneco.com**). He and his wife Karen have three children.

This article is based on concepts drawn from Life@Work *by John C. Maxwell, Stephen R. Graves, and Thomas G. Addington, published by Thomas Nelson, Inc., copyright 2005. All rights reserved.*

THE WONDER OF SKILL

FOR GROUP DISCUSSION

Prior to your small group meeting time, read and reflect on the Life@Work curriculum article you just read. Use these questions and journal pages to reflect and respond to the ideas presented. Be ready to share your thoughts at your small group gathering.

Note to small group leaders: You can download a full Leader's Guide at www.lifeatworkgroupzine.com.

- "God has made us with incredible capability," writes Dr. Stephen Graves. What skills, when you see them in action, do you celebrate? Who are some people that demonstrate those skills on a regular basis? How do you feel when you see those skills in action? Do you agree with the assertion that there is something "genuinely awe-inspiring about seeing skill in action"?

- How do you think skill should be used in your workplace? Do you tend to look at skill as if it is "a weapon"? Is skill "all about winning or ... making sure that everybody else loses?" OR do you tend to believe "God values human talent because it's one of the most important ways He builds His kingdom"? How does your answer play out in the everyday reality of your job?

- In this study, skill is defined as:
  Understanding something completely, and transforming that knowledge into creations of wonder and excellence.
  What parts of this definition do you wholeheartedly agree with? Which parts are difficult for you to see playing out in the real world? Why do you think that is?

- *Your work is an arena where you can shape and give expression to the skills and excellencies that God hard-wired into you. Your work is a place where you can become what God made you to be.* What do you think when you read these words? Does your job allow you to "give expression to the skill and excellence that God hard-wired into you"? If so, how do you ensure your job continues to allow for that? If not, what can you do to find a role that allows you to "become what God made you to be"? How do you feel when you think that opportunity might exist in the work world?

- Do you tend to fall into the false humility trap when your God-given skills are highlighted? Do agree with the argument that "it brings no glory to God for you to disparage His workmanship"? Why or why not? If false humility is your default, how can you start bringing glory to God for His gifts of talent to you? Can you do that and still remain truly humble? How?

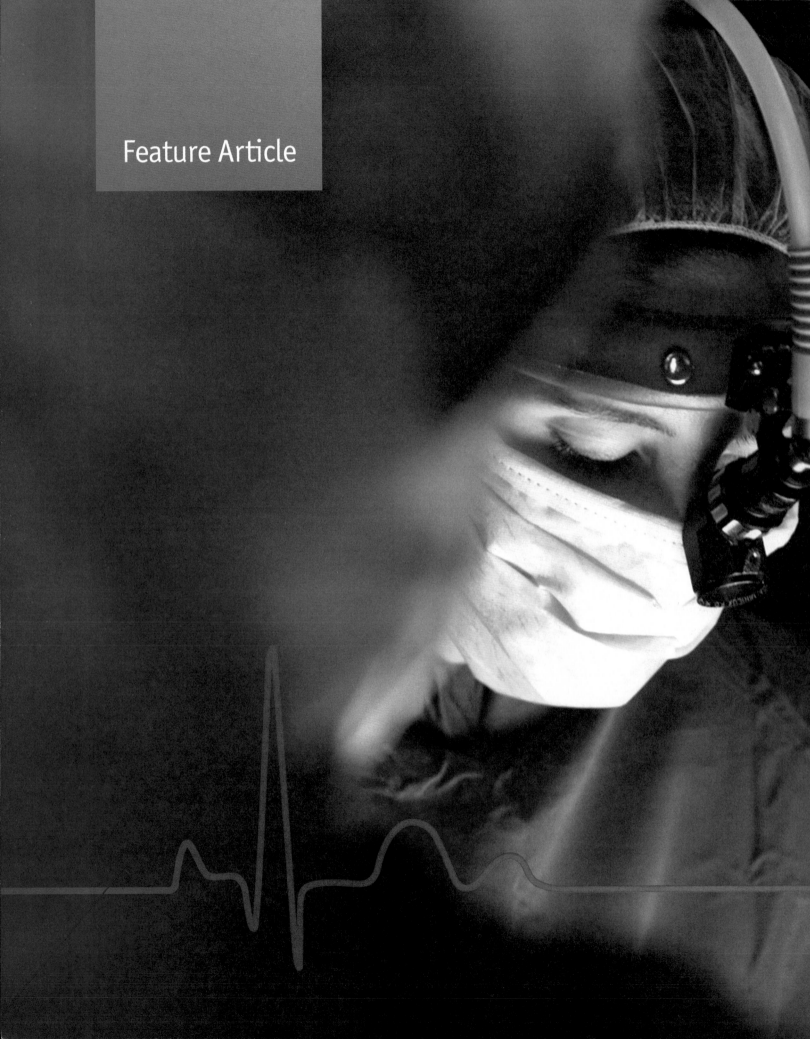
Feature Article

OPERATING WITH A MASTER'S TOUCH

Developing Your Skills Doesn't Have to be Brain Surgery

By Stephen Caldwell

The stereo system piped inspirational music into an operating room where a group of doctors hovered around Luka and Joseph Banda, conjoined twins joined at the backs of their tiny heads. As 28 hours of intense, delicate work came to a close with the successful separation of the 11-month-old babies, the "Hallelujah Chorus," as if on cue, poured through the speakers and filled the air like voices from angels.

Dr. Benjamin Carson, the world's preeminent pediatric neurosurgeon and the leader of the 20-doctor team that performed the surgery in South Africa, celebrated with his colleagues. But he knew something that perhaps no one else

while knowing that moving the wrong band at the wrong time would cause an explosion — in this case, paralysis.

When Carson examines the skills needed to handle such cases — what those skills are, where they came from, how they've been refined and how they should be used — he is careful to credit God. But he's equally quick to emphasize an individual's responsibility for managing such skills.

"I have a motto," Carson says. "Do your best and let God do the rest. But you have to do your part. You can't sit and wait and say, 'Oh Lord take care of this problem.' Man's extremity is God's

I HAVE A MOTTO.
DO YOUR BEST AND LET GOD DO THE REST.
BUT YOU HAVE TO DO YOUR PART.

knew. He had spent hours slicing through the tiniest of blood vessels to make the operation a success. Yet he knew the angels weren't singing his praises.

"That was not me," Carson says from his office on the eighth floor of Johns Hopkins Hospital. "I will admit that I have significant skills. But my skills aren't that great. That was God."

Carson, the director of pediatric neurosurgery at Johns Hopkins Children's Center, is undeniably a man of great skills. The development of his skills, intellectual and physical, helped him rise from a single-parent family in a low-income section of inner-city Detroit to become one of the top doctors in his field.

He performs as many as 400 surgeries each year, roughly twice as many as a typical neurosurgeon. Most of his patients are children. They have tumors. They have spinal deformities. They suffer from debilitating seizures. Or, on a rare occasion, they are connected to a sibling, each sharing parts of their skull, blood vessels, and tissue with the other.

He compared surgery on a seven year old's spinal column to unwrapping a bunch of rubber bands from a stick of dynamite

opportunity. But unless you do your part, it's unreasonable to expect Him to intervene."

Carson says a prayer before every operation. He prays for wisdom. He prays for guidance. And he prays for God's direct intervention should it become necessary.

With the Banda twins, Carson knew the difficulty of the case. As the surgery progressed, problems arose. Each blood vessel shared by the twins had to be identified and severed. The surgeons had to decide which child would receive each blood vessel, and then hope new collateral vessels would enlarge and assume the function of the cut vessels.

When the doctors struggled to separate the mass of abnormal blood vessels, the team took a break to discuss its options. Carson suggested they finish the surgery in stages rather than pushing forward.

"The doctors from South Africa and the doctors from Zambia told me they did not have the capability for keeping the babies alive and infection-free if we didn't complete the process," Carson says.

Translation: They might die on the operating table if the surgery continued, but they surely would die if the surgery were postponed.

"At that point, I knew that the Lord had to take over," Carson says. "We went back in there. And as I was going through those vessels, I was doing things that I normally wouldn't do. I was taking a scalpel and cutting between very thin walls, one or two cell layers thick. They were very fragile vessels that would have bled like crazy if you nicked them."

Carson made these precise cuts "for hours and hours and hours," he says. "I don't know that I personally had the ability to do that. But it was almost like I wasn't there. It was almost like I was watching me do this."

At the end of the 28 hours, one of the twins popped his eyes open and tried to pull his tube out. By the time they got to the intensive care unit, the other was doing the same thing. "We only used four units of blood," says Carson. "With the Binder twins (in 1987), it was 60."

Two days later, the twins were eating. Within two weeks, they were both crawling.

"There is a role for God to intervene when it comes to skill," Carson says. "It doesn't occur until you have reached your limit."

Carson began testing and stretching the limits of his skill when he was in the fifth grade. He was at the bottom of his class, and his prospects were bleak. But his mother devised a program. Carson and his brother would read two books each week and submit reports on them. They didn't know she only had a third-grade education and couldn't read much of what her sons wrote. They just knew they would do what their mother told them to do.

Carson read everything he could, and not just because his mother made him. His confidence soared, and he knew reading was the reason. "Reading develops the mind in the way that lifting weights

DR. BENJAMIN CARSON

THERE IS A ROLE FOR GOD TO INTERVENE WHEN IT COMES TO SKILL. IT DOESN'T OCCUR UNTIL YOU HAVE REACHED YOUR LIMIT.

develops muscles," he says. "You're not likely to develop your brain by watching other people do things or by watching television, just like you're not likely to develop muscle by watching somebody else lift weights."

Within a year, Carson was at the top of his class. Carson saw the practical benefits of developing his reading skills, especially when he read a book about Booker T. Washington.

"Here was a man who was a slave and his ideal for spending time was reading," he says. "He read everything he could get his hands on. He became so well-read that he became an advisor to presidents. The skill and the knowledge that is acquired by reading impressed me tremendously. I decided perhaps that would work for me."

It wasn't long before Carson aspired to become a doctor. Only his temper stood in his way. He once tried to hit his mother in the

lean toward him at times to keep up with the conversation. His eyes are peaceful and there's warmth in both his smile and his laugh. The idea of him harming anything, much less another person, seems ridiculous. And, in fact, Carson said he hasn't acted out of anger in years.

When Carson emerged from that schoolhouse bathroom, he saw anger as something that controlled the weak. He decided that controlling his anger would be a display of his strength.

Carson's ability to manage his emotions is a frame of mind, Carson says. "It's something that a person can make a skill if they don't have that frame of mind," he says. "They can learn to do it."

Freed from the bondage of his temper, Carson earned a scholarship to Yale. He had become a straight-A student in high school, but there was one more major academic hurdle he had to clear. And once again, it required intervention by God.

EVERYBODY MAY HAVE THE INTELLECT, BUT I DON'T THINK EVERYBODY HAS THE SKILLS. AND THERE IS A DIFFERENCE.

head with a hammer because he didn't like the clothes she had picked out for him. A youngster who attempted to close Carson's locker at school was greeted by Carson's fist — and the pad lock. His rage hit a boiling point when he was 14 and tried to stab a classmate in the stomach because the kid had changed the radio station. A metal belt buckle saved the other boy's life and kept Carson in school and out of prison.

He was so shook up by the incident that he locked himself in a bathroom, where he spent hours contemplating what he had done, reading from Proverbs and praying for deliverance from his anger.

"I recognized what a destructive emotion it is," he says.

Today, Carson is articulate, passionate and often outspoken about his beliefs. But he can be so soft-spoken that a visitor must

"All of the sudden here I am in this high-powered Ivy League institution, and I didn't have the study skills necessary to cope with that," he says. "So at the end of the first semester I was failing chemistry."

The professor decided to count the final exam twice for the students who were failing, thus offering them hope. Carson laughed at the idea of learning in one night what he hadn't been able to learn all semester. Then he turned to God.

"I said, 'Lord I've always wanted to be a doctor and I thought that's what You wanted me to be,'" Carson recalls. "'Obviously if I fail chemistry I'm not going to make it. Will You please indicate what it is You really want me to do or, alternatively and preferably, work a miracle?'"

There was no immediate answer, so Carson started going through the textbook trying to memorize formulas. It wasn't long before he fell asleep.

"I dreamed I was in an auditorium by myself, and there was a nebulous figure working out chemistry problems on the blackboard," he says. "I awakened early the next morning and the dream was so vivid that I immediately went to my textbook and started looking up the stuff I had dreamed about."

Carson felt better about the test, but he didn't feel great until he read the first question.

"I opened the booklet and looked at the first question and it was like the *Twilight Zone*," he says. "It was one of the ones I had dreamed about. And the next one and the next one and the next one. And I aced the exam. And why not? I had just seen it the night before.

"I knew at that moment that God had something special He wanted me to do in the field of medicine. I promised Him at that moment He wouldn't have to do that again. I said, 'I understand now. I have to become an in-depth studier. I have to know the materials backward and forward.' And that's what I did."

tremendous eye-hand coordination. Two, he had an ability to think in three dimensions. And, three, he enjoyed taking things apart, seeing how they worked and putting them back together.

"I started thinking back on things I was really, really good at," says Carson. "I remembered that back in college I was a champion table soccer player. I said, 'What does it require to be really good at foosball?' Hand-eye coordination."

Carson also remembered the summer he spent working in a steel plant. He became interested in the large cranes used to move steel and asked if he could operate one. To his co-workers' surprise, he was a natural. So he spent the rest of the summer working the crane.

"It's a highly skilled job where you are using multiple levers to move tons and tons of heavy steel through narrow isles and into flatbed trucks," Carson says. "I thought, 'Boy, for them to put that much confidence in a summer student, they must have had tremendous amount of confidence in my hand-eye coordination.'"

Thinking in three dimensions was a harder concept to pick out, but Carson realized he always had a good sense of where things were. He could close his eyes and picture in his mind where things were and how they were related.

I THINK GOD GIVES EVERY INDIVIDUAL SPECIAL GIFTS AND TALENTS. AND EACH PERSON HAS THE RESPONSIBILITY OF GETTING IN TOUCH WITH THOSE SPECIAL GIFTS AND TALENTS.

Carson graduated from Yale in 1973 with a degree in psychology and headed to medical school at the University of Michigan. But his undergraduate exposure to psychiatry, the field of medicine he always thought he wanted to practice, wasn't as positive as he had expected.

Faced with the critical question of what to do next, Carson took inventory of his skills. He recognized three traits. One, he had

"That obviously is very important if you're working in a substance like the brain," he says, "because everything looks pretty much the same. But you have to keep in mind where this tract is and where this function lies in the midst of all this nebulous matter."

Those skills, combined with his interest in the brain, helped him decide to practice neurosurgery. But it's another skill — the skill of innovation — that has helped separate him from many of his peers.

In high school, Carson began to look for new and better ways to do old things. It soon became a life-long pursuit.

"I worked for Ford Motor Company in the summer one year, and they had a suggestion box," Carson says. "I diagrammed and wrote out all my thoughts about a new safety restraint called the airbag."

That was in the late 1960s.

"They were supposed to give you a reward if they used your idea," Carson says with a smile. "I never heard from them. But several years later, out comes the airbag."

Carson has gotten plenty of credit for innovations in the medical profession.

"When I was in medical school I noticed that neurosurgeons were having trouble getting the needles into the *foramen ovale* (a small oval opening at the base of the skull) to achieve a certain position," he says. "I went down and got a skull and started figuring out ways to use metal rings to line up the particular area you're trying to get the needle into to make it much easier. That particular procedure has followed me throughout my career. But that started out as an interest as a medical student. I was just trying to come up with a better way and an easier way to do something."

Carson rose to prominence partly by refining a risky procedure called a hemispherectomy, a process in which half the brain is removed from a child suffering from debilitating seizures.

But not everyone can be an innovative brain surgeon, right? "Everybody may have the intellect, but I don't think everybody has the skills," Carson says. "And there is a difference."

But that difference doesn't mean others shouldn't take a similar approach to their jobs, even if their job isn't brain surgery.

"Clearly a Christian has the responsibility of developing God-given skills to the utmost," says Carson, who uses his success as a platform to challenge others to make the most of their brainpower. "I think God gives every individual special gifts and talents. And each person has the responsibility of getting in touch with those special gifts and talents.

"If you have a job to do, make sure you do it to the best of your ability. You should not be second to anyone in that area. And if that's the case, it really doesn't matter what it is that you're doing, it will be recognized. Excellence generally is."

L@W

Stephen Caldwell is a city editor for the Arkansas Democrat-Gazette and has contributed to a wide array of magazines. As a father of four, he has much fodder for his weekly "Dad Zone" column for his paper. Check out his column at **www.nwanews.com/adg/Family**.

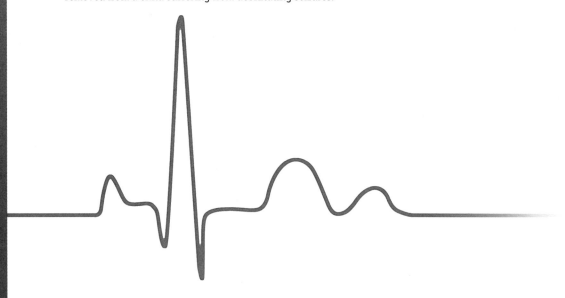

Toolbox

TOOLBOX | READING

Re-engaging in an Old Skill: Reading

By Dr. Benjamin Carson

While Dr. Benjamin Carson is best known for his skillful scalpel work, he still actively pursues a skill he learned to value in grade school: reading. He believes reading is an important way to develop mental skills.

Yet with active lives and work, family and church commitments, how can anyone find the time to regularly read? We asked Dr. Carson for a reading prescription:

"It is obviously difficult for busy people to find time to read. Over the years, I have identified some tricks that have been useful for me. These include:

• Taking reading material with me when I travel since there is a significant amount of waiting time in airports and certainly throughout the voyage.

• Keeping reading material on your person at all times since you are bound to be stuck in situations where you could be reading if you have something; otherwise you might just be wasting time.

• Having reading material in the bathroom in order to kill two birds with one stone.

• Reading for a specified amount of time in the morning before you get out of bed.

• Reading for a specified amount of time in the evening before you go to bed.

Some or all of these tips are likely to work for any busy person and should add many hours of enjoyment each week to the life of busy people." L@W

Benjamin S. Carson Sr., M.D. is the director of the director of pediatric neurosurgery at Johns Hopkins Children's Center and the author of the best-selling books *Gifted Hands, Think Big,* and *The Big Picture*. A widely respected role model, he shares motivational insights with inner-city kids and corporate executives alike. He also serves on the board at Yale University and serves on the board for the Kellogg Company and others.

Read for a specified amount of time
in the morning before you get out of bed.

No Excuses!
Debunking Five Myths about Skill

Stephen Graves

When you tackle the idea — and ideal — of skill, you often get sidetracked by one (or all) of these five myths. Take a look at each one and answer the questions to help you avoid being manipulated by myths.

1. You can't teach an old dog new tricks ... or I'm just too old to focus on my skill

What keeps most of us from improving is a settled environment that is comfortable, albeit stale and predictable. The current business landscape actually dictates, "I'm too old *not* to sharpen my skill." Every year of experience can make us that much more dated in our value to our employer if we don't maintain self-development. Things change. I must be one of those things.

What have you seen change in your profession over the past year? Five years?
What practical steps can you take to ensure that you are regularly sharpening your skills?

2. Don't wake me from my sleep ... or my particular job doesn't require any real skill

Not true. Every job has critical requirements. The other day I watched the letter carrier in my neighborhood. The skill demands of her job were easy to spot: patience, the ability to handle the mundane repetition, a high attention to detail, and better-than-average driving skills. Just think about the damage a recklessly driving letter carrier could do in a neighborhood. Every job is full of skill demands and self-development opportunities. Wake up!

Was there a time in your career where you fell into a rut? How did you get out of it? Do you look for the skills required by other people's jobs? How could you better encourage your co-workers or friends in their professional roles?

3. I wish I had Tiger's skills ... or some skills are more valuable than others

Value and self worth, in the end, are internal judgments. Even though you may not have won a gold medal, or stood in the spotlight, or had a golf shoe named after you, it doesn't mean you aren't a productive and responsible member of society. Anyway, who wants a stinky old shoe as a legacy?

Who do you admire for their skills? What is it about that skill that impresses you?
If you could have any skill set, what would you choose?

4. I was sick the day God passed out skills ... or I don't have any skills

Okay, so you might not be Oprah or Tiger, but you *are* skilled enough that if you sat down with a piece of paper, you could name three things you are good at.

What are three things you are good at? What do you value about your skills?

5. I have all the gifts ... or get a clue!

'Nuff said!

Toolbox

TOOLBOX | SKILL DEFINED

Defining Skill

The concept of skill might be as old as the earth, but the actual word — the English version — is a mere sapling. The word skill originated with Old Norse language in Scandinavia from the root words "skil," "skal," "skilja," "schil," and "scienldend."

11th century Old English: (scieldend) — function
11th century Anglo-Saxon: (schil) — distinguish
11th century Old Norse: (skal) — reason, (skilja) — to part, distinguish
12th century English: (skal) — that which is reasonable or right, differentiations, distinctions
13th century English: (skil) — the intellectual faculty, reason, awareness

Today's definitions for skill focus more on physical abilities and talents. Perhaps as helpful in figuring out the meaning of skill over time is to look at how the term has been used. **Here are a few quotes from the ages:**

BC
"I have given skill to all the craftsmen to make everything I have commanded you." — Yahweh (Exodus 31:6)

"Both hands are skilled in doing evil; the ruler demands gifts, the judge accepts bribes, the powerful dictate what they desire — they all conspire together."
— Micah (Micah 7:3)

"Natural ability is by far the best, but many men have succeeded in winning high renown by skill that is the fruit of teaching." — Greek poet Pindar (518-438 BC)

Early AD
"The greater the difficulty the more glory in surmounting it. Skillful pilots gain their reputation from storms and tempests." — Greek philosopher Epictetus (55-135)

"Therefore since we are God's offspring, we should not think that the divine being is like gold or silver or stone — an image made by man's design and skill."
— Luke (Acts 17:29)

1500s
"Skill comes so slow, and life so fast doth fly,
We learn so little and forget so much."
— Sir John Davies (1570-1626)

1700s
"The feeble tremble before opinion, the foolish defy it, the wise judge it, the skillful direct it."
— French revolutionary Jeane-Marie Roland (1754-1793)

1800s
"Intelligence is quickness to apprehend as distinct from ability, which is capacity to act wisely on the thing apprehended." — A.N. Whitehead (1861-1947)

1900s
"Ability is the art of getting credit for all the home runs somebody else hits."
— Baseball Hall of Famer Casey Stengel (1889-1975)

"The maturing of any complex talent requires a happy combination of motivation, character and opportunity. Most talent remains undeveloped."
— Writer John Gardner (1933-1982)

"Skill without imagination is craftsmanship and gives us many useful objects such as wickerwork picnic baskets. Imagination without skill gives us modern art."
— Playwright Tom Stoppard (1937-present)

"Champions aren't made in gyms. Champions are made from something they have deep inside them — a desire, a dream, a vision. They have to have the skill and the will."
— Boxing great Muhammad Ali (1942-present)

L@W

Inside Pages

MOTIVATION
Sports Can Help You Learn to Make the Most of Your Skills

By Tom Mullins

In his book *The Leadership Game,* Pastor Tom Mullins looks back on his 15 years of coaching high school and college football for insights on successful leadership. Mullins, now a senior pastor in Florida, also gleans insights through interviews with the head football coaches of eight college national championship teams, including Bobby Bowden and Tom Osborne.

In this excerpt, Mullins recalls one of his former players as he writes about how motivation can help individuals enhance their skills.

When I moved to Florida to coach high school football, I took over a team that had never experienced a winning season. The team won only four games the year before I arrived, and there were only twenty players left on the team, so I faced an immediate test.

I went to work promoting the football program among the students and local folks. I spoke in churches and community centers trying to build the team. To my surprise, about one hundred players showed up for summer ball.

> It wasn't about their talent; it was about rewarding their desire and their hearts to make a difference together.

I told them if they worked hard and remained committed, all of them would dress for the games. I issued a no-cut policy. It wasn't about their talent; it was about rewarding their desire and their hearts to make a difference together.

When it was time to hand out equipment, I lined up the former players first and then those who looked as if they had good potential. The final player to come through the line at the end of that very long day was a young man by the name of Carl Pierce. He was built like a No. 2 pencil. When he stepped forward, I asked him what position he wanted to play. "I want to be a wide receiver, Coach," he asserted. I called into the equipment room, "Hey, guys, do we have any wide receiver pads left?" "No, Coach," they called back. "We only have one pair of shoulder pads left." We'd already gone through all the varsity, junior varsity, and ninth grade equipment, trying to suit up all these kids. "Okay," I said, "just bring them out anyway. We'll make them work."

When I saw the shoulder pads, I immediately recognized who had worn them last — a defensive tackle who weighed about three hundred pounds. I put the pads on Carl, and they nearly fell down over his shoulders. He actually stuck his arm through the neck hole. "Coach," he said, "I think these are too big." "No, son," I replied. "Here's the deal. You have freedom in these pads. You can move around and won't be restricted at all — and you'll be able to catch that ball from any position." In truth, I could have twirled the pads around his neck like a propeller.

I then asked him what size helmet he needed. "A 6?" he said. When I asked the equipment guys if they had any small helmets, they called back, "No, Coach, we only have one helmet left." "Well," I said, "bring it out. We'll make it work." It was the helmet that fit that three-hundred-pound lineman — an 8-3/4. We stuffed the thing with double cheek pads and any other kind of padding we could find, but we still couldn't get it to fit right. No matter how hard we padded it up and strapped it down, it slid all over Carl's face when he started jogging. (One time I saw him running out to practice, and his nose was sticking out the ear hole.)

And of course, we had only one pair of pants left. Carl could fit both legs down one leg of the pants. We were out of belts, so he had to use shoestrings to keep the pants up. We finally got him suited, but he was a pretty sad sight.

When he ran out on the field, the other players laughed. He couldn't do much except hold onto his pants with one hand and steady his helmet with the other. Yet Carl Pierce had something fierce inside him, and he kept coming out to play.

When it was time for the first game, I had to let him dress because I made a promise to the team. I hate to admit it, but I hid him between a couple of big players so he wouldn't embarrass us when we took the field.

Our team made strides that year, and we won our first four games. One more win would set a new school record. During the fifth game we were trailing late and scored a touchdown that put us in the lead. All we had to do was kick the ball off, hold them for one defensive series, and let the clock run out. We would have five wins for the first time in school history.

As the team prepared to kick off, I counted only ten players on the field. I turned around and looked at my assistant coach and growled, "Get somebody on the field!" He turned and grabbed the first player standing next to him and threw him onto the field. It

was Carl. I started screaming to stop the play. I gave a time-out signal to the official, and he told me we had no more time-outs left.

Carl didn't even know how to line up. He didn't know any of the kickoff formations. Somehow he ended up in the contain position on the outside — one of the most crucial positions on the kickoff team. I glared at my assistant coach, and if looks could kill, he'd be dead today.

The official blew the whistle for the kickoff, and Carl took off running down the field. Pads and body parts were flapping everywhere. Then there was a huge collision at the 25-yard line, and our guys started screaming, "Fumble! Fumble!" They jumped up and started pointing and shouting, "We've got the ball! We've got the ball!" Our sideline erupted, knowing we had won the game.

And then, from the bottom of the pile emerged the hero. Sprinting to the sidelines, hugging the ball in his arms, Carl was yelling, "I got the ball, Coach! I got the ball!"

When we reviewed the game film the next morning, we saw him sprinting down the field, holding onto his pants, while his shoulder pads and helmet flopped up and down — he looked like a bobble-head doll. Then the boy returning the ball veered right into Carl. He let go of his pants and slammed into the boy, knocking the ball loose. Somebody then speared Carl in the back and knocked him onto the loose ball.

On Monday morning, I got him out of class and took him to the sporting goods store to buy him some equipment that fit. I had to go the junior department to do it, but we got him everything he needed. When I asked if there was anything else he wanted, he said, "Coach, I want some forearm pads because I want to be a special teams specialist. I want to go down and hit people!"

When he came out to practice later that day, the players cheered for him. They knew how hard they had been on Carl. He accepted their cheers graciously because he had a desire in his heart to be part of a team — despite the obstacles — and the team realized it was better for it.

I put Carl on the kickoff team for the next game because I wanted to honor him for his great effort. Wouldn't you know it — he was in on the tackle. I never took him off the special teams after that, and at the end of the season his teammates voted him the Most Improved Player. The next year they voted him captain of the special teams.

Motivation Maximizes Talent

You and I can learn a lot from Carl. His story demonstrates the sheer power of motivation to elevate common talent to an uncommon level. His body wasn't big enough, but his heart was — and that made his ability bigger than his body.

Motivation is often the only difference between the winner and the loser. This is no more evident than when two great football teams are doing battle. Sure, there are breaks and mistakes on both sides of the ball, but those can be overcome. Almost without fail, the team that ends up on top when both teams are equally talented is the team that wanted the win more than the other.

We are privy to examples every year when one team routs the same team that beat it by 3 points earlier in the year. Call the motive revenge or payback or retribution, it's still the result of one team that wants to win against one team that *will not* lose. It's the power of motivation, and a leader must learn to harness it to maximize a team's talent.

No leader understands the power of motivation better than football coaches whose players are not paid to win. The vast majority of high school and college players have no incentive to excel but for the thrill of victory and the satisfaction of accomplishment. Their motives are simple; yet maximizing them is no simple task. …

Championship coaches like Bill McCartney have a unique capacity to move a player's motives to action so that he performs at his very best. … A highly motivated athlete can outperform a more physically gifted athlete in any game. It makes sense then that the greatest leaders don't necessarily have all the greatest players. The greatest leaders know how to get the best out of every player, in every situation, which in turn produces a highly effective team.

L@W

Tom Mullins coached football for 15 years and amassed 128 victories. He is the founder and pastor for the last 21 years of Christ Fellowship, an evangelical, multi-site church of 20,000 members in Palm Beach County, Florida. He also helped found the Global Pastors Network (with the late Bill Bright).

Reprinted by permission of Thomas Nelson Inc., Nashville, from the book entitled **The Leadership Game,** *copyright 2005 by Tom Mullins. All rights reserved.*

True Story

But seek first his kingdom and his righteousness, and all these things will be given to you as well.
Matthew 6:33 (NIV)

Husbands, love your wives, just as Christ loved the church and gave himself up for her.
Ephesians 5:25 (NIV)

Fathers, do not exasperate your children; instead, bring them up in the training and instruction of the Lord.
Ephesians 6:4 (NIV)

JASON HOUSER

Jason Houser is an award-winning Country music publisher and Christian music songwriter. His favorite songs these days, however, come straight from the Bible: his series of high-energy family worship CDs entitled Seeds (**www.SeedsFamilyWorship.com**). What started as a ministry project at his church now encompasses a series of CDs and live family worship events at churches across the nation.

Harmony in Endeavors

I am involved with several companies, but the primary company that I work with is Extreme Writers Group. I am one of two senior partners of the company. We started the company in 2000. My previous role as a Creative Director at EMI taught me how to work with dynamic personalities and how to structure deals with songwriters.

Family Harmony

I have been married for 11 years. I have a great wife, Heidi, and I have seen that God can work miracles in marriages. We have three children: Benjamin (7), Brandon (4), and Abigail (2). The greatest thing I have learned from being a parent is how much God loves us and how He disciplines us *because* He loves us so much, and He wants the best for us. Our love for our children is just a shadow of the way He loves us.

Family time is always a challenge. We have not been a family that eats dinner together because of my schedule until this past year. Now doing so has made a dramatic difference for us. We also try to spend time doing a devotional and praying together before bedtime during the week. We don't get it done every day, but we are developing the habit.

Singing a New Song

I have missed so many opportunities to love people and share my faith because I have been too busy. I am trying to be more aware of the moments that God brings when someone shares what is going on. I need to be present and take the time to be with them and let other things slide.

I do not think we should try to separate our work and our faith. We need to always be ready to give the reason for the hope that we have with gentleness and respect. I am trying to keep my eyes and heart open to those things.

Singing for Eternity

As one of my company's partners, we define the culture of our company. We pray in our staff meetings and try to live out our values in how we conduct our business. We give God the credit and thanks. Our company works in both Christian and Country music ... we say that we are "Switzerland." We have a lot of contact with non-Christians. We try to share what God is doing in our company as a witness.

Having the right priorities is the strongest advice that I can give. "A man cannot serve two masters. ..." That is so challenging, but God gives us the strength. I think it's important to search your heart. If you are putting your best energy, passion, commitment, and time into your work and you don't have a real relationship with the Lord and with family and friends, then you need to make some radical changes in your life. If you don't know where to start, pray sincerely.

A Final Stanza

Life is about relationships and commitments. It is primarily about our relationship and commitment to God, and also about our relationships and commitments to others. As Jesus says: "Love the Lord your God with all your heart, and with all your soul and with all your mind, and with all your strength. ... The second is this, 'Love your neighbor as yourself'" (Matthew 22:37, 39 NIV)

L@W

Perspective

Learning from Great Churches and Great Businesses
Jim Collins helps point the way to move from *Good to Great*

By Dr. John C. Maxwell

Many church leaders have read Jim Collins' book *Good to Great*. While the book's principles about best business practices are readily transferable, I was fortunate to hear Jim talk specifically about three key things a church needs to move from good to great.

First, **keep focused on your mission.** In other words, if you want to be a great church, don't try to do everything. Find out what your calling is, find out what your opportunity is, figure out the DNA of your church, and stay focused on mission. Paul said, "This one thing I do"—not these 40 things I dabble in. Churches do way too much.

Second, **be enduring.** When a church's message is enduring, its tenure is enduring; it's been in the community for a long time and the community understands the stability that it brings to people. When those things happen, there's an enduring quality that helps take a church from good to great.

Third, **make a distinctive impact in your community.** I love that phrase, "distinctive impact in your community." In other words, Jim Collins says that the great churches are true salt and light in their neighborhoods.

Here's the question that I would ask in light of what Jim says about being a great church: If your church disappeared tomorrow, would your neighborhood miss it? If you're a live, relevant church, you'll be missed. If you're a dead, sterile, traditional church, you won't be missed. How can you tell the difference?

Live churches always have parking problems; dead churches don't. Live churches have lots of noisy kids; dead churches are quiet. Live churches are constantly planning for their future; dead churches worship their past. Live churches grow so fast that they don't know everybody's name; dead churches have known everybody's name for years. Live churches support missions heavily; dead churches keep it all at home. Live churches always need more land and buildings; dead churches need nothing. Live churches dream great dreams for God; dead churches relive nightmares. Live churches make a difference; dead churches don't.

So, what can churches learn from successful businesses... and vice versa?

What churches can learn from business:

No. 1: Excellence The corporate world has a higher standard of excellence than does the church world. Churches will tend to let things slide that the business community will not let slide.

No. 2: Commitment The business world will pay a much higher price for a dollar than we'll pay for a soul. The business world will absolutely spare no expense for a customer, for a dollar. Churches, like businesses, stop growing when they stop paying the price.

No. 3: Willingness to Change The business world will immediately change if they think there's any opportunity to seize a customer and a dollar. Churches? Our theme song is "I Shall Not Be Moved." We'd rather sit on the premises than stand on the promises.

What businesses can learn from the Church:

No. 1: Servanthood The Church understands what it really means to serve people. Jesus would teach us that leadership is servanthood. Secure leaders think of others first; insecure leaders think of themselves first.

No. 2: Value People My friend Bill Hybels has said for more than 30 years, "People matter to God." Willow Creek Community Church was built on that premise. Businesses can learn from their example.

No. 3: Operating with an Eternal Perspective The corporate community lives for today. The Church understands that we do everything in light of eternity.

Looking to move from good to great? Learn from those who are already down that pathway.

L@W

Dr. John C. Maxwell, known as America's authority on leadership, speaks in person to hundreds of thousands of people each year. He is the author of more than thirty books, including *The 21 Irrefutable Laws of Leadership,* which has sold more than a million copies. To learn more visit **www.maximumimpact.com.**

Life @ The Intersection

You have just completed Session 1. Use these journal pages to complete the following:

BIG QUESTION:
After reading this session, I'm wondering what others think about ...

NEW THOUGHT:
I just learned that ...

PERSONAL CHALLENGE:
I can't get this out of my mind. I have to figure out how to live differently so that ...

TAKE A BREAK
Think about the people you interact with everyday—your family, friends, co-workers ...even the barista at Starbucks. What skills do they demonstrate with greatness? Take some time today to recognize and appreciate them (tell them!) for the way they honor God and serve others with their skills.

Discovering Your Greatness
What Has God Uniquely Wired You To Do?

By Stephen R. Graves

Everyone knows the story of David's triumph over Goliath. When David sent that stone into the giant's forehead, he was working out of his greatness, and he was showing forth the greatness of God. In trusting God and pursuing His call, David brought incredible skill to bear on a situation he seemed to have been born for. The variety of David's talents and gifts truly was astonishing. He was handsome, athletic, poetic, charismatic, wise, full of faith, and a crack shot with a slingshot. "I am fearfully and wonderfully made," he marveled in Psalm 139:14 — and he wasn't kidding.

Yet the story of David and Goliath not only demonstrates that David discovered and exercised his greatness by doing what he was good at, but also by choosing to *not* do what he wasn't good at.

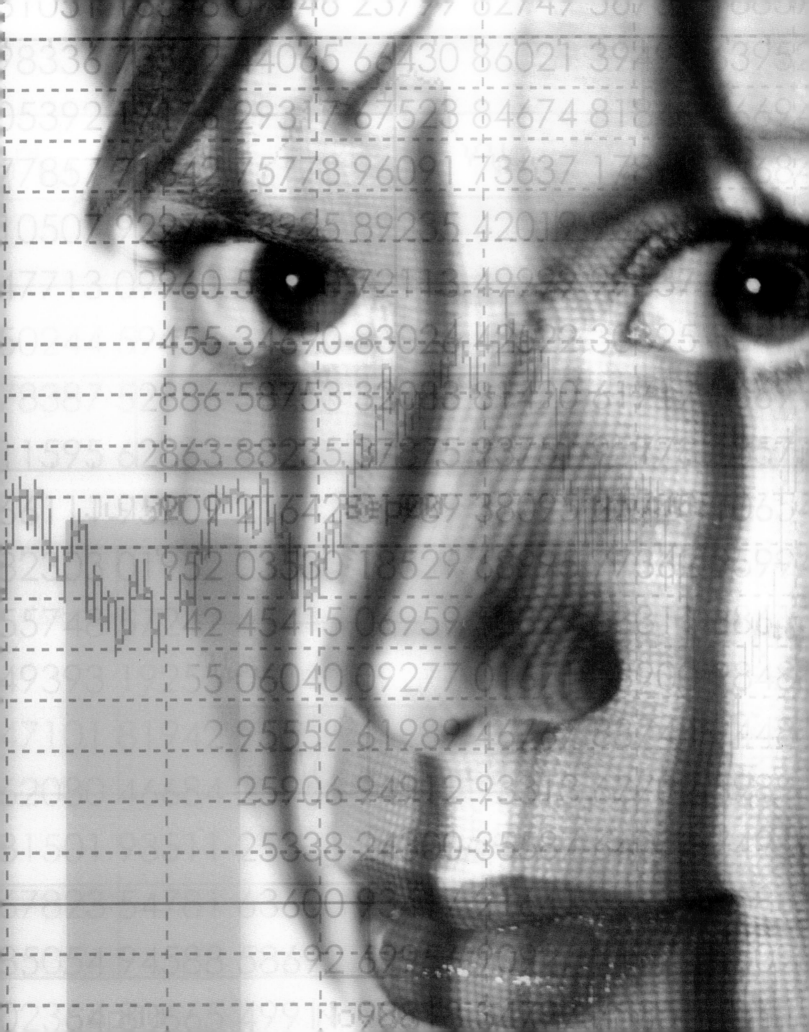

Perhaps David was in the greatest danger not when he stood before Goliath, but when he stood before his well-meaning king, who offered David the king's armor. David was designed to be a giant-killer. God made him to take on huge challenges that no one else wanted any part of. So when it came time to fight Goliath, conventional wisdom said that a giant-killer looks like a strong, well-armed soldier. He wears big armor. He has a heavy helmet. He carries a massive shield and a huge, heavy sword. This was the expectation that Saul placed on David:

> "Saul said [to David], 'Go. And GOD help you!' Then Saul outfitted David as a soldier in armor. He put his bronze helmet on his head and belted his sword over the armor. David tried to walk but he could hardly budge.

fits you. There comes a point in each of our lives when we must brush aside the expectations of others, the pressure of parents, peers, and society, in order to find who we were truly made to be. If we don't, those expectations will crush us. To put it another way, saying "yes" to your God-designed greatness requires that you say "no" to a greatness you weren't designed for.

Reverse Engineering

David knew that someone else's armor would not fit him. He also knew his sweet spot, his God-designed greatness. God has intrinsically deposited His creation fingerprints into the soul, the inner being of all of us. But how do we find out what that is? How do we discover where our greatness lies? The answer lies in reverse engineering.

God does not deliver us into this world with a label on our foreheads that reads "Artist" or "Salesperson" or "Teacher."

Part of the grand adventure of life is that God leaves it up to us to discover for ourselves what we are best at.

> "David told Saul, 'I can't even move with all this stuff on me. I'm not used to this.' And he took it all off." (1 Samuel 17:37-39 THE MESSAGE).

David had to cast aside the expectations of what others thought he should be and give himself the freedom to be who God made him to be. David knew what he was designed to do. He knew what he was good at and what he was not. He was not great at carrying heavy armor. He was too small. On the other hand, he knew that he was skillful with a rock and sling. David knew he could never do what God wanted him to do wearing someone else's armor. That was not him. You cannot freely rotate your arm in a suit of iron. It was only as he gave himself the freedom to be what God had made him that he found his greatness.

You cannot wear the armor of another, either. You must find what

What is reverse engineering, you ask? It is when you start with a final product and deduce backward, figuring out its original design.

One of the greatest triumphs of reverse engineering occurred during World War II. D-Day — the decisive event that led to Allied victory in the war — would have never succeeded without a lesser-known victory: Operation Enigma.

Operation Enigma was the Allied effort that broke the code of German encryption machines. This battle was fought secretly on an English estate called Bletchley Park. Inside its ivy-covered rock walls, cryptographers worked to decode German radio intercepts. Their real break came when they received various parts and manuals for German code machines that had been retrieved from seized German ships.

The challenge of the Allied cryptographers was to reverse-engineer the coding process, using the pieces of the code machines in their possession to reconstruct the original radio messages.

Working backward, the Allies broke the design of the German code machine, allowing them to read German radio traffic. From the intercepts the Allies were able to plot the patrol positions of German subs. With this information, the convoys of supply ships from America were able to elude the Germans and give new life to the Allied war effort. This victory in the battle of the Atlantic was crucial to the success of the later D-day invasion; and the whole thing was made possible by the reverse engineering of Operation Enigma.

We face a similar reverse-engineering challenge. God does not deliver us into this world with a label on our foreheads that reads "Artist" or "Salesperson" or "Teacher." Part of the grand adventure of life is that God leaves it up to us to discover for ourselves what we are best at. Like Operation Enigma, discovering what you were made for requires analyzing the parts of the machine.

While there are many aspects to who we are as individuals, there are two factors that are especially significant to discovering our "Sweet Spot." Our point of greatness is usually found at the intersections of what we are good at and what we like to do. Greatness requires both desire and knack. Aspiration without ability will get you nowhere. On the other hand, talent without motivation will never excel either. Greatness is an amalgam of both.

Gifting
The obvious place to start is your talents and abilities. What do you do well? Discovering what you are good at takes some thought. You're not looking for a single answer, such as "I am good at sales." Rather, you are looking for all the things that *make* you good at sales: communication, networking, relating to people, etc. These talents are all clues. They paint a picture — not a specific job, but a composite portrait of a skill set.

If you're ready to start breaking your own code, stop reading for a moment and head over to page 41. If you're not ready, hopefully you will be shortly.

To break your code, you'll need to list every job or task role that you have ever had and think through each position. What did you learn about yourself from each one? What were you really good at in each job? What were you required to do that you were bad at?

After you've done this, you'll want to write a paragraph summarizing these elements of your list:

- I like working at …
- I am good at …
- I know that I am not good at …

As you fill in the blanks from your experience, a general picture will emerge. Your history will demonstrate a pattern — your skill set … the unique package of assets that God has given you.

Passion
Being good at something, however, is not enough to propel you to greatness. It requires an accompanying passion as well. Bob Biehl says that when you get down to it, people do what they *want* to do. It takes "want-to." Biehl is right: if you are doing what you want to do, you will arrive early and stay late. On the other hand, if your job is something that you do not want to do, you will show up late and leave early.

What do you want to do? You cannot overlook your gut desires. They are part of your God-given wiring just as much as your talents and abilities.

Again, think about your job history. Are there any jobs that you hated? You do not want to go through that again, do you? But don't think of those bad work experiences as a waste of time; think of them as opportunities to learn valuable lessons. They helped you discover what you *don't* want to do. As Henry Ford said, "Failure is the opportunity to begin again, more intelligently."

When you say good riddance to a job, stop long enough to identify what it is about that position that you did not like. What do you never want to do again? What can you only tolerate in small doses? What should you avoid at all costs? The answers to these questions provide beneficial information. Now you can add another summary sentence to your paragraph: I know I need to avoid jobs that involve …

Knowing what to avoid is priceless discernment. It will save you from going down many dead-end streets. Knowing what to say no to is as critical as knowing what to say yes to.

Study your past one last time, looking for the jobs that you loved. Ask yourself what it was about those that you liked. What challenged you? What made your heart beat faster? What did you get excited about? Pull these insights into another sentence for your summary paragraph: I am drawn toward jobs that involve ... When you get this all down on paper, you will have created a mosaic of what you are good at and what you like to do. These are your motivated abilities. Maximizing your motivated abilities is the key to discovering your greatness. John Ruskin said it best: "When love and skill work together, expect a masterpiece."

Jack-of-all-Trades ... or Master of None?

A creeping mindset has been laying hold of life and work in the last few years. It is that any of us can be great in anything, and

> Being good at something is not enough to propel you to greatness. It requires an accompanying passion as well.

the way to do that is to simply assign energy toward growing each weakness into a strength. There's just one problem: that approach never works! Actually, the better thing to do is to find our strengths and optimize them in every venue of our life. God never meant us to be omni-competent. That's His job.

The problem with being a "jack-of-all-trades" is that you spread yourself too thin. As Malcolm Bane observed, "If you wait until you can do everything for everybody, instead of something for somebody, you'll end up not doing anything for anybody." You burn yourself out doing things you were never meant to handle.

You are great at *something*. Finding it will be a process of elimination. Realistically, you need to pare down your list. You will never be great until you narrow your target. Even those people among us who are generalists are not equally great at all tasks or initiatives.

Like David, you were "fearfully and wonderfully made." Discovering exactly what that means in your case — solving the mystery of your personal greatness — is one of life's true adventures.

At creation God breathes something special into each of us. What incredible design did God weave into your inward parts? He makes us to reflect a little of the wonder of who He is. We are not gods, but according to the first chapter of Genesis we were made in the image of God.

That is what makes each of us unique. We are mirrors — albeit cracked mirrors — of the image of God. That's what makes you a person and not an animal. The image of God is at least partly seen in our God-given capacity for our work on earth. To be "fearfully and wonderfully made" is to carry the fingerprints of God. He has given each of us a work that He specifically intended for us to do.

"Every calling," Oliver Wendell Holmes said, "is great when greatly pursued." How will you work out your God-designed greatness and show forth the glory of God?

L@W

Stephen R. Graves, Ph. D., is a highly sought business coach and life guide for entrepreneurs and leaders desiring to successfully make it to the finish line of life. In 1991, he co-founded the Cornerstone Group, a company built to integrate biblical wisdom and business excellence. He and his wife Karen have three children.

This article is based on concepts drawn from Life@Work *by John C. Maxwell, Stephen R. Graves, and Thomas G. Addington, published by Thomas Nelson, Inc., copyright 2005. All rights reserved.*

Looking Backwards Helps You Find Your Gifts and Passion

Gifts

List every job or task role that you have ever had. What did you learn about yourself from each job? What were you really good at in each job? What were you required to do that you were bad at? Be honest!

After you've finished listing all of your jobs, write a paragraph summarizing your list: I like working at ... I am good at ... I know that I am not good at ...

JOB/ROLE	STRENGTHS OBSERVED	WEAKNESSES OBSERVED

Passion

Go back through your list. Are there any jobs that you hated? If so, put a line through those ... but stop long enough to identify what it is about that position that you did not like. Would you ever want to do it again? Could you tolerate it in small doses? What should you avoid at all costs?

Now, add another sentence to you paragraph:
I know I need to avoid jobs that involve ...

Study your past one last time, looking for the jobs that you loved. Circle them. Now ask yourself what it was about those that you liked. What challenged you? What made your heart beat faster? What did you get excited about?

Pull these insights into another sentence for your summary paragraph: I am drawn toward jobs that involve ...

With this paragraph, you have created a mosaic of what you are good at and what you like to do. These are your motivated abilities. Maximizing your motivated abilities is the key to discovering your greatness.

John Ruskin said it best: "When love and skill work together, expect a masterpiece."

Summary Paragraph

_____

_____

_____

_____

_____

_____

_____

_____

_____

_____

_____

_____

_____

_____

_____

_____

_____

_____

_____

_____

DISCOVERING YOUR GREATNESS

FOR GROUP DISCUSSION
Prior to your small group meeting time, read and reflect on the Life@Work Study article you just read. Use these questions and journal pages to reflect and respond to the ideas presented. Be ready to share your thoughts at your small group gathering.

Note to small group leaders: You can download a full Leader's Guide at www.lifeatworkgroupzine.com.

▶ In this piece, Dr. Stephen Graves writes, "saying 'yes' to your God-designed greatness requires that you say 'no' to a greatness you weren't designed for."
  Have you ever considered that you have a "God-designed" greatness? How does that thought make you feel? What would you say your God-designed greatness encompasses? Have you gone down a career path you weren't designed for? How did you discover it was the wrong thing for you?

▶ *Our point of greatness is usually found at the intersections of what we are good at and what we like to do.*
  What are you good at? What do you like to do? Does your career focus on this integral intersection? If yes, how long did it take you to get to that intersection? If not, what can you do to get there sooner than later?

▶ In an age of multi-tasking and ever-increasing workloads, do you find yourself striving to become "omni-competent"? How can you avoid becoming a jack-of-all-trades? What can you eliminate that will allow you to focus on what you are great at?

▶ Have you ever considered that God gave you your talents? Are you happy with this gift? Do you actively use your gifts? What are your thoughts about the concept that your talents are also an investment by God? Is He currently receiving a good return on His investment in you?

▶ *In the end, your professional growth is your responsibility.*
  What have you done in the past to help you grow in your area of greatness? What are you doing now to grow in your talent? What do you think when you hear Alberta Lee Cox state, "it is not enough to be good if you have the ability to be better"? How can you ensure you are continuing to improve?

NOW, DO SOMETHING WITH YOUR STRENGTHS ...AND WEAKNESSES

AN INTERVIEW WITH BEST-SELLING AUTHOR **MARCUS BUCKINGHAM** SHEDS LIGHT ON HOW WE SHOULD KEEP OUR FOCUS ON WHAT WE MOST ENJOY DOING

He's been heralded in leading publications such as the *New York Times, USA Today,* and *Fortune* magazine. He is a valuable consulting resource for leading corporations, including Disney, Coca-Cola, and Toyota. He is a favorite at conferences, speaking to as many as a quarter-million people each year.

Marcus Buckingham has obviously found his strength. And that's helping you discover your strength.

With a Master's degree from Cambridge University, Buckingham spent nearly two decades as a senior researcher with the Gallup Organization. He is best known, however, as the author of three best-selling business books: *First, Break All the Rules; Now, Discover Your Strengths;* and *The One Thing You Need to Know.*

His latest endeavor is a series of six short films called Trombone Player Wanted. The series, and its accompanying website (**www.SimplyStrengths.com**) help leaders and their team members learn to discover their strengths and put them to work.

Buckingham heads the Marcus Buckingham Company (**www.MarcusBuckingham.com**), which is headquartered in Los Angeles. He is married and has two children.

L@W
Your research shows that more than 80 percent of people are unfulfilled in their jobs or careers. Would you say that people have settled when it comes to picking a job or a career?

Buckingham
Oh, no. I don't think people settle at all. I just think most of us don't have a clue as to how to bring the best of ourselves to work. We might have known when we were children — when our strengths were really clear and strong. You might not have called them strengths then, but when you were a kid you knew what got you out of bed every day, what process you wanted to take, and what situations kind of thrilled you and which ones you hated — and you trusted that.

But somehow, between then and now, the voice of the outside world is louder than the voice inside your head. You listen to parents tell you what job you should have, or you have to pay the bills or pay off a loan. You've got to have a boss, and the boss tells you to do this, that, and the other. And so what tends to happen is you listen to the outside world more closely than you listen to yourself … and the majority of us end up in a job where

we don't have a chance to express the best of ourselves.

In fact, only 17 percent of us say we spend most of the day playing to our strengths. So even if you get people who have 25 percent of their day filled with all that junk that we all have — the grumpy guy down the hall, or the emails you've got to do, or the tasks that just bore you or drain you — if you get people to give just a quarter of their day to fill up that stuff, that still leaves a big chunk of time that each of those could fill with activities that play to our strengths. Yet clearly less than two out of ten of us manage to.

So, I don't think we settle. I just think we aren't taught how to identify our strengths and weaknesses, and then ensure that, week by week, we're spending more time playing to our strengths and less time on activities that weaken us.

L@W
Yet most of us work for organizations that put more focus on improving our weaknesses. Why do you think people and organizations put greater focus on having people work on their areas of weakness rather than growing in areas of strength?

Buckingham
Well, my theory is that there are three myths that we believe to be true regarding weaknesses. The first myth is this: *As we grow, our personality changes.* What that means is that you can learn or acquire any personality trait you want just by working at it. The truth is, as you grow, you become more of who you already are. You might be able to change your values, your manners, or your aspirations, but in terms of the core of the positive personality, those things don't change as you grow.

Second, we believe: *We will grow the most in our weaknesses.* So we focus on our weaknesses thinking that's our area of opportunity for growth. The truth is the opposite of that — that for each of us, our greatest opportunity for growth happens in our areas of strength. And by growth, I mean we'll be most creative, most inquisitive, come up with the most new ideas, and learn the most in the areas where we're already strong. Our weaknesses are — contrary to what's written on most employee appraisals — not areas of opportunity. They are areas of *least* opportunity. In general, companies and organizations have proven themselves to be an incredibly ineffective mechanism for getting the strengths out of people.

For example, if you ask parents this question: "Your child comes home with the following grades — English, A; Social Studies, A; Biology, C; Algebra, F — which grade deserves the most attention from you?" Seventy-seven percent of parents say the F. I think that's because the school system is set up so that you say: well done on the A; now, let's dive into the F. So, right from the very early age, your weaknesses need focus, and your strengths can be sort of be patted on the head for, but you don't need to count your strengths, you need to plug your gaps. You can't ignore an F; you can't ignore your weaknesses. But that's not the question. The question is simply where do spend most of your time.

The last myth is: *To be a great team member, you should chip in and do whatever it takes to help the team.* Because, there's no "I" in "team," and therefore, to be a good teammate, you shouldn't focus on your strengths, but rather do whatever it takes to help the team. Ninety-one percent of people believe this myth. The truth is that productive team members find out what their strengths are and contribute those most of the time. That's really the most responsible thing you can do to help your team. Occasionally, you may have to step out of your strength zone, of course. But, as any great coach will tell you, that isn't the essence of teamwork; that's the exception to teamwork.

In my mind, those are three myths that we are happy to pass on to our children and are pleased with ourselves for doing so. These myths really create in the world a fascination with fixing ourselves, and an associated lack of focus on capitalizing on the particular talents that we each possess.

L@W
In your book *The One Thing*, you talk about the talents and skills required of great managers and leaders. How do you define the difference between skill and talent?

Buckingham
A skill is a technique; it is teachable. Talents are reoccurring patterns of thought, feeling, or behavior that can be productively applied with little effort or thought. They are not teachable. Arithmetic and grammar are skills. But great writing is a talent.

Checking someone into a hotel is a skill that anyone can learn. Learning someone's name and being able to say it at the right time to make that person feel welcome, that's a talent. So is being able to know exactly how to look someone in the eye so that when you tell them that you are oversold and that they don't have a room in your hotel, you do it in such a way that they feel calm, and they might actually want to come back to your hotel. A

skill is knowing the four questions you should ask a prospect when you're trying to sell them. A talent is knowing just the right moment to push in order to close.

L@W
You're on an elevator and someone asks you "What is the one thing you would tell me about strengths?" How do you answer?

Buckingham
Discover what you don't like doing and stop doing it.

Deep down, the world is basically ambivalent about you and your strengths. If it helps get something done, then people like the strengths. But as soon as your strengths move you off in a slightly different direction, then they're annoyed by your strengths. So really, the only person who's going to keep you on your strengths track is you.

But the problem with strengths is they help you get things done, and soon people start offering you new opportunities. New doors will open and you get a bigger title and more money and a bigger desk. Some of those opportunities will continue to play to your strengths, but many won't. So, really, it's your job to keep yourself sufficiently clear-headed to know which doors you shouldn't go through.

So much of this is the function of what you choose not to do; those things you manage to edit out of your life. We need to be much more disciplined and rigorous to stop doing those things that weaken us. That's what a weakness is: an activity that weakens you, that bores you, drains you, or depletes you. The annoying thing is that you might be actually quite proficient at it. Fate sometimes curses us with an ability to do something, but no appetite for it. We've all got those. They're like anti-hobbies — things you are good at and hate. So if you want to make a long and lasting contribution, you should learn how to do that, because no one else will. If you don't want to make a long and lasting contribution, then all this is irrelevant.

L@W
So then is it possible, or even realistic, for people to work toward their strengths, especially in an ever-increasing competitive work environment?

Buckingham
There's no question that the world is sufficiently varied these days, but for the grand majority of it, there is enough flexibility and

Looking for a Trombone Player

While continuing as an author and highly sought speaker, Marcus Buckingham has created a new outlet for his encouragement to people to discover their strengths. Partnering with the creative team behind Rob Bell's Nooma *series, Buckingham's first "short film series" is called* Trombone Player Wanted. *He talked about the project with Life@Work.*

"We wanted to find a way to reach more people. If you look at Google Video, Yahoo Video, YouTube, and the success of iTunes' video component, this is going to be the way that we reach Generation Y.

"While this is designed for businesses, it's going to be the way to reach school kids. I was always conscious that this message about strength is something that we need to teach people earlier than when they get into the workforce. We need to indoctrinate them really quickly because, otherwise, they can get way off track and just not contribute what they should contribute.

"And books are fine, talks are fine, but what this generation is used to are compelling, visually arresting images. Nooma was just so compelling, so beautifully done, and so intimate without being fake.

"We shot these, and I don't know what you think of the message, but as a person from the outside looking in, they sure do look pretty. My hope is that they will spread this strength message farther and faster than purely books can do. We've got to figure out a way to get these films in as many peoples' hands as possible. I'm very excited about them."

For more information, go to
www.MarcusBuckingham.com/film.

discretion in terms of where we spend our time to be able to do so ... incrementally. I don't mean finding the perfect job tomorrow, but I think all of us have the ability to, week by week by week, deliberately try to fill our days with activities that strengthen us and navigate away from the weakness. Every job, from a housekeeper in a hotel to Warren Buffet, has the chance to do that.

Look at Warren Buffet — I thought it was intriguing when he gave $31 billion to Bill Gates' foundation. The reason he gave isn't just that Bill Gates will be better at giving it away than him, which is kind of a pragmatic answer. It's interesting to me that he was quoted to say, "Philanthropy doesn't invigorate me. It's not fun for me. Fun, for me, is running a business." Fun for Bill Gates is flying to Namibia and figuring out how to give away clean needles for HIV patients, but not for Warren Buffet.

Now, that takes a huge amount of self-confidence to be able to say it that way. There's a lesson there for everybody.

L@W
Last question: Are you part of the 17 percent that feel strengthened by your job?

Buckingham
Right now, I am. About six or seven years ago I was at a place in my life where I moved way off my strengths path. It just happened incrementally over a period of about 18 months. I was never promoted. It was just that my weeks gradually filled up with a bunch of activities that weakened me. It was hard to pinpoint when and quite how it happened.

You know how you realize it when you drive home at night and notice your knuckles are white because you're grabbing the steering wheel so hard? I think it's happened to all of us at some point in our life — not because things aren't going well, because they are — and all kinds of doors are open for you.

I was lucky enough to know that I couldn't work my way out of that problem. I was aware enough to know probably because my weeks were filled up with a bunch of activities that drained me. My challenge was: "How do I cut that out and return to those activities that invigorate me?" I think I got myself back to being one of the 17 percent by thinking closely and specifically about the activities that, for no good reason at all, invigorate me.

L@W

Interview by Life@Work GroupZine editor Bob Gordon.

Toolbox

TOOLBOX | COMMUNICATION SKILLS

Skillful Communication

By Dianna Booher

Life is one series of presentations after another. Whether it's a formal speech, a client proposal, a conversation with a boss, or a personal testimony, we're always putting our ideas on display. And if we're not "on," we're off — and often out.

Here are some tips to help you improve your presentations.

Don't Let Fear Push You to Mediocrity
Don't settle for being an "average" presenter, one scared into conformity: Not too passionate. Not too loud. Not too flashy. Not too funny. Not too controversial. Not too emotional. Not too formal. Not too informal. Not too anything. Don't risk boring your audience by being average. To get attention for your information and ideas, observe what everybody else is doing — and then don't do it.

Use Fear as Fuel
Learn to perform despite nervousness — in fact, make your jitters work for you. Imagine the tension and extra adrenaline as catalysts to a great presentation — giving you the winning edge.

Focus on Your Subject
Recall and rehearse your key points rather than focus on key obstacles. Instead of thinking how you might embarrass yourself if you "go blank," concentrate on your subject. As you scan the group, think: "This information will help these people. They'll love it."

Put It in Perspective
Another trick for calming yourself is to consider the unnerving experience in light of eternity. What's the worst that can happen? Will it all matter a year from now? In fact, who will even remember it tomorrow?

The most effective speakers are not those who never experience fear. They're the ones who transform it into peak performance.

L@W

Dianna Booher, the founder of Booher Consultants (**www.booherconsultants.com**), is a popular speaker who focuses on communication and life balance issues. She has also written more than 40 books, including *Speak with Confidence!*; *Well Connected*: *Power Your Own Soul by Plugging into Others*; and *Get a Life Without Sacrificing Your Career.*

To get attention for your information and ideas, observe what everybody else is doing — and then don't do it.

An Artist's Touch
Your Creative Spark Can Lead Anywhere

By Bob Gordon

Artists have an inherent connection to skill. Find any artist — painter, sculptor, musician — and you have a living definition of skill.

Bill Strickland runs a highly successful art school. Surprisingly, however, he does not look for gifted artists to join his program.

"Artistic aptitude is not a requirement to get into the program. I don't even know what that is," Strickland says. "What I'm looking for is a flame, just a little one, and if that flame's still there, I can make it into a bonfire, with clay and ceramics and enthusiasm and sunlight and flowers."

Welcome to Bill Strickland's world. It's a little different than his contemporaries at other art schools. That's because at the Manchester Craftsmen's Guild, you will find artists that might not otherwise have a chance to succeed.

"We do clay, photography, and computer imaging for 400 kids from the public school system, all of whom are considered at risk," Strickland says. "We go into the schools, and any kid that makes the mistake of scratching their heads when we ask who's interested is in the program."

It's quite a program. Based in an under-resourced area of Pittsburgh, Manchester Craftsmen's Guild is housed in a beautiful 62,000-square-foot facility designed by a student of Frank Lloyd Wright.

Its stated mission is to:
- Educate and inspire urban youth through the arts and mentored training in life skills

- Preserve, present, and promote jazz and visual arts to stimulate intercultural understanding, appreciation, and enhancement of the quality of life for our audiences

- Equip and educate leaders to further demonstrate entrepreneurial potential

That's why in the skilled world of art, skill is not the most important ingredient at MCG.

"I'm in the attitude business, and the worst part about being poor is what it does to your spirit," Strickland says. "You never have a nice day. So my theory was, if you want to change people's lives, you have to look like the solution and not the problem.

"I'm in the attitude business, not just the training business."

IT STARTED WITH A TEACHER

Strickland personally knows the power of a changed life. He was a student at an inner-city high school in Pittsburgh in the 1960s when a walk down the school's hallway changed his life ... and the lives of countless others since.

"The art door was open and I just happened to look in," Strickland said. "I saw the art teacher making a great big old ceramic bowl. I'd never seen anything like that in my life, so I stood at the door, and I said, 'What is that?' and the art teacher said, 'Well, that's ceramics.' I said, 'Well, I want you to teach me that.'"

And that's what Frank Ross did. And then some. In addition to helping Strickland learn the ropes as a ceramic artist, Ross helped his pupil become a student. With the teacher's assistance, Strickland applied for and was accepted at the University of Pittsburgh.

Yet even before he graduated in 1969, Strickland already had a job ... make that a calling. Looking to make a difference in his hometown, he started the Guild to provide art lessons to the mainly African-American kids in his neighborhood. This was in the midst of the social unrest surrounding the murder of Dr. Martin Luther King Jr.

"I started this arts program in 1968. During the riots, the Bishop of the Episcopal Diocese took a liking to me," Strickland says. "He wrote me checks out of the bishop's discretionary fund, and that's how I got started. When he died a few years ago, his family told me that my life best represented what the bishop believed in."

With initial funding in place, the Manchester Craftsmen's Guild began making a difference in the community. It quickly was noticed by the founders of the Bidwell Training Center, which provided students with vocational technical training in the same neighborhood. For nearly 40 years, Strickland has been leading both organizations.

MAKING AN IMPACT

Since 1987, the organizations have shared a Wright-inspired building that provides areas for all of the Guild's creative training endeavors. The building has facilities and equipment for:

Ceramic Arts
Digital Imaging
Drawing and Design
Media Arts
Photography
Recording Studio
Concert Hall
Galleries

According to the organization's website (**www.manchesterguild.org**), the building's features include "natural light pouring in through windows and skylights, terracotta-toned masonry framing archways, and circular portals evoking stylistic influences of indigenous African architecture. ... Handmade objects, furniture, photographs, and paintings that adorn public and private spaces create a model environment for

behavior. Expectations are the key to this whole puzzle. You put people in a world-class training center, you can cure what's troubling them.

"We have figured out a good part of the solution to spiritual cancer. You have to bring life to people and not death, and you can do it in the worst and most difficult places in the world, where the sun doesn't normally shine."

How dark is it in Strickland's neighborhood?

"My old high school is four blocks away and they have metal detectors, armed guards, bars on the windows," he says. "In the same neighborhood, we have no guards in the building, no metal detectors. In 22 years of operation, I've never had a fight, a drug incident, an alcohol incident, zero."

BEAUTY IN ART AND MUSIC

Manchester Craftsmen's Guild offers their training for free to middle school and high school students in Pittsburgh. In addition to their after-school programs (which offers free bus transportation), they also offer summer programs, and — in partnership with the school district — school-day programs.

While the artistic opportunities are of the highest quality, they are seen as a tool, not the objective.

"The youth programs stress that success is based not only on skill and knowledge, but also on attitude and performance. Many of our alumni have gone on to successful careers in the arts, business, communications, and other fields. Young people involved in MCG learn to become creative and intellectual risk-takers," according to the website.

"I'm in the attitude business, not just the training business."

education, exhibitions, performances, and social and professional gatherings."

So, why does the building have all of these fancy elements and added features?
"It's a stunning piece of architecture in the toughest neighborhood of Pittsburgh with the highest crime rate, which is exactly where it needed to be built," Strickland says. "It's all in the way that you think about people that determines their

Some young people learn to take risks in the creative realm of jazz. MCG Jazz is a multifaceted element of the organization, offering everything from classes to concerts, lessons in the recording business to the business of recording.
Between the studio, concert hall, and Strickland's many friends, some of the most popular and gifted jazz musicians have been part of MCG Jazz.

"What I'm looking for is a flame, just a little one, and if that flame is still there, I can make it into a bonfire."

"I stood on my stage with Dizzy Gillespie on a Wednesday afternoon before the first concert, and he said, 'Bill, you don't appreciate what you've done here, but I do.' I said, 'Man, you play the great music halls of the world.' He says, 'Yeah, but a lot of times I walked down the alley and walked in the back door. Here, I walked in the front door with my head up. You ought to build one of these centers in every city in the United States of America, and I'm going to help you do it,'" Strickland says. "So Dizzy gave us the rights to the (live recording of the) music from the concert, and we now own that. He

Bill Strickland

"What we teach is enthusiasm and life over death and it works out fine."

More than vocational training, more than artistic opportunities, more than anything else, the Manchester Craftsmen's Guild and the Bidwell Training Center provide hope to under-resourced people in Pittsburgh.

"God is guiding this process, man. I can feel it," Strickland says. "I don't want to live like this in this country and in the world anymore. I'm tired of seeing poor kids hungry. Their eyes are open, but they aren't

"Now we have 600 recordings, the most important collection of contemporary jazz recordings in the world."

died a year later, but he told Wynton Marsalis what we were up to, and Herbie Hancock, and McCoy Tyner, and Billy Taylor, and the Count Basie band — so now we have 600 recordings, the most important collection of contemporary jazz recordings in the world in my center in Pittsburgh. We've won two Grammy's from our center."

The opening concert in 1987 was special to Strickland in another way as well.

"My mother and father, who are deceased, lived long enough to see their kid build this thing in their neighborhood," he says.

BEAUTIFUL RESULTS
"For the last 15 years, we've averaged over 80 percent of the kids in the program going to college, and we do not teach the academics," Strickland says. "Eight of my faculty are former kids who went through the program and are back teaching there. We have a Pulitzer Prize winner, a Fulbright scholar, and people at the Rochester Institute of Technology and Harvard University. I've got three physicians, emergency room physicians who came through the ceramics program. A welfare mother with four kids and no husband who went through the ceramics program is now an emergency room physician, and she has a life.

seeing anything. Poor kids who can't ever have a nice day, schools that don't work, and communities that are dying.

"The only thing wrong with poor people is they don't have any money — which happens to be a curable condition."

L@W

Bob Gordon is the editor of the *Life@Work GroupZine* series. He also leads Write Purpose (**www.writepurpose.com**), a writing, editing, and communication consulting company serving the needs of purposeful organizations and churches. He and his wife Carey have two kids and live near Charlotte, North Carolina.

Toolbox

TOOLBOX | SKILLS

Soft Skills Impact Work and *Home*

By Rick Packer

How corporate managers approach employee skill development greatly impacts the usability of that skill. Specifically, the approach used for hard skills development versus soft skills development is the driving force behind an employee embracing the development process. What are hard skills and soft skills?

Despite what corporate employees have been advised, it's nearly impossible to separate work life from private life — both deeply impact the other. One way to better understand this is to examine the differences between developing hard skills and soft skills — both of which are important to successful careers. Both require nurturing, development, and practice to be optimally applied.

Hard skills are technical competencies, such as data entry, implementation processes, forklift operation, etc. Soft skills are interpersonal skills, communication, presentation, relating to customers, listening, negotiation, etc.

When developing in both of these areas we have a tendency to compartmentalize the process. The majority of both hard- and soft-skills development (specifically training) is compartmentalized. And the compartment we use is work. For example, we physically conduct training sessions at *work* with co-*workers* for the purpose of benefiting *work*. This isolated training results in isolated embracement — which is only suitable only for hard skills development.

That's because hard skills are applied at work, whereas soft skills are also applied in life. It's difficult to *effectively* train soft skills in the work environment without considering the broader scope where soft skills are applied. For example, when we send an employee to "Anger Management" training, a few weeks after this soft-skill training, the employee is still angry. That's because the training is compartmentalized to focus on

anger issues at work, not anger issues in life. People are not compartmentalized. If you are angry in life you are going go to be angry at work. If you have people skills in life you use those people skills at work.

To go a layer deeper, there is a difference between being *able* and being *willing*. Soft-skills training can impact the learner's ability but not necessarily their willingness — because willingness is part of a larger equation than work. In every training setting, the learner will first filter the subject matter through their "life lens," which will indicate their willingness to embrace or reject the subject matter. If their life experiences tell them that trusting people, for example, (soft skill) is dangerous, then that impacts their willingness and therefore their ability to embrace it in the work setting.

When we compartmentalize soft-skills development, we are truncating its impact and effectiveness. When it comes to soft skills, people bring with them history and sometimes baggage that has a deep impact on how that soft skill is used in the work environment. While this is difficult, we can't overlook the tremendous impact on the learner's application of the soft skill being taught.

So what do we need to do? Corporate managers and training staffs need to work harder on bridging this gap.

To find out how organizations are filling this gap, visit **www.thepackergroup.com/skills**.

L@W

Rick Packer is president of The Packer Group, an organization that focuses on growing people, improving team cohesiveness, and developing leaders. For more info or to sign up for Rick's free newsletter, visit **www.thepackergroup.com**.

I press on toward the goal to win the prize for which God has called me heavenward in Christ Jesus.

Philippians 3:14 (NIV)

BETSY ROGERS

Betsy Rogers, Ed.D., is the School Improvement Specialist for the Jefferson County (Alabama) Board of Education (**www.jefcoed.com**). A stay-at-home mom for six years and a schoolteacher for 22 years, Betsy was recognized as the National Teacher of the Year in 2003.

Family Concerns

I am a widow; my husband died of sudden cardiac arrest at the age of 46. At the time, my two sons were in college and I had just started back to grad school. It is a loss my sons and I have never gotten over. Rick, 29, is teaching Spanish at a high school in Tennessee after completing Divinity School at Wake Forest in 2004. Alan, 28, is a personal trainer at St. Vincent's Hospital in Birmingham.

My husband and I were very intentional about our family time. We had meals together daily. I did not go back to grad school until my youngest son graduated from high school. Taking care of my family was my priority.

Real Life Lessons

When my husband and I moved our family from a more affluent neighborhood to Leeds 24 years ago, our purpose was to raise our children in an environment with a more diverse population with a rural background. Many of my colleagues do not believe it is beneficial to live in the community where you teach, but I have found this relationship with the Leeds community to be very rewarding and productive. By living and working in Leeds, I truly became a stakeholder in the community. Unfortunately, my husband's sudden death forced me to sell our small farm and leave Leeds. However, my sons and I will always consider Leeds our home and I am committed to serving the community.

Putting Beliefs to Action

From my family I learned the value of caring for others. I watched my parents and grandparents serve their church and community by teaching, visiting the sick, gathering clothes and food for the needy, celebrating births, and grieving in losses. I was taught that we are here on this earth to serve. It is this characteristic that I believe to be my greatest contribution to the children I have taught.

After taking six years to stay at home with my two sons and teaching two years in a private kindergarten, I returned to teaching at my first love — public schools. However, after an eight-year absence, I was totally unprepared for the situations that the children in my first grade class at Leeds faced. The poverty, neglect, and abuse that many of my students experienced every day overwhelmed me. I wanted to change the world for them. It took me several years to realize I could not change the world in which they lived. Understanding that school was the best place for many of these children, I became committed to making my classroom a haven of safety, as well as an environment that provided some joy to their unfortunate lives. I also made the commitment to build positive relationships with their families. I realized many of these families loved their children deeply and were often doing their best.

I felt it was vital to build a strong triangular relationship between students, parents, and myself. By helping and caring about my students' families, I believe I have made a difference in creating a classroom community that fosters growth and stability.

Teacher's Notes

I try to share my faith by being an example of a Christ-like person. I seek to show kindness and concern.

Be honest, be yourself, and stay focused on God's work.

L@W

And we know that in all things God works for the good of those who love him, who have been called according to his purpose.

Romans 8:28 (NIV)

BOB CHRISTIAN

Bob Christian retired in 2002 after an 11-year playing career in the National Football League. A twelfth-round draft pick out of Northwestern, Bob played for the Chicago Bears, Carolina Panthers, and Atlanta Falcons as a fullback and special teams player. He started 82 games, and twice was a Pro Bowl alternate. He currently volunteers his time as the Chairman of the Board for a Native American ministry called Dakota Sonshine (**www.DakotaSonshine.org**) and with the student and small group ministries at Crossroads Community Church.

Game Time

I learned so many lessons while playing football that still help me and will continue to help me as I start a new career: hard work, teamwork, perseverance, sacrifice, love, thankfulness, humility, accountability, faith, confidence, focus.

I always strove to work for God's approval first. He gave me my talent, and I wanted to give Him the performance that He expected when He gave me my abilities. I wanted Him to enjoy watching me play — not only on Sundays, but also during the week, at practice as well as in the games.

Faith in the Game

To me, that is what my life is about, my purpose: to represent Jesus and share His life-saving love with those who are lost in their sins. During my career, I always thought of myself as a missionary to the men on the teams that I played on. God gave me access to men who wouldn't go to a church.

I was always aware that in all I did at work, I was being watched by all those around me, and I wanted shine the light of Jesus in good times and bad, through failure and triumph, in the midst of pain and suffering. It was also important to me to share the gospel as God gave me opportunities. As St. Francis of Assisi said, "Preach the gospel always, and when necessary use words."

A New Teammate

I was married in 2005 and I tried to take Deuteronomy 24:5 literally: "If a man has recently married, he must not be sent to war or have any other duty laid on him. For one year he is to be free to stay at home and bring happiness to the wife he has married." Since I hadn't started a new career yet when we got married, I wanted to spend a year focusing on my wife and our marriage before getting too busy with the pressing demands of a new career. I think that it has paid big dividends, since our first year of marriage was not as difficult as we have heard it sometimes is.

Preparing for a New Game

The way you pursue success and the motivation you use is more important to God than the achievement of success. God is more pleased with a failure in which we upheld our integrity and gave our best effort within proper boundaries than if we cut a corner or shaded a truth on the way to a major success. Jesus made it simple for us when He told us the greatest commandments: "Love the Lord your God with all your heart and with all your soul and with all your mind … and love your neighbor as yourself." He wants us to work hard for the love of Him, the love of our families, our co-workers, our clientele, those we can help, and those we mentor. He is not pleased if we sacrifice our families and relationships for success at work. If we honor Him in the way we do our work, He will bless our work in His proper time.

L@W

EXECUTIVE SUMMARY
Final Thoughts On Defining Skill

SKILL IS INTENDED TO SHINE. It is God-given and awe-inspiring. It lies beneath every great creation, invention, and work of art. Exercising skill awakens the soul and enlivens the spirit.

Too often, we stifle our skills by following career paths and promotions that steer us away from what we do best. Sadly, we devote our energy and time to pursuits outside of our strength zones, and our skills are not given an outlet.

We become tired of living passionless lives and exhausted from working endless hours in roles we find dull and boring. Deep down, we know this is not how we were created to live. How can we recover the energy and excitement of expressing our skill?

IN THIS LESSON WE'VE LEARNED:

▷ Skill is understanding something completely, and transforming that knowledge into creations of wonder and excellence.

▷ Managing skill is a matter of stewardship. God has entrusted us with talent and ability, and we have been created to invest these skills for His glory.

▷ A common myth proclaims that we can acquire any skill or trait by working at it. We can see this isn't the case because as we grow, our personality doesn't change. On the contrary, growth makes us more of who we already are.

▷ Our skill is sapped when we spend time on activities that bore, drain, or deplete us. We must rigorously guard ourselves from expending too much energy in areas of weakness.

▷ We are sometimes cursed with ability to do something, but no appetite for it. Having a skill without interest will steal our enjoyment and de-motivate us.

▷ Occasionally, we must step out of our strength zones, but the essence of teamwork is to contribute in the area of our greatest skill.

▷ Our greatest opportunity for growth coincides with our area of greatest strength.

▷ We cannot be satisfied with mediocrity and still work wholeheartedly before God. Skill is more than a business necessity, it's a spiritual imperative.

▷ When we face challenges, God has a role to intervene, but He doesn't step in until we've reached the limit of our skill.

▷ God gives us our skills. Our responsibility is to locate our skills and express them in our work. When we exercise our skills, we produce excellence.

▷ The greatest leaders don't necessarily lead the most skilled people. The greatest leaders know how to get the best out of every team member, in every situation, which produces a highly effective team.

▷ Greatness requires both desire and knack. Aspiration without ability will get you nowhere. Likewise, talent without motivation will never excel.

▷ God never intended for us to be omni-competent. Only He can be that. The adventure in life lies in finding our strengths and optimizing them in every venue of our lives.

Notes

_____
_____
_____
_____
_____
_____
_____
_____

NEXT STEPS

You are responsible for discovering your skills and relentlessly pursuing them. The first step of this journey is to identify your strengths zone — the intersection between what you do well and what you love to do.

- → Think about your current and most recent jobs. In what areas do you consistently excel? Identify three activities you do well and with ease. Identify three activities that you don't do well or that drain you.

- → Ask five family members, coworkers, or close friends what they perceive as your strengths. Compare their responses and look for commonalities.

- → Go to your local or online bookstore or the library and pick up a copy of Marcus Buckingham's book *Now Discover Your Strengths*. Take the Strengths Finder test online, and study the profile of your top five strengths.

According to Buckingham, to play to your strengths you must: "Discover what you don't like doing and stop doing it."

↻ **Below, list the activities you currently spend time doing at work. When your list is complete, review it, and circle the activities you don't like doing.**

↻ **Next, list work activities you would enjoy doing, but which are not part of your present role.**

- → Over the next month, take steps to eliminate the items circled on the page and replace them with the new activities listed.

- → Make the time to repeat this exercise monthly to cut down on the activities that drain you, and to explore opportunities you find fulfilling.

CALLING@WORK

Calling: God's personal invitation for me to work on His agenda, using the talents I have been given in ways that are eternally significant

PICK UP THE PHONE

Will You Answer God's Call In Your Life?

By Stephen R. Graves

The Bible includes many verses that speak of a calling connected to our work. What may surprise you is that fewer than half of these verses have anything to do with a full-time Christian vocation. Most refer to God's calling of somebody to the marketplace: to cut jewelry, dig ditches, build roads, nurse the sick, take notes as a scribe, play music, shepherd, rule a kingdom. God still calls us to design websites, decide court cases, deliver copy machines.

Calling, in its fullness, is an idea too good to be true — unless and until Jesus is involved in the conversation. When He calls, He does so with great precision. Not only does He know what needs to be accomplished and how that task fits within eternal boundaries, He also knows the one He is calling. After all, He made that person *specifically* to do what he or she is being called to do.

In his book *The Rest of God*, Mark Buchanan writes: "Virtually any job, no matter how grueling or tedious — any job that is not criminal or sinful — can be a gift from God, through God, and to God. The work of our hands, by the alchemy of our devotion, becomes the worship of our hearts."

How does your view of work match up to that standard?

On Purpose

The rat race. The treadmill. The old grind. Surely God has something better in mind for your Life@Work than the futility and tedium implied by some of our most familiar synonyms for the workaday life. We human beings weren't designed to go around in circles, as on a treadmill. We were made to move toward a purpose. We were made to grow. The thought of purposelessness strikes horror in us; the huge appeal of books like Rick Warren's *The Purpose-Driven Life* should come as no surprise. We need to know we're a part of something larger than ourselves. We need to know there's more to our work than "another day, another dollar." God has a grand design for the universe He created. The work we do from 9 to 5 is — or should be — one of the most important ways we take part in that grand design. That's what calling means. The knowledge that we are working out a calling imbues our work with a dignity and joy that go well beyond the goods we produce and the services we render.

What is Scripture's definition of calling? Calling is:

God's personal invitation for me to work on His agenda, using the talents I have been given in ways that are eternally significant.

To be called means I know that what I am doing is what God wants me to do. God calls every one of us to a specific work assignment at any given time. When Paul was speaking to philosophers in Athens, he made it clear that God had a very precise plan for individual lives: "From

one man he made every nation of men, that they should inhabit the whole earth; and *he determined the times set for them and the exact places where they should live*" (Acts 17:26 NIV, emphasis added). God designed *me* to do something for *Him*.

WE HUMAN BEINGS WEREN'T DESIGNED TO GO AROUND IN CIRCLES, AS ON A TREADMILL. WE WERE MADE TO MOVE TOWARD A PURPOSE. WE WERE MADE TO GROW.

We are men and women who do consulting, banking, truck driving, plumbing, doctoring, full-time parenting, teaching, pastoring, and a host of other things. God calls individuals to all kinds of careers. The common factor that we all share, however, is the One who has called us all.

Anchored in eternal reality, we are freed to view our work from a perspective above the constant changing of day-to-day business. At the same time, we are not "above it all," exempted from or unchallenged by the ever-changing realities of the work world before us, temporary as that work may be. God throws us in to join the fray. We plant eternal seeds in the ground of the everyday. Our work involves the implementation of God's agenda in history.

When we come to grips with the idea and magnitude of God's calling, we are less tempted to define success as a promotion to the seventeenth floor or a vacation in the Swiss Alps. In our work we are called to higher, more attainable realities and to a deeper fulfillment and sustaining significance.

Looking Outside Ourselves

It's true that knowing yourself — your skill set, your limitations, your passions — is an important part of pursuing your calling. But ultimately, calling isn't about getting in touch with yourself so much as it's about letting God touch you. This is an important point. There's nothing wrong with looking deep inside. But calling is about being part of something that's a whole lot bigger than you: God's purposes — and not just His purposes for your life, but His purposes for everything else too. Your calling reaches beyond you, and pursuing your calling means responding to a big God in ways that always expand your boundaries.

Let's look at two of the most dramatic cases of calling in the Bible: Moses and Paul. When Moses encountered God in the burning bush, his career had been in a 40-year freefall. He had once been a prince of Egypt, but a moment of violent anger destroyed all that and sent him running to the desert. In the desert, it had been his job to take care of his father-in-law's sheep. Talk about going nowhere! Then came the unmistakable call of God: "I will send you to Pharaoh that you may bring My people, the children of Israel, out of Egypt" (Exodus 3:10 NKJV).

Moses was doubtful that God had the right man. Years of working for his father-in-law, far from the privilege and honor of his old station in life, had done a number on his self-confidence. But he answered the call anyway, and as time went on, it became obvious that this kind of leadership was what he was born for. He had all the advantages of being raised and educated in the house of Pharaoh. He had a heart for the sufferings of the Hebrew people — as evidenced by his rash killing of an Egyptian overseer who was oppressing them. And his 40-year banishment to the desert was vital training for the 40 years he would spend leading his people in a similar desert.

Paul — or Saul, as he was known at the time — was on a much different career path when he heard God's call. He was a

He was on his way, in fact, to stomp out more Christians when he saw the light — or more precisely, he was blinded by it. His call from God was as specific as Moses':

"I have appeared to you for this purpose, to make you a minister and a witness both of the things which you have seen and of the things which I will yet reveal to you. I will deliver you from the Jewish people, as well as from the Gentiles, to whom I now send you, to open their eyes, in order to turn them from darkness to light, and from the power of Satan to God, that they may receive forgiveness of sins and an inheritance among those who are sanctified by faith in Me" (Acts 26:16-20 NKJV).

Once Paul responded to God's call, it became obvious that everything in his life up to that point had been preparing him for this work. The drive and energy and focus that had made him such a formidable enemy of the early Church made him an even more formidable force in the growth of the Church during extremely difficult times. In Paul's epistles, which are so important in the definition of the truths of Christianity, you can see the logic and rhetorical skill that had been sharpened during his training under Judaism's leading lights.

One thing to note: the word *calling* isn't just Christian-ese for career. No career counselor would have looked over Moses' resume and said, "Have you ever thought about facing down the most powerful ruler in the world and leading three million slaves to freedom?" No corporate headhunter would have thought to take Saul out to lunch and recruit him to take the lead in shaping the Christian Church as we know it.

In retrospect, it's obvious that Moses and Paul were the men for the jobs God gave them. But they could have filled out

GOD DESIGNED **ME** TO DO SOMETHING FOR **HIM.**

rising star among Jewish religious professionals. He had all the qualifications of birth and had been trained by some of the greatest scholars of the Jewish faith. He had ambition, drive, smarts, and single-minded commitment to the cause. He had become the Pharisees' go-to guy for stomping out the latest threat to their religious hegemony: the Christians.

personality profiles and self-evaluations until the cows came home, and they would have never found inside themselves the incredible things God would do through them. One looked like an abject failure and one looked like a wild success, but for Moses and Paul alike, the act of responding to God's call focused a lifetime of misdirected energy into a career of mind-boggling significance.

Settled Calling

So what does life look like when you're pursuing your calling? There's no single answer to that question, but there are at least a few guidelines. There's a certain settled-ness about a person who is pursuing his or her calling. You've seen people who are always looking over the fence, people who get a little too excited about every new possibility, whose interest is piqued a little too much by every conversation. That's not a person who has settled into his or her calling. When you've answered God's call, you're able to live in the now. You can enjoy what God is doing in the present; you can look forward to the future too, but in a way that rests in God's sovereignty. You don't have that luxury if you don't feel settled.

Living out your calling involves obeying Christ's command to "abide" in Him. In the Greek, "abide" is related to the idea of a bowstring when it's not pulled tight. To abide in Christ is to be released from the constant tension of being unsettled and discontent. That doesn't mean your life will be struggle-free. Of course there still will be challenges to be met. Sometimes you've got to pull back the bowstring and let fly. But you always return to a state of rest. Max Lucado calls it living in

YOUR CALLING REACHES BEYOND YOU, AND PURSUING YOUR CALLING MEANS RESPONDING TO A BIG GOD IN WAYS THAT ALWAYS EXPAND YOUR BOUNDARIES.

your sweet spot: "A zone, a region, a life precinct in which you were made to dwell. He tailored the curves of your life to fit an empty space in His jigsaw puzzle."

When you're pursuing your calling, you're not constantly trying to convince God to go along with your plan. Instead, you find out what God is doing,

and you join Him. A sense of calling gives you a relaxed view of God's sovereignty. You're in your spot, doing your part, but you realize there's a lot more going on than your

FOR MOSES AND PAUL ALIKE, THE ACT OF RESPONDING TO GOD'S CALL FOCUSED A LIFETIME OF MISDIRECTED ENERGY INTO A CAREER OF MIND-BOGGLING SIGNIFICANCE.

one-person drama. It's your job to grow and go, to be sure you're who you ought to be as a person. It's God's job to weave your life into the larger tapestry of His purpose. If God sees fit to make you the next Warren Buffett or Bill Gates or John Grisham or Michael Jordan, that's great. If He chooses to use your talents on a smaller stage, that's great too. There's real rest in that realization.

Calling need not be a lifetime mystery. God intended from the beginning to unfold His plans and desires for each us with specificity. If there is anything that ought to sound good in today's world, it is this: work can have eternal purpose, and our lives can have fullness of meaning through the work we do.

L@W

Dr. Stephen R. Graves is a highly sought business coach and life guide for entrepreneurs and leaders desiring to successfully make it to the finish line of life. In 1991, he co-founded the Cornerstone Group, a company built to integrate biblical wisdom and business excellence. He and his wife Karen have three children.

This article is based on concepts drawn from Life@Work *by John C. Maxwell, Stephen R. Graves, and Thomas G. Addington, published by Thomas Nelson, Inc.*

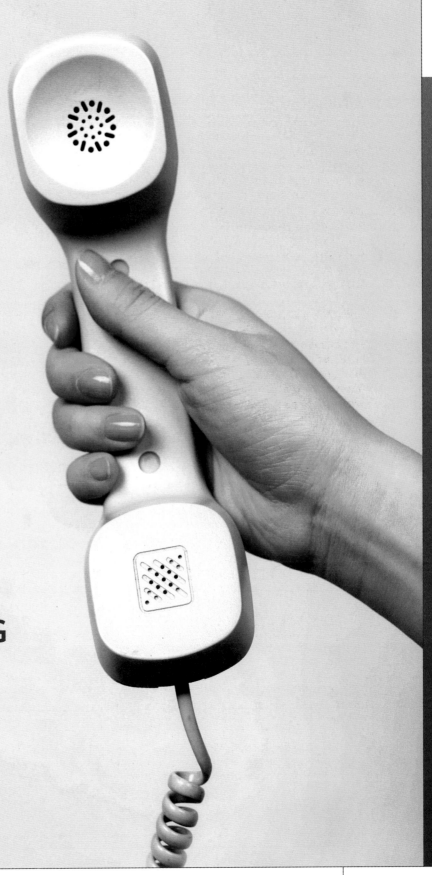

WHEN YOU'RE **PURSUING** YOUR CALLING, YOU'RE NOT CONSTANTLY TRYING TO CONVINCE **GOD** TO GO ALONG WITH YOUR PLAN.

PICK UP THE PHONE

FOR GROUP DISCUSSION

Prior to your small group meeting time, read and reflect on the Life@Work Study article you just read. Use these questions and journal pages to reflect and respond to the ideas presented. Be ready to share your thoughts at your small group gathering.

Note to small group leaders: You can download a full Leader's Guide at www.lifeatworkgroupzine.com.

- *Calling is God's personal invitation for me to work on His agenda, using the talents I have been given in ways that are eternally significant. To be called means I know that what I am doing is what God wants me to do.*
    What do you think of this description of calling? Have you bought into the idea that "calling" only refers to a role in ministry? Do you believe your current job is a calling? If so, how did you know you were called to it? If not, what do you think your calling is?

- *God throws us in to join the fray. We plant eternal seeds in the ground of the everyday. Our work involves the implementation of God's agenda in history.*
    Read that statement again. Have you ever stopped to consider that your work is playing a role in God's history? How does that make you feel? If you began working with this perspective, what would have to immediately change about how you do your job? How would you then handle successes? Failures?

- Think about Moses' career. Here was a man destined for greatness as the son of Pharaoh, yet he spent much of his career tending to sheep in the wilderness. Eventually, though, he was true to his calling when he led the Israelites out of Egypt.
    At this point in your career, do you feel more like Moses the sheep-watcher or Moses the people-mover? Are you in your calling's sweet spot? How would you describe your sweet spot? If you're not there, how does Moses' life provide you with inspiration?

- *There's a certain settled-ness about a person who is pursuing his or her calling. You've seen people who are always looking over the fence, people who get a little too excited about every new possibility, whose interest is piqued a little too much by every conversation. That's not a person who has settled into his or her calling.*
    On a continuum, with 1 being that you are always looking over the fence and 5 being a certain settled-ness, where would you say you are in terms finding your calling? What are you willing to do career-wise in order to take a further step toward your calling?

- *A sense of calling gives you a relaxed view of God's sovereignty. You're in your spot, doing your part, but you realize there's a lot more going on than your one-person drama.*
    What is your reaction to this view of your calling? Do you have a more relaxed view of God's sovereignty? Are you able to look at your role in the bigger picture of what God is doing? If not, what steps can you take to move beyond your one-person drama?

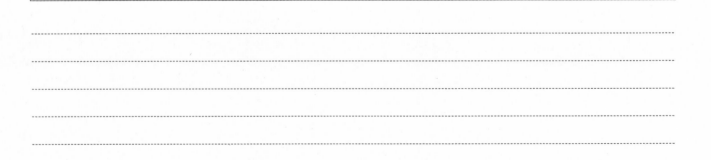

Feature Article

Creative Calling

When Creativity Reigns, Callings Can Be Multi-Faceted

By Bob Gordon

Steve Taylor started out as a youth pastor, made a name for himself in Christian music, and now is a movie director and screenwriter. Marcy Walker found fame and fortune as a soap opera star and now, as Marcy Smith, can be found leading a dynamic children's ministry at a church in North Carolina.

When it comes to the issue of calling, creativity adds a unique element. Oftentimes, even when they are engaging their gifts and talents, creatives sense an internal unrest that can be both challenging and daunting.

As gifted artists, Steve Taylor and Marcy Smith have followed their individual callings to award-winning levels in New York, Los Angeles, and Nashville — the centers of the entertainment industry.

Yet what has kept them both centered is their calling to follow God.

All in God's Timing
Skill, experience, and connections all play an important role for someone looking to get their break in the world of professional acting. Of course, there is something to be said for divine providence — even when the person being led doesn't yet know God.

Marcy Walker Smith had graduated from high school and was working in an office with a team of middle-aged women who smoked. A lot. She knew that job was something she didn't want to do the rest of her life; what she didn't know was what she did want to do.

> *Oftentimes, even when they are engaging their gifts and talents, creatives sense an internal unrest that can be both challenging and daunting.*

She had enjoyed being part of school drama productions, so she decided to talk with the drama department head at nearby Southern Illinois University-Edwardsville. As she walked into his office for their scheduled meeting, he was on the phone. "I heard him say, 'There's a girl in my office that looks like she could play the part,'" Smith recalls. "I had no idea who he was talking to or what he was talking about."

It turned out that a graduate of the university's drama department was helping cast a television movie based on Mark Twain's *Life on the Mississippi* that was going to be filmed in nearby Peoria, IL. Despite having no professional experience, an agent, nor even a portfolio, Marcy went to the audition. She wore her only dress for her big day.

The only thing that caught the director's and the producer's eyes more than her inexperience was her genuine naivety. Fortunately, the key characteristic of the movie's teenage Southern belle Emmeline was her genuine naivety. "I came to find out later that they had never met anyone so naïve in their lives. I was Emmeline; they found her in me," Smith says.

At 17, she had her first professional role. Soon afterward, she moved to New York and tasted more quick success in commercial work (she filmed more than 50 national commercials). That helped lead to an audition for "All My Children."

Still in her teens, she became "Liza Colby" in 1981. Liza became a central character on the popular program as a leading villainess, "I was a bad girl ... just nasty," she says. "It was the beginning of a youth movement in daytime soap operas. We hit it right at the right time. The show was a huge success."

While quickly becoming a star, Smith dealt with fans that had trouble separating reality from fiction. "They only knew me as Liza, not Marcy," she says. "I would get verbally beaten up by fans. It was a wild ride for someone who came from where I came from."

And the ride was only beginning. After playing Liza until 1984, Smith was hired as one of the lead characters in a new soap opera, "Santa Barbara." As Eden Capwell, she would earn a Daytime Emmy as Outstanding Leading Actress in 1989. Marcy stayed with the show, which was filmed in California, until 1991. After making a handful of television movies, she headed back to New York to play Tangie Hill on "The Guiding Light" from 1993-95.

In 1995, her acting career came full circle as she returned to "All My Children" as Liza, a role she would play for another decade.

While her career was on a roll, her real life was not. Having grown up in an unchurched home, Marcy found life in the fast lane much to her liking ... and much to blame for her troubles.

"I remember one time going to buy a Porsche and not being able to decide between two colors. So I bought them both," she says.

"When I moved back to the East Coast, I had done it all and seen it all, and I was in my 30s. I saw a lot of friends die of AIDS, overdoses, anorexia. Here was the pinnacle of success and years later, you see the consequences of choices that had been made. There was a lot of emptiness."

Along the way of her own poor choices, Marcy was befriended by a pen-pal ... a Christian woman who had stumbled onto a soap opera and felt compelled to pray for Marcy.

Having grown up in an unchurched home, Marcy found life in the fast lane much to her liking ... and much to blame for her troubles.

"She prayed for me for six years before I asked her about God," Smith says. "She never gave up on me." Neither did God. In time, Marcy became a Christ-follower and soon afterward began serving in the children's ministry of her new church home. Her shooting schedule allowed her a lot of flexibility. As time went on, she found herself longing to be at the church more than in New York filming her scenes.

In 2004, nearly a quarter century after first playing Liza, Marcy finally said good-bye to "All My Children." Her calling had changed: she became the children's director at her church in Connecticut. Eventually, her passion for children's ministry led her to take the role as the children's ministry director at Lake Forest, a growing church in suburban Charlotte, NC, where she's been since 2005.

When she attends a children's ministry conference at another church or even when a visitor comes to her own church, it's not uncommon for Marcy to be asked, "Aren't you? ..."

It's an easy answer: Yes — in life's first act.

"My agent still calls me every once in a while. It's always attractive to experience something new and the money would be nice," Marcy says. "I'm not closing any door. But to go back only to acting ... no, I wouldn't.

"I'm exactly where I'm supposed to be."

An Action-Packed Career

As the senior pastor's son, Steve Taylor was the natural choice to be the youth pastor. The previous leader had left, so Steve returned home to Denver to finish college while serving the students at his dad's church.

All the while, he knew that wouldn't be his life's calling.

"I really liked being a youth pastor, but I couldn't imagine having to sit through all of those church board meetings," he says. "Those meetings would go on and on and on."

His college classes thus were focused on his twin passions. "When I was in high school, I thought I would like to do something with music or filmmaking. In college, I studied both."

He was willing to head in either direction after college, but when he quickly earned a recording contract with Sparrow Records, his course was set.

"I looked at music as an extension of youth ministry," Taylor says. "The kids were getting their values from music. It was a great way to communicate to them."

As Christian music was becoming more popular in the early 1980s, Steve Taylor was an alternative to the somewhat standardized sound of CCM. His music, which has been described as socially relevant, clever, and passionate, earned two Grammy nominations. He won a Dove Award for best video album in 1985, the first of five that he's won.

Yet as a creative, he found himself wondering what else was out there. After recording five CCM albums (along with a greatest hits) between 1983-1987, Taylor joined with other Christian musicians who were intrigued by the idea of creating music targeted for mainstream audiences and airwaves. They birthed a band called Chagall Guevara, whose lone album has become a cult classic. But at the time of the album's release in 1991, "we were too edgy for Christians and too Christian for some of the rock establishment."

When the band broke up, Taylor returned to his roots and recorded two more CCM albums between 1993-1995. Since his last album, he has written and produced for a number of artists — he was the lyricist on many of the Newsboys' most popular songs, including "He Reigns." All along, he kept honing his moviemaking craft by directing music videos.

"The first one I did was my own because my label said they didn't have any money to hire a professional director," he says. "They gave me $5,000. The results turned out really well, so I was asked to do other artists' videos."

After years of creative projects — writing, producing, video directing —Taylor found himself in a completely different role: the head of a start-up, independent record label, Squint Entertainment.

"I was approached by Sixpence None the Richer to produce their record, but their label went bankrupt," Taylor says. "We went ahead

> "*What* I wanted to do was work with fellow Christians whose music needed to be heard by the larger world."

and did the album ... kind of on my credit card. I started a record label so that Sixpence would have a home.

"I certainly didn't have any business experience. It was a major shift and a major learning experience."

That experimental experience lasted from 1997 until the label was sold in 2001. While Squint no longer exists, the label was in many ways a success. Sixpence's "Kiss Me" was a No. 1 radio song and the Taylor-directed video of the song earned heavy play on MTV and VH1. In addition, Squint helped launch the careers of Chevelle, Burlap To Cashmere, The Insyderz, Waterdeep and L.A. Symphony.

"What I wanted to do was work with fellow Christians whose music needed to be heard by the larger world," he says. "It was challenging."

Always up for a challenge, Taylor decided his next move should be into the moviemaking business. His start came with the co-writing, directing, and producing of The Second Chance, which starred Michael W. Smith. This independent film, which was distributed by Sony Pictures in 2006, was a challenge to the church to examine its heart in matters of social justice and race.

"I always wanted to make a movie. One of the movie's other writers suggested having Michael W. Smith in the cast," Taylor says. "Once I had the combination of the script and Michael, I thought it would be easy to find the money to make the film. Man, was I wrong. The process was really frustrating."

Taylor and his wife took out a second mortgage on their home to help finance the film.

"I'm hoping it's easier the next time around," Taylor says. "But the process of making the movie was very enjoyable. It was long, hard work, but it was really fun."

The movie had many similarities to his music career: it was a challenging topic for people in the church, and a bit too church-y for those outside. Its limited release may have had limited commercial success, but it had Taylor's creative knack for making people think.

While his current plans are to remain in the movie business (he's wrapping up the screenplay for a comedic film), a new creative wind might lead him elsewhere down the line. Wrestling with issues of faith and how they play out in the creative realm will always be the common denominator in his calling.

"I did a song on my album Squint called 'Sock Heaven' that talks about the tension of being caught in two worlds," Taylor says. "As an artist, I love expressing my faith and my Christian worldview in whatever I'm working on. But I don't really like having external forces telling me how to do that.

"It's where I've lived my artistic life — right in that tension. For the most part, it's really rewarding ... but it's never been easy."

L@W

Bob Gordon is the editor of the *Life@Work GroupZine* series. He also leads Write Purpose (**www.writepurpose.com**), a content editing, editorial, and communication consulting company serving the needs of purposeful organizations and churches. He and his wife Carey have two kids and live near Charlotte, North Carolina.

Toolbox

TOOLBOX | ANSWER

Be the Answer

By Bishop Dale Bronner

In Matthew 13, Jesus explains the parable of the sower and the seeds to His disciples. Jesus said to the disciples, "He who sows the good seed is the son of man. The field is the world, and the good seeds are the sons of the kingdom, but the tares are the sons of the wicked one, and the enemy who sold them is the devil. The harvest is the end of the age, and the reapers are the angels."

Our great commission is to restore lost relationships. Christianity is really about relationships. We can't impact our community until we build relationships with others. They don't care to know how much we know, until they know how much we care. As we build powerful relationships, it begins to touch the world in a wonderful way.

In the parable, Jesus says that the seed is sown into the field. The field, He explains, is the world, not the church. We are to be sown into the world. We are the Church, the *ecclesia*, the called-out ones.

Sometimes I believe that we've gotten the direction wrong. We thought that we were just called out *of* the world, but I believe that we are called out *to* the world, because we are to be light and salt in a dark and thirsty world. To impact our communities, our workplaces, we need to be the answer that God has called us to be.

You have been called to be an answer. The world is not looking for another problem. We have enough problems. We are looking for answers. It is one thing to pray and ask God for an answer. It's another thing to receive an answer. But the highest thing is to be an answer, and I believe that we are called to be an answer.

I see too many Christians that begin to complain about being the only one saved on their job. Good! It means that you've got your work cut out for you. What a wonderful opportunity to be able to disciple people and lead them to Jesus Christ and be paid by the world to do it.

But let me tell you: don't try to do that until you are serving on your job with excellence. I believe you shouldn't even tell people that you're a Christian until they tell you that you do great work. So that we don't bring reproach on the name of Jesus Christ, but that we serve with excellence, and so we are good seed.

We are called to be an answer. God's answer to every problem is always a person.

L@W

Bishop Dale C. Bronner is the founder and Senior Pastor of Word of Faith Family Worship Cathedral (**www.woffamily.org**), an interdenominational ministry with more than 10,000 members that was founded in 1991. He is the author of several books, including *Get A Grip* and *Guard Your Gates.* He also ministers locally and nationally via television and radio. Bishop Bronner, his wife Nina, and their four daughters and one son live in Atlanta.

> To impact our communities, our workplaces, we need
> to be the answer that God has called us to be.

Over-Thinking Your Calling

By Regi Campbell

I am just about the only person I know who hasn't struggled with what to do with my life. I never changed majors in college, every job I had was somehow connected to the central thread of my profession, and I've never gotten bored with my work. When I went back to get an MBA, I chose the same area as my focus. Weird, huh?

Virtually everybody I know struggles with happiness in their work. People change careers as often as they trade cars. Almost nobody ends up working in the field they are educated for. Lawyers become doctors ... doctors become teachers ... teachers become real estate agents.

So why am I different? Why did this not happen to me? Is there anything I can figure out here that might help someone else?

Necessity is the Mother of ...

From third grade, I knew I wanted to be in sales. No kidding. All I could ever visualize for myself was "sales and marketing." As long as I can remember, I've loved the challenge of getting the deal. I love to meet new people, to tell them my story, to ask lots of questions, and get to know what their situation is. When I can introduce them to some product or service that will help them, I get a real rush — both from knowing that I've helped them and from making a sale.

But how did a 10-year-old get a career orientation — one that set the course of his entire work life?

Answer: I wanted a car.

I loved cars. I had always loved cars. My sister tells me that I could identify and say the make, model and year of every car on the road ... when I was only five years old!

Even though I was very young, I dreamed of the day I would buy my first car. My dad had made it clear to me that I would pay for my first car and that I had plenty of time to save up for it. How soon I got it depended on how much money I made and saved.

So what do you do to make money as a 10 year old? You sell stuff. My parents helped me get started selling a weekly newspaper which the folks in my neighborhood loved, but had trouble getting. From there, I moved on to a daily paper route, knocking on doors and adding new subscribers. When I finally bought that

first car, I could now transport a lawn mower, so I started selling people on letting me cut their grass. Then it was magazine subscriptions, then greeting cards, then encyclopedias. Selling success built my self-esteem *and* gave me money to do what I wanted to do ... a powerful combination.

So work started out for me as a means to an end. It was something *I had to do* to get what I wanted. And my job choice was easy because there weren't other choices. As I succeeded in sales, I found that I liked it. I got better at it and I liked it more.

Necessity will beat out preference every time. We do what we have to do to make the living that we want, and that is very often the place where we "find our niche." In the abundance of Western society, we've gravitated toward an unrealistic and unsustainable idea that we can all just do what we enjoy, and if we don't enjoy our work, it's because we missed our "calling." I contend that's not realistic, and not biblical either!

In our quest to do what we really enjoy, we've lost sight of basic economic truth. If we want certain things, or to have a standard of living that is at a certain level, we have to do what we're good at and what the market needs to have done. We have to work in a job where we're needed and where we add value, if we are expecting the financial rewards that come with success.

Now we can whine, "that's just not right," and "that's not fair," and "that's not the way it should be." But that's how our economy works.

Expectations ... Ours and Others'

Here's another thing that makes the career choice thing so stinking difficult: The things required for "the good life" cost so much that we don't think we can afford to do what we really enjoy. By the time you add up the cost of owning a nice house, a new car or two, an up-to-date computer, DSL, cable, cell phones, wireless Internet, furniture, health club memberships, and acceptable clothes, half the professions we could pursue are out of the question.

that you would rather just leave alone? Are you being forced into situations where you are having to trust God, because you're pressed way beyond your area of comfort or confidence? Maybe, just maybe, God is using your current job to stretch you, to teach you some things about yourself or about Him.

God didn't create you to be anyone else's clone. You weren't built to be some compilation of your parents' or other people's expectations. You and I were "fearfully and wonderfully made" in

> So work started out for me as a means to an end. It was something I had to do to get what I wanted. ... As I succeeded in sales, I found that I liked it. I got better at it and I liked it more.

And right along with that goes the social and parental expectations of success. A law school graduate who decides he wants to be a freelance photographer might be an embarrassment to his parents or in-laws. And his circle of friends will shake their heads and say "What an idiot. I guess he just wants to be poor." He'll feel their rejection and judgment, even if it isn't spoken.

On the other hand, you can't help but admire a young person who says "You know, I may live in a smaller house, drive an older car, and take fewer and less spectacular trips than anyone else my age, but I want to be a teacher. I love kids ... I love teaching; I'm good at it, and that's what I want to do!"

Look Inside

Another huge factor in my story is my personality. As a kid, I wanted to be liked and accepted in the worst kind of way. When someone would welcome me at the door, be nice to me, buy my product, and welcome me back again the next week, I was affirmed deep in my soul. I wanted that affirmation so badly that I would take the overt rejection that came when the door was slammed. (Or, even worse, when they wouldn't come to the door but you knew they were home!) I am an extrovert — I love interacting with people, learning from people, helping people, and being a part of people's lives. So a sales career was a natural for my personality style.

I don't believe that God makes mistakes. You are in the job you're in for a reason. Is the job requiring you to grow parts of yourself

His image ... to share in His creativity and to do work that reflects well on Him. Like any good father, God wants you to grow and develop. He wants you to be challenged in your work, and He wants you to collaborate with Him in every aspect of life.

But What About My "Calling"?

Unquestionably, God "calls" or "sets apart" some people for vocational ministry. I totally believe that to be true, even though I don't understand it.

But for everyone else, I believe He gives us talents and skills, and He gives us access to wise counsel. He tells us to be wise and God-honoring in all our decisions and then gives us free will to do whatever we want. Will He guide us along the way? Absolutely. Will He give us unique opportunities? Yes. Will He allow doors to slam in our face to move us on to other places and things? He has certainly done that for me and to others that I know! Consider Jesus' disciples.

In his book *Velvet Elvis,* Rob Bell tells us how the brightest young students in Jesus' day were invited by rabbis to follow them by becoming the rabbis' disciples. Once selected, they would continue in their studies of the Talmud and on the career path of the Jewish rabbinical "clergy." If a young man wasn't so chosen by a rabbi at the age of 13 or 14, then he would follow his father or uncle into the family trade, become an apprentice, and ultimately make his living doing what his dad or uncle did.

We can assume, based on their professions (fishermen, tax collector, etc.) that Jesus' disciples were "rejects" as career religious leaders. They hadn't been called by a rabbi, yet they had to make a living somehow. So out of necessity, they followed in the career footsteps of their fathers … until Jesus said "follow me" and called them to be His disciples. Were they really "rejects" or failures until then? No. Did they stop being fishermen after Jesus called them? No. As best we know, they continued to do what they needed to do to make a living until the demands of apostleship finally took them to far away places and most, to eventual martyrdom.

In Romans 8:28, we see that Christians are "called according to His purpose." We are *all* called to be disciples and to make disciples, to know Christ and make Him known, no matter what profession we pursue. But as with most things, we can only know God's individual will for our lives retrospectively. We'd like to know *in advance* that things are going to work out perfectly (in other words: exactly how we want them to work out!).

what you've got, and trust God for the outcome." Shamgar started where he was — there were 600 Philistines attacking the Israelites nearby. He killed them all (he did all he could). Not with nuclear weapons … he had an oxgoad (a stick) … so he used what he had. And finally, he trusted God for the outcome. There were a lot more than 600 Philistines, and the Bible never says that Shamgar saved the children of Israel. It says that God did. We do what we can do, trust God for the outcomes, and deflect *all* the credit for outcomes to Him, since He's the one who decides how it all turns out.

Don't spend your life over-thinking your calling. If you're called to vocational ministry, you'll know it. You won't be able to resist that calling. But otherwise, use your noggin. Use your skills and your experience. Use your network. Take advantage of the wise counselors that God has put in your life, and most importantly, give a job a chance. Just because it's hard, or because your boss is hard to work for doesn't mean that it's not exactly where God wants you to be.

Like any good father, God wants you to **grow and develop.** He wants you **to be challenged** in your work, and He wants you **to collaborate with Him** in every aspect of life.

But unfortunately, God's will isn't always wrinkle free, pain free, or struggle free. It's often quite the opposite. As country artist Garth Brooks sings, "Some of God's greatest gifts are unanswered prayers." It's after things happen, decisions are made and events occur that we can look back and see the hand of God in them.

When I look back on my career, I can clearly see God's guiding hand. I wasn't conscious of it along much of the way, but He was clearly there … providing the next opportunity, nudging me on when the results were poor and I wanted to give up, and reminding me that it was Him who brought that new job or that huge sale.

Be Like Shamgar!
Dan Cathy, president of Chick-Fil-A, tells his people to be like Shamgar, the Israelite who "… killed six hundred Philistines with an oxgoad. And He [God] also delivered Israel" (Judges 3:31 NKJV).

Cathy explains: "Start from where you are, do what you can, use

Pursue being the unique person that God created you to be. Be grateful for the job you have. Do your work heartily, as to the Lord, and trust God for outcomes. You are where you are for a reason. Go and be an ambassador for Christ through your unique position and personality. Make God smile.

L@W

Regi Campbell is businessman with more than 20 years of experience in learning and implementing strategies for becoming a spiritual leader at work in companies small and large. He is the author of *About My Father's Business* (**www.amfb.com**) (Multnomah, 2005). Campbell operates Seedsower Investments, which invests in start-up technology-enabled service companies. He also serves on the boards of Good Samaritan Health Center of Cobb; High Tech Ministries; and as an elder at North Point Community Church. Campbell and his wife Miriam live in Atlanta.

True Story

JIM MORIARTY

Jim Moriarty is the executive director of Surfrider Foundation (**www.Surfrider.org**), a non-profit environmental organization with 60 chapters that was founded in 1984. It is dedicated to the protection and enjoyment of the world's oceans, waves, and beaches through preservation, activism, research, and education. Following a 15-year business career, Jim has fronted Surfrider since 2005.

Beach-Bound Techie

I hold a BS in Information Systems from Ohio State University. I've worked at tech companies large and small, working alongside brilliant people who worked insanely hard to make an idea become a reality. That concept can translate to environmental organizations and Christian organizations. It's about moving an idea from a novel concept to a notable action to a cultural movement. Christ's love and grace are ideas that continue to be impactful when they move from the concept stage into real actions.

I'm also currently Chairman of the Board for a biotech search engine company called Notiora. It enables genetic scientists to mine databases in the formative stages of genetic and chemical research. It is used by a gaggle of big pharmaceuticals.

Surfin' with the Kids

I've been married to Andrea for 20 years. We have 12-year old twins, a boy and a girl. My family time is tightly guarded; when I'm home my cell is usually off and my PC is off. Achieving these two things is not easy. What is easy, and quite powerful, is the fact that we disconnected our TV ten years ago (with the exception of DVDs). I think one of the most important decisions I've made in my life is to "just say no" to TV.

I also mentor students on a weekly basis with the high school ministry at Solana Beach Presbyterian Church. For the past few years I have led snowboarding trips to the Sierras and surfing trips to Baja. High school students and I seem to gel pretty well; it's probably because we both listen to The Ramones.

Work, Faith, and Faith at Work

A big part of getting the gospel message across is first earning the right to be heard; most of us forget this part and therefore lose our audience just as we're starting. Walk a mile in their shoes and earn their trust as a friend who cares about them. Only with authentic trust and credibility can people connect. For me, faith is a natural extension of who a person is. If it's non-threatening, it's more authentic and in the end, more transferable, more contagious, and more enticing.

Sharing my faith is important to me and it is as unique as my fingerprint. Most of my friends are non-Christian and are not looking to join a church. They are inquisitive about the larger meaning of life. I see many seekers being put off by "Christian-ese" — Christianity isn't some exclusive club. Christianity is meeting someone where they are (as Christ did) and investing in them, loving them. Doing this in the work place is actually quite simple since it doesn't have to involve sermonizing.

Honoring God at Work

Each of us has something different to bring to the table. God created me with leadership skills, creativity, tenacity, and a love of surfing. I have the simple goal of using and building on these gifts. At Surfrider Foundation I am seeing firsthand that God's creation hasn't been managed well. This isn't abstract to me anymore; it becomes concrete when you walk polluted beaches. I'm working alongside some great and dedicated people to try and correct these collective wrongs.

L@W

Perspective

Answering the Call

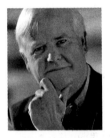

By Os Guinness

Calling is the truth that God calls us to Himself so decisively that everything we are, everything we do, and everything we have is invested with a special devotion, dynamism, and direction lived out as a response to His summons and service.

Our primary calling as followers of Christ is by Him, to Him, and for Him. First and foremost we are called to Someone (God), not to something (such as motherhood, politics, or teaching) or to somewhere (such as the inner city or Outer Mongolia).

Our secondary calling, considering who God is as sovereign, is that everyone, everywhere, *and in* everything *we should think, speak, live, and act entirely for Him.* We can therefore properly say as a matter of secondary calling that we are called to home-making or to the practice of law or to art history. But these and other things are always the secondary, never the primary calling. They are "callings" rather than the "calling." They are our personal answer to God's address, our response to God's summons. Secondary callings matter, but only because the primary calling matters most.

This vital distinction between primary and secondary calling carries with it two challenges—first, to hold the two together and, second, to ensure that they are kept in the right order. In other words, if we understand calling, we must make sure that first things remain first and the primary calling always comes before the secondary calling. But we must also make sure that the primary calling leads without fail to the secondary calling. The Church's failure to meet these challenges has led to the two grand distortions that have crippled the truth of calling. We may call them the "Catholic distortion" and the "Protestant distortion."

The first distortion may be called the "Catholic distortion" because it rose in the Catholic area and is the majority position in the Catholic tradition. The early writings of Eusebius argues that Christ gave "two ways of life" to His Church. One is the "perfect life"—dedicated to contemplation and reserved for priests, monks, and nuns. The other is "permitted"—a secular life dedicated to action and open tasks such as soldiering, governing, farming, trading, and raising families. Sadly, this "two-tier" or "double life" view of calling flagrantly perverted biblical teaching by narrowing the sphere of calling and excluding most Christians from its scope. Whereas the Catholic distortion is a spiritual form of dualism, elevating the spiritual at the expense of the secular, the Protestant distortion is a secular form of dualism, elevating the secular at the expense of the spiritual.

Under the pressure of the modern world, the "Protestant distortion" serves to sever the secular from the spiritual altogether and reduces vocation to an alternative word for work. The seeds can be traced back to the Puritans themselves as words such as work, trade, employment, and occupation came to be used interchangeably with calling and vocation. As this happened, the guidelines for calling shifted; instead of being directed by the commands of God, they were seen as directed by duties and roles in society. Eventually the day came when faith and calling were separated completely. The original demand that each Christian should have a calling was boiled down to the demand that each citizen should have a job.

At least two things are required to overcome the Protestant distortion: 1) We must refuse to play the word games that pretend calling means anything without a Caller; and 2) We must restore the primary calling to its primary place by restoring the worship that is its setting and the dedication to Jesus that is its heart.

In sum, we must avoid the two distortions by keeping the two callings together, stressing the primary calling to counter the Protestant distortion and secondary callings to counter the Catholic distortion. Whereas dualism cripples calling, a holistic understanding releases its power—the passion to be God's concentrates the energy of all who answer the call.

L@W

Dr. Os Guinness is an internationally renown speaker and the author of numerous books, including *The Call*, *Journey Home*, and *Time for Truth*. He is the co-founder and regular moderator of The Trinity Forum (**www.ttf.org**).

You have just completed Session 3. Use these journal pages to complete the following:

BIG QUESTION:
After reading this session, I'm wondering what others think about...

NEW THOUGHT:
I just learned that...

PERSONAL CHALLENGE:
I can't get this out of my mind. I have to figure out how to live differently so that...

TAKE A BREAK

Ask your child (or the next small child you see), "What do you want to be when you grow up?" Really listen to their response. Lift up a prayer for that child, asking God to give them clarity of calling, and to courageously grow into the man or woman He has designed them to be. Reflect and pray on your own personal calling as well.

CALLED by DESIRE

Don't Ignore Your Passions When Seeking Your Calling

By Stephen R. Graves and Thomas G. Addington

People's callings become obvious to them in various ways. Abraham, Samuel, Moses, Paul, and other biblical figures were *called by name*. If God ever appears to you in a burning bush, you'd do well to pay attention to what He says about your future path. Your unique set of talents and skills offer another clue to God's plan for your life. If you can hit a 97-mile-per-hour fastball, you might have missed your calling if you're not playing baseball in the big leagues.

Some people are *called by a path*. Prince Charles of England, like many people who stand to inherit the family business, has a pretty clear idea of where his path is taking him.

Another important means of discerning your calling is to *listen to your desires*. What is it that you want out of life? What truly matters to you? If you're seeking God's calling for your life, those desires might be your next clue.

Christians are often suspicious of desire. Misguided desires, after all, are the cause of all kinds of trouble. Yet just as wrong desires can lead you down the wrong path, right desires are signposts to the right path. "Delight yourself also in the LORD," said the psalmist, "and He shall give you the desires of your heart" (Psalm 37:4 NKJV). Saint Augustine said the same thing in a different way: "Love God, and do as you please." If your desires are in harmony with God's desires for you, why wouldn't He give you the desires of your heart?

C.S. Lewis is frequently quoted on the subject of desire. His remarks in the sermon "The Weight of Glory" are worth repeating:
> "It would seem that our Lord finds our desires not too strong, but too weak. We are half-hearted creatures, fooling about with drink and sex and ambition, when infinite joy is offered to us, like an ignorant child who wants to go on making mud pies in the slum because he cannot imagine what is meant by the offer of a holiday at the sea. We are far too easily pleased."

You may be asking too little of your Life@Work. The irony of the career track is that we usually expect too much of it and too little of it — all at the same time! We expect a paycheck or a promotion or a job title to provide the kind of fulfillment they could never provide. Then we feel disappointed and restless when our careers aren't fulfilling. And yet the workplace affords the opportunity to enjoy a fulfillment that a paycheck can't even touch. You have the opportunity to live out your calling, to do your part in God's grand design of building His kingdom.

Our desires and longings are homing signals, calling us back to the One who alone can fulfill every desire. True, we often get off track, settling for things that fall well short of our true desire. Nevertheless, desire is one of the chief ways God calls His people to the work He would have them do. That longing you feel for something more in your work — perhaps it's not simple (and sinful) discontent. Perhaps it's the call of God on your life. If you're not pursuing God's call in your work, you can be sure you'll feel discontent at work. That doesn't necessarily mean you need to quit your job and get a new one. It might mean you need to line up your efforts with God's purposes right where you are. Whatever the case, you do well to pay attention to your desires if you're seeking to answer God's call.

The Agitation of Calling

Consider the case of Nehemiah. He was one of the Jews who were living in exile, far from their beloved homeland of Judah, in the fifth century B.C. Defeated by the Babylonians, the brightest and best of the Jews were carried into captivity in Babylon. The Babylonians were soon defeated by the Persians. Nehemiah enjoyed tremendous career success at the court of Artaxerxes, the Persian king. Nehemiah rose all the way to the position of cupbearer to Artaxerxes. He seemed pretty well set as far as his career went. He had direct access to the world's most powerful ruler, which gave him tremendous influence. He was wealthy. He was a keeper of state secrets.

If your **desires** are in harmony with God's desires for you, why wouldn't He give you the desires of your **heart?**

But Nehemiah's career trajectory was changed completely by a conversation with his brother, who brought news from the land of their ancestors:
> "Hanani, one of my brothers, came from Judah with some other men, and I questioned them about the Jewish remnant that survived the exile, and also about Jerusalem. They said to me, 'Those who survived the exile and are back in the province are in great trouble and disgrace. The wall of Jerusalem is broken down, and its gates have been

If you're not pursuing God's call in your work, you can be sure you'll feel discontent at work.

burned with fire.' When I heard these things, I sat down and wept" (Nehemiah 1:2–4 NIV).

A new variable rocked Nehemiah's world. His status quo was shattered by news from his homeland that tore at his heartstrings. That is to say, his desires changed completely when he heard what was happening in Judah.

What Nehemiah heard troubled him deeply. The walls around Jerusalem lay in rubble. Nehemiah wept. He mourned. He cried some more. For over four months he fasted and prayed. This was no "here today, gone tomorrow" burden. Nehemiah was affected to the core of his being.

Noted nineteenth-century French writer Honore de Balzac commented on such heartfelt callings: "Vocations which we wanted to pursue, but didn't, bleed, like colors, on the whole of our existence."

At work, Nehemiah had every reason to put on his game face. You never wanted to offend a Persian king. They were known for their capricious ruthlessness. Those at their court were expected to enter the king's presence with nothing less than a countenance of joy. After all, who would not be thrilled to stand in his presence? Nehemiah, however, could not hide his heavy heart. For months after he was given the truth of the sorry state in Jerusalem, he descended into such heartache that he could not hide his anguish from the king.

Nehemiah's heart must have skipped a beat when the king asked what was the matter. By then Nehemiah had a firm sense of his calling and did not let even the potential threat of a king's wrath stand in the way of pursuing his mission:

"I was very much afraid, but I said to the king, 'May the king live forever! Why should my face not look sad when the city where my fathers are buried lies in ruins, and its gates have been destroyed by fire?'
The king said to me, 'What is it you want?'
Then I prayed to the God of heaven, and I answered the king, 'If it pleases the king and if your servant has found favor in his sight, let him send me to the city in Judah where my fathers are buried so that I can rebuild it.'
Then the king, with the queen sitting beside him, asked me, 'How long will your journey take, and when will you get back?' It pleased the king to send me" (Nehemiah 2:2–6 NIV).

The biblical story of Nehemiah makes no mention of God speaking audibly to the man he called. God spoke to Nehemiah through his desires. And yet it's obvious that Nehemiah was truly following the call of God when he went to Jerusalem to rebuild the wall. The same natural talents that attracted the attention of Artaxerxes, sharpened by years of service in the palace — not to mention the goodwill of the world's most powerful man — qualified Nehemiah for the challenges of managing a massive building project in the dangerous setting that was Jerusalem. And why was Artaxerxes so agreeable to Nehemiah's plan? He had nothing to gain. The only explanation is that this was a God thing. The burden Nehemiah felt was God's undeniable call to a very specific task.

How Do I Know I'm Called by Desire?

When you encounter someone who is called by desire, you generally meet a highly focused person. She knows what she is about, and she is tenacious about getting there. Sidney Madwed advised, "If you want to be truly successful, invest in yourself to get the knowledge you need to find your unique factor. When you find it and focus on it and

When you **encounter** someone who is called by desire, you generally meet a highly **focused** person.

persevere, your success will blossom." You cannot know your calling if you do not first know yourself. Calling is a process of definition, identifying both what you are and what you are not. To determine if a desire is a genuine, God-given direction, here are some filters:

It might be calling by desire if the sense of urgency is persistent and relatively longstanding. A calling is more than a passing fancy. Life always has its zigs and zags. We are not talking here about a "passion of the moment." No, a calling is an abiding passion of your soul. When God places a desire on your heart and then uses that desire to call you to do something specific, it is usually something that builds and is seasoned over time, not something that just shows up on your doorstep today for you to do tomorrow.

It is probably not calling by desire if I am completely unequipped to get the job done. God equips whom He calls and calls whom He equips. If I feel called to do something that is outside the bounds of who God has made me, then it

probably is not a calling after all. Calling is more about doing than it is about thinking. Calling requires that I take action that results in accomplishing something. It is not primarily about ideas that I just roll through my mind. Many people have dreams that they equate with God's call; but calling is about doing, not dreaming. Dreaming is often part of the equation, but the dream must result in tangible motion.

J. K. Rowling had a dream to write a book. In that regard, she is not particularly unique. One day she sat down at a keyboard and began to write. The difference is that she had what it takes to do it, and she sat down and did it. Of her own journey, she said, "It does not do to dwell on dreams and forget to live." A calling is not something you just dream; it is something you must be capable of bringing to fruition.

It is probably not calling by desire if I quit when I encounter significant hurdles. Life is seldom a cakewalk for one who hears God call by desire. A calling is tenacious. It works itself out despite the obstacles. Robert Morrison, the first Protestant missionary to China, was a man called by desire. He was 25 years old when he arrived in China, in 1807. He was filled with a driving passion to see the Chinese people come to know Jesus. He died 27 years later a very discouraged man. Over his entire career he had only baptized ten Chinese. He considered his work a failure. Yet his influence continues in the Chinese church to this day. Why? Because Robert Morrison translated the Bible into Chinese.

How hard was it for Morrison to fulfill what was obviously a calling by desire? First, his mother made him promise that he would not leave his native Scotland as long as she was alive, so he did not leave until she died. Then, to travel to China, he was forced to go by way of the United States, because

Many people have **dreams that they equate with God's call; but calling is about doing, not dreaming.**

the English East India Company, which controlled all travel between England and China, refused passage to missionaries. They were afraid that the evangelizing of Chinese would hurt business. It was no easier when he finally arrived in Canton to work. William Milne, the first assistant to join him, said: "To acquire the Chinese [language] is a work for

The work of Christ in your life changes what you want out of life.

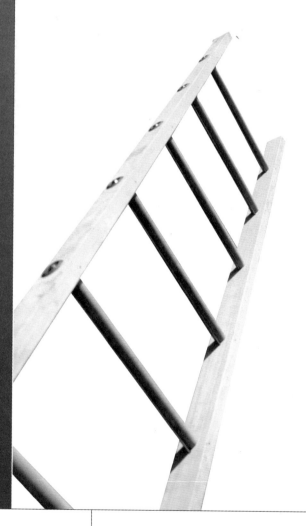

men with bodies of brass, lungs of steel, heads of oak, hands of spring steel, eyes of eagles, hearts of apostles, memories of angels, and lives of Methuselah." The Chinese Bible is a testament to Robert Morrison's persistent pursuit of his calling despite all odds.

Two Kinds of Calling

As Os Guinness discusses in his excellent book *The Calling*, theologians distinguish between two main kinds of calling — a primary calling to salvation, and secondary callings to specific roles and tasks within the kingdom of God. That primary calling is the same for all believers: God calls you out of the darkness of a sin-dominated life into the light of a Christ-dominated life. But you also have multiple secondary callings that are unique to you. All of those other callings — your calling to parenthood, to fellowship in a local church, to community involvement, to specific work — grow out of that big, primary calling. That's because the work of Christ in your life changes what you want out of life. You have bigger dreams than a big paycheck or success as the world defines it. You want to be a part of what God is doing in the world. Your deepest desire is to respond to God's invitation to work on His agenda, using the talents you have been given in ways that are eternally significant.

L@W

Dr. Stephen R. Graves is a highly sought business coach and life guide for entrepreneurs and leaders desiring to successfully make it to the finish line of life. In 1991, he co-founded the Cornerstone Group, a company built to integrate biblical wisdom and business excellence. He and his wife Karen have three children.

Dr. Thomas G. Addington is the co-founder of Cornerstone Consulting Group and WellSpring Group. He advises senior corporate leaders, helps organizations and their boards formulate strategic solutions, and assists leadership as they chart the future and navigate new realities. He and his wife Susan have three children.

This article is based on concepts drawn from Life@Work by John C. Maxwell, Stephen R. Graves, and Thomas G. Addington, published by Thomas Nelson, Inc.

Reflect

4 WAYS GOD CALLS US TO WORK

1 GOD CALLS ME DIRECTLY BY NAME

GOD AUDIBLY CALLS ME BY MY NAME

MOSES (EXODUS 3:1-10)

GOD TELLS ME WHAT MY WORK WILL LOOK LIKE

PAUL (ACTS 9:4-6)

2 GOD PLACES A DESIRE IN MY HEART

I FEEL A RESPONSIBILITY TO ACCOMPLISH A TASK AND TO MEET A NEED

ISAIAH (ISAIAH 6)

NEHEMIAH (NEHEMIAH 1)

3 GOD ARRANGES MY PATH

I HAVE NO LIST OF OPTIONS, NO CHOICES

JOSIAH (2 KINGS 22)

IT IS ALL PRE-ARRANGED FOR ME

JOHN THE BAPTIST (MARK 1:2-7)

4 GOD PREPARES AN ATTRACTIVE OPTION

I HAVE BEEN LED TO CHOOSE AN OPPORTUNITY

ELISHA (1 KINGS 19:20-21)

IT IS NOT A MATTER OF COINCIDENCE, BUT IT MAY SEEM THAT WAY

STEPHEN (ACTS 6:2-4)

CALLED BY DESIRE

FOR GROUP DISCUSSION
Prior to your small group meeting time, read and reflect on the Life@Work Study article you just read. Use these questions and journal pages to reflect and respond to the ideas presented. Be ready to share your thoughts at your small group gathering.

Note to small group leaders: You can download a full Leader's Guide at www.lifeatworkgroupzine.com.

⋗ *Christians are often suspicious of desire. … Yet just as wrong desires can lead you down the wrong path, right desires are signposts to the right path.*

With this in mind, what are the right desires in your life? What are you passionate about? Does your passion area tie into your professional area? If so, how did you get to this point? If not, what can you begin doing to match your desires with your skills?

⋗ *That longing you feel for something more in your work — perhaps it's not simple (and sinful) discontent. Perhaps it's the call of God on your life. If you're not pursuing God's call in your work, you can be sure you'll feel discontent at work.*

Do you feel discontent at work? In what ways does that play out daily? In what ways does it play out in the bigger picture of your life? If your discontent really is the call of God on your life, what can you do differently to follow that calling? Would you need to find a new job? Or could you "line up your efforts with God's purposes right where you are"?

⋗ *"Vocations which we wanted to pursue, but didn't, bleed, like colors, on the whole of our existence."*

What is a vocation you wanted to pursue but didn't? Why didn't you pursue it? Does the hurt of not pursuing that vocation "bleed, like colors, on the whole of (y)our existence"? What might God be telling you with that heartache?

⋗ *God spoke to Nehemiah through his desires. And yet it's obvious that Nehemiah was truly following the call of God.*

Do you agree with the assessment that a true call by desire needs to be persistent and longstanding? Why or why not? What is a longstanding desire of your heart? If that currently isn't part of your work situation, how could you move closer to using your skills with your desires?

⋗ *Your deepest desire is to respond to God's invitation to work on His agenda, using the talents you have been given in ways that are eternally significant.*

If you could choose one thing to do with your gifts and desires that would help God further His agenda, what would you want to be doing? What can you do to move closer to that desire?

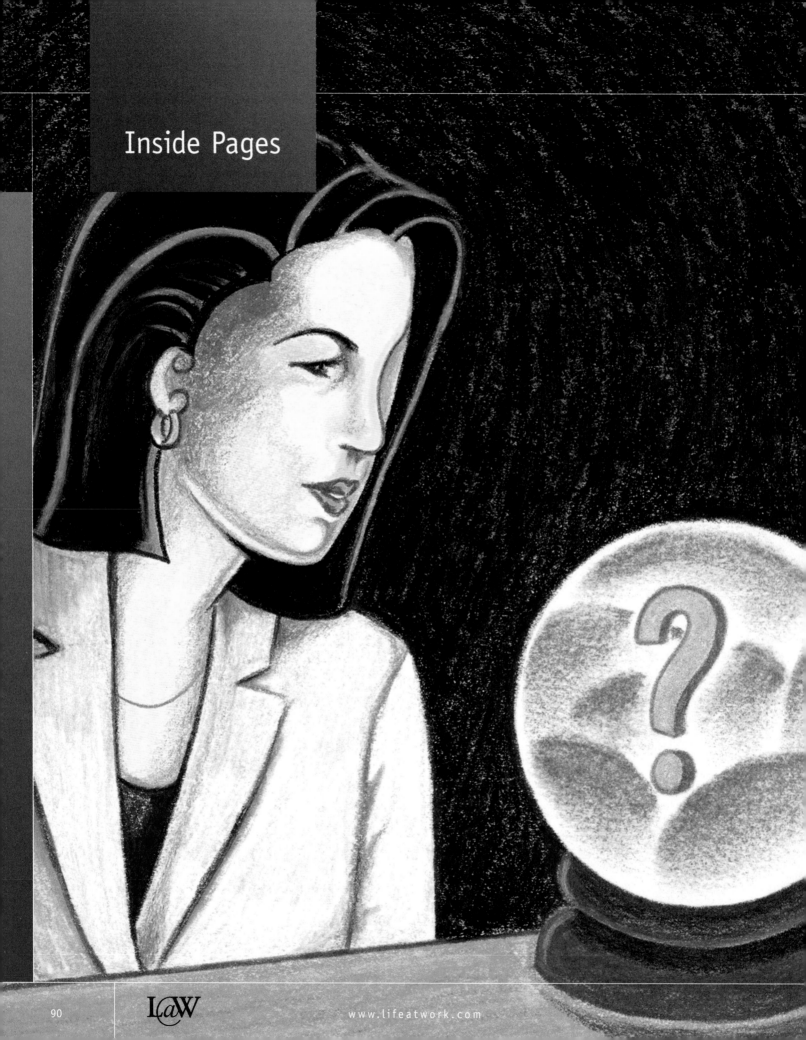

LAUNCH
WHERE DO WE GO FROM HERE?

By Margaret Feinberg

What the Heck Am I Going to Do with My Life? If we're honest, this is a question most of us have asked ... at multiple stages of our lives! It's also the title of Margaret Feinberg's book that looks at the difficulties often associated with discerning your calling. The good news is that Feinberg believes it's never too late to pursue your passion and calling.

In this excerpt, Feinberg gives readers permission to ask themselves what they want to do with their lives ... and shares the experiences of people who have wrestled deeply with this question.

I basically grew up trying to answer the question, *What the heck am I going to do with my life?* At the time that I needed the answer the most—during college, when you have to declare a major—I had no idea what I wanted to do. ...

As graduation approached, *What the heck are you going to do with your life?* became the topic of choice for nearly everyone that my parents and I encountered. It was exhausting.

Unsure of which direction to go, I sent out applications to anywhere that piqued my interest. I applied to Hebrew University in Israel, graduate school, and an internship at a small religious magazine in Florida. All the doors closed except for the internship—which turned out to be with a sister magazine to the one I had applied for—so I spent a summer sweating it out in Orlando. Afterward, I went on a weeklong mission trip that lasted more than a month and then returned for a second stint, where I discovered the hard way that I simply wasn't missions material.

I came back to the United States nearly a year after I graduated and faced the doomsday question yet again. I was living at home and working as a ski instructor, kids' adventure-camp counselor, and nanny. I asked myself a different question: *If I could do anything with my life, assuming that time and money were no object, what would I choose to do?*

The answer came almost instantly. From the deepest part of my being, I wanted to write.

Then I had to face the follow-up question: *What is stopping me from doing it?*

At that moment, the insecurities and fears rose to the surface. What if, like mission work, writing didn't work out? What if I couldn't get published? What if I didn't have the discipline? What if I couldn't feed myself doing it? What if I had to live with Mom and Dad forever?

As I bounced between the emotions related to every concern, I realized that my desire to write was greater than any fear or insecurity I had. I went to the library and researched publishing opportunities. I sent off clips to several Christian magazines and asked if I could write small reviews for the backs of their publications. All but one said yes. Over the next five years, I grew from writing reviews to news stories to feature stories to magazine cover stories. In 2002, Relevant Books published my first book, *God Whispers: Learning to Hear His Voice.*

Do We Every Really **Know?**

Today, when people ask what the heck I'm going to do with my life, I have my fallback answer: I am going to write. I'm a writer. That's what I do. Yet even with what most people would consider a career, I can't help but wonder if there's something more. I can't help but revisit the basic questions I have been wrestling with since those days when I could still fit into a pair of Underoos: *What am I going to do with my life? What's next? What's around the corner? What more could I be doing? What could I be doing better now?*

I have asked these questions so many times that I am convinced I should have the answers by now. The problem is that just as soon as I develop an answer, something radically changes in my life or I'm introduced to something new, and I'm forced to revisit the questions again.

I know that I am not alone. I have interviewed more than one hundred people of all ages and backgrounds from around the country, and everyone I've spoken with has wrestled with this question in one form or another.

Even those who have known what they wanted to do since they were knee-high to a grasshopper still admit to struggling and second-guessing along the journey.

Those in their twenties and thirties are particularly vulnerable to soul-searching, but they are joined by people of all ages.

Beth's Story

Beth, a twenty-five-year-old, says that when she enrolled in college, she realized it was time to finally answer the question,

What do you want to be when you grow up? The only problem was that she didn't have an answer.

"I think I put a lot of pressure on myself feeling that my job would be my life's purpose, so I wanted it to be something I really had a passion for and would enjoy doing," she says. "I took a lot of different classes my first few years of college trying to figure it all out. I envied my roommate and others who just knew from the time they were small and were on their way to doing it. I, on the other hand, would spend much time wondering and praying what I would do."

In college, Beth took an Introduction to Social Work class and felt that out of everything she studied, the subject matter was the closest she could come to picking a career once she graduated. "Deep down I think I knew that wasn't the best thing, but it was the best thing at the time," she says.

She graduated with a degree in social work and worked in the field for a few years. "I loved the work and the children I worked with and felt like when I went home and laid my head down at night, I had spent the day doing something worthwhile [for] society and purposeful. But I became burned out from working way too many hours in very stressful situations and realized that I could not continue the pace and demands that social work required for the rest of my life."

Beth began to wonder what else she could do with her life. "There I was again, wondering what in the world I wanted to be and do and a bit frustrated to be in that place again. I began fervently praying and seeking God's direction and knew that even though I had no idea, He had formed and made me and knew the answers I was searching for. So I prayed and waited."

In the meantime, she quit her job and moved home with her parents to rest and de-stress for a month. She continued praying and began substitute teaching to pay the bills. "[God] began to put the field of nursing on my heart," she recalls. "I looked into it, and I am now completing my first semester of nursing school. I'm starting over, wondering what in the heck I'm doing in nursing school but feeling a remarkable peace."

Beth says she has come to terms with the fact that life is too complex to figure it all out. "I wish someone had told me when I

was in school the first time that it was okay if I didn't know. At that age it is kind of hard to know what you want to do with the rest of your life. I really had to go out into the world and get some life into me before I really could see and know what all is out there to be and do. I think I put way too much pressure on myself and didn't enjoy the process of not knowing and discovering what I liked and might be good at doing."

It's a Question Worth Asking

I can identify all too well with the stress and pressure Beth describes. Figuring out what to do with your life isn't easy because even after landing a job or finally earning a few years' work experience to put on the résumé, the questions about what you are going to do don't always disappear. They just keep resurfacing. Singles, newlyweds, oldlyweds, empty nesters, retirees—anyone at any age or stage in life—can wrestle with these questions and struggle to find answers. No one is immune.

That's one reason I think *What the heck am I going to do with my life?* is one of the greatest questions we will ever ask ourselves. Not just because it is the question that won't go away, but because it forces us to examine ourselves in a new light—who we are today and who we are called to be tomorrow. The question challenges us to look at the core of who we are as individuals, discover our talents and gifts, and come to terms with our weaknesses. When we dare to ask, we step into a realm where anything—including growth, transformation, and change—is possible. Risk, failure, and loss are all potential outcomes, but so are success, innovation, and building a legacy that lives beyond us.

What the heck am I going to do with my life? isn't a safe question, but it has the power to awaken dormant dreams and silent desires. It has the ability to both compel and propel us to fulfill our lifelong calling and purpose. And that makes it a question worth asking.

L@W

Margaret Feinberg (**www.margaretfeinberg.com**) is an author and speaker who lives in Juneau, Alaska, with her husband Leif. She has written nearly 1,000 magazine articles and has written more than a dozen books, including *Twentysomething: Surviving & Thriving in the Real World* ; *God Whispers: Learning to Hear His Voice*; and *Just Married: What Just Might Surprise You About the First Few Years of Marriage.*

Adapted from What the Heck am I Going to Do With My Life*?
Copyright ©2006 by Margaret Feinberg, Tyndale House Publishers.
Used by Permission.*

God's Three-Dimensional Purpose

THE RIGHT PATH *CAN* BE FOUND

By Dr. Kenneth Boa

"Just turn right after the railroad tracks. You can't miss it." Locals have a quaint way of giving directions to lost motorists. They make a lot of assumptions. "Go past the Johnson's old farm to where the grocery store used to be." They forget about the fork in the road or the new traffic signal. "You can't miss it," they insist. But the problem is that while *they* may not be able to miss it, *we* often do. And, after traveling 15 or 20 miles out of our way, we have to turn around, go back to that last intersection and ask for directions again.

Sometimes we move through life thinking we can't miss it. The next turn will be so obvious. There can't be any doubt which way to go at the next junction. But how many times have we discovered, to our chagrin, that we're completely lost and should have taken the other fork 20 miles back?

There's an old story about a pilot who came over the intercom and said, "Good news, ladies and gentlemen: We've got a very strong tailwind and are making excellent time. The bad news is that our navigation equipment has gone down, so we have no idea where we are." Perhaps this is a fitting analogy for many of us. We're making great time on a road to nowhere. We're on the fast track, but we don't really know where all of this is headed. When we finally get what we've wanted all these years, we discover that it wasn't really what we wanted after all. So, we hop on another treadmill, but it leads to the same disillusionment. How far do we have to travel, before we turn around, go back to that last intersection and ask for directions again?

A well-known poem whose author's identity has been forgotten says it like this:

> Across the fields of yesterday,
> He sometimes comes to me
> A little lad just back from play —
> The boy I used to be.
> He looks at me so wistfully
> When once he's crept within
> It is as if he hoped to see
> The man I might have been.

It is interesting to go back to the days of idealistic youth and recall the things we hoped for, the kind of person we thought we might become. But such nostalgic recollections can be depressing. We wonder where the years have gone and what happened. Could it be that we took the wrong turn somewhere along the line? Is it too late to rectify an error in judgment?

As followers of Jesus, we say that the answer is, "No! It's never too late." We always have the opportunity of turning back and getting on the right track. Our source of direction is far greater than the people who say, "You can't miss it." There is a source that can tell us what life is really about. Found in the pages of Scripture, particularly the wisdom literature, are directions not just to "live and learn" but to "learn and live." The promise of skillful living is made to all those who will "listen to advice and accept instruction" (Proverbs 19:20). God

Could it be that we took the wrong turn somewhere along the line?

has revealed truths about life; the Bible is a guidebook of sorts, a blueprint to living, the foundation of a well-built life and a roadmap through the maze of confusion that our days often resemble. There is purpose and meaning, clarity and fulfillment in this life. But it is only found as we navigate by the wisdom contained in the Word of God.

Three Dimensions of God's Purpose for Us

While Scripture provides us only glimpses of God's *ultimate* purposes in creating the cosmos, the Word does reveal God's *universal* purpose for believers. In short, this purpose is to know Christ and to make Him known. God does not want anyone to perish, but desires that everyone come to repentance and enter into a relationship with Him through the new birth in Christ (2 Peter 3:9). Once a person is born-again as a child of God, God wants that person to grow in Christ and be "conformed to the likeness of his Son" (Romans 8:29). Thus, God's purpose for each of us is edification

There is purpose and meaning, clarity and fulfillment in this life.

(spiritual growth) and evangelism (spiritual reproduction). God also has a *unique* purpose for each of us, and this relates to our distinctive temperaments, abilities, experiences, spiritual gifts, education, and spheres of influence. Why do you get out of bed in the morning? What is your life purpose? Few people can articulate a clear purpose statement for their

lives. It is ironic that people tend to put more effort into planning a two-week vacation than they do in thinking about the destiny of their earthly journey. In Paul's second letter to the church at Corinth we find more of an eternal perspective on this temporal journey:

> Therefore we do not lose heart. Though outwardly we are wasting away, yet inwardly we are being renewed day by day. For our light and momentary troubles are achieving for us an eternal glory that far outweighs them all. So we fix our eyes not on what is seen, but on what is unseen. For what is seen is temporary, but what is unseen is eternal (2 Corinthians 4:16-18 NIV).

This passage provides the context for God's unique purposes for our lives, and reminds us to develop an eternal perspective so that we will have a passion to give our lives in exchange for the things that God tells us will endure.

Biblically speaking, there are two things on this planet that are going to endure: people and the Word of God.

Biblically speaking, there are two things on this planet that are going to endure: people and the Word of God. If we take God's eternal word and invest it in eternal people, then we're leveraging the temporal for eternity. We're actually sending something ahead of us into eternity. It's not what we leave behind that's important; it's what we send ahead.

Our little piles of goods will fall into someone else's hands after we're gone. Someone else will take our possessions and our positions. The world will go on without us, and we will be quickly forgotten. This might be a major cause of depression if it weren't for the fact that God calls us to place our hope on that which lasts and to invest in that which will endure. It's not enough for leaders to have purpose and passion; they need to be passionate about the right things. Leaders must come to view this world from eternity's perspective.

With this perspective, we will place more value in people than in possessions. Rather than using people to gain possessions, we will use our possessions to gain people. The marketplace becomes an arena in which we can accomplish things that will last forever. Our associations become areas of influence where we can alter a person's eternal trajectory. There is no secular part of life. When we view others the way God views them, every place becomes holy ground, a place where God is working in us and through us to accomplish His universal purpose of bringing about the abundant life of Christ in men and women. We become people who minister to others by manifesting eternal values and by loving and serving people with eternal things in mind.

Relationships are the currency of heaven. Being rightly related to God and rightly related to others—this is true righteousness. God, who loved us first, makes it possible for us to love Him. Loving Him makes it possible for us to love others and dwell in a community of believers, united in our love for Christ and one another.

What is your purpose for being on this planet? If you have not developed a purpose statement for your life, ask God to guide you in the process of creating one that fits with your passion and gifts. A biblical purpose is an unchanging reason for

God also has a unique purpose for each of us, and this relates to our distinctive temperaments, abilities, experiences, spiritual gifts, education, and spheres of influence.

being. Your purpose statement must include something of the transcendent. Don't settle for a purpose that only includes excellence in the temporal arena. This is something that will animate you whether you're young or old, single or married, have children or not. This is not something that ends in retirement or changes according to circumstances or season of

life. Put this purpose in a transcendent context by adding a spiritual dimension to why you're doing what you're doing. Then you can be sure you're embracing the things that are worth embracing.

L@W

Dr. Kenneth Boa is engaged in a ministry of relational evangelism and discipleship, teaching, writing, and speaking (**www.kenboa.org**). Dr. Boa is the President of Reflections Ministries, an organization that seeks to encourage, teach, and equip people to know Christ, follow Him, become progressively conformed to His image, and reproduce His life in others. He is also President of Trinity House Publishers. Sign up for his free monthly teaching letter at **www.reflectionsministries.org**.

Toolbox

Fully Using Your Gifts

By Valorie Burton

If you received a wonderful gift for your birthday, what would you do with it? Use it joyfully, right? How are you utilizing in the workplace the gifts God has given to you? We asked author Valorie Burton to offer some tips for putting your gifts more fully into play.

Identify Your Gifts

What are you excellent at? What is it that you do without even noticing that time is passing? With what resources are you blessed in abundance? By looking into your childhood, you can probably identify a gift that has been with you your entire life. Gifts can range from innate talent, to resources such as money, contacts, or even your personality. Make a list of your unique gifts. If you have a hard time identifying your gifts, ask someone close to you what they think your greatest gifts are.

Pinpoint Your Passion

The desires of your heart — the things about which you are passionate — are a gift. Follow your passion and you will tap into your gifts at the highest level.

Seek Ways to Serve

If each of us used his or her gifts to serve others, the world would move closer to being a better place. Each of us was sent here for a purpose — using our gifts to serve one another. The reason you receive so much joy when you follow your passion and use your gifts is because that is the mission you were created to fulfill. Many people are shy about sharing their gifts, but the truth is that it is selfish not to share your gifts. Don't keep them to yourself and deprive others of the gifts you have to share!

Improve Your Gift(s)

When something comes naturally to you, it can be easy to "rest on your laurels." But those who make the biggest impact on others are those who are continually seeking ways to do what they do even better. Learn and improve upon your gifts and talents. Seek role models and mentors, read books, practice, and stretch yourself. It will be the difference between being good at your gift, and becoming truly great at it. Maximize your potential by improving one day at a time.

So, use your gifts … you and those around you will be better for it.

L@W

Valorie Burton is a life coach and speaker, and the author of a number of books, including *Listen to Your Life*; *Rich Minds, Rich Rewards*; and her latest, *What's Really Holding You Back*? Subscribe to her free inspirational e-newsletter at **www.valorieburton.com**.

> Those who make the biggest impact on others are those who are continually seeking ways to do what they do even better.

How God Molds Fishermen

By Os Hillman

We all have a calling that we share: "'Come, follow me,' Jesus said, 'and I will make you fishers of men'" (Matthew 4:19 NIV).

This calling has three distinct stages, which we can see in the lives of the many called before us to become mature fishers of men, greatly impacting God's Kingdom.

First, there is the gestation period. This is the development stage of our lives. It may involve years of normal work experiences. You may be a Christian during this time, or you may be following after worldly success as a non-Christian. Paul spent years in religious and political training, persecuting believers most of his early life. Moses spent years in the court of Pharaoh and 40 years tending flocks in the desert. Jesus spent 30 years living at home and working in His father's carpentry business. However, all these years were part of their preparation.

Next is the crisis stage. Sooner or later, God calls you into relationship with Him. For some, like Paul, it comes through dramatic encounters like being knocked off a horse, blinded, and spoken to personally by God. Some people are more difficult than others to reach and so they require this level of crisis. This is a time when major changes are required by God so that you follow Him fully. It can be a time in which God harnesses years of experience for a new life purpose. Paul's earthly experiences would be used in his calling to the religious and political leaders of his day. For Moses, the burning bush experience would begin his journey in which he would discover his ultimate calling after years of preparation. For Peter, it was his denial of Jesus three times that allowed him to face his shallow commitment to Christ. For Jesus, it was the cross. These were benchmark turning points for men who made an impact on their world.

Last is the fruit-bearing stage. In it, God's power is manifested in your life like never before. God takes all your experiences and uses them to build His Kingdom in and through your life. Your obedience to this final call results in fruitfulness you could never imagine without the long preparation process. For Abraham, it resulted in becoming the father of many nations. For Paul, it resulted in bringing the gospel to the Gentiles. And for Peter, it meant becoming the rock the Church was built on. For Jesus, it was salvation for the entire world.

What does God want to achieve through your life? God has a plan that is so incredible you cannot comprehend it. It requires only that you love Him and follow Him. Then you will become fishers of men like the world has never known.

L@W

Os Hillman is an internationally recognized speaker on the subject of faith and work and writes on various faith and work related subjects. He has authored ten books including *The Faith @ Work Movement: What Every Pastor & Church Leader Should Know*. He is also founder and director of the International Coalition of Workplace Ministries (ICWM), president of Aslan Group Publishing, and directs the website **faithandworkresources.com**. He and his wife Angie live outside of Atlanta with their daughter.

I have brought you glory on earth by finishing the work you gave me to do.

John 17:4 (NIV)

JEFF HENDERSON

Jeff Henderson is the Campus Pastor of Buckhead Church (**www.BuckheadChurch.org**), a campus of North Point Ministries. After a 15-year career in marketing and advertising, Jeff moved into his fulltime ministry role in 2003. He and his wife Wendy have a daughter Jesse (7) and a son Cole (4).

Game Time

I managed the beverage and sports marketing efforts of Chick-fil-A, Inc., a quick-service restaurant company with 1,250 locations and $1.9 billion in annual sales. I've also held marketing positions with the Atlanta Braves, Callaway Gardens, and Lake Lanier Islands Resort.

Chick-fil-A instilled in me a passion for continuous improvement, both personally and professionally. I learned the two ways a person improves: through the books they read and the people with whom they interact. I now have a reading book list each year of at least 40 books and a team of people I meet with for learning, accountability, and personal improvement.

Modeled Leadership

I had the opportunity to observe and learn from Truett Cathy, Chick-fil-A's founder, and his sons (and company executives) Dan and Bubba Cathy. They modeled servant leadership in such a way that it became contagious. I also learned that if you succeed in your career but fail at home, you can't consider that a success. As Truett taught me, "You can be a success at both business and at home. In fact, you must be!"

I work a Sunday through Thursday schedule, so I have Fridays and Saturdays off. I'm also home by 6 p.m. during the week. This allows me to have quantity time with Wendy and the kids. What I have discovered is the beauty of quantity time. It's different from quality time. Quality time is great. However, quantity time is full of surprises because it is in those "routine" moments that some wonderful memories can happen.

To create this quantity time requires me to have a laser-like focus on what I want to accomplish each week. As a result, I spend 15–20 minutes every Sunday afternoon planning out the week ahead. I use a tool developed by the 1% Club called The Weekly Focus. It allows me to determine what is most important and who is most important so that I can have the maximum impact in the week ahead. In addition, I have a planning day once a quarter with a team of people to determine our goals, progress, opportunities for improvement, and plan of action for the upcoming quarter.

Leadership Modeled

At Buckhead Church, one of my ultimate aims is to create an irresistible work environment. I want my staff to know that I care more about them as an individual than I do as an employee. Some employers believe "People are there to get the work done." That's flawed thinking. Instead, they should think, "Work is there to get the people done." In other words, the management of a company should ultimately be concerned with the people first, and the work second. And one of the primary reasons is because it's a fantastic business strategy. Show me a company, church, or organization that has a passionate, loyal, talented, committed staff and I will show you a thriving organization.

Our work is part of our worship of God. How we approach our work, deal with staff members, follow through on action items, and strive for excellence is all a reflection of where we are spiritually. As believers in Christ, not only should our character and integrity be above reproach, but we should also set the pace for our industry and culture. Faith isn't an excuse not to work hard, diligently and with excellence. Instead, our faith should motivate us to even higher levels than those who don't believe.

L@W

"For I know the plans I have for you," declares the Lord, "plans to prosper you and not harm you, plans to give you hope and a future."

Jeremiah 29:11 (NIV)

And we know that in all things God works for the good of those who love him, who have been called according to his purpose.

Romans 8:28 (NIV)

MARY BANKS

Mary Banks is the founder and president of Women of Wisdom (W.O.W) Consulting Group (www.wowconsultinggroup.com). A graduate of Oral Roberts University with a Master's degree from Houston Baptist, Mary was an award-winning corporate human resources executive when she started her firm in 2003. She moved into fulltime consulting in 2006.

Relating to Humans

As a human resources executive, I developed many skills in the area of people development, people management, and strategic planning in people initiatives. These skills have been instrumental in increasing my adaptability to a consulting role in which the key areas that I consult on are typically people issues.

I was Senior Vice President/Managing Director of Employee Relations Compliance for JP Morgan Chase; Senior Vice President and National Director of Employee Relations for Bank One Corporation; and Vice President and National Director of Change Management at Bank One. All of my other previous roles were also in the field of human resources management.

Relating to Family

I am married and I have one child, Elise, who is

18. During the initial stages of my career, it was sometimes difficult to factor in quality time with my family. However, I developed the ability to carve out time by using the same time-management principles that I use in business. I make my family a priority by being sure that family time and family events are placed on my calendar before all other events.

Relating to Others

Currently I sit on the board of Spaulding for Children, a non-profit organization that specializes in adoptions and foster care for special needs and abused children. Previously, I have sat on a number of other boards, including the Texas Commission on Human Rights. (I was appointed by the governor for a six-year term as Commissioner and was appointed Chair of the Commission in 2002.)

My husband and I are on the teaching team at Lakewood Church in Houston. We teach couples Bible study and marriage preparation courses. I am also a volunteer and frequent speaker in the women's ministry at Lakewood.

Relating to God at Work

Put God first in your career. Really seek Him out in making career decisions and apply the golden rule lavishly by treating others as you would want to be treated.

My faith is an integral part of my work. I believe that my occupation is also my vocation and that I am set apart to do my work under God's authority. As a result, I see myself as working "unto the Lord" and know that since God is my ultimate CEO, I am accountable to Him for my results and for the way I conduct myself in any business transaction.

When I was working for other firms, my role was to demonstrate my faith by my actions primarily rather than by my words. In a secular work environment, it is important to demonstrate the gospel versus verbalizing the gospel because of the perception that people of faith have a tendency to spend work time evangelizing others. Employers want to get what they are paying for and frankly, many do not believe that they are paying me or others to "spread the gospel;" nor do they believe that it is appropriate to mix religion and business. I try to respect that and use wisdom when sharing the gospel in a business setting, knowing that how I live has a greater impact than what I say.

The best way that I can honor God with my work is to do it excellently. I always want my clients to believe that I delivered the best results possible. I believe this is the best way to honor God.

EXECUTIVE SUMMARY
Final Thoughts On Defining Calling

CALLING GIVES FULFILLMENT. It's our reason for being; it's why we are created. God breathed life into each of us for a specific purpose. Through our calling, we join God's plan of redeeming humanity.

Immersion in day-to-day business threatens to drown out our divine calling. As our attention becomes focused on the tasks of selling widgets and making gadgets, we can easily lose the sense of our ultimate purpose.

We crave meaning. We hunger to be a part of a grander story than our own. Yet through the demands of our fast-paced work environments, we struggle to connect our work with a higher calling. How can we latch onto an eternal perspective in the midst of our daily routines?

IN THIS LESSON WE'VE LEARNED:

▷ Calling is God's personal invitation for us to work on His agenda, using the talents we have been given in ways that are eternally significant.

▷ The knowledge that we are working out a calling adds a dignity and joy that transcends the goods we produce and the services we render.

▷ We plant eternal seeds in the ground of the everyday. Our work involves the implementation of God's agenda in history.

▷ Knowing ourselves — our skill sets, limitations, passions — is an important part of pursuing calling. Yet ultimately, calling is less about getting in touch with ourselves and more about letting God touch us.

▷ Calling reaches beyond us, and pursuing calling means responding to a big God in ways that always expand our boundaries.

▷ For Moses and Paul alike, the act of responding to God's call focused a lifetime of misdirected energy into (eventually) a career of mind-boggling significance.

▷ When we pursue our calling, we aren't constantly trying to convince God to go along with our plan. Instead, we search out what God is doing and join Him.

▷ Work can have eternal purpose, and our lives can have fullness of meaning through the work we do.

▷ When seeking God's calling for our lives, our desires may be clues to His master plan. Our desires and longings are homing signals, calling us back to the One who alone can fulfill every desire.

▷ Rather than using people to gain possessions, we ought to use our possessions to gain people.

▷ If we take God's eternal Word and invest it in eternal people, then we're leveraging the temporal for eternity. It's not what we leave behind on this earth that's important, it's what we send ahead to eternity.

▷ When we view others the way God views them, every place becomes holy ground, where God is working in us and through us to accomplish His universal purpose of bringing about the abundant life of Christ in men and women.

Notes

_____

_____

_____

_____

_____

_____

_____

_____

_____

_____

NEXT STEPS

"The child is the father of the man." *William Wordsworth*

"What we do in life echoes in eternity." *Maximus*, in *The Gladiator*

⤷ Sadly, we are quick to trade dreams for dollars. We work where we are best compensated rather than daring to reach for our deepest desires. If you could do anything professionally with your life, assuming that time and money were no object, what would you choose to do?

⤷ Oftentimes, our childhood is filled with clues and hints of the talents and desires God has placed within us. What were you like as a small boy or girl? How did you spend your time in play? What hobbies did you have? What were your dreams?

⤷ Fast forward to your funeral: write your own eulogy. How do you want to be remembered? What do you want others to say about you when you pass from this life?

⤷ If we forget the ultimate, we become slaves to the immediate. In the absence of an eternal perspective, our daily routine absorbs us. Read Luke 4:18-19. What was Jesus' purpose statement? Draft your own purpose statement. It should be concise — no more than two sentences — so that you can readily articulate your calling.

SERVING@WORK

Serving: The art of focusing on someone
else's interest instead of your own

SESSION FIVE

Serving Up a
New Work Model

Putting Others First Brings Meaning to What You Do

By Stephen R. Graves

Service is one of the most important buzzwords of our contemporary business climate. Our economy, after all, is increasingly service-based; better customer service is a serious business advantage. No wonder you hear so much about "service with a smile" and "putting the customer first."

But for all the talk about service, the underlying principle can still be self-interest: business gurus encourage you to focus on customer service because serving others is a good way to get what you want out of them. People who feel that you care about them are more likely to fork over their money.

That's true enough, but a biblical view of service — including the concept of Serving@Work — calls you to a whole new motivation.

Serving others doesn't come naturally. We are born bent in the opposite direction. Instead of having fine-tuned radar directed outward toward other people's needs and betterment, we are usually focused on taking care of ourselves. We are skilled at arranging information,

opportunities, even relationships around our self-interested grid. "What's in it for me?" is often the single criterion.

"Let nothing be done through selfish ambition or conceit," the apostle Paul wrote to the Philippians, "but in lowliness of mind let each esteem others better than himself. Let each of you look out not only for his own interests, but also for the interests of others" (Philippians 2:3-5 NKJV). That's not a "you scratch my back, I'll scratch yours" mentality. It's a 180-degree turn from the way we naturally interact with other people.

It's a question of motivation, a question of focus. What is your true motivation for serving other people? Is it to oblige them, so they will "owe you one"? Is it to build your own reputation? Is it just a shrewd maneuver to trigger a boomerang effect of focus back to you? Or does your service to other people really grow out of a selfless desire to see another person benefit? That's God's standard for service—the habit of forgetting about yourself, your career trajectory, your bottom line in order to take care of somebody else.

The work that God intends us to do always involves a mindset of service to others. A spirit of service can express itself in a million ways, but when you boil it down to its essence, **serving is the art and act of focusing on someone else's interests, not my own.**

THE WORK THAT GOD INTENDS US TO DO ALWAYS INVOLVES A MINDSET OF SERVICE TO OTHERS.

"Serving" Best Practices

Serving is so foreign to us that we hardly know what it looks like. Thankfully, God did not leave us to our imaginations; He rolled up His sleeves, came down on the shop floor, and said, "I'll go first. Let Me show you how it is done." Listen to these words from *The Message* that give the job-focus sheet of Jesus, the Servant of all servants: "Whoever wants to be great must become a servant. Whoever wants to be first among you must be your slave. That is what the Son of Man has done: He came to serve, not to be served" (Mark 10:43–45). Jesus' words are powerful because they were backed up by a life to match.

Consider the last night Jesus spent on earth before His crucifixion. His disciples had been arguing among themselves about who was the greatest. Imagine their surprise when Jesus, the greatest of all, took off His robe, wrapped a towel around His waist, and began washing their feet. The CEO of the universe, wiping dust and sweat and camel dung off the feet of those under Him. Don't rush by this too quickly. You don't think Donald Trump fixes clogged toilets in the lobby of Trump Towers, do you?

Bear in mind, Jesus was entering the last hours of His life on the earth. What was the single greatest, most important lesson Jesus wanted to emphasize in this, His last opportunity to communicate with His disciples? A quick scan of all of the Old Testament personalities? No. A fast recap of how to preach or perform miracles? No. It was not even a review of the high points of theology. It was a never-to-be-forgotten object lesson on serving.

Every person needs to be served. There were no clean feet in the days of Jesus. Everyone who was physically able walked the dirty streets and trails in open-sandaled feet. These roads were often covered with trash and sewage. It wasn't just the servants' job to wash feet in Jesus' time: it was the job of the lowest-ranking servants. It was a bit of a scandal to see Jesus kneeling down washing someone else's feet; but what better example of serving could He have given?

The disciples had been preoccupied with the question of who was going to be the greatest. Jesus was asking them to reorient their point of reference outward to others. Everyone gets dirty. Everyone has needs. To meet them, the disciples would have to disrobe, take off their prerogatives, be willing to get a little dirty, and put aside their desire to be great in the kingdom of God.

Service is an action, not just an idea. Jesus did not tell them about foot washing on the flip chart or pass out notes on the steps for effective foot washing. He stood up, disrobed, knelt down, grabbed the stinky and dirty feet of His followers, and washed them.

Service to Others

That attitude changes the way we think about work. We have the opportunity, through simple acts motivated by a spirit of service, to participate with God in the day-to-day

THE CEO OF THE UNIVERSE, WIPING DUST AND SWEAT AND CAMEL DUNG OFF THE FEET OF THOSE UNDER HIM.

spinning of His world. In this sense, the plumber, the preacher, the policeman, and the pool keeper all stand on level ground. Whether he or she unclogs drains or souls or streets or filters, each person contributes a necessary good to the world through that act.

This utilitarian component of work has nothing to do with "me and my needs." We are supposed to be part of that big "work" machine in life. Our work somehow makes the world a

REAL SERVICE ALWAYS **GROWS** OTHERS. ITS BOTTOM LINE MUST BE **MEASURED** IN THE LIVES OF THOSE AROUND ME.

better place. At the end of the day, if it is all about me and my money, then we have left something out: service to humanity. With ability comes reciprocal responsibility. As Barbara Sher has noted, "Being gifted creates obligations,

WORK CAN EITHER BE SOMETHING THAT SHRINKS ME DOWN TO AN EVEN MORE SELF-CENTERED EXISTENCE, OR IT CAN **OPEN** ME UP TO THE LARGER WORLD AROUND **ME.**

which means you owe the world your best effort at the work you love. You too are a natural resource."

Why drag yourself back to the office for another day? Because for one thing, the daily grind of work is a "service offering" to the world God created. Work can either be something that shrinks me down to an even more self-centered existence, or it can open me up to the larger world around me.

Add Serving to Your Job Description

Is serving risky? Yes, it is. People are messy. The closer you get to them, the higher your chances of getting dirty. Your service will not always be noticed or appreciated. It will often be taken for granted. It will drain you. Serving is literally spending yourself. Yet in the process, we will be stretched. Investing in others, we are enriched. As Bob Moawad suggests, "Help others get ahead. You will always stand taller with someone else on your shoulders."

How do we know if we are serving others? Robert Greenleaf, in the book *On Becoming a Servant-Leader*, takes a look from the other side of serving. He suggests that we ask, "Do those being served grow as persons: do they, while being served, become healthier, wiser, freer, more autonomous, more likely themselves to become servants?" Real service always grows others. Its bottom line must be measured in the lives of those around me.

Your work is either serving or self-serving. Christ-like service is the art of building someone else up, not pumping up your own balloon. J. B. Phillips explained the role of selfless serving in Christ's revolutionary equation of life this way: "Christ regarded the self-loving, self-regarding, self-seeking spirit as the direct antithesis of real living. His two fundamental rules for life were that 'love energy,' instead of being turned in on itself should go out first to God, and then to other people."

What would our work lives look like if they were restructured upon such a foundation? One thing is for sure: our places of work would not be the same.

A Paradigm Shift

Approaching your career with a servant's heart calls for a total paradigm shift. It requires that you think differently about everything. But has the old way of thinking about work really been working for you? Maybe self-seeking has helped you climb the career ladder; sometimes it does. But has a self-seeking attitude ever made your work more meaningful? Has it ever achieved anything of lasting, eternal value?

There's one main problem with seeking your own happiness first: it doesn't work. Ironically, self-seeking never manages to find the happiness it's looking for. But when you serve others in the service of God, you discover that what used to be the rat race is now the pursuit of something meaningful and gratifying.

Colossians 3:22 is one of those Bible verses whose reputation has long been in need of rehabilitation: "Bondservants, obey in all things your masters according to the flesh, not with eye service, as men-pleasers, but in sincerity of heart, fearing God" (NASB). For centuries this verse was used to justify the practice of slavery. But Paul wasn't advocating slavery in this verse: he was advocating liberty. Consider what happens to a slave who serves not by the master's compulsion, but out of gratitude to the God who Himself became a servant. That slave suddenly enjoys more freedom than his or her earthly master.

This passage continues with another well-known passage: "Whatever you do, do it heartily, as to the Lord and not to men, knowing that from the Lord you will receive the reward of the inheritance; for you serve the Lord Christ" (Colossians 3:23-24 NKJV). There's your motivation, and there's your focus: you serve the Lord Christ. That means you're nobody's servant ... it also means you're everybody's servant. You love others because Christ first loved you. You serve others because you're a servant of Christ.

It is Christ who will reward you, not your customers and clients, not your boss or your shareholders. You can serve at work for selfish reasons. You can even be rewarded for it, with a growing business and a growing reputation. But there's so much more at stake than that. In the Sermon on the Mount, Jesus said, "When you do a charitable deed, do not sound a trumpet before you as the hypocrites do ... that they may have glory from men. Assuredly I say to you, they have their reward"(Matthew 6:2 NKJV). If the glory of men is reward enough for you, it's easy enough to get. But that's paltry stuff compared to "the reward of the inheritance" that is yours in Christ. Are you willing to serve even when nobody sees you doing it? Are you willing to serve people who have no way of paying you back?

Servanthood isn't a matter of giving up all hope of meaningful work. It's just the beginning of true freedom and purpose. Only as we learn of the life and character of Jesus

THERE'S **ONE** MAIN PROBLEM WITH SEEKING YOUR **OWN** HAPPINESS FIRST: IT DOESN'T **WORK**.

can we begin to reflect His words and deeds in our own work. Slowly, He re-creates us into the people we were originally created to be: fully human, uniquely gifted,

natural in worship, and tirelessly productive. Our work begins to work ... as a light does in a dark place.

L@W

Dr. Stephen R. Graves is a highly sought business coach and life guide for entrepreneurs and leaders desiring to successfully make it to the finish line of life. In 1991, he co-founded the Cornerstone Group, a company built to integrate biblical wisdom and business excellence. He and his wife Karen have three children.

This article is based on concepts drawn from Life@Work by John C. Maxwell, Stephen R. Graves, and Thomas G. Addington, published by Thomas Nelson, Inc.

NEW WORK MODEL

FOR GROUP DISCUSSION

Prior to your small group meeting time, read and reflect on the Life@Work Study article you just read. Use these questions and journal pages to reflect and respond to the ideas presented. Be ready to share your thoughts at your small group gathering.

Note to small group leaders: You can download a full Leader's Guide at www.lifeatworkgroupzine.com.

‣ *"Let nothing be done through selfish ambition or conceit, but in lowliness of mind let each esteem others better than himself. Let each of you look out not only for his own interests, but also for the interests of others."* (Philippians 2:3-4 NKJV)

  Paul says this is what true serving should look like. Do you ever find yourself serving in hopes of receiving recognition for your efforts? Have you ever served thinking it might help you get ahead at work ... or even at church? How can you make sure you are looking out for the interests of others when you serve?

‣ *The CEO of the universe, wiping dust and sweat and camel dung off the feet of those under Him. Don't rush by this too quickly. You don't think Donald Trump fixes clogged toilets in the lobby of Trump Towers, do you?*

  What do you think Trump's underlings would think if they saw their boss cleaning toilets? Why do you think that, in general, the higher up someone is in an organization, the less likely they are to serve others? Do you think employees would be more motivated to serve others if they saw it modeled by senior leadership? Why or why not?

‣ *Service is an action, not just an idea. Jesus ... stood up, disrobed, knelt down, grabbed the stinky and dirty feet of His followers, and washed them.*

  Name a time when you put service into action and it really impacted you. How were you impacted? Why do you think it made such a difference in your life? What area or areas are you currently serving the needs of others? How do you feel when you are serving?

‣ What can you do to add serving to your job description? Do you see serving at work as a one-time event or a regular occurrence? What are practical ways you can ensure that you bring a servant's heart to the workplace every day?

‣ *Real service always grows others. Its bottom line must be measured in the lives of those around me.*

  Are you willing to measure your impact as a servant? On a scale of 1 (low) to 5 (high), what kind of score would you currently receive from those you work with? Those you work for? Those who work for you? Do you think those three scores should be consistent? Why?

L@W

www.lifeatwork.com

THIS IS WHAT I WAS MADE FOR

Experiencing the Volunteer Revolution

By Bill Hybels

For more than three decades, Bill Hybels has been challenging people to live *The Volunteer Revolution*. It's something he understands extremely well … he and the core that started Willow Creek Community Church in 1975 were *all* volunteers. In this book about serving, Hybels shares insights and stories of gifted, talented people who've discovered a deeper connection to God and others by serving at their local church. No matter how much (or little) satisfaction you receive from your job, there's always a place to serve at your church, knowing you are helping people and honoring God with your gifts and talents.

Some years ago a new staff member of our church asked me how I had the gall to ask people who are already busy at work or in the home to get involved as volunteers at church.

"I mean, don't you feel a little guilty doing this?" he asked. "Isn't it hard to heap such a burden on people?"

He had a point. But I knew I had a bigger point:

> You and I get to invite these people to be used by God in ways they never imagined.

"During the next few months you're going to meet people who stand at drill presses, ten hours a day, five or six days a week. When they go home at night, few of them sense the pleasure, meaning, and purpose of life they've heard advertised in commercials for beer or computer systems. They're godly, conscientious people, and they feel thankful for their jobs. But they don't find satisfaction for their souls at the drill press. "And you're going to meet fine, hardworking people in real estate who show thirty homes a week. If they're lucky, one buyer will make an offer, but they're not lucky every week. Many are extroverts who love showing property and helping families find the right home, but even then they probably don't arrive home at night filled with deep inner joy because of their latest showing.

"You'll meet insurance salespeople who have been selling policies for twenty years. While they feel grateful that the insurance business puts food on their table and sends their kids to college, the thought of selling one more policy likely doesn't float their emotional boat.

"You're going to meet car dealers and stockbrokers and bricklayers and police officers and plumbers who, despite their commitment to their careers and jobs, are honest enough to

admit that their secular vocation does not offer enough meaning to satisfy the deeper needs that stir in their souls.

"Some of them love their jobs; they feel stimulated and energized by their work. Some of them even leave their workplace each day knowing that they have honored God by their work and their love for people. But few of them would say: *This is what life is all about.*"

I looked directly into the eyes of my young friend. "You and I get to invite these people to be used by God in ways they never imagined. We have the opportunity to empower them to develop gifts they didn't know they had. We can cheer them on as they courageously assume new levels of Kingdom responsibility that fill their hearts to overflowing. And we get to see the look on their faces when they realize God has used them to touch another human being.

> It's as if God has work gloves on. And He calls us to roll up our sleeves and join Him with our talents, our money, our time, and our passion.

"No," I said, "I never really feel guilty inviting people to become volunteers in our church. Never."

On A Mission

When the writer of the book of Ecclesiastes decided to determine his purpose in life, he started by accumulating a vast sum of money, only to discover that it didn't provide the meaning he had hoped for. Then he sought power, attained it, and discovered that it too failed to satisfy. Next came a scandalous pursuit of pleasure. Then fame and celebrity. Finally, at the end of all his efforts, he uttered his famous words: "Vanity, vanity, all is vanity." Or as another translation says, "All of this is like chasing the wind."

We were not created to chase the wind.

We are created to join God on a mission. Some people think of God as hanging around beyond the edges of the universe somewhere, listening to really good worship music. The Bible sees it much differently. It teaches that God is at work 24/7, all over our world, filling His followers with grace and mercy and power to reclaim and redeem and fix this broken planet.

It's as if God has work gloves on. And He calls us to roll up our sleeves and join Him with our talents, our money, our time, and our passion. He wants His mission to become ours. "If you're into chasing the wind," He tells us, "you can keep right on doing that. Or you can hook up with Me, and together we'll transform this hurting planet."

What would it feel like to lay your head on your pillow at night and say, "You know what I did today? I teamed up with God to change the world"?

The desire to be a world-changer is planted in the heart of every human being, and that desire comes directly from the heart of God. We can suffocate that desire in selfishness, silence it with the chatter of competing demands, or bypass it on the fast track to personal achievement. But it's still there. Whenever we wonder if the daily eight-to-five grind or our round-the-clock parenting tasks are all there is to life, that divine desire nudges us. Whenever we feel restless and unsatisfied, the desire whispers in our soul. Whenever we wonder what a life of real purpose would feel like, the desire calls us to something more.

> When it comes to sports, it's a lot more exciting to be a participant than a spectator.

A Transformed World

Jesus made it pretty clear what God's idea of a transformed world would look like, first within the community of believers called the Church and then as the values of that community spread out into the world:

- When Jesus said we should *love the Lord our God with all our heart and soul and mind and strength, and our neighbor as ourselves*, he was calling us to trade a ritualized religion for a genuine love relationship with God and to offer to others the same kind of attention, honor, and compassion we give ourselves.

- When Jesus punctuated His teaching with *concern for the poor, the powerless, and the oppressed*, He was describing a new value system.

- When He said, *Take up your cross and follow Me*, He was telling us in graphic terms that following Him would require sacrifice, hardship, and death to something selfish inside of us.

- When He said, *Go into all the world and preach the gospel, baptizing in My name and telling people all that you have heard from Me*, He was making it clear that His will for us includes the call to worldwide mission. Our call to love our neighbor as ourselves includes our neighbor across the globe as well as the one next door.

The transformation God longs for transforms everything: marriages, families, friendships, economic, and political systems. It lifts up the humble, humbles the proud, and draws people together across racial, social, and cultural divides. It calls us to live in such a way that, as pastor Rob Bell from Mars Hill Bible Church says, *love wins*—in the discussion with our spouse, in the conversation with our neighbor, in the encounter with a stranger, in the decision we make, in the response to one in need, in the attitude toward our enemy ... in the choice we make to serve.

A Powerful Moment

When I ask long-term volunteers when they became "lifers"—people who decide to serve in God's mission for as long as He gives them breath—they almost always point back to a specific serving moment that sealed their commitment. "In that moment," they say, "I felt the God of heaven and earth use me, and I discovered that there's nothing in the world like that. It beats anything else I've ever experienced!"

Whether they taught a child how to pray, guided someone toward faith, helped a husband and wife reconcile, served a meal to a homeless person, or produced an audio tape that puts the Christian message in somebody's hand, they knew their lives would never be the same.

Acts 13:36 speaks about the Old Testament character David. It says simply, "And David served the purposes of God in his generation." I love the clarity of that single sentence. David didn't waste time chasing the wind. He devoted himself single-mindedly to God's mission and died knowing that his one and only life had served its highest purpose.

A Participant Or A Spectator?

I've never been a great athlete, but I've played enough to learn that when it comes to sports, it's a lot more exciting to be a participant than a spectator.

For five years in the early '80s, I played with a group of friends in a park district football league. Most of the teams we played against had big guys in construction jobs who hit the bars hard after work. By the time they got to the park, they just wanted to hit people hard.

We church guys weren't big or inebriated, but with speed and deception we did rather well. Several times we won the Tuesday night park district championship.

> People who let God lead them to where He wants them to serve find an incredible sense of satisfaction and joy.

During those same five years, I served as the chaplain for the Chicago Bears football team. Several times the team gave me premier tickets for games at Soldier Field during the Bears' spectacular charge toward the Super Bowl.

Sometimes on Sunday afternoons or Monday evenings I'd be at Soldier Field, in seats on the fifty-yard-line, watching the world championship Bears cream their opponents. I'd try to focus on the game, but I'd see somebody catch a spiraling pass … and I'd wish it was Tuesday night so I could be catching one myself. I'd watch somebody throw a beautiful block … and I'd recall the cruncher a big guy put on me the previous week. Despite the bruises I had to show for my participation, I wished I could trade Soldier Field for the hard-packed field at the park district. I wanted to be *in* the action, not just watching it.

My current recreational passion is sailing. Three times, by God's grace, I've had the opportunity to watch the premier sailboat-racing event in the world, the America's Cup. Seated on the deck of a friend's boat in the spectacular waters just north of Auckland, New Zealand, I saw the top racing boats and crews under sail on one racecourse.

But the whole time I thought, *I'd rather participate in one of our local Lake Michigan regattas, on my used, banged-up sailboat with my eight buddies, than be a spectator at the America's Cup Finals.*

Spectating never compares with the thrills and chills of being in the middle of the action. I'd much rather get a little beat up participating in a regatta than sip a lemonade from the comfort of a deck chair on a spectator boat. And I don't think I'm the only one who feels that way.

Every local churchgoer has a choice to make. He can park in his usual spot in the church parking lot, make his way to a comfortable seat in a favorite row, watch a good service, chat with friends, and then go home. That choice makes for a nice, safe Sunday morning experience. Or he can throw himself into an adventure by rolling up his sleeves, joining a team of like-minded servants, and helping to build the local church God has called him to be a part of.

I get letters and emails all the time from volunteers who have discovered that serving is far more satisfying than spectating. Here's an example:

> Three years ago you challenged me to get involved as a volunteer. I was hesitant at first, but you wouldn't let up. Now I can't thank you enough. The meaning I derive, the sense of ownership I feel, the friendships I have built, the spiritual growth I've experienced—it's all directly related to finding my niche in serving. I will be grateful to you for the rest of my life for inviting me into the game.

Scattered throughout this book you'll find dozens of excerpts from actual emails I've received from volunteers at our church and elsewhere who found the purpose of their lives when they finally committed themselves to serving.

Most of them didn't find the perfect volunteer niche overnight. A lot of them served faithfully in less-than-ideal situations before they discovered what they're really good at. Some of them didn't have a clue where to start. But they started anyway. They experimented. Even though they felt scared or thought they had little to offer, they decided to take a first small step.

A few of those you'll read about tried through the years to silence the voice calling them from self-absorption into servanthood. But God didn't quit. And now they have become the most enthusiastic proponents of serving.

One man wrote the following:

My life used to be about one thing: me. I was a self-serving guy who had neither purpose nor passion. I was leading a miserable life, throwing away time and money on beer and cheap thrills. Then one day I walked into a church and heard the message of Christ: Give your life away to others and you will find your life. I didn't have much to give up so I decided to give it a shot. That's when my life started to change and Christ became more real to me. I started serving teenagers and found a purpose … a reason for my existence.

It was twenty-one years ago that I wandered into that church. Today my life is richer than I ever believed it could be. Serving others made the difference. It was one of the best decisions I ever made.

Here's the experience of a woman named Marty:

Two years ago I started volunteering in our ministry for children experiencing divorce. I had been divorced myself and clearly remembered what it was like for me as a single parent, struggling with all that was happening in my life and having very little energy left for my children. When I heard about this ministry I was convinced God was calling me to get involved.

Every week I see children come in struggling with anger and fear and leave with hope and peace. How I wish my own kids had been served in this way.

So many people hesitate to volunteer because they are afraid of failing. I felt that way too. But when we let God lead us to where He wants us to serve, we find an incredible sense of satisfaction and joy. I wouldn't give that up for the world.

Why don't I feel guilty asking people to volunteer in the local church? Because I know that what Marty says is true. People who let God lead them to where He wants them to serve find "an incredible sense of satisfaction and joy."

What about you? Is it time for you to get up from the grandstands, crawl over a couple of benches, suit up, and get out on the playing field? I guarantee, it's far more exhilarating to be a participant than a spectator. Why watch others change the world when you can join them?

Your move.

L@W

Bill Hybels is the founding pastor of Willow Creek Community Church (**www.willowcreek.org**) near Chicago. He also serves as chairman of the Willow Creek Association, a ministry that serves more than 10,000 churches worldwide. He is the bestselling author of more than 20 books including *Courageous Leadership*, *The Volunteer Revolution,* and *Just Walk Across the Room: Simple Steps Pointing People to Faith* .

Taken from The Volunteer Revolution, *copyright © 2004 by Bill Hybels. Used by permission of Zondervan Publishers.* (**www.zondervan.com**)

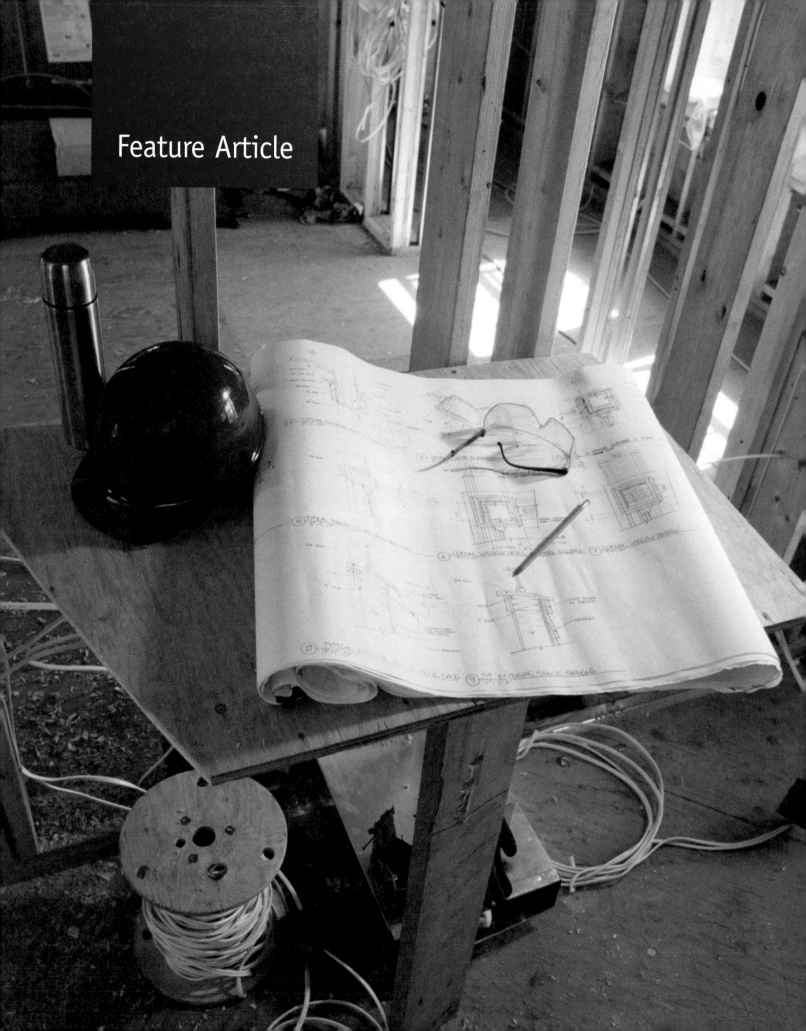

Building Strong Foundations

Habitat For Humanity Provides a Home for Volunteers Around the World

By Christine Willard

Habitat is dedicated to eliminating substandard housing and homelessness worldwide and to making adequate, affordable shelter a matter of conscience and action.

"Building Lives. Building Community." A nice-sounding tagline … and a tough task to accomplish. Yet that's the goal of Habitat for Humanity International, one of the most recognized non-profit organizations in the United States, and also the 17th largest homebuilder in the nation.

Based in Americus, Georgia, Habitat was founded in 1976 by Millard and Linda Fuller. In its first thirty years, the ministry has built or rehabbed more than 200,000 houses that have provided affordable housing for more than 1 million people.

The organization describes itself on its website (**www.Habitat.org**) as "a nonprofit, ecumenical Christian organization dedicated to eliminating substandard housing and homelessness worldwide and to making adequate, affordable shelter a matter of conscience and action. Habitat is founded on the conviction that every man, woman and child should have a simple, decent, affordable place to live in dignity and safety."

Utilizing independent local organizations, there are more than 2,000 Habitat affiliates in all 50 states and more than 90 nations. Wherever the location, Habitat's call is to extend a hand and serve a neighbor.

Making Affordable Housing

One Habitat affiliate is based in the Atlanta area's Gwinnett County. Jim Hallberg, the developmental director of Gwinnett Habitat for Humanity, says the organization's main goal is "to move families from being unstable to stable." The families that Habitat helps are living in unstable conditions, including substandard rentals that may have poor plumbing, too few rooms for too many people, or poor construction. The desire is to build affordable homes for working families.

"Habitat is a hand-up, not a hand-out," says Charles Craig,

executive director of the Gwinnett Habitat. "This is not a charity — people are working for it."

Habitat's unique structure requires that families who receive a new house must pay the interest-free mortgage on their home. In addition, families must be willing to partner with Habitat by working with what the ministry refers to as "sweat equity." In other words, families that receive houses must work on the construction of their homes as well as the houses of other Habitat families.

"This draws them into the process," Hallberg says. "The homeowners see what we are building together."

The Business of Serving

It takes about 300 volunteers to build one Habitat home. So where does Habitat find all of these volunteers? One source of Habitat's volunteers is corporations that have caught a vision of making an impact in their community.

According to Craig, businesses serve Habitat in several ways. The most powerful way is by providing full sponsorship of a house. That includes a financial commitment to cover the cost of a house and a resources commitment to provide enough volunteer workers to build the house.

Other times, businesses will allow their employees to volunteer part of their workweek with Habitat. Still other businesses serve Habitat homeowners by having their people serve on committees that help Habitat families learn important tasks including managing a budget.

Scientific Atlanta has been one of Gwinnett Habitat's most dedicated corporate partners over the years. Bill McCargo, the company's vice president of Community Relations, recalls that one of his company's first Habitat team-building ventures was building a house in conjunction with the 1996 Atlanta Olympics. The company bussed in groups of people to complete the house near Turner Field. In the years that followed, the neighborhood within sight of the Olympic Stadium took on a new look and feel.

"It gives us the opportunity to help the community on multiple levels," McCargo says. "We can renovate the community we live in and let our people satisfy their desire to volunteer and give back to their community."

McCargo says that Scientific Atlanta employees especially appreciate the impact that Habitat is having on families. At a company party, employees saw a video of a mom and her children in their new home.

"They were able to see this woman who could normally not afford a house standing in front of one with her two kids," McCargo says. "The experience at Habitat whets their appetite. It makes them want to keep serving. You learn by doing."

Serving Beyond the Walls
Churches are also active when it comes to laying bricks and breaking ground with Habitat. Crossroads Community Church in suburban Atlanta has partnered with Gwinnett Habitat over the years. Mark Knap, who works in Crossroad's Compassion Ministry, has volunteered for three years, helping coordinate the church's "Faith Build."

That's what Crossroads calls their partnerships with other churches that use combined resources to purchase and construct a Habitat home. During Faith Build, Crossroads is assigned five specific Saturday workdays to help build the house.

Typically, Crossroads has between 200 and 250 volunteers working on the Faith Build house. One year, the churches worked on a house for a family of Kosovo refugees. Knap says the people of Crossroads that serve with Habitat are stretched as they serve others.

"There is a group of people for whom compassion is difficult to express. They may not be good at doing that one on one," he says. "But they may be gifted with their hands. Habitat does an incredible job of making an accessible way for people to serve."

And even if someone is not gifted in the area of construction, there are other ways for them to serve with Habitat. Crossroads sends a hospitality team to the site of each workday, providing drinks and sandwiches.

"Habitat fits the heart of those wired to do things such as building homes, but it also makes it accessible to those not wired that way," Knap says. "Individuals can serve in the unique ways they have been gifted."

And some of the people they are serving with are the people that will call the house under construction their home. As Knap says, "This is different than a food drive where you don't get to interact with the people you are helping."

"With Habitat, you get to know them, care about them, and demonstrate the love of Christ to them." Habitat can also help teach people the true meaning of service, even those who have been in the church for a long time.

"It takes Habitat pushing you beyond the four walls of the church," Knap says. "It is an entry point for people into service. For some, that's where they'll stay. For others, it will be the first step — they will go on and do other missions. Service becomes more than a program. It becomes their lifestyle."

Building Up the Kingdom
Habitat for Humanity volunteers build houses. They also build community. But perhaps the most important thing they build is eternal. Laying a foundation of love, trust, and true service to our neighbors through Habitat for Humanity provides a clear picture of the kingdom of God.

The kingdom impact is noticeable when a family from Kosovo finds true refuge under one roof — their own. It's seen with a single mother's dream realized of a safe, affordable home for her children. It's seen in a company's commitment to its community … and a church's impact beyond its own walls.

Habitat is service; it is true commitment.

"It is a big commitment to grab a hammer and nails and push concrete around," Hallberg says. "But, this is what Christ called His people to do."

Habitat's goal is to change people's lives for the better —helping them live better, helping them be better. But it is not only changing the lives of the Habitat homeowners, it is changing the lives of those who pour out and give of their time, money, and abilities.

People who serve with Habitat discover the true meaning of serving your neighbor, no matter where that person may live.

What begins with a plot of land ultimately becomes a home … and a glimpse of our home that awaits us.

L@W

Christine Willard is a freelance writer who lives in Atlanta with her husband Tim. After graduating from Grace Theological Seminary with a Master of Arts in Theological Studies, Christine began focusing on Women's Ministries. She enjoys traveling the country with her husband, mountain biking, writing, and teaching the Bible to women.

Toolbox

A Call to All to Serve

By Bob Coy

... Since I, the Lord and Teacher, have washed your feet, you ought to wash each other's feet. I have given you an example to follow. Do as I have done to you.

John 13:13-15 NLT

The human heart cannot be conquered by authority; it must be won by humility. Jesus knew this. That's why this passage from John gives cause for pause in my busy day. The thought of God Almighty, the Creator of the Universe, the Sovereign I Am, kneeling to wash the feet of mere men is more than my mind can sometimes imagine.

The danger, however, of being stunned by the humility of divinity is that we can stop there and miss the point altogether. Jesus said that He humbled Himself as an example for us to follow. And while foot washing requires humility on either end, I truly don't believe that was all He had in mind. I think He had a more universal application for all of us.

I believe Jesus wanted us to know that although we may find ourselves at times in a position of great authority, we are never too important to serve those who are under our authority. It is because of this principle that the writers of the New Testament chose words to describe ministers or leaders of the church that meant "servant." God was underscoring the fact that those who lead should do so with the heart and mindset of service.

Of all the people on the face of this earth, those who should be the most gracious, the most loving, the most humble, and the most considerate of others are those in whom dwells the kneeling Savior who washed His disciples' feet. Not because we want to look like Jesus, but because we have the life of Christ living in and through us.

I don't know what platform of authority God has given you in this life. I do know that whether you are a mom who oversees her kids or the CEO of a billion-dollar corporation, the purpose for your position is to display Him to the world around you—as a loving Lord, who isn't too high and mighty to serve. It will be His divine humility through you that compels a loyalty to you that no amount of tyranny, threats, or time-management courses could ever hope to gain. As 2 Corinthians 5:14 says, "For the love of Christ compels us. ..."

L@W

Bob Coy is the Senior Pastor of Calvary Chapel Fort Lauderdale (**www.calvaryftl.org**), which was named by *Church Growth* magazine as one of the largest and fastest-growing churches in America. Bob communicates God's Word without compromise, connecting with each generation in a relevant and engaging manner. He can be heard and seen on the Active Word (**www.activeword.org**) radio and television program.

> Jesus wanted us to know that ... we are never too important to serve those who are under our authority.

Sunday Service

By Todd Duncan

When I met Mona I was in a hurry. I was leaving the country in less than twenty-four hours and I needed a couple of pairs of pants for the trip. Mona approached me to help and quickly had me in two good-looking pairs. There was only one problem. The hems were unfinished and it was Sunday.

Mona intuitively excused herself. She returned shortly thereafter with a promise that my pants would be ready by five o'clock that evening. I was surprised and delighted. Then she went overboard.

"You're probably going to be very busy packing for your trip," she said, "so rather than you coming back here, why don't I just deliver them to your home? Would that be okay?"

"You'll do that?" I replied. She assured me it would be her pleasure.

It was 4 p.m. later that day and I was packing when I heard a car drive up. I walked to the front door and met Mona as she approached the house. "I'm confident these will fit perfectly," she said and handed me the hangers holding my new pants. "But just in case, why don't you try them on. The tailor is available until 9 p.m."

I hurried to the bedroom and slid into both pair and then returned to the front and gave Mona the thumbs up. She smiled and shook my hand and I expressed my sincere gratitude—she didn't have to do all this, I told her, but I was thankful she did.

I walked her down the drive and she explained that this was her way of doing business. "Todd," she said, "I hope you buy from me for the rest of your life."

I held open the driver side door and said thanks again, assuring her that I'd ask for her every time I visited the store.

As she backed out of the driveway I noticed other items hanging in plastic in her back seat—a few more home deliveries still to be made. I smiled and waved and as she pulled away I noticed her license plate. I nodded. It read, "SERVE."

A customer is far more impressed by someone who is willing to serve him despite the sale than by someone who adjusts her service according to the size of the sale. The first person is focused on earning trust; the second person on earning money. Expect people to notice the difference. I do. And I return to people like Mona every chance I get.

L@W

Todd Duncan is the *New York Times* best-selling author of *Time Traps*. He's also the *Businessweek* best-selling author of *High Trust Selling*. He is one of America's most sought-after motivational speakers and sales trainers. He is the founder and chairman of The Duncan Group, an Atlanta-based international leadership, sales training, and personal development company that is dedicated to helping business leaders and salespeople succeed both professionally and in life. Todd, his wife Sheryl, and their two sons live in La Jolla, California.

> I expressed my sincere gratitude—she didn't have to do all this, but I was thankful she did.

KATHERINE LEARY

Katherine Leary is the Executive Director of the Center for Faith and Work at Redeemer Presbyterian Church (**www.Redeemer.com**) in New York City. With an MBA from the University of Virginia's Darden School (and a BA from Wittenberg), Katherine spent 20 years in the high tech industry. In 2002, Redeemer—the church where she met Christ 10 years before—asked her to return to New York City to start up a faith and work ministry.

The Right Background

The Center for Faith and Work was launched in 2003 to equip, connect, and mobilize professionals in all fields to renew the culture around us with the truth and love of the gospel. Prior to that, I served in leadership roles — from head of sales and marketing to CEO — for several hardware, software, and Internet-based technology companies from 1990–2002. These roles prepared me for my current work in many ways:

- The passion exhibited by workers in the high-tech industry to develop products that improve the way the world works is a beautiful picture of how God intended us to work. I long to see all Christians approach their work with equal passion.
- I led start-ups — companies making something of value out of nothing. The faith and work initiative is a start-up: we don't have many models to follow. We have lots of early adopters eager to buy the "product," but we don't know what it will take to develop a sustainable program, and we have to create much of the materials ourselves. The key is to find good people to build a leadership team with you and be willing to take risks and learn from your mistakes.
- As someone who became a Christian at mid-career, I am deeply aware of how hard it is to be a Christ follower and Christ ambassador in our workplaces. I personally experienced the need for a ministry such as the one we are creating.

God has given me some unique gifts and experiences and I seek to put them to use with as much excellence as I can muster.

I seek to mobilize others to creatively address some of the problems in our culture. And I hope, through God's grace, to draw others to Him by the evidence of His work in my life — hammering away at my sin and idols and refining me to be a more faith-full person.

Faith in the Workplace

While in leadership positions in high tech, I tried to be sensitive to the many other faiths in our workplace. I was open about being Christian, that I went to church, and that I really believed it. Beyond that I attempted to exhibit the grace and humility of the Christian life.

It's important that we redefine success so that it syncs up with the way God defines it. God wants us to work and work well, and He even wants us to prosper. However it seems that success in ways the world would define it is the antithesis of a God-honoring life. It has to be about Him, His purposes, and His way. For example, the world around us celebrates the individual who can make it on his own. In the Christian life, we need to guard against doing it alone. We need the accountability and encouragement of others to get past our self-deceit and selfishness, in order to be open to how God wants to use us.

Finally, it's important to think about how what you do impacts the world around you ... not just the person sitting next to you or your spouse or child. God gave us responsibility for the earth He created, therefore, we need to expand our scope and be concerned, informed, and engaged in what's happening all around us. Think about the world around you as God would and get involved, as an ambassador for Christ.

L@W

Perspective

More Than Just Words

By Matthew Barnett

I remember watching my dad shake every last hand at the door after services. As Senior Pastor, it didn't matter how tired and ready to get home he must have been; it only mattered that he was there to meet each person who walked up wanting to talk or needing some encouragement. While it seemed like a small act of service to me at the time, he knew for many people how big it could be.

Sometimes I would watch to see how he would react to the people who were dressed nicely and who I thought were "important" in the church — against those who came in on a bus or from one our outreaches. To him it was clear they were *all* important. And at the moment he met them and shook their hand, he made sure they knew it too. He wasn't a leader to these people because he was their boss or because he was in a high position. He was a leader in their lives because he cared and was willing to serve them. This was one of my first pictures of leadership and serving.

People often aspire to be a leader because they think there is power or perks to leadership positions — and sometimes there is. But true leadership is not about being more important than others; it is about having more responsibility for others. The greatest leaders I've seen are always the most humble and the ones most ready to serve.

The greatest example of servanthood for me is the picture of Jesus Christ, on the floor, washing the feet of those He was leading. Great leaders always work to be nothing more than great servants.

One of the keys I have found in serving is finding out where the other person is coming from and the needs they are facing. In 1993, we started with the vision of building an inner-city church. It was not until we got involved in the lives of the people that we really knew what the church should be. What is now the Dream Center emerged as a response to the needs of a hurting, hopeless community. It was very different from our original vision, and yet it includes everything and more than I could have imagined.

When the Dream Center first started, it was not an immediate success. The people in the community around us were skeptical. They needed to know they could trust us. They needed to know we cared about them.

As I got to know the people, I saw what they were actually facing and it helped me know how to serve them. I found any and every way to serve people — from helping them clean-up their homes, to bringing food, to just sitting and being with them.

Our Adopt-a-Block program, food truck, and life-rehabilitation programs were all born out of trying to find a way to serve. I realized I could talk about hope all I wanted, but for anyone to believe it and be willing to follow my leading, it would take more than just words. I needed to go to their door, look them in the eye, look at where they lived and what they were facing, and still be able to share that there was hope for *them*.

Is it easy to stare straight into the face of a homeless mother with her three little kids … or the woman with the black eye from her husband … or the man who had tried unsuccessfully for the last five years to stay sober, and inspire them that there really is hope for their lives to be better? It's never easy. But I see my job as creating a space for others to grow and succeed — to lift them up to reach their dreams.

Leading is more than supervising the tasks; it is about the people. And when people know you care because they see it in your actions toward them, when they see you serving them, they will respond in great ways.

A pipe that allows liquid to flow through it is called a leader. I believe that is how Jesus led. I encourage you to lay yourself out for people as a guide to direct them, and serve as a passage to get where God is taking them.

L@W

Pastor Matthew Barnett is the Co-Founder of the Dream Center in Los Angeles (**www.dreamcenter.org**). Recognized by President George W. Bush for its successful work in the inner-city, hundreds of Dream Centers around the world have been launched off this example. An author and speaker, he is also the Senior Pastor of Angelus Temple (**www.angelustemple.org**).

Life @ The Intersection

You have just completed Session 5. Use these journal pages to complete the following:

BIG QUESTION:
After reading this session, I'm wondering what others think about ...

NEW THOUGHT:
I just learned that ...

PERSONAL CHALLENGE:
I can't get this out of my mind. I have to figure out how to live differently so that ...

TAKE A BREAK

Make a list of the needs of people in your community (church, work, or neighborhood). Choose one need and create a list of action steps. Then ask yourself, "What is one thing I can do today to serve this need." Then do it.

Life@Work Study

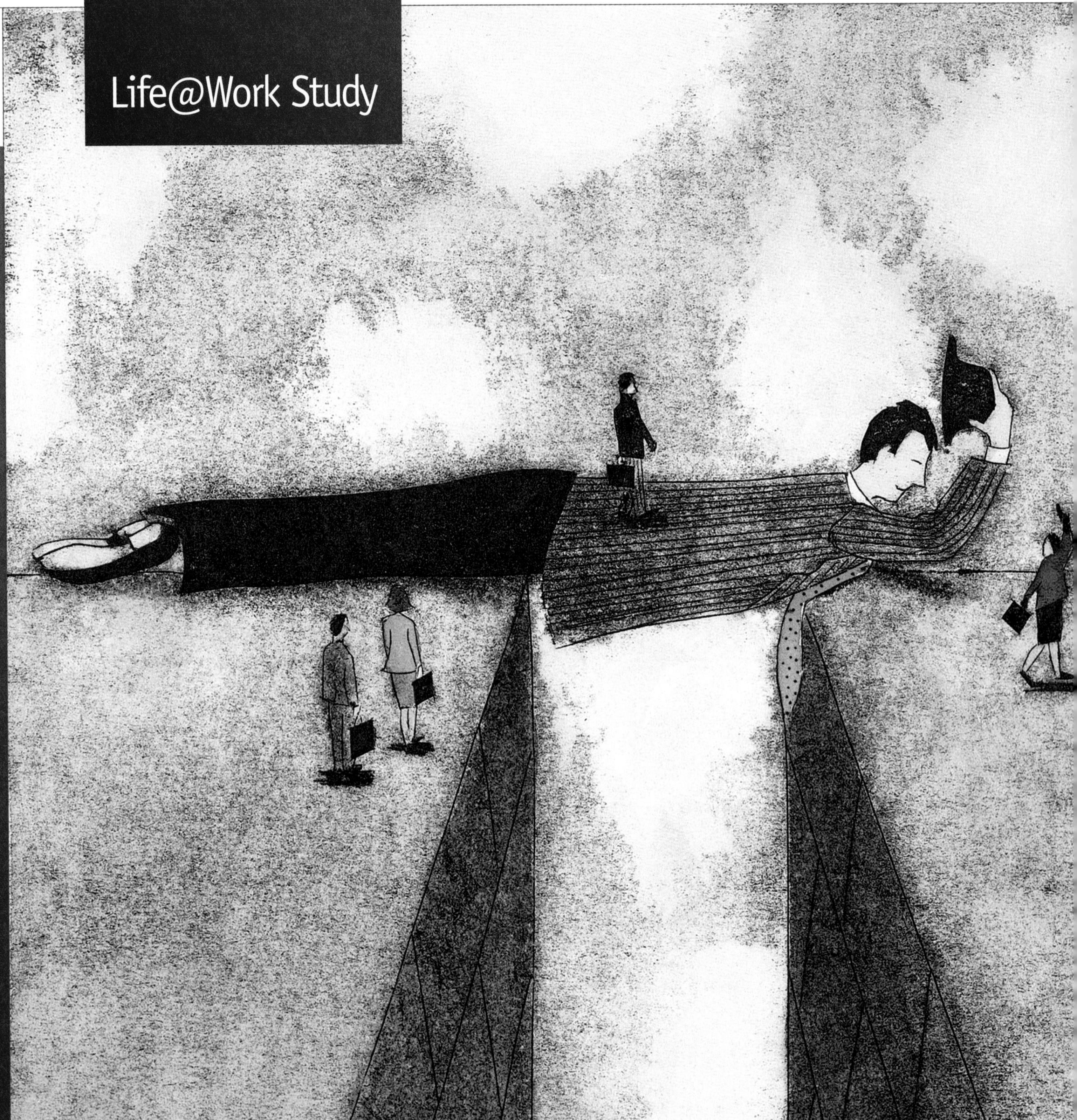

SESSION SIX

The Good Samaritan laid aside his own agenda and laid out his own resources to serve a person in need.

Everyday Samaritans

Serving Others with God's Heart of Compassion

By Stephen R. Graves

It's one of the oldest tricks in the fisherman's book: when you get your picture taken with your catch, hold the fish way out in front of you at arm's length so it's a lot closer to the camera than you are. With that little trick of perspective, you can make a little bluegill look as if it's big enough to swallow you whole.

Similarly, if you're keeping other people at arm's length, their troubles seem pretty small. By comparison, up close your own preoccupations look enormous. The result? You walk on by, passing up opportunities to serve others in the way God calls you to.

That's what happened in Jesus' parable of the Good Samaritan. A man lay broken and bleeding, half dead by the side of the road. Two very religious, highly respected men walked right past him. It's not that they didn't see him. They actually went to the trouble of walking to the other side of the road to put more distance between themselves and the suffering man.

No doubt the priest and the Levite had their reasons for not helping the man. Perhaps they were in a hurry, trying to get to scheduled appointments. It's not good form, after all, to keep someone waiting when you've made a commitment. Also, the road between Jerusalem and Jericho was famously dangerous. To stop would have put themselves in peril for the sake of a man they didn't know — who might have even been bait in a bandit's trap. Then there was the fact that it would have compromised their ceremonial cleanness to touch the man if he turned out to be dead already. The hassle of all that washing and days of being unfit to serve in the Temple would have truly been a burden.

These were all legitimate concerns. But none of them outweighed a person's moral responsibility to a dying man in need of help. It was a trick of perspective. Comparatively small preoccupations towered over the dire needs of a man whom they kept at arm's length.

to provide. Jesus calls you and me to be "Everyday Samaritans."

Seeing Like an Everyday Samaritan

How could two highly religious men walk right past the man lying by the side of the road, and so violate one of the most cherished tenets of the faith they professed? They had serious vision problems. When they looked at the man, they only saw a ceremonially unclean body, which, if touched, would make them ceremonially unclean as well. They had a blind spot that was created by their own self-styled religion.

My neighbor is anyone who crosses my path and who needs help that I can afford to provide.

The hero of the story, of course, is a man who was able to step back and see that his own concerns and preoccupations — whatever they might have been — were small compared to the needs of a broken man he could help. The Good Samaritan laid aside his own agenda and laid out his own resources to serve a person in need.

Jesus told the story of the Good Samaritan in answer to a lawyer's question: *who is my neighbor?* Jesus wanted His followers to realize that the scope of serving goodwill to others is much broader than two or three best friends. Every day, you are also faced with the question, who is my neighbor? You see people who need help. A colleague scrambling to meet a client's eleventh-hour demand. An office mate whose car will not start. A competitor in the next convention booth who gets sick at a trade show. A client who asks for help on something you don't get a commission on.

Who exactly qualifies as my neighbor? The implicit question is, do I have to help *them?* The answer was unmistakable in the first-century story, and it is undeniable today. My neighbor is anyone who crosses my path and who needs help that I can afford

The Samaritan saw a fellow human being in trouble; he saw an opportunity to serve.

We can have blind spots to those around us as well, passing by needy people every day. It is easy to have eyes and yet not see. The power of observation is something that must be learned. It is not something that just comes naturally.

Too often we walk blindly through our workday, passing by innumerable opportunities to serve others. One huge blind spot is busy self-absorption. Everyone is busy. We are all on the go. Wireless technology means we have no uninterrupted private time anymore. It's not just information overload we experience anymore, but *nonstop* information overload, following us everywhere we go. In such a context it is particularly hard to see the living, breathing, thinking, feeling human beings around us. Such a frenzied existence doesn't foster a lifestyle of service. That's why we need to retrain our eyes to see all the lives that we are walking right by.

Feeling Like an Everyday Samaritan

Why did the Samaritan stop when the two religious professionals didn't? Jesus said it was deep sympathy that drove the Samaritan to help. One translation calls it *pity* or *compassion.* He was moved deep down in his heart with empathy and care. Empathy requires you to connect with the interior of your own life, and offer more than a surface, shallow sympathetic frown.

In their excellent book titled *Leadership Presence*, Belle Linda Halpern and Kathy Lubar isolate the ability to reach out in empathy as one of the four elements of effective modern leadership. Someone once observed, "The greatest feats of love are performed by those who have had much practice in performing daily acts of kindness." It takes empathy to do that.

Empathy, however, is not an easy flower to cultivate. There is much in our culture and current business climate that works against it. Empathy is rarely heralded or rewarded in the workplace. It has no year-end bonus tied to it. But can you imagine how the American workplace would be transformed if we all learned to empathize with co-workers, with employees, with bosses, with customers, with vendors? "Rejoice with those who rejoice, and weep with those who weep," wrote the apostle Paul in Romans 12:15 (NKJV). That's the basis of true interpersonal connection, and it's a serious motivator for the kind of service that God looks for in His people.

Acting Like an Everyday Samaritan

We already know that only one traveler stopped and provided help. The Samaritan saw the man in need; he empathetically felt his pain and stopped to help the injured man. What did it take for the Samaritan to put feet to his

Christian faith. John Stott, one of this age's leading Christian statesmen, observed, "Social responsibility becomes an aspect not of Christian mission only, but also of Christian conversion. It is impossible to be truly converted to God without being thereby converted to our neighbor."

Action requires intentionality.

- *It takes initiative.* The Samaritan took a relational chance. He knew he was probably hated by the Jewish victim in the road, but he took the risk anyway. He stopped and reached out his hand, not knowing what the response might be.

- **It takes adjustment.** The Samaritan obviously was going somewhere himself. I doubt seriously he was roaming around Jericho, looking for assault victims to help. He obviously missed his appointment and had his schedule wrecked that day. Effective serving sometimes means accepting inconvenience.

- *It takes sacrifice.* The Samaritan gave his time, his money, and his compassion. He obviously got his hands dirty helping clean up the stripped, beaten man. The story as told by Jesus even says that he instructed the innkeeper to keep a tab of the cost to convalesce the assaulted man and that he would take care of the entire debt.

In business we deal in goods every day, yet we often miss their moral role in meeting needs. As Saint Clement of Alexandria remarked, "Goods are called good because they

Empathy is rarely heralded or rewarded in the workplace. It has no year-end bonus tied to it.

feelings? More to the point, how can you practically serve others as you go through your workday?

Sentiments mean nothing without deeds that do something about it. Such service of others is at the heart of a life of

can be used for good: they are instruments for good, in the hands of those who use them properly." Goods are only good when they are taken off the shelf and put into circulation to meet real needs. Serving means spending. It will cost you some goods.

Detours From Acting Like a Samaritan

Two people walked by the injured man. They detoured to the other side just to avoid him. They both had their reasons. Action always meets resistance. We each have our internal script that suggests excuses for why we would be better off to just pass on by. Doing the right thing always has a mental enemy. Our status quo does not like to be bothered. Its inertia takes several forms.

suddenly felt he was obligated to travel the road day and night looking for mugged and wounded victims to service. He did not quit his job and become a full-time, one-man mobile hospital outfit. He saw someone hurt, felt compassion, and responded on the spot.

Sometimes we miss life opportunities because we make them out to be more complex in our minds than they really are. Paranoia makes every person in need a grafter trying to

Goods are only good when they are taken off the shelf and put into circulation to meet real needs.

Ruts and Routines

Routines can be a good thing. They can also blind our perspective. I have some friends who seem to never get beyond their same old circle of cronies. They have become comfortable in their little circle. They have become very ingrown and unaccepting of outsiders. You will meet few needs and do little service if you never leave your comfort zone.

Fear of Getting Too Involved

The Samaritan accepted the full liability and related costs to mend his neighbor. He did not over-think his situation. Nowhere does the story give us any hint that the Samaritan

extract nourishment from you and every stranded traveler a serial killer. Every employee with a personal problem is not a lawsuit waiting to happen. The Samaritan saw the situation for what it was. A man had been attacked and needed help. He saw one man on the side of one road and he responded with the resources he could give.

Relational Laziness

There are many of us who are too passive in relationships. Such people always think that it is the other person's job to initiate. They never make the first step toward other people — maybe not even the second or third step. They have

become accustomed to people pursuing them, and except for selfish pursuit of powerful people, they are all but dead in their ability to initiate towards others.

Stopping to serve is incompatible with relational laziness. It is always easier to cross to the other side of the street. Yet

your wounds. We need more dogs at work and fewer cats. Which are you?

Being an everyday Samaritan begins with the ability to get a little distance from your own preoccupations and get a little closer to the difficulties faced by another person. Sometimes

We need more dogs at work and fewer cats.

you will never truly live if you do not daily connect with the reality of your fellow human beings. Initiative means asking, "How are things at home?" It means calling the person who was laid off six months ago and checking to see how his or her job search is going. It means introducing yourself to someone you see regularly, but whom you have not met.

Haddon Robinson, one of America's best preachers, likes to say that there are two kinds of people in this world: cats and dogs. A "cat," according to Robinson, is a "here I am" person. Dogs, on the other hand, live as "there you are" people. Cats arch their backs to be noticed and to get stroked. They make you come to where they are. Dogs come to you, wagging their tails, getting up into your lap, and licking you. They have no inhibitions, walking right into your world and plopping down beside you. A cat is always busy burying its own poop, while a dog will come and lick

you really aren't in a position to help. That's fine. But too often we're too busy looking at our bluegill of a problem through a close-up lens to see the sharks that are threatening to swallow our neighbors whole.

L@W

Dr. Stephen R. Graves is a highly sought business coach and life guide for entrepreneurs and leaders desiring to successfully make it to the finish line of life. In 1991, he co-founded the Cornerstone Group, a company built to integrate biblical wisdom and business excellence. He and his wife Karen have three children.

This article is based on concepts drawn from Life@Work by John C. Maxwell, Stephen R. Graves, and Thomas G. Addington, published by Thomas Nelson, Inc.

EVERYDAY SAMARITANS

FOR GROUP DISCUSSION

Prior to your small group meeting time, read and reflect on the Life@Work Study article you just read. Use these questions and journal pages to reflect and respond to the ideas presented. Be ready to share your thoughts at your small group gathering.

Note to small group leaders: You can download a full Leader's Guide at www.lifeatworkgroupzine.com.

- *Every day, you are also faced with the question, who is my neighbor? You see people who need help. ... Who exactly qualifies as my neighbor? The implicit question is, do I have to help them?*

    Jesus answered this "dilemma" by telling the story of the Good Samaritan. When was a time you, like the Samaritan, stopped along your path to serve the needs of someone at work? How did you feel? When was a time, like the priest or the Levite, you diverted your attention away from another's needs? How did that experience feel?

- *It's not just information overload we experience anymore, but nonstop information overload, following us everywhere we go. In such a context it is particularly hard to see the living, breathing, thinking, feeling human beings around us. Such a frenzied existence doesn't foster a lifestyle of service.*

    What keeps you overloaded? How many different ways do people have to reach you? Do you have set times you will and won't check email and voicemail? What can you do to slow down? What can you *really* do to *really* slow down?

- Empathy and compassion compel people to serve one another. Where would you rank yourself on a scale of 1 (not very compassionate) to 5 (highly compassionate)? How would your spouse or best friend rate your compassion level? How about the people you work with?

- *Sentiments mean nothing without deeds that do something about it. Such service of others is at the heart of a life of Christian faith.*

    How can you practically serve others as you go through your workday? Who can help you stay true to your desire to serve others? Are you willing to be accountable and let them ask you the hard questions?

- Pastor Haddon Robinson says there are two kinds of people: cats and dogs. Cats are "here I am" people. Dogs, on the other hand, live as "there you are" people.

    If you are honest with yourself, are you a cat or a dog? How can you become more doglike when it comes to having compassion to serve others?

Feature Article

L@W

SERVANT LEADERSHIP CAN
RADICALLY CHANGE THE WAY
YOU DO BUSINESS

By Ken Blanchard and Phil Hodges

Lead as He Led

The world desperately needs a new leadership role model. We have all seen how destructive self-serving leaders can be to organizations and people. No matter what your role is in life, you can be a servant leader. How? Because leadership is an influence process! Any time you influence the thoughts and actions of others — in either your personal or professional life — you are engaging in leadership. Leading like Jesus means aligning your **heart**, your **head**, your **hands**, and your **habits** together in a way that allows you to carry out God's perfect vision.

Leading like Jesus is more than an announcement: it is a commitment to lead in a different way. It is a transformational journey.

through you? True success in life is the fulfillment of the life mission God planned for you. Your success depends on your relationship with Christ and what level of control you will let Him have in your life.

Jesus demonstrated His desire to please only the Father and settled this matter following His baptism during the ordeal in the wilderness. Then when Satan came to tempt Him, He was ready! He lived by the mission His Father had given Him for the accomplishment of His Father's purpose.

Once leaders have settled the personal leadership perspective through self-examination, they are then ready to begin

LEADERS OFTEN DEMONSTRATE WHOSE THEY ARE BY HOW THEY DEFINE SUCCESS IN TODAY'S WORLD.

Effective leadership starts on the inside — it is a heart issue. Before you can hope to lead anyone else, you have to know yourself. This is called **personal leadership** because it involves choice. You first have to answer two questions:
- Whose am I?
- Who am I?

The answer to these questions will provide the sure foundation to becoming a servant leader. Leaders often demonstrate whose they are by how they define success in today's world. Scripture teaches us that ultimately, we are created to please God.

The second question — Who am I? —deals with your life purpose. Why are you here? What does the Lord want to do

developing trusting relationships with others. Without trust, it is impossible for any organization to function effectively.

Jesus as Our Example

We can turn to Jesus as our example of servant-hearted, **one-on-one leadership**. After spending time in the wilderness, where His life purpose and perspective were refined by trials and temptations, Jesus began the process of calling His disciples. Once they agreed to follow Him, He spent three years building a culture of trust with those men. This trust between Jesus and His disciples would not have developed if Jesus had not first spent time in the wilderness.

In life-role leadership, trust is the stream on which vulnerability, caring, commitment, and grace flow between parents and children, husbands and wives, brothers and sisters, friends and fellow citizens. Trust pours first from loving hearts committed to serve and support one another, through promises kept, to encouragement and appreciation expressed, through support and acceptance, to repentance and apologies accepted to reconciliation and restoration. Trust is a stream with a fragile ecological balance: once it is polluted, it will take time and effort to restore.

As leaders develop a trusting relationship with people in the one-on-one leadership arena, they become trustworthy. Then they are ready for **team leadership** by developing people through empowerment. Effective leaders working at the team

level realize that to be good stewards of the energy and efforts of those committed to work with them, they must honor the power of diversity and acknowledge the power of teamwork.

start with the organizational level when He was on earth, but by valuing both relationships and results, Jesus created the environment for developing an effective organization. Jesus

> ## When we UNDERSTAND the characteristics of Jesus' leadership, we can be a SERVANT leader too.

Once again, we look to Jesus as our model. After Jesus spent time personally teaching and modeling the type of leadership He wanted the disciples to adopt, He sent them out to minister in teams of two (see Mark 6). In doing so, Jesus empowered them to act on His behalf to support one another in accomplishing the work they had been trained to do. Trust is also a key factor at the team level. Individuals in the group will not empower each other to accomplish an assigned task if they do not trust each other.

When it comes to team leadership in the family, things really get interesting. The leader's efforts and aspirations to serve the best interests of others often come in direct conflict with his or her own immediate priorities and demands. The rewards of family leadership are most apt to be found in the subtle fashioning of loving relationships and the slow growth of personal character. The family leader's example determines how family members treat people of all ages and conditions; how they view success, failure, and adversity; how they solve problems; and how they communicate love and self-worth. If the family leader demonstrates humility, grace, and an open reliance on God,

clearly identified the purposes for His followers and their organizations when He gave us the Great Commission and the Great Commandment.

When organizational leadership enters into the arena of **community leadership**, it calls for the leader to willingly extend service for the common good. It focuses on finding common ground and reconciliation with people of diverse opinions, backgrounds, priorities, and spiritual perspectives. Community leadership requires love to be spoken in truth and courage, with good will and tolerance without wandering from moral and ethical conviction.

One of the primary mistakes that leaders make today, when called to lead, is spending most of their time and energy trying to improve things at the organizational level before ensuring that they have adequately addressed their own credibility at the individual, one-on-one, or team leadership levels.

Getting Practical
So, then, how do we lead like Jesus? His mandate for all of us was to be servant leaders. As He said, "The Son of Man did not

> ## TRUST is a stream with a fragile ecological balance: once it is polluted, it will take TIME and EFFORT to restore.

His Word, and His promises, these traits are likely to flow into the family members.

Whether a leader can function well in the **organizational leadership** arena depends on the outcome of perspective, trust, and community attained at the first three levels in his or her transformational leadership journey. The outcome of focusing on this level is organizational effectiveness, both high performance and high human satisfaction. Jesus did not

come to be served; but He came to serve others" (Matthew 20:28 NLT). Before we can model our behavior after His perfect servant leadership example, we must first learn to be like Jesus. When we understand the characteristics of His leadership, we can be a servant leader too. We describe servant leadership as it relates to four domains: *heart*, *head*, *hands*, and *habits*.

Heart relates to your character. Are you leading to serve, or to

serving@work   L@W   141

be served? When your heart is wrong, you quickly lose your way on the leadership journey. The journey of life is to move from a self-serving heart to a serving heart. You finally become an adult when you realize that life is about what you give, rather than what you get. When Jesus talked about the heart He was referring to the center of our spiritual nature — our EGO. The EGO can stand for Edging God Out. When the ego edges God out, the heart is overshadowed, and you become a self-serving leader.

EGO can also stand for Exalting God Only. When the ego exalts God only, the heart recognizes the priority to "seek first the Kingdom of God and His righteousness ..." (Matthew 6:33 NKJV).

with a clear and compelling vision of the future that excites passion and commitment. Jesus explained His vision of the future in Matthew 28:19-20: "Go, therefore, and make disciples of all nations, baptizing them in the name of the Father and of the Son and of the Holy Spirit, teaching them to observe everything I have commanded you ..." (NKJV).

Moving from the *heart* and the *head* to the *hands* is where most leadership methodologies fail. Once the *heart* and *head* are transformed, there must be a change in behavior (*hands*)!

Hands are important because "Leading like Jesus" is more than a theory; it's about changing the way you lead others. It means making a commitment to change your behavior to

---

THE JOURNEY OF SERVANT LEADERSHIP STARTS IN THE HEART WITH MOTIVATION AND INTENT.

The journey of servant leadership starts in the *heart* with motivation and intent. Then it must travel through the *head*, which is the leader's belief system and perspective on the role of the leader.

Head focuses on your beliefs and assumptions about leadership. Effective leaders have clear leadership points of view that they are willing to teach others. All great leaders have a specific leadership point of view that defines how they see their role and their relationships to those they seek to influence. Leaders are willing to teach their point of view to others.

be more like Jesus. It means starting to ask yourself, "What would Jesus do?" before you act as a leader. The *Hands* transmit your leadership character as you interact with those who are under your influence. A key activity of an effective servant leader is to act as a performance coach. When Jesus called His disciples to follow Him, He pledged them His full support and guidance as they developed into fishers of men. This is the duty of a servant leader — the ongoing investment of the leader's life into the lives of those who follow.

ON A DAILY BASIS, EFFECTIVE SERVANT LEADERS RECALIBRATE AND RENEW THEIR COMMITMENT TO SERVE RATHER THAN TO BE SERVED.

Jesus was completely focused on pleasing His Father as His audience of One! He sent His disciples to help people understand the good news and live according to the values of God's Kingdom, not just do whatever they wanted. Jesus made it very clear that what He was asking His followers to do, in His name, would not please everyone.

Jesus continually taught His disciples about servant leadership. He emphasized that servant leadership begins

Your decision-by-decision behavior can make or break your relationships and your ability to inspire trust. Here is where good intention and right thinking start to bear good fruit, and real discipleship is truly tested. That was the power of Jesus' leadership — the leaders He trained, went on to change the world when He was no longer with them in bodily form. But He promised them and promises us: "surely I am with you always, to the very end of the age." (Matthew 28:20 NIV).

Through His hands, Jesus was able to transmit to His disciples what was in His heart and head about servant leadership.

Habits enable you to renew your daily commitment to develop into a valuable servant leader. On a daily basis, effective servant leaders recalibrate and renew their commitment to serve rather than to be served. That's exactly what Jesus did. He used solitude, prayer, understanding of Scripture, and faith in the unconditional love of His Father to keep Him on track. He formed a small support group with Peter, John, and James, in which He could be more vulnerable and share the plans His Father had for Him.

Leading like Jesus means we must be like Jesus and allow Him to align our *heart, head, hands,* and *habits* in a way that reflects His character to the world. People everywhere will be drawn to Jesus because of those who lead like Him!

L@W

Ken Blanchard is the Chief Spiritual Officer of The Ken Blanchard Companies, a full-service managment consulting and training company that he and his wife Margie founded in 1979. Ken is one of today's most sought-after authors, speakers, and business consultants, and he is co-founder and chairman of the National Board of The Center for Faithwalk Leadership (now known as Lead Like Jesus). He has authored and co-authored numerous books, including *The One Minute Manager*, *Raving Fans*, and *Gung Ho!*

Phil Hodges currently serves as co-founder and director of product development at Lead Like Jesus. He is a co-author of several books including *Leadership by the Book* with Ken Blanchard and Bill Hybels and *Lead Like Jesus: Lessons from the Greatest Leadership Role Model of All Time* with Ken Blanchard. Phil and his wife Jane Kinnaird Hodges live in Southern California.

Used by permission of Lead Like Jesus, a non-profit ministry committed to inspiring and equipping people to Lead Like Jesus. For more information, visit **www.leadlikejesus.com**.

PURPOSE MATTERS

Joy at Work is Possible

By Dennis W. Bakke

According to the subtitle of Dennis Bakke's book *Joy at Work*, readers will discover "a revolutionary approach to fun on the job." And at the heart of that revolution is service. As the co-founder and later president and CEO of The AES Corporation, Bakke puts his principles in play in the real world every day. As the book's jacket says, "*Joy at Work* offers a model for the 21st-century company that treats its people with respect, gives them unprecedented responsibility, and holds them strictly accountable—because it's the right thing to do." Talk about revolutionary!

The historic Chesapeake & Ohio Canal towpath runs along the Potomac River for 184 miles from Washington, D.C. to Cumberland, Maryland. In Washington's Georgetown neighborhood, a commemorative plaque gives credit to George Washington for having inspired the canal. Long before he became our first president, he came up with the idea of building a series of locks around the falls just north of Washington that were blocking commercial navigation. He formed the Patowmack Co., a profit-making corporation with investors, to carry out his scheme.

> When a company gives a high priority to serving society, its employees are energized.

What was Washington's primary motivation for starting the company? To make money for himself? To make money for investors? To make a name for himself? To test his engineering skills? To open the river to navigation for the betterment of Maryland and Virginia and their citizens? From what I have read of Washington, I suspect his purpose was primarily to improve navigation and only secondarily to make profits.

I have learned that one measure of a good society is that it makes doing good deeds easy and makes bad behavior difficult. Shouldn't a company be the same way?

During the past several centuries, large organizations could choose from a wide variety of missions, goals, and purposes.

. . . . .

Capitalists tend to assume that the primary purpose of a company is making profits for shareholders. This mission is besmirched by some executives who use their enterprises to make themselves rich, powerful, and profligate, or all three. In the old Soviet Union, most large organizations had yet a different mission. They were primarily a means of carrying out state policy. In the United States, the rhetoric and behavior of some government leaders suggest they believe the primary purpose of profit-making companies is to generate tax revenues to fund government programs. Other government officials believe businesses exist to create jobs. Finally, some not-for-profit organizations write lofty mission statements about helping society, without any reference to their own economic activities.

People tend to act in ways that are consistent with their personal goals. Similarly, a company's primary purpose—the real one, which isn't necessarily the one written in official documents or etched on wall plaques—guides its actions and decisions.

If board members and senior executives react with enthusiasm when the stock price goes up and turn grim when it drops, the organization's uppermost priority quickly becomes clear to its top executives. Did the goal of maintaining a high stock price or increasing profits lead some Enron officials to bend or break the rules? I can't say for certain, but I do know that goals and missions tend to shape the behavior of organizations and the people in them.

Nineteenth-century philosopher and economist John Stuart Mill said, "Those only are happy who have their minds trained on some object other than their own happiness—on the happiness of others... on the importance of mankind, even on some act or pursuit followed not as a means for profits, but as in itself an ideal."

Selecting a mission is crucial because it becomes an organization's definition of success. If a company chooses as its primary goal "adding value for shareholders," then success is typically defined by stock price. If a publicly traded company chooses the goal of creating long-term value for shareholders, success would probably be measured by stock price plus cash dividends paid. Jim Collins, for example, used stock price appreciation over 15 years to separate the "good" companies from "great" companies in his book *Good to Great*. Unfortunately, stock price appreciation is, at best, an incomplete definition of greatness. At worst, it is misleading or even dangerous because it encourages executives to make decisions that are not in the overall interests of the company or society.

If a company states that its main goal is providing good jobs and employee satisfaction, growth of the workforce will probably

define success. If a firm's goal is providing a certain vaccine to children, it will most likely measure itself by how many children it inoculates. If an organization decides that its primary goals are to act with integrity and create a great working environment, it will grade itself according to how well it achieves those intangibles.

Every organization has a unique mission. Still, every modern, progressive, and socially responsible organization should strive to achieve three goals:

- To serve society with specified services or products;
- To operate in an economically sustainable manner;
- To achieve these results while rigorously adhering to a defined set of ethical principles and shared values.

The goal of meeting a need in society should be central to every organization incorporated by the state. Most firms and the people who work in them acknowledge that their organization exists to do something useful for society. Unfortunately, the current fad of putting shareholder value at the forefront of mission statements has made serving society a secondary goal, at least for many publicly traded corporations. Many executives forget that "value" doesn't necessarily have a dollar sign in front of it.

Some companies seem to exist only for profits. Selling a product becomes the means to that end. In my opinion, a much better case can be made for reversing the means and ends. The end should be selling a product, and the means to keep doing so should be making a profit.

Both investor-owned and nonprofit organizations have been given special status by the state, with associated rights and responsibilities. Both types of organizations exist to manage resources in such a way that a useful product or service will result. Serving society is an organization's main reason for existing. This is why I prefer the words "serving" and "stewardship" to "selling" and "management." The distinction in language makes clear that employees are guardians of resources, not owners. In the workplace, I make no distinction between "managers" or "management" and other employees. All employees are managers; all managers are employees. All are stewards. This is the ethos I tried to instill at AES, as articulated in our goal of making "every person a business person."

The manager/employee is a caretaker. "This is not mine, but I will steward it as if it were" is the proper perspective of every person who works in a moneymaking operation. "Serving" conveys an element of humility that is absent from "selling." A manager's work should be of service to someone else. Service not only helps an enterprise succeed; it also satisfies the altruistic impulse that is in all of us.

The concept of service is crucial to the creation of a joyful workplace. As I've already mentioned, people want to be part of something greater than themselves. They want to do something that makes a positive difference in the world. Most employees do not consider making a profit for shareholders, or even making money for themselves, sufficient to satisfy this goal. My hope was that the people at AES would be motivated primarily by the satisfaction of meeting the electricity needs of others, not by a desire to make profits or to fulfill the requirements of their jobs. One AES person described this as "love in work clothes."

When a company gives a high priority to serving society, its employees are energized. At AES, our people took satisfaction from being stewards, and many became passionate about their work. They incorporated as their own the organization's goal to serve society. Most did whatever it took to ensure that the company accomplished this goal.

There is another argument for making serving society the cornerstone purpose of every business. It is nothing less than the survival of private enterprise. I fear that free capitalist societies will one day reject their own systems if economic gain is the only goal of business. Sooner or later, societies will demand an end to the selfishness that in recent years has motivated so many companies, shareholders, and senior executives. Corporations exist at the sufferance of society and consequently must have a broader and more meaningful purpose than simply making money.

L@W

Dennis W. Bakke (**www.dennisbakke.com**) graduated from the University of Puget Sound, Harvard Business School, and the National War College. He co-founded The AES Corporation in 1981 and served as its president and CEO from 1994 to 2002. He is now president and CEO of Imagine Schools, a company that operates elementary and secondary (K-12) charter schools in 10 states. He and his wife Eileen live in Virginia.

Adapted from Joy@Work: A Revolutionary Approach to Fun on the Job, *copyright © 2005 by Dennis W. Bakke, PVG. Used by permission.*

Dennis Bakke's Top 10 Steps Toward Joy at Work

1. When given the opportunity to use our ability to reason, make decisions, and take responsibility for our actions, we experience joy at work.

2. The purpose of business is not to maximize profits for shareholders *but* should be to steward our resources to serve the world in an economically sustainable way.

3. Attempt to create the most fun workplace in the history of the world.

4. Eliminate management, organization charts, job descriptions, and hourly wages.

5. Fairness means treating everybody differently.

6. Principles and values must guide all decisions.

7. Put other stakeholders (shareholders, customers, suppliers, etc.) equal to or above yourself.

8. Everyone must get advice before making a decision. If you don't seek advice, "you're fired."

9. A "good" decision should make all the stakeholders unhappy because no individual or group got all they wanted.

10. Lead with passion, humility, and love.

Toolbox

What Can You Give?

By Mark Sanborn

People who want to make a positive difference in the world around them often wish to give of their time, expertise, money, and skills.

Nonetheless, giving, for many people, is harder than it first appears. *USA Today* recently published a poll that asked people to finish the line, "I'd give more, but ..." The results?

> **84 percent** said they doubted their donation would be put to good use
> **80 percent** said job demands left them no time to participate
> **79 percent** said they had no excess income to give
> **70 percent** said family commitments consumed their extra time

From the responses above, do you recognize your own reason to give less of yourself that you'd like?

So, why do people give of themselves?

Giving teaches us to look beyond ourselves. It breaks down our preoccupation with "self," our absorption with how do "I" look, and how do others perceive me. It reminds us that we are part of a larger community, and that our navel is not the center of the universe.

Giving teaches us to be of greater service in helping others. Giving is an art. That requires practice. After all, what is the point of having physical and emotional reserves if you don't share them?

Giving makes the world a better place. Capitalism can be a great force for good. Having a generous spirit is an even

stronger source for good. Together they make a powerful combination.

Giving makes us feel good. We don't do good because we feel good. We feel good because we do good.

Remember, there are many ways to give. One easy way to give is to donate money. It's not hard to identify worthwhile charities and non-profits that do an efficient job of putting the funds they receive to good use. If you're concerned that a donation won't be used properly, consider getting personally involved in the organization that you're donating money to as a way of tracking its use. Or fund your own project. Enlist your employer as a sponsor. Many organizations match dollars, and some make time available for community service.

If you don't have extra money to give, you can give of your time, expertise, or skills. However you give—of your money, time or talents—you help make the world a better place.

L@W

Mark Sanborn is president of Sanborn & Associates, Inc., (**www.marksanborn.com**) an idea studio for leadership development. He is an internationally recognized speaker and author of the bestselling book *The Fred Factor: How Passion In Your Work and Life Can Turn the Ordinary Into the Extraordinary.*

Excerpted from You Don't Need a Title to be a Leader: How Anyone, Anywhere Can Make a Positive Difference by *Mark Sanborn, © September 2006, Currency.* (**www.YouDontNeedaTitle.com**)

TOOLBOX | BRAVE HEART

Having a Brave Heart at Work

By Randy Kilgore

"You have bled with Wallace, now bleed with me!"

In this stirring scene from the movie *Braveheart*, Robert the Bruce heads a Scottish army still mourning the death of William Wallace. With these words, even members of movie audiences were ready to jump out of their seats and join the battle.

What is it about humankind that makes us able to offer our lives for ideas of justice and freedom, but fails us when called upon to represent our true King, Jesus Christ? It is largely, I think, because we fail to see our routine daily efforts as part of the "living sacrifice" Paul calls us to in the text from Romans. We must commit ourselves not merely to surviving in the work culture that feeds our family, but to minister there, perhaps even to shape that culture.

But how? Where do we start? First, seek out other believers in your workplace and build relationships with them. An employer once told me he could tell when two of his employees were in love by the "electricity between them." He continued, "I don't sense love between you Christians; you shoot your wounded!"

Christians are often defined not by what binds them together, but rather by what separates them. The hope that is in us (Christ Jesus) shines ever brighter when bound to others with that same hope! While it's true even one person can make a difference in a culture, it's equally true a team of people often have better success in accomplishing difficult tasks.

Consider these five advantages to knowing and respecting other Christians in the workplace:

- We are able to fellowship, offering encouragement steeped not only in our common Savior, but also in our common understanding of the setting where God calls us to work.

- We are able to pray for each other with greater insight than are people outside that workplace.

- We may be able to seek counsel from, and offer counsel to, each other on matters relating to the particular department or company where we work.

- We are able to hold each other accountable in ways pastors, friends, and family members cannot during the workday.

- There may be opportunities for us to coalesce in shaping or influencing the work culture.

Our world has ample evidence of the bonds of firefighters and other professions. It is time for you and me to show the bond of the believers, who hear Christ's words in John 14:1: "...(you) believe in God, believe also in Me."

Like the Scottish warriors, may we be moved by His mercy to become living sacrifices every minute of our day.

L@W

Randy Kilgore is workplace chaplain and senior writer for Marketplace Network, Inc. (**www.marketplacenetwork.com**) a ministry to career-minded Christians headquartered in Boston. He writes a weekly devotion for working Christians, *Marketplace Moments,* and is the author of a six-book series of Bible studies entitled *"30 Moments Christians Face in the Workplace".*

Reprinted by permission from Talking About God In the 21st Century Marketplace *by Randy Kilgore, © 2003.*

Be joyful always; pray continually; give thanks in all circumstances, for this is God's will for you in Christ Jesus.

1 Thessalonians 5:16-18 (NIV)

BETH LUDLUM

Beth Ludlum is the Manager of National Partnerships for the Points of Light Foundation and Volunteer Center National Network (**www.PointsofLight.org**). The mission of the Foundation, which has been recognized by President George W. Bush as a leader in volunteerism, is to engage more people and resources more effectively in volunteer service to help solve serious social problems.

A Point of Light

Prior to joining the Points of Light Foundation in 2005, my work included interning in the office of Sen. Pat Roberts (Republican, Kansas) and teaching English at a university in northeast China. This variety of experiences provided me with insight into what I wanted to do and gave me a new view on the world and on America, which has continually proven useful in my work.

The spirit of service I learned from my family and church is also a highlight of my current workplace and greatly directs my life outside of work. Since arriving in D.C., I have taught English as a second language through my church and tutored children at a local homeless shelter.

A Strong Network

Education has played a huge role in my life. I have a B.S. in Agriculture Communications from Kansas State University. I am currently working on a Master's in Theological Studies at Wesley Theological Seminary. Although taking evening and weekend classes is sometimes difficult, I find that my studies continually equip me to grow and minister in my church, work, and relationships.

Although I am single, community is essential to me. In the area, I have many close friends, a sister, and three great roommates. I have found that by regularly making time to share meals, particularly breakfasts and dinners, I am able to maintain strong relationships with these people in spite of being busy.

A Strong Faith

Primarily, I believe that my faith should be exemplified through my attitude toward work and my co-workers. With God's help, I work "as unto the Lord," asking God for the motivation, vision, and attitude to direct and advance the work that I do. Each day, I also work closely with co-workers, constituents, and the public, and I pray that I might glorify God through those interactions.

Sharing my faith is always very important. To paraphrase Mother Theresa, sometimes sharing requires the use of words, and sometimes it doesn't. My co-workers all know that I am committed to Christ, and that makes a difference in our interactions. I try to make myself available to those who are having struggles or challenges, personally or on the job. I pray with my co-workers when the opportunity arises. I work with a nearby church that provides lunchtime Bible studies and I encourage my co-workers to come with me.

A Strong Commitment

I try to honor God in all of these ways, but especially through my attitude. I have discovered how easy it is to complain or gossip about work or co-workers, and I try to avoid negative talk. However, I also believe that I honor God by helping my co-workers to remember that this is just a job. We should do our work to the best of our ability, but our work is not what defines us. It is a gift from God, but there are things in our lives that are much more important.

No matter what happens, God must come first in every aspect of our lives. I think that life is a continual struggle to climb down from the altar of "self" and give everything up to God. Work is no different. Success will look different to each and every person, depending on what God has called them to do. I believe that it is important to keep work in perspective; with God first, everything else will fall into place.

L@W

He who calls you is faithful; he will surely do it.
1 Thessalonians 5:24 (ESV)

SHELLEY GIGLIO

Shelley Giglio is the manager of sixstepsrecords (**www.sixstepsrecords.com**), a worship record label that is home to artists/worshippers Chris Tomlin, Charlie Hall, David Crowder*Band and Matt Redman. Shelley and her husband, Louie, launched sixstepsrecords in 2000. They are also the founders of Passion Conferences (**www.268generation.com**), a movement among college students that challenges students to live for God's glory and to spread His fame to all the earth. In relation to working with her husband, Shelley comments, "we work together, play together, live together ... it never gets old!"

Preparation for Passion
I have one of those roles with Passion that continually evolves ... at the moment I lead the team that is responsible for creating great worship and exporting it to the world in many different formats.

After I received my bachelor's degree in business from Baylor, my first job out of college was at an Egyptian-Arabian horse farm outside of Waco, Texas. I know ... you are thinking you can definitely see how that prepared me for what I do now! Funny, huh?

I have also worked in the insurance world. Amazingly all of these roles have prepared me to be better in the position I currently hold.

A Passion for Work
In every way I look to honor God with my work. I want to live a life of distinction and focus. I'm determined to make God huge in my little part of His story.

We've received various awards through the years, but most recently we received the Gospel Music Association Impact Award for 2006 for the organization or people who are having an impact in the world of Christian Music.

My faith and my work are the exact same thing. I try to do all things with God in view, making much of Him is what I am called to do here on earth. Through my work is the perfect place to let Him shine.

It is pretty comforting to know that the same God who has called us into action is the God who will work through us to complete it. Basically, it's up to Him on all fronts — we just make ourselves available ... smart, smart God!

A Passion for People
The people I work with are believers for the most part, but sharing God at work is still so important: encouraging believers to live up to the potential that God has placed in us is vital ... and continually reminding ourselves of what we are here for. Outside of work, sharing my faith is overt — it's the crux of who I am, so that comes out!

It is possible to work well and honor well. It's the little choices that make honoring God possible: making the right decisions ... being wise about the investments of our time ... living uniquely and in the abundance of God that has been given to us.

The better we work and the better the quality of our work, the more people notice and start to inquire as to the difference. It's nice that God is central to that whole process ... He ends up getting credit instead of us.

L@W

EXECUTIVE SUMMARY
Final Thoughts On Defining Serving

SERVING SETS US FREE — free from selfishness, free from our ego, free from isolation. Serving expands us from the smallness of self-interest and liberates us from the shackles of selfishness.

In the marketplace, we are bombarded with me-first messaging. The drive to get ahead is embedded within our nature. Serving takes sacrifice, and sacrifice runs contrary to our instincts.

Servant leadership forces us to die to self. Instead of climbing the corporate ladder, we stoop and wash the feet of those around us.

IN THIS LESSON WE'VE LEARNED:

▷ Serving is the art and act of focusing on someone else's interests, not my own.

▷ If we are to follow God on our journey of life, we need to make a decision to move from a self-serving heart to a servant's heart.

▷ Servant leadership begins with a clear and compelling vision of the future that excites passion and commitment.

▷ On a daily basis, effective servant leaders recalibrate and renew their commitment to serve rather than to be served.

▷ Servant leaders are able to view their own concerns and preoccupations — whatever they may be — as small compared to the brokenness and needs around them.

▷ It is easy in our "busy-ness" to not see opportunities to serve. The power of selfless observation must be learned or our self-absorption will blind us.

▷ It is impossible to be truly converted to God without thereby being converted to our neighbor.

▷ The habit of serving doesn't develop on its own accord. A life of service springs from intentional initiative, the readiness to adjust our agendas, and the willingness to sacrifice our self-interests.

▷ Our servant leadership will have a small scope if we refuse to venture outside our comfort zones.

▷ God is at work 24/7 all over our world, filling His followers with grace, mercy, and power to reclaim and redeem this broken planet through lives of service.

▷ When Jesus called us to take up our cross and follow Him, He was telling us in graphic terms that following Him would require sacrifice, hardship, and death to the self-focus inside of us all.

▷ Work can shrink us down to a self-centered existence, or it can open us to the larger world around us. The difference is our willingness to serve.

▷ Our service will not always be noticed or appreciated and will often be taken for granted. At times, our service will be sweaty, tiring, and stretching. Yet by investing in others, we are enriched; in losing our lives, we experience life most fully.

▷ Servant leadership isn't a detour from our more meaningful work; it's our central assignment ... and the beginning of true freedom and purpose.

▷ God intends for our service to be more than an isolated act or program. He beckons us to a lifestyle of service.

▷ As managers and employers, we ought to view ourselves as caretakers. Company resources are not ours, but we should steward them as if they were.

Notes

NEXT STEPS

In our time-starved society, we are much more likely to donate our money than our minutes. You have to be intentional to fight that in your own life.

→ Look for a volunteer opportunity that allows you to do something you enjoy at a church, charity, or shelter this coming Saturday.

→ Once a week for a month, visit a nursing home, prison, or orphanage. Showing the forgotten that you care may seem to be a simple act, but you'd be surprised at its significance.

→ In your daily schedule, set aside 15 minutes to serve a co-worker. During this time, focus your energy and attention on how you can make his or her day easier. If no practical ways of assistance come to mind, take the time to write a sincere note of encouragement to your co-worker.

→ Find an untidy common area in your workplace. Maybe it's the microwave oven in the break room, the office-supplies cabinet, or the storage closet. Take initiative to serve everyone by thoroughly cleaning and organizing that area.

→ On a note card, write out Philippians 2:3-5 and Mark 10:43-45.
Each morning before heading to work, recite these verses. Then, think of one act of service you could perform during the day. Jot it down and make it a point to do it.

CHARACTER@WORK

Character: The sum of my behaviors, public and private, consistently arranged across the spectrum of my life

From the Inside Out

YOUR CHARACTER SPEAKS VOLUMES FROM DEEP WITHIN

By Stephen R. Graves

Do you equate math with character? Perhaps you should. *Integer* is a mathematical term for a whole number — no decimals, no fractions, just a straightforward number. What you see is what you get. It's undivided. It's whole.

The word *integrity* comes from the same root as *integer*. A man or woman of integrity is a "whole" person — a person of authenticity and transparency. A person of integrity lives out in deed what he or she believes in the heart and the head. That is to say, a person of integrity is undivided. What you see is what you get. Don Galer defined integrity this way: "what we do, what we say, and what we say we do." The key is consistency between all three.

The word for "character" in the Bible comes from the Greek term describing an engraving instrument. The picture is of an artist who wears a groove on a metal plate by repeatedly etching the same place with a sharp tool. After repeated strokes, an image begins to take shape. My character is forged as a set of distinctive marks that, when taken together, draw a portrait of who I really am. Everyone has character and it can be described as bad or good, shifty or sturdy, sordid or sterling.

You've seen rocks in a river-cut or canyon that have been etched and engraved by water and wind. No single wave, no day of wind can make any discernible difference in the face of the rock. But centuries of waves and wind make indelible marks. So it is with character. Everything we do — every thought, every choice — is a wave with ripple effects. It is easier to see the immediate effect on others than it is to see the consequence on the rock core of our own character. Yet if you will look at the contours of your life, you will clearly see the grooves shaped by the pattern of your past.

Every time you make a decision, you cut a groove. Every time you react to a crisis, you cut a groove. When you hold your tongue and practice self-control or when you let it run loose and speak your mind, you are carving your character. When you say yes or no to a reckless temptation, stand up to peer pressure, hold the line on truth, or return kindness for cruelty, you are cutting the pattern of your character. Anthony Robbins was right on the mark when he said, "It is in your moments of decision that your destiny is shaped."

Hooking Up the Heart

The grooves of character that mark us most deeply, however, are those that are made when no one is looking. These moves of our minds and hearts tend to make the deepest ruts — for good or ill. That is why Jesus' message to His followers almost always focused on hooking up the internal attitude with the external action.

You might say that the Sermon on the Mount was Jesus' orientation seminar for His disciples. He laid out a whole new way of thinking about righteousness: "Unless your righteousness exceeds the righteousness of the scribes and Pharisees, you will by no means enter the kingdom of heaven" (Matthew 5:20 NKJV). That must have come as a shock to the disciples. Who could out-righteousness the scribes and Pharisees? But it quickly became apparent that Jesus wasn't talking about the externalities of the scribes and Pharisees' religiosity. He was talking about their hearts. And there the religious professionals of Jesus' day weren't so impressive. At another time, Jesus compared them to whitewashed tombs — gleaming moral: of or relating To principles of right and wrong (2) conforming To a Standard of right behavior

morality: Ties To moral conduct

Question? is the absence of bad behavior that makes someone good, or the presence of good behavior

white on the outside, but full of rot within. Or to put it in modern-day terms, they constantly ran their cars through the carwash to keep the exteriors clean, while the interiors remained a rolling trash heap.

True morality, Jesus preached, is a matter of the heart. It's good that you've never murdered anybody. But if you've ever been angry with a person without cause, you're guilty. You've never committed adultery? Good. But if you've ever lusted, you've already committed adultery in your heart. It's our natural tendency to ask for a list of rules to follow — actions we can perform or avoid, checklists by which we can judge ourselves … and others. That's what the scribes and Pharisees did, and their rules grew so complex that nobody but the scribes and Pharisees could ever hope to follow them.

Matt 5:17

Jesus wasn't having any of that. It's not that He came to abolish all those laws; He came to complete them. However, the laws of the Old Testament were only signposts, not the destination as the scribes and Pharisees seemed to believe. The religious professionals were obsessed with food and drink, with what was clean and unclean, what would defile and what was okay. But Jesus knew that holiness comes from the inside out: "Not what goes into the mouth defiles the man, but what comes out of the mouth, this defiles a man" (Matthew 15:11 NKJV). Sin and righteousness both are simply the overflow of what's inside a person. To put it another way, "doing" always follows "being."

consequence (all sin is serious)

When a friend or colleague falls into serious sin, it often feels like a sudden thing. The guy's an upstanding citizen, everything seems to be rocking along okay, and suddenly he's sleeping with his secretary or suddenly it turns out he's been embezzling.

But sin is never sudden. A person might suddenly get caught. He might even suddenly act on an urge. But there has already been something happening on the inside before the sin makes itself obvious on the outside. Our actions are the overflow of our hearts. To be a person of integrity and character is to be the same person inside and out.

Errant Brush Strokes

True character doesn't mean you have a perfect record. None of us is perfect. It is not perfection, but the overall pattern, that is the point. Painters have at least one wrong stroke on the canvas by the time their paintings are done. Writers used to go through bottles of Wite-Out® until someone invented the delete button.

King David was no exception. He needed Wite-Out, just like the rest of us. He had a wild, misguided stroke on his character canvas. There are two opposite reports that give us a conflicting view of the life of David. One is the comment that David was "a man after God's own heart." The other is the fact that David committed adultery with Bathsheba and killed her husband to cover it up. How could David be characterized as a man with a heart for God when he was a murderous adulterer?

We all would agree that David botched his canvas. He stumbled and failed in a big way. Nevertheless, when we see David in the book of Acts, it is not his failure that is remembered. In chapter 13 we are told, "I have found David, the son of Jesse, a man after my own heart" (verse 22 NKJV). Verse 36 says David "served God's purpose in his generation." So it was not the rogue brushstroke of adultery chronicled in the book of Acts. Yes, he sinned, and yes, he stumbled. But one stumble is not a groove, and my character is bigger than a slip and fall — even a major one. It is the pattern of my life that defines character. For David that overall pattern was a man who pursued the heart of God.

if you don't admit your error you may repeat it.

I'm not excusing or ignoring the blotches on David's character. It took him almost a year to come to grips with the right steps of recovery. He had to carry some consequences of his sin the rest of his life. But there is a difference between slipping once and repeating the behavior over and over, creating a groove in your character. As columnist Marilyn vos Savant said, "An error becomes a mistake when we refuse to admit it." Proverbs 24:16 agrees: "Though a righteous man falls seven times, he rises again" (NIV). David got back up. Character is not perfect, but when it falls, it gets back up.

Matt 6:14+15

Repenting Your Way to Better Character

How do you build better, stronger character? Lesson One from David is to learn how to practice genuine repentance and accept genuine forgiveness. Many of David's psalms — Psalm 51 in particular — chronicle David's prayers of confession and his thanksgiving for God's forgiveness.

We must realize that we *are* going to mess up. It is what we do with that mess-up that cuts the groove in our character. Abraham Lincoln once said, "My great concern is not whether you have failed, but whether you are content with your failure." Do you cover up failure, ignore it, deny it? Or do you admit it, walk toward it and embrace personal change?

THE **GROOVES OF CHARACTER** THAT MARK US **MOST DEEPLY** ARE THOSE THAT ARE MADE WHEN **NO ONE IS LOOKING.**

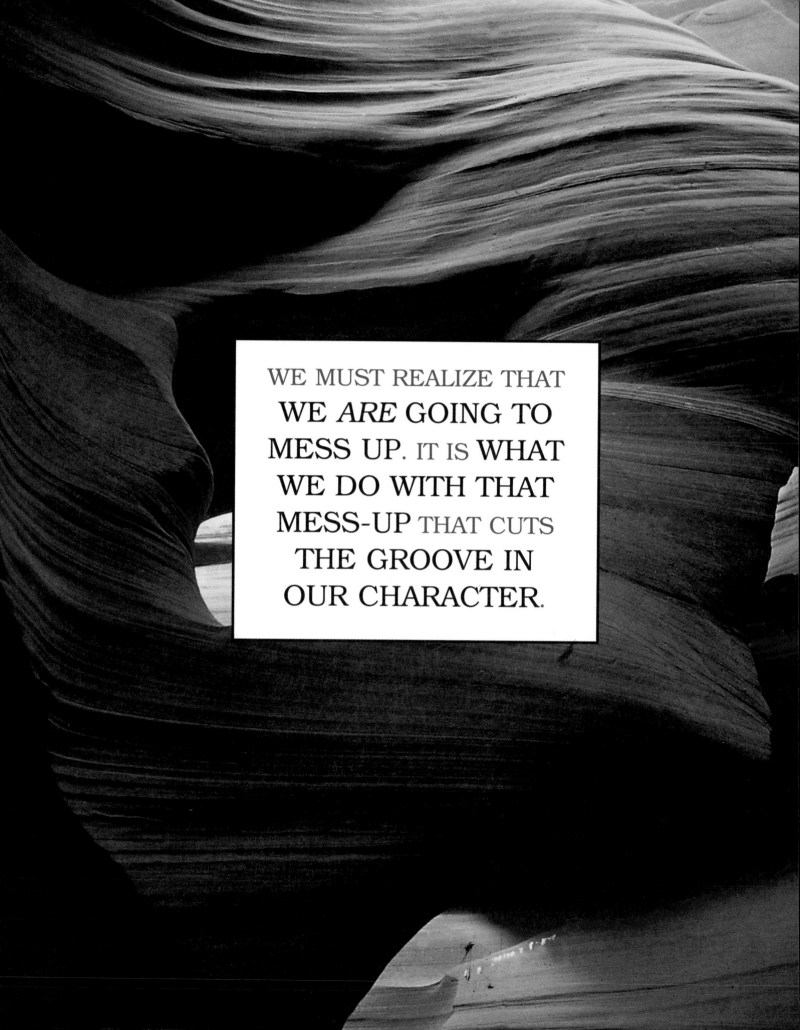

WE MUST REALIZE THAT WE *ARE* GOING TO MESS UP. IT IS WHAT WE DO WITH THAT MESS-UP THAT CUTS THE GROOVE IN OUR CHARACTER.

Oswald Sanders pointed out that "How men react *after* they have been sifted by Satan is a revelation of their true character. For over a year and maybe longer, David remained in stubborn unwillingness to confess his sin. But ultimately the enormity of his sin was matched by the depth of his repentance." Despite David's serious sins, the way he dealt with those sins and with his relationship to God and with other people gives us a picture of a man after God's own heart.

Over-manage Your Achilles   *over-view*

Homer's *Iliad* tells the story of Achilles, one of the most famous warriors of Greek mythology. At his birth, his mother dipped him in the River Styx in order to make him invulnerable to his enemy's spears and arrows. Her planned worked, except for one thing: she held baby Achilles by the heel to dip him in the river, so that heel never touched the magic waters. In that one spot, he was as vulnerable as anybody else. He met his end when an enemy's arrow struck Achilles' heel.

Each of us has an Achilles heel. It is crucial to our character that we know what it is and how to protect ourselves from its weakness. It has been my observation that we all struggle with one or two sins of the heart that are unique to our makeup. Although we are all theoretically vulnerable to all kinds of sin, there is almost always one sin of the heart that persistently stalks us.

That sin is different for everybody. As Oswald Sanders observed, "David's sensitive and artistic nature laid him open to temptation that would have bypassed one of a different texture." This was David's Achilles' heel. What is yours? Know your Achilles' heel. Then manage it. Build boundaries to protect yourself from your own weakness.

It's Yours to Build and Keep

Governing your character is different from knowing your gift mix and internal wiring. Those were built into you by God when He created you. You are gifted and wired to be able to do certain things incredibly well. You are attracted to certain tasks and repelled by others. No matter how hard you work at improving your ability in certain areas, you may never be able to do them as well as someone else who is gifted and wired in different ways. You do have control, however, over your character. You can improve it, modify it, or compromise it. In a world where we seem to have little control, we call the shots when it comes to whether or not our character is diminished. Job said to his friends, "I will not deny my integrity. I will maintain my

righteousness and never let go of it; my conscience will not reproach me as long as I live" (Job 27:5–6 NIV).

If my character goes down, I am the only one who can be blamed. No other person apart from me can allow my character to be compromised. The first time I read this passage from Job, it hit me like a thunderbolt. I cannot blame anyone for my character erosion but myself. Nobody can steal it from me. Only I can give up my character.

Character, it has been said, means doing the right thing even when nobody is watching. Character changes the way you do your work. In his book *The Call*, Os Guinness articulates the furniture-making philosophy of the Shakers, whose handiwork has outlasted them by hundreds of years:

> "Make every product better than it has ever been done before. Make the parts you cannot see as well as the parts you can see. Use only the best of materials, even for the most everyday items. Give the same attention to the smallest detail as you do to the largest. Design every item you make to last forever."

"Make the parts you can't see as well as the parts you can see." You couldn't describe Character@Work any more concisely than that.

L@W

Dr. Stephen R. Graves is a highly sought business coach and life guide for entrepreneurs and leaders desiring to successfully make it to the finish line of life. In 1991, he co-founded the Cornerstone Group, a company built to integrate biblical wisdom and business excellence. He and his wife Karen have three children.

This article is based on concepts drawn from Life@Work by John C. Maxwell, Stephen R. Graves, and Thomas G. Addington, published by Thomas Nelson, Inc.

FROM THE INSIDE OUT

FOR GROUP DISCUSSION

Prior to your small group meeting time, read and reflect on the Life@Work Study article you just read. Use these questions and journal pages to reflect and respond to the ideas presented. Be ready to share your thoughts at your small group gathering.

Note to small group leaders: You can download a full Leader's Guide at www.lifeatworkgroupzine.com.

> ▶ *Don Galer defined integrity this way: "what we do, what we say, and what we say we do." The key is consistency between all three.*
>   Why is it so important for there to be consistency in what we do, say, and say we do? Do you consider yourself a person of integrity? Do you think others consider you that way? Why or why not?
>
> ▶ *True morality, Jesus preached, is a matter of the heart. ... It's our natural tendency to ask for a list of rules to follow — actions we can perform or avoid, checklists by which we can judge ourselves ... and others.*
>   If you used the 10 Commandments as your checklist, how are you doing with true morality? If you used your heart — your true thoughts and feelings — how are you doing then?
>
> ▶ *"Though a righteous man falls seven times, he rises again." (Proverbs 24:16)*
>   When was a time you fell? Does this verse, and the story of David's ability to "bounce back" from his sinful actions to be seen as a man after God's heart, give hope to you? Or do you feel like you can't be forgiven? Explain.
>
> ▶ *Abraham Lincoln once said, "My great concern is not whether you have failed, but whether you are content with your failure."*
>   Do you cover up your failure, ignore it, or deny it? Or do you admit it, walk toward it, and embrace personal change? Which way is easier? What failure or sin do you need to genuinely repent of and receive God's forgiveness? How can you begin to more readily admit your failure or sin?
>
> ▶ What is your Achilles' heel? What boundaries are building to protect yourself from this weakness? Who are you talking with honestly about your Achilles' heel? Does it encourage you to know that you have control over your character?

A COACH FOR LIFE

UCLA's **John Wooden** Built a Successful Career on Fundamentals

By anyone's definition, John Wooden is a success. As a player, he won a high-school state championship in Indiana, where he was a three-time all-state player. He then won a national championship in college at Purdue, where he was a three-time all-America player. He was named the collegiate player of the year in 1932.

After 11 years as a high school coach, he moved to the college ranks. After two winning seasons at Indiana State, he was hired by UCLA in 1948. He would coach the Bruins until 1975, winning 620 games, including an NCAA record of 88 consecutive games. His teams won 10 national championships, including seven in a row from 1966-73.

John Wooden was enshrined in the Naismith Basketball Hall of Fame—twice! First for his playing in 1961 and then for his coaching in 1973.

When John Maxwell, Tom Addington, and Steve Graves sat down for Life@Work with the man known simply as Coach, their discussion started in an obvious place:

L@W
Long ago, you created a Pyramid of Success. What is your definition of success?

COACH WOODEN
In my early days of teaching English, I was a little unhappy with what parents seemed to consider success. If the students didn't make an A or B, there were many parents who would make them feel that they, or the teacher, had failed. I didn't think that was proper. I don't think the good Lord created us all equal as far as intelligence is concerned, any more than we're the same in size or appearance. And I wanted to come up with something that I hoped would make me a better teacher and give those under my supervision something to which to aspire, other than just a higher mark in the classroom or perhaps more points in some athletic endeavor. I wanted to come up with my own definition, and three things entered into it.

My father, when I was in grade school, tried to teach me and my brothers to **never try to be better than someone else**. You have no control over that. Another was to **learn from others**, because you can learn something that you didn't know. The last and most important element is **never cease trying to be the best you can be**.

Then I ran across a very simple verse—I love poetry—and this little verse said, "That God's footstool to confess a poor soul now then, bowed his head. 'I failed,' he cried. The Master said, 'Thou didst thou best. That is success.'" And from those things, I coined my own definition of success:

> **Success is peace of mind attained only through self-satisfaction, knowing you made the effort to do the best of what you're capable.**

L@W
How important do you think it is to have a correct definition of success?

COACH WOODEN
I think you need something. Don't be thinking about scoring somebody. Let that be a byproduct. This is success: when you have that peace within yourself. If you don't have peace with yourself, I don't think you have much of anything, and you're the only one that knows that. It's like character and reputation. Your character is what you are—and you're the only one that really knows that. And your reputation is what you're perceived to be by others, and the two are not always the same. So, I think it's very important that you have a goal, in a sense, of what you're trying to achieve.

L@W
Sustained success is a little harder than a one-time flash of success. Talk about the concept of success over time.

COACH WOODEN
You can't live in the past. Today is the only day that really matters. I tried to get that across to my youngsters. One of the points in the Seven-Point Creed that my father gave me when I graduated from grade school was: **make each day your masterpiece**. You can do nothing about yesterday and you only attract the future by what you do today. So, I tried to teach that and tried to use that. I love poetry and many of my players write me poems. Part of one was,

> "Coach, you're a hunter and a seeker;
> Not for silver or for gold;
> Not for treasure or for pleasure
> Or for anything that's sold.
> You're a connoisseur of living
> As you move along life's way,
> With no worries of tomorrow,
> For you have found today."

You've got to forget the past. You can't live in the past. Just learn from it. Then you can learn what to do and what not to do, from the past.

L@W
Coach, you referenced your father twice so far. Is that where your bedrock beliefs come from?

COACH WOODEN .
Unquestionably. Abraham Lincoln once said, "There's nothing stronger than gentleness." My father had only a high school education, but I think he's one of the most intelligent people I've ever known. Maybe I didn't think so when I was a youngster, but as I look back, he was a good man. He never spoke an ill word of another person. He never used a word of profanity. He gave us sets of rules, in a sense, he said, "Don't whine, don't complain, don't make any excuses—just do the best you can." And he felt that there's a time for play—after the chores and the studies are done. But there is a time for it and you should make a time for it. He was just a very, very wise man.

L@W
Talk a little bit about the wisdom that your father specifically imparted to you when you were a youngster.

COACH WOODEN
He gave me a little card when I graduated from grade school, and all he said was, "Son, try to live up to these." There was a verse by Reverend Henry Van Dyke that said, "Four things a man must learn to do, if he would make his life more true. To think without confusion clearly. To love his fellow man sincerely. To act from honest motives purely. To trust in God and heaven securely."

Then on the other side of the card was a Seven-Point Creed that he used. It said:

> **Be true to yourself**
> **Help others**
> **Drink deeply from good books, especially the Bible**
> **Make friendship a fine art**
> **Make each day your masterpiece**
> **Build a shelter against a rainy day**
> **Give thanks for your blessings and pray for guidance every day**

L@W
That's great, Coach. With these as a basis, how does a leader build a company or a corporate value system?

COACH WOODEN
By giving due credit to those under your supervision. I think a leader must make all those under his or her supervision understand they're working with you, not for you. If you make them feel they're working for you, in my opinion, they'll be there on time and they'll punch in on time and they'll punch out on time. But if they're working with you, they'll go further than that. They'll stay over. They'll be early. They'll do the extra things. **A leader must give others credit.** They must get across that we're going for a common goal, and we have to work together.

L@W
Your players are very important to you and you continue relating to them. You see them, you talk to them. Do you have a system for regularly staying in touch with them?

COACH WOODEN
No system, I would say. I just stay in contact as much as possible with anyone that I've had under my supervision or with whom I have worked. And if they know you care for them, they'll care for you. And I say it's not friendship when they're under your supervision. It becomes friendship after they're out from under your supervision.

L@W
How does a manager or a coach or some other leader balance the soft side of relationship with the harder edge of relationship?

COACH WOODEN
Well, **I think one of the greatest motivations is the pat on the back. But sometimes it has to be a little lower and a little harder. But never personal—never personal.** Let's see if I can recall something that I heard: "Criticism, I agree, does have its proper place. But nothing gives a person more than pure and honest praise."

I think that is true. And I think you establish relationships at practice. That's the important thing. I used to equate our practices with a statement by Cervantes, who said, "The journey is better than the end." Games are the end; practices are the journey. You're not going to reach the end unless you do well in the practice. So, it's the journey that's important. After retiring,

I missed practices. I don't miss games, I don't miss tournaments—I miss practices. That's where you get to know your young men. You establish a rapport, you establish a relationship that's going to be important years after they're gone from the team.

L@W
How do you know, as a coach, when to push somebody out of their comfort zone, in order to improve their performance?

COACH WOODEN
Well, you must remember that they're all different. There's no formula. What works with one, won't necessarily work with another. As I mentioned, some need a pat on the back more, and others need a little lower and a little harder. I have many examples of players on the same team. You have to study those under your supervision. It's so important that you study and know each one and know what button to push for one and know that it has to be something else for a different one.

Treating everybody alike shows partiality. You should give each individual the treatment they earn and deserve. You have to make the decision, and decision-making isn't easy. We're all imperfect and we'll be wrong at times, but I think you're more wrong if you try to treat everybody alike.

L@W
That's an interesting way to look at things. How about competition … is it healthy?

COACH WOODEN
No, not all competition. It could be. I've said that athletics builds character. But it doesn't always. It reveals character more so than it builds it, in my opinion. But in a sense, **life itself is competition and we have to learn to face things and know that there's going to be obstacles and blocks along the road.** We have to know how to react to them. You have to know how to keep trying and so, competition can be good. But it isn't a fight to show I'm better than somebody else. It should be the effort to come as close as possible to your own particular level of competency and you could hope that would be better than others—but you have no control over others.

L@W
So, do you think that everyone can be a success?

COACH WOODEN
I think that is true. It's within ourselves. If you make the effort to do the best of what you're capable and whatever you're trying to do, no one could do more than that. There may be people more gifted. But I know in my teaching of basketball, I've had players that I thought were more successful than some all-Americans I had. That's because I thought they came closer to realizing their full potential.

Coach Wooden, thanks for sharing your wisdom!

L@W

This interview was edited for print.

The Pyramid of Success
John Wooden's Winning Approach to Life

For 14 years, John Wooden worked on what has become known as his Pyramid of Success, which is on display here. In addition to what you see on the Pyramid, we've added thoughts from Coach Wooden's interview with John Maxwell, Tom Addington, and Steve Graves.

"I gave each position a lot of thought—and made a lot of changes through the years. But the first two blocks I chose were the true cornerstones. And if any structure is to have any strength or solidity, it must have a strong foundation— cornerstones that anchor—and mine are industriousness and enthusiasm."

John Wooden

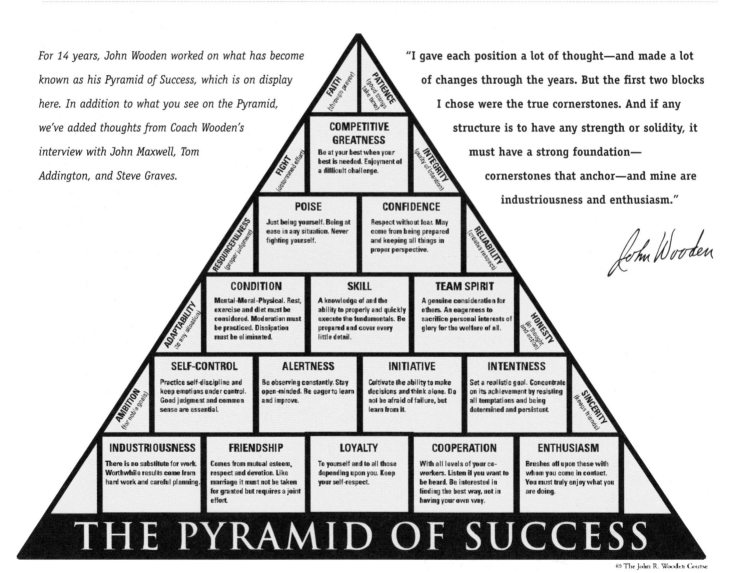

FAITH (through prayer)

PATIENCE (good things take time)

COMPETITIVE GREATNESS
Be at your best when your best is needed. Enjoyment of a difficult challenge.

FIGHT (determined effort)

INTEGRITY (purity of intention)

POISE
Just being yourself. Being at ease in any situation. Never fighting yourself.

CONFIDENCE
Respect without fear. May come from being prepared and keeping all things in proper perspective.

RESOURCEFULNESS (proper judgment)

RELIABILITY (creates respect)

CONDITION
Mental-Moral-Physical. Rest, exercise and diet must be considered. Moderation must be practiced. Dissipation must be eliminated.

SKILL
A knowledge of and the ability to properly and quickly execute the fundamentals. Be prepared and cover every little detail.

TEAM SPIRIT
A genuine consideration for others. An eagerness to sacrifice personal interests of glory for the welfare of all.

ADAPTABILITY (to any situation)

HONESTY (in thought and action)

SELF-CONTROL
Practice self-discipline and keep emotions under control. Good judgment and common sense are essential.

ALERTNESS
Be observing constantly. Stay open-minded. Be eager to learn and improve.

INITIATIVE
Cultivate the ability to make decisions and think alone. Do not be afraid of failure, but learn from it.

INTENTNESS
Set a realistic goal. Concentrate on its achievement by resisting all temptations and being determined and persistent.

AMBITION (for noble goals)

SINCERITY (keeps friends)

INDUSTRIOUSNESS
There is no substitute for work. Worthwhile results come from hard work and careful planning.

FRIENDSHIP
Comes from mutual esteem, respect and devotion. Like marriage it must not be taken for granted but requires a joint effort.

LOYALTY
To yourself and to all those depending upon you. Keep your self-respect.

COOPERATION
With all levels of your co-workers. Listen if you want to be heard. Be interested in finding the best way, not in having your own way.

ENTHUSIASM
Brushes off upon those with whom you come in contact. You must truly enjoy what you are doing.

THE PYRAMID OF SUCCESS

© The John R. Wooden Course

Industriousness

"There is no substitute for work. Sometimes we look for the easy way. And might get by for a spell too. But you're not developing the talents that lie within when you do that. There is no substitute for work."

Enthusiasm

"If you don't enjoy what you're doing, there is no way can you be functioning anywhere near your level of competency — you have to enjoy what you're doing."

Friendship

"Don't take it for granted. You have work at making friendships flourish."

Loyalty

"I believe each and every one of us needs to have someone to whom — and something to which — we must be loyal if we're ever going to come close to realizing our own potential."

Cooperation

"This has always been essential. But now, with the world getting smaller and smaller, we see things happening on the other side of the world as they're happening. That wasn't true in my younger days. As the world gets smaller, it's essential that we get along with others."

Self-Control

"You must maintain self-control in whatever you're doing. Whether it's playing golf, making key decisions, or disciplining someone under your supervision, you must maintain self-control."

Alertness

"Be alert and alive; there's something going on around us all the time from which we can learn. My favorite American, Abraham Lincoln, said he'd never met a person from whom he did not learn something."

Initiative

"Don't be afraid to fail. Goodness gracious, we're all imperfect and we're going to fail on occasions. But we should learn from our failures and not repeat them over and over. But the greatest failure of all is failure to act when action is necessary."

Intentness

"I might have said determination. I might have said persistence. I might have said perseverance. I'm not even sure intentness is in the dictionary. But you have to have goals and you have to be intent on reaching on the goals. Don't give up."

Conditioned

"There are different kinds of conditioning — you have to be conditioned for whatever you're doing. Practice moderation."

Skills

"You must know how to do things. But that's not enough. Even though you may know what to do, you have to be able to do it quickly. You have to be able to do things not only properly, but quickly. It's so essential."

Team Spirit

"Consideration for others is team spirit. I once heard it defined as a willingness to lose oneself for the group, for the welfare of the group. And I liked that, but I had to change one word — drop willingness and insert eagerness. If you're eager to do something, you really want to do it."

Poise

"Just being yourself — that's all. You're not acting. You're not pretending. You're not trying to be something you're not. You are yourself. Therefore, you're going to function on your own particular level of competency."

Confidence

"You can't have confidence unless you're prepared. Failure to prepare is preparing to fail. So, you must have poise and confidence."

Competitive Greatness

"There's joy in being involved in something that is difficult, and there is no great pleasure in doing the easy things. But whatever we're doing, we should do it to the best of our ability — whether it's difficult or not."

"From this last block of the Pyramid, leading up to the apex, I have **patience** on one side and **faith** on the other side. You must have patience. Good things take time, and should. We don't want them to, but they should. And we must have faith. We must believe that things will turn out as they should, providing, of course, that we do what we're capable of doing, to help that become reality. All the blocks below, I think, lead up to this. Remember to have faith and patience — they're essential."

Learn more about the **John R. Wooden Course,** the professional and personal development curriculum based on the principles of legendary basketball coach John Wooden, at **www.woodencourse.com.** Developed in collaboration with Coach Wooden, the course delivers a teachable point-of-view on the most important fundamentals required to develop your players and empower your team to achieve and maintain extraordinary levels of performance.

L@W

FOOLISH OR WISE...
IT'S OUR CHOICE

By Ted Haggard

 Ted Haggard believes that God wants us to be wise, free, and full of power ... and he's got the Scripture passages to back up his argument. Using Paul's letter to the Galatians as his starting point, Haggard also utilizes the wisdom of Proverbs to help argue the case that God gives us the choice to be wise ... or foolish. Wondering what advice readers receive from the president of the National Association of Evangelicals and pastor of a large church in Colorado Springs? The title of the book says it all: *Foolish No More.*

In the spiritual dimension—which impacts everything we think, feel, say, and do—there are clearly marked paths that will result in wise or foolish living. It's up to us. If we want to be foolish no more, we need to take to heart words like these:

You foolish Galatians! Who has bewitched you? Before your very eyes Jesus Christ was clearly portrayed as crucified. I would like to learn just one thing from you: Did you receive the Spirit by observing the law, or by believing what you heard? Are you so foolish? After beginning with the Spirit, are you now trying to attain your goal by human effort? (Galatians 3:1-3)

> In the Bible, the book of Proverbs is a gold mine of information on the topics of foolishness and wisdom.

The Bible has a lot to say about these two ways of life. Decision after decision, large or small, we decide, "Will I be foolish or wise?" Being foolish is more than just saying dumb things to one another when we are angry or frustrated. There really is a state of foolishness—no, it's not California—and it's inside our heads and hearts! Some people, based on an ongoing pattern of how they think and act, are bona-fide, card-carrying, certified fools. On the opposite pole, there are people who make good decisions and do the right thing most of the time. They deserve to be called wise.

How do we know whether we are wise or foolish? Well, we

determine on a daily basis what path we will follow. We must constantly ask ourselves, "Okay, am I gaining wisdom? Is my life getting better? Do I know how to gain wisdom, or am I just living life hoping that good things will happen to me? Do I really want to grow in wisdom and enjoy the life God has planned for me? Is my life random or intentional? God created an orderly universe with wisdom; is my life becoming orderly with wisdom as well?"

In the Bible, the book of Proverbs is a gold mine of information on the topics of foolishness and wisdom. If you will study and apply to your life even the first nine chapters of Proverbs, you will earn the equivalent of a bachelor's degree in wisdom.

In Proverbs, wisdom and folly are personified as two women who call out to a group of people called "the simple." If you are wondering who "the simple" are, well, let's pause for a moment and pull out our picture IDs! This is one club that bars no one based on any social, economic, racial, gender, or religious distinctions. "Y'all come down," is this group's mantra. We're all insiders, so don't be embarrassed by the label. But we "simples" must decide whether to respond to the call of wisdom or the call of folly. We can't just wander through life and hope it turns out okay. We can't be passive. That's about the best way possible to end up at Camp Folly. Proverbs 9 introduces Lady Wisdom first:

> Wisdom has built her house;
> she has hewn out its seven pillars.
> She has prepared her meat and mixed her wine;
> she has also set her table.
> She has sent out her maids, and she calls
> from the highest point of the city.
> "Let all who are simple come in here!"
> she says to those who lack judgment. ...
> "Leave your simple ways and you will live;
> walk in the way of understanding." (verses 1-4,6)

The other female recruiter in Proverbs shows up a few verses later:

> The woman Folly is loud;
> she is undisciplined and without knowledge.
> She sits at the door of her house,

> on a seat at the highest point of the city,
> calling out to those who pass by,
> who go straight on their way.
> "Let all who are simple come in here!"
> she says to those who lack judgment.
> "Stolen water is sweet;
> food eaten in secret is delicious!"
> [She's talking about immoral and other sinful behavior.]
> But little do they know that the dead are there,
> that her guests are in the depths of the grave.
> (verses 13-18)

Please get the picture that Proverbs is painting for us. The simple wander by and hear two voices. Both offer seemingly desirable things. Both are certainly attractive. But Wisdom draws people to life and God's destiny for them, while Folly welcomes others to pressure, worry, anxiety, disappointment, and ultimately death.

> Wisdom draws people to life and God's destiny for them ...

So that we know precisely what to look for, let's take a closer look at the two options for "the simple."

The Foolish and the Wise
Following are some insights from Scripture on foolishness and wisdom. You'll observe that the majority of the verses dealing with wisdom relate to how a person receives instruction, responds to discipline or to a harsh word, or uses his or her tongue. A wise person is someone who is humble, not arrogant. As for the foolish, well, you'll get a pretty good sense of them in these verses.

> The fool says in his heart,
> "There is no God."
> They are corrupt, and their ways are vile;
> there is no one who does good. (Psalm 53:1)

As if to give the point special emphasis, twice the Bible says, "The fool says in his heart, 'There is no God'" (see also Psalm 14:1). So when you hear somebody at work or in the media or anywhere say something like, "There is no God!"—well, you can count on the fact that this person does not embrace wisdom. It's interesting to me that those who claim to be wise, who believe that reason, science, or their own intellects have concluded that there is no God, are so obviously foolish. Often they will claim to be freethinkers when in reality they have wandered into the oldest trick—believing that they have the ability to comprehend an infinite God with their finite minds and proclaim that He doesn't exist. There is empirical evidence all around us that points to God as Creator. Only a person determined to deny facts and embrace fantasy can deny the existence of God. As a result, those who think of themselves as thoughtful and wise are instead, often notably, great fools.

> A fool spurns his father's discipline,
> but whoever heeds correction shows prudence.
> (Proverbs 15:5)

> A mocker resents correction;
> he will not consult the wise. (verse 12)

Accepting discipline is not just for kids, either. That's why you and I need to seek spiritual accountability with godly mentors and acquire a taste for correction in life. Wise people know how to respond to authority in society, in the family, in the church, and in the workplace. Fools, however, often find themselves in consternation over governmental authorities, become destructive forces within their families, are unable to cooperate in a community of faith, or are a burden to their supervisors at work. As I mentioned earlier, God has established His creation in order. As a result, the wise see God's hand in creation and appreciate evidence, research, science, and order. Fools deny that order and believe the universe is chaotic. God has established order for relationships. Fools challenge God's order in society, the family, the church, and the workplace, while the wise understand it, work with it, and utilize it to provide strength and safety for people.

> A fool finds pleasure in evil conduct,
> but a man of understanding delights in wisdom.
> (Proverbs 10:23)

Stay away from people who like to push the evil edge in what they watch on television, what they do with their free time, or what they talk and joke about. Fools don't comprehend how destructive personal behavior destroys their futures, their families, and the communities around them. Those who have

gained wisdom, on the other hand, appreciate the constraints required by responsibility, so they can joyfully approach their futures as they live honorable lives that provide stability and consistency and communicate trustworthy life messages to others. Wisdom instructs people in joyful honor, while foolish living is selfish and unstable.

> The wise in heart accept commands,
> but a chattering fool comes to ruin. (Proverbs 10:8)

> The way of a fool seems right to him,
> but a wise man listens to advice. (Proverbs 12:15)

A wise person is connected to other people who are respected and know something—and he or she acts on what they say. Fools say, "Just do it!"—whatever seems right at the time. They listen only to themselves, sometimes because they're jabbering so much no one else can get a word in edgewise.

> You and I need to seek spiritual accountability with godly mentors and acquire a taste for correction in life.

> A wise man fears the LORD and shuns evil, but a fool
> is hotheaded and reckless. (Proverbs 14:16)

I've always told my kids that nothing good happens after midnight. By that I mean, "Stay home and away from evil." It's reckless to be places where, time after time, bad things tend to happen. Pay attention to this principle. It could save your life.

> The wise inherit honor,
> but fools he [the Lord] holds up to shame.
> (Proverbs 3:35)

God wants to give us honor; He wants to bless us. But He will reveal fools for what they are.

> Do not rebuke a mocker or he will hate you;
> rebuke a wise man and he will love you.
> Instruct a wise man and he will be wiser still;
> teach a righteous man and he will add to his learning.
> (Proverbs 9:8-9)

Again, wise people are open to criticism and instruction. Foolish people have a more difficult time imagining that they are wrong.

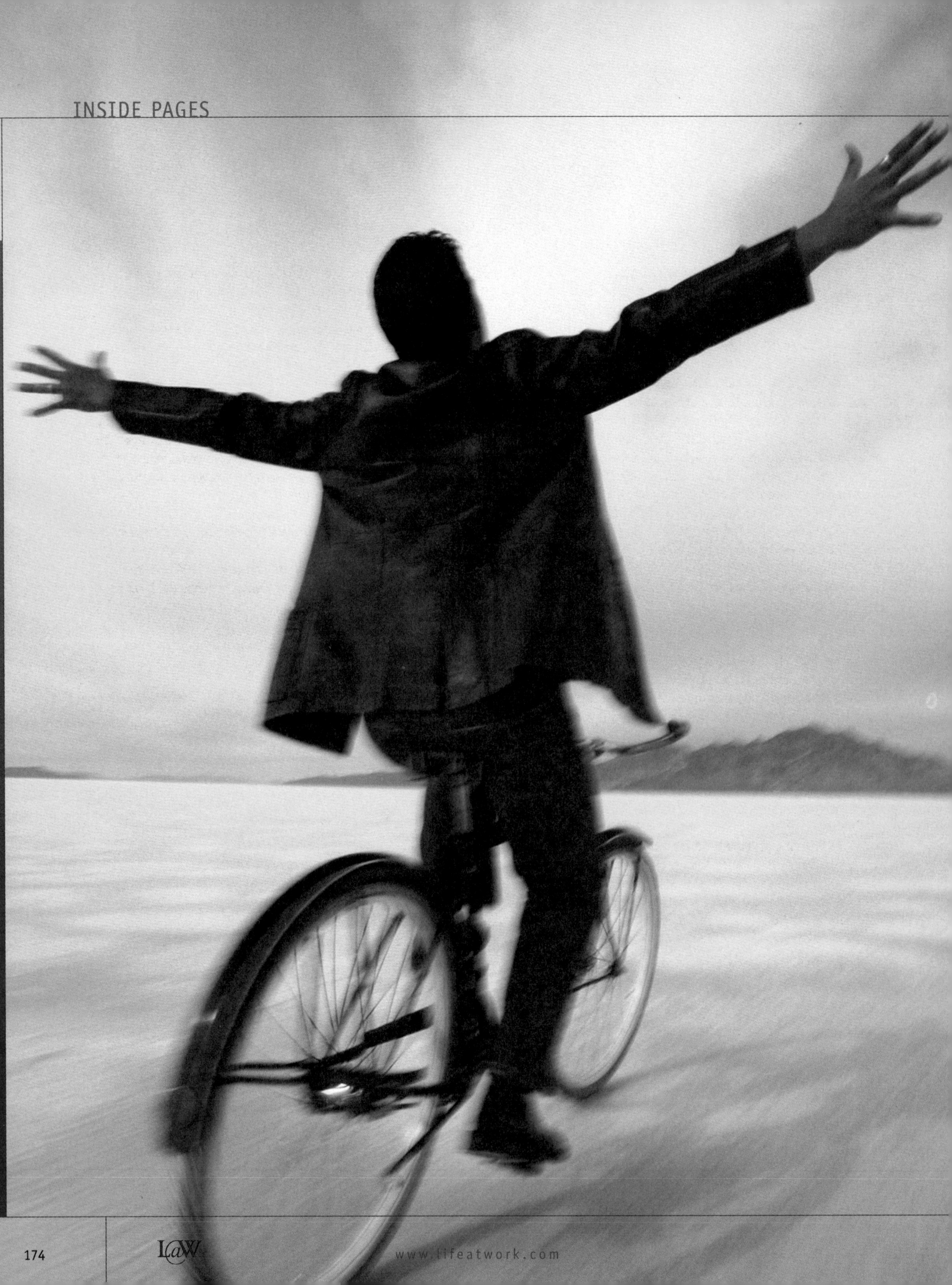

A wise son brings joy to his father,
but a foolish son grief to his mother.
(Proverbs 10:1)

Do you have kids? Have you ever been someone's kid? 'Nuff said.

I am amazed as I grow older and see the incredible delight that comes to parents when their children love them and honor them. I'll never forget the first time our two oldest children, Christy and Marcus, were back from college and wanted to stay home with us instead of going out with their friends. I would never have expected it, but it did so much for both Gayle and me. I am becoming convinced that one of the greatest blessings in life for parents is to be able to be proud of their children. This applies to children of all ages. Our charge: Live lives of wisdom so that we will be a blessing to our parents and our family name.

The wise woman builds her house,
but with her own hands the foolish one
tears hers down. (Proverbs 14:1)

Wise women contribute positively to those around them, including their husbands and children, and thus build up their houses. They are usually thoughtful and intentional in the process. I've observed that a foolish woman who is tearing down her house—that is, wrecking her marriage and family with some type of destructive behavior—often doesn't know or admit to what she's doing. She just can't see it because she thinks she's in the right. Fools often displace responsibility and seldom find fault within themselves.

The lips of the wise spread knowledge;
not so the hearts of fools. (Proverbs 15:7)

Fools have not attained wisdom, so how can they pass along anything helpful or of value to others?

Let the wise listen and add to their learning,
and let the discerning get guidance. (Proverbs 1:5)

The wise are not too proud to keep learning. The greatest leaders in the world are simply great students who now articulate what they have learned.

That's just a sampling of verses related to wisdom and foolishness, but I'm going to stop because I think you get the point. Scripture goes on and on and on about this subject. Why? Because it's essential.

I urge you to explore all the Bible has to say on these topics. You will be amazed at the benefits.

L@W

Ted Haggard is the president of the National Association of Evangelicals (NAE). He is also the senior pastor of New Life Church in Colorado Springs, an 11,000-member church that he founded in 1985. He is the author of seven books. He and his wife Gayle have five children.

All scriptures referenced from the New International Version.

Toolbox

Modus Operandi Par Excellence

By Amy C. Baker

Modus operandi is a Latin phrase, approximately translated as "mode of operation," and commonly used to describe someone's habits. Our habits at work—how we operate not just what we do—say a great deal about our integrity. Consider these aspects of our days in the marketplace and you will see what I mean:

- Do I always arrive rushing in or late for my shift or for meetings, or do I get there in time to relax and prepare for what lies ahead?
- Do I plan out my day the afternoon before so I am certain I'm ready for any deadlines, conference calls, or encounters I know I will have the following day?
- Do I complete my projects on time and under budget, to the best of my ability?
- How do I respond when I don't know the answer to a question? Do I make something up or say, "I need to get back to you," and then really follow up?
- Do I behave consistently with my company's culture?

The list could go on and on. These are just a few of the basic work habits that can convey our commitment to excellence in all things and therefore a level of integrity that is too often missing in the workplace today. These are ways we put feet on our faith and at the same time solidify our standing as a valuable employee.

In 2 Timothy 2:14–16 we are given some advice on how we should present ourselves, and it isn't hard to see how this applies to our work life. Paul writes, "Warn them before God against quarreling about words; it is of no value, and only ruins those who listen. Do your best to present yourself to God as one approved, a workman who does not need to be ashamed and who correctly handles the word of truth. Avoid godless chatter, because those who indulge in it will become more and more ungodly." (NIV)

We are called to present ourselves to God as workmen — that means we are doing our work. Our actions speak for themselves. Yes, we have earth-bound managers and roles and responsibilities, and we should do our work with pride and excellence. But ultimately, we are presenting our work to the Lord. We rely on His strength and timing, and we should definitely avoid godless chatter, especially if it is about us!

Though the title may be tantalizing, the last thing we want to do is talk ourselves into a position or a set of responsibilities that we are not really qualified to handle. That's grandstanding that leads to not only a huge lapse of integrity, but career disaster as well!

L@W

Amy C. Baker has 20 plus years of experience in human resources and communications. She is a dynamic professional speaker and writer with her own communications consulting practice, Logos Strategies (**www.logosstrategies.com**). She and her husband live in Austin, Texas with their two children. For more information, visit **www.amycbaker.com**.

Adapted from Succeeding at Work without Sidetracking Your Faith: 7 Lessons of Career Excellence for Women, © *2006 by Amy C. Baker. Used with permission of New Hope Publishers.* (**www.wmustore.com**)

TOOLBOX | BUILD WEALTH

Build Wealth ... Build Character

By Dave Ramsey

Andrew Carnegie said, "Surplus wealth is a sacred trust which its possessor is bound to administer in his lifetime for the good of the community."

No doubt about it—wealth is a big responsibility. When you learn the steps to build effectively toward your future, you will absolutely become wealthy in 20 to 40 years. The problem with becoming wealthy is that you stand a chance of becoming enamored with wealth. It's easy to start worshiping money after you have some.

The wealthy person who is ruled by his stuff is no freer than the debt-ridden consumer. There is a real spiritual danger to having great wealth, and that danger is old-fashioned materialism. Some people who become affluent seek happiness, solace, and fulfillment in consuming stuff, trying to get things to do something they weren't designed to do. Stuff is great ... go ahead and get yourself some stuff. Just don't let the pursuit of wealth become your god.

Instead, be concerned that your wealth becomes a blessing and not a curse to others—especially your children. Think about it: if you get this wealth-building stuff right, you're going to leave an incredible inheritance to your children. Teach them that stuff doesn't equal happiness, because if they don't know how to handle money and how to view possessions, the wealth you leave them will ruin their lives.

Good things can happen as a result of a money makeover only if we have the spiritual character to recognize that wealth is not the answer to life's questions. The reality of wealth is that it actually only magnifies the character you already have.

Let that one sink in for a minute. If you are a jerk and you become wealthy, you will be king of the jerks. If you are kind, wealth will allow you to show kindness in immeasurable ways.

If you are a Christian, it is your spiritual duty to possess riches so that you can do with them things that bring glory to God. Managing money wisely allows you to do good with it. And, if you continue building character as you build wealth, you'll enjoy the incredible blessings that wealth can be to your family, your community, and future generations.

L@W

Dave Ramsey, a personal money management expert, is an extremely popular national radio personality and author of the New York Times best-sellers *The Total Money Makeover* and *Financial Peace*. Ramsey knows first-hand what financial peace means in his own life—living a true riches to rags to riches story. Since rebuilding his own financial life, he now devotes himself full-time to helping ordinary people understand the forces behind their financial distress and how to set things right—financially, emotionally, and spiritually. For more information visit **www.daveramsey.com**.

The reality of wealth is that it actually only magnifies the character you already have.

No weapon that is formed against thee shall prosper; and every tongue that shall rise against thee in judgment thou shalt condemn. This is the heritage of the servants of the Lord, and their righteousness is of me, saith the Lord.

Isaiah 54:17 (KJV)

GLORIA JOHNSON GOINS

Gloria Johnson Goins is an attorney by trade, and has served as General Attorney for BellSouth Cellular. She eventually headed up Cingular's diversity efforts. In 2003, she became the Vice President of Diversity and Inclusion at The Home Depot (**www.HomeDepot.com**), the largest home-improvement retailer in the world (and the world's second-largest retailer). She is responsible for creating and implementing company-wide diversity and inclusion initiatives.

A Diverse Career

I have been an attorney for 18 years and have worked at private firms and served as in-house counsel for a large corporation. This work prepared me to be an advocate and to represent people and issues with passion and professionalism. While my job as Vice President of Diversity at Cingular Wireless certainly helped prepare me for my current job, my work as a lawyer honed my ability to analyze problems, find creative solutions and build bridges.

I earned my bachelor's degree at Stanford University, my juris doctorate at the University of Pennsylvania law school and my MBA at Mercer University's Atlanta campus. I am a member of the Florida and Georgia Bars, the National Bar Association, and the American Bar Association.

Building a Family

My husband and I have a daughter, Grace Princess Goins. She is 2-years-old. I do my very best to put God and my family first. They are my top priorities, and I make sure to spend quality time with my family. Sometimes it's tough, but I make sure it happens.

Helping Out, Getting Noticed

Over the course of my career, I have served on 14 nonprofit boards. I currently sit on the board of The Home Depot Foundation and SER Jobs for Progress (the nation's leading employment agency for Hispanics).

The Atlanta chapter of the National Society of Hispanic MBAs named me Professional of the Year in 2005. Also in 2005, I won the Business Advocate of the Year Award from the U.S. Hispanic Chamber of Commerce. In 2004, I won the Sister 2 Sister Intergenerational Award for Mentoring Young People. In 1998, I received a commendation from the President of the State Bar of Georgia for outstanding service to the Georgia Bar Journal.

I actively volunteer with the United Negro College Fund, The Atlanta Business League, Girls Inc., and New Birth Missionary Baptist Church. I make a point of helping as much as possible. It's my true passion.

Honoring God at Work

I honor God with my work by being ethical, professional, and responsible when performing my duties. I always strive to deliver superior results in everything I do at work.

It's important to always keep in mind that you work for God, regardless of what is going on around you. You are there to always maintain your high standards of quality and ethics.

I use my faith to help me execute and perform at a high level at work. My faith serves as a guidepost for providing service to others at and outside of work.

L@W

Perspective

Living Holy Lives

It's Possible... IF You Avoid Behavioral Modification Plans

By John Ortberg

Jesus' Sermon on the Mount provides us with magnificent teachings, including:

Blessed are the poor in spirit, for theirs is the kingdom of Heaven.
Blessed are those who mourn, for they will be comforted.
You are the salt of the earth. You are the light of the world.

People love these words from Matthew 5. They put them on plaques and hang them up on their walls.

However, Jesus' sermon gets a little uncomfortable after that. He talks about the sin that holds us back. Jesus takes sin really seriously. He says some tough things:

> "You have heard it said you shall not murder. I say to you if you are nursing contempt for somebody in your heart, you are in trouble with God. ... You have heard it said you should not commit adultery. I say to you if you choose to cultivate lust in your heart, you are in trouble with God" (Matthew 5:21-22; 27-28 NIV).

And if that's not striking enough, Jesus then says:

> "If your right eye causes you to sin, gouge it out and dispose of it. It is better for you to lose one part of your body than for your whole body to be thrown into Hell. And if your right hand causes you to sin, cut it off. It is better for you to lose part of your body than for your whole body to go into Hell" (Matthew 5:29-30 NIV).

Have you ever seen *those* words hanging on the wall?

In this section of the Sermon on the Mount, Jesus is engaged in a fundamental disagreement with the prevailing view in His day about what makes someone "good" in God's eyes. It seems those people were on a "Behavioral Modification Plan."

Of course, you hear this same kind of thing going on a lot in our day. When people think about holiness, they think about behavior modification. They think, "As long as I'm not engaged in forbidden behaviors, then I'm on the right track." They see God as a severe guy with a checklist. We get so mechanical about this.

To be "holy" does not mean that I get real good at not doing things I really want to do. Developing lots of will power to override my desires is not holiness.

Holiness means that I become the kind of person who actually wants to do what is right and good and noble and beautiful and true. Jesus says, "What God wants to do is to change something

inside of you so you become the kind of person who just naturally does good things with My help because I'm with you."

That's holiness.

Jesus' invites us to "Abide in Me as I abide in you. Just as the branch cannot bear fruit by itself unless it abides in the vine, neither can you. You'll never be able to make that change in your heart. You'll never be able to do good stuff on your own unless you abide in Me. Be My student. Talk to Me. Ask for My help. Be My companion. Be My friend."

That's holiness.

There are two practices that we need to cultivate that naturally flow out of holiness. The first one is what I call "Adventures in Obedience." One of the things Jesus says is, "If you love Me, you will keep My commandments" (John 14:15 NASB). In other words: you'll actually try to do whatever I say. Jesus will be with us, and as we seek to do the things that He tells us over time, He begins to rewire us.

Another thing that happens when I try to obey by the power of my own will — the realization that it isn't in me. So I need to confess. We try to hide our sin. It's tempting to think, "If I don't get caught, it doesn't really matter." But it does matter. Because we live in a spiritual universe, my sin damages other people, it corrodes my soul, and it wounds God. It matters.

So followers of Jesus who seek to live this holy life commit themselves to the practice of confession. "Confess your sins one to another" (James 5:16 NASB). Every time there's a great movement of the Spirit of God, one of the things that happen is that there is confession. People come out of hiding.

Because, as Jesus taught us, "blessed are those who hunger and thirst for righteousness."

L@W

John Ortberg is the Teaching Pastor of Menlo Park Presbyterian Church in Northern California. (**www.mppcfamily.org**) He is a former teaching pastor at Willow Creek Community Church and senior pastor at Horizons Community Church. John is the author of a number of best-selling books, including *The Life You've Always Wanted* and *If You Want to Walk on Water, You Have to Get Out of the Boat*.

Life @ The Intersection

You have just completed Session 7. Use these journal pages to complete the following:

BIG QUESTION:
After reading this session, I'm wondering what others think about ...

NEW THOUGHT:
I just learned that ...

PERSONAL CHALLENGE:
I can't get this out of my mind. I have to figure out how to live differently so that ...

TAKE A BREAK

We all mess up, but what do we do about it? Reflect over the past 24 hours. Are there any relationships that were damaged or strained as a result of foolishness or lack of character? Go to the person and ask forgiveness. Ask God to help you restore that relationship.

SESSION EIGHT

THE INFRASTRUCTURE OF CHARACTER

BEING PREPARED ENSURES THAT YOUR MORAL SHELVES ARE STOCKED

By Stephen R. Graves

You could list numerous reasons why Wal-Mart is the leading retailer, but one of the most important is its system of warehousing and distribution. You will never see an empty shelf at Wal-Mart. Nor will you see the merchandise on the shelves — either in the store or at the warehouse — sitting there for long. That's because of Wal-Mart's system of distribution centers, which move a staggering number of products from all over the world with incredible efficiency.

A Wal-Mart warehouse and distribution center is a wonder to behold. There are 800,000 square feet of warehousing space on 50 acres of land. Truckloads of goods never cease coming in and out at its 45-plus shipping docks. Six hundred employees work day and night receiving freight, tracking it, and dispatching it as needed to go directly to store shelves. On any given day, a single Wal-Mart warehouse handles $10 million worth of inventory. In a year, Wal-Mart's warehouses ship over $244 billion worth of merchandise worldwide.

Wal-Mart invests $55 million to construct each of its distribution centers. There's one reason they make such a large investment: you have to stock before you can sell. You cannot retail what you have not invested in wholesale.

This principle is just as true for our work lives. Character has to have a moral warehouse from which to draw. Constructing a

moral infrastructure is critical for God-intended Life@Work. Are you regularly investing in your infrastructure? If we have not put systems in place that keep our souls well stocked, we should not be surprised when we show up at the store one day and find the shelves empty.

A moral warehouse is not static virtue. As in warehousing and distribution, character depends on an ongoing process. It must constantly be replenished. Its inventory needs ongoing management.

Too often those who discuss moral character only talk about the virtues themselves — honesty, loyalty, perseverance, courage, etc. Yet we also need to focus on the process by which these personal strengths are acquired and built into one's life. Sam Walton knew that if he built the infrastructure, the goods would flow. Similarly, building a moral infrastructure is more about life habits that stock character than it is about the specific character qualities themselves.

IF WE HAVE NOT PUT SYSTEMS IN PLACE THAT KEEP OUR SOULS WELL STOCKED, WE SHOULD NOT BE SURPRISED WHEN WE SHOW UP AT THE STORE ONE DAY AND FIND THE SHELVES EMPTY.

Four activities are helpful in the construction, utilization, and replenishment of your moral infrastructure:
- Constructing personal convictions
- Capturing transformational moments
- Conducting Scripture memory
- Connecting with people of character

Constructing Personal Convictions

It has been said that an opinion is something you hold, whereas a conviction is something that holds you. Character begins with having sound, solid, personal principles by which to live. We call those convictions. What is a conviction? A conviction is a category of God's thinking on a particular area or issue that I wholeheartedly embrace and act upon with determination.

Your warehouse needs to be stocked with timeless values that do not change. There is only one place to get an unbiased perspective not subject to human whim: God's Word. Building a conviction begins with discovering exactly what God thinks and has had to say about a topic or issue that you might be wrestling with. If you're going to make the Bible the guideline for your everyday life, bear in mind two guidelines. First, remember that there is not a specific verse for every occurrence in life to give you a black-and-white guidebook on your journey. Second, yet almost every core area of life is touched on by principle, proverb, or illustration somewhere in the Bible.

There is no such thing as an inactive conviction. Character is never passive. Every personal conviction needs to show up to fight. Every personal principle eventually will be called out and tested. Moral challenges are always battles won or lost by the will. You need clearly defined convictions because the heat of the moment is the wrong time to decide what kind of person you are going to be. Better decide who exactly you are, what exactly you hold to be true and important, in times of quiet, when there's ample opportunity for reflection.

When it comes time to make a decision, you always choose what you want most at the moment of choosing. The problem, of course, is that you want conflicting things. Almost everybody you've ever met wants to do the right thing. So why don't people do the right thing more often? Because the right thing isn't the only thing they want. Very often they want something else even more.

BUILDING A MORAL INFRASTRUCTURE IS MORE ABOUT LIFE HABITS THAT STOCK CHARACTER THAN IT IS ABOUT THE SPECIFIC CHARACTER QUALITIES THEMSELVES.

Settled convictions give you guideposts for navigating the twisting swamp of your own wants and desires. You're surrounded by messages that aim to convince you that you want something other than what God wants for you. I don't care who you are, it can start to get to you. You begin to feel maybe you don't have enough stuff or the right kind of stuff, or your spouse isn't exciting enough, or there's no point in being the only person in your office who doesn't cheat on your income taxes. Without some serious convictions, how are you ever going to do the right thing consistently?

Constructing your personal convictions begins with taking charge of your thought life. Rather than marinating your mind in thoughts and images that are contrary to God's standards, fill your mind with the things that will strengthen your satisfaction in the things of God. Paul put it this way:

> "Finally, brethren, whatever things are true, whatever things are noble, whatever things are just, whatever things are pure, whatever things are lovely, whatever things are of good report, if there is any virtue and if there is anything praiseworthy — meditate on these things" (Philippians 4:8 NKJV).

The idea is to pack your mind so full with things that build you up that there's no room left for things that tear you down.

Of course you can't control every thought that wanders into your mind. But you do have some control over the things you dwell on. As the old proverb says, you can't keep a bird from flying over your head, but you can keep it from building a nest in your hair. Your convictions are under constant attack. You fight back by taking control of your thought life.

Capturing Transformational Moments of Life

There are moments in life that are pregnant with meaning. These are those times that hit us in the gut: the birth of a child, graduations, weddings, funerals, promotions, layoffs, achievements, failures. These life milestones usually happen when something externally has caused us to pull over internally for some reflection. We pause and drink in life a little slower than usual. We call these *transformational encounters.*

Life's significant moments are opportunities, and you shouldn't miss them. They provide the chance to inventory your moral warehouse.

It could be a close call or an accident. It could be a scare or a thrill. It could be simply an evening on the porch, watching the sun go down. It could be attached to a day away or a vacation. A song can trigger it. A memory can hit the switch. An annual review could do it.

Transformational moments may be tragedies, they may be personal triumphs, or they may be something in between. The point is not the drama, but the teachable moment that life provides us. We pause and inhale and contemplate. A transformational moment is a time when you reorder your private world, a time when you realign your belief systems

THERE IS NO SUCH THING AS AN INACTIVE CONVICTION. CHARACTER IS NEVER PASSIVE.

with your behavior. It is at these moments in life that you do some of your best character review and alignment.

Conducting Scripture Memory

I do not think it is an overstatement to suggest that we now have a whole cohort growing up without a firsthand knowledge of the Scriptures. I love modern worship, and I love progressive churches. I prefer practical sermons and fun, creative narratives. But I am concerned that we too rarely engage the Scriptures directly.

Scripture memory is not difficult. Like working out, it just requires an investment of a few minutes each day. There are many resources designed to get you started. But you can easily begin on your own. Stop and make a list of the current concerns on your plate of life, whatever they may be: perhaps a difficult boss, your son's bad grades, conflict with your husband over finances, a scary lab report, the uncertainty of a job transition. Now take these concerns to Scripture. You might be surprised to find how much the Bible has to say directly about the things you are facing.

Connecting with People of Character

Good character keeps good company. We all know this to be true when we are young; we just forget that it's still true as we get older. I can remember my mom instructing me to stay away from Jimmy down the street. "He's a rotten apple," she would say. We all know what that means. It means the same thing that Paul meant when he said decisively, "Bad company corrupts good character" (1 Corinthians 15:33 NIV). But who cautions us of rotten apples when life graduates us to our

IT'S EXTREMELY TEMPTING TO COMPROMISE YOUR CONVICTIONS HERE OR THERE IN THE WORKPLACE.

twenties, thirties, forties, and beyond?

For some reason, we've relegated peer pressure to the realm of teenage problems. But you probably know adults who become different people depending on who they are around. There's just so much more at stake in your adult relationships than there ever was when you were in high school. It's extremely tempting to compromise your convictions here or there in the workplace. You don't want to lose the deal; you don't want to let the firm down. You don't want to alienate the person who does your annual review. So you conform to the world instead of being transformed and being an agent of transformation.

"Do not be unequally yoked with unbelievers" (2 Corinthians 6:14a NKJV). We typically think of that as wedding advice, but nothing in the context suggests that Paul was directing his remarks specifically at people thinking about getting married. That's good advice any time you're forming a business partnership or seeking capital or entering into any relationship in which another person has significant leverage in your decision-making process.

Keeping the Vital Lifeline Growing

Southern California is a veritable paradise. Its balmy weather and rolling hills overlooking the Pacific Ocean have attracted ever-increasing numbers of transplants from across America. Swanky neighborhoods with their irrigated green grass and lush landscaping make it an enticing place to move.

Los Angeles' growth, however, has had one principal problem from the very beginning: water. Its annual rainfall is insufficient for its needs. There is no reservoir within its city limits to quench its growing suburban thirst. One hundred

years ago its citizens and civic leaders realized they needed a reliable outside supply of water. Plenty of water existed in the watershed of western America. It just did not flow to Southern California. To get it there would require an artificial infrastructure. Southern Californians began buying water rights and building canals and pipelines to get the water they needed from the mountains to their growing urban metropolis. These aqueducts are the lifelines of Southern California. They deliver over 4.5 billion gallons of water per year.

It is a simple fact that you cannot grow what you do not water. Furthermore, you cannot water where you have no irrigation system. The same is true with character. Integrity requires an infrastructure. It must be constantly nurtured and re-supplied. Doing so requires intentional lifelong investment. It means building character-sustaining habits. There is no shortcut. There is no point of arrival. Personal growth always requires an ever-deeper reservoir.

Southern California cannot grow without an infrastructure supplying it water. Wal-Mart cannot sell without a distribution infrastructure. You will never have any character to display if

THERE IS NO SHORTCUT. THERE IS NO POINT OF ARRIVAL. PERSONAL GROWTH ALWAYS REQUIRES AN EVER-DEEPER RESERVOIR.

you do not first have a moral infrastructure. Start building yours today.

L@W

Dr. Stephen R. Graves is a highly sought business coach and life guide for entrepreneurs and leaders desiring to successfully make it to the finish line of life. In 1991, he co-founded the Cornerstone Group, a company built to integrate biblical wisdom and business excellence. He and his wife Karen have three children.

This article is based on concepts drawn from Life@Work *by John C. Maxwell, Stephen R. Graves, and Thomas G. Addington, published by Thomas Nelson, Inc.*

INFRASTRUCTURE OF CHARACTER

FOR GROUP DISCUSSION

Prior to your small group meeting time, read and reflect on the Life@Work Study article you just read. Use these questions and journal pages to reflect and respond to the ideas presented. Be ready to share your thoughts at your small group gathering.

Note to small group leaders: You can download a full Leader's Guide at www.lifeatworkgroupzine.com.

- *There is only one place to get an unbiased perspective not subject to human whim: God's Word. Building a conviction begins with discovering exactly what God thinks and has to say about a topic or issue that you might be wrestling with.*

    How often are you turning to God's Word these days? Is it more frequently or less frequently than at this time last year? What can you do to be more disciplined in your reading and studying of the Bible? How often do you memorize Scripture? Why is that important to do?

- *Moral challenges are always battles won or lost by the will. You need clearly defined convictions because the heat of the moment is the wrong time to decide what kind of person you are going to be.*

    Name a time you failed in the heat of the moment. Did it surprise you at the time that this occurred? Looking back on it now, do you have a different perspective? Do you agree with the assertion that you need to decide ahead of time what type of person you are? Why or why not?

- *"Finally, brethren, whatever things are true, whatever things are noble, whatever things are just, whatever things are pure, whatever things are lovely, whatever things are of good report, if there is any virtue and if there is anything praiseworthy — meditate on these things." (Philippians 4:8 NKJV)*

    How often do you find yourself thinking — meditating — on things that are true, lovely, virtuous, praiseworthy? What are some things that fit these categories? What could you do to keep your mind on the good and away from the bad? Are you regularly doing these things?

- *Life's significant moments are opportunities, and you shouldn't miss them. They provide the chance to inventory your moral warehouse.*

    When was the last significant moment — the birth of a child, a graduation, wedding, funeral, promotion, layoff, achievement, failure — in your life? Did you use that occasion as a chance to take inventory? Why do you think these occurrences are natural moments to pause and contemplate?

- *Good character keeps good company. We all know this to be true when we are young; we just forget that it's still true as we get older.*

    Who were some of the kids your mom warned you about when you were a kid? Who are some of the people in your life you should spend less time with now? Who are the good-character people in your world that you should be spending more time with? What are you willing to change in your schedule to allow that to happen?

Feature Article

When I graduated from college in 1977, I was hired as a sales rep for Texas Instruments. The funny thing is, I was a history major and I'd never sold anything before, let alone anything in the technology realm. I was a bit overwhelmed, so I went to somebody I considered a business mentor, and I said, "I'm going to be a sales person. What advice do you have for me?"

We were sitting at lunch and he looked at me and he said, "Well, I only have one piece of advice." I'm thinking, "Oh boy, this is going to be the key to my business success."

He said, "Learn to tell the truth. If you learn to tell the truth you will absolutely stand out from all of your peers."

We finished that lunch and I started my career. But the funny

> I decided that I was going to make that one of my lifetime goals —
> ## I WAS GOING TO BE A TRUTH TELLER.

thing is those words kept ringing around in my head. I decided that I was going to make that one of my lifetime goals — I was going to be a truth teller.

Along the way, I've learned three lessons about telling the truth:
- No. 1: Consider the cost, because the price tag might be high
- No. 2: People are attracted to the truth
- No. 3: It's a lot easier to tell the truth if you know the Author of the truth

I've come to the conclusion that telling the truth should be a lot like the golden rule: we should tell to others what we personally would want to be told.

Lesson No. 1: Consider the cost, because the price tag might be high

During the first part of my career, I was with Texas Instruments, a highly ethical company. During the years I was there, every employee worldwide went through ethics training annually.

I decided to leave there in the mid-1980s to join a startup

that was founded by a brilliant retired professor. I was lucky enough to be the first sales person they hired, employee number 17. We had great technology, which we turned into a fantastic product. After two years we were able to take the company public. We had some of the best venture money in the world behind it and we were on a rocket. I really felt like I had won the lottery. I tasted the upside of the Silicon Valley and I really liked it.

There was, however, a problem in how the CEO dealt with people. It was pretty unpleasant. He had a nasty habit of pitting the management team against each other. And he would normally pit the team against a person who wasn't in the room.

He decided to start one particular meeting by making an accusation about the one senior manager that wasn't in the room. He said this guy had done something the previous week to intentionally damage the company.

Well, it was one of those things that not only wasn't true, it was so outrageous that people didn't even want to acknowledge it. The CEO decided he was going to call on each one of us to see if we agreed with him. I was sitting to his immediate right, but he started on his left. He literally went around to each of the people at the table, looked them in the eye, and said, "This is what I believe. Do you agree with me?" I sat there and watched every senior exec crumble under the pressure of the CEO.

> ## THERE I WAS, ON THE STREET
> looking for a job, wondering what had happened to me.

I was thinking, "What am I going to say?" The words that came to my mind were, "Be a truth teller. Tell the truth." So I decided to do that. When it was finally my turn, he looked at me and said, "Do you agree with me and everyone else?"

Being the sales guy that I am, I attempted a little humor. Nobody was laughing. So I swallowed hard and I looked him in the eye and I said, "Well, actually if you really think he did

To Tell the Truth

Honestly, Can You Trust Anyone at Work?

By John Brandon

that intentionally to damage the company, I disagree. I was there when the situation happened. And by the way, I'm personally really uncomfortable that we're talking about one of the senior managers that's not here to defend himself."

I wish I could say that at that moment the CEO jumped up and said, "Finally, an honest man. I'm looking for my successor and you will be the next CEO of this company." That's what I was hoping. It's not what happened. He kind of glared at me, changed the subject, and finished the managers' meeting.

The next morning the CEO's administrative assistant called me. She said, "John, you need to know: he started a search this morning to replace you."

Ninety days later I'm out of the company. I had my tail between the legs; I was all chewed up. I was trying to figure it all out: "Lord what in the world are You doing in my life? Haven't You noticed we're wearing the same color jersey? I thought I was on Your team."

There I was, being chased out the company that I had worked so hard for, wondering what had happened to me.

Lesson No. 2: People are attracted to the truth

People are desperate for the truth. I've learned over the years that telling the truth is an amazing thing. Even if they don't do it themselves, people want the truth to be told to them. And they almost expect it.

At Adobe, we were committed to annual reviews for every employee. But even though we would train our managers, they didn't do a very good job with it.

There's a dirty little secret that's part of the culture of corporate America. While many companies are committed to annual reviews, most managers won't tell the truth in the reviews. They won't tell the employee how they are truly viewed.

I was developing a reputation that I'd tell employees the truth, so I would find around review time, employees in completely different parts of the organization would want to meet with me.

They would walk in and say, "I'm desperate to know the truth. I got my review. I don't believe it. What's going on?"

Some of them I had to look in the eyes and say, "I'll tell you why. We view you as a brilliant engineer, but you're so difficult to do business with nobody wants to be on your team, let alone let you lead a team. Go back and ask your boss, 'How are my people skills?' Get some honest feedback."

After a great 10-year run at Adobe, I got a phone call from one of the most powerful and influential venture capitalist in the world. He offered me the opportunity to become the CEO of a company he was involved with. So I became a CEO for the first time.

I showed up on my first day of work and met my new team. The second day, we worked through all of the presentations for the board meeting, which would be held the next day. The

THE ROOM GOT QUIET.
One of them handed me an email from the controller that basically said the numbers that we had used to raise our money were bogus.

When I left that company completely beaten up, I took the best job that I could find with a little software company that was trying to decide if they were going to go get in the application software business. That company was Adobe Systems. Adobe was a highly ethical company, just the opposite of the experience I had come out of with that start-up company.

Later on, all my friends thought I was brilliant, but I was just desperate for a job because I was married with two little kids and trying to make a mortgage.

third day, we go to the board meeting. My new team goes through the presentations and they've got all the answers to every question. It could not have gone any better.

At the end of the day, I called all of the execs back into my office and said, "I thought you guys did a really good job today. I'm really proud of you. Let's go over a few of the numbers. I just want to go over the risk one more time." The room got quiet. One of them handed me an email from the controller that basically said the numbers that we had used to raise our money were bogus.

Years ago, I decided that my best chance of success at being a truth teller and living a life of integrity was to share my life with a handful of guys. I have a very strong support system. I actually have two accountability groups: one with guys that are in the marketplace, the other with the elder board of our church.

There is no major decision or anything that happens in my life that I don't share with those guys. I've just made that part of a decision grid that with every major decision, I run it through those guys.

Those groups have told me the most difficult things I've ever heard about myself. But we made a covenant with each other that we love each other enough to tell each other the truth.

Do not walk this path alone.

— John Brandon

I said, "Guys, I have a big problem with this." One of the company's cofounders looked at me and said, "You really don't get it, do you? If you let them know these numbers are wrong, we won't get this next round of funding. We're living on a bridge loan. It's going to run out in less than 30 days. You're going to lay off every employee in the company."

I looked at him and said, "Actually I do get it and you need to know we are not going to take people's money based on things we know are not true."

I didn't sleep very well that night. The next morning at 7:30, I called the lead venture capitalist. I said, "I just went over the numbers. Contrary to what you heard at the board meeting, they're not correct. There's enormous risk in them. We need to be upfront." Needless to say, he was angry.

He said, "I need you to call all the rest of the investors, especially the new lead investor in this round." He was a CEO in New York. I called him. If the first guy was angry, this guy was really angry.

When I finally got to the last investor, she said, "You're calling about the numbers aren't you?" I said, "How did you know?" She said, "We did our due diligence and we knew the numbers were squishy. We just wanted to find out how long it was going to take you to find out how squishy they were and when you were going to tell us."

Amazingly we closed the round at the same valuation and took the company forward. But the really amazing thing is that through a rough set of circumstances, I discovered a team of

PEOPLE ARE ATTRACTED TO THE TRUTH
because they're finding it too rare these days.

investors that was attracted to the truth. People are attracted to the truth because they're finding it too rare these days.

Lesson No. 3: It's a lot easier to tell the truth if you know the Author of the truth
Even though I've got some interesting war stories, I still

struggle all the time with telling the truth. I'm just not that good. I still struggle about wanting to make up excuses when I'm late for dinner. Or why I've not called somebody back. Or why I haven't done something that I've committed to.

I've found my only hope comes out of my relationship with Jesus. It's the only hope. Jesus said, "I am the way, the truth,

> ## I STILL STRUGGLE ALL THE TIME
> with telling the truth.
> I'm just not that good.

and the life. No man comes to the Father but by Me."

I decided that I am going to take Him at His word ... and I've found that it's true. I have found that no matter what the circumstances, out of my relationship with Him, I somehow am able to step up to this issue of being a truth teller.

If you're going to live in the marketplace, if that's where the Lord has placed you, you're going to get challenged about issues of telling the truth every day of your existence. If you think you can do it on your own, if you think people are going to step up because they're basically good and they have good intentions, you're going to be disappointed.

But if you realize that there is hope in a relationship with Jesus, there is true hope. And there is truth.

L@W

John Brandon has served as Vice President of the Americas and Asia Pacific for Apple Computer since 2001. Before joining Apple, he spent 24 years with other high-technology companies. He also leads a team of Silicon Valley executives who speak at the nation's top business schools on the subjects of integrity and business ethics. John lives in Atherton, California with his wife and three children.

Inside Pages

I WAS A TEENAGE GREED-HEAD

By Andy Stanley

Andy Stanley wants to know how your heart is doing. Don't think he's heartless because he isn't concerned about your physical fitness program. It's just that he knows that life can be hard on our hearts ... and when it is, we can let our hearts get hardened. In his book *It Came from Within!* Stanley encourages readers that there is hope that our hearts can grow healthy despite regular battles with guilt, anger, greed, and jealousy. Andy Stanley is a popular author, speaker, and the Senior Pastor at North Point Community Church near Atlanta.

Quick review. Guilt says, "I owe you." Anger says, "You owe me." The third hideous beast on our list is greed.

Greed says, "*I owe me.*"

Bottom line, the greedy people believe they deserve every good thing that comes their way. Not only that, but they believe they deserve every good thing that could *possibly* come their way. Their mantra is, *What's mine is mine because I've earned it—and I've got a lot more coming.* Consequently, it is hard to get a greedy person to part with money or stuff. Why? Because it's theirs. And they are scared.

> Although it may be difficult to spot greed in the mirror, it isn't difficult at all to see in the people around us.

Like the angry man or woman, greedy people usually have a story to tell. And like the angry person, this story explains their propensity toward greed. For example, being raised in a home with little or no financial security might explain why a man or woman tends to hold tight to whatever amount of money comes their way. Similarly, it's easy to understand why someone who once lost everything would cling to what they have now.

But greed is a different breed than the other three enemies of the heart we will discuss. Greed disguises itself. In fact, while reading these last couple of paragraphs you may have already had a thought along the lines of, *Here's one issue I don't struggle with.* You may even have been tempted to skip ahead. After all, you may have the occasional angry outburst and you may harbor a few guilty secrets, but you certainly aren't greedy. Right?

Seeing the Invisible

Now that I think about it, I have never *met* a greedy person. By that I mean I have never known a man or woman who would look me in the eye and admit, "I struggle with greed." What they say is, "I'm careful."

The truth is, we've made it almost impossible to identify greed in our own lives. Unlike anger or guilt, greed hides behind several virtues. Greedy people are savers, and saving is a good thing. Greedy people are often planners, and planning is a good thing. Greedy people want to make sure their financial future is secure, and that's a good thing as well. Right?

> Then it hit me: I was far, far more concerned with the condition of my guitar than I was the soul of that young man.

Greed is easy to hide—from ourselves. But the people around us know. Because although it may be difficult to spot greed in the mirror, it isn't difficult at all to see in the people around us. In fact, we can identify it almost instantly in someone else:

Greedy people talk a lot and worry a lot about money.
Greedy people are not cheerful givers.
Greedy people are reluctant to share.
Greedy people are poor losers.
Greedy people quibble over insignificant sums of money.
Greedy people talk as if they have just enough to get by.
Greedy people often create a culture of secrecy around them.
Greedy people won't let you forget what they have done for you.
Greedy people are reluctant to express gratitude.
Greedy people are not content with what they have.
Greedy people try to control people with their money.

Greed knows no socio-economic boundaries. I've met greedy poor people and greedy rich people. Greed is not a *financial* issue; it is a *heart* issue. Financial gain doesn't make greedy people less greedy. Financial gain or loss doesn't change anything, because greed emanates from the heart.

The Monster in the Mirror

Is this an issue for you? Is it hard for you to give away money? Are you quick to make excuses? Do you ask questions intended to make you look like a careful steward when in fact you are looking for an excuse not to give? When you do give, do you feel like the recipient owes you something in return? In other words, are there always strings attached to your gifts?

If this is a heart issue for you, then I can assure you that your family feels like they're competing with your stuff. At times they will feel like you value your stuff over them. They may feel like they have to beg you for whatever they get out of you financially. They see and feel the strings. They hate bringing up financial issues around you. Sound familiar? Remind you of any conversations you've had lately?

Consider this warning issued by Jesus himself:

"Watch out! Be on your guard against all kinds of greed; a man's life does not consist in the abundance of his possessions" (Luke 12:15 NIV).

Be on your guard? Why? Because of the four heart conditions we will discuss, greed is the most subtle of all.

And take special note of this statement: "a man's life does not consist in the abundance of his possessions." For the greedy person, stuff equals life. They have bought into the lie, "My stuff is my life." And so to tamper with or ask for or damage their stuff is … well, it's personally threatening. Their stuff is an extension of who they are.

I know a bit more about this than I would like to admit. In fact, I distinctly remember the first time I was confronted with my greed. I was twenty-seven and working as the student pastor at my dad's church. I wasn't making a lot of money, and if anyone had accused me of being greedy I would have laughed.

The incident took place during our summer camp. As it happened, I was the worship leader for the week, which required me to bring my guitar to camp with me. But I didn't want a bunch of teenagers touching my precious guitar, so I brought two guitars. One I kept on stage and the other one—the nice one, the one that was an extension of me—I kept locked in a case off to the side. Any time a student asked me if he or she could play my guitar, I would say, "Sure!" And then I would point them to the cheap guitar I left out on stage. Pretty good system. Actually, I saw it as good stewardship: I was protecting an asset God had given me to manage.

About halfway through the week, however, a kid walked up and asked if he could play my *good* guitar. The jig was up; they were on to me. I remember standing there trying to come up with a plausible reason why that wasn't such a good idea. I considered lying and telling him that I left the key to the case in my cabin. Greed will make you do that kind of stuff, you know. But seeing as I was there to teach kids not to lie ... I swallowed hard, forced a smile, and said, "Sure."

I carefully lifted my precious guitar out of its case and handed it gingerly to this lanky eighth-grader. He sat down and began playing while I stood right there beside him. After a few minutes I realized how stupid I must look, so I wandered off to another part of the room, pretending to be busy, but all the time keeping my eyes on little Eddie Van Halen and my *good* guitar.

Well, as fate or God or bad luck would have it, somebody ran into the room yelling for the kid to hurry out to do something and he jumped up, leaned my guitar against a railing, and hustled toward the door. As he bounded down the steps from the stage, I watched in horror, helpless, as MY good guitar slowly toppled sideways and crashed to the stage floor.

When I reached it there was a dent in the wood and a scratch about an inch long. I was devastated. My perfect guitar wasn't perfect anymore. I was so mad, I wanted to strangle the kid. And then it hit me: I was far, far more concerned with the condition of my guitar than I was the soul of that young man. My heart was exposed. I was so ashamed of myself. I wasn't just being careful—I had a greed problem. I had placed greater value on a possession than on a person. That's the nature of greed.

Here's the real irony of the story. That kid who was responsible for dinging my guitar grew up to become one of the most sought-after worship leaders in America. Not only that, but he has written some of today's most popular worship songs. His name is Todd Fields.

Driving Force

Fear is the driving force behind greed. Fear fuels greed. Why didn't I want anybody messing with my good guitar? I was afraid of what might happen to it. Greed is supported by an endless cast of what ifs. What if it gets scratched? What if it gets lost? What if there's not enough? What if I don't get my fair share? What if she has more? What if the economy collapses?

People with greed lodged in their heart fear that God either can't or won't take care of them. More to the point, they're afraid that God won't take care of them in the fashion or style in which they want to be cared for. And the gap between what they suspect God might be willing to do and what they want becomes a major source of anxiety. So greedy people shoulder the burden to acquire and maintain everything they need to provide the sense of security they desire.

But therein lies the problem: There's never enough. Greedy people can never have enough to satisfy their need to feel secure in light of every conceivable eventuality. There's always another what if that drives them to acquire more. Their appetite cannot be satisfied. So they never feel like they have quite enough, which of course is the very thing they fear. Consequently, greedy people are rarely at peace with others and never at peace with themselves. Greed eventually strains their relationships at every level, eroding long-term relationships over stuff that has a use-life of only a few years. The guitar I mentioned earlier? I don't even own it anymore. In fact, I ended up giving it away to a college student whose guitar had been stolen.

Maybe I learned something after all.

L@W

Andy Stanley is the lead pastor of North Point Community Church in Atlanta, Georgia. (**www.northpoint.org**) He is the bestselling author of *Visioneering, The Next Generation Leader, The Best Question Ever*, and the recent *It Came from Within!*. Andy and his wife, Sandra, live in Atlanta with their two sons and daughter.

Excerpted from It Came From Within *by Andy Stanley, copyright © 2006 by Andy Stanley. Used by permission of Multnomah Publishers.* (**www.multnomahpublishers.com**)

Do-Right Rules

A famous football coach once claimed that he had only one rule for his players: Do right. The "do-right" rule, of course, is easier said than lived. First, you have to know what is "right." Second, you have to "do it" no matter what others say or do.

Another famous football coach used to start every season going back to the basics. Before you get back in the game, here are some "Do-Right" basics for you to consider … and do!

———

Building an ethical framework begins by identifying ethical models, determining your personal standards, and making a commitment that includes accountability.

Effective organizational ethics are the result of careful reflection and cultivation, and they require guidance, planning, discipline, and practice.

While there has been an increased focus and commitment on corporate ethics, culturally accepted ethical behavior doesn't always line up with biblically acceptable ethical behavior.

An organization that starts on a foundation of greed and mistrust cannot sustain its momentum for long. In fact, its very existence is questionable in the long term.

Businesses should have a policy for dealing with the inevitable convergence of a worker's moral beliefs and professional duties.

Companies must be willing to accept the characteristics that make for good employees. If they want employees who are

not afraid to act ethically when it would benefit the organization, these same employees must be given reasonable leeway when the exercise of conscience may not be in the direct interests of the company.

Core values aren't worth much if the people within an organization don't believe in them. It is critical to incorporate ethical concerns into an organization's philosophy and sense of mission. Allowing employees to participate in defining ethical standards helps ensure buy-in.

Leading by example remains a crucial component for integrating ethical behavior into a corporate culture.

Our convictions are tested when we are detached from a Christ-centered subculture.

Friendships are a key part of shaping and maintaining biblical convictions.

The display of godly convictions isn't always overt.

Ethical standards must be applied consistently to all areas of life.

There is a correlation between how we deal with ethical dilemmas and how effective we are as leaders and as witnesses for God.

Faith is essential for holding to biblical convictions regardless of the consequences.

Ethical behavior is not a last-minute decision.

L@W

Lessons Learned While Grieving

By David Roth

This particular day was like most other days. Life, in all its personal and professional busyness, was at full tilt. Then, at about 9:30 a.m. the phone rang and my life changed forever. Dean Ramsey, my best friend since the day I was born, had suffered cardiac arrest and was in the ER. By the time I got there, he was dead.

From that moment, I have been observing life through a different lens. You may have been through similar life-changing experiences and now see through this same lens. Allow me to put aside grief for the moment and share with you some encouraging life lessons. As I reflect on these lessons, it occurs to me that they are apropos whether you are dealing with tragedy or other crises that we all experience at different times in our personal and professional lives.

God is good
Through this tragedy, I have seen Him influence so many people's lives. This gives me great hope.

Adversity is our friend
Whether it is life altering, such as death or serious illness, or simply the daily challenges we experience at work, adversity will either make us stronger or weaker. Many good things come through adversity. Spiritually, mentally, and physically we get stronger through adversity, yet we fear it. The Bible has much to say on this subject.

What is success?
John Wooden, the legendary basketball coach of the UCLA Bruins, is one of my greatest heroes. His definition of success is different than others, and very compelling. Spend some time marinating over this definition and what it means to you. "Success is *peace of mind*, which is a direct result of self-satisfaction in knowing you did your best to become the best that you are capable of being."

Relationships are the marrow of life
Whether it is your best friend or an associate at work, relationships matter. I want to be more intentional in my relationships ... with my wife, with my two boys, with coworkers, with friends, and with Jesus. Each day is precious. The greatest commandment, as seen in Matthew 22:37-39, makes this simple.

Balance is elusive, but our legacy is at stake
Work matters. For many people it is a passion. And that is good. For others it defines who they are. That isn't. Coach Wooden said balance is keeping things in perspective. I want to battle every day to create balance in my life.

"Is this heaven?"
My favorite line in one of my favorite movies, *Field of Dreams,* has been on my mind lately. If I die today, will I spend eternity in heaven? And if I do, will my life be something Jesus is proud of?

L@W

David M. Roth is President of WorkMatters, Inc, a nondenominational outreach launched in Fayetteville, Ark., in April 2002. It is made up of Small Groups who meet regularly to discuss issues, share ideas and enjoy the support of a peer group—all in a workplace setting. Check out their free newsletter and other info at **www.workmatters.com**. Roth resides in Fayetteville with his wife Theresa and their two sons.

That if you confess with your mouth, "Jesus is Lord," and believe in your heart that God raised him from the dead, you will be saved. For it is with your heart that you believe and are justified, and it is with your mouth that you confess and are saved.

Romans 10:9-10 (NIV)

FRANK TURNER

Frank Turner is the co-anchor of the 5 p.m. and 7 p.m. newscasts on WXYZ-TV, Channel 7 in Detroit. He has been an anchor and reporter for the station since 1990 and a broadcaster since 1977, having also worked in radio. Frank (**www.FrankTurner.org**) is also an evangelist, pointing people to Christ from the pulpit ... and the television set.

Faith on the Air
I am known as "America's First Evangelical Anchorman" because of my bold proclamations of salvation by faith in the Lord Jesus Christ on the air, including during regular nightly commentaries on my 7 p.m. broadcast.

Work is merely another mission field where God has "sown" believers to lead people to salvation by faith in Christ for the "harvest" upon His return. Obviously we are to serve our employers with diligence as the Bible commands (Colossians 3:22). However, we are also to serve the Lord and His purposes in our lives, demonstrating His love, preaching His gospel, and proclaiming His return. For me, this is a particular challenge because I also proclaim my faith "on-air" as well as off.

Never be afraid, ashamed, or hesitant to share with everybody the truth of what the Lord Jesus Christ has done for you. Sharing my faith at work is very important to me, but no more or less important than sharing it in any other venue. I do not believe that Christians should live compartmentalized lives where we separate work, faith, and service to God. This is why I have no hesitation to proclaim Christ on the air.

Family and Ministry Matters
I have been married since 1999 to my wonderful and beautiful wife Annick. We have two children together: Allyson, who is 4, and Rachel, 2. I also have two children from my wife's first marriage: Austin 19 and Andrea 21. We are very guarded when it comes to protecting family time and building it into my schedule. My wife is largely credited with helping me stay focused on the children and making sure work and ministry doesn't interfere with family time.

I provide Christian guidance and biblical counseling to people in drug and alcohol treatment programs and provide biblical instruction for marriage, parenting, and relationships for several churches, organizations and individuals.

On-Air Excellence
I attended Columbia College, a small school in downtown Chicago. I left school to take my first reporting job in Omaha midway through my senior year and did not graduate.

I have received two Emmy awards from the Michigan Chapter of the National Academy of Television Arts and Sciences, several awards from the Michigan Association of Broadcasters, Associated Press Broadcasters, New York Festivals Television, and the Radio and Television News Directors Association's Michelle Clark Fellowship award.

Honoring God at Work
I try to honor God with my work by the way I treat my co-workers, by the level of quality I bring to my job, and by the effect I can have on my broadcasts to hinder or counteract the glorification of anything that opposes God.

The best way to honor God and be successful at work is to refuse to compromise either God or work, and maintain the credibility of being honest. Never compromise in your dedication to your work or in your zeal to ensure the quality of your work is always the highest you can provide. However, you must never compromise your faith and must always be true to God, proclaim His reality and goodness, proclaim in word and deed your allegiance to and worship of Him, and honor Him first and foremost in your employment service. Finally you must maintain your credibility through honesty.

L@W

Whatever you do, work at it with all of your heart, as working for the Lord, not for men, since you know that you will receive an inheritance from the Lord as your reward. It is the Lord Christ you are serving.

Colossians 3:23–24 (NIV)

CONNIE KITTSON

Connie Kittson is a National Sales Director for Mary Kay, Inc. (**www.MaryKay.com**). She has been an independent Mary Kay representative since 1987 and one of 200 women to serve as a National Sales Director since 2003. Mary Kay is committed "to use the Golden Rule as a business guide and to help women live a balanced life by placing God first, family second, and career third."

From Plumbing ...

After graduating from Arizona State, I went to work for my dad "short term" in our chain of family-owned industrial and electrical supply showrooms, KIE Supply. Seven years later, I was still there! I managed a showroom ... it was a great experience. It taught me a great deal. It is a wholesale and retail supplier of electrical, plumbing, irrigation, cabinet, and lighting. Basically, I worked construction. I drove a forklift. I could load your cabinets onto your truck.

To Diapers ...

I worked there until the day my daughter Kristin was born. She's 25 and is now with Mary Kay. My son Scott is 21 and in college. I was home with them for five years and became a professional volunteer. I started a preschool at the church across the street. I did the curriculum, hired the teacher, bought the toys, and helped set up the board.

I've done it all, from VBS to Sunday school to Awana. You name it, I did it. You search for what is your thing. I never really found my niche. I never did until Mary Kay.

To Beauty Products

I was a single mom. I started with Mary Kay out of necessity ... I needed to support my kids. I knew Mary Kay was a good match for me. I always wanted to help kids and I realized if I can help the mother, I can help the children.

I had some success as a volunteer. I needed that success in church so that I could start doing bigger things. I was ready to soar when I started with Mary Kay. I moved up pretty rapidly. This company was a nurturing company.

Family Matters

Anyone who knows my dad would say he's as honest as the day is long. My dad gave me the good business savvy. My mother never met a stranger; she loves people. It's a good combination. Our family business started in our backyard. As kids, we'd go down to the showroom and sweep the floors, clean the bathrooms.

I integrated my kids in my business. I needed them to feel that this was their business, not mine. They've been a part of this all along. You have to make your family a priority.

Faith at Work

Mary Kay Ash was a phenomenal Christian woman. She showed us it was okay to give God the praise and glory for success. Being a single parent, God took on a bigger role in my life. God's really blessed my work since I took Him as my business partner in 1987.

I can't separate my faith from the rest of my life. I'm a mom and a Christian and a Mary Kay National Sales Director all at the same time. I want people to know I'm a Christian by the way I treat people and my acts of service. It starts with treating people with dignity and respect.

I really mentor the women I lead. I have a real loyalty from them because of how much I give to them. I tell them that when their lives are in order, starting with God, everything else is good. I coach them to greatness.

L@W

EXECUTIVE SUMMARY
Final Thoughts On Defining Character

CHARACTER GUIDES BEHAVIOR. It's the moral beacon lighting our way through a maze of conflicting value systems. It influences our ethics. It steers us safely away from the pitfalls of dishonesty, manipulation, and untruth. It empowers our conscience with resolve.

In the marketplace, character is challenged daily. The pressure of turning a profit and the drive to dominate the competition can easily coax us toward character compromise.

We want to do what is right, but our best intentions can easily fall prey to the allure of shortcuts and half-truths. How do we safeguard against ethical slips? Is it possible to construct solid convictions and develop airtight moral character?

IN THIS LESSON WE'VE LEARNED:

▷ Character must have a moral warehouse from which to draw. Constructing a moral infrastructure is critical for leading a God-intended Life@Work.

▷ Character is not a static virtue. It must constantly be replenished through an ongoing process of renewal.

▷ Character begins with having convictions — sound, solid, personal principles by which to live.

▷ An opinion is something we hold; a conviction is something that holds us.

▷ Convictions form when we wholeheartedly adopt God's position toward an issue and choose to act in accordance with that position.

▷ We need to have clearly defined convictions because we can't decide what kind of person we are going to be in the heat of the moment.

▷ Settled convictions give us guideposts for navigating our wants and desires.

▷ Constructing personal convictions begins with taking charge of our thought life.

▷ Just as when we were kids, good character keeps good company.

▷ The grooves of character that mark us most deeply are those that are made when no one is looking.

▷ Integrity must be constantly nurtured and re-supplied. Doing so requires lifelong investment in character-sustaining habits. There are no shortcuts.

▷ Never try to be better than someone else. Never cease trying to be the best you can be.

▷ Success is peace of mind attained through self-satisfaction.

▷ Reputation is who others perceive us to be. Character is who we are — and we're the only ones that can truly gauge our own character.

▷ Leaders build value systems by giving due credit to those under their supervision.

▷ Don't be afraid to fail. We're all going to fail on occasion. We should learn from failures and avoid repeating them, but the greatest failure of all is failure to act when action is necessary.

▷ A person of integrity lives out in deed what he or she believes in the heart and the head. A person of integrity is undivided.

▷ A person of integrity and character is the same both within and without.

▷ We cannot blame anyone else for our character erosion.

▷ Greed is not a financial issue; it's a heart issue. Financial gain or loss doesn't change anything, because greed emanates from the heart.

NEXT STEPS

Character is formed each day. We never graduate from having to make moral decisions, and we are never immune to assaults against our character.

→ Every line of work has unique temptations. Salespeople may be enticed to mislead customers; accountants may find it convenient to ignore standards and transparent reporting. In your present role, what areas are you likely to face an attack on your character? What steps will you take to handle such temptations honorably? Remember: the heat of the moment is the worst moment to choose your values.

→ Take 10 minutes at the end of each workday and replay it in your mind. Monitor your heart for any moments in which you exercised poor moral judgment. Seek to make right anything you have done wrong.

→ Keeping our word is a simple character-forming step. Always have a notepad available in meetings and phone calls, and write down any promises you make. Promptly follow through on any actions you said you would take.

→ Nothing undercuts greed like unseen generosity. Make an anonymous donation to an organization or friend in need.

NELSON IMPACT
A Division of Thomas Nelson Publishers
Since 1798

The Nelson Impact Team is here to answer your questions
and suggestions as to how we can create more resources
that benefit you, your family, and your community.

Contact us at Impact@thomasnelson.com